# ENCYCLOPEDIA OF
# GLOBAL RESOURCES

# ENCYCLOPEDIA OF
# GLOBAL RESOURCES

## Volume 2
### Environment and Natural Resources Division - Mica

*Editor*

**Craig W. Allin**

*Cornell College*

SALEM PRESS
Pasadena, California          Hackensack, New Jersey

*Editor in Chief:* Dawn P. Dawson

*Editorial Director:* Christina J. Moose
*Manuscript Editor:* Christopher Rager
*Acquisitions Editor:* Mark Rehn
*Research Supervisor:* Jeffry Jensen
*Photo Editor:* Cynthia Breslin Beres

*Production Editor:* Andrea E. Miller
*Page Design and Layout:* James Hutson
*Additional Layout:* Mary Overell and
William Zimmerman
*Editorial Assistant:* Brett Weisberg

*Cover photo:* ©Tebnad/Dreamstime.com

**Library of Congress Cataloging-in-Publication Data**

Encyclopedia of global resources / Craig W. Allin, editor.
    p. cm.
    Includes bibliographical references and index.
    ISBN 978-1-58765-644-6 (set : alk. paper) — ISBN 978-1-58765-645-3 (vol. 1 : alk. paper) — ISBN 978-1-58765-646-0 (vol. 2 : alk. paper) — ISBN 978-1-58765-647-7 (vol. 3 : alk. paper) — ISBN 978-1-58765-648-4 (vol. 4 : alk. paper)  1. Natural resources.  I. Allin, Craig W.
    HC85.E49 2010
    333.703—dc22

2010001984

**Mixed Sources**
Product group from well-managed forests, controlled sources and recycled wood or fiber
www.fsc.org  Cert no. SGS-COC-005368
© 1996 Forest Stewardship Council
**FSC**

30%

PRINTED IN THE UNITED STATES OF AMERICA

# Contents

# Common Units of Measure

Common prefixes for metric units—which may apply in more cases than shown below—include *giga-* (1 billion times the unit), *mega-* (one million times), *kilo-* (1,000 times), *hecto-* (100 times), *deka-* (10 times), *deci-* (0.1 times, or one tenth), *centi-* (0.01, or one hundredth), *milli-* (0.001, or one thousandth), and *micro-* (0.0001, or one millionth).

| UNIT | QUANTITY | SYMBOL | EQUIVALENTS |
|---|---|---|---|
| Acre | Area | ac | 43,560 square feet<br>4,840 square yards<br>0.405 hectare |
| Ampere | Electric current | A *or* amp | 1.00016502722949 international ampere<br>0.1 biot *or* abampere |
| Angstrom | Length | Å | 0.1 nanometer<br>0.0000001 millimeter<br>0.000000004 inch |
| Astronomical unit | Length | AU | 92,955,807 miles<br>149,597,871 kilometers<br>(mean Earth-Sun distance) |
| Barn | Area | b | $10^{-28}$ meters squared<br>(approx. cross-sectional area of 1 uranium nucleus) |
| Barrel (dry, for most produce) | Volume/capacity | bbl | 7,056 cubic inches; 105 dry quarts; 3.281 bushels, struck measure |
| Barrel (liquid) | Volume/capacity | bbl | 31 to 42 gallons |
| British thermal unit | Energy | Btu | 1055.05585262 joule |
| Bushel (U.S., heaped) | Volume/capacity | bsh *or* bu | 2,747.715 cubic inches<br>1.278 bushels, struck measure |
| Bushel (U.S., struck measure) | Volume/capacity | bsh *or* bu | 2,150.42 cubic inches<br>35.238 liters |
| Candela | Luminous intensity | cd | 1.09 hefner candle |
| Celsius | Temperature | C | 1° centigrade |
| Centigram | Mass/weight | cg | 0.15 grain |
| Centimeter | Length | cm | 0.3937 inch |
| Centimeter, cubic | Volume/capacity | cm³ | 0.061 cubic inch |
| Centimeter, square | Area | cm² | 0.155 square inch |
| Coulomb | Electric charge | C | 1 ampere second |

| Unit | Quantity | Symbol | Equivalents |
|------|----------|--------|-------------|
| Cup | Volume/capacity | C | 250 milliliters<br>8 fluid ounces<br>0.5 liquid pint |
| Deciliter | Volume/capacity | dl | 0.21 pint |
| Decimeter | Length | dm | 3.937 inches |
| Decimeter, cubic | Volume/capacity | dm$^3$ | 61.024 cubic inches |
| Decimeter, square | Area | dm$^2$ | 15.5 square inches |
| Dekaliter | Volume/capacity | dal | 2.642 gallons<br>1.135 pecks |
| Dekameter | Length | dam | 32.808 feet |
| Dram | Mass/weight | dr *or* dr avdp | 0.0625 ounce<br>27.344 grains<br>1.772 grams |
| Electron volt | Energy | eV | $1.5185847232839 \times 10^{-22}$ Btus<br>$1.6021917 \times 10^{-19}$ joules |
| Fermi | Length | fm | 1 femtometer<br>$1.0 \times 10^{-15}$ meters |
| Foot | Length | ft *or* ' | 12 inches<br>0.3048 meter<br>30.48 centimeters |
| Foot, cubic | Volume/capacity | ft$^3$ | 0.028 cubic meter<br>0.0370 cubic yard<br>1,728 cubic inches |
| Foot, square | Area | ft$^2$ | 929.030 square centimeters |
| Gallon (British Imperial) | Volume/capacity | gal | 277.42 cubic inches<br>1.201 U.S. gallons<br>4.546 liters<br>160 British fluid ounces |
| Gallon (U.S.) | Volume/capacity | gal | 231 cubic inches<br>3.785 liters<br>0.833 British gallon<br>128 U.S. fluid ounces |
| Giga-electron volt | Energy | GeV | $1.6021917 \times 10^{-10}$ joule |
| Gigahertz | Frequency | GHz | — |
| Gill | Volume/capacity | gi | 7.219 cubic inches<br>4 fluid ounces<br>0.118 liter |

| Unit | Quantity | Symbol | Equivalents |
|---|---|---|---|
| Grain | Mass/weight | gr | 0.037 dram<br>0.002083 ounce<br>0.0648 gram |
| Gram | Mass/weight | g | 15.432 grains<br>0.035 avoirdupois ounce |
| Hectare | Area | ha | 2.471 acres |
| Hectoliter | Volume/capacity | hl | 26.418 gallons<br>2.838 bushels |
| Hertz | Frequency | Hz | $1.08782775707767 \times 10^{-10}$ cesium atom frequency |
| Hour | Time | h | 60 minutes<br>3,600 seconds |
| Inch | Length | in *or* ″ | 2.54 centimeters |
| Inch, cubic | Volume/capacity | in³ | 0.554 fluid ounce<br>4.433 fluid drams<br>16.387 cubic centimeters |
| Inch, square | Area | in² | 6.4516 square centimeters |
| Joule | Energy | J | $6.2414503832469 \times 10^{18}$ electron volt |
| Joule per kelvin | Heat capacity | J/K | $7.24311216248908 \times 10^{22}$ Boltzmann constant |
| Joule per second | Power | J/s | 1 watt |
| Kelvin | Temperature | K | −272.15 Celsius |
| Kilo-electron volt | Energy | keV | $1.5185847232839 \times 10^{-19}$ joule |
| Kilogram | Mass/weight | kg | 2.205 pounds |
| Kilogram per cubic meter | Mass/weight density | kg/m³ | $5.78036672001339 \times 10^{-4}$ ounces per cubic inch |
| Kilohertz | Frequency | kHz | — |
| Kiloliter | Volume/capacity | kl | — |
| Kilometer | Length | km | 0.621 mile |
| Kilometer, square | Area | km² | 0.386 square mile<br>247.105 acres |
| Light-year (distance traveled by light in one Earth year) | Length/distance | lt-yr | 5,878,499,814,275.88 miles<br>$9.46 \times 10^{12}$ kilometers |
| Liter | Volume/capacity | L | 1.057 liquid quarts<br>0.908 dry quart<br>61.024 cubic inches |

| Unit | Quantity | Symbol | Equivalents |
|---|---|---|---|
| Mega-electron volt | Energy | MeV | — |
| Megahertz | Frequency | MHz | — |
| Meter | Length | m | 39.37 inches |
| Meter, cubic | Volume/capacity | m³ | 1.308 cubic yards |
| Meter per second | Velocity | m/s | 2.24 miles per hour<br>3.60 kilometers per hour |
| Meter per second per second | Acceleration | m/s² | 12,960.00 kilometers per hour per hour<br>8,052.97 miles per hour per hour |
| Meter, square | Area | m² | 1.196 square yards<br>10.764 square feet |
| Metric. *See* unit name | | | |
| Microgram | Mass/weight | mcg *or* μg | 0.000001 gram |
| Microliter | Volume/capacity | μl | 0.00027 fluid ounce |
| Micrometer | Length | μm | 0.001 millimeter<br>0.00003937 inch |
| Mile (nautical international) | Length | mi | 1.852 kilometers<br>1.151 statute miles<br>0.999 U.S. nautical miles |
| Mile (statute or land) | Length | mi | 5,280 feet<br>1.609 kilometers |
| Mile, square | Area | mi² | 258.999 hectares |
| Milligram | Mass/weight | mg | 0.015 grain |
| Milliliter | Volume/capacity | ml | 0.271 fluid dram<br>16.231 minims<br>0.061 cubic inch |
| Millimeter | Length | mm | 0.03937 inch |
| Millimeter, square | Area | mm² | 0.002 square inch |
| Minute | Time | m | 60 seconds |
| Mole | Amount of substance | mol | $6.02 \times 10^{23}$ atoms or molecules of a given substance |
| Nanometer | Length | nm | 1,000,000 fermis<br>10 angstroms<br>0.001 micrometer<br>0.00000003937 inch |

| Unit | Quantity | Symbol | Equivalents |
|------|----------|--------|-------------|
| Newton | Force | N | x<br>0.224808943099711 pound force<br>0.101971621297793 kilogram force<br>100,000 dynes |
| Newton meter | Torque | N·m | 0.7375621 foot-pound |
| Ounce<br>(avoirdupois) | Mass/weight | oz | 28.350 grams<br>437.5 grains<br>0.911 troy or apothecaries' ounce |
| Ounce<br>(troy) | Mass/weight | oz | 31.103 grams<br>480 grains<br>1.097 avoirdupois ounces |
| Ounce<br>(U.S., fluid or liquid) | Mass/weight | oz | 1.805 cubic inch<br>29.574 milliliters<br>1.041 British fluid ounces |
| Parsec | Length | pc | 30,856,775,876,793 kilometers<br>19,173,511,615,163 miles |
| Peck | Volume/capacity | pk | 8.810 liters |
| Pint<br>(dry) | Volume/capacity | pt | 33.600 cubic inches<br>0.551 liter |
| Pint<br>(liquid) | Volume/capacity | pt | 28.875 cubic inches<br>0.473 liter |
| Pound<br>(avoirdupois) | Mass/weight | lb | 7,000 grains<br>1.215 troy or apothecaries' pounds<br>453.59237 grams |
| Pound<br>(troy) | Mass/weight | lb | 5,760 grains<br>0.823 avoirdupois pound<br>373.242 grams |
| Quart<br>(British) | Volume/capacity | qt | 69.354 cubic inches<br>1.032 U.S. dry quarts<br>1.201 U.S. liquid quarts |
| Quart<br>(U.S., dry) | Volume/capacity | qt | 67.201 cubic inches<br>1.101 liters<br>0.969 British quart |
| Quart<br>(U.S., liquid) | Volume/capacity | qt | 57.75 cubic inches<br>0.946 liter<br>0.833 British quart |
| Rod | Length | rd | 5.029 meters<br>5.50 yards |

| Unit | Quantity | Symbol | Equivalents |
|---|---|---|---|
| Rod, square | Area | rd$^2$ | 25.293 square meters<br>30.25 square yards<br>0.00625 acre |
| Second | Time | s *or* sec | $\frac{1}{60}$ minute<br>$\frac{1}{3600}$ hour |
| Tablespoon | Volume/capacity | T *or* tb | 3 teaspoons<br>4 fluid drams |
| Teaspoon | Volume/capacity | t *or* tsp | 0.33 tablespoon<br>1.33 fluid drams |
| Ton<br>(gross or long) | Mass/weight | t | 2,240 pounds<br>1.12 net tons<br>1.016 metric tons |
| Ton<br>(metric) | Mass/weight | t | 1,000 kilograms<br>2,204.62 pounds<br>0.984 gross ton<br>1.102 net tons |
| Ton<br>(net or short) | Mass/weight | t | 2,000 pounds<br>0.893 gross ton<br>0.907 metric ton |
| Volt | Electric potential | V | 1 joule per coulomb |
| Watt | Power | W | 1 joule per second<br>0.001 kilowatt<br>$2.84345136093995 \times 10^{-4}$ ton of refrigeration |
| Yard | Length | yd | 0.9144 meter |
| Yard, cubic | Volume/capacity | yd$^3$ | 0.765 cubic meter |
| Yard, square | Area | yd$^2$ | 0.836 square meter |

# Complete List of Contents

## Volume 1

# Volume 2

# Volume 3

# Volume 4

# ENCYCLOPEDIA OF
# GLOBAL RESOURCES

# Environment and Natural Resources Division

CATEGORY: Organizations, agencies, and programs
DATE: Established 1909 as Public Lands Division

*The Environment and Natural Resources Division of the U.S. Department of Justice represents the U.S. government in a wide variety of litigation, both civil and criminal, involving the environment, natural resources, and public lands. It litigates cases for the Environmental Protection Agency.*

## DEFINITION

The Environment and Natural Resources Division of the U.S. Department of Justice litigates cases ranging from the protection of endangered species to the cleaning up of hazardous waste sites. In other words, it serves as the nation's environmental lawyer. It enforces civil and criminal environmental laws to protect human health and the environment. It also defends the government against legal challenges to its environmental programs and attempts to ensure that the laws are applied fairly. The division represents the U.S. government in matters concerning the protection, use, and development of natural resources and public lands, wildlife protection, Indian rights and claims, and the acquisition of property by the government. The division, formerly known as the Land and Natural Resources Division, and before that as the Public Lands Division, is organized into nine sections.

## OVERVIEW

The Environmental Crimes Section prosecutes individuals and corporations who violate environmental protection laws; it works with the Federal Bureau of Investigation and with investigators from the Environmental Protection Agency (EPA). Among the statutes it enforces are the Clean Air Act, the Resource Conservation and Recovery Act, and the Comprehensive Environmental Response, Compensation, and Liability Act (CERCLA, or "Superfund"). The Environmental Enforcement Section is responsible for bringing civil litigation on behalf of the EPA, for claims for natural resource damage filed by government agencies, for claims regarding contamination of public land, and for the recoupment of money spent to clean up oil spills on behalf of the U.S. Coast Guard. Its role is to provide a credible deterrent against violation of environmental statutes.

The Environmental Defense Section represents the government—primarily the EPA—in suits challenging its administration of federal environmental laws. These suits include claims by industries that regulations are too strict and, conversely, by environmental groups claiming they are too lax. Suits are also sometimes brought by states or individuals alleging that federal agencies themselves are not complying with environmental regulations. The Wildlife and Marines Resources Section tries civil and criminal cases involving federal wildlife laws and laws protecting marine life. Smugglers and black-market dealers in protected wildlife are prosecuted. Civil litigation involving the Endangered Species Act may pit the requirements of species protection against the interests of either private concerns or government agencies.

The Policy, Legislation, and Special Litigation Section advises and assists the U.S. assistant attorney general regarding policy issues. It also directs the division's legislative program—testimony before congressional committees and representation of the division in congressional and interagency policy meetings. The division undertakes specially assigned projects and serves as the division's ethics office. The Appellate Section handles appeals of cases tried in lower courts by any of the division's other sections. It drafts briefs for any division cases that reach the U.S. Supreme Court. The Executive Office is the administrator of the division, providing financial management, personnel, planning, and litigation support services.

The division's General Litigation Section is responsible for litigation involving federally owned public lands and natural resources. Cases may arise regarding more than eighty laws covering land management and natural resources. Issues include water rights, land-use plans, timber and mineral production, landowner compensation, and trust obligations to Indian tribes. The Indian Resources Section represents the United States in its trust capacity regarding Indian tribes. Suits include such issues as water rights, hunting and fishing rights, damages for trespassing on American Indian lands, and reservation boundaries and land rights. The Land Acquisition Section acquires land for the government through purchase or condemnation proceedings. Land is acquired for a variety of purposes, ranging from parks to missile sites. A number of issues may be raised in such cases, including balancing the rights of individual property owners against the needs of the government, ascertaining the fair market value of property, and determining the applicability of local zoning regulations.

*Vincent M. D. Lopez*

WEB SITE

U.S. DEPARTMENT OF JUSTICE
Environment and Natural Resources Division
http://www.usdoj.gov/enrd/

SEE ALSO: Clean Air Act; Clean Water Act; Endangered Species Act; Environmental law in the United States; Environmental Protection Agency; Public lands; Superfund legislation and cleanup activities.

# Environmental biotechnology

CATEGORIES: Plant and animal resources; scientific disciplines; social, economic, and political issues

*Environmental, or "white," biotechnology, seeks to accomplish three major goals: bioremediation, pollution abatement, and the generation of renewable resources. These goals are typically achieved using either naturally occurring or genetically engineered plants and microorganisms as well as specific chemical substances that have been obtained from these organisms.*

## BACKGROUND

Biotechnology has been defined as the use of living organisms to achieve human goals. Because these goals cover such a broad range of possibilities, biotechnology is often subdivided into three major categories, namely those with medical, agricultural, and environmental applications. Some have even gone as far as to color-code these categories, referring to them as red, green, and white biotechnology, respectively. Historically, the former category has received the most attention. Measured in terms of capital investments, it has overshadowed the other two by a factor of nearly 20 to 1 since the use of modern biotechnology began in earnest in the 1980's. The latter categories, however, have seen steady growth in the twenty-first century and may someday be able to close this gap. Each of these categories of biotechnology can, in turn, be further subdivided according to its specific goals. Environmental biotechnology, for instance, can be thought of as encompassing bioremediation (cleaning up contaminated environments), pollution abatement (preventing the discharge of pollutants from currently existing industries), and the production of renewable chemicals and biofuels. Bioremediation has garnered the most interest over time, while the latter two categories, although less developed, appear to be gaining in popularity over time.

## BIOREMEDIATION

Environmental biotechnology has become increasingly popular in waste treatment and remediation because it has several desirable characteristics. It is a "green" technology: It uses natural systems and naturally occurring organisms to detoxify environmental pollutants. The final products (usually carbon dioxide and inorganic elements) are harmless. It is not a particularly new and, therefore, uncertain technology, so there are few unintended consequences of its use. Natural bioremediation of pollution is constantly occurring in the environment; otherwise, past pollution would never have gone away. Bioremediation is inexpensive compared with other treatment technologies. If one can provide the proper environment and nutrients for the remediating organisms, relatively little other infrastructure is involved. It can be done on-site without having to move hundreds of cubic meters of contaminated material. It can even be done in contaminated aquifers and soils that cannot be moved.

Environmental biotechnology typically involves using either plants or microorganisms to achieve its stated aims. Using plants to bioremediate an environment is referred to as "phytoremediation." Phytoremediation is typically used when the environment is contaminated by heavy metals such as lead, mercury, or selenium. Certain plants (*astragalus*, for example) are able to accumulate high concentrations of metals such as selenium in their tissue. The plants can be harvested, the tissue can be burned, and the metal-contaminated ash can be stored in a hazardous-waste facility.

Bioremediation most commonly refers to the use of soil microorganisms (bacteria and fungi) to degrade or immobilize pollutants. It can be used with a wide variety of wastes, including some nuclear wastes such as uranium. In bioremediation one generally has two options. First, the environmental engineer can simply make the contaminated site as favorable for microbial growth as possible by adding nutrients (nitrogen and phosphorus, for example), keeping the area moist, and mixing the contaminated site periodically (if it is soil) to make sure it has sufficient air (or pumping air into the system if it is an aquifer). Then, the engineer waits for microbes already present on the site to start growing and use the waste as a food source.

Frequently there are wastes that cannot be used as a food source by microorganisms. However, they can still be biodegraded by a process called cometabolism. In cometabolism, wastes are biodegraded during the growth of the microbes on some other compound. For example, trichloroethylene (TCE), one of the most common groundwater contaminants, is cometabolized during the growth of bacteria that use methane for their food source. Many other wastes, such as dichloro-diphenyl-trichloroethane (DDT), atrazine, and polychlorinated biphenyls (PCBs), are cometabolized by microbes in the environment.

Waiting for organisms to grow can take a long time (especially in winter), so environmental engineers often try to speed the process by adding microorganisms they have grown in the laboratory. These microorganisms are special because they have already been grown on various pollutants. Therefore, when they are added to the environment in high numbers, they start bioremediating the pollutants immediately. This process is called "seeding."

Sometimes a waste is so toxic or is present in such high concentration that neither plants nor microorganisms can survive in its presence. In this case, enzymes are sometimes used to try to degrade the waste. Enzymes are proteins with catalytic activity—that is, they make chemical reactions occur faster than they normally would. Enzymes are not alive in a strict sense, but they come only from living organisms. They have an advantage over living organisms in that they can retain their catalytic activity in environments that are other-

wise lethal. For example, horseradish peroxidase is a plant enzyme that has been used to treat chlorinated compounds. The peroxidase causes the chlorinated compounds to bind together. When they do that, they become less soluble, and if they become less soluble and precipitate, then they are much less likely to enter the food chain of an ecosystem.

Bioremediation has been used on a large scale

*Scientists examine contaminated mud samples at a Superfund site in Texas. Bioremediation is one aspect of environmental biotechnology.* (Getty Images)

mostly to treat oil spills. The best example of this was during the *Exxon Valdez* oil spill in Alaska in 1989. Rather than try to remove oil from beaches physically (by steam spraying or absorbing it into other materials), engineers had several beaches sprayed with a nutrient solution that helped naturally occurring oil-degrading microbes in the environment to multiply and begin decomposing the pollutant. The experiment was so successful that the U.S. Environmental Protection Agency recommended that Exxon expand its bioremediation efforts to more of the affected beaches.

Environmental biotechnology is a growing industry, and numerous venture capital firms have started to supply remediation technology for various types of wastes. One application of this technology is "designer microbes" for sewage treatment facilities receiving industrial pollutants. Another activity involves creating unique microorganisms, using genetic engineering techniques, that have the ability to degrade new types of pollutants completely. The first living thing to be patented in the United States, a bacterium that was genetically engineered at General Electric, was created specifically to degrade petroleum from oil spills.

## POLLUTION ABATEMENT

Preventing pollution from occurring in the first place is much more desirable than allowing it to happen with the hopes of using biotechnology to clean it up afterward. Microorganisms, for instance, have been used to remove a portion of the carbon dioxide ($CO_2$) found in the emissions resulting from the burning of fossil fuels. One example of an organism being used for pollution control is the microscopic aquatic algae called phytoplankton. In nature, the phytoplankton make up a large portion of the carbon fixation cycle by converting $CO_2$ to sugars during photosynthesis, then sinking to the bottom of the ocean upon their death, effectively removing this carbon from global circulation. Scientists have passed effluents from power plants that burn fossil fuels through columns filled with algae in order to reduce their $CO_2$ emissions. While the subsequent deposition of these algae to the bottom of the ocean is not entirely practical, burning the dried algal pellets for fuel effectively results in more energy being obtained while ultimately releasing the same amount of $CO_2$ emissions as the untreated effluent.

These same abatement principles apply to the treatment of water effluents as well. Some factories have installed anaerobic bioreactors, vessels where microbial digestion of wastes is allowed to take place in the absence of $O_2$. Under these conditions, particular microbes that are present in the bioreactor release methane, which can then be captured and used to run the boilers in the factory and/or provide electricity for the plant. In this case, the treated water is usually pure enough to release directly into a nearby water source. Both aerobic and anaerobic bioreactors have been used to treat sewage, agricultural, and industrial waste.

## PRODUCTION OF RENEWABLE RESOURCES

It is not always the organisms themselves which are of interest to biotechnologists, but certain metabolic by-products that are given off by, or at least easily purified from, the organism in question. The specific enzymes in bioremediation as well as other enzymes can often be purified from the organism that produced them and used in industrial processes involving green chemistry, the practice of chemistry with the aim of reducing the use and generation of hazardous substances. In addition to enzymes, certain organisms are also known to produce small organic compounds known as secondary metabolites, so named because they do not play central roles in the growth or development of the organism in question. These compounds, which often possess pharmaceutical properties, are instead hypothesized to play signaling or defensive roles in the cells that produce them. The production of secondary metabolites and their derivatives form much of the foundation for medical biotechnology based on natural products. Compounds that can be used as a renewable source of fuel represent another class of materials that is produced by living organisms that holds great promise for environmental biotechnology. The direct use of biomass for fuel in the case of dried algal pellets is not practical for use in machinery such as automobiles. Therefore, organisms are typically treated to produce alcohols, oils, or gases that can more easily be used for such purposes. The widespread use of nonfossil fuels to power automobiles dates from the 1970's, when fuel-grade ethanol was first mass-produced in the United States and Brazil. The former purified the ethanol from the fermentation of corn by microbes and used it as an additive to petroleum-based fuels, while the latter used sugarcane in the fermentation process and used the ethanol as a complete replacement for fossil fuels. Research is ongoing into the use of plant waste for ethanol production so that fuel production does not directly compete with the use of crops for food.

An alternative to the production of ethanol via fermentation of a particular biomass is the direct use of plant oils, sometimes called biodiesel, in specifically designed engines. While the adoption of biodiesel as fuel has been relatively slow, the use of soybean oil and rapeseed oil in conjunction with certain public transportation fleets in the United States and Europe, respectively, has steadily increased. Another alternative biofuel that could be adapted for use in automobiles is hydrogen. This biofuel has the added advantage of producing no carbon emissions whatsoever, but it is in the early stages of development, in terms of both its efficient production by microorganisms and the development of engines designed to burn this fuel.

*Mark S. Coyne, updated by James S. Godde*

### FURTHER READING

Alexander, Martin. *Biodegradation and Bioremediation.* San Diego, Calif.: Academic Press, 1994.

Bhattacharyya, Bimal C., and Rintu Banerjee. *Environmental Biotechnology.* New York: Oxford University Press, 2007.

Clark, David P., and Nanette J. Pazdernik. "Environmental Biotechnology." In *Biotechnology: Applying the Genetic Revolution.* Burlington, Mass.: Academic Press/Elsevier, 2009.

Jordening, Hans-Joachim, and Josef Winter, eds. *Environmental Biotechnology: Concepts and Applications.* Weinheim, Germany: Wiley-VCH, 2005.

Scragg, Alan. *Environmental Biotechnology.* 2d ed. New York: Oxford University Press, 2004.

Singh, Ajay, and Owen P. Ward, eds. *Biodegradation and Bioremediation.* New York: Springer, 2004.

Singh, Shree N., and Rudra D. Tripathi, eds. *Environmental Bioremediation Technologies.* New York: Springer, 2007.

Skipper, H. D., and R. F. Turco, eds. *Bioremediation: Science and Applications.* Madison, Wis.: Soil Science Society of America, 1995.

Wainwright, Milton. *An Introduction to Environmental Biotechnology.* Boston: Kluwer Academic, 1999.

### WEB SITES

U.S. ENVIRONMENTAL PROTECTION AGENCY
Treatment/Control: Treatment Technologies, Bioremediation
http://www.epa.gov/ebtpages/treatreatmenttechnbioremediation.html

U.S. GEOLOGICAL SURVEY
Bioremediation: Nature's Way to a Cleaner Environment
http://water.usgs.gov/wid/html/bioremed.html

SEE ALSO: Biofuels; Biotechnology; Environmental Protection Agency; Hazardous waste disposal; Oil spills; Superfund legislation and cleanup activities.

# Environmental degradation, resource exploitation and

CATEGORIES: Environment, conservation, and resource management; pollution and waste disposal

*The needs of human beings for food, shelter, clothing, and other material goods are most often met by extracting raw materials from the natural physical environment. In the process of undertaking this extraction, the quality of the environment is often degraded. Through gaining an understanding of the nature of this degradation and the ability of the environment to regenerate, laws and regulations may be developed to satisfy the human needs in environmentally compatible ways.*

### BACKGROUND

The satisfaction of human resource needs and desires often involves intense interaction with the natural physical environment. Such interaction may involve resource extraction, transportation, and processing. Each of these events has the potential to degrade the environment while meeting human resource needs. Yet instances of environmental degradation also carry with them the potential for solving the problems in ways that may provide long-term satisfaction of resource needs in an environmentally compatible manner. Four examples—damage to wildlife, forests, and soil, and the degradation caused by surface mining—illustrate the circumstances under which such problems have developed and the methods by which environmental restoration has been undertaken.

### SURFACE MINING

Surface mining for resource extraction has a long history. The primary modern procedure is to use large-scale machinery to remove the overlying earth material to expose the economically valuable mineral

*Two State Natural Resources employees stand atop a pile of waste coal in Ohio in 2006. Landscapes in coal districts have been severely degraded through mining.* (AP/Wide World Photos)

resource beneath. Once the mineral is exposed, it can be removed, transported, and refined for use. The most widespread application of surface mining has been in the mining of bituminous coal. During the mining process, numerous undesirable disruptions in land use, water quality, and a community's social fabric can occur. Generally, surface mining is seen as aesthetically undesirable, as large areas of exposed earth material degrade the landscape. The premining land uses are also disrupted, and once-productive lands (farms, forests) are taken out of production. The exposed earth material, if left unprotected, is subject to erosion by both water and wind. If the land is left in an unreclaimed state, the mined land is slow to revegetate and remains an unproductive source of eroded materials and an eyesore.

Water pollution problems may also result from such mining. Most commonly, the removal of coal may expose iron pyrites, which, when exposed to air and water, contribute acid mine drainage to the regional water supply. This acid drainage, along with silt washed from the eroding surface, clogs stream channels, kills aquatic life, and lowers the overall water quality. In cases in which streams are large enough for dams and navigation, the silt fills in reservoirs and clogs the machinery to operate navigation locks. Structural features such as bridge piers, dams, and locks may be damaged from extreme stream acidity.

In the areas where mining occurs, the social organization may also be disrupted. Roads are relocated, farms and houses removed, and, in some cases, entire villages may be removed for mining to take place. The surface mining of coal, therefore, may contribute to many social and environmental problems in the areas where it takes place.

Because of these many disruptive qualities, states

where mining occurs and the federal government have taken steps to remedy the problems and provide a framework for mining the coal needed to meet U.S. energy needs in a more environmentally compatible way. During the 1940's, 1950's, and 1960's, such states as Ohio, Pennsylvania, and Illinois began to pass legislation to curtail surface-mining-related problems by requiring mined land reclamation. The success of these efforts coupled with the need for a national effort to establish a consistent reclamation program led to the passage of the federal Surface Mining Control and Reclamation Act of 1977. The Office of Surface Mining Reclamation and Enforcement in the Department of the Interior is responsible for administering the programs of the act, reviewing state programs for reclamation, and enforcing the act's provisions.

Current mining operations are subject to the provisions of the act, and money is provided to reclaim those lands left unreclaimed and abandoned in the past. Through a series of standards, requirements, and enforcement policies, this act, in conjunction with state laws, has directed the once environmentally destructive process of surface mining into a pattern of energy resource acquisition, mined land reclamation, productive land creation, and post-mining environmental restoration.

## WILDLIFE

A second example in which resource exploitation has led to environmental degradation is wildlife. Wildlife populations depend on a complex set of interacting factors such as food, water, protective habitat, migration routes, and breeding areas. As human populations have grown and expanded on the land surface of the Earth, wildlife populations have been displaced. This displacement has been the result of habitat removal, water pollution, air pollution, the introduction of alien species, hunting, and changing land uses. All these activities have led to declining wildlife populations while meeting human needs for food, shelter, and living space. The declines have led to the extinction of some species and declines in the population of others to the point at which they are considered endangered. At the same time that these declines have occurred, recognition of the problems confronting wildlife populations has led to human responses in areas of habitat preservation and restoration, wildlife management, and the development of a legal framework for wildlife protection.

Perhaps best known of the organizations concerned with wildlife is the National Audubon Society, but it is only one of a large number of national, state, and local wildlife organizations. Such groups undertake a variety of wildlife-related projects such as maintaining preserves and refuges, stocking streams and habitat areas, cleaning waterways, and educating the public. Such activities promote citizen participation and establish a grassroots base for wildlife preservation.

As a complement to these activities there are those functions and programs that result from governmental actions. Federal, state, and local governments are all involved in wildlife activities. While it would be impossible to list all activities, the broad categories of habitat protection, species protection and restoration, and wildlife management are all part of governmental concern. Much of the early concern of the federal government for wildlife was voiced as part of action on other issues such as forest protection, soil erosion, and water pollution control. A federal tax on sporting guns and ammunition passed in the 1930's devoted resources to the purchase of land for wildlife conservation. In 1960, the Multiple Use-Sustained Yield Act specified that wildlife and fish be part of the overall administrative concern. The Endangered Species Act of 1973 gave the federal government direct involvement in dealing with the problems of endangered species through the Office of Endangered Species in the Department of the Interior. The expansion of habitat areas by various agencies of the government has also been a positive move toward preserving and restoring wildlife. At the international level, a variety of laws, treaties, and agreements to protect wildlife are in place. There are also numerous international wildlife organizations.

The 1946 formation of the International Whaling Commission is a good example of such an international organization. It was formed to regulate whale harvesting so that overkilling did not result in species elimination. Such regulation, however, is not binding by law, and countries can withdraw from the commission. More specific regulations are found in the Migratory Bird Treaty. This treaty involves the United States, Canada, and several other countries in habitat protection, wildlife hunting regulation, and international cooperation. Globally, there is a wide variety of laws, treaties, agencies, and organizations aimed at wildlife protection, habitat preservation, and achievement of a balance between the human use of the world's resources and wildlife needs.

## FORESTS AND FORESTRY

A third area of resource exploitation that is useful to review in the context of environmental degradation is forests. At the time that European settlers began to exploit the resources of the United States, forests covered about two-thirds of the land. To the settlers, these forests were both a resource and an impediment. As a resource, the forests met their needs for structural material, fuel, fencing, implements, and windbreaks. As an impediment, the forests had to be cleared to make way for agriculture, farmsteads, roads, and towns. To many of the early settlers, these forests seemed endless, so cutting, burning, and removal went on without concern for the decline in forest cover. Not until the late 1800's did people begin to perceive problems arising from the overuse and abuse of U.S. forests. These concerns reached such a level of importance that in 1897 an act was passed by Congress to allow the establishment of national forests.

Along with land earlier set aside, lands declared national forests established a basis for preserving and conserving the national forest resources. Management of these resources developed along lines that began to recognize two crucial qualities of forestlands: Forestlands could provide a sustained yield, and they could serve a multiple-use purpose. In the first case, if the rate of losses caused by cutting, fire, and insect damage could be offset by planting and land-use management, then the forest's yield could be managed on a sustainable basis. Second, forestlands offer splendid potential to be used in a multiple-use context. Forests offer protection to the soil to slow or prevent erosion, slow runoff, and retain moisture for release during periods of reduced precipitation. Forests therefore provide very good watershed protection.

Forests also serve as an important part of wildlife habitat. They provide cover, food, nesting sites, and space, all essential to wildlife continuation. The recreational benefits of forests—as places for camping, hiking, and other outdoor activities—are also part of a multiple-use approach. In a multiple-use context, therefore, forest management seeks to balance the sustainable yield of forest products with the provision of recreation, wildlife, and watershed protection values. This concept of multiple use, sustained yield was formalized with the passage by Congress of the Multiple Use-Sustained Yield Act of 1960. This act integrated the ideas and concepts of multiple use with those of sustained yield to provide an overall management approach to forest use. While these approaches have not removed all problems from forestry, they have helped to balance the problems resulting from exploitation with the ability to achieve a higher quality environment.

## SOIL

A fourth resource that has suffered degradation as a result of exploitation is soil. The degradation has been the result of a combination of improper agricultural practices, careless rangeland use, thoughtless forestry techniques, and unplanned urban growth. All of these have led to an overall deterioration of U.S. soil resources and a decline in farmland. In many ways, the soil losses have mirrored the decline in forest productivity. The early settlers cleared the forests to make way for agriculture. Impressed with the size of the trees and the extent of the forest cover, they often viewed the soil beneath the forests as very fertile and nearly inexhaustible. In the humid East, the forests were replaced by clear tilled-row agriculture that exposed the soil to rain and did little to slow runoff. The result was erosion and the subsequent loss of the productive topsoil.

As the settlement frontier moved westward, eastern agricultural practices followed. These practices, developed in areas with more than 50 centimeters of rainfall per year, were inappropriate for the dryer conditions encountered west of the Mississippi River. Combined with crops ill suited for the new conditions, they led to crop failure and, in years of drought, severe erosion of the soil by blowing wind. Similarly, overgrazing of the rangelands of the western United States led to soil exposure and subsequent soil losses. Thoughtless forestry techniques have also left the topsoil exposed to erosion by running water. Urban expansion on the landscape removes the vegetative cover and leaves the soil exposed to erosion by both wind and rain. As a result of these combined problems, by the 1930's serious concern existed regarding soil erosion and losses.

The severe drought of that decade, which resulted in the Dust Bowl conditions of the Great Plains, stirred people to action. Land rehabilitation was given great assistance through the actions of the Civilian Conservation Corps (CCC). Participants in this program planted trees and built soil erosion control structures and dams, all aimed at slowing the rate of erosion and loss of soil. This growing concern was given greater attention in 1935, when Hugh Hammond Bennett was appointed head of the Soil Conservation Service. This service, a part of the U.S. Department of Agriculture, was designed to assist farmers in developing farm plans to reduce soil erosion. Contour farming, land terracing, farm pond construction, and conservation planting all assumed important roles in soil erosion prevention. Congress also passed, in 1934, the Taylor Grazing Act, which had as part of its provisions the establishment of rangeland use and regulation to curb soil abuses and losses.

## CONTEXT

The preceding four examples depict some of the problems associated with human exploitation of the resource base. Certainly, this exploitation has involved considerable cost in the form of resource use, misuse, and loss and has had a severe impact on the environment. However, recognition of the problems has also meant that some solutions have been found. Extinct species can never be recovered, and careless exploitation continues today, but a legal and administrative framework has been established to help correct past mistakes and to attend to humankind's resource needs in a more environmentally compatible fashion in the present and future.

*Jerry E. Green*

## FURTHER READING

Buchholz, Rogene A. *Principles of Environmental Management: The Greening of Business.* 2d ed. Upper Saddle River, N.J.: Prentice Hall, 1998.

Chiras, Daniel D., and John P. Reganold. *Natural Resource Conservation: Management for a Sustainable Future.* 10th ed. Upper Saddle River, N.J.: Pearson Prentice Hall, 2009.

Cutter, Susan L., and William H. Renwick. *Exploitation, Conservation, Preservation: A Geographic Perspective on Natural Resource Use.* 4th ed. Danvers, Mass.: J. Wiley, 2004.

Dodds, Walter K. *Humanity's Footprint: Momentum, Impact, and Our Global Environment.* New York: Columbia University Press, 2008.

Ehrenfeld, David. *Becoming Good Ancestors: How We Balance Nature, Community, and Technology.* New York: Oxford University Press, 2009.

Goudie, Andrew. *The Human Impact on the Natural Environment: Past, Present, and Future.* 6th ed. Malden, Mass.: Blackwell, 2006.

Leopold, Aldo. *A Sand County Almanac, and Sketches Here and There.* Illustrated by Charles W. Schwartz. 1949. Reprint. New York: Oxford University Press, 1987.

Liotta, P. H., and Allan W. Shearer. *Gaia's Revenge: Climate Change and Humanity's Loss.* Westport, Conn.: Praeger, 2007.

Petulla, Joseph M. *American Environmental History: The Exploitation and Conservation of Natural Resources.* 2d ed. Columbus, Ohio: Merrill, 1988.

Sedjo, Roger A., ed. *Perspectives on Sustainable Resources in America.* Washington, D.C.: Resources for the Future, 2008.

## WEB SITE

U.S. GEOLOGICAL SURVEY
Materials in the Economy: Material Flows, Scarcity, and the Environment
http://pubs.usgs.gov/circ/2002/c1221

SEE ALSO: Coal; Deforestation; Drought; Dust Bowl; Forest management; Mining wastes and mine reclamation; Soil management; Species loss; Surface Mining Control and Reclamation Act; Wildlife.

# Environmental engineering

CATEGORY: Environment, conservation, and resource management

*Environmental engineering encompasses a number of disciplines in which experts analyze data and make recommendations regarding activities that affect the environment in general and public health and welfare in particular.*

## BACKGROUND

"Environmental engineering" is a term that emerged during the 1960's to describe the curricula of, and the activities of graduates from, certain engineering and public health schools. The subject matter addressed by environmental engineering continues to evolve, reaching into the disciplines of civil engineering, public health, ecology, and ethics. Specialization and fragmentation of university programs have resulted in the subject matter being treated in departments ranging from hydrology to chemical engineering to biology. The major areas covered by environmental engineering are water and wastewater pollution and treatment, air pollution control, solid and hazardous waste management and remediation, noise pollution, ecosystem management, and environmental ethics. Such a broad interdisciplinary program often makes it difficult for students to acquire the necessary knowledge and skills in many universities that are largely structured in the traditional disciplines. Prior to the use of the term "environmental engineering," much of the subject matter and basic concepts were covered in sanitary engineering programs.

## RISK ANALYSIS

Many of the activities performed by environmental engineers are associated with evaluating the risks to the environment and to public health from various hazards. Environmental engineers are often asked both to evaluate current risks and to predict future risks. They determine how science, engineering, and technology can be used to prevent or lower risks. Environmental risk analysis and the design of suitable approaches to lower risk involve a working knowledge of many disciplines.

## WATER AND SOLID WASTES

A thorough understanding of water resources and the pollutants that can be associated with them as well as knowledge of how to remove or reduce pollutants to acceptable levels are central to the skills of the environmental engineer. This involves a thorough understanding of the common sources of water, its means of conveyance to a user, and typical sources of contamination. Water suitable for one use may be unsuitable for another, and the environmental engineer knows of the various means used to treat the water to make it suitable for any use. Environmental engineers also learn how to handle sewage and other solid wastes. They learn to process sewage and wastewater so that the water can be reused or dispersed into the environment without harmful effects. The processing of the solids from sewage as well as solids in garbage is a major problem.

Solutions to the handling of these materials must be suitable technically, economically, legally, politically, and socially. The environmental engineer often operates under considerable scrutiny from many sectors of society. The environmental engineer is often situated somewhere between environmentalists and business interests in providing the technical input used for setting limits on various pollutants released into water, soil, and the air. The limits need to be such that the environment is not unduly affected while industry is allowed to operate and produce the products needed by society.

## RESOURCE REUSE

Some environmental engineers develop various reuse, recycling, and resource recovery programs. Finding effective means to clean polluted water, soil, and air as well as ensuring that current and future activities do not unduly pollute them are major areas in the profession. The environmental engineer is asked to examine pollution that has occurred in the past from spilled chemicals, leaking landfills, and scattered radioactive waste and determine how sites can best be cleaned, reduced, or stabilized. Many of these broad analyses must draw upon a solid understanding of microbiology, chemistry, physics, physiology, public health, and other areas.

## AIR POLLUTION

Air pollution is an area receiving more attention from environmental engineers than it has in the past. Environmental engineers provide technical input to assist in the development of laws and regulations that set thresholds or levels for chemicals and pollutants in the air. They also quantify the amount of various pollutants in the air and compare these to the limits to determine the risk to the public. After legislation is enacted, the amount and types of pollutants that a business releases into the air are compared with the laws and regulations to determine whether the business is in compliance, whether fines are required, or whether the business activity is to be ordered to cease operation. Pollutant management plans are often developed by environmental engineers.

## NOISE POLLUTION

Noise pollution is another area where environmental engineers provide technical input for use in setting acceptable noise levels in laws and regulations. They also measure the emitted noise levels of noise sources to determine whether they are in compliance with regulations. In addition, they often develop noise management plans.

## ENVIRONMENTAL IMPACT STATEMENTS

Environmental engineers are often involved in developing environmental impact statements associated with any proposed activity that might have a negative impact on the environment. They draw on their knowledge of the natural functioning of the ecosystems composing the environment to determine the effects of the proposed activity. They are also often asked to estimate the economic impact of these proposed activities on the community, surrounding area, society, or other businesses. These analyses may transcend pure data, touching on ethical issues and giving views about what is best for society. Decisions on activities that interact with and affect the environment need to be made in a complex arena, and those making the decisions are often aided by input from environmental engineers trained in many disciplines.

*William O. Rasmussen*

### FURTHER READING

Davis, Mackenzie L., and David A. Cornwell. *Introduction to Environmental Engineering.* 4th ed. Boston: McGraw-Hill, 2008.

Masters, Gilbert M., and Wendell P. Ela. *Introduction to Environmental Engineering and Science.* 3d ed. Upper Saddle River, N.J.: Prentice Hall, 2008.

Nazaroff, William W., and Lisa Alvarez-Cohen. *Environmental Engineering Science.* New York: Wiley, 2001.

Ray, Bill T. *Environmental Engineering.* New York: PWS, 1995.

Reible, Danny D. *Fundamentals of Environmental Engineering.* Boca Raton, Fla.: Lewis, 1999.

Vallero, Daniel A., and Chris Brasier. *Sustainable Design: The Science of Sustainability and Green Engineering.* Hoboken, N.J.: John Wiley, 2008.

Vesilind, P. Aarne, J. Jeffrey Peirce, and Ruth F. Weiner. *Environmental Engineering.* 3d ed. Boston: Butterworth-Heinemann, 1994.

Vesilind, P. Aarne, and Susan M. Morgan. *Introduction to Environmental Engineering.* 2d ed. Belmont, Calif.: Thomson/Brook/Cole, 2004.

Wallace, Bill. *Becoming Part of the Solution: The Engineer's Guide to Sustainable Development.* Washington, D.C.: American Council of Engineering Companies, 2005.

SEE ALSO: Air pollution and air pollution control; Hazardous waste disposal; Incineration of wastes; Nuclear waste and its disposal; Waste management and sewage disposal; Water pollution and water pollution control.

# Environmental ethics

CATEGORY: Social, economic, and political issues

*Environmental ethics encompasses a variety of perspectives on the relationship between humans and their environment, ranging from anthropocentrism to individualism to ecofeminism; each perspective has its own view of the appropriate ways to use the Earth's resources.*

### BACKGROUND

Ethics is concerned with what people value; specifically it is concerned with proper behavior toward things with intrinsic value. Things valued in and of themselves are said to have intrinsic value; human beings, for example, generally are considered to have intrinsic value. (Things valued for what they can help humans accomplish—money, for example—are said to have instrumental value.) Environmental ethics is the field of inquiry that evaluates the ethical responsibilities humans have for the natural world, including natural resources. There are many different, and often conflicting, perspectives on appropriate human responsibilities toward nature and natural resources; each has strengths and weaknesses, and each can be advocated by thoughtful and articulate scholars.

### ANTHROPOCENTRISM

Anthropocentrism is a human-centered philosophy whose adherents believe that moral values should be limited to humans and should not be extended to other creatures or to nature as a whole. A justification for this perspective is that moral relationships are sets of reciprocal rules followed by humans in their mutual relationships. Nonhumans cannot participate in these relationships because they lack comprehension of the rules; moreover, to the extent their behaviors can be understood, they often appear to live by different rules. Anthropocentrists also argue that, from an evolutionary perspective, successful species do not work for the net good of another. Species behave purposefully for their own survival; those that failed to do so have become extinct.

Some anthropocentrists oppose restrictions on natural resource use because restrictions seem to have negative impacts on human well-being—impacts such as the loss of jobs or products beneficial to humans. However, other anthropocentrists stress that the natural world is a critical life-support system for humans and a significant source of aesthetic richness; such anthropocentrists advocate careful environmental controls so that the natural world and its resources will maintain their full value for present and future generations. This anthropocentric regard for the environment is based on the belief that the natural world has important instrumental value for meeting human needs rather than on a belief in the intrinsic value of the natural world.

### INDIVIDUALISM

An individualist perspective is that humans should extend moral concern beyond humans to encompass individual animals of certain species. Examples of individualists include adherents of the animal liberation and animal rights movements. Individualists accept that all humans have intrinsic value; they argue further that the distinctions between humans and nonhumans are often vague and that many of the qualities valued in humans, such as rationality, complex communication, intelligence, or self-awareness, are shared to some degree by other species. Thus it becomes arbitrary to include all humans but exclude all nonhumans from moral concern. Rather, individualists say that humans have a duty to identify and respect the morally relevant qualities of all species. Animal liberationists define the capacity for pleasure and pain (sentience) as the morally relevant feature to be most considered. Animal rightists value more complex features including desires, self-consciousness, a sense of the future, intentionality, and memories, which they associate with most mammals.

Like anthropocentrists, individualists generally are not directly concerned with the environment; rather, they are concerned with the well-being of individuals of those species they believe deserve moral concern. Individualists would not be concerned about natural resource use unless that resource use involved a direct threat to individuals of a species deserving moral concern, as through hunting or trapping.

### ECOCENTRISM

Ecocentrism is based on the perspective that the natural world has intrinsic value. The term ecocentrism has been applied to both the land ethic and deep ecology. Land ethic advocates believe that moral concern should be extended beyond humans and individual animals, with a major focus on natural units such as ecosystems, watersheds, habitats, and bioregions. In contrast to anthropocentrism and individualism, in which an emphasis often is placed on the rights of individuals deserving moral concern, land ethic advocates emphasize respect for the natural world. Moral concern for the natural world and the environment may be justified by drawing on insights from evolu-

tionary theory and ecology. From evolutionary theory, it is evident that all living things have a common origin and history. From ecology it is argued that all living things are connected and interdependent in the biosphere. These notions of common origin and history and of interdependence in the natural world are viewed as analogous to the human concept of "family." Ecocentrists view humans as members of a very large family comprising all of nature. Family relationships entail not only privilege but also responsibilities for the well-being of the other family members and their environment. Thus, humans are responsible for the natural world.

Impact on land health is an important criterion by which natural resource use is assessed according to a land ethic. Aldo Leopold, one of the first to articulate a land ethic, stated, "A thing is right when it tends to preserve the integrity, stability, and beauty of the biotic community. It is wrong when it tends otherwise." Land health can be assessed by the occurrence of natural ecological functioning; examples include maintenance of soil fertility, absence of erosion, and having all the original species properly represented at a site (biodiversity). Natural resource use should have minimal long-term impact on land health, or even enhance land health, from a land ethic perspective.

Deep ecology also is an ecocentric perspective. However, rather than containing specific ethical rules of behavior, deep ecology often is viewed as an "ecosophy"—an ecological wisdom that calls for a deep questioning of lifestyles and attitudes. While there are no specific ethical rules, several precepts regularly occur among its adherents; these include living lives that are simple in means but rich in ends, honoring and empathizing with all life-forms, and maximizing the diversity of human and nonhuman life. Supporters of deep ecology advocate a lifestyle of minimal impact on the Earth, including the way natural resources are used.

### ECOFEMINISM

A perspective that has emerged relatively recently is ecofeminism. Many ecofeminists believe that a desire for domination is an underlying problem in Western society. Environmental problems are tied to a desire to dominate nature, and this desire is closely linked with the problem of the domination of women and other groups in Western society. Ecofeminists believe that these problems would decline with a transformation in societal attitudes from dualistic, hierarchical, and patriarchal thinking to an enrichment of underlying relationships and a greater focus on egalitarian, nonviolent, and empathetic attitudes. Ecofeminism also calls for a greater integration of nature and culture, reason and feeling, mind and body, and theory and practice. Ecofeminism emphasizes less intrusive and more gentle use of natural resources.

## ENVIRONMENTAL ETHICS IN ESTABLISHED CULTURES AND RELIGIONS

Many westerners have reexamined established cultural and religious perspectives for inspiration and insights in developing an environmental ethic. American Indian cultures often are seen as a source of moral insights on human relationship to the environment. Although it is difficult to generalize for such a large and complex set of cultures, several perspectives appear common to many American Indian groups. These include a strong sense of identity with a specific geographic feature such as a river or mountain. Another common theme is that all the world is inspirited: Everything has being, life, and a self-consciousness. In many cultures, the Earth itself is perceived as a living being deserving respect. Further, most American Indian groups have developed a strong sense of kinship with the natural world. Such views generally have led to relatively harmonious relations with the natural world and have reduced the impact of American Indians on natural resources.

Judaism, Christianity, and Islam share common traditions; each has elements that scholars have drawn upon for insights into environmental responsibility. Some scholars emphasize portions of Genesis in which the world is seen as God's creation, and they interpret that as meaning that humans should be free to use and enjoy the environment; subjugation, use, and development are acceptable, but one must also appreciate and protect the land as belonging to God. Others emphasize the special role of humans as caretakers or stewards. Some scholars draw on themes of Francis of Assisi and advocate close relationships to the natural world. Still others have used the Promised Land story as a metaphor for viewing the natural world as generously given to an undeserving people who have an opportunity to show their gratitude by obedience to God and care for the creation. Additional themes emerging in more recent literature include pantheism and process theology. Attitudes toward the natural world and natural resource use may vary widely within various subgroups of Jews, Christians, and Muslims.

Some Eastern philosophies contain insights for environmental ethics. Daoism includes nature as a part of a great impersonal reality that links all being in an equal-status relationship and encourages a sense of virtuous behavior toward nature. Buddhism, which focuses on reducing human suffering, leads to a gentle and nonaggressive attitude toward nature, including a focus on reducing the desire for material gain.

*Richard G. Botzler*

## FURTHER READING

Armstrong, Susan J., and Richard G. Botzler, eds. *Environmental Ethics: Divergence and Convergence.* 3d ed. Boston: McGraw-Hill, 2003.

Jamieson, Dale. *Ethics and the Environment: An Introduction.* Cambridge, England: Cambridge University Press, 2008.

Jenkins, Willis. *Ecologies of Grace: Environmental Ethics and Christian Theology.* New York: Oxford University Press, 2008.

Kheel, Marti. *Nature Ethics: An Ecofeminist Perspective.* Lanham, Md.: Rowman & Littlefield, 2008.

Minteer, Ben A., ed. *Nature in Common? Environmental Ethics and the Contested Foundations of Environmental Policy.* Philadelphia: Temple University Press, 2009.

Pierce, Christine, and Donald VanDeVeer, eds. *People, Penguins, and Plastic Trees: Basic Issues in Environmental Ethics.* 2d ed. Belmont, Calif.: Wadsworth, 1995.

Pojman, Louis P., ed. *Environmental Ethics: Readings in Theory and Application.* 4th ed. Belmont, Calif.: Thomson/Wadsworth, 2005.

Traer, Robert. *Doing Environmental Ethics.* Boulder, Colo.: Westview Press, 2009.

VanDeVeer, Donald, and Christine Pierce. *The Environmental Ethics and Policy Book: Philosophy, Ecology, Economics.* Belmont, Calif.: Wadsworth, 1994.

Zimmerman, Michael E., et al., eds. *Environmental Philosophy: From Animal Rights to Radical Ecology.* 4th ed. Upper Saddle River, N.J.: Pearson/Prentice Hall, 2005.

SEE ALSO: Conservation; Deep ecology; Environmental degradation, resource exploitation and; Environmental law in the United States; Environmental movement; Leopold, Aldo.

# Environmental impact statement

CATEGORIES: Environment, conservation, and resource management; government and resources

*An environmental impact statement (or environmental impact report) is a document that evaluates the probable environmental effects of any planned program or project that might seriously affect the environment.*

## DEFINITION

In the United States, people have a reasonable expectation that their government will provide a safe and habitable environment. Most assume that government will protect its citizens against polluted water, toxic waste, and excessive radiation. On the other hand, many activities sanctioned by the government to create jobs and sustain economic growth produce damage to the environment. In attempting to satisfy these competing demands, lawmakers must decide how much pollution or environmental damage is acceptable and must consider what obligations need to be imposed on the sources of pollution.

Any agency of the United States government that plans to build facilities such as large-scale residential or commercial construction projects, highways, dams, or power plants must issue an environmental impact statement (EIS), a report that assesses the probable environmental effects of any planned program or project.

## OVERVIEW

The National Environmental Policy Act of 1970 requires that every U.S. government agency issue an environmental impact statement on any project it plans to undertake, regulate, or fund. The purpose of the report is to ensure that any federal agency planning to build facilities consider fully the possible environmental damage that might result from projects under its jurisdiction. A federal agency must also issue an environmental impact statement for any large state, local, or private project that it will regulate or support financially. The Environmental Protection Agency (EPA), established in 1970, reviews all federal environmental impact statements to ensure that they comply with the law.

The particular federal agency under whose jurisdiction a proposed project falls must also consider alternatives to the project under consideration. The agency then decides, basing its decision on established federal guidelines, whether the project is to be pursued or abandoned. For example, before a proposed highway can be built, the appropriate federal agency must study how pollution generated by vehicles that will use this highway will affect the surrounding area. The agency prepares a preliminary environmental impact statement and submits it to federal, state, and local agencies as well as to the general public. Once reactions from these groups are reviewed, the federal agency makes its decision and issues a final environmental impact statement.

Environmental impact statements are intended to make environmental quality a serious factor in federal planning and legislation, but some people have argued that the reports are a hindrance to economic growth or are too vague to provide a strict standard for environmental control. Individuals and groups have used these reports in filing lawsuits to delay or stop projects they consider harmful. For example, the Endangered Species Act, which is designed to protect rare animal and plant species, has been used several times to block projects that might destroy wildlife habitats. Likewise, projects involving the drilling of oil wells and the construction of harbors and power plants have often been legally blocked or delayed based on the content of environmental impact statements.

*Alvin K. Benson*

SEE ALSO: Environmental degradation, resource exploitation and; Environmental ethics; Environmental law in the United States; Environmental Protection Agency; National Environmental Policy Act; Waste management and sewage disposal; Water pollution and water pollution control.

# Environmental law in the United States

CATEGORIES: Environment, conservation, and resource management; government and resources; laws and conventions; social, economic, and political issues

*Environmental regulation in the United States derives primarily from federal and state legislation and is nor-*

*mally implemented by administrative agencies. Environmental law protects human health and property and natural ecosystems from air and water pollution, toxic contamination and exposure, and other harms arising from myriad commercial, industrial, and governmental activities.*

BACKGROUND

Environmental law in the United States comprises a complex patchwork of federal, state, and local statutes and regulations, along with the traditions of common law. Most statutory environmental programs emerged in the second half of the twentieth century. In the 1960's, writings such as Rachel Carson's *Silent Spring* (1962) fueled environmental awareness in the United States; the first Earth Day, celebrated on April 22, 1970, symbolized the birth of a national environmental consciousness. Federal environmental law entered a new era in 1970, when President Richard Nixon created the Environmental Protection Agency and the U.S. Congress passed the National Environmental Policy Act and the 1970 Clean Air Act Amendments. In the next decade, the Federal Water Pollution Control Act Amendments (1972), the Coastal Zone Management Act (1972), the Federal Insecticide, Fungicide, and Rodenticide Act (FIFRA, 1972), the Endangered Species Act (1973), the Toxic Substances Control Act (1976), the Resource Conservation and Recovery Act (1976), the Surface Mining Control and Reclamation Act (1977), and the Comprehensive Environmental Response, Compensation, and Liability Act, or "Superfund" law (1980), formed the body of modern environmental law.

Federal environmental law brings into focus the constitutional and historical relationship between the states and the federal government. Protection of the health and welfare of citizens is generally the province of the states under their police powers. However, because air and water pollution cannot be contained within state borders and because even seemingly local activity such as mining can have interstate effects, Congress deemed it appropriate to impose environmental regulation pursuant to its powers under the "commerce clause" of the U.S. Constitution. Congress also recognized that the establishment of national standards could reduce the potential for a "race of laxity" in which states compete for economic development by offering the most lenient regulatory climate. To preserve the balance of state and federal power where nonfederal lands or activities are in-

volved, federal environmental programs embraced the model of "cooperative federalism" whereby Congress and the relevant federal agencies establish national standards but allow each state to regulate within its borders through a federally approved plan that implements—at a minimum—the federal requirements. State governments may impose additional requirements and enact environmental laws consistent with federal statutory or constitutional provisions; many have done so in programs relating to solid waste control and disposal, groundwater, land use, zoning, and other activities of local concern.

Implementation and enforcement typically occur at the agency level. Administrative agencies promulgate regulations to interpret the law and to handle such matters as permit issuance, inspections, and enforcement. Such agencies are usually empowered to issue cease-and-desist orders, civil penalties, and various remedial requirements. Criminal penalties for known violations of environmental laws are imposed by state and federal courts.

COMMON LAW

Long before the enactment of modern environmental programs, courts were empowered to protect the rights of landowners and the general public in cases brought under the common law of nuisance and related doctrines. Although the laws of individual states vary, courts generally define a "private nuisance" as the intentional and unreasonable interference with the use and enjoyment of private property. A public nuisance is the intentional and unreasonable interference with rights shared by the public.

Nuisance law has not been entirely supplanted by modern environmental statutory programs. Activity that is unregulated or in compliance with existing statutes or regulations may nevertheless be considered harmful and unreasonable in a particular locale and may therefore constitute an actionable nuisance. A wide variety of conditions—air and water pollution, land contamination, and even noise and odors—can be redressed in a lawsuit brought against common-law nuisance. Courts can award money damages to compensate for the devaluation or loss of use and enjoyment of property and for personal injuries, and they can issue injunctive relief to prevent or abate a nuisance. Nuisance law is a mainstay of modern "toxic tort" litigation because it enables courts to grant not only these traditional forms of relief but also innovative remedies such as requiring medical surveillance of persons exposed to toxic chemicals. Other common-law doctrines—including the law of trespass, negligence, strict liability for ultrahazardous activity, and riparian rights—are also used to protect health and property from environmental harm on a case-specific basis.

## FEDERAL PROGRAMS: AIR POLLUTION

The Federal Air Pollution Control Act, or Clean Air Act (CAA), comprises a complex group of interlocking programs designed to address the nationwide problem of air pollution. The basic structure of the CAA emerged in the 1970 amendments to the Air Quality Act of 1967, and the program was substantially revised through amendments enacted in 1977 and 1990.

The CAA charged the Environmental Protection Agency (EPA) with the task of dividing the country into Air Quality Control Regions, establishing air quality criteria based on health and environmental studies, and publishing National Ambient Air Quality Standards (NAAQS) for certain "criteria pollutants" so that safe levels for such pollutants could be set and maintained. The EPA is required to establish criteria if emissions of a pollutant "will cause or contribute to air pollution which may reasonably be anticipated to endanger public welfare" and come from "numerous and diverse mobile or stationary sources." Six pollutants have been included in this category: sulfur dioxide, particulates, carbon monoxide, ozone, nitrogen oxides, and lead. NAAQS for these criteria pollutants include primary standards, set at a level to protect public health with a margin of safety for those who suffer from respiratory ailments, and secondary standards to protect the public welfare in regard to more generalized environmental well-being.

The CAA requires the states to assure compliance with the NAAQS by formulating EPA-approved State Implementation Plans (SIPs). Each state determines whether the air quality in its Air Quality Control Regions meets the NAAQS, designating them "attainment" or "nonattainment" areas for each criteria pollutant. After conducting an inventory of all existing sources, states establish emission limitations for each such source or category of sources to achieve the NAAQS before the relevant statutory deadline. These limitations are included in various permits for new, modified, or existing sources, which provide for various pollution controls in conformity with applicable regulations.

Beginning in 1970, the Clean Air Act was amended periodically to address the problem of nonattainment. In 1977, Congress added strict permitting requirements as well as deadlines for nonattainment areas to ensure that reasonable progress was made toward compliance and required new and modified major sources to offset existing pollutants and to achieve "lowest achievable emission rates." Amendments in 1990 further tightened the permit requirements for nonattainment areas, requiring retrofitting of existing sources in some instances. SIPs must also include a program for prevention of significant deterioration to assure that areas that have better air quality than required for attainment are not allowed to become appreciably worse.

Although the NAAQS are the heart of the Clean Air Act, other programs coexist with and supplement these requirements. Source Performance Standards require all major emitting facilities to employ the "best available control technology." Hazardous air pollutants are governed by National Emissions Standards for Hazardous Air Pollutants (NESHAPs), requiring major sources of listed hazardous pollutants to meet "maximum achievable control technology" standards.

In 1990, Congress responded to the problem of "acid rain" by creating an emissions trading program for sulfur dioxide under which coal-burning power plants accumulate, buy, and sell emissions allowances; thus polluters who can most economically reduce emissions may sell unused allowances to those who need them, while the overall number of annual allowances is steadily reduced by 9 million metric tons from 1980 levels.

There is also a program to protect visibility in national parklands. In 2003, the George W. Bush administration backed the Clean Skies Act, an amendment to the Clean Air Act that proposed to reduce sulfur dioxide, mercury, and nitrogen oxide emissions. The bill stalled in the Senate. In 2009, the Environmental Protection Agency was given the mandate of setting mercury emission standards for oil- and coal-fired power plants by 2011.

Finally, mobile sources such as automobiles and other vehicles are covered by strict provisions in Title II of the Clean Air Act, which requires manufacturers to reduce emission rates drastically in their new models within specified time frames. California, afflicted with the worst automobile pollution in the United States, has stricter requirements for automobile emission reduction and is an exception to the national standards imposed in those provisions. In 2002, the California Air Resources Board instituted stricter emission standards for cars and trucks to encourage the use of and continued development of low-emission vehicles.

## WATER POLLUTION

The Clean Water Act (CWA) took shape in the Federal Water Pollution Control Act Amendments of 1972, and it was revised and strengthened in the 1977, 1982, and 1987 amendments to the CWA. Several proposed amendments have sought to define specifics of the CWA more clearly. These include the Clean Water Protection Act (a House of Representatives bill introduced in 2009), which concerns mountaintop removal mining and the discharge pollutants the procedure produces, and the Clean Water Restoration Act (a Senate bill introduced in 2009), which focuses on the protection of rivers and wetlands. The focal point of the CWA is the National Pollutant Discharge Elimination System (NPDES). An NPDES permit is required for discharges into any "navigable water" from a "point source," defined as "any discernable, confined, and discrete conveyance . . . from which pollutants are or may be discharged." Non-point sources such as agricultural or silvicultural runoff or area pollution do not require NPDES permits and are for the most part unregulated under the program. Stormwater and publicly owned treatment works are subject to special provisions under the Clean Water Act; public water supply systems are regulated separately under the Safe Drinking Water Act (1974) and by some state groundwater statutes.

The NPDES permit system imposes technology-based effluent limitations on dischargers. Effluent levels for toxic and "nonconventional" pollutants are based on "best available technology economically achievable," while conventional nontoxic pollutants must meet "best conventional pollution control technology" standards. To implement these requirements, the EPA promulgates mandatory effluent "guidelines" for each industry, setting forth the pollution reduction required. These, in turn, are incorporated into permit conditions by the permitting authority—usually a state agency—specifying the permissible discharge for each source. Additional New Source Performance Standards may also be required in the permit.

In addition to technology-based effluent limitations, the Clean Water Act provides for water quality standards, which focus on the designated use and quality of the receiving water. State water quality standards existed before the NPDES permit system, but they were ineffective and took a secondary role after the implementation of technology-based emission limitations in the 1972 program. In 1987, the provisions of the Clean Water Act relating to toxic pollutants were substantially strengthened, requiring the EPA and the states to establish and implement strict water quality criteria for listed toxics. Thus permits may include both technology-based and specific water-quality-based effluent limitations depending on the pollutant and the use and quality of the water into which it is discharged.

The Clean Water Act also contains provisions relating to wetlands such as swamps, marshes, bogs, and similar areas. Although the U.S. Army Corps of Engineers has long regulated dredge and fill activities in navigable waters under the Rivers and Harbors Act of 1899, the Clean Water Act expands this by regulating point source discharges of dredge and fill materials into wetlands. Land developers who use fill material to create viable construction sites on swampy soils and others who deposit excavated material into wetlands must obtain permits from the Army Corps of Engineers for such activity, and they may be required to demonstrate the absence of available nonwetland sites or practicable alternatives that would have less adverse impact on aquatic ecosystems.

## HAZARDOUS AND TOXIC POLLUTANTS

A major component of environmental regulation responds to the health hazards associated with toxic and hazardous substances in the environment. Emissions or discharges of such substances are limited in the Clean Water Act and the Clean Air Act. Some toxic substances have been removed from commerce under the Toxic Substances Control Act (TSCA) of 1976, and pesticides must be registered and controlled under the Federal Environmental Pesticide Control Act (FEPCA). Beyond these regulations, however, an increasing awareness of the quantity of hazardous material produced by U.S. industry, combined with the public outcry accompanying the discovery of toxic dumps near residential neighborhoods, caused Congress to create specific programs intended to control hazardous waste disposal and to remove and remediate contaminated areas.

The first of these programs, created in 1976 and substantially amended in 1984 and 1986, was the Resource Conservation and Recovery Act (RCRA). Although RCRA relates to solid waste generally, its key regulatory provisions are found in Subtitle C, which imposes "cradle to grave" controls on hazardous waste. Strict regulatory controls apply when material falls within the definition of "hazardous waste." Some wastes are specifically listed as hazardous, while others may be determined to be so based on the presence of a hazardous characteristic such as toxicity, reactivity, corrosivity, and ignitability. In general, household waste is excluded from the program. There are also separate provisions regulating underground storage tanks such as those used for gasoline and other hazardous liquids.

Under Subtitle C, generators of hazardous wastes are subjected to strict recordkeeping and reporting as well as to specifications for containment and labeling.

*Activists rally in 1985 at the U.S. Capitol for the passage of amendments to Superfund legislation, a group of U.S. laws focused on hazardous waste remediation. (Time & Life Pictures/Getty Images)*

Transporters are required to comply with a manifest system which identifies the waste and assures that it is taken to a permitted facility for treatment, storage, or disposal (TSD). TSD facilities must comply with elaborate permitting requirements, usually issued and enforced by a state agency, including not only technical standards but also financial responsibility and background review. Under the 1984 amendments, land disposal is regarded as the "least favored method for managing hazardous wastes" and is severely restricted. Landfills may be permitted, provided they meet strict technical requirements such as double plastic liners and leachate collection systems. Treatment systems are preferred; they must meet "best demonstrated available technology" standards.

The RCRA regulates hazardous wastes prospectively. Although RCRA provides for injunctive relief to eliminate "imminent and substantial endangerment to the health or environment," Congress addressed in another program, the Comprehensive Environmental Response, Compensation, and Liability Act (CERCLA), the need for cleaning up areas which are already contaminated. Sometimes referred to as "Superfund" because of the trust fund created by the act to fund cleanups, CERCLA is a comprehensive approach to hazardous chemical dump and spill sites. It authorizes the president of the United States, through the EPA, to clean up facilities at which hazardous substances have been released. Hazardous substances subject to the act are identified predominantly by cross-reference to lists established under the Resource Conservation and Recovery Act, Clean Water Act, and Clean Air Act. Petroleum substances not otherwise contaminated or listed as hazardous are exempted from the purview of the act. CERCLA requires persons in charge of certain facilities to report releases of hazardous substances, subject to strict penalties for failure to do so. It also created a system of listing hazardous sites, a National Contingency Plan (NCP), setting forth the protocols and standards of remedial investigation, feasibility study, removal and long-term remediation, and a National Priorities List listing the cleanup sites in order of priority.

Under CERCLA, hazardous substance removal and site remediation is accomplished in two ways: first, the EPA can issue an order requiring potentially responsible parties (PRPs) to clean up a site; alternatively, the EPA can clean up the site itself and bring a cost recovery action against the PRPs for response costs and natural resource damages. Private parties who have incurred response costs may also seek reimbursement. CERCLA's cost recovery provisions impose "strict liability"—without any required showing of fault—upon present and past owners and operators of facilities from which there has been a release or threatened release of hazardous substances, upon those who "arranged for disposal," and upon transporters who took part in site selection. Although cost recovery must be consistent with the National Contingency Plan, there are only a few very limited defenses to liability, and the act's provisions tend to encourage voluntary settlements and cleanups. Nevertheless, litigation often occurs among PRPs who are jointly and severally liable for the full amount but may apportion their liability in actions for contribution. In 2002, the Small Business Liability Relief and Brownfields Revitalization Act amended CERCLA. Brownfields are derelict commercial or industrial complexes that can be revitalized for new uses. The amendment provides funds for the cleanup of these areas.

### ENDANGERED SPECIES

The Endangered Species Act (1973) was elevated to national debate by a small fish, the snail darter, the threatened demise of which caused the U.S. Supreme Court to cease construction of the Tellico Dam on the Little Tennessee River. In *Tennessee Valley Authority v. Hill* (1978) the Court held that there are no exceptions to the Endangered Species Act command that all federal agencies ensure that actions authorized, funded, or carried out by them do not jeopardize the continued existence of an endangered or threatened species or result in the destruction or modification of habitat of such species. Congress amended the statute in 1978 to provide some flexibility, but the prohibitions of the Endangered Species Act remain strong. The act prohibits the importation, exportation, and "taking" of endangered species; the Department of the Interior, which administers the Endangered Species Act, has defined "taking" not only to prohibit such predatory activities as hunting, pursuing, shooting, wounding, killing, trapping, or capturing endangered species but also to outlaw harming such species by "significant habitat modification or degradation where it actually kills or injures wildlife by significantly impairing essential behavioral patterns, including breeding, feeding, or sheltering." A narrow exception is made for "incidental taking" of species in pursuit of otherwise lawful activity. Since its enactment, the Endangered Species Act has remained a contentious political issue; presidential administrations have often differed substantially on their stances on this issue. The Reagan administration attempted to limit protective status for certain species, a policy that hampered the enforcement of the act and caused more than a decade of legal battles that resulted in the expansion of the designation of critical habitat. The Clinton administration enacted the Safe Harbor agreement that encouraged landowners to make their territories friendlier to endangered species. Nearly fifty species previously considered endangered have been removed from the protection of the Endangered Species Act, an indication that the act has been generally successful.

### NATIONAL ENVIRONMENTAL POLICY ACT

The National Environmental Policy Act (NEPA), enacted in 1970, was designed to force federal decision makers to take a "hard look" at the environmental consequences of their actions. NEPA provides that "all federal agencies shall include in any recommendation or report on any proposal for legislation or other major federal action significantly affecting the quality of the human environment a detailed statement . . . on environmental impact . . . any adverse effects which cannot be avoided . . . alternatives to the proposed action," and other considerations. Environmental impact statements (EISs), conforming to regulations promulgated by the Counsel on Environmental Quality, may be required for a variety of governmental activities—including the construction of airports, dams, and highways; the issuance of federal licenses or permits; and decisions regarding the management and use of federal lands and resources. NEPA is regarded as a procedural statute because it imposes no substantive requirements. Despite much debate over its effectiveness as a tool to protect the environment, it has been emulated by some state environmental policy acts and in international law as well.

*Joshua I. Barrett*

### FURTHER READING

Ashford, Nicholas A., and Charles C. Caldart. *Environmental Law, Policy, and Economics: Reclaiming the Environmental Agenda.* Cambridge, Mass.: MIT Press, 2008.

Brooks, Karl Boyd. *Before Earth Day: The Origins of American Environmental Law, 1945-1970.* Lawrence: University Press of Kansas, 2009.

Buck, Susan J. *Understanding Environmental Administration and Law*. 3d ed. Washington, D.C.: Island Press, 2006.

Findley, Roger W., and Daniel A. Farber. *Environmental Law in a Nutshell*. 7th ed. St. Paul, Minn.: Thomson/West, 2008.

Kubasek, Nancy K., and Gary S. Silverman. *Environmental Law*. 6th ed. Upper Saddle River, N.J.: Pearson Prentice Hall, 2008.

Manheim, Frank T. *The Conflict over Environmental Regulation in the United States: Origins, Outcomes, and Comparisons with the EU and Other Regions*. New York: Springer, 2009.

Pearson, Eric. *Environmental and Natural Resources Law*. 3d ed. Newark, N.J.: LexisNexis Matthew Bender, 2008.

Schnaiberg, Allan, and Kenneth Alan Gould. *Environment and Society: The Enduring Conflict*. New York: St. Martin's Press, 1994. Reprint. Caldwell, N.J.: Blackburn Press, 2000.

Vietzen, Laurel A. *Practical Environmental Law*. New York: Aspen, 2008.

Weinberg, Philip, and Kevin A. Reilly. *Understanding Environmental Law*. 2d ed. Newark N.J.: LexisNexis Matthew Bender, 2008.

### WEB SITE

WildLaw: A Nonprofit Environmental Law Firm
Statutes, Regulation, and Help
http://www.wildlaw.org/Eco-Laws/start.html

SEE ALSO: Clean Air Act; Clean Water Act; Endangered Species Act; Environment and Natural Resources Division; Environmental impact statement; Environmental Protection Agency; National Environmental Policy Act; Superfund legislation and cleanup activities; Takings law and eminent domain.


# Environmental movement

CATEGORY: Historical events and movements

*In the United States, the environmental movement can be divided a number of distinct periods of development, each of which is noteworthy for the level of activism and the impact the movement has had on natural resource policy.*

### BACKGROUND

Although a handful of environmental organizations were founded in the late nineteenth and early twentieth centuries, they were not influential enough to comprise a social movement. For example, the Sierra Club (founded in 1892), the National Audubon Society (1905), and the National Parks Association (1919, now the National Parks Conservation Association) had specific political agendas, and their memberships were relatively small. The environmental movement did not begin to coalesce until after World War II, with public concern about the management of resources and growing apprehension about pollution.

### THE AGE OF ECOLOGY

The 1960's have been called the age of ecology because the decade brought conflict between those who sought to enhance postwar industrial growth and those who sought government regulation over the by-products of growth—smog in cities such as Los Angeles and London, water pollution in virtually every major urban area, and environmental crises such as the oil spill off the coast of Santa Barbara, California, which received extensive media coverage in 1969.

Public awareness of the magnitude of environmental degradation was magnified by the work of two authors. Rachel Carson's exposé on the dangers of pesticides, *Silent Spring* (1962), and Paul Ehrlich's warnings about population growth in *The Population Bomb* (1968) lent credence to the groups that were just beginning to have an impact on the policy-making process.

During the 1960's, the environmental movement began to have an impact on the U.S. Congress, which realized that environmental problems were rapidly becoming a salient political issue. Most of the hallmark pieces of 1960's legislation, such as the Clean Air Act (1963), Clean Water Act (1965), Endangered Species Conservation Act (1966), and National Environmental Policy Act (1970), can be traced directly to one or more of the environmental groups pushing for their passage.

The decade also marked a tremendous expansion in the number of environmental groups and political strategies. The Environmental Defense Fund (founded in 1967), for example, used litigation as a powerful tool, while the more venerable organizations such as the Sierra Club focused on public education. From 1952 to 1969, the Sierra Club's membership grew tenfold, while the Wilderness Society's membership grew from twelve thousand in 1960 to fifty-four thousand in 1970.

At the same time, new organizations such as the African Wildlife Foundation (1961) and the World Wildlife Fund (1961, now the World Wide Fund for Nature) began to broaden their approach to include environmental issues of global concern. While the majority of groups were dedicated to preserving wildlife and their habitats, there also began to be a parallel growth of organizations in Europe that were dealing with pollution in their own regions. These groups became the core of what later became an international environmental movement.

### EARTH DAYS AND CRISES

If one event could be said to have galvanized the environmental movement, it would be the observance of Earth Day on April 22, 1970. An estimated twenty million Americans participated in events ranging from protests and demonstrations to educational seminars to call attention to the declining health of the environment. That year also was the beginning of an exceptional period of development for new groups, including Friends of the Earth, the League of Conservation Voters, the Natural Resources Defense Council, and the Center for Science in the Public Interest. A year later, the American branch of Greenpeace was founded, along with the environmental watchdog organization Public Citizen.

Although public opinion polls showed that Americans were deeply concerned about the environment during the period immediately before and after Earth Day 1970, that interest was partially replaced over the following fifteen years by the Vietnam War, the 1973 Arab oil embargo, and a declining economy. The environmental movement seemed to lose much of its early momentum as both legislators and the public turned to other issues. Although Congress enacted several significant pieces of legislation, such as the Marine Mammal Protection Act (1972) and the Toxic Substances Control Act (1976), by 1980 the pace of legislative activity had slowed considerably—and with it the growth of the environmental movement.

From 1970 to 1990, the environ-

mental movement's ebb and flow seemed tied to crisis or controversy. When an accident at the Three Mile Island nuclear power plant near Harrisburg, Pennsylvania, triggered a meltdown, environmental groups opposed to nuclear power gained prominence. Groups associated with fighting toxic waste gained new members in 1978 when the media reported that homes and a school at Love Canal, New York, had been built in an area previously used as a toxic dumping ground by a chemical company. A deadly leak of poisonous gas at a Union Carbide plant in Bhopal, India, in 1984, led to legislative initiatives in the United States, such as the reauthorization of the Comprehensive Environmental Response, Compensation, and Liability Act, better known as Superfund. Pressure by the environmental movement's leaders led Congress to investigate whether a Bhopal-type incident could occur at a similar Union Carbide facility in Institute, West Virginia.

### THE REAGAN AND CLINTON ERAS

In one sense, the environmental movement's lowest ebb may have been during the administration of President Ronald Reagan, whose policies of deregulation, budget and personnel cuts, and conservative political appointments scaled back the implementation and enforcement of the prior decades' environmental laws. However, it also galvanized the movement, creating a common enemy for environmentalists to rally against. Through their lobbying efforts, they forced the president to fire his secretary of the interior,

*Greenpeace activists in France protest to call attention to the danger of radioactive waste.* (AFP/Getty Images)

James G. Watt, and the head of the Environmental Protection Agency, Anne M. Burford.

The most noteworthy trend within the environmental movement in the early 1990's was the globalization of issues and participants. The 1992 Earth Summit in Rio de Janeiro brought together the largest group of environmental organizations ever assembled and reiterated the need to view issues in global, rather than local, terms. It also forced groups to focus their attention on a wide spectrum of emerging environmental issues, such as global climate change and transboundary pollution, and highlighted disputes over whether developed nations should help pay for the cleanup of degraded environments (like those of the former Soviet Union) or for new pollution control technology in developing countries.

### The Bush Era: Rollbacks, Repudiation, and Redemption

As the twenty-first century commenced, so too did the presidency of George W. Bush. For environmentalists, the eight Bush years were characterized by the "three R's": rollbacks, repudiation, and redemption. Environmentalists witnessed rollback of environmental legislation and regulations of the past, repudiation of scientific findings on global warming in particular, and a final act of redemption—the designation of nearly 520,000 square kilometers of the Pacific Ocean and all of the marine life within as national monuments a few days before Bush left office. The rollbacks occurred on several fronts: Clean Water Act and Clean Air Act tampering; the curtailing of funds for clean-up programs at hazardous waste sites; the weakening of the Endangered Species Act and removal of animals, such as grizzly bears, from the list of protected species; endorsement of commercial whaling, which causes severe depletion rates because of technologically sophisticated hunting and harvesting apparatuses; the opening of protected lands to mining, logging, and oil and gas drilling; and the elimination of obstacles to mountaintop removal mining. Status quo economics, especially in the energy industry, received preference over support for research and development for green alternatives to the use of finite fossil fuels.

The repudiation of scientific findings on global warming and the reluctance to sponsor studies of its effects on animal species proved demoralizing to science professionals in several federal agencies. The Bush administration was accused of ignoring or suppressing credible scientific studies on numerous environment issues.

### Environmental Nongovernmental Organizations (NGOs)

The environmental problems of the Bush era were balanced by two counterweights. While the environmental movement in the United States went on the defensive during the first decade of the twenty-first century, it also inspired the international upsurge of environmental nongovernmental organizations (NGOs). The upsurge in NGOs became an international phenomenon, occurring in many countries, both rich and poor, democratic and despotic. Dedicated groups of citizen activists allied with scientific experts emerged to focus attention on local, national, and global environmental concerns. Impressive NGO fund-raising capabilities, aided by the Internet, meant independently sponsored scientific research, educational initiatives, the monitoring of hazardous conditions, and remediation of contaminated sites. Such activities often supplemented government projects or acted in place of them in developing nations. Some NGOs, like Greenpeace or the World Wide Fund for Nature, have supranational status, but others, such as China's Friends of Nature or Brazil's SOS Mata Atlântica (SOS Atlantic Forest), exist with localized mandates. Over time, countless efforts to amend environmental damage caused by humans on both small and grand scales created a climate of awareness that Earth was in trouble. In turn, this created a climate of receptivity for advisories issued about global warming and the need for worldwide cooperation to reverse it.

### Al Gore and the Environmental Movement

The power of the individual to make a difference in the world still exists. Before Al Gore was a citizen soldier in Vietnam, journalist, businessperson, senator, or U.S. vice president, he was an environmentalist. In 1967, he enrolled in a life-changing course called "climate science" at Harvard University. During that class, he learned about the seriousness of global warming and the need for action to halt it. As a legislator in Congress for many years, he focused on the need for the United States to redirect its dependence on fossil fuels to renewable energy options. The scientific community had convincingly established that fossil fuel emissions from automobiles and factory smokestacks raised carbon dioxide levels with dire planetary consequences.

As his political career waned, Gore became an international spokesman for the twin concerns of global warming and the need for green energy relief. Gore used his ability to explain complex scientific issues to the general public in the documentary film *An Inconvenient Truth* (2006). The film garnered an Academy Award for Best Documentary Feature in 2007. A companion book entitled *An Inconvenient Truth: The Planetary Emergency of Global Warming and What We Can Do About It* (2006) became a best seller. However, the greatest recognition of his efforts came in 2007. Gore, along with the Intergovernmental Panel on Climate Change, was awarded the Nobel Peace Prize.

### THE KYOTO PROTOCOL AND BEYOND

All of these strands of human endeavor—efforts to maintain the status quo and actively stave off challenges to it, or calls for sweeping, planetary change—converge in the Kyoto Protocol. The United Nations Framework Convention on Climate Change (UNFCCC) began the process of voluntary emission reduction in 1992. All of the accords and protocols that succeeded it led to the Kyoto Protocol, calling for a mandatory 55 percent global reduction of carbon dioxide based on 1990 levels by all signatories. The United States signed the treaty in 1997 but agreed to only a 6 percent reduction at the time; Bush refused to ratify the treaty in 2001. A nineteenth century business model based on short-term profit margins that once brought the United States unrivaled prosperity and world hegemony bumped up against twenty-first century reality, in which global interdependence holds sway and all life is threatened by self-indulgence. Despite Bush's contrarian approach to the environment, several states and cities in the United States have enacted Kyoto-inspired provisions to circumvent the last stand of the guardians of old energy. In the meantime, the Kyoto Protocol took effect on February 16, 2005.

As the Bush administration came to an end and a new Democratic president, Barack Obama, took office in 2009, scientific evidence for human contributions to climate change were mounting and forming a consensus in the minds of many—scientists and the public alike—that international action must be taken to avert (or at least prepare for) the more catastrophic effects of global warming. However, the contentiousness surrounding international cooperation was highlighted in December, 2009, as representatives of 193 nations met in Copenhagen, Denmark, to decide whether to extend or replace the Kyoto Protocol, due to expire in 2012. Kyoto had obligated only signatory developed (industrialized) nations to meet carbon emissions standards. Some representatives of developing and poorer nations at Copenhagen strongly objected to the new call for all nations to curb emissions, pointing out that the industrialized nations (particularly the United States), with their disproportionately high emissions, were more responsible for climate change and should bear the brunt of its mitigation. Al Gore urged participants to reach an agreement, and the secretary-general of the North Atlantic Treaty Organization (NATO), Anders Fogh Rasmussen, warned that climate change could lead to crop failure and, in turn, "rebellions which eventually could fuel radical movements, extremism and terrorism."

*Jacqueline Vaughn Switzer, updated by JoEllen Broome*

### FURTHER READING

Dewey, Scott Hamilton. *Don't Breathe the Air: Air Pollution and U.S. Environmental Politics, 1945-1970*. College Station: Texas A&M University Press, 2000.

Dowie, Mark. *Losing Ground: American Environmentalism at the Close of the Twentieth Century*. Cambridge: Massachusetts Institute of Technology Press, 1995.

Dunlap, Riley E., and Angela G. Mertig, eds. *American Environmentalism: The U.S. Environmental Movement, 1970-1990*. Philadelphia: Taylor & Francis, 1992.

Egan, Michael, and Jeff Crane, eds. *Natural Protest: Essays on the History of American Environmentalism*. New York: Routledge, 2009.

Kline, Benjamin. *First Along the River: A Brief History of the U.S. Environmental Movement*. 3d ed. Lanham, Md.: Rowman & Littlefield, 2007.

Lytle, Mark Hamilton. *The Gentle Subversive: Rachel Carson, "Silent Spring," and the Rise of the Environmental Movement*. New York: Oxford University Press, 2007.

Merchant, Carolyn. *The Columbia Guide to American Environmental History*. New York: Columbia University Press, 2002.

Mongillo, John, and Linda Zierdt-Warshaw. *Encyclopedia of Environmental Science*. Phoenix, Ariz.: Oryx Press, 2000.

Nash, Roderick Frazier, ed. *American Environmentalism: Readings in Conservation History*. 3d ed. New York: McGraw-Hill, 1990.

Philippon, Daniel J. *Conserving Words: How American Nature Writers Shaped the Environmental Movement*. Athens: University of Georgia Press, 2004.

Rome, Adam. *The Bulldozer in the Countryside: Suburban*

*Sprawl and the Rise of American Environmentalism.* New York: Cambridge University Press, 2001.

Shabecoff, Philip. *A Fierce Green Fire: The American Environmental Movement.* Rev. ed. Washington, D.C.: Island Press, 2003.

Victor, David G. *The Collapse of the Kyoto Protocol and the Struggle to Slow Global Warming.* Princeton, N.J.: Princeton University Press, 2001.

WEB SITE

ECOLOGY HALL OF FAME
Environmental Movement Timeline
http://www.ecotopia.org/ehof/timeline.html

SEE ALSO: Climate Change and Sustainable Energy Act; Conservation; Conservation International; Earth Summit; Endangered species; Environmental ethics; Friends of the Earth International; Gore, Al; Greenpeace; Intergovernmental Panel on Climate Change; Kyoto Protocol; Montreal Protocol; National Audubon Society; Natural Resources Defense Council; Sierra Club; United Nations climate change conferences; United Nations Convention on Long-Range Transboundary Air Pollution; World Wide Fund for Nature.

# Environmental Protection Agency

CATEGORY: Organizations, agencies, and programs
DATE: Established 1970

*The U.S. Environmental Protection Agency is charged with administering various environmental regulatory and distributive programs in the United States as well as conducting environmental research activities.*

BACKGROUND
From the inception of the Environmental Protection Agency (EPA) in 1970, the organization has been beset by differing conceptions of its mission as the primary U.S. government environmental regulatory agency. The EPA expanded during the 1970's but came under severe attack in the 1980's, particularly during Anne Gorsuch's tenure as director. The agency was revitalized and its mission expanded in the late 1980's and early 1990's, only to suffer setbacks during the second Bush administration in the early twenty-first century. The EPA aims to protect the health of the human population by reducing the pollution of the environment. It has attempted to achieve this goal primarily through enforcing congressional legislation and issuing regulations.

ORGANIZATION AND MISSION
The EPA is headed by a director appointed by the president and has its central headquarters in Washington, D.C. It also has ten regional offices, each headed by a regional administrator. Although regional offices deal with all manner of environmental issues, national offices, each with a commissioner as head, deal with specific issues. These offices include the Air Pollution Control Office, the Pesticide Office, the Radiation Office, and the Solid Waste Office. In addition, the Council on Environmental Quality coordinates federal and international environmental efforts. This group of three is appointed by the president and works closely with, though is independent of, the EPA. In some cases the implementation of the EPA's regulatory burden is entrusted to state environmental agencies. The major regulatory tasks assigned to the agency include air quality, water quality, disposal of hazardous and radioactive wastes, the regulation of chemicals (including pesticides), and the setting of noise levels for construction equipment, transportation equipment, motors, and electronic equipment. Legislation that the EPA is charged with implementing includes the Federal Insecticide, Fungicide, and Rodenticide Act (1947), the Clean Air Act (1963), the Clean Water Act (1965), the Endangered Species Act (1973), the Resource Conservation and Recovery Act (1976), the Toxic Substances Act (1976), the Comprehensive Environmental Response, Compensation, and Liability Act ("Superfunds," 1980), and the Energy Policy Act (2005).

The EPA suffers from overload and has found implementing its various mandates difficult and in some cases impossible. In part this inability stems from congressional action. Congress has often specified unrealistic deadlines with various statutory penalties attached should the EPA not comply and given detailed management instructions for action. In addition, some members of Congress have used environmental legislation (for example, Superfund) as political pork barrels so that the EPA is not always able to allocate its funds in the most efficient fashion. In addition, as Marc Landy, Marc Roberts, and Stephen Thomas point out in *The Environmental Protection Agency: Asking the Wrong Questions from Nixon to Clinton* (1994), the

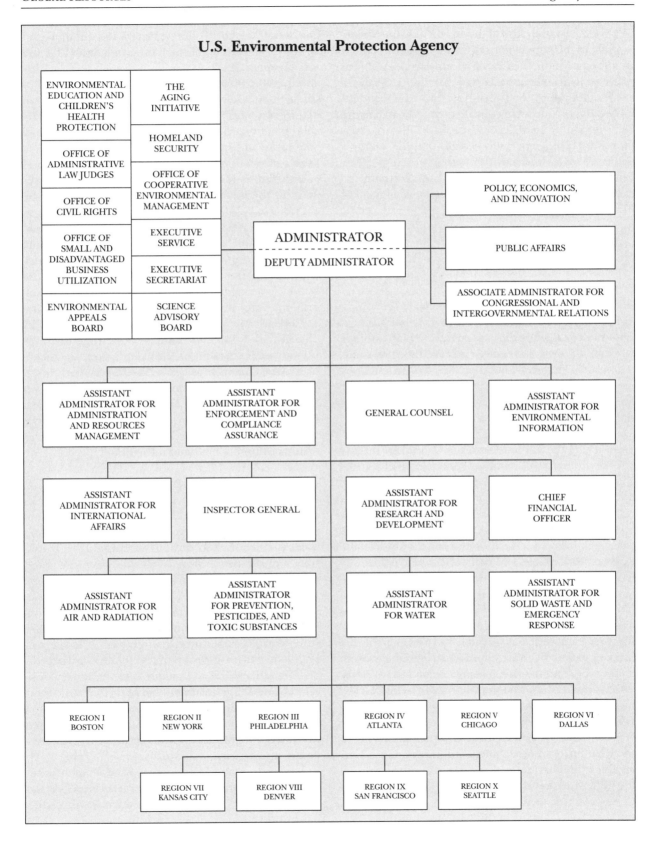

EPA itself has often "asked the wrong questions" concerning its mission. By concentrating on enforcement from its inception, the EPA has not always been able to establish its scientific credentials in order to lend scientific credibility to its actions. The EPA has also missed opportunities to educate the public regarding environmental issues, and therefore citizens often have unrealistic expectations regarding the agency's ability to deal with environmental problems. The leadership of the EPA has not always been attentive to the need to develop a strategic perspective in dealing with environmental issues, a failing that is fostered by leaving conceptual ambiguities unresolved. At times factionalism has also detracted from the accomplishment of the EPA's mission.

### THE IMPACT OF POLITICS

Public support for the EPA's mission has shifted since its founding in 1970. In the early 1970's, many Americans thought that the EPA was not moving fast enough to clean up environmental problems. By 1980, some people had begun to question the cost of environmental regulation, saying that the EPA had become too stringent. During the 1990's public opinion shifted in the direction of a more supportive stance for environmental regulation. This stance continued even during the administration of George W. Bush.

One difficulty that continues to beset the EPA is the changing national political climate. Many aspects of the organization's mission are highly charged politically. Therefore, the agendas of each presidential administration have affected the ability of the agency to carry out its mission. Until the presidency of Ronald Reagan (1981-1989), presidents and much of the public demanded tough enforcement of environmental laws. At times, the EPA had difficulty keeping up with public opinion in trying to clean up various environmental problems. During the Reagan administration the approach shifted as Gorsuch and Secretary of the Interior James G. Watt opposed stringent environmental regulation, often placing agency staff at odds with its leadership. The presidency of George H. W. Bush turned slightly to tough environmental regulation. The Clinton administration (1993-2000) heightened this tough stance. Carol M. Browner, who headed the EPA during much of the Clinton presidency, was an able administrator with a clear idea of the role of the EPA. Also, she enjoyed support within the agency.

The election of George W. Bush in 2000 marked a return to presidential hostility to much of the EPA's mission. Christine Todd Whitman, the onetime governor of New Jersey, became the head of the EPA and tried to maintain several initiatives, such as regulating mountaintop removal in the coal fields of West Virginia. Soon after, she was politically marginalized and was forced out in 2003 by opponents of environmental regulation. Vice President Dick Cheney played an important role in trying to base environmental regulation in economic reasoning favorable to business rather than in scientific reasoning.

With the election of Barack Obama in 2008, the presidential philosophy regarding the EPA moved in the opposite direction of the Bush administration. Lisa P. Jackson, the head of the EPA in the Obama administration, came to the post with a strong environmental record. The agency shifted back to using scientific reasoning in tandem with economic considerations in its decision-making processes.

Related to the mission challenges imposed by changing political climates has been a high turnover rate in the leadership of the agency. From its inception to the Obama presidency, the EPA has had eleven different administrators, most of whom have served for short periods of time. Browner served the longest, from 1993 to 2001, but several of the other administrators served for only two years. Thus, maintaining leadership continuity has been difficult.

### PUBLIC HEALTH AND THE EPA

Protecting the public's health is at the core of EPA's mission. Regulating human contact with and possible ingestion of dangerous pesticides and improving water quality are two obvious examples of this mission. Cancer prevention, while not always a stated goal, has been one of the key concerns of the agency. In the late 1970's, the EPA, the Food and Drug Administration, the Occupational Safety and Health Administration, and the Consumer Product Safety Commission worked together through the Interagency Regulatory Liaison Group to formulate standards for dealing with chemicals that might cause cancer. However, the resulting document did not enunciate a clear standard of risk assessment, nor did it establish a sound level of cancer risk. It also failed as an attempt to educate the public concerning cancer risks and scientific uncertainty.

By contrast, the EPA's efforts at regulating water and air pollution have led to several successes. Water quality has improved in the United States. Air quality has improved in some areas. In both cases the EPA had a clear mandate that it was able to implement and, therefore, was more easily able to achieve its goals.

The risk of cancer also underlay the public controversy concerning the implementation of Superfund legislation. Part of the problem with Superfund was Congress's inability to set cleanup priorities or cleanup levels for Superfund sites. The EPA was deficient in providing Congress with the detailed information necessary to make these decisions. Because Superfund was conceptually deficient, the EPA often had to react to what the public perceived as crisis situations, such as the Times Beach, Missouri, dioxin cleanup in the early 1980's. Such actions were not always based on reliable research and often displayed an inability to educate the public regarding environmental risk.

IMPACT ON RESOURCE USE
Although public health concerns have been the stated rationale for much of the EPA's actions, further concerns have been the protection of the environment and resource conservation. Enhancing water quality, for example, has obvious benefits for aquatic life. Controlling the negative impact of pesticides has an impact from the bottom to the top of the food chain. The threat of acid deposition to forest products and water quality in some regions of the country is substantial; the EPA's efforts to establish air-quality standards under the 1990 revisions of the Clean Air Act attempted to deal with this issue. Indirectly, the EPA's regulations dealing with improving automobile mileage have decreased the consumption of both steel and oil. The question of mileage requirements remains a hotly debated issue, as the EPA has expanded its emphasis to encourage innovative types of automobiles as a means of decreasing pollution. The goal of much of the EPA's regulatory efforts has been waste reduction. By its very nature, waste reduction lowers the amount of natural resources consumed by the economy.

The 1984 revisions of the Resource Conservation and Recovery Act (RCRA) directed the EPA to advocate conservation as a means of dealing with hazardous materials. RCRA stated that the placement of hazardous wastes in landfills was the least favored option in dealing with these materials. The most favored approach was for industry to generate less of the material, thus practicing resource conservation. In the early 1990's, many industries continued to generate large amounts of hazardous wastes, although some industries were beginning to find substitutes for hazardous materials. In the early twenty-first century, disposal of these wastes continued to be a problem that was further complicated by the efforts of some polluters to ship their wastes abroad.

In all likelihood the EPA will continue to be beset by political changes. Because its regulatory power touches many aspects of American life, various groups will continue to try to influence EPA policy directly and indirectly. Many of the EPA's decisions have economic impacts, and the agency faces continual challenges from, on one hand, groups and individuals who desire economic growth and, on the other hand, those who see environmental protection as more important than short-term economic gain.

In addition to continuing to deal with the environmental issues of the past, the EPA will be challenged by evolving issues. One of the concerns has to do with environmental equity: Are environmental hazards being imposed on the less-advantaged in American society? The EPA will need to balance questions of environmental protection and social justice in its decisions.

Part of the EPA's mission overlaps with that of other agencies in regard to climate change and its impact. EPA regulators have become increasingly concerned with the issue of carbon dioxide and other greenhouse-gas emissions. These issues are related to sustainable development and the use of natural resources, an issue that is at the heart of the American environmental movement. The EPA will continue to coordinate with other agencies and cabinet departments that have oversight roles for natural resource management. Because many resource questions, such as global warming, affect more than the United States, the EPA will need to develop better means for coordinating its actions with the world community.

*John M. Theilmann*

FURTHER READING
Collin, Robert W. *The Environmental Protection Agency: Cleaning Up America's Act.* Westport, Conn.: Greenwood Press, 2006.

DeLong, James V. *Out of Bounds, out of Control: Regulatory Enforcement at the EPA.* Washington, D.C.: Cato Institute, 2002.

Jasper, Margaret C. "The Environmental Protection Agency." In *Environmental Law.* 2d ed. Dobbs Ferry, N.Y.: Oceana, 2002.

Klyza, Christopher McGrory, and David J. Sousa. *American Environmental Policy, 1990-2006: Beyond Gridlock.* Cambridge, Mass.: MIT Press, 2008.

Landy, Marc Karnis, Marc J. Roberts, and Stephen R. Thomas. *The Environmental Protection Agency: Asking the Wrong Questions from Nixon to Clinton.* New York: Oxford University Press, 1994.

McMahon, Robert. *The Environmental Protection Agency: Structuring Motivation in a Green Bureaucracy— the Conflict Between Regulatory Style and Cultural Identity.* Portland, Oreg.: Sussex Academic Press, 2006.

Portney, Paul R., and Robert N. Stavins, eds. *Public Policies for Environmental Protection.* 2d ed. Washington, D.C.: Resources for the Future, 2000.

Rosenbaum, Walter A. *Environmental Politics and Policy.* 7th ed. Washington, D.C.: CQ Press, 2008.

Samuel, Peter. *Lead Astray: Inside an EPA Superfund Disaster.* San Francisco: Pacific Research Institute, 2002.

Yeager, Peter Cleary. *The Limits of Law: The Public Regulation of Private Pollution.* New York: Cambridge University Press, 1991.

WEB SITE

U.S. ENVIRONMENTAL PROTECTION AGENCY
http://www.epa.gov

SEE ALSO: Carbon; Clean Air Act; Clean Water Act; Climate Change and Sustainable Energy Act; Ecosystem services; Endangered species; Environment and Natural Resources Division; Environmental impact statement; Environmental law in the United States; Hazardous waste disposal; National Environmental Policy Act; Superfund legislation and cleanup activities; United Nations Convention on Long-Range Transboundary Air Pollution; Watt, James.

# Erosion and erosion control

CATEGORY: Environment, conservation, and resource management

*Erosion is the gradual wearing away of the land surface by natural agents of water, wind, and ice. Eroded sediments are a major water pollutant. The land is degraded because the soil that remains is of lower productivity, and the sediment may damage crops or aquatic environments. Therefore, the control of erosion is an important soil conservation and water quality protection practice.*

BACKGROUND

Erosion is a natural process in which water, wind, and ice remove soil particles from the land surface and redeposit them somewhere else. Sediment pollution is the water pollutant comprising the largest volume or mass. Erosion also causes the soil to be less productive because the remaining soil is more coarsely textured and of lower fertility. Nutrients and pesticides can be released from eroded sediments into streams and lakes.

There are three erosion processes: detachment, transportation, and deposition. Detachment is the removal of soil particles from the soil mass. Transportation carries detached particles away from the soil mass. The distance can be a few centimeters or hundreds of kilometers. After the soil is transported, the particles are then redeposited somewhere else (deposition).

CLASSIFICATION OF EROSION

Erosion can be classified in a number of ways. Geological erosion is the natural, slow rate of erosion that occurs when the land is protected by its native vegetation. Rates are in the range of grams to a few kilograms per hectare per year. This kind of erosion is responsible for many important present-day land formations. Accelerated erosion is the rapid erosion that occurs when the native vegetation is removed. These rates are in the range of metric tons per hectare per year.

The two most important agents of accelerated erosion are water and wind. Kinds of water erosion are raindrop splash, sheet, rill, and gully erosion. Raindrop splash occurs when raindrops strike soil particles and dislodge them from the rest of the soil mass. Falling raindrops have considerable kinetic energy and can easily dislodge particles from bare soils. In sheet erosion a thin layer of soil is removed fairly uniformly across the land surface. Rill erosion occurs when small channels (rills) form in the soil. These rills are usually parallel to one another, are narrow and shallow, and can be easily removed by ordinary tillage and cultivation practices. Rill erosion is responsible for the greatest quantities of soil loss. Gully erosion occurs when deep, wide channels form that cannot be removed by ordinary tillage and cultivation practices.

*Following a June, 2008, flood, this cornfield in Indiana suffered significant erosion.* (AP/Wide World Photos)

It is the most spectacular because the gullies are easily seen.

Wind erosion is classified according to the way the soil particles are transported. Surface creep is a rolling of large particles across the surface. Saltation is a bouncing of intermediate-sized particles and is responsible for the largest amount of erosion by wind. Suspension occurs when small particles are picked up by the wind and carried long distances. It is the most spectacular because the resulting dust cloud is easily seen.

Erosion damage occurs both on-site and off-site. On-site damage occurs because the eroded land is degraded by the removal of the most productive parts of the soil. The eroded parts are usually finer textured and higher in organic matter than the remaining parts. The soil that is left behind is usually coarser textured. Off-site damage occurs because the transported soil causes damage somewhere else. Examples are smothered crops, decreased storage of drinking water reservoirs, and the filling in of harbors. Sediment also drastically alters the aquatic life of rivers

and lakes. The costs for correcting some of these off-site effects are usually borne by society.

### EROSION CONTROL

Strategies for erosion control involve preventing detachment or encouraging deposition before the soil travels very far. The most effective and cheapest methods of erosion control are to keep the soil in place and reduce water runoff. Erosion control methods may be divided into cultural practices and mechanical control. Cultural practices include cropping rotations, tillage methods, and residue management. Mechanical control includes terraces, sediment control basins, and silt fences. A guiding principle in erosion control is to keep the soil covered, either with growing vegetation or with the remains of vegetation in the form of mulch. Another principle is to shorten the slope length. Reducing the steepness of a slope is not practical.

Erosion control in farming includes contouring, whereby all tillage, planting, and harvesting operations are done across the slope instead of up and down the slope. This practice is most effective for gentle slopes, with a gradient of between 2 and 6 percent. Strip cropping is alternately planting a strip of a row crop such as corn, soybeans, or cotton and then a strip of a close-growing crop such as small grain or forage. Field strip cropping is planting the strips straight and parallel without regard to the slope. Contour strip cropping, planting the strips across the contour of the slope, will provide erosion control for steeper slopes up to about 18 percent. Terraces are constructed channels across a slope that reduce the slope length. The channel is at a slight grade so the water is removed slowly and safely. Terraces may be cropped or in permanent vegetation.

Grassed waterways are vegetated channels constructed where water would cause a gully. The channel is at a slight grade; the grass stabilizes the soil. A water and sediment control basin is a riser pipe connected to a subsurface drain. A small dam and an orifice plate in the riser pipe allow the water to pond for no more than twenty-four hours, which allows sedimentation before the water enters the riser pipe. Conservation tillage is a method of planting crops in which last year's old crop residue (in the form of straw, stalks, and so on) is not completely incorporated into the soil but instead is left on the surface as a mulch. At least 30 percent of the soil surface must be covered by residue to qualify as conservation tillage. No-till is a form of conservation tillage where the crop is planted without any previous tillage. Special planting equipment is necessary in order to plant through the crop residue. Weed pests are controlled by herbicides rather than by cultivation. No-till is very effective at reducing soil loss.

Erosion control for developments and construction sites includes saving existing vegetation and disturbing only as much land as can be reasonably developed in a few months. Other methods include temporary seedings, straw mulch, sedimentation basins, silt fences (plastic sheets staked into the ground), and straw bales staked in erosive channels.

*Tom L. Zimmerman*

FURTHER READING

Blanco-Canqui, Humberto, and Lal Rattan. *Principles of Soil Conservation and Management.* London: Springer, 2008.

Brady, Nyle C., and Ray R. Weil. *The Nature and Properties of Soils.* 14th ed. Upper Saddle River, N.J.: Prentice Hall, 2008.

Montgomery, David R. *Dirt: The Erosion of Civilizations.* Berkeley: University of California Press, 2007.

Morgan, R. P. C. *Soil Erosion and Conservation.* 3d ed. Malden, Mass.: Blackwell, 2005.

Schwab, Glenn O., Delmar D. Fangmeier, and William J. Elliot. *Soil and Water Management Systems.* 4th ed. New York: Wiley, 1996.

Toy, Terrence J., George R. Foster, and Kenneth G. Renard. *Soil Erosion: Processes, Prediction, Measurement, and Control.* New York: John Wiley & Sons, 2002.

WEB SITES

SCHOOL OF GEOGRAPHY, QUEEN'S UNIVERSITY BELFAST, NORTHERN IRELAND
Soil Erosion Site
http://soilerosion.net

U.S. DEPARTMENT OF AGRICULTURE
Soil Quality Resource Concerns: Soil Erosion
http://soils.usda.gov/SQI/publications/files/sq_two_1.pdf

U.S. GEOLOGICAL SURVEY
Erosion
http://www.usgs.gov/science/science.php?term=353

SEE ALSO: Conservation; Deforestation; Dust Bowl; Environmental degradation, resource exploitation and; Farmland; Land management; Soil; Soil management.

# Ethanol

CATEGORIES: Products from resources; plant and animal resources

WHERE FOUND
Ethanol, a biofuel, is produced by carbohydrate fermentation processes, hydration of ethylene, and, to a lesser extent, reduction of acetaldehyde obtained from acetylene.

PRIMARY USES
Ethanol—also known as ethyl alcohol, grain alcohol, or spirits—has traditionally found many uses in the chemical industry: for the preparation of numerous esters vital to many polymer industries, for the pro-

duction of diethyl ether (also called ether or ethyl ether), and as a major solvent and extractant. However, it has been best known for thousands of years as the primary alcohol component in alcoholic beverages and, since the 1970's, as a potentially significant source of transportation fuel, either as a gasoline replacement or as a blend fuel stretching available petroleum supplies.

### TECHNICAL DEFINITION

Ethanol is a colorless liquid with a mild and characteristic aroma and taste. It has a boiling point of 78.3° Celsius and a melting point of −114.5° Celsius. At 20° Celsius it has a density of 0.7894 gram per milliliter and a refractive index of 1.3614. Its molar mass is 46.07 grams. Ethanol is completely soluble in water and most organic solvents. It has a flash point of 8° Celsius and is thus highly flammable.

### DESCRIPTION, DISTRIBUTION, AND FORMS

Alcohol obtained from fermentation processes is generally included with other fermentation products and extracts from the carbohydrate-rich grains, fruits, and so on that are the raw materials for the multitudinous alcoholic beverages produced and consumed on Earth. Alcohol produced by yeast fermentation is obtained at a maximum concentration of 14 percent; therefore, alcoholic beverages other than beer and nonfortified wines require the addition of concentrated alcohol, which is obtained by distilling dilute alcohol from the fermentation of molasses and other sugar sources. In the United States and other highly industrialized countries, the alcohol added to beverages has increasingly been produced by other methods.

Ethanol is also used in large quantities for chemical synthesis in the organic chemical industry. It is used for the preparation of numerous esters vital to many polymer industries and for the production of diethyl ether (also called ether or ethyl ether), a major solvent and extractant. Other synthetic procedures lead to the manufacture of acetaldehyde, acetic acid, ethyl halides, and acetonitrile, which are in turn employed for the preparation of drugs, explosives, adhesives, pesticides, detergents, synthetic fibers, and other substances. Ethanol itself is used in vast quantities as an extractant or solvent.

For some time, ethanol has been added to gasoline in winter to reduce air pollution, an advantage of ethanol that has been viewed as particularly valuable since the Kyoto Protocol (1997) and other international agreements obligated their signors to reduce the carbon emissions associated with internal combustion engines. Thus, the United States and other oil-importing countries have frequently explored and, to some degree, pursued the "gasohol" option of combining ethanol with varying amounts of gasoline.

### HISTORY

The fermentation of various fruits and other products of the soil into drinking alcohol can produce pleasant tastes and, in the minds of people throughout the globe and for a very long part of history, a pleasurable effect. Based on archaeological discoveries, there is evidence of alcoholic imbibing as early as the sixth century B.C.E.

Historically, ethanol has been used as a home fuel source, albeit more recently than as a beverage. In the 1820's, for example, a blend of ethanol and turpentine was utilized as lamp fuel in the majority of American homes. Subsequently, natural gas and electricity displaced ethanol in home use in the United States and Europe, but it is still used in rural areas of the developing world for lighting and cooking. It is also widely employed as a part of everyday life in American and European homes as rubbing alcohol and as a solvent in chemical products.

Ethanol was used to power cars—especially in Western Europe—well before the Model T rolled off the first assembly line in 1908, driven by a motor based on an 1860 internal combustion engine developed in Germany to run on ethanol. However, before the first Model T was produced, the discovery of oil in the United States in the 1880's and the high tax that Congress enacted on industrial alcohol during the Civil War had combined to render the production of ethanol for transportation purposes both uneconomical and unnecessary. Both the Prohibition era in the United States (1919-1933), which tainted the home production of ethanol for fuel purposes as "closet moonshining," and the discovery of deep pools of cheap oil in the Middle East during the period between World War I and World War II pushed ethanol further off the market as a source of transportation fuel until the 1973 energy crisis.

### OBTAINING ETHANOL

Beverage alcohol is produced from a great variety of sources, including grains, potatoes, and fruit, but fermentation-based industrial alcohol is almost entirely

*A worker in Brazil harvests sugarcane, which can be used to produce ethanol fuel.* (AP/Wide World Photos)

obtained by yeast fermentation of molasses. Molasses (50 percent sucrose residue from sugar processing or cornstarch) is diluted with water to approximately 15 percent and under slightly acidic conditions is fermented by yeast to give 14 percent ethanol. Fractional distillation of the solution yields the commercial product: 95 percent ethanol. Approximately 9 liters of blackstrap molasses are needed to make 3.785 liters of 190-proof ethanol.

Although ethylene hydration was known in the early part of the nineteenth century, it did not become an industrial process until 1929; today, it is the dominant method of producing ethanol. Ethylene, obtained from the thermal cracking of petroleum fractions or from natural gas separation processes, is treated with complex phosphoric acid-based catalysts at temperatures above 300° Celsius and steam at pressures of thousands of kilograms per square centimeter. The ethanol can be fractionally distilled, and the residual ethylene can be recycled. Ethylene can also be passed into concentrated sulfuric acid, and after

hydrolysis, the ethanol can be distilled from the diluted sulfuric acid.

## USES OF ETHANOL

Despite ethanol's importance in the production of alcoholic beverages and its continued employment in various sectors of the chemical industry, its utility as a means of reducing petroleum dependency has commanded the most commentary and controversy since 1973, when Arab states embargoed oil shipments to countries supporting Israel in the Yom Kippur War.

Whether corn or sugarcane is used as ethanol's feedstock, concern exists that the expanded cultivation of both of these crops will greatly increase both air and water pollution. The indictment is especially levied against corn, because its cultivation requires the most pesticides and insecticides of any crop grown in the United States. The "pesticide cocktail"—composed of four weed killers, three insecticides, and two fungicides—produces a toxic effect known to kill wildlife, and its runoff damages subsoil streams and, hence, threatens U.S. supply of drinking water. Increasing the production of ethanol increases environmental costs. So too does burning it in internal combustion engines, in which—depending on the gasohol mixture of ethanol and petroleum—ethanol fuels can produce more than twice as much ground ozone as gasoline. Meanwhile, in the short term, reallocating existing corn production to meet a growing demand for ethanol inflates the cost of corn and of everything depending on it. This includes the price of corn-fed beef, milk drawn from corn-fed dairy cows, and the powdered milk that the United States exports to meet nourishment needs in poor countries of the developing world. Nonetheless, the United States, which has subsidized biofuels since 1978, is committed, under its Energy Independence and Security Act of 2007, to the goal of producing 136 billion liters of ethanol by 2022—a fourfold increase over the amount produced in 2008.

Issues also exist concerning the actual fuel savings available from an E90 (10 percent ethanol, 90 percent petroleum) gasohol mixture used in the United States. Planting and harvesting corn and processing it into ethanol involve significant use of fuel, which has to be considered in assessing overall petroleum savings through the widespread use of ethanol-petroleum solutions as gasoline. There is also the issue of kilometers-per-liter savings in ethanol versus conventional gasoline. Ethanol burns cleaner than traditional gasoline in terms of carbon gases, but it also burns faster, meaning that it requires more energy to provide the same energy output as its fossil-fuel kin. Brazil has evaded these efficiency issues by utilizing sugarcane harvested by cheap labor as its feedstock and by mandating the sale after 2007 of only flexible fuel vehicles (FFVs) capable of burning fuels containing very high levels of ethanol (up to 85 percent ethanol and beyond). Consequently, coupled with its domestic oil production, Brazil has become independent of foreign oil. For other countries, and especially those locked into E90 or even E85 mixtures, concerns over actual fuel savings as well as environmental damage from the use of corn- and sugarcane-derived ethanol continue to linger.

In the democratic world of pluralistic bargaining in public policy, these feedstocks that have nonetheless been favored over the use of switchgrass and other cellulosic sources of ethanol in the production of gasoline, despite the two to three times greater reduction in greenhouse gases possible by using cellulosic biofuels. Existing internal-combustion-engine automobiles and trucks can run, without major modifications, on E85, so the automotive industry has had reasons to support the development of the fuel, especially when alternatives have involved government mandates to retool to produce solar- or electric-powered cars. The petroleum industry, too, supports ethanol, which will maintain the demand for petroleum, as opposed to alternative energy technologies in the transportation field, in which more than one-half of all petroleum used in the United States is consumed. Above all, agricultural states with an interest in reviving their sagging agricultural communities and the large farming corporations that own most farming land in the United States have had reason to lobby diligently on behalf of the ethanol industry. Thus, whenever the focus has been on the high cost of imported fuels or reducing carbon emissions associated with automobile use, bills requiring the use of corn-based ethanol have been introduced in the U.S. Congress and have been enacted into law.

*William J. Wasserman, updated by Joseph R. Rudolph, Jr.*

## FURTHER READING

Blume, David. *Alcohol Can Be a Gas! Fueling an Ethanol Revolution for the Twenty-first Century.* Santa Cruz, Calif.: International Institute for Ecological Agriculture, 2007.

Boudreaux, Terry. *Ethanol and Biodiesel: What You Need to Know.* McLean, Va.: Hart Energy, 2007.

Brune, Michael. *Coming Clean: Breaking America's Addiction to Oil and Coal.* San Francisco: Sierra Club Books, 2008.

Freudenberger, Richard. *Alcohol Fuel: A Guide to Making and Using Ethanol as a Renewable Fuel.* Gabriola Island, B.C.: New Society, 2009.

Goettemoeller, Jeffrey, and Adrian Goettemoeller. *Sustainable Ethanol: Biofuels, Biorefineries, Cellulosic Biomass, Flex-Fuel Vehicles, and Sustainable Farming for Energy Independence.* Maryville, Mo.: Prairie Oak, 2007.

Minteer, Shelley, ed. *Alcoholic Fuels.* Boca Raton, Fla.: CRC/Taylor & Francis, 2006.

Mousdale, David M. *Biofuels: Biotechnology, Chemistry, and Sustainable Development.* Boca Raton, Fla.: CRC Press, 2008.

Pahl, Greg. *Biodiesel: Growing a New Energy Economy.* 2d ed. White River Junction, Vt.: Chelsea Green, 2008.

Paul, J. K., ed. *Ethyl Alcohol Production and Use as a Motor Fuel.* Park Ridge, N.J.: Noyes Data, 1979.

Rothman, Harry, Rod Greenshields, and Francisco Rosillo Callé. *Energy from Alcohol: The Brazilian Experience.* Lexington: University Press of Kentucky, 1983.

Shaffer, Brenda. *Energy Politics.* Philadelphia: University of Pennsylvania Press, 2009.

## WEB SITES

ALTERNATIVE FUELS AND ADVANCED VEHICLES DATA CENTER, U.S. DEPARTMENT OF ENERGY
Ethanol
http://www.afdc.energy.gov/afdc/ethanol/index.html

ECONOMIC RESEARCH SERVICE, U.S. DEPARTMENT OF AGRICULTURE
Ethanol Expansion in the United States: How Will the Agricultural Sector Adjust?
http://www.ers.usda.gov/Publications/FDS/2007/05May/FDS07D01/fds07D01.pdf

SEE ALSO: Biofuels; Brazil; Corn; Energy economics; Energy Policy Act; Gasoline and other petroleum fuels; Internal combustion engine; Oil and natural gas chemistry; Peak oil; Petrochemical products; Petroleum refining and processing; Plant domestication and breeding; Resources for the Future; Synthetic Fuels Corporation.

# European Union Natura 2000

CATEGORIES: Laws and conventions; organizations, agencies, and programs

DATE: Birds Directive, April 2, 1979; Habitats Directive, May 21, 1992

*Natura 2000 was established to protect endangered species and regions in the European Union.*

## BACKGROUND

The geography of the European Union includes nine different biogeographical regions. This large diversity of European ecosystems and landscapes offers a variety of different habitats for fauna and flora: arctic and high-alpine rocks and glaciers, areas of moderate climate, marine ecosystems, and arid areas and deserts. Estimates indicate that more than 40 percent of mammals, 15 percent of bird species, and 45 percent of reptiles in Europe are endangered or threatened.

While policies for environmental protection and nature conservation in protected areas have a rather long history, environmental protection and nature conservation policies were not accounted for in the founding documents of the European Union, such as the Treaty of Rome (1958). At the beginning of the 1970's, after the United Nations Conference on the Human Environment in Stockholm, the European Commission finally developed environmental policy programs. The Single European Act (1985) and, later, the Treaty of Amsterdam (1997) included environmental protection in the European treaties. The Birds Directive, emphasizing the conservation of birds, was passed in 1979; however, the Habitats Directive, establishing a European network of protected areas, was not established until 1992. Hence, the European Union's Natura 2000 stipulations are part of the European Union's Sustainable Development Strategy and of the Environment Action Programme of the European Community, the latter of which has multiple editions. The importance of biodiversity conservation also has been widely acknowledged in many European Union policies of other fields, such as in the European Spatial Planning Strategy and the Common Agricultural Policy.

## PROVISIONS

The Birds Directive and the Habitats Directive can be considered the fundamental documents of joint European Union nature conservation policies. The Habitats Directive is based on two policies. A network of protected areas (Natura 2000 network) has been established in all member countries, and a strict framework for species conservation has been instituted. Individual member countries are no longer free to decide which nature conservation policies should be pursued if the ecosystems or species endangered or threatened are of community interest. However, all member states established their own legal regulations regarding nature conservation much earlier than the joint European framework.

The Habitats Directive aims at maintaining biodiversity by means of a common framework for the conservation of wildlife (fauna and flora) and of habitats of community interest. Member states are obliged to protect "special protection areas" (SPAs) and "sites of community interest" (SCIs). The directive includes several appendixes where biodiversity elements of community interest are listed, such as natural habitats, animal and plant species, and the definition of "priority" or "strict protection" habitats and species. European Union member countries who find habitats or species of community interest on their territory are obliged to set up conservation areas and management plans and to report to the European Commission about the concrete conservation policies. For instance, SPAs (Natura 2000 sites) are established based on the annex of the Habitats Directive, reported by the member state to the European Commission, which includes the site in a list of habitats of community interest. When this has been done, the area is established as protected. Failure of any EU member country to report sites of community interest is subject to charges before the European Court of Justice.

An important provision of Natura 2000 is that member states are obliged to guarantee that habitats of community interest are conserved and any deterioration of the habitat is avoided. Member states also have to initiate the management of landscapes and habitats of special importance for the migration, dispersal, and genetic exchange of wildlife; establish strict protection of threatened fauna and flora; explore possibilities of reintroducing extinct wildlife; and prevent the nonselective taking, killing, or capturing of wildlife listed in the directive. Even if the member state does not formally establish a Natura 2000 site for a priority habitat or species, it is nevertheless protected under European Union law.

The Natura 2000 regulations not only provide for

the conservation of biodiversity but also establish the possibilities for co-financing conservation measures. Implementation of Natura 2000 is estimated to cost about 6.1 billion euros ($8.6 billion) per year. One of the financial instruments set up for co-financing is the "LIFE+ Nature and Biodiversity" program. It is specifically designed to contribute to the implementation of Natura 2000 in member states and to support the establishment and management of protected areas.

The European Union and its member states are signatories of the Convention on Biological Diversity (CBD). The European Union has also committed itself to the goal of halting biodiversity loss. In order to support this goal, the European Commission adopted a Biodiversity Action Plan in 2006, which followed earlier strategies such as the Biodiversity Strategy of 1998. The strategy encompasses the European Union's commitment to conserving global biodiversity, addressing issues of biodiversity and climate change, and implementing a comprehensive knowledge base regarding the conservation of biodiversity. Natura 2000 may serve as a nature conservation model for other parts of the world.

## IMPACT ON RESOURCE USE

The Natura 2000 regulations are progressive in terms of their strict regulatory framework and the concept of establishing a consistent, coherent, and representative European ecological network of protected areas. Furthermore, the number of sites set up is impressive. The following are based on 2008 figures: In terms of the Birds Directive, there are 5,044 SPAs covering an area of 517,896 square kilometers (10.5 percent of the area of the European Union and 531 marine sites covering 66,084 square kilometers. The Habitats Directive has 21,612 SCIs covering an area of 655,968 square kilometers (13.3 percent of the area of the European Union) and 1,294 marine sites covering an area of 87,505 square kilometers. However, the application of the directives in the individual member states varies and ranges from around 7 percent of the national territory for SCIs (United Kingdom) up to 31.4 percent (Slovenia). While the Natura 2000 frameworks provide a coherent and strong basis for conserving biodiversity, they need to be implemented effectively in all member states. Many areas of community interest are still "paper parks" without concrete management plans or funds for administering the European Union directives' requirements. The

Biodiversity Action Plans, published assessments of the EU's biodiversity policies, revealed that it was unlikely that the European Union would be able to meet its aims of halting biodiversity loss by 2010. Policies therefore have to concentrate on the finalization of the Natura 2000 network, provide adequate financial resources for establishing and managing the sites, and implement the necessary action and management plans in the member countries. Of specific importance in this context is the support of Natura 2000 sites in the new European Union member countries in Central and Eastern Europe that significantly contribute to the natural endowment of the European Union. Funding programs for capacity building is important because the management of protected areas is an emerging interdisciplinary professional field.

*Michael Getzner*

## FURTHER READING

Bromley, Peter. *Nature Conservation in Europe: Policy and Practice.* New York: Spon, 1997.

European Communities. *The European Union's Biodiversity Action Plan: Halting the Loss of Biodiversity by 2010—and Beyond.* Luxembourg: Office for Official Publications of the European Communities, 2008.

Keulartz, Jozef, and Gilbert Leistra, eds. *Legitimacy in European Nature Conservation Policy: Case Studies in Multilevel Governance.* New York: Springer, 2008.

Rosa, H. D., and J. M. Silva. "From Environmental Ethics to Nature Conservation Policy: Natura 2000 and the Burden of Proof." *Journal of Agricultural and Environmental Ethics* 18, no. 2 (2005): 107-130.

## WEB SITES

### EIONET

The European Topic Centre on Biological Diversity
http://biodiversity.eionet.europa.eu/

### EUROPEAN COMMISSION

Nature and Biodiversity
http://ec.europa.eu/environment/nature/index_en.htm

SEE ALSO: Austria; Belgium; Biodiversity; Denmark; Endangered species; France; Germany; Greece; Italy; The Netherlands; Norway; Poland; Portugal; Spain; Sweden; United Kingdom.

# Eutrophication

CATEGORY: Pollution and waste disposal

*Eutrophication is the overenrichment of water by nutrients; it causes excessive plant growth and stagnation, which leads to the death of other aquatic life such as fish.*

## DEFINITION

The word "eutrophic" comes from the Greek *eu*, which means "good" or "well," and *trophikos*, which means "food" or "nutrition." Eutrophic waters are well nourished and rich in nutrients; they support abundant life. Eutrophication refers to a condition in aquatic systems (ponds, lakes, and streams) in which nutrients are so abundant that plants and algae grow uncontrollably and become a problem. The plants die and decompose, and the water becomes stagnant. This ultimately causes the death of other aquatic animals, particularly fish, that cannot tolerate such conditions. Eutrophication is a major problem in watersheds and waterways such as the Great Lakes and Chesapeake Bay that are surrounded by urban populations.

## OVERVIEW

The stagnation that occurs during eutrophication is attributable to the activity of microorganisms growing on the dead and dying plant material in water. As they decompose the plant material, microbes consume oxygen faster than it can be resupplied by the atmosphere. Fish, which need oxygen in the water to breathe, become starved for oxygen and suffocate. In addition, noxious gases such as hydrogen sulfide ($H_2S$) can be released during the decay of the plant material. The hallmark of a eutrophic environment is one that is plant-filled, littered with dead aquatic life, and smelly.

Eutrophication is actually a natural process that occurs as lakes age and fill with sediment, as deltas form, and as rivers seek new channels. The main concern with eutrophication in natural resource conservation is that human activity can accelerate the process and can cause it to occur in previously clean but nutrient-poor water. This is sometimes referred to as "cultural eutrophication." For example, there is great concern with eutrophication in Lake Tahoe. Much of Lake Tahoe's appeal is its crystal-clear water. However, development around Lake Tahoe is causing excess nutrients to flow into the lake and damaging the very thing that attracts people to the lake.

The nutrients that cause eutrophication usually come from surface runoff of soil and fertilizer associated with mismanaged agriculture or from domestic and industrial wastes discharged into rivers and lakes. Phosphorus (P) and nitrogen (N) are two of the nutrients most limiting to plant growth in water. When they are supplied, plant growth can explode and eutrophication can occur. Phosphorus was one of the major causes of eutrophication in Lake Erie during the 1960's. Before preventative action was taken, the lake was considered to be dying. These preventative actions included banning phosphates from laundry detergent and imposing stricter conservation practices on farmers to reduce soil erosion in the watersheds draining into Lake Erie. Many areas now restrict the total amount of phosphorus that can be applied to land that drains into waterways. Preventative action also forced sewage treatment facilities to start chemically removing phosphorus from the water they discharged. As a result of these actions, phosphorus loading into Lake Erie was cut in half from the 1960's to the early 1990's; however, total phosphorus content in Lake Erie rose slightly over the subsequent decade and a half.

*Mark S. Coyne*

SEE ALSO: Ecosystems; Erosion and erosion control; Lakes; Streams and rivers.

# Evaporites

CATEGORY: Mineral and other nonliving resources

*Evaporites are sedimentary deposits of salt minerals that crystallize from marine and continental brines. Common evaporite minerals include halite (sodium chloride, or table salt), gypsum (hydrated calcium sulfate), calcite (calcium carbonate), dolomite (calcium-magnesium carbonate), and various borate minerals.*

## DEFINITION

Evaporites form in environments where evaporative water loss from a body of water exceeds, at least periodically, the rate of inflow to the body. Evaporites occur in all the major continents; the most extensive deposits are found in North and South America, Europe, and the Middle East. Notable North American localities are the Michigan Basin and the Permian Basin of Texas and New Mexico. Most rock salt (halite) is mined from evaporites, as is the gypsum used in wallboard and other construction materials. Borate minerals are used in cleaning agents and in other industrial uses. Other evaporite minerals are important sources for industrial metals such as magnesium and strontium.

## OVERVIEW

Evaporites are stratified sedimentary deposits consisting of minerals precipitated from salt brines (highly concentrated salt water). These deposits have formed on every continent and throughout geologic time, although the Silurian (438 to 408 million years ago) and Permian (286 to 248 million years ago) periods were the most prolific times of evaporite formation. In recent times evaporite deposition has been relatively rare. The chief factors influencing evaporite formation are aridity and a closed basin environment in which water inflow is restricted. High air temperatures generally accompany these conditions, but this is not always the case. For example, recent minor evaporites are known from the arid regions of Antarctica.

Evaporite minerals crystallize from seawater in a certain order, depending on their relative solubilities. Calcite generally crystallizes first as the amount of water is reduced by evaporation. Gypsum follows, with halite precipitating when only about one tenth of the original solution is left. More soluble minerals crystallize in the final liquid, including sylvite (potassium chloride). This process produces concentrated crystalline layers that consist of only one or two major minerals.

World evaporite bodies can be divided into marine deposits, the thickest and most extensive in origin, and continental deposits. Marine evaporites may form in marginal lagoons closed off from the sea by a sandbar or other barrier. Another important environment is the sabkha, a shallow margin of a sea or ocean in an extremely arid climate, as occurs, for example, in the Persian Gulf. Continental deposits most commonly form in temporary desert lakes called playas. Evaporite minerals in playas are derived from streams that leach marine brines trapped in sedimentary rocks from surrounding mountains.

Major evaporite localities in North America are the Michigan Basin (Salina deposits), the Permian Basin of Texas and New Mexico, the Midcontinent field centered in Kansas and adjacent states, and the borate deposits of Death Valley and adjacent areas. The first three of these localities are mostly known for halite and gypsum production. They are primarily marine deposits formed in shallow continental seas during Silurian times (Michigan Basin) or during the Permian period (Permian Basin and Midcontinent). The Death Valley area is famous for its borate deposits, minerals that were deposited in playas.

*John L. Berkley*

SEE ALSO: Borax; Boron; Carbonate minerals; Deserts; Gypsum; Limestone; Magnesium; Oceans; Salt; Salt domes; Sedimentary processes, rocks, and mineral deposits; Strontium; Water.

*Gypsum-selenite is one example of an evaporite.* (USGS)

# Exclusive economic zones

CATEGORY: Government and resources
DATE: December 10, 1982

*Although the concept of a conservation zone off national coasts was not new, the exclusive economic zone (EEZ), created by the United Nations Convention on the Law of the Sea, was a legal and political achievement because it was the result of a consensus by all the world's states.*

## BACKGROUND

Part V of the United Nations Convention on the Law of the Sea of December 10, 1982, established the exclusive economic zone of a coastal state as "an area beyond and adjacent to the territorial sea" which is under the jurisdiction of the coastal state for specific purposes. The convention, the work of more than fourteen years of negotiation, is a comprehensive legal document that created an ordered system for the use of ocean space and for the protection of the natural resources of the oceans.

According to customary use of the seas, the area beyond the territorial waters of a state had been considered "high seas," open to use by all and under no nation's jurisdiction. The territorial waters had been generally accepted as extending 4.8 kilometers from the coast into the sea. Then, in the Truman Proclamation of September 28, 1945, the United States claimed the right to extend its jurisdiction over "conservation zones" in the high seas contiguous to the U.S. coast. Other countries followed, establishing their own zones and extending their economic jurisdiction into the high seas. Many maritime nations feared that the tradition of open seas and free navigation would end. Thus in 1967 the United Nations General Assembly established an ad hoc committee to begin studying peaceful uses of the seas in preparation for convening the Third United Nations Convention on the Law of the Sea.

## PROVISIONS

A dispute over coastal rights and claims versus the freedom of all to use the seas erupted at the first session of the conference in Caracas, Venezuela. The creation of an economic zone of protection for a coastal state's offshore resources was one of the first agreements negotiated at the conference. The EEZ part of the convention was put together as a smaller part within the overall package, which was a carefully negotiated compromise document. The EEZ extends up to 200 nautical miles from a baseline drawn along the low-water line of a coast.

## IMPACT ON RESOURCE USE

Within that zone the coastal state acquires sovereign economic rights over living and nonliving resources for the purpose of exploitation, conservation, and resource management, including the right to establish the allowable catch of living resources. All other states retain their rights under the freedom of the seas concept and retain access to the EEZ for the purpose of exploiting those resources that the coastal state does not use.

Should disagreements arise with respect to the EEZ area, the convention calls for them to be settled on the basis of equity, and in the interests of all parties and of the international community as a whole. An international tribunal is provided for the settlement of disputes that may arise regarding the use of ocean space and EEZ resources.

*Colleen M. Driscoll*

SEE ALSO: Fisheries; Law of the sea; Marine mining; Oceans; United Nations Convention on the Law of the Sea.

# *Exxon Valdez* oil spill

CATEGORY: Historical events and movements
DATE: March 24, 1989

*The* Exxon Valdez *oil spill, in which 42 million liters of crude oil spilled into Prince William Sound off the Alaskan coast, demonstrated the destructive power of oil. It contaminated approximately 2,100 kilometers of pristine shoreline, killing and endangering wildlife. Twenty years later, oil was still surfacing in some areas and two species had not recovered, while others still struggled to recover.*

## BACKGROUND

At 12:04 A.M. on March 24, 1989, the oil tanker *Exxon Valdez* plowed into Bligh Reef about 161 kilometers off the coast of Alaska. The 301-meter tanker had diverted course out of the narrow shipping lane to avoid icebergs but hit the reef before turning back on course. Of the more than 200 million liters of crude oil it carried, 42 million flowed into Prince William Sound. The close proximity to the shore, stormy seas, and high winds all contributed to the contamination of 322 kilometers of shoreline. The slick stretched 740 kilometers, reaching the village of Chignik on the Alaskan Peninsula.

Response efforts were delayed and inadequate. Little of the oil was scooped from the waters, because a response barge was out of service. Not enough skimmers and booms designed to contain a spill were available. Dispersants used to break up the oil for easier cleanup were not effective, because of weather conditions. Though the seas calmed in the following days, the oil slick spread, lightly coating another 684 kilometers of shoreline. In all, an estimated 250,000 seabirds, 2,800 sea otters, 250 bald eagles, 22 killer whales, 300 harbor seals, and billions of fish were killed. The col-

_Workers use pressure washers to remove oil from a Smith Island beach in Alaska following the 1989_ Exxon Valdez _oil spill._ (Bob Hallinen/MCT/Landov)

lapse of the Pacific herring fishery, which devastated local economies, is blamed on this event.

IMPACT ON RESOURCE USE

The _Exxon Valdez_ Oil Spill Trustee Council was established to oversee restoration efforts in the sound. Cleanup efforts took six months at a cost of about $2.1 billion to Exxon Corporation. Though no longer listed as one of the top fifty oil spills in terms of the amount of oil expelled, this event remains one of the most devastating oil spills in terms of environmental impact.

This incident established changes in response and recovery. Practice response drills are held in Prince William Sound twice yearly. Seven barges are available in case of a spill, and 64 kilometers of boom and a stockpile of dispersants are on hand. The U.S. Coast Guard now monitors vessels passing through the narrow shipping lane in the sound, and two vessels accompany fully laden tankers to offer assistance in emergencies. In addition, Congress enacted a law requiring tankers traveling through Prince William Sound to be double-hulled. The oil industry now uses double- and triple-hulled tankers.

Despite the devastation and far-reaching effect of the oil spill, the environment was expected to recover within several years. Areas of shoreline that were lightly coated did recover. In 1994, five years after the accident, the _Exxon Valdez_ Oil Spill Trustee Council compiled an official list of resources and services affected by the spill. Twenty years after the spill, areas most heavily contaminated still showed oil surfacing from beneath rocks and pebbles. Only ten, or one-third, of the resources and services listed are considered "recovered." Recovery of many of these resources and services is dependent on recovery of others. Oil spills are no longer considered acute, short-term environmental threats.

_Lisa A. Wroble_

SEE ALSO: Alaska pipeline; American Petroleum Institute; Bureau of Reclamation, U.S.; Ecology; Ecosystems; Oil industry; Oil spills; Organization of Petroleum Exporting Countries; Species loss.

## Fabrics. *See* Textiles and fabrics

## Farmland

CATEGORY: Ecological resources

*Agricultural soil able to produce sufficient food and fiber to feed and clothe the growing human population is one of the world's most important natural resources.*

Farmland, like this field in Wyoming, composes a significant portion of the American Midwest. (©iStockphoto.com)

BACKGROUND

Land suitable for agriculture is not evenly distributed throughout the world; it tends to be concentrated in limited areas. In order to be considered arable, land must be located in an area with the right combination of environmental conditions. First, the land must be located at the proper elevation and slope. Because the soil supplies all the mineral nutrients required for plant growth, it must also have the appropriate fertility, texture, and pH level. Approximately 64 percent of the world's land has the proper topography, and about 46 percent has satisfactory soil fertility.

Plants require large amounts of water for photosynthesis and access to soil nutrients; therefore, farmland must have an adequate supply of moisture, either as rainfall or as irrigation water. About 46 percent of the world's land has adequate and reliable rainfall. Because plant growth is dramatically affected by temperature, farmland must be located in areas with growing seasons sufficiently long to sustain the crop from planting to harvest. Approximately 83 percent of the world's land has favorable temperatures. Plants also require sufficient sunlight and atmospheric carbon dioxide levels to support the photosynthetic process necessary for growth and development. Virtually all the world's land has adequate sunlight and sufficient carbon dioxide to support plant growth. Crop production requires the right combination of all these factors, but only about 7 percent of the world's land has the proper combination of these factors to make the production of crops feasible without additional technological advances.

FARMLAND IN THE UNITED STATES

With its temperate climate, the United States devotes considerably more of its land area to agriculture than do many other countries. About 45 percent of the land in the United States is utilized for various forms of agriculture; however, not all this land is devoted to crop production. Only about 20 percent of the land is actual cropland. Approximately 4 percent is devoted to woodlands, and the other 21 percent is used for other purposes, such as pastures and grasslands. Of the farmland devoted to crop production, only 14 percent is used at any given time to produce harvestable crops. Approximately 21 percent of this harvested cropland is used to produce food grains for human consumption. Another 31 percent is used to grow feed grains for feeding livestock, and the remaining 48 percent of harvested cropland is devoted to the production of soybeans, oil, seed, fiber, and miscellaneous crops.

Seven major agricultural regions exist in the United States. The dairy region is located in the North Atlantic states and extends westward past the Great Lakes and along the Pacific coast. The wheat belt is centered in the central and northern Great Plains and in the Columbia basin of the Northwest. The general and self-sufficient regions primarily made up of small, family-owned farms are found mostly in the eastern highlands region, which includes the Appalachian Mountains—a few hundred kilometers inland from the Atlantic Coast—and the Ozark-Ouachita mountains west of the Mississippi River. The corn and livestock belt is found throughout the midwestern states. The range-livestock region of the western United States stretches in a band from 800 to 1,600 kilometers wide and extends from the Canadian border to Mexico. The western specialty-crops area is primarily composed of irrigated land in seventeen western states and produces the vast majority of the nation's vegetable crops. The cotton belt, located in the southern states (most notably Georgia, Alabama, and Mississippi), contains more counties with more farmers than any other region. While this area has been known historically for its cotton production, many other goods—including tobacco, peanuts, truck crops, livestock, and poultry—are also produced in the South. In addition to these major regions, smaller farming areas are located throughout the country. Tobacco is produced in localities throughout Kentucky, Virginia, Tennessee, and North and South Carolina. Apples and other fruits are grown in a variety of places, including the Middle Atlantic seaboard, around the Great Lakes, and in the Pacific Northwest. Potatoes are produced in Maine, Minnesota, Idaho, North Dakota, and California. Citrus is grown in southern Texas, Florida, and California. Sugarcane is grown in southern Louisiana and Florida.

## CANADA

In addition to the rich farmland of the United States, good farmland exists in neighboring Canada. Although the arable land percentage in Canada is only 4.57, that amount is sufficient to produce large yields of wheat, barley, oilseeds (including flax and sunflower), tobacco, fruits, and vegetables. Canada also is a large producer of dairy products from its many dairy farms and seafood products from both Atlantic and Pacific fisheries.

## EURASIA

On the Eurasian continent, important farmland regions are found in the Ukraine, Russia, China, and India. Ukraine has one of the largest areas of arable land in the world, with 53.8 percent of its land total considered suitable for farming. However, only 1.5 percent of the country's production is in permanent crops, a possible indication that more farming might occur in the country if economic conditions are more stable. Ukraine is a large producer of sugar beets, sunflower seeds, vegetables, beef, and milk.

Neighboring Russia, which has long been considered one of the world's "breadbaskets," grows the same crops as Ukraine, but on only 7.17 percent of its area. Some of Russia's farmland has been lost to development and desertification as well as rendered unsafe by excess and improper uses of agricultural pesticides.

China owes more than 43 percent of its gross domestic product to agricultural production and is a leading producer of rice, wheat, potatoes, corn, peanuts, and tea. Millet, barley, apples, cotton, and oilseeds are produced in China in smaller amounts but are nevertheless important to the country's economy. China has only 1.27 percent of its land in permanent crops, and 14.86 percent of the country's land is considered arable. However, China is facing a very serious problem in that at least one-fifth of its agricultural land has been lost since the 1950's, primarily because of soil erosion and economic development. China has therefore passed laws that exact severe penalties for the conversion of farmland to any type of development in an attempt to conserve remaining agricultural lands.

India, like Ukraine, has one of the highest proportions of arable land in the world, with 48.83 percent of usable farmland in the country. Rice, wheat, oilseeds, cotton, jute, tea, sugarcane, potatoes, and livestock are produced on 2.8 percent of land devoted to permanent agricultural use. A rapidly growing population and severe water pollution are two problems detrimental to farming in India.

## SOUTH AMERICA

Brazil is the third largest agricultural producer in the world behind the United States and the European Union. On approximately 6.93 percent of its total land area and with less than 1 percent devoted to permanent crops, Brazil is number one in the world in exports of coffee, frozen orange juice, and sugar. It is the world's second largest producer of soybeans, tobacco, beef, and poultry. Brazil's problems with habitat fragmentation, water pollution, and non-farm development plague this important South American nation in terms of its ability to continue to be a major agricultural producer.

Argentina is another important producer of crops in South America. It produces soybeans and cereal grains, including corn and wheat. The country has been a major producer of beef for many years. Cereal crops and cattle are produced on about 10 percent of the country's land area.

## FARMLAND DEGRADATION

All of the developed and developing countries around the world are encountering many of the same problems involving the loss or degradation of farmland. Within developed countries the most serious problems are outright destruction of farmland by development. Urban, suburban, and residential developments destroy thousands of hectares of farmland daily, and unless governments act to preserve farmland within their countries, it is unlikely that agricultural production will be able to keep pace with the exploding world population.

In the United States, both the amount of land devoted to farming and the number of farmers began decreasing after 1965. The amount of good farmland worldwide has also decreased. Most of this decrease is attributed to a combination of urbanization and poor agricultural methods that have led to loss of topsoil through water and wind erosion. Historically, large tracts of farmland have been located near major metropolitan areas. In recent times, these urban centers have grown outward into large suburban areas, and this sprawl has consumed vast areas of farmland. Erosion destroys thousands of hectares of farmland every year, and desertification—the conversion of productive rangeland, rain-fed cropland, or irrigated cropland into desertlike land with a resulting drop in agricultural productivity—has reduced productivity on more than 80 million hectares since the 1960's. In many cases, the desertified land is no longer useful as farmland. Because most of the world's available farmland is now in production, steps must be taken to preserve this valuable resource, or the world could suffer mass food shortages in the future.

Degradation of world farmland is occurring at a rapid pace. Desertification of formerly fertile areas is taking place on every continent that has farmland. Water pollution, from both industrialized areas and agricultural runoff, is a serious concern in most countries. In addition to water pollution, the loss of water available for irrigation is affecting many farming areas. Global climate change is altering rainfall patterns throughout the world, with some areas receiving too much rainfall and others too little. Throughout many parts of the United States, for instance, the water table has fallen drastically, as too much water has been withdrawn for both urban and agricultural uses. Governments, whether national or local, must continue to search for reasonable ways to balance water use among competing interests in order for agricultural production to continue.

*D. R. Gossett, updated by Lenela Glass-Godwin*

## FURTHER READING

Acquaah, George. *Principles of Crop Production: Theory, Techniques, and Technology.* 2d ed. Upper Saddle River, N.J.: Pearson Prentice Hall, 2005.

Beattie, Bruce R. "The Disappearance of Agricultural Land: Fact or Fiction?" In *Agriculture and the Environment: Searching for Greener Pastures,* edited by Terry L. Anderson and Bruce Yandle. Stanford, Calif.: Hoover Institution Press, 2001.

Caldwell, Wayne, Stew Hilts, and Bronwynne Wilton, eds. *Farmland Preservation: Land for Future Generations.* Guelph, Ont.: Ontario Farmland Trust, 2007.

Daniels, Tom, and Deborah Bowers. *Holding Our Ground: Protecting America's Farms and Farmland.* Washington, D.C.: Island Press, 1997.

Fish, Robert, et al. *Sustainable Farmland Management: New Transdisciplinary Approaches.* Cambridge, Mass.: CABI, 2008.

Ho, Peter. *Institutions in Transition: Land Ownership, Property Rights, and Social Conflict in China.* New York: Oxford University Press, 2005.

Johnston, Robert J., and Stephen K. Swallow. *Economics and Contemporary Land Use Policy: Development and Conservation at the Rural-Urban Fringe.* Washington, D.C.: Resources for the Future, 2006.

Kipps, M. S. *Production of Field Crops: A Textbook of Agronomy.* 6th ed. New York: McGraw-Hill, 1970.

Metcalfe, Darrel S., and Donald M. Elkins. *Crop Production: Principles and Practices*. 4th ed. New York: Macmillan, 1980.

Millington, Andrew, and Wendy Jepson, eds. *Land Change Science in the Tropics: Changing Agricultural Landscapes*. New York: Springer, 2008.

Olson, Richard K., and Thomas A. Lyson, eds. *Under the Blade: The Conversion of Agricultural Landscapes*. Boulder, Colo.: Westview Press, 1999.

WEB SITES

AMERICAN FARMLAND TRUST
http://www.farmland.org

U.S. DEPARTMENT OF AGRICULTURE
Conservation Policy: Farming Land and Grazing Land Protection Programs
http://www.ers.usda.gov/Briefing/ConservationPolicy/farmland.htm

U.S. DEPARTMENT OF AGRICULTURE
Major Uses of the Land in the United States, 2002
http://www.ers.usda.gov/Publications/EIB14

SEE ALSO: Agriculture industry; Argentina; Brazil; Canada; China; Department of the Interior, U.S.; Desertification; Erosion and erosion control; Food shortages; Horticulture; India; Land ethic; Monoculture agriculture; Rangeland; Russia; Seed Savers Exchange; Slash-and-burn agriculture; Soil; Ukraine; United Nations Convention to Combat Desertification; United States.

# Federal Energy Regulatory Commission

CATEGORY: Organizations, agencies, and programs
DATE: Established 1978

*The Federal Energy Regulatory Commission regulates a number of aspects of energy, including hydroelectric power, oil and natural gas, and wholesale sales of electricity, in which interstate commerce is involved.*

BACKGROUND
The Federal Energy Regulatory Commission (FERC) was established in 1978. At that time, as part of the new cabinet-level Department of Energy (established

in 1977), the responsibilities of several different agencies dealing with energy issues were combined and given to one independent regulatory commission. The Federal Power Commission (FPC), the most direct predecessor to the FERC, had been responsible for overseeing interstate issues involving the generation and transmission of electricity and the development and regulation of hydroelectric facilities. The FERC continues to regulate electricity, but it also oversees a variety of other energy resources if interstate commerce is involved.

The FERC's regulation of hydroelectric development is historically the oldest component of the agency's responsibilities. The Federal Water Power Act of 1920 centralized authority for federal oversight of water power development in one agency, the FPC. The agency as originally established was both small and weak, consisting of only one permanent employee, an executive secretary. Support staff were borrowed from other agencies, and engineering reviews of proposed projects were performed by consulting engineers. Still, the FPC managed to establish guidelines that prevented wildcat speculations and conserved federal wilderness areas.

Congress reorganized and gradually strengthened the FPC several times in the following decades. In 1935, the Federal Power Act added regulation of the interstate transmission and wholesale sale of electricity to the FPC's responsibilities, while the Public Utility Regulatory Policies Act (PURPA), passed during the energy crisis of the 1970's, added provisions to encourage cogeneration and alternative energy resource development. More recently, the Energy Policy Act (2005) clarified regulation of natural gas and oil transported across state lines.

IMPACT ON RESOURCE USE
The FERC's responsibilities include regulating the transmission of natural gas and oil by pipeline in interstate commerce and the transmission and sale of electricity in interstate commerce. FERC licenses and inspects private, municipal, and state hydroelectric projects and oversees related environmental matters. The FERC's mission in overseeing wholesale sales of electricity is to ensure that utilities charge reasonable rates and that federal public utility regulations regarding officers and directorships of utility companies are obeyed. Rates set by federal power generating agencies, such as the Bonneville Power Administration, are also reviewed by the FERC. The retail rates

paid by consumers are regulated within the individual states by public utilities commissions.

The FERC consists of five members appointed by the president. Members serve for five years. When the commission was established, terms of office were staggered so that only one member's term would expire each year. The president of the United States designates the chairperson for the FERC, and, in the event that a vacancy occurs on the commission, anyone appointed to fill that vacancy serves only the remainder of that particular term. Although no specific qualifications were set for commission members, the legislative mandate does require that the president appoint to the commission persons who are familiar with energy issues and procedures.

In overseeing natural gas and oil, the FERC regulates the construction of pipelines and other methods used in interstate transportation of these resources as well as the facilities at wellheads and at distribution points. At one time, the FERC was required to establish ceiling prices for natural gas, but the Natural Gas Wellhead Deregulation Act of 1993 eliminated that practice.

*Nancy Farm Männikkö*

WEB SITE

FEDERAL ENERGY REGULATORY COMMISSION
http://www.ferc.gov/

SEE ALSO: Dams; Department of Energy, U.S.; Electrical power; Energy economics; Energy politics; Hydroenergy; Oil industry.

# Federal Water Quality Act. *See* Clean Water Act

# Federalism and resource management

CATEGORIES: Environment, conservation, and resource management; social, economic, and political issues

*Natural resources management plays a key role in conserving and enhancing those goods and services pro-*

*vided by nature. Management practices in the United States are guided by the federalism model, providing an integrated mode of management structured around the needs and capabilities of local, state, and national efforts.*

BACKGROUND

Federalism refers to the institutional framework that divides decision-making power between the national government and individual states. In this framework, both national governments and states develop laws and public policies.

Before the United States ratified its constitution, the states acted autonomously. In the immediate aftermath of the signing of the Constitution in 1787, the national government dealt primarily with national issues, such as defense. Over time, changes in this balance of power occurred directly in the form of amendments to the Constitution and legislative actions. As an example of an explicit allocation of decision-making power, the Tenth Amendment to the U.S. Constitution declares, "powers not delegated to the United States . . . are reserved to the States. . . ." The U.S. national government has increased its power over time, especially in response to large national events, such as the Civil War and the Great Depression.

As a subset of federalism, environmental federalism refers to a dynamic balance of power between the states and the federal government, which is determined by the nature of the role played in establishing environmental protection and managing natural resources. Natural resources include both renewable and nonrenewable resources: soil, minerals, forests, water, fisheries, and energy. In response to natural resource scarcity and the degradation of environmental quality, Congress has designed environmental programs that allow for implementation of policies to manage and protect these resources on the federal, state, and local levels.

HISTORY OF NATURAL RESOURCE POLICY AND
     MANAGEMENT
William Lowry describes the evolution of natural resource policies as divided into the following three eras: an era from colonial times to the end of the nineteenth century in which government did not get involved in resource extraction and most viewed resources as abundant; an ongoing era in which government determines natural resource policies; and a new era in which policies are determined by synthesizing

the preferences and perspectives of different, often competing, stakeholders.

Before the shift to government involvement in the allocation of natural resources, a majority of the public perceived natural resources to be abundant. As the public began to utilize the expansive resources of the United States, it became evident that a lack of natural resource and public land management was leading to the exploitation of numerous types of natural resources, including wildlife, rangelands, and forests. In response to this exploitation, the federal government increased its role in the management of these resources.

For much of the twentieth century and into the twenty-first century, natural resource policy and management focused on the management of individual resources rather than taking a more holistic view of public resources. As a result of this segmented approach, management responsibilities are divided among an array of state and federal agencies. The division of management between the federal government and state and local governments is often described as a vertical division. Within the U.S. government, the largest land and resource management agencies are the Bureau of Land Management, the U.S. Fish and Wildlife Service, the National Park Service, and the U.S. Forest Service. These four agencies manage roughly 250 million hectares of land. Other federal agencies also play key roles in managing natural resources, including the U.S. Army Corps of Engineers, the Minerals Management Service, and the National Oceanic and Atmospheric Administration. State and local governments also play an important role in land management, with roughly 23 million hectares under management. These estimates do not include the 11.7 million square nautical kilometers of ocean under U.S. jurisdiction.

## PUBLIC POLICY AND NATURAL RESOURCES MANAGEMENT

Public policy refers to government action or inaction in response to some type of social problem. Management either involves day-to-day efforts on the ground (or water) or the efforts to control agencies that oversee those day-to-day efforts. Management represents a distinct form of policy implementation. It can be conceptually divided into two separate categories: strategic management and operational management. Strategic management refers to those efforts that determine the organizational/institutional structure; operational management refers to on-the-ground actions of the agencies.

Natural resource management is not a science. Ideally, natural resource management will be guided by both natural and social sciences but influenced by a host of other factors, including the values and the subjective processes of managers and resource stakeholders. Managers have the difficult task of bridging gaps between management, policy, and science.

## GENERAL ISSUES IN ENVIRONMENTAL FEDERALISM

One topic garnering continued discussion is the proper way to evaluate the balance of power between the federal government and the state governments. This requires determining how the vertical divisions of decision making influence the management of natural resources. Which level of government has the best claim on the management of the resource and which level of government can manage the resource most efficiently are two factors that must be determined.

Several benefits of lower-level, or local (state, city, and county), government jurisdiction exist. Local governments promote citizen involvement in self-governance, are often more responsive to the needs and preferences of local citizens, and tend to be more cost-effective. Skeptics of local government effectiveness point out that they often do not have the necessary resources to perform well. In addition, detractors also assert that some environmental issues are larger than local jurisdictional boundaries. For example, air pollution is not likely to stay in certain geographical boundaries, because of natural shifts in global wind patterns.

One of the ongoing debates over environmental federalism concerns the correct balance of power. Researchers have found that different levels of government produce different policies. One major cause can be attributed to the perceived consequence of localized versus national decision making. In some instances, lower levels of government are more likely to encourage developmental policies, like economic growth, over redistributive policies. This can be traced to fears that residents may move to nearby locations with more pro-growth policies. On a national level, redistributive policies, such as those protecting environmental quality and natural resource abundance, can be more effective because individuals and firms are less likely to move beyond national boundaries.

Theorists have described this localized tendency to

favor development, as it affects environmental quality and natural resources, as a "race to the bottom." This refers to situations in which state and local governments favor development over environmental quality, allowing for lower environmental standards. This perception has been disputed in academic literature. In some cases, states have exceeded existing federal standards. In practice, states and local governments have actually developed a whole host of innovative policies. On the localized level, state and local governments benefit from having the ability to tailor policies to meet the specific needs of a given area. Local levels of government also tend to be more cost-effective than the federal government.

The federal government has played a key role in the development of laws protecting the environment and natural resources. However, the federal government does not always have the ability or the knowledge to tailor policies to meet regional or localized needs. The federal government is well suited to address issues that are large in scale or that cross more localized jurisdictional boundaries.

## COLLABORATIVE OUTPUTS OF NATURAL RESOURCE POLICY

In application, there are numerous cases in which states and the federal government collaborate in the management of natural resources. One example of this occurs via the management of marine fisheries in the United States. Marine fisheries represent a unique natural resource requiring both state and federal attention, because some fish exist locally, but other fish have large migration patterns crossing numerous jurisdictional boundaries. Marine fisheries are a type of common-pool resource which, without oversight, are often depleted. In most cases, states control waters out to 5.6 nautical kilometers (the exceptions are Texas, Florida's Gulf coast, and Puerto Rico, which control waters out to 16.7 nautical kilometers), and the federal government controls waters out to 370 nautical kilometers. Of course, environmental systems do not adhere to these types of jurisdictional boundaries, thus necessitating collaborative efforts.

In response to these challenges, Congress passed the Magnuson-Stevens Fishery Conservation and Management Act of 1976 (amended in 1996 and reauthorized in 2006) to outline principal goals in conservation and management of fish, while simultaneously promoting safety and efficiency.

The Magnuson-Stevens Act relies on collaboration between state and federal governments. The National Marine Fisheries Service (NMFS) acts as the lead federal agency for the management of fisheries in federal waters. The act also designated regional management councils to advise the NMFS in this management effort. These management councils are composed of representatives from state fisheries management agencies, mandatory appointees from coastal states, at-large appointees from states in the region, and the regional directors of NMFS. The fisheries management councils have the vital responsibilities of creating Fisheries Management Plans (FMPs), which designate fish in need of management, analyze factors (both natural and social) influencing the fishery, and prepare the FMP to balance environmental, social, and economic goals. In the case of fisheries, states have the important role of managing fish in their jurisdiction as well as participating in regional management responsibilities, such as educating commercial and recreational fishermen and promoting the safe, legal fishing practices outlined in the Magnuson-Stevens Act.

## CONTEXT

Federalism is the operating system used by the United States to manage its natural resources. Considering the goals for resource management, such as conservation and protection, good working relationships between federal and local agencies are necessary to ensure the most efficient and most effective supervision. Goals at the local and national levels are intertwined, creating opportunities to work together to maximize benefits to and from the natural resources available.

*Joelle D. Godwin*

## FURTHER READING

Kay, Robert, and Jackie Alder. *Coastal Planning and Management.* New York: Taylor and Francis, 2005.

Koontz, Tomas M. *Federalism in the Forest: National Versus State Natural Resource Policy.* Washington, D.C.: Georgetown University Press, 2002.

Lowry, William R. "Natural Resource Policies in the Twenty-first Century." In *Environmental Policy: New Directions in the Twenty-first Century,* edited by Norman J. Vig and Michael E. Kraft. 4th ed. Washington, D.C.: Congressional Quarterly Press, 1999.

Magnun, William R., and Daniel H. Henning. *Managing the Environmental Crisis: Competing Values in Natural Resource Administration.* Durham, N.C.: Duke University Press, 1999.

Rabe, B. G. "Power to the States: The Promise and Pitfalls of Decentralization." In *Environmental Policy: New Directions in the Twenty-first Century*, edited by Norman J. Vig and Michael E. Kraft. 4th ed. Washington, D.C.: Congressional Quarterly Press, 1999.

Scheberle, Denise. "Partners in Policymaking: Forging Effective Federal-State Relations." *Environment* 40, no. 10 (1998): 14.

SEE ALSO: Bureau of Land Management, U.S.; Department of Agriculture, U.S.; Department of Energy, U.S.; Department of the Interior, U.S.; Ecozones and biogeographic realms; Environmental law in the United States; Fish and Wildlife Service, U.S.; Fisheries; Forest Service, U.S.; Land management; Land-use regulation and control; Public lands; Rangeland.

# Feldspars

CATEGORY: Mineral and other nonliving resources

*Feldspars are the most common minerals on the Earth's surface. They are a major component in most igneous rocks, available in inexhaustible supply.*

## WHERE FOUND

The largest concentration of feldspars occurs in igneous pegmatites, where zones of pure orthoclase that are greater than 30 meters thick are common. China, France, Italy, Mexico, Spain, Thailand, Turkey, and the United States together produce roughly 75 percent of the world's feldspar; most U.S. feldspar is obtained in North Carolina.

## PRIMARY USES

Feldspar is ground for use in industries as scouring soaps, ceramics, glassmaking material, and pottery. A plagioclase feldspar called labradorite and an alkali feldspar called moonstone show such a strong "play of colors" that they are used as semiprecious gemstones.

## TECHNICAL DEFINITION

The common feldspars are expressed in terms of mixtures of three end-member compositions; orthoclase, $KAlSi_3O_8$; albite, $NaAlSi_3O_8$; and anorthite, $CaAl_2Si_2O_8$. A feldspar that is a mixture of orthoclase and albite is called an alkali feldspar, and any member that is a mixture of albite and anorthite is known as a plagioclase feldspar. Orthoclase feldspar will change its crystal shape when exposed to prolonged periods of higher or lower temperatures; the high-temperature form is named sanidine, and the low-temperature form is microcline. Good cleavage in two directions at an angle of 90° is characteristic of all feldspars. The hardness of feldspars ranges from 6 to 6.5, and the specific gravity, excluding barium feldspars, is 2.55 to 2.76.

## DESCRIPTION, DISTRIBUTION, AND FORMS

Feldspar is the name given to members of a group of closely related anhydrous aluminum silicate minerals that vary in the chemical percentages of potassium, sodium, calcium, or, more rarely, barium in their formulas.

The internal atomic arrangements of the elements in all feldspars is similar except for aluminum. Its distribution in the structure depends on the temperature of formation of the feldspar. High-temperature sanidine shows a random distribution of aluminum within the atomic sites where aluminum and silicon occur, whereas low-temperature microcline shows a completely ordered arrangement of the aluminum ions.

The mining and processing of feldspar do not cause major disturbances to the environment. Feldspar is highly concentrated in the mined rock, so there is relatively little dump material and only a small pit needing reclamation. There are relatively few toxic chemicals utilized in the mining and processing of the rock, thereby restricting the possibilities for polluting the environment. The primary crushing of feldspar is done outside, so prolonged respiratory intake of silica dust can be avoided. Indoor dry milling requires the use of sufficient artificial ventilation to guard against dust inhalation.

## HISTORY

Feldspars appear to have been mined by American Indians before the discovery of the Americas by Europeans. Feldspar or feldspathic sand is evident in prehistoric pottery. It is thought that feldspar obtained from American Indians was shipped from what is now the state of North Carolina to Europe in 1744. Commercial feldspar production started in Connecticut in 1825, with the mining of alkali feldspar from an igneous pegmatite. The feldspar was hand-sorted, packed into barrels, and shipped to the United Kingdom. In 1850, a mill was constructed in Middletown, Connect-

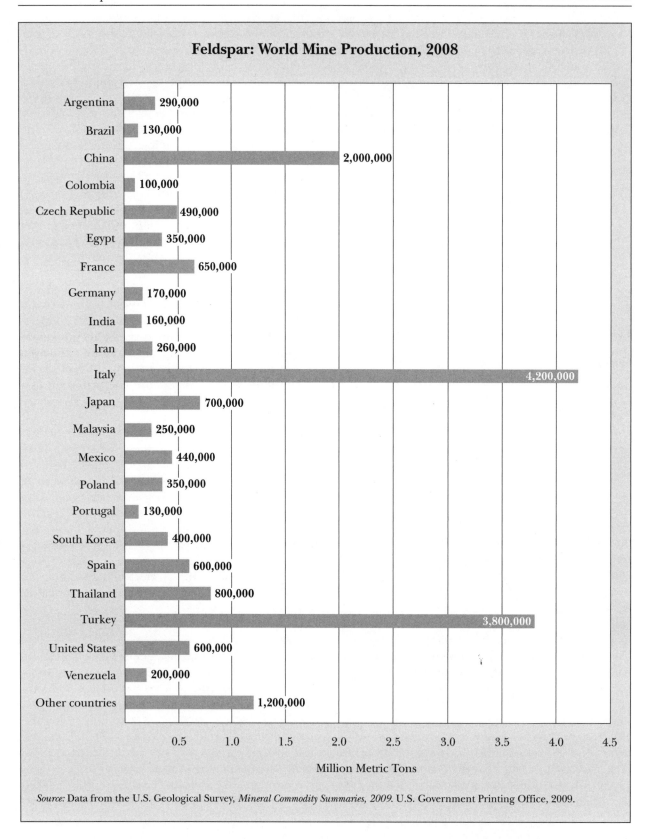

Feldspar: World Mine Production, 2008

| Country | Production |
|---|---|
| Argentina | 290,000 |
| Brazil | 130,000 |
| China | 2,000,000 |
| Colombia | 100,000 |
| Czech Republic | 490,000 |
| Egypt | 350,000 |
| France | 650,000 |
| Germany | 170,000 |
| India | 160,000 |
| Iran | 260,000 |
| Italy | 4,200,000 |
| Japan | 700,000 |
| Malaysia | 250,000 |
| Mexico | 440,000 |
| Poland | 350,000 |
| Portugal | 130,000 |
| South Korea | 400,000 |
| Spain | 600,000 |
| Thailand | 800,000 |
| Turkey | 3,800,000 |
| United States | 600,000 |
| Venezuela | 200,000 |
| Other countries | 1,200,000 |

Million Metric Tons

*Source:* Data from the U.S. Geological Survey, *Mineral Commodity Summaries, 2009.* U.S. Government Printing Office, 2009.

icut, to grind feldspar for the newly developed pottery industry in the United States.

The largest production of feldspar in the United States is in North Carolina, followed by Virginia, California, Oklahoma, Georgia, Idaho, and South Dakota. Crude feldspar is also produced by at least thirty-eight other countries. China, Turkey, Italy, and Thailand jointly produce approximately 60 percent of the world's total feldspar. U.S. production of crude feldspar is about 3 percent of the world total.

### OBTAINING FELDSPAR

The method used to obtain feldspar depends on the type of deposit to be mined. Most feldspar can be quarried by open-pit mining. Some feldspars are mined by boring down through distinct zones within pegmatite dikes, but many deposits require the use of explosives and drills. Dragline excavators are used to mine feldspathic sands. High-grade feldspar can be dry-processed. It is sent through jaw crushers, rolls, and oiled pebble mills, and is finally subjected to high-intensity magnetic or electrostatic treatments that reduce the iron content to acceptable levels.

Feldspathic sands are crushed and rolled, then processed by a three-step froth flotation sequence that removes mica, extracts the iron-bearing minerals, and finally separates the quartz residuals. Sometimes the last flotation procedure is omitted so that a feldspar-quartz mixture can be sold to the glassmaking industry. The feldspar is ground to about twenty mesh for glassmaking and to two hundred mesh or finer for ceramic and filler applications.

### USES OF FELDSPAR

Feldspar is used in the manufacturing of soaps, glass, enamels, and pottery. As a scouring soap, its intermediate hardness, angular fracture, and two directions of cleavage cause it to form sharp-edged, gritty particles that are hard enough to abrade but soft enough not to cause damage to surfaces. In glassmaking, feldspar brings alumina, together with alkalies, into the melt. This enhances the workability of the glass for shaping and gives it better chemical stability.

Feldspar is used primarily as a flux in ceramics mixtures to make vitreous china and porcelain enamels. The feldspar is ground to a very fine state and mixed with kaolin or clay and quartz. The feldspar fuses at a temperature below most of the other components and acts as a vitreous binder, cementing the material together. Fused feldspar is also used as the major part of the glaze on porcelain ware.

*Dion C. Stewart*

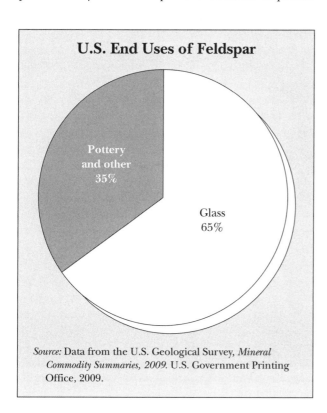

**U.S. End Uses of Feldspar**

Pottery and other 35%

Glass 65%

*Source:* Data from the U.S. Geological Survey, *Mineral Commodity Summaries, 2009.* U.S. Government Printing Office, 2009.

### FURTHER READING

Chatterjee, Kaulir Kisor. "Feldspar." In *Uses of Industrial Minerals, Rocks, and Freshwater.* New York: Nova Science, 2009.

Deer, W. A., R. A. Howie, and J. Zussman. *Framework Silcates: Feldspars.* Vol 4A in *Rock-Forming Minerals.* 2d ed. London: Geological Society, 2001.

Klein, Cornelis, and Barbara Dutrow. *The Twenty-third Edition of the Manual of Mineral Science.* 23d ed. Hoboken, N.J.: J. Wiley, 2008.

Kogel, Jessica Elzea, et al., eds. "Feldspars." In *Industrial Minerals and Rocks: Commodities, Markets, and Uses.* 7th ed. Littleton, Colo.: Society for Mining, Metallurgy, and Exploration, 2006.

Ribbe, R. H., ed. *Feldspar Mineralogy.* 2d ed. Washington, D.C.: Mineralogical Society of America, 1983.

Smith, Joseph V., and William L. Brown. *Feldspar Minerals.* 2d rev. and extended ed. New York: Springer, 1988.

Wenk, Hans-Rudolf, and Andrei Bulakh. *Minerals: Their Constitution and Origin.* New York: Cambridge University Press, 2004.

WEB SITES

U.S. GEOLOGICAL SURVEY
Feldspar
http://minerals.er.usgs.gov/minerals/pubs/
    commodity/gemstones/sp14-95/feldspar.html

U.S. GEOLOGICAL SURVEY
Feldspar: Statistics and Information
http://minerals.usgs.gov/minerals/pubs/
    commodity/feldspar

SEE ALSO: Abrasives; Ceramics; China; France; Igneous processes, rocks, and mineral deposits; Italy; Mexico; Pegmatites; Plutonic rocks and mineral deposits; Spain; Thailand; Turkey; United States.


# Fermi, Enrico

CATEGORY: People
BORN: September 29, 1901; Rome, Italy
DIED: November 28, 1954; Chicago, Illinois

*Fermi was an Italian physicist known for his work on the first nuclear reactor and his theory of beta decay. He contributed to quantum theory, statistical mechanics, and nuclear and particle physics. He conducted investigations on the atom's nucleus and experimented with uranium, which led to his observation of nuclear fission. His discovery of a methodology to release nuclear energy earned him the Nobel Prize in Physics in 1938.*

## BIOGRAPHICAL BACKGROUND

Enrico Fermi was born in Rome, Italy, the son of a railroad official and a schoolteacher. He excelled in school, sharing his interests with his older brother, Giulio, who died in 1915 after minor throat surgery. After high school, Fermi studied at the University of Pisa from 1918 to 1922, completing his undergraduate degree and Ph.D. in physics. Fermi solved the Fourier analysis for his college entrance exam and published his first scientific work on electrical charges in transient conditions in 1921.

Fermi received a fellowship to work at the University of Göttingen in Germany in 1924. He taught math at the University of Rome and the University of Florence, where he researched what

would later be called the Fermi-Dirac statistics. Fermi studied at Leyden in the Netherlands and married Laura Capon in 1928. Their daughter, Nella Fermi Weiner (1931-1995), and son, Giulio (1936-1997), both obtained Ph.D.'s. Fermi was one of the only physicists of the twentieth century to excel in both theoretical and applied nuclear physics. He died from stomach cancer, resulting from radiation exposure, on November 28, 1954.

After his death, his lecture notes were transcribed into books, and schools and many awards were named in his honor. Three nuclear reactor installations were named after him, as was "fermium," the one hundredth element on the periodic table.

## IMPACT ON RESOURCE USE

Fermi's research at the University of Rome led to the discovery of uranium fission in 1934. In 1939, on the Columbia University campus, the first splitting of the uranium atom took place. Fermi's focus was on

*Enrico Fermi's work with radioactive isotopes led to the development of the atomic bomb. (NARA)*

the isotope separation phase of the atomic energy project. In 1942, he led a famous team of scientists in lighting the first atomic fire on earth at the University of Chicago. His studies led to the construction of the first nuclear pile, called Chicago Pile-1, whereby he assessed the properties of fission, the key to extracting energy from nuclear reactions.

Another example of his impact was noted on July 16, 1945, when Fermi supervised the design and assembly of the atomic bomb. Fermi dropped small pieces of paper as the wave of the blast reached him and then measured the distance those pieces were blown. This allowed him to estimate the bomb's energy yield. The calculations became known as the "Fermi method." His discovery of how to release nuclear energy encouraged the development of many peaceful uses for nuclear energy.

Fermi discovered induced radioactivity (radioactive elements produced by the irradiation of neutrons) and nonexplosive uranium, which is transmuted into plutonium (a vital element in the atomic and hydrogen bombs and the first atomic submarine). His research led to the creation of more than forty artificial radioactive isotopes, and his theory of neutron decay became the model for future theories of particle interaction.

*Gina M. Robertiello*

SEE ALSO: Hydrogen; Nobel, Alfred; Nuclear energy; Nuclear Energy Institute; Uranium.


# Ferroalloys

CATEGORY: Mineral and other nonliving resources

## WHERE FOUND

Ferroalloy production occurs in many countries around the world, but the primary ferroalloy-producing countries are China, South Africa, Ukraine, Russia, and Kazakhstan. These five countries produce more than 74 percent of the world's ferroalloy supply. However, because the various ferroalloys contain a number of different elements, many parts of the world supply minerals important in ferroalloy production.

## PRIMARY USES

Ferroalloys are used extensively in the iron and steel industry. The type of alloy produced depends upon the properties of the element that is added to the iron. Stainless steel, high-strength steels, tool steels, and cast irons are the major ferroalloy products. Some ferroalloys are also used to produce metal coatings, catalysts, electrodes, lighting filaments, aerospace and marine products, medical implants, and household batteries.

## TECHNICAL DEFINITION

Ferroalloys constitute a wide variety of alloyed metals that combine a large percentage of iron with a smaller percentage of one or more elements. Combining other elements with iron imparts superior strength to these alloys, and this increased strength enables the metals to be used in many important products within the metallurgical industry. Ferroalloys have lower melting points than do the pure elements that form them; therefore, they are incorporated more easily into molten metal. Manganese, chromium, magnesium, molybdenum, nickel, titanium, vanadium, silicon, cobalt, copper, boron, phosphorus, niobium, tungsten, aluminum, and zirconium are the primary elements mixed in varying proportions with iron to produce ferroalloys. Ferroalloys are produced primarily in electric arc furnaces; the nonferrous metal combines with the iron at high temperatures to produce the various types of steel.

## DESCRIPTION, DISTRIBUTION, AND FORMS

Much of the stainless-steel production of Europe, Asia, and North and South America is possible because of ferrochromium. In 2007, approximately 29 metric tons of stainless steel were produced throughout the world. Most chromite ore mining takes place in China, India, South Africa, Russia, Turkey, and Kazakhstan. The majority of chromite ore is smelted in electric arc furnaces to produce ferrochromium, which is then exported to the countries that manufacture stainless steel.

Ferromanganese and silicomanganese are primary ingredients in steelmaking. Most of the U.S. supply of these alloys is imported from South Africa, although China, Brazil, India, and Ukraine are also important producers. The United States also produces some ferromanganese at a plant near Marietta, Ohio. Besides being a key component in steel manufacturing, manganese is used in the production of household batteries. Silicomanganese production at plants in New Haven, West Virginia, the United Kingdom, and Ukraine has been vital to steelmaking for a number of years.

Ferrosilicon is a deoxidizing agent in cast iron and steel production. China, Brazil, and Russia are the main producers of ferrosilicon, with China producing more than four times as much as the other two countries.

More than 99 percent of ferronickel use within the United States is for stainless steel and heat-resistant steel. Stainless-steel cooking pots, pans, and kitchen sinks are products of the ferronickel industry. The United States does not produce any primary nickel but instead produces a remelt alloy with small percentages of chromium and nickel from recycled materials. Japan, New Caledonia, Colombia, Greece, Ukraine, Indonesia, the Dominican Republic, and Venezuela lead the world in ferronickel production.

Another major ferroalloy is ferromolybdenum, a component of stainless steels, tool steels, and cast iron. About 80 percent of world production of ferromolybdenum takes place in Chile, China, and the United States, while the remainder occurs in Canada, Mexico, and Peru.

Ferrotitanium plays a large role in the steel industry as a deoxidizing and stabilizing agent as well as an alloy that assists in controlling the grain size of steel. Titanium is not naturally found in metallic form but instead is mined from titanates, oxides, and silicotitanites. Ferrotitanium is then produced by an induction melting process. Steels with a high titanium content include stainless, high-strength, and interstitial-free (space-free) forms. Other important ferrotitanium uses include catalysts, pigments, floor coverings, roofing material, aerospace products, medical implants, armor, and marine industrial goods. Major producers of ferrotitanium include China, India, Japan, Russia, the United Kingdom, and the United States.

Ferrovanadium, used in the manufacture of catalysts and chemicals, is produced in the United States mostly from petroleum ash and residues as well as from tar sands. China and South Africa contribute 71 percent of the world's supply of ferrovanadium, while Russia makes up most of the remaining supply.

## HISTORY

Steel has been produced by a number of methods since before the fifteenth century, but only since the seventeenth century has it been produced efficiently. The Bessemer process, invented in the mid-1800's by Sir Henry Bessemer, enabled steel to be mass-produced in a cost-effective manner. Improvements on the Bessemer process included the Thomas-Gilchrist process and the Siemens-Martin process of open-hearth steel manufacture. Basic oxygen steelmaking, also known as the Linz-Donawitz process, was developed in the 1950's, and although the Bessemer process and other processes continued to be used for a few more years, basic oxygen steelmaking soon became the process of choice for modern steel manufacture.

## CREATING FERROALLOYS

Ferroalloys have been used in the steel manufacturing industry primarily since the 1960's. In the twentieth century, metallurgists discovered that adding varying amounts of manganese, silicon, or aluminum to the molten steel pulled oxygen away from the melted material, thus allowing for sound castings without bubbles or blowholes. The other ferroalloys—those containing chromium, tungsten, molybdenum, vanadium, titanium, and boron—provide a method for making specialty steels other than ordinary carbon steel. By adding small amounts of the other metals, high-strength, heat-resistant steels, such as stainless steel, can be produced.

The amount of steel that a country produces is often considered to be an important indicator of economic progress. Therefore, the production of ferroalloys within the iron and steel manufacturing industry is also a key factor of the economy of the countries in which it takes place. In the twenty-first century, the economic booms in China and India brought about a large increase in demand for steel products and a corresponding need for a large number of workers in this industry. The top producers of steel in the world are, in order of metric-ton production per year, China, Japan, Russia, and the United States. Each of these countries has many thousands of workers in its steel industry and in the mining industries, which supply the raw materials for iron and steel production.

## USES OF FERROALLOYS

The primary use of ferroalloys is in the manufacturing of iron and steel. Combining various metallic elements with iron results in a strong, stable product vital to many industries. Stainless and heat-resisting steels are produced from ferrochromium, ferrotitanium, and ferronickel. Ordinary carbon steel rusts, but stainless steel resists corrosion because of the chromium oxide film it contains. In general, at least 11 percent chromium must be added to the steel in order to produce the stainless quality. Up to 26 percent chromium must be added if the stainless steel is to be exposed to harsh environmental conditions. Although stainless steel has a huge number of applications in modern society, it is mostly used for cutlery, appliances, surgical instruments, cooking equipment, and aerospace parts. Because stainless steel is also resistant to bacterial growth, it is important in the cooking and medical industries. Stainless steel is also used in jewelry and firearm production.

Ferrochromium is used in the chemical industry as a surface treatment coating for metals. Besides the primary uses of ferroalloys in steelmaking, these substances are also used to produce catalysts in catalytic converters, pigments in paint, grinding and cutting tools, lighting filaments, and electrodes. Ferrosilicon is used by the military to produce hydrogen for balloons in a process that combines sodium hydroxide, ferrosilicon, and water.

*Lenela Glass-Godwin*

## FURTHER READING

Corathers, Lisa A. "Manganese." *USGS Minerals Yearbook* (2007).

Dunkley, J. J., and D. Norval. "Atomisation of Ferroalloys." In *Industrial Minerals and Rocks*, edited by Jessica Elzea Kogel. 6th ed. Littleton, Colo.: Society of Mining, Metallurgy, and Exploration, 2004.

Jones, Andrew. "The Market and Cost Environments for Bulk Ferroalloys." In *International Conference on Innovations in the Ferroalloy Industry.* New Delhi: The Indian Ferro Alloy Producers' Association, 2004.

Papp, J. F. "Chromite." In *Industrial Minerals and Rocks*, edited by Jessica Elzea Kogel. 6th ed. Littleton, Colo.: Society of Mining, Metallurgy, and Exploration, 2004.

## WEB SITE

U.S. GEOLOGICAL SURVEY
Minerals Information: Ferroalloys Statistics and Information
http://minerals.usgs.gov/minerals/pubs/commodity/ferroalloys/

SEE ALSO: Aluminum; Bessemer process; Boron; Chromium; Cobalt; Copper; Magnesium; Manganese; Molybdenum; Nickel; Niobium; Siemens, William; Silicon; Steel; Steel industry; Titanium; Tungsten; Vanadium; Zirconium.

# Fertilizers

CATEGORIES: Plant and animal resources; products from resources

*Fertilizers, those materials that are used to modify the chemical composition of the soil in order to enhance plant growth, represent an important use of natural resources because agricultural systems are dependent upon the ability to retain soil fertility. Among the essential nutrients provided in fertilizers are calcium, magnesium, sulfur, nitrogen, potassium, and phosphorus.*

## BACKGROUND

It has been said that civilization owes its existence to the 15-centimeter layer of soil covering the Earth's landmasses. This layer of topsoil represents the root zone for the majority of the world's food and fiber crops. Soil is a dynamic, chemically reactive medium, and agricultural soils must provide structural support for plants, contain a sufficient supply of plant nutrients, and exhibit an adequate capacity to hold and exchange minerals. As plants grow and develop, they remove the essential mineral nutrients from the soil. Since normal crop production usually requires the removal of plants or plant parts, nutrients are continuously being removed from the soil. Therefore, the long-term agricultural utilization of any soil requires periodic fertilization to replace these lost nutrients. Fertilizers are associated with every aspect of this nutrient replacement process. The application of fertilizer is based on a knowledge of plant growth and development, soil chemistry, and plant-soil interactions.

## SOIL NUTRIENTS

Plants require an adequate supply of both macronutrients (calcium, magnesium, sulfur, nitrogen, potassium, and phosphorus) and micronutrients (iron, copper, zinc, boron, manganese, chloride, and molybdenum) from the soil. If any one of these nutrients is not present in sufficient amounts, plant growth and, ultimately, yields will be reduced. Because micronutrients are required in small quantities and deficiencies in these minerals occur infrequently, the majority of agricultural fertilizers contain only macronutrients. Although magnesium and calcium are utilized in large quantities, most agricultural soils contain an abundance of these two elements, either derived from parent material or added as lime. Most soils also contain sufficient amounts of sulfur from the weathering of sulfur-containing minerals, the presence of sulfur in other fertilizers, and atmospheric pollutants.

The remaining three macronutrients (nitrogen, potassium, and phosphorus) are readily depleted and are referred to as fertilizer elements. Hence, these elements must be added to most soils on a regular basis. Fertilizers containing two or more nutrients are called mixed fertilizers. A fertilizer labeled 10-10-10, for example, means that the product contains 10 percent nitrogen, 10 percent phosphorus, and 10 percent potassium. Since these elements can be supplied in a number of different forms, some of which may not be immediately useful to plants, most states require that the label reflect the percentage of nutrients available for plant utilization. Fertilizers are produced in a wide variety of single and mixed formulations, and the percentage of available nutrients generally ranges from a low of 5 percent to a high of 33 percent. Mixed fertilizers may also contain varying amounts of different micronutrients.

## FERTILIZER PRODUCTION

Nitrogen fertilizers can be classified as either chemical or natural organic. Natural organic sources are derived from plant and animal residues and include such materials as animal manures, cottonseed meal, and soybean meal. Since natural organic fertilizers contain relatively small amounts of nitrogen, commercial operations rely on chemical fertilizers derived from sources other than plants and animals. The major chemical sources of nitrogen include both ammonium compounds and nitrates. The chemical fixation of atmospheric nitrogen by the Claude-Haber ammonification process is the cornerstone of the modern nitrogen fertilizer manufacturing process. Once the ammonia is produced, it can be applied directly to the soil as anhydrous ammonia, or it can be mixed with water and supplied as a solution of aqueous ammonia and used in chemical reactions to produce other ammonium fertilizers or urea, or converted to nitrates that can be used to make nitrate fertilizers.

Some organic fertilizers contain small amounts of phosphorus, and organically derived phosphates from guano or acid-treated bonemeal were used in the past. However, the supply of these materials is scarce. Almost all commercially produced agricultural phosphates are applied as either phosphoric acid or superphosphate derived from rock phosphate. The major phosphate component in commercially important deposits of rock phosphate is apatite. The apatite is mined, processed to separate the phosphorus-containing fraction from inert materials, and then treated with sulfuric acid to break the apatite bond. The superphosphate precipitates out of the solution and sets up as a hard block, which can be mechanically granulated to produce a fertilizer containing calcium, sulfur, and phosphorus. Potassium fertilizers, commonly called "potash," are also obtained from mineral deposits below the Earth's surface. The major commercially available potassium fertilizers are potassium chloride extracted from sylvanite ore, potassium sulfate produced by various methods (including extraction from langbeinite or burkeite ores or chemical reactions with potassium chloride), and potassium nitrate, which can be manufactured by several different chemical processes. Although limited, there are sources of organic potassium fertilizers such as tobacco stalks and dried kelp.

While the individual nitrogen, phosphorus, and potassium fertilizers can be applied directly to the soil, they are also commonly used to manufacture mixed fertilizers. From two to ten different materials with widely different properties are mixed together in the manufacturing process. The three most common processes utilized in mixed fertilizer production are the ammonification of phosphorus materials and the subsequent addition of other materials, bulk blending of solid ingredients, and liquid mixing. Fillers and make-weight materials are often added to make up the difference between the weight of fertilizer materials required to furnish the stated amount of nutrient and the desired bulk of mixed products. Mixed fertilizers have the obvious advantage of supplying all the required nutrients in one application.

## BENEFITS AND COSTS

For every crop there is a point at which the yield may continue to increase with application of additional nutrients, but the increase will not offset the additional cost of the fertilizer. Therefore, considerable care should be exercised when applying fertilizer. The economically feasible practice, therefore, is to apply the appropriate amount of fertilizer to produce maximum profit rather than maximum yield. Moreover, since excessive fertilization can result in adverse soil reactions that damage plant roots or produce undesired growth patterns, overfertilization can actually decrease yields. If supplied in excessive amounts, some of the micronutrients are toxic to plants and will dramatically reduce plant growth. Fertilizer manufacturers must ensure that their products contain the specified amounts of nutrients indicated on their labels and that there are no contaminants that could adversely affect plant yield directly or indirectly through undesirable soil reactions.

The environment can also be adversely affect by overfertilization. Excess nutrients can be leached through the soil into underground water supplies and/or removed from the soil in the runoff water that eventually empties into streams and lakes. High levels of plant nutrients in streams and lakes (eutrophication) can result in abnormal algal growth, which can cause serious pollution problems. Water that contains excessive amounts of plant nutrients can also pose health problems if it is consumed by humans or livestock.

## IMPORTANCE TO FOOD PRODUCTION
Without a doubt, the modern use of fertilizer has dramatically increased crop yields. If food and fiber production is to keep pace with the world's growing population, increased reliance on fertilizers will be required in the future. With ever-increasing attention to the environment, future research will primarily be aimed at finding fertilizer materials that will remain in the field to which they are applied and at improving application and cultivation techniques to contain materials within the designated application area. The use of technology developed from discoveries in the field of molecular biology to develop more efficient plants holds considerable promise for the future.

*D. R. Gossett*

## FURTHER READING
Altieri, Miguel A. *Agroecology: The Scientific Basis of Alternative Agriculture.* Boulder, Colo.: Westview Press, 1987.

Black, C. A. *Soil-Plant Relationships.* 2d ed. Malabar, Fla.: R. E. Krieger, 1984.

Brady, Nyle C., and Ray R. Weil. *The Nature and Properties of Soils.* 14th ed. Upper Saddle River, N.J.: Prentice Hall, 2008.

Elsworth, Langdon R., and Walter O. Paley, eds. *Fertilizers: Properties, Applications, and Effects.* New York: Nova Science, 2008.

Engelstad, Orvis P. *Fertilizer Technology and Use.* 3d ed. Madison, Wis.: Soil Science Society of America, 1986.

Follett, Roy H., Larry S. Murphy, and Roy L. Donahue. *Fertilizers and Soil Amendments.* Englewood Cliffs, N.J.: Prentice-Hall, 1981.

Hall, William L., Jr., and Wayne P. Robarge, eds. *Environmental Impact of Fertilizer on Soil and Water.* Washington, D.C.: American Chemical Society, 2004.

Havlin, John L., Samuel Tisdale, Werner Nelson, and James D. Beaton. *Soil Fertility and Fertilizers: An Introduction to Nutrient Management.* 7th ed. Upper Saddle River, N.J.: Pearson Prentice Hall, 2005.

## WEB SITES

AGRICULTURE AND AGRI-FOOD CANADA
Manure, Fertilizer, and Pesticide Management in Canada
http://www4.agr.gc.ca/AAFC-AAC/display-afficher.do?id=1178825328101&lang=eng

ECONOMIC RESEARCH SERVICE, U.S. DEPARTMENT OF AGRICULTURE
U.S. Fertilizer Use and Price
http://www.ers.usda.gov/Data/FertilizerUse

SEE ALSO: Agriculture industry; Eutrophication; Green Revolution; Guano; Horticulture; Hydroponics; Monoculture agriculture; Nitrogen and ammonia; Potash; Slash-and-burn agriculture; Soil degradation.

# Fiberglass

CATEGORY: Products from resources

*Fiberglass has many practical uses, especially in structural applications and insulation, because its fibers are stronger than steel and will not burn, stretch, rot, or fade.*

## DEFINITION
Fiberglass consists of fine, flexible glass filaments or fibers drawn or blown directly from a glass melt. These fibers may be many times finer than human hair.

## OVERVIEW
Fiberglass is typically made in a two-stage process. Glass is first melted and formed into marbles in an electric furnace, and then fibers are drawn continuously through holes in a platinum bushing and wound

onto a revolving drum like threads on spools. The drum can pull out more than 3 kilometers of fibers in a minute, and up to 153 kilometers of fiber can be drawn from one glass marble that is 1.6 centimeters in diameter. For a given set of operating conditions, the size of the fibers is uniform, with diameters varying from approximately 0.00025 centimeter to 0.00125 centimeter, depending on the application. Some ultrafine fibers have diameters of 0.0000762 centimeter or less. A typical composition of fiberglass (E glass) is 54 percent silica, 15 percent alumina, 16 percent calcia, 9.5 percent boron oxide, 5 percent magnesia, and 0.5 percent sodium oxide by weight. Because of its low alkali (sodium) content, this type of fiberglass has good durability and strength, and because of the boron, it can be melted at reasonably low temperatures.

Coarse glass fibers were used by the ancient Egyptians to decorate dishes, cups, bottles, and vases. At the Columbian Exposition in Chicago in 1893, Edward Drummond Libbey exhibited a dress made of fiberglass and silk. During World War I (1914-1918), the Germans produced fiberglass in small diameters as a substitute for asbestos. In 1938, the Owens-Corning Fiberglass Corporation was formed in the United States, and fiberglass production was soon started on a commercial scale.

Fiberglass wool, made of loosely intertwined strands of glass with air pockets in between, is an excellent insulator against heat and cold. It is used as a thermal insulator in the exterior walls and ceilings of homes and other buildings, as a thermal and electrical insulator in furnaces, ovens, water heaters, refrigerators, and freezers, and as a thermal and sound insulator in airplanes. Fiberglass is commonly combined with plastic polymers to produce laminates that can be formed into complex shapes for use in automobile and truck bodies, boats, carport roofs, swimming pool covers, and other items requiring light weight, strength, and corrosion resistance. In addition, fiberglass is woven into a variety of fabrics, tapes, braids, and cords for use in shower curtains, fireproof draperies, and electrical insulation of wire and cable in electric motors, generators, transformers, meters, and electronic equipment.

*Alvin K. Benson*

SEE ALSO: Aluminum; Boron; Glass; Petrochemical products; Sedimentary processes, rocks, and mineral deposits; Silicates; Silicon; Textiles and fabrics.

# Fires

CATEGORY: Environment, conservation, and resource management

*Wildfire is an integral part of wilderness life cycles, helping keep ecosystems healthy and diverse in plant and animal life. Controlled human-set fires aid farmers, ranchers, and foresters in making their lands more productive.*

## BACKGROUND

Fire is both inevitable and necessary to most land ecosystems. Every day, lightning strikes the ground about eight million times globally, and one stroke in twenty-five can start a fire. Even so, lightning accounts for only about 10 percent of ignitions; humans are the leading agent in setting fires. Fire was one of the first tools humans used to shape their environment, and it has remained among the most common tools ever since. Add to lightning and humans as agents the molten rock from volcanoes and the sparks sometimes caused by rock slides, and not surprisingly millions of hectares of land burn worldwide every year.

Because fire is so prevalent, ecosystems have evolved tolerance to it or even a symbiotic dependence on it. Wildfires foster decomposition of dead material, recycle nutrients, control diseases by burning infected plants and trees, help determine which plant species flourish in a particular area, and in some cases even play a role in germinating seeds. Purposefully set fires, today called controlled burns, have flushed game for hunters since prehistoric times and are still put to work fertilizing fields and clearing them of unwanted plants, pruning forests, combating human and animal enemies, and eliminating dead, dry materials before they can support a destructive major fire.

## TYPES OF FIRE

Not all fires are equal. Scientists distinguish five basic types in increasing order of intensity and destructive potential: those that smolder in deep layers of organic material; surface backfires, which burn against the wind; surface headfires, which burn with the wind; crown fires, which advance as a single front; and high-intensity spotting fires, during which winds loft burning fragments that ignite separate fires. Moreover, the intensity, likelihood, and range of fires for any locale depend upon the climate, season, terrain, weather (es-

*Wildfires, like this one in 1996 in Calabasas, California, are integral aspects of the natural cycles of life, but too often and increasingly they encroach on places in which humans dwell.* (AP/Wide World Photos)

pecially the wind), relative moisture, and time since a previous burn. The dominant species of plant also affects which type of fire an ecosystem can support.

### TUNDRA AND FAR-NORTHERN FORESTS

Fires visit northern ecosystems infrequently because they retain a great deal of moisture even during the summer: There are intervals of sixty to more than one hundred years between fires for forests and several centuries for tundra. Caused primarily by lightning, light surface fires are most common. Crown fires are rare. The seeds of many northern tree species, such as pine and spruce, germinate well only on soil that a fire has bared. Fire does not occur in high Arctic tundra and plays only a minor role in the development of low Arctic tundra.

### GRASSLANDS

Grasslands of all kinds rebound from surface fires in about three years. In shortgrass and mixed-grass prairies, grass species, especially buffalo grass and blue grama, survive fires well, while small cacti and broadleaf plants succumb easily, assuring dominance of the grasses. For this reason, cattle ranchers frequently burn the prairies to remove litter and inedible species, thus improving the distribution of grazing fodder. In tallgrass prairies, big bluestem, Indian grass, and switchgrass increase after a fire, whereas cold-season grasses, such as Kentucky bluegrass, are devastated, and fires prevent invasions of trees and woody shrubs.

### SEMIDESERT AND DESERT REGIONS

Similarly, surface fires control shrubs in semidesert grass-shrub lands on mesas and foothills, while allowing the fire-resistant mesquite to flourish. Desert sagebrush areas in the intermountain West have a surface fire about every thirty-two to seventy years. A burned area takes about thirty years to recover fully, although horsebrush and rabbitbrush come back quickly.

## CHAPARRAL-DOMINATED LANDS

The chaparral of temperate coastal climates, such as that in Southern California, ignites easily and is likely to burn from surface fires every ten to fifteen years. In fact, without fire, chaparral fields, which also support manzanita, scrub oak, and coyote brush, become choked, and many nonsprouting shrubs die. Light fires every twenty to thirty years are therefore necessary to species survival. Unburned for longer than that, the fields accumulate so much dead debris that the chances for a tremendously destructive fire soar.

## FOREST FIRES

Great diversity in tree types and, accordingly, fire frequency and intensity, exists among evergreen and deciduous forests. Forests can fall prey to all types of fire; crown and high-intensity spotting fires are most common in Douglas fir-dominated areas, while mature stands of pure juniper are nearly impossible to burn. In general, fire helps maintain the dominance of pines by preventing hardwoods, which burn more readily (with the exception of some oak species), from invading. Several pine and spruce species, most notably ponderosa pine, require fire-cleared soil to germinate seeds. Wildfire intervals range from five to ten years for ponderosa pines and up to five hundred years for redwoods.

Beginning in the 1960's, government land managers used controlled burns and unopposed wildfires to clear away underbrush and dead trees in public forests. However, since such fires destroy public timber resources and sometimes, out of control, ravage private lands and human residential areas, the practice has been controversial, especially after the devastating Yellowstone National Park fire of 1988.

The political as well as economic infeasibility of controlling overgrowth may have contributed to Southern California's "Station Fire" of 2009, which ravaged roughly two hundred square miles of the Angeles National Forest and adjacent residential interface areas (an area the size of San Francisco) during the largest forest fire in the history of Los Angeles County. The region, normally prone to fires driven by Santa Ana winds, instead underwent a fuel-driven fire that threatened lives and destroyed approximately one hundred homes as well as vast areas of wildlife habitat. Australia experienced similar massive fires during this period.

Such events, while part of a natural cycle, pose immediate threats not only to ecological and other natural resources but also to human infrastructure when development has encroached on the areas subject to burning. Combined with evidence of global warming and concomitant trends toward droughts and longer or unbroken "fire seasons," such fires can be expected to increase the strain on economic and human resources.

*Roger Smith*

## FURTHER READING

Carle, David. *Introduction to Fire in California.* Berkeley: University of California Press, 2008.

DeBano, Leonard F., Daniel G. Neary, and Peter F. Ffolliott. *Fire's Effects on Ecosystems.* New York: J. Wiley, 1998.

Pyne, Stephen J. *Awful Splendour: A Fire History of Canada.* Vancouver: University of British Columbia Press, 2007.

_____. *Fire in America: A Cultural History of Wildland and Rural Fire.* 1982. Reprint. Princeton, N.J.: Princeton University Press, 1988.

_____. *World Fire: The Culture of Fire on Earth.* New York: Holt, 1995.

Quintiere, James G. *Fundamentals of Fire Phenomena.* Chichester, England: John Wiley, 2006.

Rossotti, Hazel. *Fire.* New York: Oxford University Press, 1993.

Wein, Ross W., and David A. MacLean, eds. *The Role of Fire in Northern Circumpolar Ecosystems.* New York: Published on behalf of the Scientific Committee on Problems of the Environment of the International Council of Scientific Unions by Wiley, 1983.

Whelan, Robert J. *The Ecology of Fire.* New York: Cambridge University Press, 1995.

Wright, Henry A., and Arthur W. Bailey. *Fire Ecology: United States and Southern Canada.* New York: Wiley, 1982.

## WEB SITES

CANADIAN FOREST SERVICE, NATURAL RESOURCES CANADA
Canadian Wildland Fire Information System
http://cwfis.cfs.nrcan.gc.ca/en_CA/index

U.S. GEOLOGICAL SURVEY
Natural Hazards: Wildfires
http://www.usgs.gov/hazards/wildfires

SEE ALSO: Erosion and erosion control; Forest fires; Forest management; Forestry; Grasslands; Rangeland; Slash-and-burn agriculture.

# Fish and Wildlife Service, U.S.

CATEGORY: Government and resources
DATE: Established 1940

*The U.S. Fish and Wildlife Service, a part of the U.S. Department of the Interior, is the primary federal agency charged with protecting the nation's fish, wildlife, and associated habitats.*

## BACKGROUND

The U.S. Fish and Wildlife Service (FWS) grew out of two agencies: the Bureau of Fisheries (1871) in the Department of Commerce and the Bureau of Biological Survey (1885) in the Department of Agriculture. Each held specific duties designed to protect the country's fishing, game hunting, and other natural resources. Under Presidential Reorganization Plan 111, Franklin D. Roosevelt consolidated the agencies and created the FWS in 1940.

## IMPACT ON RESOURCE USE

Under the Fish and Wildlife Act of 1956, the Fish and Wildlife Service was given legislative status and divided into two divisions: the Bureau of Commercial Fisheries and the Bureau of Sport Fisheries and Wildlife. The latter eventually took over the agency when the commercial division moved into the Department of Commerce in 1970. The FWS is a bureau of the Department of the Interior. It seeks to enforce legislation pertaining to wildlife and to protect associated natural resources. A director, under the umbrella of the secretary of the interior, is in charge of the nearly nine thousand employees of the FWS.

To fulfill its duties, the FWS developed a three-pronged approach: conservation, research, and enforcement. Conservation relates to the 38 million hectares in more than seven hundred areas of the National Wildlife Refuge System that fall under FWS jurisdiction. In addition, the FWS maintains the National Fish Hatcheries System and provides support to state and local agencies seeking federal funding or intervention. Its research activities involve a national network of field agents and biologists who work to protect wildlife and its surroundings. FWS policy maintains that the protection of habitat through conservation and research is essential to the survival of animals. Its mission includes particular attention to endangered species.

The agency's approach to enforcement has evolved through the years. In addition to its central administrative office it has eight regional offices and almost seven hundred field offices. Through its regional offices and hundreds of field stations, the FWS has increased the numbers of animal species under its care. From regulating migratory bird hunting and issuing duck-hunting licenses to setting limits on fish catches and enforcing the protection of threatened wildlife, the FWS has greatly expanded its role over its history. Eventually "wildlife" came to represent a traditional definition of animal life as well as fresh and anadromous fish, certain marine mammals, and identified endangered species. In the late twentieth century, as national policy extended to include a more conservational and environmental approach, the FWS responded with improved regulation of wetlands and the wildlife refuge system. Legislative support brought increased research into the water, air, and plant life of wildlife habitats. In addition to preservation, one of the most important tasks of the FWS is education in wildlife and conservation, particularly geared to the youth of the United States. The FWS features numerous programs addressing issues of wildlife. The FWS has a law enforcement division aiming to stop crimes against wildlife and those committed on its lands. The FWS also has the world's only forensics laboratory devoted to solving and preventing crimes against wildlife.

The 38-million-hectare National Wildlife Refuge System is the only collection of federal lands managed exclusively for the benefit of wildlife. This beautiful ecosystem includes diverse water, land, and forest habitats. About 750,000 hectares of wetlands, essential to the health and welfare of wildlife and humans, are included in this total. More than thirty-nine million tourists visit the National Wildlife Refuge System annually. Despite the importance of this system, the FWS managed these habitats for decades without an organic law. "Organic law" means a fundamental constitution or law that outlines the basic principles of government. Without an organic law, the FWS oversaw the National Wildlife Refuge System by means of piecemeal legislation and regulation. Congress passed numerous important pieces of legislation affecting FWS throughout the second half of the twentieth century. For example, the Federal Aid in Sport Fish Restoration Act (Dingell-Johnson Act), enacted in 1950, established a program to improve the fishery resources of the nation. The National Wildlife Refuge

System Administration Act, enacted in 1966, served to protect the refuge areas from damaging uses. The Endangered Species Act, enacted in 1973, entrusted FWS with responsibility over many endangered species. The Alaska National Interest Lands Conservation Act, enacted in 1980, greatly expanded the National Wildlife Refuge System, adding more than 21 million hectares of land.

A watershed moment for the FWS came in 1997 with the passage of perhaps the most important legislation in its history. The National Wildlife Refuge System Improvement Act of 1997 was a major legislative scheme affecting federal use and oversight of wildlife lands. Congress passed the act as Public Law 105-57. President Bill Clinton signed the act on October 9, 1997. The National Wildlife Refuge System Improvement Act provided the organic law for the FWS. In other words, all of the actions of the FWS should follow from this act. It represents a comprehensive set of legislation that mandates the responsibilities and actions of the FWS as it relates to the National Wildlife Refuge System. The act is divided into ten parts, covering such topics as hunting, trapping, and fishing; concerns relating to live wildlife and fish; the sale, purchase, and transport of wild animals; and licensing, enforcement, penalties, and regulations. Perhaps most important, the act gave a strong mission statement to guide the Department of the Interior and the FWS. This mission statement emphasizes the mandate to protect wildlife and maintain the diversity, health, and outstanding qualities of the habitats. The act required a new process to determine which recreational activities are appropriate in the refuges. The act also recognized that traditional activities such as fishing, hunting, and wildlife observation are appropriate public uses of the National Wildlife Refuge System, as long as they do not harm the environment. Finally, the National Wildlife Refuge System Improvement Act required the FWS to devise a comprehensive plan to conserve all of the refuges under its management.

The FWS received $280 million under the American Recovery and Reinvestment Act of 2009 to complete projects that enhance the wildlife habitats while providing jobs and stimulating the economy. This measure harked back to the days of the Civilian Conservation Corps (CCC). The CCC (1933-1942) was created as a project of the New Deal, both to provide jobs in a time of economic crisis and to develop and conserve natural resources in the United States. In late 2009, the FWS released a strategic plan to help the wildlife and habitats under its management to survive the impact of global climate change.

In its efforts to conserve, research, and protect through enforcement, the FWS often faces opposition from business interests and conservation groups. The logging industry, for example, has criticized certain protective measures, claiming that they place more importance on animals than humans. Conservation groups, on the other hand, have criticized the FWS for allowing controlled predatory animal reductions on federal refuge land. In all such instances, the FWS finds itself faced with balancing national policy with wildlife interests.

The FWS provides a vital link between the U.S. government, U.S. citizens, and the natural world. The FWS prides itself on managing the largest and most impressive wildlife habitat in the world. Through its protective as well as investigative functions, the FWS works to maintain a strong level of biodiversity in the United States.

*Jennifer Davis, updated by Howard Bromberg*

FURTHER READING

Bean, Michael. *The Evolution of National Wildlife Law.* 3d ed. Westport, Conn.: Praeger, 1997.

Fischman, Robert. *The National Wildlife Refuges: Coordinating A Conservation System Through Law.* Washington, D.C.: Island Press, 2003.

Freyfogle, Eric, and Dale Goble. *Wildlife Law: A Primer.* Washington, D.C.: Island Press, 2009.

SEE ALSO: Conservation; Department of the Interior, U.S.; Endangered species; Endangered Species Act; Fisheries; Wetlands; Wildlife.

# Fisheries

CATEGORIES: Plant and animal resources; environment, conservation, and resource management

*Fisheries, places where fish or other aquatic foods are caught or taken, provide an important source of protein. Fishing technologies range in scope from simple hook-and-line fishing in small ponds to industrial operations that use huge nets stretching behind seagoing trawlers. Many experts believe overfishing has placed fisheries throughout the world in danger of ecosystem collapse.*

## BACKGROUND

Oceans cover nearly 71 percent of the Earth and contain 86.5 percent of the Earth's water (510 million cubic kilometers). Freshwater areas cover an additional 1 percent of the Earth. Most life exists in ecosystems at or below the surface of water. Aquatic ecosystems have a distinct advantage over land-based ecosystems because their life-forms are not limited by a lack of water. Nutrient-rich areas of the ocean are green with lush plant growth, and can produce more food than cultivated farmland. Even polar ocean areas with pack ice most of the year are rich with algae growing in open areas and inside ice. Furthermore, "blue-water deserts"—ocean regions with low nutrient levels—produce more biomass (total weight of plants and animals) per unit of surface than land deserts.

Food resources from water include finned fish, shellfish, crustaceans (such as shrimp, krill, and lobster), cephalopods, some marine mammals and reptiles, and plants. Water plants should be included in a discussion of fisheries because they are the ultimate source of food for animals that are fished and because some mixture of plants and animals are often harvested. World fisheries and aquaculture supply more than 145 million metric tons of high-protein food each year, which is more than beef, pork, or poultry. Globally, fishing is a $92-billion-a-year industry directly employing nearly 38 million people and indirectly employing an additional 162 million people. (Subsistence fishers in tropical areas are probably undercounted in numbers but estimates suggest about nineteen million fishers; financial measures are hard to apply.) In the United States, commercial fishing annually harvests roughly 3.65 billion kilograms of fish and shellfish worth more than $4 billion. In the United States alone, the secondary market and consumption value of seafood have an annual value of more than $195 billion.

## OCEANIC PLANT LIFE

Sunlight drives photosynthesis, by which plants supply almost all food on Earth, either directly or indirectly, through the animal life feeding on them. Because the top several hundred meters of ocean water absorb virtually all sunlight hitting it, these uppermost waters contain the oceans' supporting photosynthetic plants. Below the oceans' illuminated zone, animal life becomes progressively scarcer, and animals feed on living and dead matter drifting down to them.

Biologically productive areas of oceans occur mostly in coastal regions, where minerals and nutrients are washed from land and where currents and winds dredge nutrient-rich sediments from the near-shore ocean floor. Similarly, nutrients from the deep ocean can be brought to coastal regions by differing ocean temperatures meeting to form convergent zones, resulting in upwelling—warm water rising to the surface and bringing with it conditions favorable for plant and animal life. Less than 1 percent of ocean areas are occupied by coastal ecosystems, yet these areas are twenty times more productive than the open ocean. Near-shore waters are home to mangrove swamps, salt marshes and tidal wetlands, coral reefs, and estuaries. Between 95 and 98 percent of commercial fishery species spend their early lives in fertile estuary ecosystems. Coral reefs harbor more plant and animal phyla than any other ecosystem; and tidal wetlands are the rearing grounds for vast numbers of crustaceans and mollusks. These near-shore waters are the primary areas for marine life, and three-quarters of the world's fish harvest occurs within 9 kilometers of continental shorelines.

A number of freshwater and near-shore plants are similar to land plants, including species such as eelgrass, turtle grass, and kelp, beds of which are often called ocean forests. Many near-shore plants, such as nori in Japan, are eaten directly. Others are harvested for use as food additives. For instance, giant kelp (or bull kelp) off the west coast of North America is harvested by clipping barges (which could be described as floating lawnmowers) for agar and alginate, used for stabilizing ice cream and beer foam.

Semiaquatic plants such as mangrove trees, cattails, and other swamp plants also have a tremendous effect on fisheries. Many fish spawn and spend their early lives around these types of plants. The areas where they are found are sometimes considered wasteland, but they are actually crucial to many fished species, including shrimp. In fact, river estuaries, mangrove swamps, and salt marshes produce more organic material per unit area than any other areas on Earth.

Away from shallow water, most oceanic plants are drifting algae barely large enough to be seen without magnification. In freshwater and near-shore waters, algae may comprise a large or small part of the ecosystem. In the deep ocean, phytoplankton (from the Greek words for "plant" and "wanderer") is one of the only food supplies for many marine animals. Although individually small, phytoplankton numbers are so great that they represent most of the vegetable mass in the oceans: an estimated new growth of 18 billion metric tons per year. Phytoplankton eaten by tiny animals, such as zooplankton, are food for small schooling fish, such as sardines, pilchard, herring, capelin, and anchovy. In turn, these fish are eaten by higher predators in the food chain, such as cod and mackerel, which are eaten by "top predators," such as tuna, sharks, and porpoises. In each stage from phytoplankton to top predators, about 90 percent of the food content is lost.

FISHERY LOCATIONS

The richest fisheries have traditionally been along continental shelves. Continental shelves are gently sloping regions transitioning between the continents and the deep ocean. Continental shelves represent only 8 percent of the ocean expanse. Roughly 16 percent of the ocean expanse is continental slopes with gradients about ten times steeper than the gently sloping shelves. Continental slopes drop off 500 to 3,000 meters into the ocean depths. Along these continental slopes, nutrient-rich upwelling occurs. Where the continental shelves are broad, major fisheries exist—or did exist before they were damaged by human activities. Three-quarters of all marine organisms spend at least a portion of their lives along a continental shelf.

Major shelf fisheries include the waters around Iceland, the Patagonian shelf (extending to the Falkland Islands), the Sea of Okhotsk, the shelf around Alaska, island chains and coastal waters from Indonesia through Japan, the Persian Gulf, and the Grand Banks east of North America. Major shelf fisheries that were important but have declined because of overfishing and pollution include the North Sea, the Baltic Sea, the Black Sea, Chesapeake Bay, and many areas in the Mediterranean.

Coral reefs, which have some similarities to land ecosystems, are actually colonies of tiny animals that contain algae within their bodies. Reefs are areas of high productivity. The algae provide oxygen and food to the coral, while waste matter and carbon dioxide from the coral are nutrients to the algae. This symbiosis allows reef ecosystems to be as productive as nearshore waters, even though nutrient levels are typically lower for reefs in tropical waters. However, this symbiosis also makes reefs vulnerable to excessive fertilization from pollutants, particularly phosphates from fertilizers and detergents. Reefs are also highly sensitive to changes in turbidity, saline variation, and water temperature.

Corals actually rebuild their environment to survive, and, in the process, create a more productive fishery. Like shellfish, corals grow their own calcium-carbonate living environment, in which living layers build atop the remains of older generations. The coral reefs grow with many gaps and fissures, allowing water to flow continually to the live corals. These gaps provide hiding places and nests for many small and juvenile creatures, many of which help defend the corals from predators. Because of corals, the islands of Polynesia have many small but rich fisheries. The Great Barrier Reef on the north side of Australia is enriched by corals and has the added advantage of a broad shelf area.

Other natural areas of high productivity are created where deep water rises to the surface in an upwelling. Exceptionally cold meltwater from Antarctica is heavier than the bottom water, so bottom water is pushed toward the surface. Consequently, one of the largest areas of high biomass is along the continental slopes of the Antarctic.

Another area of upwelling exists west of Peru, where a current from the north meets a current from the south, and the combined current flows west. The resulting gap is filled by an upwelling that supports anchovy production. Periodically, an increase in warmer water (the El Niño current) weakens this upwelling, causing a drastic fall in plankton, and hence anchovy, production. A "crash" of this fishery in the early 1970's, a result of an El Niño, was made worse by overfishing. Similar current-induced upwelling occurs along the Moroccan and Namibian coasts. Waters off Alaska have upwelling and large shelf areas, making them especially fertile.

Most of the deep ocean away from land is abyssal plain or "blue-water desert" with low productivity; this is especially true near the equator. These waters have sufficient nitrates and phosphates to support higher levels of marine life but lack trace amounts of iron, a mineral vital for phytoplankton survival.

EXISTING FISHERIES

The evolution of fisheries has involved both the availability of fish and the public's taste in seafood. Top predators, such as tuna, are prized for their taste, but schooling fishes that feed on zooplankton are harvested in the greatest tonnage. Another factor in the evolution of fisheries is that species tend to decline as they are overfished, so new species must be fished. The schooling fish that generally represent the highest tonnage of fish caught are a cheap source of protein. As such, roughly 25 percent of the fin catch is processed into fishmeal for livestock, and an additional 50 percent of fishmeal is consumed by aquaculture. Also, 70 percent of all fish oil is consumed by aquaculture. Invertebrates are much lower in tonnage than finned fish, but they make up a significant percentage of the value of the fisheries trade. They include prized crustacean species such as lobster, king crab, and shrimp. They also include shellfish such as clams, abalone, and scallops.

Krill are small zooplankton crustaceans similar to shrimp. Krill are the primary food for baleen whales, which strain water for their tiny prey. Some limited krill fishing has been done to provide fishmeal. (It has been noted that people may be slow to accept krill in their diets on a significant scale because cooked krill look similar to maggots.) The largest krill population is in waters around Antarctica, where the krill population is estimated at 600 million metric tons. Further estimations indicate that a sustainable yield for krill would be one-tenth of this total. These same Antarctic waters also support a large population of whales, which survive on krill. Any overharvesting of krill would have an adverse effect on whales. The northern polar region has the largest single-species fishery in the world—pollock, which thrive in the Bering Sea near Alaska. The world's largest remaining cod fishery is in the Barents Sea of northern Europe. The Barents Sea fishery is threatened by pollution, mineral exploration, busy shipping lanes, overfishing, and illegal fishing. Unsustainable commercial fishing practices, in combination with an illegal catch estimated at 90 million metric tons per year, are pushing the Barents Sea cod fishery toward collapse.

FISHING TECHNOLOGIES

Fishing can be done with hooks, traps, or nets; all three of these fishing methods are used by subsistence fishers and small fishing operations. For large-scale, industrial fishing operations, nets are the most practical and efficient tools. Large fishing operations radically changed fishing and the world's fisheries in the twentieth century.

Although some mechanized fishing was done in the nineteenth century, commercial fishing production was only around 2.5 million metric tons at the beginning of the twentieth century and had reached 18 million metric tons at the beginning of the 1950's. Then a combination of insecticides, newly introduced medicines, and better hygiene reduced disease, allowing a rapid growth in human population, which created a growing market for food. At the same time, better transportation allowed rapid shipment of premium catches, so lobsters, for instance, would never again be considered food for poor people along the coast. The greater fish market was met by investments in technology. First came large boats, followed by sonar navigation equipment, spotter aircraft, and nylon nets, which are nearly invisible to fish and are more resistant to rotting than natural fibers. More important, large factory ships allow processing of the catch at sea. A factory ship need not steam back to port frequently, but can stay out fishing until its hold is full. Factory ships also allow profitable fishing farther from shore, which is important because these ships often deplete nearby fisheries. In one hour a factory ship can harvest as much fish as a sixteenth century fishing boat took in a season.

There are three major categories of nets: trawl nets, purse seines, and drift nets. Trawl nets are conical nets dragged across the bottom with the big, open-end first, funneling fish into the closed point of the cone. Purse seines are nets held as vertical walls by floats at the top and weights at the bottom until the wall can surround an area of the water and the bottom can be pulled together. In the 1970's and 1980's, commercial fishing fleets began using large drift nets, many as long as 50 kilometers. These massive nets "vacuumed" or "swept" vast swaths of ocean, collecting everything in their range. Though the nets were intended for cod, tuna, and squid harvest, their use resulted in massive "bycatches" of nontarget species, including sharks, dolphins, whales, and sea turtles. Such large drift nets were banned for use outside a nation's 370-kilometer exclusive economic zone (EEZ), within which a country has exclusive control of all marine resources. Forty percent of the world's oceans are under control of individual nations claiming EEZs, but nets as large as 2 kilometers are still in use on the open ocean.

Large, high-tech operations (plus smaller but nevertheless highly capitalized operations) directly employ more than one million people worldwide and take about two-thirds of the world's harvest. Some nineteen million subsistence fishers and small operations take the balance. The small operators are often poor, but they spend much less per unit catch and use

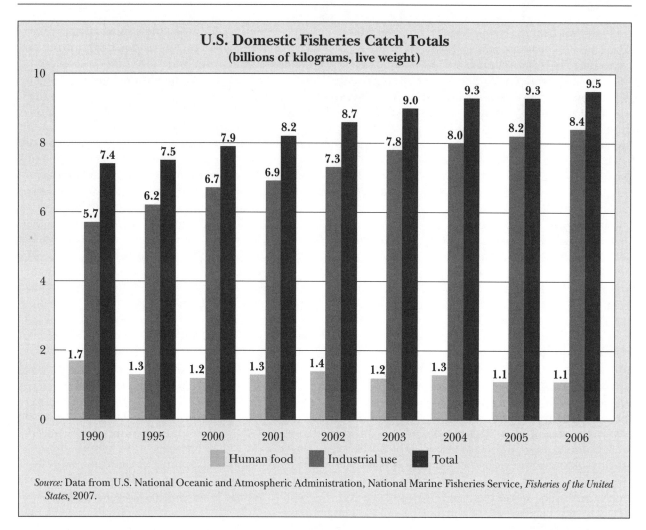

**U.S. Domestic Fisheries Catch Totals**
(billions of kilograms, live weight)

Source: Data from U.S. National Oceanic and Atmospheric Administration, National Marine Fisheries Service, *Fisheries of the United States*, 2007.

most of what they catch. This contrasts with industrial fishing operations, which tend to specialize in a single species. As a result there are often "unwanted" catches referred to as "bycatch." Bycatch can be fish that are too young, nontarget species, or over-quota. However, bycatch fish are usually dead from being netted and dropped in a hold, sitting for minutes or hours during the sorting process. The bycatch is discarded back into the sea and equates to more than 20 million metric tons per year. This dead and dumped bycatch affects fish populations present and future.

THE DEATH OF TRADITIONAL FISHING
By the early twenty-first century, fishing had become a troubled industry, its many successes having led to a string of related fishery collapses. The basic problem with fishing as it evolved in the latter twentieth cen-

tury was that it was a hunter-gatherer operation rather than an agricultural one: Fishers do not nurture and protect schools of fish as farmers protect herds of cattle. This fact alone limits productivity. For instance, there is little investment in habitat for fish, such as in maintaining wetlands for juveniles of many species or clear rivers and estuaries for salmon and other river-spawning fish.

Worse, fisheries management according to the hunter-gatherer dynamic is based on the idea that the fish are common property, with each fishing operation competing with the others for the fish. Any fishers who hold back in catching fish to save breeding stock for the future lose catch to other fishers willing to take the fish. In 1976, Garrett Hardin applied the term "the tragedy of the commons" to the problem of overfishing. The term has also been applied to the grazing of cattle; however, cattle can at least be counted, but fish populations are more likely to be gauged by catch. Thus, fishers using advanced equipment to catch the dwindling numbers of fish can create the illusion of a stable population. An entire fish species may ultimately be fished to near extinction, and the fishery may collapse, but the worst offenders will be the most profitable until the disaster occurs.

Furthermore, many fishing practices have dire effects on other species. More powerful boats and trawl nets equipped with "rock-hoppers" and better controls can drag rough-bottom areas with less danger of snagging the nets. Trawlers can work rough areas that fishers have avoided before and can fish steadily deeper-hunting bottom fish (such as cod, flounder, eels, and turbot). However, the sea bottom is also habitat for the young of many species and has food for many others. In a manner similar to coral reefs, the bottom ecosystem functions best when old shells, worm tunnels, and sponges and other attached organisms provide a complex environment where juvenile animals can hide from predators. A one-metric-ton boom dragging across the bottom kills attached animals, compacts the sediment so that worms cannot burrow well, silts some animals to death, and generally grinds the area down to wasteland. Years later, the lost production on the bottom manifests itself as missing adults elsewhere.

Finally, the areas closest to land, which are usually the richest fisheries, are subject to poisoning by pollutants. The Chesapeake Bay produces only a fraction of the life that early settlers found there. The Black Sea, naturally darkened by anaerobic decomposition (rotting without oxygen), is blacker because of fertilizer runoff and toxic contaminants. In 1991, three thousand people in Peru died from cholera linked to sewage-contaminated seafood.

Many human excesses were overmatched by the vastness of the oceans until the late twentieth century. By the mid-1990's, production exceeded the estimated 90-million-metric-ton sustainable yield of a wild ocean; by 2002, the yield had dropped to 63 million metric tons. The best fishing grounds have moved progressively farther from the ports of the fishing fleets, so production increases are largely confined to the last frontiers in the Indian Ocean. Virtually every fishing region of the world is overexploited or under pressure.

In the 1990's, the Grand Banks (east of Canada) began collapsing noticeably. In 1992, the Canadian government halted cod fishing in Canadian waters because there were virtually no cod of spawning age. Human-induced climate change will surely and seriously affect ocean fisheries and commercial fishing. As warming and cooling surface waters disrupt currents and phytoplankton populations, additional fresh water entering the marine habitat from melt-ice will alter regional salinity; increases in water depths will inundate estuaries and tidal zones, altering breeding and rearing habitats; and deepening coastal waters will drop coral reefs below the vital photic zone, stressing their ability to survive.

Nonetheless, production has been maintained by various subsidies for bigger and more sophisticated boats going farther and fishing deeper to catch dwindling fish stocks. Many subsidies are given to fishing fleets simply to help cover the cost of fuel to run the boats and processing operations. It is estimated that a cumulative worldwide annual investment of around $34 billion in subsidies is helping to deplete the global fishery, with the subsidies accounting for 20 percent of the value of the annual commercial harvest. Japan provides the largest annual subsidies to fishers (about $2 billion). The result of such subsidized fishing is that one-half of all major fish stocks are close to their capable limit, with another 15 percent identified as overfished.

The delayed crisis in the marine fishery, when it arrives, will probably be painful for the world's fishing fleets. Nations are increasingly limiting fishing by foreign boats so they can rebuild production. Meanwhile, unregulated waters are being overfished. At some point the collapse of the Grand Banks fishery will be repeated in a number of areas. The continued large investment and subsidies of large fishing fleets have increased marine harvests for decades, but in most regions fish harvests have exceeded estimated sustainable yields. Fish stocks have collapsed in many regions of the globe and many fishing businesses have gone bankrupt. High-gain commercial fishing has devastated some of the most traditionally productive fisheries. To meet demands for fishmeal and table fish, fish not previously sought are being harvested at unsustainable rates. By the late 1990's, the U.S. government had reported that for three hundred species of harvested fish for which data were available, one hundred were being fished beyond sustainable yields. When fish stocks reach critical levels of depletion and unsustainability, many nations put fishing bans into effect. In 1992, along the Georges Bank, stock levels of haddock, cod, and flounder became so low their harvest was banned. In 2003, Pacific coast rockfish became so endangered an emergency ban on all bottom fishing was enacted. In 2008, Pacific salmon stocks had become so low a ban on their commercial harvest was put into place.

The loss of viable fisheries has also resulted in armed conflict between nations. As fish stocks decrease from overfishing, territorial waters have become aggressively monitored to stop other nations from harvesting within those zones. During the late 1950's and mid-1970's, Britain, Iceland, and several other European countries with commercial fishing fleets engaged in what has been called "the cod wars." Because Iceland is highly dependent on fish exports, it extended its territorial waters to protect its regional fish harvests; to ensure its extended boundaries, Iceland patrolled the waters with naval gunboats. Great Britain did not recognize Iceland's territorial waters claims and sent its own naval warships to support the British fishing fleets venturing into the disputed waters. These "cod wars" were the impetus for the United Nations Convention on the Law of the Sea (UNCLOS), which, in 1982, established global territorial waters limits and the extent of EEZs. During the mid-1990's, a similar fishing conflict between the United States and Canada resulted in "the salmon war." While no naval fleets were involved in "the salmon war," back-and-forth retaliatory fishing quotas and retaliatory unlimited harvest practices resulted in an intense diplomatic battle and, eventually, a Canadian fishing-boat blockade of an American ferry in Prince Rupert harbor. In 1999, the two governments signed a treaty to coordinate management of the Pacific salmon fishery.

## REGULATION, AQUACULTURE, AND MARICULTURE

The mechanized hunting by unsupervised fishing fleets is as inherently problematic as the whaling and buffalo hunting of the nineteenth century that drove these hunted species to commercial extinction. Eventually these fleets will have to be replaced by regulated fishing and organized mariculture in which marine-water-living plants and animals are bred, protected, and cultured. As with agriculture on land, this shift will increase production many times.

Regulated or rationalized fishing is simply managing ordinary fishing so the catch is sustainable. Regarding the taking of freshwater fish, states sell limited numbers of licenses and limit fishing catches. Similar limitations are increasingly set within the EEZ. Controlled harvesting has allowed the Norwegians to maintain fish production at sustainable yields. It should have allowed the United States and Canadian governments to maintain a smaller sustainable yield than they have attempted. Ultimately, treaties must apply to international waters in addition to domestic waters.

Along with the controlling of production, fish habitats must be protected or repaired. British Columbia invested in reducing silt runoff from logging, and the reward was a rebound in salmon production. Treating some of the world's presently untreated sewage would have important health benefits for people as well as for fisheries. Suggestions have been made that fishing

| U.S. Aquaculture Production, 2006 | | | |
|---|---|---|---|
| | THOUSANDS OF POUNDS | METRIC TONS | THOUSANDS OF DOLLARS |
| *Finfish* | | | |
| Baitfish | — | — | 38,018 |
| Catfish | 566,131 | 256,795 | 498,820 |
| Salmon | 20,726 | 9,401 | 37,439 |
| Striped bass | 11,925 | 5,409 | 30,063 |
| Tilapia | 18,738 | 8,500 | 32,263 |
| Trout | 61,534 | 27,912 | 67,745 |
| *Shellfish* | | | |
| Clams | 12,564 | 5,699 | 72,783 |
| Crawfish | 80,000 | 36,288 | 96,000 |
| Mussels | 962 | 436 | 4,990 |
| Oysters | 13,711 | 6,219 | 92,602 |
| Shrimp | 8,037 | 3,646 | 18,684 |
| *Miscellaneous* | — | — | 254,738 |
| **Totals** | **794,328** | **360,305** | **1,244,145** |

*Source:* Data from the National Oceanic and Atmospheric Administration, National Marine Fisheries Association.

*Note:* Miscellaneous includes ornamental and tropical fish, alligators, algae, aquatic plants, eels, scallops, crabs, and others.

rentals or production taxes be used to support controls and habitat improvement. They would also help reduce the excess capacity in the industry.

Aquaculture is culturing fish and plants in fresh water. It has been practiced for centuries in Asia. In rice culture, small fish can be raised in the paddies during the water-covered stage and caught when the paddies are drained. Hatcheries have long been used throughout the world to increase the numbers of sport fish or commercially fished species (although stocking has risks of reducing genetic diversity, and hence the viability of the wild stocks). From hatcheries, it was a short step to fish farming of salmon, trout, catfish, carp, tilapia, and shrimp. Fish farming is a fast-growing source of production, having profits of more than $1 billion dollars per year in the United States.

There is some commercial production of freshwater algae, such as spirulina, which was eaten by the ancient Aztecs and is still harvested and eaten around Lake Chad in Africa. As with plankton, the production per unit of area is greater than any land plant. Water hyacinths (water lily) and certain other water plants could also be used for livestock forage and even for human food. Once again, culturing of the plants could be combined with water animal production.

Aquaculture, too, has risks and costs. Fish-pond wastes can pollute neighboring waters, and, as with stocking, a risk exists of weakening the species by reducing genetic diversity. Another risk is that economics would naturally drive fish farmers toward high concentrations of animals, thus increasing the risk of disease. Antibiotics can be used, but routine antibiotic use can create antibiotic-resistant microbes. There are also probable environmental costs; for example, shrimp farmers in undeveloped countries have often destroyed mangrove swamps to make their farms, thus destroying wild stocks of shrimp and other species that start life in the mangrove swamps. The loss of the mangroves also makes shorelines susceptible to devastating erosion from storms.

Mariculture is essentially agriculture in the ocean. Once again, Asian countries have pioneered many processes. Some edible plants are cultured on nets. Shellfish such as oysters are grown on ropes suspended from rafts. Because they do not touch the bottom, these shellfish are safer from starfish and other bottom-dwelling predators. A few commercial operations in the West are pioneering fish cages in the open ocean, where vast distances allow nearly unlimited clean-water input and waste disposal. Australia has several successful open-ocean operations for the rearing of tuna.

More speculative proposals for the future include vast networks of cables and netting that would provide holdfast points for near-shore plants such as kelp. Beds of plants, in turn, would provide food and habitat for sea animals. Such marine plantations could be fertilized by chemicals or perhaps by artificial upwellings connected with oceanic power stations.

While aquaculture and mariculture help provide fish and seafood, the fish-feed required for this type of operation to be successful puts pressure on wild fisheries. It requires almost 1 kilogram of fishmeal derived from wild fish to produce one-half kilogram of farmed salmon. In 2001, fish farming required one-third of the world's production of fishmeal. Estimates indicated that this proportion was approaching one-half in 2010.

*Roger V. Carlson, updated by Randall L. Milstein*

### FURTHER READING

Charles, Anthony T. *Sustainable Fishery Systems.* Malden, Mass.: Blackwell Science, 2001.

Clarke, Arthur C. *The Challenge of the Sea.* Illustrated by Alex Schomburg. New York: Holt, Rinehart and Winston, 1960.

Clover, Charles. *The End of the Line: How Overfishing Is Changing the World and What We Eat.* London: Ebury, 2004.

Earle, Sylvia Alice. *Sea Change: A Message of the Oceans.* New York: Putnam, 1995.

Ellis, Richard. *The Empty Ocean: Plundering the World's Marine Life.* Washington, D.C.: Island Press/Shearwater Books, 2003.

Kura, Yumkio, Carmen Revenga, Eriko Hoshino, and Greg Mock. *Fishing for Answers: Making Sense of the Global Fish Crisis.* Washington, D.C.: World Resources Institute, 2004.

Pew Oceans Commission. *America's Living Oceans—Charting a Course for Sea Change: A Report to the Nation—Recommendations for a New Ocean Policy.* Arlington, Va.: Pew Oceans Commission, 2003.

Rogers, Raymond A. *The Oceans Are Emptying: Fish Wars and Sustainability.* New York: Black Rose Books, 1995.

Stickney, Robert R. *Aquaculture: An Introductory Text.* Cambridge, Mass.: CABI, 2005.

United Nations Food and Agriculture Organization, Fisheries Department. *The State of World Fisheries and Aquaculture, 2008.* Rome: Author, 2009.

SEE ALSO: Agriculture industry; Biodiversity; Coral reefs; Coral reefs; El Niño and La Niña; Exclusive economic zones; Fish and Wildlife Service, U.S.; Food chain; Integrated Ocean Drilling Program; Law of the sea; Oceans; Sea Shepherd Conservation Society.

# Flax

CATEGORY: Plant and animal resources

## WHERE FOUND
Flax, also known as linseed, common flax, or *Linum usitatissimum* in Latin, is native to the region stretching from the eastern Mediterranean to India. Flax was probably first domesticated in the Fertile Crescent and was cultivated extensively in ancient Egypt.

## PRIMARY USES
Common flax is grown for both its versatile fibers and its nutritionally rich seeds. It is also cultivated as an ornamental plant in gardens. Various parts of the plant have been used to produce a variety of products, including dye, fabric, paper, linen, ropes, fish nets, medicines, and health foods. Flax seeds contain omega-3 fatty acids, which are believed to possess anticancer properties, to lower the risk of cardiovascular diseases, and to lessen the severity of diabetes.

## TECHNICAL DEFINITION
Flax is a member of the genus *Linum*, in the Linaceae family. It is an erect annual with slender stems and lanceolate leaves. The plant can grow up to 1.2 meters tall, with leaves 2-4 centimeters long and 0.3 centimeter wide. The flower color varies, ranging from bright red to purple or pale blue, each with five petals 1.5-2.5 centimeters in diameter. When mature, each plant produces round, dry capsules of 0.5-0.9 centimeter in diameter, each containing several seeds. The glossy flax seeds, either brown or golden yellow in color, contain high levels of lignans and omega-3 fatty acids, both of which are believed to have health benefits. Flax stems are wrapped around by bast fibers of high cellulosic content.

## DESCRIPTION, DISTRIBUTION, AND FORMS
In ancient times, some flax plants were cultivated for both their fiber and their nutrient-rich seeds. Modern-day flax cultivars have diverged into two separate lines, one for high seed yield and another for superior fibers. The plants for seed production are more branched. Seed flax is an erect annual that grows up to 91 centimeters tall and has a distinct main stem and several branches at the top that produce flowers. The branched taproot system may penetrate a depth of about 1 meter in the soil. A flax flower has five petals, producing a fruit of a five-chamber capsule. Each capsule contains an average of six to eight seeds. The capsules may split open or remain tightly closed at maturity, depending upon genetic variations. Cultivars with tight capsules resist seed shattering better than those with split capsules and thus are less likely to suffer damage from bad weather.

Flax is mostly a self-pollinated crop with occasional cross-pollination by some insect species. The extent of cross-pollination varies with cultivars and environmental conditions. Flax flowers typically open soon after sunrise on clear days, and their petals fall within five to six hours after opening. Flower color may vary from white to pink, blue, or different shades of purple. However, most modern-day cultivars bear blue petals. Seed colors also vary from various shades of yellow, brown, greenish-yellow, and greenish-brown to nearly black.

Flax is well adapted to fertile, fine-textured clay soil at near neutral pH levels (6.0-6.5) and with a considerable amount of organic matter. Sandy, coarse-textured peat or muck soils are not ideal for flax cultivation. Adequate moisture and cooler temperatures, especially during the reproductive phase (from flowering to seed maturity), are beneficial for high oil content and superior oil quality. The seed coat of flax can easily be damaged in harvest or during handling. Even slight, often invisible damage will make seeds susceptible to decay because of their high oil and protein content. For this reason, seeds with no damage should be carefully selected for planting. In addition, treating seeds with fungicides before planting is critical to ensure a high germination rate. A well-prepared seedbed similar to those for seeding lawn grasses is also important for obtaining good seedling stands.

The plants from which fibers are extracted are tall annuals with few branches. Since ancient times, flax fibers have been used to make many products. Ropes, cords, tents, sails, fishing nets, and carpets can be traced back at least three thousand years. Flax fibers are extracted from the stem and are called bast fibers. Bast fibers from flax are naturally smooth and straight, containing small, regular lumens and regular diameters with a clockwise twist. Flax fibers are two to three times stronger than cotton fibers. Linen, the textile made from flax, has long been prized for its durability.

## HISTORY

Flax is regarded as one of the first crops domesticated by humans. Its proposed Mediterranean origin was supported by uncovered remains of a flax species in ancient settlements occupied by the Swiss Lake Dwellers about ten thousand years ago. Archaeological evidence showed the use of flax for both fiber and seeds by people of the Stone Age. Egyptian mummies in ancient tombs dated to more than five thousand years ago were wrapped in linen cloth made from flax fiber. In the 1990's, excavations in eastern Turkey found impressions of a linen fiber carbon-dated to nine thousand years ago. In addition, carvings in Egyptian tombs recorded flax cultivation along with the cultivation of figs, olives, and wheat. The ancient Greeks also used linen, while the Romans are considered responsible for spreading the cultivation of flax across Europe.

In the United States, the early colonists began to cultivate flax on a small scale, primarily for home uses. The commercial production of flax did not begin until 1753. With the invention of the cotton gin by Eli Whitney in 1793, flax cultivation began to decline and was nearly driven to extinction by the 1940's. In the latter part of the twentieth century in North America, flax regained some momentum as an alternative crop for health food. Flax production for oil-rich seeds occurs primarily in Canada (34 percent), China (25 percent), India (9 percent), the United States (8 percent), and Ethiopia (3.5 percent), with a combined total production of approximately 1.4 metric tons. Flax cultivation for commercial textiles is in Europe (France, Belgium, the Netherlands, Spain, Russia, and Belarus), Egypt, and China.

## OBTAINING FLAX

After flax is planted, the initial growth of the crop is somewhat slow, with seedlings reaching 10-15 centimeters in six weeks. Thereafter, however, the growth rate accelerates to several centimeters a day. The time span from planting to harvest is about seventy to one hundred days, depending upon the climate. At maturation, plants are cut with mowing equipment. Fruit capsules are separated from the stalk, and seeds are

*A worker in Germany prepares flax for use in the textile industry.* (AP/Wide World Photos)

released by gentle threshing. Oil is pressed from flax-seeds and further extracted using a petroleum solvent.

Strands of fiber are attached longitudinally to the stem, between the epidermis and the central woody core. The flax fiber, with a very high cellulose concentration, is extracted by retting and scutching. Retting begins with submerging the flax stems in water and ends with rotting away the inner stalk, leaving the outer fibers intact. Following retting, the stalk is sun- or wind-dried and then broken into short bits, leaving the fiber unharmed. The scutching scrapes the straw away from the fiber and combs non-fiber residue out of the fiber.

## USES OF FLAX

Flaxseed (linseed) is produced primarily for the value of its oil. Linseed oil is one of the oldest commercial oils used by humans. Flax has been cultivated as a commercial oilseed crop in the United States and Canada for more than one century. In general, however, solvent-processed oil from brown flax has been used for many centuries in paints and varnishes, although it has not been usable for food or feed. The linseed meal, a by-product after oil extraction, however, is often used in animal feed and organic fertilizers.

Use of flaxseed as a food has increased in recent years because of its beneficial health effects from three major components: a high omega-3 fatty acid content, high dietary fiber, and the highest lignan content of all plants. Although color variations can range from golden yellow to brown, seeds have similar nutritional values and equal amounts of omega-3 fatty acids. Omega-3 fatty acid, similar to that which is found in fish like salmon, acts to lower total cholesterol and low-density lipoprotein (LDL) levels, improve cardiovascular health, and promote skin health. The high fiber content also helps lower cholesterol and reduce colon and stomach cancers. Lignan acts as both a phytoestrogen and an antioxidant, which reduces the risk of various cancers. In addition, a very low amount of carbohydrates makes flaxseed ideal for diabetes and weight loss and maintenance. These potential health benefits have resulted in a steady increase in consumption of whole seeds, ground seeds, and linseed oil.

Flax stem fiber is soft, lustrous, and flexible; it is stronger than cotton fiber but less elastic. The top quality flax fibers are used for linen fabrics. Lower grades are used for the manufacturing of twine and ropes. Other products made from flax fibers include cigarette paper, paper for banknotes, reinforcing materials in plastics, erosion control mats, and interior panels and mats in automobiles. A growing demand for natural fibers exists in Europe. Fibers extracted from flax, hemp, and jute are blended with synthetic fibers to make automotive head liners and other interior components. A composite material composed of flax fiber and polypropylene combines excellent strength and durability with moisture resistance, which is suitable for use in carpet backings, filters, insulation, geotextiles for erosion control, and upholstery padding.

*Ming Y. Zheng*

## FURTHER READING

Beutler, Jade. *Flax for Life! 101 Delicious Recipes and Tips Featuring Fabulous Flax Oil.* Vancouver: Apple, 1996.

Foulk, J. A., et al. "Flax Fiber: Potential for a New Crop in the Southeast." In *Trends in New Crops and New Uses*, edited by Jules Janick and Anna Whipkey. Alexandria, Va.: ASHS Press, 2002.

Joiner-Bey, Herb. *The Healing Power of Flax.* Topanga, Calif.: Freedom Press, 2004.

Moquette-Magee, Elaine. *The Flax Cookbook: Recipes and Strategies for Getting the Most from the Most Powerful Plants on the Planet.* New York: Marlowe, 2004.

Reinhardt-Martin, Jane. *Flax Your Way to Better Health.* Silvis, Ill.: Author, 2001.

## WEB SITE

FLAX-SEED.ORG
Flax Seed Oil
http://www.flax-seed.org/

SEE ALSO: Cotton; Deforestation; Forestry; Global Strategy for Plant Conservation; Hemp; Paper, alternative sources of; Plant fibers; Plants as a medical resource; Renewable and nonrenewable resources; Textiles and fabrics; Wheat.

*Survivors of a deadly flood in Ecuador struggle to salvage their belongings in knee-deep waters.* (Xinhua/Landov)

# Floods and flood control

CATEGORIES: Environment, conservation, and
resource management; geological processes and
formations

*Floods can have both devastating and positive effects
on natural resources and human infrastructure.*

## BACKGROUND

Floods happen with any high flow of surface waters
that overtop normal confining banks and cover land
that is usually dry. Floods occur naturally along most
river systems. Low-lying areas and areas downstream
of dams are most at risk. Flooding causes loss of human and animal life; structural damage to bridges,
buildings, roadbeds, and utilities; soil erosion; destruction of property; and destruction of livestock
and crops that provide food for people. As a result,
famines may follow floods, with large numbers of people dying from starvation. Floodwaters are typically
contaminated with raw sewage, including both hu-

man and animal waste, and may contain dangerous
levels of bacteria, leading to outbreaks of waterborne
illness.

Floods also can have positive impacts. Floods recharge natural ecosystems; provide abundant fresh
water for agriculture, health, and sanitation; and deposit nutrient-rich sediment on floodplains, enhancing crop yields. The importance of floods to aquatic
ecosystems is demonstrated by the artificial flooding
in the Grand Canyon of the Colorado River in the
United States.

However, floods are the most devastating of all geological agents, surpassing earthquakes and volcanic
eruptions in terms of loss of life and property damage.
In developing countries, floods cause a large number
of deaths, whereas in developed countries, floods
cause billions of dollars worth of property damage.
Each year there are between fifty and three hundred
inland floods worldwide, impacting an estimated 520
million people and causing as many as 25,000 deaths.
Since 1985, inland floods have killed approximately
130,000 people (not including loss of life from storm

surge and tsunami-related floods). Floods and other water-related disasters cost the world economy as much as $50 to $60 billion per year. Globally, the greatest potential for flooding exists in Asia, where more than 1,200 floods occurred between 1900 and 2006, claiming an average of 5,300 lives and costing up to $207 billion in losses. As urbanization increases, particularly in flood-prone areas, the potential for flooding rises because of land-use changes (such as deforestation and the covering of once-permeable ground with concrete, asphalt, and buildings). Climate change and sea-level rise also lead to increased flooding. Nearly 1 billion people, about one-sixth of the world's population, live in areas prone to flooding. Many of these people are among the world's poorest inhabitants, depending on fertile floodplain soils and wetlands for agriculture and economic opportunity.

## FLOODPLAINS

Most streams are naturally bordered by flat, low-lying areas known as floodplains. Floodplains have been carved into the landscape by stream erosion and are covered in fine-grained sand, silt, and clay deposited by floodwaters. Some streams have natural levees, moundlike deposits of sediment that border the stream channel. Natural levees form as floodwaters leave the channel and spread onto the floodplain. As rushing water leaves the channel, its velocity drops, and coarser sediment is deposited adjacent to the stream. Man-made levees may be built along streams in an attempt to control flooding. However, if the water in a stream is allowed to spread over its natural floodplain, the impact of downstream flooding is lessened.

## TYPES OF FLOODS

Floods occur when a drainage basin (or watershed) receives so much water that stream and river channels cannot handle the flow. After a rain, some water infiltrates the soil, some evaporates or is used by plants, and the remainder (about 30 percent) becomes runoff, flowing across the ground surface.

Riverine floods occur when heavy rainfall or spring thaws (melting snow and ice) increase water levels in a drainage basin. Heavy rainfall may be the result of a hurricane, a tropical cyclone, a monsoonal rain, or a prolonged period of unusually wet weather, as in the case of the Great Midwest Flood of 1993 in the central United States, which impacted nine states along the

Mississippi River and lasted more than four months.

In cold climate areas where rivers freeze in the winter, spring thaws bring ice jams and associated flooding. Rising water levels lift river ice, which breaks into large sheets that float downstream and pile up near narrow passages or against obstructions such as bridges. When the ice stops moving because of a jam, floodwaters rapidly spread over the riverbanks upstream from the jam and may cover vast areas of usually dry land, flooding roads and causing property damage. When the ice jam breaks, a sudden flood of water is released. Ice jam flooding occurs in Canada, the northern United States, Europe, Russia, Kazakhstan, China, and other countries.

Flash floods are associated with intense storms that release large amounts of rain into small drainage basins in a relatively short period of time. Flash floods occur with little or no warning and can reach peak levels within minutes, carrying a deadly cargo of rocks, trees, and other debris. Fifteen centimeters of swiftly moving water can sweep people off their feet, and cars can be swept away by 0.6 meter of water. A notable flash flood occurred July 31, 1976, along the Big Thompson River near Denver, Colorado, after an unusually heavy rainstorm. A wall of water 5.8 meters high roared down a canyon where people were camping. The flood killed 140 people and caused millions of dollars in property damage. Flash floods may even occur in dry streambeds on sunny days when small but heavy rainstorms occur upstream kilometers away.

Storm surge floods (coastal floods) occur when onshore winds and hurricanes cause the sea level to rise over low-lying coastal areas. If storm surges happen during high tide, leading to a tidal surge, the devastation can be catastrophic. Sometimes during hurricanes coastal areas are affected simultaneously by storm surges and riverine floods. In May, 2008, Cyclone Nargis struck Myanmar (Burma) with storm surge, flooding up to 4 meters in the densely populated Irrawaddy Delta region. The death toll was estimated to be more than 100,000.

Coastal flooding can also occur as a result of a tsunami or seismic sea wave following an earthquake. On December 26, 2004, a magnitude 9.3 earthquake off the coast of the Indonesian island of Sumatra produced a tsunami in the Indian Ocean that flooded coastal areas across Southeast Asia, Sri Lanka, India, and other nations bordering the Indian Ocean, including Australia and several African countries. The tsunami, which was up to 25 meters high, killed nearly

300,000 people and left more than 1.5 million home-less. Billions of dollars worth of property damage occurred, and several islands were completely sub-merged.

Floods can also be caused by human interference with a drainage basin. The most obvious example is the bursting of dams or levees. Dam failures represent potentially the worst flooding event in terms of sud-den, catastrophic loss of life and destruction of prop-erty. Dam failures are primarily caused by neglect, poor design, or structural damage caused by an earth-quake or other event. The deadliest flood in U.S. his-tory was the result of a dam failure on the Little Conemaugh River in Johnstown, Pennsylvania, on May 31, 1889. A wall of water 12 meters high killed 2,200 people.

### NOTABLE FLOODS

Near the end of the last ice age, about thirteen thou-sand years ago, glacial-related ice jam flooding in the northwestern United States formed prehistoric Lake Missoula along the Clark Fork River in Montana. When the ice jam broke up, the water in the lake, which was about 600 meters deep with a volume of about 2,500 cubic kilometers, was released cata-strophically, flowing westward and both creating the Channeled Scablands and eroding immense chan-nels across the Columbia Plateau.

The worst natural disasters in history, in terms of loss of life, have been floods along Chinese rivers. The Huang River (also known as the Yellow River) in China has killed more people than any other natural feature. Over the past three to four thousand years, it has flooded 1,593 times. The river's English name de-rives from the ochre-yellow color of the silt carried by the river. Millions of metric tons of silt deposited on the riverbed choke the channel and displace the water, and, over time, the river level rises. To prevent flooding and to keep the river within its banks, the Chinese built levees or earthen embankments along the sides of the river. As the sediment accumulated in the river channel, the levees had to be built higher and higher. In places, the riverbed is higher than the surrounding countryside, with levees towering 9 me-ters or more above the floodplain. In 1887, heavy rains over a period of months caused the river level to rise. The levees broke catastrophically, spilling flood-waters 3 meters deep over the surrounding country-side and covering an estimated 129,500 square kilo-meters. The flooding claimed between 900,000 and 6

million lives (estimates vary widely; the larger figure includes deaths from flood-induced famine). A flood on the same river in 1931 killed nearly 4 million peo-ple. The longest river in China, the Chang (also known as the Yangtze), has also flooded numerous times. In 1911, a flood on the Chang River claimed 100,000 lives. In 1931, the river crested at nearly 31 meters above its normal level and killed 145,000, but as many as 3,700,000 died as a result of starvation be-cause the flooded area normally produced nearly one-half of China's grain. Other more recent floods on the Chang occurred in 1954, killing 30,000, and in 1998. In an effort to control flooding along the Chang, as well as to generate electricity, the Three Gorges Dam was completed in 2006.

Hurricane Katrina, which struck the southeast-ern United States in August, 2005, caused flooding along the coast of the Gulf of Mexico from Florida to Texas. Federal disaster declarations covered an area of 233,000 square kilometers. Much of the damage was caused by the highest storm surge in U.S. history (8.2 meters) as the hurricane approached the Missis-sippi coast. However, the most severe damage was in New Orleans, Louisiana, where the man-made levees and floodwalls along the Mississippi River failed in more than fifty places, flooding 80 percent of the city. Floodwaters covered the area for weeks, and at least 1,836 people were killed and 705 were missing. This was the costliest natural disaster in U.S. history, with damage estimates near $100 billion.

### HUMAN INFLUENCES ON FLOODING

Human activities along waterways can increase flood-ing inadvertently. Paving and building on floodplains and surrounding areas decrease infiltration of rainwa-ter into the soil and, as a consequence, increase run-off. Runoff also increases when forests are cleared or when wetlands are destroyed by construction or infilling. Agriculture decreases the ability of soil to re-tain water and therefore increases runoff. Rapid run-off causes soil erosion. Sediment-clogged streams can-not support normal levels of aquatic life, and wildlife habitats are destroyed. Sediment deposition in stream channels also leaves little room for water and leads to the likelihood of flooding.

### EFFECTS OF FLOODING

People are attracted to floodplains because floods de-posit nutrient-rich topsoil, eroded from upstream, pro-ducing fertile land for agriculture. In Egypt, for exam-

*Father and son paddle through flooded streets after heavy rains in Poquoson, Virginia, in 2009. (AP/Wide World Photos)*

ple, floods and deposition of nutrient-rich sediment from the Nile River have increased agricultural yields for perhaps five thousand years. Floodplains tend to be flat, making them easy to cultivate, and near water, making them easy to irrigate. In addition, the nearby source of water is useful for transportation of agricultural products. Flooding is beneficial to streams as well: It serves to maintain both local and regional environmental balance, affecting water quality and aquatic life. Floods also recharge groundwater supplies.

Floods can be considered human-caused disasters in that people build on floodplains, refusing to consider the risk. Dangers of flooding include losses of both human and animal lives; structural damage to bridges, buildings, roadbeds, dams, and utilities; agricultural losses; severe soil erosion (sometimes even unearthing coffins in cemeteries and washing them downstream); and property destruction. Most flood deaths are attributable to drowning, and in the United States, more than one-half of them are associated with motor vehicles being driven into areas covered by water.

When water filtration facilities are inundated, floods spread waters polluted by industrial contaminants and human waste. Polluted floodwater can also contaminate wells and water supplies. Wild animals, including poisonous snakes, often come into homes with rising floodwater. Disease spread by waterborne pathogens and insects such as mosquitoes, in addition to famine due to crop damage and loss of food supplies, can cause great loss of life. Additional long-term problems include homelessness and losses to commerce, employment, and education.

FLOOD CONTROL

Floods can be controlled in two ways: by controlling the waters or by controlling floodplain development. To minimize the effects of flooding, engineers build dams, levees, and floodwalls along rivers. Dams can store water during periods of heavy runoff and release it gradually during periods of low flow. Artificial levees and floodwalls are built along streams to confine floodwaters and to keep them from covering the floodplain. As more communities build levees, however, river levels rise because floodwaters cannot spread out. The river deposits its sediment in the channel instead of on the floodplain, raising the riverbed and displacing the water. Artificial levees must be heightened because of rising water levels over time.

Levees are by no means a foolproof solution to flood prevention. Floodwaters occasionally overflow levees, burst through them, or go around their upstream ends. Where levees or floodwalls are built on only one side of a river, towns on the other side experience higher flood levels than normal. Other methods of flood control include restoring vegetation, instituting soil conservation measures, constructing floodways to divert floodwaters, widening rivers to accommodate more water, and purposely flooding certain areas to prevent flooding in others.

## FLOOD FREQUENCY

Flood frequencies are described in statistical terms to estimate the chance of a particular flood level. For example, the term "one-hundred-year flood" means that a flood of a particular level will have a 1 percent chance of occurring within a given year. It does not mean that a flood of this level would happen only once in one hundred years. A one-hundred-year flood can occur any time. Similarly, a "ten-year flood" has a 10 percent chance of occurring in a given year. In some cases, the difference between a ten-year and a one-hundred-year flood is only a few centimeters.

Around the world, the number of catastrophic inland floods was twice as large per decade between 1996 and 2005 as it was between 1950 and 1980. Property damage was five times as large. The increase is primarily attributed to socioeconomic reasons such as population growth and changes in land use, including increased building on floodplains.

## FLOODS AND GLOBAL WARMING

With global climate change and predictions about increases in temperature, the potential exists for the hydrologic cycle to intensify, leading to more extremes in climate. For every 1° Celsius in temperature rise, the capacity of the atmosphere to hold water increases by 7 percent. This creates the potential for more intense precipitation and, as a consequence, more intense flooding. In recent years, changes also have occurred in the timing of floods, including a decrease in the number of ice-jam floods in Europe.

During the twentieth century, sea level rose 10-20 centimeters. Sea level is expected to rise 9-88 centimeters by the end of the twenty-first century, suggesting that coastal flooding will become more widespread. This will have a significant impact on coastal inhabitants; more than 70 percent of the world's population lives on coastal plains. Increasingly, islands are affected by sea-level rise. The Pacific island nation of Kiribati, which has already lost two islands to rising seas, is a prime example. In early 2005, several other islands in Kiribati were flooded by high spring tides that damaged buildings, contaminated wells with salt water, and eroded farmland. A sea-level rise of 1 meter would have a devastating effect on some of the world's poorest countries, displacing tens of millions of people and flooding low-lying areas used for growing rice and other food crops.

*Pamela J. W. Gore*

## FURTHER READING

Doe, Robert. *Extreme Floods: A History in a Changing Climate.* Stroud, England: Sutton, 2006.

Erickson, Jon. *Quakes, Eruptions, and Other Geologic Cataclysms: Revealing the Earth's Hazards.* New York: Facts On File, 2002.

Hoyt, William G., and Walter B. Langbein. *Floods.* Princeton, N.J.: Princeton University Press, 1955.

Miller, E. Willard, and Ruby M. Miller. *Natural Disasters—Floods: A Reference Handbook.* Santa Barbara, Calif.: ABC-CLIO, 2000.

Mogil, H. Michael. *Extreme Weather: Understanding the Science of Hurricanes, Tornadoes, Floods, Heat Waves, Snow Storms, Global Warming, and Other Atmospheric Disturbances.* New York: Black Dog & Leventhal, 2007.

Nuhfer, Edward B., Richard J. Proctor, and Paul H. Moser. *The Citizens' Guide to Geologic Hazards: A Guide to Understanding Geologic Hazards, Including Asbestos, Radon, Swelling Soils, Earthquakes, Volcanoes, Landslides, Subsidence, Floods, and Coastal Hazards.* Arvada, Colo.: American Institute of Professional Geologists, 1993.

O'Neill, Karen M. *Rivers by Design: State Power and the Origins of U.S. Flood Control.* Durham, N.C.: Duke University Press, 2006.

Reice, Seth R. "Disturbance Ecology and Flood Control." In *The Silver Lining: The Benefits of Natural Disasters.* Princeton, N.J.: Princeton University Press, 2001.

Woods, Michael, and Mary B. Woods. *Floods.* 2d ed. Minneapolis: Lerner, 2009.

WEB SITES

DARTMOUTH FLOOD OBSERVATORY
Space-Based Measurement of Surface Water for
Research, Educational, and Humanitarian
Applications
http://www.dartmouth.edu/~floods/

FEDERAL EMERGENCY MANAGEMENT AGENCY
Flood
http://www.fema.gov/hazard/flood/index.shtm

PUBLIC BROADCASTING SERVICE NOVA ONLINE
Flood!
http://www.pbs.org/wgbh/nova/flood/

UNITED NATIONS EDUCATIONAL, SCIENTIFIC AND
CULTURAL ORGANIZATION (UNESCO)
International Flood Initiative
http://unesdoc.unesco.org/images/0015/001512/
151208e.pdf

UNITED NATIONS EDUCATIONAL, SCIENTIFIC AND
CULTURAL ORGANIZATION (UNESCO)
Third United Nations World Water Development
Report, 2009: Water in a Changing World
http://www.unesco.org/water/wwap/wwdr/wwdr3/
pdf/24_WWDR3_ch_12.pdf

U.S. GEOLOGICAL SURVEY
Floods
http://www.usgs.gov/science/science.php?term=398

SEE ALSO: El Niño and La Niña; Hydrology and the hydrologic cycle; Monsoons; Streams and rivers; Wetlands.


# Fluorite

CATEGORY: Mineral and other nonliving resources

## WHERE FOUND

Fluorite is a common mineral that is found worldwide. It occurs in hydrothermal veins associated with the ore minerals of lead, silver, and zinc. It commonly is the most abundant mineral in the vein and can occur as the only mineral in some veins. Fluorite is also found in cavities of sedimentary rocks, in hot-water deposits near springs, and in water-rich igneous pegmatites. Fluorite is associated with many different minerals, including calcite, dolomite, gypsum, barite, quartz, ga-lena, sphalerite, topaz, and apatite. In the United States, the most important sources are in Illinois, Kentucky, Ohio, New Mexico, and Colorado. Worldwide, fluorite is found in China, Kenya, Mexico, Mongolia, Morocco, Namibia, Russia, South Africa, and Spain.

## PRIMARY USES

Fluorite is an excellent flux and is used extensively in the production of iron, steel, and aluminum. Fluorite is the chief ore for elemental fluorine gas and related fluorine chemicals. It is used in the chemical industry in the production of hydrofluoric acid (HF). This acid is the primary ingredient used to produce almost all organic and inorganic fluorine-bearing chemicals. Fluorite is also used in manufacturing of glass, fiberglass, pottery, and enamel.

## TECHNICAL DEFINITION

The mineral fluorite, called fluorspar in the mining industry, has a formula of $CaF_2$ and is the index mineral on the Mohs hardness scale at 4.0. Fluorite displays a glassy luster and a perfect cleavage that yields octahedral fragments. Fluorite crystallizes in the isometric system and commonly forms perfect to near-perfect cubes.

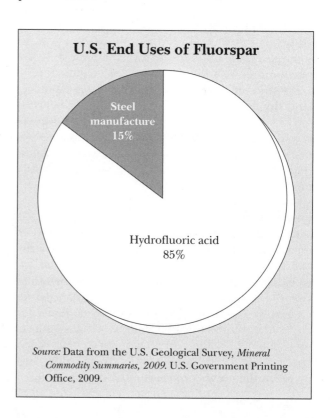

**U.S. End Uses of Fluorspar**

Steel manufacture 15%

Hydrofluoric acid 85%

*Source:* Data from the U.S. Geological Survey, *Mineral Commodity Summaries, 2009.* U.S. Government Printing Office, 2009.

## DESCRIPTION, DISTRIBUTION, AND FORMS

Fluorite has a structural defect in its atomic arrangement called a "color center," where an electron fills a "hole" from a missing ion. This defect causes fluorite to display a wide variety of colors, including deep purple, light green, bluish green, yellow, and less commonly colors of rose, blue, or brown. A single slab or crystal can show distinct color banding, commonly with four or more different colors being present. Fluorite can also be colorless and perfectly transparent. The property of "fluorescence," a luminescence caused by exposure to ultraviolet light, is common and pronounced in fluorite to the point that fluorite is the namesake of this spectacular property.

## HISTORY

The name fluorite comes from the Latin word *fluere*, which means "to flow," referring to its ancient use as a flux in smelting iron. Fluorite has a long history of use as an ornamental material; fluorite carvings are among the earliest Chinese works of art. A red-blue-colorless-dark purple sequentially banded variety of fluorite from Derbyshire, England, known as "Blue John," was used by the Romans for cups and dishes. Early American Indians carved artifacts from purple fluorite from southern Illinois.

In the early 1940's, scientists determined that in drinking water a sodium fluoride concentration of 1 part per million was high enough to cause a decrease in dental cavity formation but low enough not to cause the mottling of teeth that higher levels were known to cause. Early fluoridation programs were instituted in Michigan and Wisconsin in 1945. Fluoridation was controversial from the beginning, with its more radical opponents deeming it a communist plot against the United States. Nonetheless, as tests seemed to validate fluoride's effectiveness as an antidecay agent, its use spread throughout municipal water districts in the United States. In the past, some debated whether fluoridation was truly effective or whether other factors (such as better nutrition and oral hygiene) might be responsible for the decrease in tooth decay seen beginning in late 1940's. However, the scientific community widely accepts that fluoridation does indeed reduce decay.

## OBTAINING FLUORITE

Mining of fluorite for industrial and chemical applications began in the eighteenth century in the United States. There are three principal market grades of fluorite: acid, ceramic, and metallurgical. The specifications are in regard to purity. Acid grade is 97 percent pure, ceramic grade is about 94 percent pure, and metallurgical grade is between 60 and 90 percent pure.

## USES OF FLUORITE

Chlorofluorocarbons (CFCs) were made from acid-grade fluorite by having the hydrofluoric acid react with chloroform or carbon tetrachloride. These fluorocarbons performed outstandingly as refrigerants, aerosol propellants, and solvents. However, the diffusion of CFCs into the upper atmosphere is believed to be responsible for damage to the ozone layer, and production of these fluorine-based chemicals was banned by the Montreal Protocol in 1987.

Artificial fluoridation of drinking water and toothpaste is another widespread use of fluorine compounds, or fluorides. In the 1930's, researchers discovered that the presence of sufficient amounts of fluorine occurring naturally in drinking water could lead to a low level of tooth decay and dental cavities.

*Dion C. Stewart*

### WEB SITE

U.S. GEOLOGICAL SURVEY
Minerals Information: Fluorspar Statistics and Information
http://minerals.usgs.gov/minerals/pubs/commodity/fluorspar/

SEE ALSO: Aluminum; Ceramics; Crystals; Iron; Mohs hardness scale; Montreal Protocol; Ozone layer and ozone hole debate; Steel.

# Food chain

CATEGORIES: Ecological resources; plant and animal resources

*The food chain concept allowed ecologists to interconnect the organisms living in an ecosystem and to trace mathematically the flow of energy from plants through animals to decomposers. The concept provides the basic framework for production biology and has major implications for agriculture, wildlife biology, and calculating the maximum amount of life that can be supported on the Earth.*

## BACKGROUND

As early as 1789, naturalists such as Gilbert White described the many sequences of animals eating plants, and animals being eaten by other animals. However, the use of the term "food chain" dates from 1927, when Charles S. Elton described the implications of the food chain and food web concept in a clear manner. His solid exposition advanced the study of two important biological concepts: the complex organization and interrelatedness of nature, and energy flow through ecosystems.

## FOOD CHAINS IN ECOSYSTEM DESCRIPTION

Stephen Alfred Forbes, founder of the Illinois Natural History Survey, contended in 1887 that a lake comprises a system in which no organism or process can be understood unless its relationship to all the parts is understood. Forty years later, Elton's food chains provided an accurate way to diagram these relationships. Since most organisms feed on several food items, food chains were cross-linked into complex webs with predictive power. For instance, algae in a lake might support an insect that in turn is food for bluegill. If unfavorable conditions eliminate this algae, the insect might also disappear. However, the bluegill, which feeds on a wider range of insects, survives because the loss of this algae merely increases the pressure on the other food sources. This detailed linkage of food chains advanced agriculture and wildlife management and gave scientists a solid overview of living systems. When Arthur G. Tansley penned the term "ecosystem" in 1939, it was food-chain relationships that described much of the equilibrium of the ecosystem.

Most people still think of food chains as the basis for the "balance of nature." This phrase dates from the controversial 1960 work of Nelson G. Hairston, Frederick E. Smith, and Lawrence B. Slobodkin. They proposed that if only grazers and plants are present, grazing limits the plants. However, with predators present, grazers are limited by predation, and the plants are free to grow to the limits of the nutrients available. Such explanations of the "balance of nature" were commonly taught in biology books throughout the 1960's and 1970's.

## FOOD CHAINS IN PRODUCTION BIOLOGY

Elton's explanation of food chains came only one year after Edgar Nelson Transeau of Ohio State University presented his calculations on the efficiency with which corn plants converted sunlight into plant tissue. Ecologists traced this flow of stored chemical energy up the food chain to herbivores that ate plants and on to carnivores that ate herbivores. Food chains therefore undergirded the new "production biology" that placed all organisms at various trophic levels and calculated the extent to which energy was lost or preserved as it passed up the food chain.

With data accumulating from many ecologists, Elton extended food chains into a pyramid of numbers. The food pyramid in which much plant tissue supports some herbivores that are in turn eaten by fewer carnivores is still referred to as an "Eltonian pyramid." In 1939, August Thienemann added "decomposers" to reduce unconsumed tissues and return the nutrients of all levels back to the plants. Early pyramids were based on the amount of living tissues or biomass.

Calculations based on the amount of chemical energy at each level, as measured by the heat released (calories) when food is burned, provided even more accurate budgets. Because so much energy is lost at each stage in a food chain, it became obvious that this inefficiency is the reason food chains are rarely more than five or six links long and why large, fierce animals are uncommon. It also became evident that because the Earth intercepts a limited amount of sunlight energy per year, there is a limit on the amount of plant life—and ultimately upon the amount of animal life and decomposers—that can be fed. Food chains are also important in the accounting of carbon, nitrogen, and water cycling.

## VALUE OF FOOD CHAINS IN ENVIRONMENTAL SCIENCE

Unlike calories, which are dramatically reduced at each step in a food chain, some toxic substances become more concentrated as the molecules are passed along. The concentration of molecules along the food chain was first noticed by the Atomic Energy Commission, which found that radioactive iodine and strontium released in the Columbia River was concentrated in tissue of birds and fish. However, the pesticide dichloro-diphenyl-trichloroethane (DDT) provided the most notorious example of biological magnification: DDT was found to be deposited in animal body fat in ever-increasing concentrations as it moved up the food chain to ospreys, pelicans, and peregrine falcons. High levels of DDT in these birds broke down steroid hormones and interfered with eggshell formation.

Because humans are omnivores able to feed at several levels on the food chain, it has been suggested that a higher world population could be supported by humans moving down the food chain and becoming only vegetarians. A problem with this argument is that much grazing land worldwide is unfit for cultivation, and therefore the cessation of pig or cattle farming does not necessarily free up substantial land to grow crops.

While the food chain and food web concepts are convenient theoretical ways to summarize feeding interactions among organisms, real field situations have proved far more complex and difficult to measure. Animals often switch diets between larval and adult stages, and they are often able to shift food sources widely. In real life, it is often difficult to draw the boundaries of food chains and food webs.

*John Richard Schrock*

FURTHER READING

Colinvaux, Paul. "The Efficiency of Life." In *Why Big Fierce Animals Are Rare: An Ecologist's Perspective*. Princeton, N.J.: Princeton University Press, 1978.

Golley, Frank Benjamin. *A History of the Ecosystem Concept in Ecology: More than the Sum of the Parts*. New Haven, Conn.: Yale University Press, 1993.

Lowenfels, Jeff, and Wayne Lewis. *Teaming with Microbes: A Gardener's Guide to the Soil Food Web*. Portland, Oreg.: Timber Press, 2006.

Pimm, Stuart L. *Food Webs*. New York: Chapman and Hall, 1982. Reprint. Chicago: University of Chicago Press, 2002.

Rooney, N., K. S. McCann, and D. L. G. Noakes, eds. *From Energetics to Ecosystems: The Dynamics and Structure of Ecological Systems*. Dordrecht, the Netherlands: Springer, 2007.

Schilthuizen, Menno. *The Loom of Life: Unravelling Ecosystems*. Berlin: Springer, 2008.

SEE ALSO: Biosphere; Carbon cycle; Ecology; Ecosystems; Lithosphere; Nitrogen cycle; Phosphorus cycle; Sulfur cycle.

# Food shortages

CATEGORY: Social, economic, and political issues

*Throughout human history, civilizations have been plagued by malnutrition, hunger, and famine. The growth of the human population, the ecological disasters the world is facing, and continued warfare and civil strife have all been named as contributors to the problem in modern times.*

BACKGROUND

The procurement of food is one of the necessities of all societies. For thousands of years this was accomplished by hunting and gathering. While people were able to find and to use a variety of types of food, they were not always able to acquire the items they needed in the quantities that were required. With the onset of the agricultural revolution and the advent of organized farming, the problem was alleviated to a certain extent. Individuals and societies had more control over what their food supply might be at a given time. While this fact did not eradicate the problems caused by natural disasters that could destroy food sources, it did help to mitigate those catastrophes.

Other important developments were the scientific and technological advances that occurred beginning in the sixteenth century. The results of this scientific progress were applied to agricultural endeavors, medical practice, and industry. The knowledge gleaned from science enabled farmers to grow additional crops and to increase the productivity of the land on which they grew them. The advances in medical science increased the life expectancy of people and thus created additional demands for the foodstuffs that were produced. The Industrial Revolution also led to the invention of fuels and machines. These fuels provided the energy to run the factories that created farm equipment and machinery. They later served as a source of energy for farm equipment.

POPULATION

By 2009, the global population was approximately 6.8 billion. Very poor people continue to have large families for a variety of cultural and religious reasons. Large families provide labor; in some countries children as young as six years of age are part of the family's labor pool. Besides providing more income, having many family members may mean more clout in community affairs. Extra children also provide additional hands to care for parents in their old age.

It would be tempting simply to blame the problem of food shortages on the world's increasing population, but population increase alone is by no means responsible for the hunger that exists in the world. Rather, food shortages are caused by a combination of

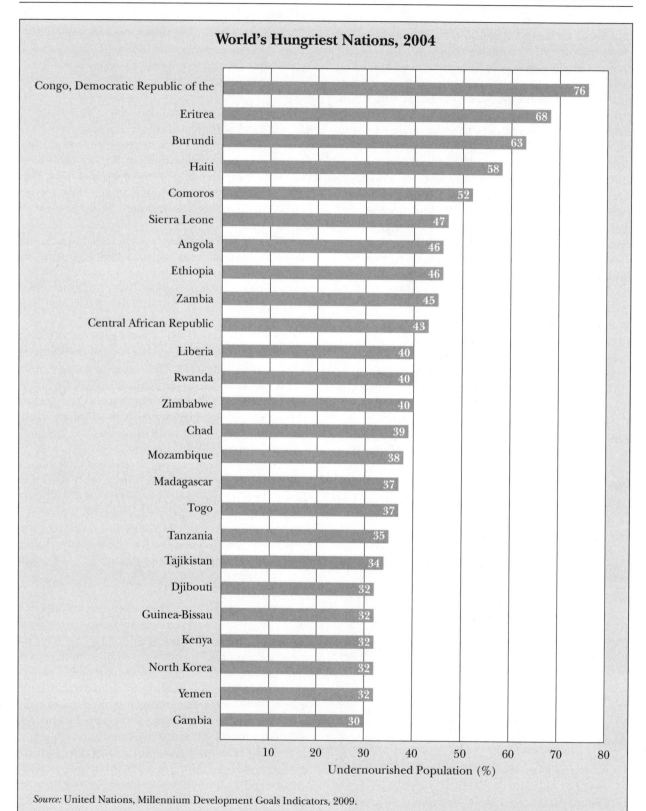

**World's Hungriest Nations, 2004**

| Nation | Undernourished Population (%) |
|---|---|
| Congo, Democratic Republic of the | 76 |
| Eritrea | 68 |
| Burundi | 63 |
| Haiti | 58 |
| Comoros | 52 |
| Sierra Leone | 47 |
| Angola | 46 |
| Ethiopia | 46 |
| Zambia | 45 |
| Central African Republic | 43 |
| Liberia | 40 |
| Rwanda | 40 |
| Zimbabwe | 40 |
| Chad | 39 |
| Mozambique | 38 |
| Madagascar | 37 |
| Togo | 37 |
| Tanzania | 35 |
| Tajikistan | 34 |
| Djibouti | 32 |
| Guinea-Bissau | 32 |
| Kenya | 32 |
| North Korea | 32 |
| Yemen | 32 |
| Gambia | 30 |

*Source:* United Nations, Millennium Development Goals Indicators, 2009.

elements that contribute to block access to the tools that would enable people or cultural groups to break the cycle of hunger.

### EXTENT AND CAUSES OF HUNGER

Estimates indicate that at least one billion people are hungry at any given time. Almost sixteen thousand children die of hunger-related diseases each day. Malnutrition, or not getting the proper nutrients, is one of these related syndromes. Malnutrition often leads to other diseases, such as goiter, as is the case in Bangladesh, where people have great iodine deficiencies. Pellagra, another malnutrition-related disease, is caused by a lack of the amino acid tryptophan. Pellagra is found in countries where the diet consists mainly of maize and *jowah*, a type of sorghum eaten mainly in India. Nutritional blindness also is a side effect of malnutrition. Infantile marasmus and kwashiorkor are two protein-deficiency diseases that cause lethargy, edema, and a number of other medical problems. These are brought on by a lack of protein in the diet and are prevalent in West Africa.

One of the easiest methods of ascertaining the extent of hunger worldwide is to examine infant mortality rates. In countries where hunger is greatest, the infant mortality rate tends to be high. It is often as high as 50 deaths per every 1,000 births; in Angola, the infant mortality rate is 180. In developed countries, in contrast, the rate is far lower. Singapore has the lowest rate at 2.31. In less developed countries, the infant mortality rate averages 90 per 1,000; in more developed countries it averages 8. (In all countries the rate varies from area to area.) The developed, or highly industrialized, countries are able to feed their own populations and generally have additional supplies of food to send to other nations. Developing countries, however, include more than two-thirds of the world's population and account for more than 90 percent of the hunger that exists in the world. Estimates indicate that 14 to 18 million people die each year from hunger. The World Health Organization states that more than 820 million people in developing countries suffer from malnutrition.

There are a number of explanations for hunger throughout the world. Many experts believe that hunger arises not so much from overpopulation as from the inequitable distribution of food supplies. In other words, a small number of people are responsible for the production of food and are obliged to apportion it to the world. Political scientist Susan George argues this viewpoint and states that it is not only the ineffective or inequitable distribution of food that leads to hunger; in addition, the inequitable income distri-

*Women in Pakistan buy rice discounted for Ramadan. The reduced price of the rice is a humanitarian gesture by the government of a country beset by food shortages.* (Mohsin Raza/Reuters/Landov)

bution among the peoples of the world leads to the inability to purchase food. Poverty leads to hunger, and the causes of poverty throughout the world are many. Large numbers of people are poor because they have no access to land or to the means of production. Many people have no way to earn a living, and many are forced to migrate to other places—which often offer no relief for their suffering. Hunger occurs when there are societal dislocations; Arline T. Golkin summarizes these as "disorders in food production, distribution, earning capacity, medical care, and levels of development." Hunger exists in rich nations as well as poor.

Environmental factors such as soil erosion, deforestation, and desertification lead to a diminution of farmland, a situation that eventually leads to food shortages and hunger. Deforestation leads to the washing away of soil. Forests are often destroyed to provide fuel; in other cases, forests are reduced or washed away completely by flooding. The Food and Agriculture Organization of the United Nations estimates that some 70 percent of global drylands, which are 30 percent of the globe, are already degraded, with much of the farmland becoming desert annually. Desertification is caused by periods of exceptional dryness in an already tenuous climate. Desertification is found in a number of African countries as well as in Russia, Ecuador, Nepal, and other nations. For all these reasons there is a shortage of usable farmland, which translates into hunger as a chronic condition for millions of people throughout the world.

When hunger persists in a region for an extended period of time and leads to increased mortality from disease or starvation, famine exists. These periods can last for several years, and often more than a food shortage is involved. Major famines have occurred throughout history. Since 1970, famines have occurred in Ethiopia, Nigeria, the Democratic Republic of the Congo, Sudan, the Sahel region in northern Africa, and North Korea. In Ethiopia, the cause was drought. In the Democratic Republic of the Congo and Nigeria, civil war was primarily responsible. Frequently, a famine is indicative of many underlying structural malfunctions within a society. A long and deep recession in a rural area, for example, can cause dislocation in employment, income, and production. The people who are most subject to displacement by this process are those who own no land, artisans, and those who trade in goods and services.

In times of famine, people are unable to pay for artisans' services and products. As John Osgood Field states, "famine occurs not only because a chain of events disposes to a famine outcome but also because nothing, or at least nothing effective, is done to break the process." Most of the countries that are subject to famine do not have the resources with which to break the cycle of famine, and often the ecosystem is out of balance in a number of ways. While societal problems may lead to famines, they can also be the outgrowth of famines. When groups of people suffer from famine, they frequently migrate elsewhere if they are able; they then become part of the throng of people in overcrowded cities. The result can be significant numbers of people hoarding, huge increases in the price of food, and concomitant violence.

*Judy Arlis Chesen*

FURTHER READING

Bennett, Jon. *The Hunger Machine: The Politics of Food.* New York: Polity Press in association with B. Blackwell, 1987.

Devereux, Stephen, ed. *The New Famines: Why Famines Persist in an Era of Globalization.* New York: Routledge, 2007.

Field, John Osgood, ed. *The Challenge of Famine: Recent Experience, Lessons Learned.* West Hartford, Conn.: Kumarian Press, 1993.

George, Susan. *How the Other Half Dies: The Real Reasons for World Hunger.* New York: Penguin, 1976.

George, Susan, and Nigel Paige. *Food for Beginners.* New York: W. W. Norton, 1982.

Golkin, Arline T. *Famine, a Heritage of Hunger: A Guide to Issues and References.* Claremont, Calif.: Regina Books, 1987.

Patel, Rajeev. *Stuffed and Starved: Markets, Power, and the Hidden Battle for the World Food System.* Toronto: HarperCollins, 2007.

Roberts, Paul. *The End of Food.* Boston: Houghton Mifflin, 2008.

Southgate, Douglas, Douglas H. Graham, and Luther Tweeten. *The World Food Economy.* Malden, Mass.: Blackwell, 2007.

Stanford, Claire, ed. *World Hunger.* Bronx, N.Y.: H. W. Wilson, 2007.

SEE ALSO: Desertification; Developing countries; Drought; Earth First!; Earth Summit; Environmental degradation, resource exploitation and; Green Revolution; Land ethic; Land-use regulation and control; United Nations Convention to Combat Desertification.

# Ford, Henry

CATEGORY: People

BORN: July 30, 1863; Springwells township (now Dearborn), Michigan

DIED: April 7, 1947; Dearborn, Michigan

*The "automobile age" of the twentieth century owes its existence largely to Henry Ford's vision of the automobile as a utility vehicle for the masses rather than as a wealthy individual's luxury. Ford's development of the Model T instituted some of the greatest and most rapid changes in the history of modern civilization.*

## BIOGRAPHICAL BACKGROUND

Henry Ford's conception of mass-produced automobiles manufactured at a rapid rate changed the world's concept of crucial resources. An American inventor, world-famous industrialist, and technological genius, Ford learned about internal combustion engines when he was nineteen. In 1896, he built his first "horseless carriage," the four-horsepower Quadricycle. In 1899, he formed the Detroit Automobile Company (later reorganized as the Henry Ford Company) and built several racing cars, including the "999."

Ford left the Detroit Automobile Company to start the Ford Motor Company, which was incorporated in 1903. The company's first automobile on the market was the Model A, built in 1903. Realizing the Model A was not the car that he believed the United States needed, he declared, "I will build a motor car for the great multitude." In October, 1908, he announced the birth of the Model T, an automobile that was built with the most advanced production technology conceived to that point. The car arrived on the market the following year.

The establishment of a constantly moving main production line in Highland Park, Michigan, that eventually reduced the assembly time of a car from twelve hours to one and one-half was the cause of the spectacular success of the Model T, of which nearly seventeen million were sold over a period of nineteen years. It took a number of years to perfect this assembly line. Ford's production methods were intensively studied. In 1914, after the Model T was a success, Ford startled the world by announcing a $5 daily wage (compared with an average of $2.34).

Ford established small village factories and built

*Henry Ford's technological contribution to the transportation industry helped generate America's love affair with the automobile. (Library of Congress)*

schools that emphasized vocational training. His holdings eventually went into the Ford Foundation, the richest private foundation in the world. Henry Ford worked intuitively, and he spent most of his life making headlines, both positive and negative.

## IMPACT ON RESOURCE USE

Without the twenty-four-hour assembly line and its utilization in the creation of millions of affordable automobiles, resources such as petroleum, rubber (both natural and artificial), and the metals used to produce automotive components would not have the importance they do in contemporary society. Ford's influence reached far beyond the automotive world, in that other industries adapted his efficient assembly-line technique to their own needs.

*Mysore Narayanan*

SEE ALSO: Gasoline and other petroleum fuels; Internal combustion engine; Oil industry; Rockefeller, John D.; Rubber, natural; Steel.

# Forest fires

CATEGORY: Environment, conservation, and resource management

*Forest fires can be natural or caused by humans. They destroy life and property and devastate thousands of hectares, but they are also vital to the health of the forest.*

## BACKGROUND

Evidence of forest fires is routinely found in soil samples and tree borings. The first major North American fires in the historical record were the Miramichi and Piscataquis fires of 1825. Together, they burned more than 1 million hectares in Maine and New Brunswick. Other U.S. fires of significance were the Peshtigo fire in 1871, which raged over 500,000 hectares and took fourteen hundred lives in Wisconsin; the fire that devastated northern Idaho and northwestern Montana in 1910 and killed at least seventy-nine firefighters; a series of fires that joined forces to sweep across a third of Yellowstone National Park in 1988; and the "Station Fire" of 2009, the largest in the history of Los Angeles County.

## FIRE BEHAVIOR

Fires need heat, fuel, and oxygen. They spread horizontally by igniting particles at their edge. At first, flames burn at one point, then move outward, accumulating enough heat to keep burning on their own. Topography and weather affect fire behavior. Fires go uphill faster than downhill because warm air rises and preheats the uphill fuels. Vegetation on south- and west-facing slopes receives more sunlight and so is drier and burns more easily. Steep, narrow canyons will pull heat up them like a chimney, increasing heat intensity.

For several reasons, only one-third of the vegetation within a large fire usually burns. This mosaic effect may be caused by varied tree species that burn differently, old burns that stop fire, strong winds that blow the fire to the leeward side of trees, and varied fuel moisture.

## FOREST MANAGEMENT

One of the early criteria of forest management was fire protection. In the second quarter of the twentieth century, lookout towers, firebreaks, and trails were built to locate fires as quickly as possible. Low fires that typically would have burned through the forest at ground level and cleared out brush every five to twenty-five years were suppressed. As a result, the natural cycle of frequent fires moving through an area was broken. Fallen trees, needles, cones, and other debris collected as kindling on the forest floor rather than being incinerated every few years.

It took foresters and ecologists fifty years to realize that too much fire suppression was as bad as too little. Accumulated kindling burns hot and fast and explodes into treetops. The result is a devastating crown fire, a large fire that advances as a single front. Burning embers of seed cones, as well as sparks borne by hot, strong winds created within the fire, are tossed into unburned areas to start more fires.

In the 1970's, prescribed burning was added to forest management techniques used to keep forests healthy. Fires set by lightning are allowed to burn when the weather is cool, the area isolated, and the risk of the fire exploding into a major fire low. More than 70 percent of prescribed burning takes place in the southeastern states, where natural fires would burn through an area more frequently than in the West.

## CAUSES OF FIRES

Forest fires may be caused by natural events or human activity. Most natural fires are started by lightning strikes. Dozens of strikes can be recorded from one lightning storm. When a strike seems likely, fire spotters watch for columns of smoke, and small spotter planes will fly over the area looking for smoke. Many of the small fires simply smolder and go out, but if the forest is dry because of drought or any period of hot, dry weather, multiple fires can erupt from a single lightning storm.

The majority of forest fires are human-caused, and most are the result of carelessness rather than arson. Careless campers may leave a campsite without squelching their campfire completely, and winds may then whip the glowing embers into flames; a smoker may toss a cigarette butt from a car window; sparks from a flat tire riding on the hub may set fire to vegetation alongside the highway; and the Sun shining through a piece of broken glass left by litterers may ignite dry leaves.

Prescribed fires may be natural or human-caused. In some areas they are set in an attempt to re-create the natural sequence of fire, as in Florida, where prescribed burns provide wildlife habitat and open up groves to encourage healthy growth. Other prescribed fires start accidentally but are allowed to burn until they reach a predetermined size.

## BENEFITS OF FIRE

Some tree species require very high temperatures for their seed casings to split for germination. When fire periodically sweeps through the forest, seeds will germinate. Other species, such as the fire-resistant ponderosa pine, require a shallow layer of decaying vegetable matter in which to root. Fires burn excess debris and small trees of competing species, leaving an open environment suitable for germination. Dead material on the forest floor is processed into nutrients more quickly by fire than by decay, and in a layer of rich soil, plants will sprout within days to replace those destroyed in the fire, thus providing feed for wildlife.

Fire intervals vary. Without human intervention, spacious ponderosa pine forests will burn every five to twenty-five years. Lodgepole pine, which grows in dense stands, will burn every two hundred to four hundred years. Southern pines, if fire is not suppressed, are cleared every three to five years.

## DISADVANTAGES

Erosion is one of the devastating effects of a fire. If the fuels burn hot, tree oils and resins can be baked into the soil, creating a hard shell that will not absorb water. When it rains, the water runoff gathers mud and debris, creating flash floods and extreme stream sedimentation. Culverts and storm drains fill with silt, and streams flood and change course. Fish habitat is destroyed, vegetation sheltering stream banks is ripped away, and property many kilometers downstream from the forest is affected.

When a fire passes through timber, it generally leaves pockets of green, although weakened, stands. Forest pests such as the bark beetle are attracted to the burned trees and soon move to the surviving trees, weakening them further and destroying them. Healthy trees outside the burn area may also fall to pest infestation unless the burned trees are

salvaged before pests can take hold. The ash and smoke from hot, fast-burning forest fires can be transported for kilometers, affecting the air quality of cities many kilometers from the actual fire.

## RELATIONSHIP TO TIMBER RESOURCES

Although a prescribed fire is an attempt to duplicate natural fire, it is not as efficient, because private and commercial property within the fire path must be protected. Once a fire has occurred, burned timber deteriorates quickly, through either insect infestation or blueing—a mold that stains the wood. Private landowners can move quickly to salvage fire-damaged trees and plant new seedlings to harness erosion. On federal land, regulations governing the salvage of trees can delay logging of the burned snags until deterioration makes it uneconomical to harvest them.

## FIRE FIGHTING

Bulldozers are used to cut fire lines ahead of the approaching fire, and fuels between this line and the fire are backburned. Helicopters and tanker planes drop water with a fire-retardant additive or bentonite, a clay, at the head of the fire to smother fuels. Firefighters are equipped with fire shelters in the form of aluminized pup tents, which they can pull over themselves if a fire outruns them. Despite technological advances, one of the best tools for fighting fires—along

*A firefighter gives directions as a backfire is set during the devastating Station Fire that burned uncontrollably in the Los Angeles National Forest during the summer of 2009.* (AP/Wide World Photos)

with the shovel—remains the Pulaski, a combination ax and hoe, first produced commercially in 1920. This tool, in the hands of on-the-ground firefighters, is used to cut firebreaks and to throw dirt on smoldering debris.

## PUBLIC POLICY AND PUBLIC AWARENESS

Beginning in the early twentieth century, forest fires engendered public policy. In the aftermath of major fires in 1903 and 1908 in Maine and New York, state fire organizations and private timber protective associations were formed to provide fire protection. These, in turn, contributed to the Weeks Act of 1911, which permitted cooperative fire protection between federal and state governments.

People who make their homes in woodland settings in or near forests face the danger of forest fire, and government agencies provide information to help the public safeguard themselves and their property. Homes near forests should be designed and landscaped with fire safety in mind, using fire-resistant, noncombustible materials on the roof and exterior. Landscaping should include a clear safety zone around the house, and hardwood trees, less flammable than conifers, should be planted.

*Jill A. Cooper*

FURTHER READING

Carle, David. *Burning Questions: America's Fight with Nature's Fire.* Westport, Conn.: Praeger, 2002.

Fuller, Margaret. *Forest Fires: An Introduction to Wildland Fire Behavior, Management, Firefighting, and Prevention.* New York: Wiley, 1991.

Omi, Philip N. *Forest Fires: A Reference Handbook.* Santa Barbara, Calif.: ABC-CLIO, 2005.

Pyne, Stephen J. *Awful Splendour: A Fire History of Canada.* Vancouver: University of British Columbia Press, 2007.

_____. *Fire in America: A Cultural History of Wildland and Rural Fire.* 1982. Reprint. Princeton, N.J.: Princeton University Press, 1988.

_____. *Smokechasing.* Tucson: University of Arizona Press, 2003.

Rothman, Hal K. *Blazing Heritage: A History of Wildland Fire in the National Parks.* New York: Oxford University Press, 2007.

Wuerthner, George, ed. *The Wildfire Reader: A Century of Failed Forest Policy.* Washington, D.C.: Island Press, 2006.

WEB SITE

NATIONAL INTERAGENCY FIRE CENTER
Fire Information: Wildland Fire Statistics
http://www.nifc.gov/fire_info/fire_stats.htm

SEE ALSO: Erosion and erosion control; Fires; Forest management; Forestry.

# Forest management

CATEGORY: Environment, conservation, and resource management

*Forest management is the process of planning, organizing, and implementing activities designed to produce and maintain a mix of resources in the forest that will meet the goals and objectives of landowners and society.*

## BACKGROUND

In 1967, the Society of American Foresters defined forestry as "the science, the art, and the practice of managing and using for human benefit the natural resources that occur on and in association with forestlands." In 1971, the same organization redefined forest management as "generally, the application of scientific, economic, and social principles to the administration and working of a forest estate for specified objectives" and "more particularly, the branch of forestry concerned with a) the overall administrative, economic, legal, and social aspects, and b) with the essentially scientific and technical aspects, especially silviculture, protection, and forest regulation."

Forests include or provide many things of value to humans: water, wildlife, grazing, timber, and recreation. Forest structure and composition can be designed to produce different mixtures of these things; one aspect of forest management is the determination of the mixture of goods and services that will best satisfy the goals and objectives of landowners and society. Forest managers have the responsibility to plan, schedule, and implement activities in the forest to achieve the management objectives.

## SILVICULTURE

Ralph Nyland, in *Silviculture: Concepts and Applications* (2d ed., 2001), defines silviculture as "the science and art of growing and tending forest crops" and particu-

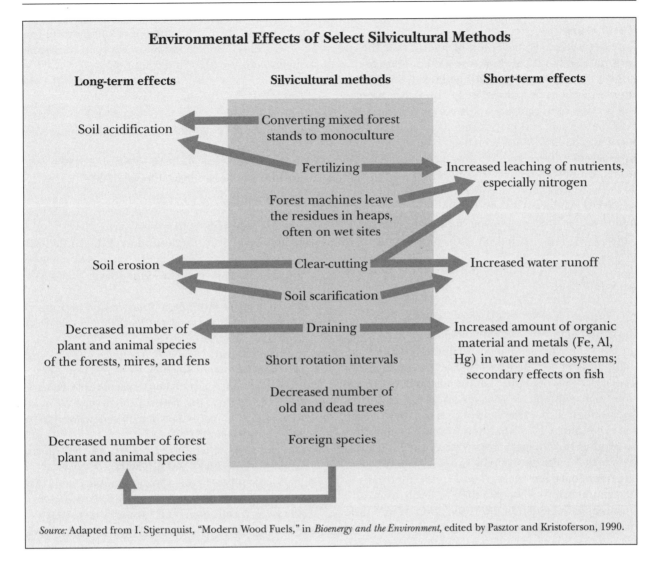

## Environmental Effects of Select Silvicultural Methods

| Long-term effects | Silvicultural methods | Short-term effects |
|---|---|---|

Soil acidification

Converting mixed forest stands to monoculture

Fertilizing

Increased leaching of nutrients, especially nitrogen

Forest machines leave the residues in heaps, often on wet sites

Soil erosion

Clear-cutting

Increased water runoff

Soil scarification

Decreased number of plant and animal species of the forests, mires, and fens

Draining

Increased amount of organic material and metals (Fe, Al, Hg) in water and ecosystems; secondary effects on fish

Short rotation intervals

Decreased number of old and dead trees

Decreased number of forest plant and animal species

Foreign species

*Source:* Adapted from I. Stjernquist, "Modern Wood Fuels," in *Bioenergy and the Environment*, edited by Pasztor and Kristoferson, 1990.

larly as "the theory and practice of controlling the establishment, composition, character, and growth of forest stands to satisfy specific objectives." Silviculture is distinct from forest management. Forest management is concerned with the establishment of management goals and objectives and the administrative activity to support the achievement of these goals, while silviculture is concerned with the detailed prescriptions for individual forest management units required to achieve the goals set for the larger area. The types of resources to emphasize and the mix of goods and services to produce are forest management decisions; specific measures to achieve these goals and the development of prescriptions for individual areas are the province of silviculture.

### PROTECTION

Forest protection is the branch of forestry concerned with minimizing damage to forests from both abiotic and biotic factors. Abiotic factors such as wind, floods, and fire can directly kill trees and affect the achievement of management goals. Biotic factors such as pests, pathogens, herbivores, livestock, and humans also affect tree mortality and health. The amount and type of material and human resources to allocate to fire protection, for example, are management decisions. Forest management is concerned with the allocation of financial, material, and human resources to manage all of these risk factors in such a way as to balance the costs of control measures with the benefits of maintaining forest health and productivity.

## REGULATION

Forest regulation is the process of determining the appropriate size and age structure of the forest over a large area to ensure the continued production of resource values in perpetuity. Regulation also refers to the process of organizing a forest to meet social and economic goals and constraints. One such requirement may be to produce a relatively even flow of forest products over time; another may be to ensure a continued supply of high-quality water from a municipal watershed. An industrial forest manager may be required to produce a certain level of fiber to supply a billion-dollar mill employing hundreds of people. The appropriate size and age distributions of trees to best achieve this goal may be quite different from those required to maximize the habitat for a particular animal species.

## BIOLOGICAL AND ECOLOGICAL CONSIDERATIONS

Physical, chemical, and climatic factors place limits on both the types of plants and animals that can inhabit an area and their productive potential. Forest managers must recognize and be able to develop possible management alternatives given the biological and ecological characteristics of an area. These define the types and mix of products and values that may be produced. Managers must work within these limits to determine the appropriate mix to best meet management goals. For every resource, it is important to determine appropriate production levels to ensure sustainable production over the long term while maintaining ecosystem structure and function. This is complicated by the fact that production is measured in different units for different resources. For water, it may be the annual volume of water per year from a watershed that meets certain quality standards. For wildlife it may be the population levels an area can sustain.

## INTEGRATION

Forest management, therefore, deals with the integration of biological and ecological potential with human economic and social goals and objectives. Some forested areas are managed to produce a mix of commodities and services, while others are managed to maximize the production of a single item. Designated wilderness areas, national parks, and national wildlife refuges, for example, are all managed largely to optimize the production of a relatively narrow set of resources, but they still produce a mix of other resources. Forest managers are concerned with the

production of the whole range of resources from forest ecosystems in such a way as to maintain ecosystem structure and function in perpetuity.

*David D. Reed*

FURTHER READING

Barnes, Burton V., et al. *Forest Ecology.* 4th ed. New York: Wiley, 1998.

Bettinger, Peter, et al. *Forest Management and Planning.* Boston: Academic Press/Elsevier, 2009.

Davis, Lawrence S., et al. *Forest Management: To Sustain Ecological, Economic, and Social Values.* 4th ed. Boston: McGraw-Hill, 2001.

Food and Agriculture Organization of the United Nations. *Global Forest Resources Assessment 2005: Progress Towards Sustainable Forest Management.* Rome: Author, 2006.

Gane, Michael. *Forest Strategy: Strategic Management and Sustainable Development for the Forest Sector.* Dordrecht, the Netherlands: Springer, 2007.

Humphreys, David. *Logjam: Deforestation and the Crisis of Global Governance.* Sterling, Va.: Earthscan, 2006.

Hunter, Malcolm L., Jr. *Wildlife, Forests, and Forestry: Principles of Managing Forests for Biological Diversity.* Illustrated by Diane Bowman. Englewood Cliffs, N.J.: Prentice-Hall, 1990.

Nyland, Ralph D. *Silviculture: Concepts and Applications.* 2d ed. Boston: McGraw-Hill, 2002.

Sauer, Leslie Jones, and Andropogon Associates. *The Once and Future Forest: A Guide to Forest Restoration Strategies.* Washington, D.C.: Island Press, 1998.

Smith, David M., et al. *The Practice of Silviculture: Applied Forest Ecology.* 9th ed. New York: Wiley, 1997.

SEE ALSO: Ecology; Ecosystems; Forestry; Forests; Land management; Multiple-use approach; Sustainable development; Timber industry; Wood and timber.

# Forest Service, U.S.

CATEGORY: Organizations, agencies, and programs
DATE: Established as Division of Forestry, 1897; renamed United States Forest Service, 1905

*The United States Forest Service manages and conserves U.S. national forestlands and grasslands with a mission of ensuring resource use by the public for recreation and by industry for logging and ranching. The*

*U.S. Forest Service is a recognized international leader in forest and ecosystem research and in natural resource protection and conservation and serves as a model for similar agencies in developing nations.*

## BACKGROUND

The U.S. Forest Service, a division of the U.S. Department of Agriculture, is responsible for managing approximately 77 million hectares of national forest as well as 1.6 million hectares of grassland located in forty-four states, Puerto Rico, and the Virgin Islands. The agency's history dates back to the early 1890's, when President Grover Cleveland proclaimed seventeen federal forest reserves, totaling 7,087,500 hectares. In the nineteenth century, the timber industry had become notorious for stripping an area of all its marketable timber and then moving on, leaving behind a barren, eroded landscape and deserted towns. At the beginning of the nineteenth century, the forest resources of the North American continent appeared so inexhaustible that the forest products industry gave little thought to conserving forests or practicing what is now known as sustainable forestry. By the 1880's, however, the fact that forest reserves were disappearing was clear. Public concerns about excessive harvesting contributed to fears that the nation's supply of timber would be exhausted before the turn of the century. Conservation leagues formed, and newspapers and magazines of the time published numerous articles warning of a coming timber famine.

One of President Cleveland's final acts as president in 1897 was to sign legislation providing funding for the administration of the reserves and creating the Division of Forestry within the Department of the Interior. Not all members of the public supported the Division of Forestry's creation: Many business interests responded to the initial creation of the federal forest reserves by urging that President Cleveland be impeached. The act stood, however, and in 1905, responsibility for the federal forest reserves was transferred from the Department of the Interior to the Department of Agriculture. At that time the agency's name changed from the Division of Forestry to the United States Forest Service.

President Theodore Roosevelt appointed a personal friend, renowned forester and conservation advocate Gifford Pinchot, to serve as the agency's first director. Pinchot had studied forestry in France, where forests had been managed for hundreds of years, and had also observed forestry practices in other European countries. The initial mission of the U.S. Forest Service was to conserve forest resources for future generations and to protect the nation's watersheds and riverways by preventing erosion. That is, the U.S. Forest Service attempted to manage the forest reserves in a way that would allow for both sustained-yield harvesting and the prevention of soil run-off from hillsides into waterways. One of the consequences of excessive timber harvesting was heavy silt deposits that choked formerly navigable rivers. Rain falling on forested hillsides is slowed or absorbed by vegetation; rain falling on barren hillsides tends to run off quickly, washing soil with it and contributing to both erosion and flooding.

## IMPACT ON RESOURCE USE

Under Pinchot, the U.S. Forest Service practiced forest management that allowed for harvesting in a manner that attempted both to be ecologically sound and to create a solid economic base for logging towns. Sustained-yield harvesting would allow permanent communities to grow; families could flourish as lumbering and related industries provided stable, year-round employment.

In addition to managing forest reserves, the U.S. Forest Service established regional research stations to investigate issues such as silviculture, reforestation, fire suppression, and harvesting practices. Although referred to as stations, the locations of research efforts were not actually centralized but instead took place in a variety of settings, including controlled laboratory environments and forests. The U.S. Forest Service also supported research performed by scientists at universities by funding grants and participating in cooperative research agreements with academia and industry. Research conducted or supported by the Forest Service has led to a better understanding of forest ecology and to subsequent changes in management by both government agencies and private industry. Research continued into the twenty-first century with activities such as the Forest Inventory and Analysis program, which conducts research on both public and private lands to assess the conditions of U.S. forests and to detect future trends.

The U.S. Forest Service is also responsible for overseeing twenty national grasslands. National grasslands were established during the Great Depression of the 1930's, when the Great Plains were devastated by the Dust Bowl, an ecological disaster caused by a combination of drought and farming practices unsuited for a prairie ecosystem. Farmers especially were affected by the country's economic woes, resulting in thousands of farms being abandoned by farmers unable to make mortgage payments or pay property taxes. As part of national relief efforts, the federal government acquired millions of hectares of submarginal farmland that included both forest tracts and grasslands. Land more suited for forests than for farming was incorporated into national forests, such as the Oconee National Forest in Georgia, and planted with trees. Prairie lands were restored to grasslands, such as Buffalo Gap National Grassland in South Dakota. Because land for many forests was often acquired in small, noncontiguous blocks as it became available rather than through condemnation, many forests and grasslands remain a patchwork of private and public ownership with irregular boundaries. Like national forests, national grasslands are managed for multiple use, including recreation, wildlife habitat, and livestock forage.

Also in the 1930's, the U.S. Forest Service began to provide more recreational opportunities in national forests. Civilian Conservation Corps members developed campgrounds, picnic areas, and hiking trails. The agency also instituted leasing programs that allowed the public to lease lots within national forests on which they could build recreational cabins for seasonal use. The U.S. Forest Service provided guidelines that set size limits and specified the materials, such as types of exterior siding, that could be used. Although these recreational opportunities were viewed originally as secondary to the agency's primary mission of ensuring a sustainable timber supply, over time recreation assumed a more important role. As the threat of a timber famine faded, the public's understanding of forest conservation and the appropriate role of the U.S. Forest Service changed.

This change has been reflected in significant pieces of twentieth century federal legislation, such as the Wilderness Act (1964), the National Environmental Policy Act (1970), and the National Forest Management Act (1976). Congress originally created the Forest Service for conservation, that is, to promote the wise use of forest resources. Subsequent legislation has resulted in the Forest Service becoming a diverse agency with multiple missions relating to natural and cultural resources in the United States. The National Forest Management Act in particular redefined the agency's mission by making multiple use an explicit rather than an implicit requirement. In the twenty-first century, in addition to managing forests for a sustained yield available to the commercial forest products industry, the Forest Service also is charged with protecting critical wildlife habitat, providing outdoor recreational opportunities for the general public, and protecting cultural resources, such as historic buildings or archaeological sites, that fall within national forest boundaries.

Thus the Forest Service is occasionally embroiled in controversy when one mission, such as providing recreational opportunities for the public, conflicts with other missions, such as protecting critical habitat for endangered species. Nonetheless, as part of the Department of Agriculture, the Forest Service still oversees national forests as reserves of timber which have been set aside for eventual sale to private industry.

For administrative purposes the U.S. Forest Service is divided into ten geographic regions. The boundaries for these regions have changed over time to reflect changes in administration policies and goals. Similarly, improvements in office automation, communications, and transportation technology have led to management of individual forests becoming more centralized. In Wisconsin, for example, the formerly separate Nicolet National Forest and Chequamegon National Forest are now managed as the Chequamegon-Nicolet National Forest, while in Texas four national forests (the Angelina, Davy Crockett, Sabine, and Sam Houston) and two grasslands (Caddo and LBJ) are supervised from a central office.

*Nancy Farm Männikkö*

FURTHER READING

Arnold, R. Keith, et al. *View from the Top: Forest Service Research.* Durham, N.C.: Forest History Society, 1994.

Clary, David A. *Timber and the Forest Service.* Lawrence: University of Kansas Press, 1986.

Lewis, James G. *The Forest Service and the Greatest Good: A Centennial History.* Durham, N.C.: Forest History Society, 2005.

Steen, Harold K. *Origins of the National Forests: A Centennial Symposium.* Durham, N.C.: Forest History Society, 1992.

WEB SITE

U.S. FOREST SERVICE
http://www.fs.fed.us

SEE ALSO: Conservation; Forestry; Forests; Multiple-use approach; Pinchot, Gifford; Timber industry.

# Forestry

CATEGORY: Environment, conservation, and
    resource management

*Billions of people, industrialists, and the economies
of many nations rely on forests, which cover approximately 30 percent of the world's landmass. The practice of forestry can ensure that there will be sustainable
forests to support all living things with timber and
wood products, energy resources, animal ranges, wildlife habitats, recreational opportunities, water resources, oxygen, and climate control.*

## BACKGROUND

Forestry, considered both a science and an art, has its
origins in China, while the Western world formalized
the practice of forestry during the Middle Ages. By the
sixteenth century, Germany and Japan were leaders
in developing systematic forest management, and
German foresters established many of the earliest
forestry schools in the eighteenth and nineteenth
centuries. Royalty often promoted forest management
through mapping, harvesting, and reforestation. An
example of such early forestry practices was Great
Britain's Broad Arrow Policy of 1691, which required
reservation for the navy of all trees on public lands
with a diameter of 60 centimeters or greater. These
trees were used in large part for building ship masts—
one of the significant commercial enterprises that
made use of forest products in the seventeenth century.

The German influence was felt in North America
by 1898, when German Carl Schenck established one
of the first American schools of forestry in North Carolina. The New York State College of Forestry was also
established at Cornell University in the same year.
Schenck, who initially came to the United States to replace Gifford Pinchot in managing the forests of the
Biltmore Estate in Asheville, North Carolina, utilized
many of the German forestry methods in his education program. Pinchot, who was trained in France, was
appointed by President William McKinley as the head
of what became known as the United States Forest
Service.

## THE BEGINNINGS OF FORESTRY

Initially, forestry involved finding ways to cultivate
trees and plant materials quickly because of the depletion of wood products caused by war but also necessi-
tated by the spread of settlements throughout the
world. People used wood not only for construction of
buildings and fences but also as the main source of energy. Thus, as population increased, the demand for
wood products increased. The settlers in the New
World began shipping substantial amounts of logs
and lumber to the Old World, where many forests had
already been depleted, often as a result of practices
such as clear-cutting—the cutting of all trees in a
stand with little concern for underlying plants, soil,
and water resources.

As the population in the United States spread in
the eighteenth and nineteenth centuries from New
England south through the Appalachian forests and
west to the forests surrounding the Great Lakes, early
settlers practiced little forest management or conservation. Most of the settlers believed there was an endless supply of trees; not until the second half of the
nineteenth century did influential politicians and authors begin to advocate for forest management and
conservation. However, the United States did little to
manage its forests until after many trees had been
clear-cut for commercial purposes, including building railroads, and soil had been degraded through
erosion.

The scientific methods employed in early forestry
involved managing and improving existing forests
through cutting, pruning, and thinning of forests and
controlling erosion, diseases, and pests. To foster forest continuity, loggers modified their previous "cut
out and get out" approach to logging and also applied
science in order to protect the soil, water, and young
trees in areas where timber harvesting was taking
place. Many of these early scientific methods are still
practiced. In addition, during the nineteenth and
twentieth centuries, many nations began to adopt
laws and regulations to conserve forests, protect watersheds, and establish forest reserves. In many cases,
these laws were a reaction to the commercial slash-
and-burn practices of the past and the technologies
being employed by the logging and paper industries.

As the nineteenth century began, Pinchot philoso-
phized that forests could be used wisely while also being preserved for the enjoyment of future generations. This multiple-use philosophy, that there can
be a balance between economic and environmental
factors to meet both present and future needs, is
known as sustainable forestry. The debate, however,
continues in modern forestry—should forests be pre-

served or managed for commercial timber production?

MODERN FORESTRY PRACTICES

Modern forestry not only employs the early scientific methods and management practices but also utilizes many new mechanized and science-based techniques. Today's foresters use tools such as portable computers to maintain and organize forest inventory databases and to generate financial and harvest-yield models. Forest scientists link computer mapping technologies with satellite resources such as geographic information systems that allow remote sensing. Combining mapping and sensing data allows evaluation of forests, such as insect damage, forest erosion, and potential harvest yields throughout the globe. Global Positioning Systems are also important in pinpointing exact locations of forest resources that may have been identified through aerial photography or remote-sensing technologies.

Today's forest management also involves specialization. Silviculture is the main specialty that concerns management of forests and their surroundings to establish healthy tree populations and plant materials for commercial harvesting. Silviculturalists develop forest management plans in order to ensure healthy and profitable yields, while recognizing that forests are in constant states of change, which is known as succession. In addition, genetic engineers are conducting global research to improve species that can withstand pests, diseases, and drought in specific geographic areas. Controlled or prescribed forest burning to reduce the amount of fuel available for fires, soil conservation and watershed management to ensure that soils are adequate to support a forest and to prevent soil erosion, protection of forest ecosystems

*A forest employee uses a chainsaw to clear a felled tree.* (©iStockphoto.com)

and biodiversity enhancement, water quality management and pollution control, pest and disease control, and climate control by ensuring sufficient plant materials to create a sink for atmospheric carbon dioxide and oxygen restoration through photosynthesis are all prominent features of modern-day forestry practice and education.

The commercial enterprise of plantation forestry, much like single-crop farming, involves establishing monocultures or single varieties of trees and plant materials usually started from seeds or seedlings. Christmas tree farms and nurseries are examples of plantation forestry. Urban forestry is practiced in highly populated areas where urban living environments are enhanced through the creation of green spaces and the planting of shade tree species and other plant materials appropriate for a geographic location. Another specialty branch of forestry is tropical forestry, which takes place in equatorial forests and involves harvesting of woods popular in furniture manufacturing, such as mahogany and teak.

## COMMERCE VS. PRESERVATION

Forests have substantial commercial value not only for wood and paper products such as plywood and as a renewable energy source but also for many manufactured products that are derived from trees and plant materials. Many of these manufactured products begin with a wood source that is turned into a useful product through the application of chemicals. These products include rayon, cellophane, adhesives, photo film, paints, household cleaners, baby food, ice cream, cosmetics, and food flavorings. Many pharmaceutical products also come from forest sources. Economics is important in forestry, and foresters must have an understanding of how to ensure that forest products will have sufficient quantity and quality to maintain a profitable business.

Global forestry initiatives have taken place for many years. The World Forestry Congress has met almost every six years since 1926, and the 2009 meeting in Buenos Aires, Argentina, concerned ways to achieve a balance between preserving tropical rain forests and allowing for development. Moreover, since the 1980's, many international entities, including the United Nations, the World Bank, and the European Forest Institute, have begun to formulate and implement global conservation-oriented forestry strategies and initiatives.

However, not all of the world leaders agree that conservation is the best policy, as national development varies globally from hunter-gatherer societies to industrialized nations that place an emphasis on the commercial value of forest products. Many developing nations believe in maximum use of their forests to fuel their development in the same manner that industrialized nations overused their forests to enhance their economies. Although overuse of forests and lack of forest management in one area of the globe will impact other areas, the many international agencies trying to resolve the global forestry debate between deforestation for economic development and preservation are not likely to come to an easy resolution.

*Carol A. Rolf*

FURTHER READING

Achard, Frédéric. *Vital Forest Graphics.* Nairobi, Kenya: United Nations Environment Programme, 2009.

Berger, John J. *Forests Forever: Their Ecology, Restoration, and Protection.* Chicago: Center for American Places, 2008.

Burton, L. DeVere. *Introduction to Forestry Science.* 2d ed. Clifton Park, N.Y.: Thomson Delmar Learning, 2008.

Dietrich, William. *The Final Forest: The Battle for the Last Great Trees of the Pacific Northwest.* New York: Penguin, 1993.

Lele, Uma, ed. *Managing a Global Resource: Challenges of Forest Conservation and Development.* World Bank Series on Management and Development, Volume 5. New Brunswick, N.J.: Transaction, 2002.

McEvoy, Thomas J. *Positive Impact Forestry: A Sustainable Approach to Managing Woodlands.* Covelo, Calif.: Island Press, 2004.

Morsbach, Hans W. *Common Sense Forestry.* White River Junction, Vt.: Chelsea Green, 2002.

Palo, Matti, and Jussi Uusivuori. *World Forests, Society, and Environment.* Boston: Kluwer Academic, 1999.

Perry, David A., Ram Oren, and Stephen C. Hart. *Forest Ecosystems.* 2d ed. Baltimore: Johns Hopkins University Press, 2008.

WEB SITES

EUROPEAN FOREST INSTITUTE
http://www.efi.int/portal/

FOOD AND AGRICULTURE ORGANIZATION OF THE UNITED NATIONS
Forestry Information Centre
http://www.fao.org/forestry/library/en/

SEE ALSO: Forest management; Forest Service, U.S.; Forests; Multiple-use approach; Pinchot, Gifford; Timber industry; Wood and charcoal as fuel resources; Wood and timber.

# Forests

CATEGORY: Plant and animal resources

*Forests are complex ecosystems in which trees are the dominant type of plant. Both humans and animals depend on forests for food, shelter, and other resources.*

## BACKGROUND

Forests once covered much of the world and are still found from the equator to the Arctic regions. A forest may vary in size from only a few hectares to thousands of square kilometers, but generally any natural area in which trees are the dominant plant type can be considered a forest. For a plant to be called a tree, the standard definition requires that the plant must attain a mature height of at least 2.4 meters, have a woody stem, and possess a distinct crown. Thus, even though apples and roses are otherwise close botanical relatives, size dictates that roses grow on shrubs and apples grow on trees.

## TROPICAL, TEMPERATE, AND BOREAL FORESTS

Foresters generally divide the forests of the world into three general categories: tropical, temperate, and boreal. (See "Rain forests" for a discussion of the tropical rain forest.) In brief, the tropical forest consists of a dizzying variety of trees that remain green year-round, shrubs, and other plants. The growth is lush and usually includes both a dense canopy formed by the crowns of the largest trees and a thick understory of smaller trees and shrubs. Growth is often continuous, rather than broken into periods of dormancy and active growth, so that fruiting trees are occasionally seen bearing blossoms and mature fruit simultaneously.

The temperate forest lies between the tropical forest and the boreal, or northern, forest. The forests of the Mediterranean region of Europe as well as the forests of the southern United States are temperate forests. Trees in temperate forests can be either deciduous or coniferous. Although coniferous trees are generally thought of as evergreen, the distinction between types is actually based on seed production and leaf shape. Coniferous trees, such as spruces, pines, and hemlocks, produce seeds in cones and have needle-shaped leaves. Deciduous trees, such as maples, poplars, and oaks, have broad leaves and bear seeds in other ways. Some conifers, such as tamarack, do change color and drop their needles in the autumn, while some deciduous trees, particularly in the more southerly regions of the temperate forest, are evergreen. Deciduous trees are also referred to as hardwoods, while conifers are softwoods, a classification that refers more to the typical density of the wood than how difficult it is to nail into it. Softwoods are lower in density and will generally float in water while still green. Hardwoods are higher in density on average and will sink.

Like the tropical forest, the temperate forest can be quite lush. While the dominant species vary from area to area, depending on factors such as soil types and available rainfall, a dense understory of shade-tolerant species often thrives beneath the canopy formed by taller trees. Thus, a mature temperate forest may have thick stands of rhododendrons 6 to 9 meters high thriving in the shade of 25-meter oaks and tulip poplars. As the temperate forest approaches the edges of its range and the forest makes the transition to boreal, the understory thins out, disappearing almost completely or consisting only of low shrubs. Even in temperate forests, the dominant species may prevent an understory from forming. Stands of southern loblolly pine, for example, often have a parklike feel as the thick mulch created by fallen needles chokes out growth by other species.

The boreal forest, which lies in a band across the northern United States, Canada, northern Europe, and northern Asia, is primarily a coniferous forest. The dominant species are trees such as white spruce, hemlock, and white pine. Mixed stands of northern hardwoods, such as birch, sugar maple, and red oak, may be found along the southern reaches of the boreal forest. As the forest approaches the Arctic, trees are fewer in type, becoming primarily spruce, birch, and willows, and smaller in size. The understory is generally thin or nonexistent, consisting of seedlings of shade-tolerant species, such as maple, and low shrubs. Patches of boreal-type forest can be found quite far south in higher elevations in the United States, such as the mountains of West Virginia, while the edge of the temperate forest has crept steadily northward following the retreat of the glaciers at the end of the Ice Age twenty thousand years ago.

### FOREST ECOLOGY AND RESOURCES

In all three types of forests a complex system of interrelationship governs the ecological well-being of the forest and its inhabitants. Trees and animals alike have evolved to fit into particular environmental niches. Some wildlife may need one resource provided by one species of tree in the forest during one season and a resource provided by another during a different time of year, while other animals become totally dependent on one specific tree. Whitetail deer, for example, browse on maple leaves in the summer, build reserves of fat by eating acorns in the fall, and

survive the winter by eating evergreens. Deer are highly adaptable in contrast with other species, such as the Australian koala, which depends entirely on eucalyptus leaves for its nutritional needs. Just as the animals depend on the forest, the forest depends on the animals to disperse seeds and thin new growth. Certain plant seeds, in fact, will not sprout until being abraded as they pass through the digestive tracts of birds.

Humans also rely on the forest for food, fuel, shelter, and other products. Forests provide wood for fuel and construction, fibers for paper, and chemicals for thousands of products often not immediately recognized as deriving from the forest, such as plastics and textiles. In addition, through the process of transpiration, forests regulate the climate by releasing

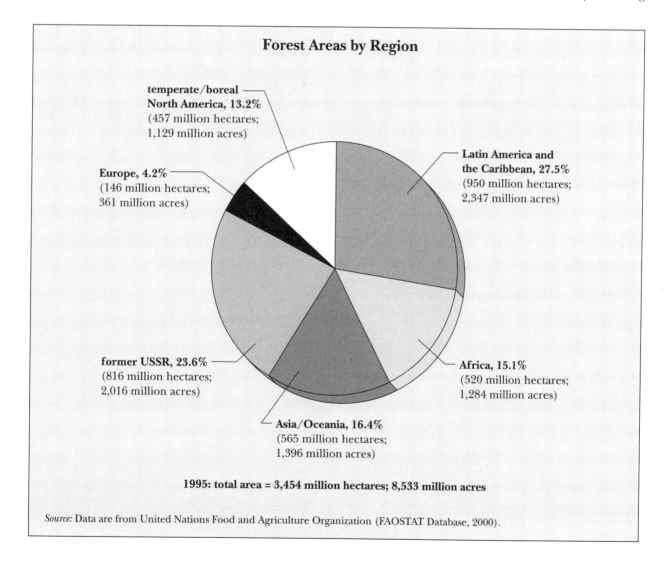

**Forest Areas by Region**

temperate/boreal
**North America, 13.2%**
(457 million hectares;
1,129 million acres)

**Europe, 4.2%**
(146 million hectares;
361 million acres)

**Latin America and
the Caribbean, 27.5%**
(950 million hectares;
2,347 million acres)

**former USSR, 23.6%**
(816 million hectares;
2,016 million acres)

**Africa, 15.1%**
(520 million hectares;
1,284 million acres)

**Asia/Oceania, 16.4%**
(565 million hectares;
1,396 million acres)

**1995: total area = 3,454 million hectares; 8,533 million acres**

*Source:* Data are from United Nations Food and Agriculture Organization (FAOSTAT Database, 2000).

water vapor into the atmosphere while removing harmful carbon compounds. Forests play an important role in the hydrology of a watershed. Rain that falls on a forest will be slowed in its passage downhill and is often absorbed into the soil rather than running off into lakes and rivers. Thus, forests can moderate the effects of severe storms, reducing the dangers of flooding and preventing soil erosion along streams and riverbanks.

## THREATS TO THE FOREST

The primary threat to maintaining healthy forests around the world is the rising rate of human population growth. As the population grows, three types of pressure are placed on the existing forest. First, forests are cleared to provide land for agriculture or for the construction of new homes. This process has occurred almost continuously in the temperate regions for thousands of years, but it did not become common in tropical regions until the twentieth century. Often settlers level the forest and burn the fallen trees to clear land for farming without the wood itself being utilized in any way. Developers tend to see the forest as a nuisance to be removed as quickly as possible. As a result, the exposed land often becomes infertile for farming within a few years. After a few years of steadily diminishing crops, the land is abandoned. With the protective forest cover removed, it may quickly become a barren, eroded wasteland.

Second, rising populations in developing nations often depend on wood or charcoal as their primary fuel for cooking and for home heat. Forests are destroyed as mature trees are removed for fuel wood faster than natural growth can replace them. As the mature trees disappear, younger and younger growth is also removed, and eventually the forest is gone completely.

Finally, growing populations naturally demand more products derived from wood, which can include everything from lumber for construction to chemicals used in cancer research. Market forces can drive forest products companies to harvest more trees than is ecologically sound as stockholders focus on short-term individual profits rather than long-term environmental costs. The challenge to foresters, ecologists, and other scientists is to devise methods that allow humanity to continue to utilize the forest resources we need to survive without destroying the forests as complete and healthy ecosystems.

*Nancy Farm Männikkö*

## FURTHER READING

Food and Agriculture Organization of the United Nations. *Forests and Energy: Key Issues.* Rome: Author, 2008.

_____. *Global Forest Resources Assessment 2005: Progress Towards Sustainable Forest Management.* Rome: Author, 2006.

Holland, I. I., and G. L. Rolfe. *Forests and Forestry.* 5th ed. Danville, Ill.: Interstate Publishers, 1997.

Kimmins, Hamish. *Balancing Act: Environmental Issues in Forestry.* Vancouver: University of British Columbia Press, 1992.

Nyland, Ralph D. *Silviculture: Concepts and Applications.* 2d ed. Boston: McGraw-Hill, 2002.

Page, Jake. *Forest.* Alexandria, Va.: Time-Life Books, 1983.

Sands, Roger. *Forestry in a Global Context.* Cambridge, Mass.: CABI, 2005.

Sharpe, Grant W., John C. Hendee, and Wenonah F. Sharpe. *Introduction to Forests and Renewable Resources.* 7th ed. Boston: McGraw-Hill Higher Education, 2003.

Walker, Laurence C., and Brian P. Oswald. *The Southern Forest: Geography, Ecology, and Silviculture.* Rev. ed. Boca Raton, Fla.: CRC Press, 2000.

## WEB SITES

### ENVIRONMENT CANADA
Welcome to the Western Boreal Conservation Initiative
http://www.pnr-rpn.ec.gc.ca/nature/ecosystems/wbci-icbo/index.en.html

### NATURAL RESOURCES CANADA
Canada's Forests
http://canadaforests.nrcan.gc.ca/?lang=en

### U.S. FOREST SERVICE
Forest Inventory and Analysis National Program
http://www.fia.fs.fed.us

### U.S. GEOLOGICAL SURVEY
Forest Ecosystems
http://www.usgs.gov/science/science.php?term=410

SEE ALSO: Clear-cutting; Deforestation; Forest fires; Forest management; Forestry; Hydrology and the hydrologic cycle; Rain forests; Reforestation; Timber industry; Wood and charcoal as fuel resources; Wood and timber.

# France

CATEGORIES: Countries; government and resources

*France ranks regularly among the top five countries in the global production of wheat and other cereals, sugar beets, potatoes, and wine grapes because of its rich soils. France also exports significant amounts of vegetables, beef, and dairy products as well as some timber and fish.*

## THE COUNTRY

France benefits from its geographic location between northern and southern Europe, possessing coastal openings on both the Atlantic Ocean and the Mediterranean Sea. The river systems of the Seine, Loire, Garonne, and Rhone favor interior communication, with only the Massif Central considered an internal natural obstacle. Although France has limited mineral resources, it has abundant fertile soils, receives ample rainfall, and has an equable climate. Historically, the nation has been known for its agricultural products.

After World War II, however, France industrialized rapidly under extensive governmental promotion of such development, and in the twenty-first century the French are recognized for their high-tech products in such areas as public transportation, defense, and power generation. Among European countries, France ranks the lowest in the material intensity measure of its gross domestic product (GDP)—at 0.7 kilogram per euro—which some researchers believe is a measure of technological and environmental efficiency but also reflects the service and agricultural orientation of France's mixed economy.

In 2008, France had the eighth largest GDP in the world—measured in terms of purchasing power parity—at $2.1 trillion, with 20 percent coming from the production of items such as machinery, chemicals, pharmaceuticals, automobiles, metallurgical materials, aircraft, electronics, textiles, and beverages. A little more than 2 percent comes from agriculture (including wheat and other cereals, sugar beets, potatoes, and wine grapes), beef, dairy products, and fish. The global recession of 2008 slowed French GDP growth to 0.7 percent, with an estimated −8 percent in industrial production. France is one of the world's most popular tourist destinations, attracting approximately 75 million foreign visitors every year.

## MINERALS AND ORES

The mining sector, which began declining in the 1990's, typically contributes around 7 percent to the French GDP and employs less than 1 percent of the workforce. In 2006, France produced an estimated 13 million metric tons of stone, sand, and gravel; 21 million metric tons of hydraulic cement; 9.4 million metric tons of salt (rock, refined brine, marine, and in solution); 3.5 million metric tons of crude gypsum and anhydrite; 300,000 metric tons of marketable kaolin and kaolinitic clay; 650,000 metric tons of crude feldspar; 40,000 metric tons of marketable fluorspar; 30,000 metric tons of barite; 65,000 metric tons of kyanite, andalusite, and related materials; 20,000 metric tons of mica; and 420,000 metric tons of crude talc. France has also mined copper, gold, silver, powder tungsten, sponge zirconium, elemental bromine, ball and refractory clays, diatomite, lime, nitrogen, and iron oxide pigments as well as thomas slag phosphates, pumice (pozzolan and lapilli), and soda ash and sodium sulfate.

Phosphorous iron deposits found along the Moselle in Lorraine constitute the largest vein in Western Europe. They once produced 50 million metric tons per year but were increasingly hard to exploit profitably; the last mine was closed in 1998. Bauxite, discovered in the village of Les Baux in Provence, also was once mined extensively, but the deposits are nearly exhausted, and France ceased production in 1993. Similarly, potassium carbonate (potash), important in the production of fertilizer, once came abundantly from the mines of Alsace, but production was stopped because of ecological concerns and the depletion of the resource. During a decade of neoliberal policies, the government ceased subsidizing unprofitable operations. In 2000, mining production in France was 76 percent of what it was in the 1990's. In fact, since 1985, the European Union as a whole has imported more industrial minerals and ores, including fossil fuels, than it has extracted.

Nevertheless, from 2003 to 2007, the French metal and mining industries grew by 5.5 percent because of concerns about foreign dependency for certain alloys and ores needed in industrial production. In 2007, companies in heavy industry reached a total value of $19 billion and were forecast to continue to grow into the next decade. Sales of iron and steel—including crude steel, pig iron, and direct reduced iron—accounted for 87 percent of the industry's overall value. Other metal and mineral products include aluminum, composing 7 percent of total revenues in the

# France: Resources at a Glance

*Official name:* French Republic
*Government:* Republic
*Capital city:* Paris
*Area:* 248,447 mi²; 643,427 km²
*Population (2009 est.):* 64,057,792
*Language:* French
*Monetary unit:* euro (EUR)

## ECONOMIC SUMMARY:

*GDP composition by sector (2008 est.):* agriculture, 2%; industry, 20.4%; services, 77.6%
*Natural resources:* metropolitan France: coal, iron ore, bauxite, zinc, uranium, antimony, arsenic, potash, feldspar, fluorspar, gypsum, timber, fish, timber products
*Land use:* arable land, 33.46%; permanent crops, 2.03%; other, 64.51%
*Industries:* machinery, chemicals, automobiles, metallurgy, aircraft, electronics, textiles, food processing, tourism
*Agricultural products:* wheat, cereals, sugar beets, potatoes, wine grapes, beef, dairy products, fish
*Exports (2008 est.):* $601.9 billion
*Commodities exported:* machinery and transportation equipment, aircraft, plastics, chemicals, pharmaceutical products, iron and steel, beverages
*Imports (2008 est.):* $692 billion
*Commodities imported:* machinery and equipment, vehicles, crude oil, aircraft, plastics, chemicals
*Labor force (2008 est.):* 27.97 million
*Labor force by occupation (2005):* agriculture, 3.8%; industry, 24.3%; services, 71.8%

## ENERGY RESOURCES:

*Electricity production (2007 est.):* 570 billion kWh
*Electricity consumption (2007 est.):* 480 billion kWh
*Electricity exports (2007):* 67.6 billion kWh
*Electricity imports (2007):* 10.8 billion kWh

*Natural gas production (2007 est.):* 953 million m³
*Natural gas consumption (2007 est.):* 42.69 billion m³
*Natural gas exports (2007 est.):* 966 million m³
*Natural gas imports (2007 est.):* 42.9 billion m³
*Natural gas proved reserves (Jan. 2008 est.):* 7.277 billion m³

*Oil production (2007):* 71,400 bbl/day
*Oil imports (2005):* 2.465 million bbl/day
*Oil proved reserves (Jan. 2008 est.):* 122 million bbl

*Source:* Data from *The World Factbook 2009.* Washington, D.C.: Central Intelligence Agency, 2009.
*Notes:* Data are the most recent tracked by the CIA. Values are given in U.S. dollars. Abbreviations: bbl/day = barrels per day; GDP = gross domestic product; km² = square kilometers; kWh = kilowatt-hours; m³ = cubic meters; mi² = square miles.

sector; coal (anthracite, bituminous, and lignite) and base metals (lead, zinc, copper, nickel, and tin), making up 5.6 percent of sales; and precious metals (gold, silver, platinum, palladium, rhodium, and industrial diamonds), amounting to 0.1 percent. In 2007, the value of France's metal and mining industries was 5.8 percent of the total European value in the category, behind Germany (17.5 percent) and near the production level of Great Britain.

## Fossil Fuels

As of 2009, 500 to 600 million metric tons of coal were estimated to be under French soil. However, because of the poor quality of the coal and the effort needed to remove it, extraction has largely ceased. The major coal-mining operations in the Nord were closed in 1991, and the last mines in Lorraine and Provence were closed in 2004. France continues to import some coal for its steel industry and coal-fired power stations.

Hydrocarbon reserves, found in the regions of Aquitaine and Seine-et-Marne, also are limited. Natural gas deposits also are on the verge of exhaustion. In 2007, estimates indicated that France had about 122 million barrels of oil reserves; production was only 71,400 barrels a day, while consumption was almost 2 million barrels a day. Clearly, the nation must import most of its needs, as crude oil and French oil refining capacity amount to about 1.9 million barrels per day. The multinational corporation Total is the world's fourth largest petroleum company, with assets in Africa, Latin America, and the North Sea, and was formed in 1999-2000 by mergers of the French companies Total and Elf Aquitaine with Belgium's Petrofina. Natural gas reserves were estimated to be only about 7.3 billion cubic meters in 2008, while consumption was at 42.7 billion cubic meters in 2007, most of which was imported.

At one time, uranium, one of France's principal energy sources, was extracted from mines at Bessines and La Crouzille (Limousin). Production in the 1990's was around 80,000 metric tons, or 3 percent, of the world's uranium supply, but the last mine was closed in 2001. France still relies heavily on nuclear power production of electricity and is third globally among countries in terms of nuclear waste disposal, behind only the United States and Canada.

## Energy

France is the tenth largest producer of electricity in the world, producing about 570 billion kilowatt-hours (kWh) and exporting 67.6 billion kWh in 2007. It is second to the United States in the production of nuclear energy, amounting to 77 percent of domestic production and 47 percent of European Union production of electricity. The nation has fifty-eight reactors. About 15 percent of energy production comes from natural gas. Hydroelectricity is also well developed in France but is short of French energy needs. In 2000, energy consumption in France was 54 percent fossil fuels, 39 percent nuclear, 3 percent renewable sources (biomass, geothermal, solar, wind, and tidal), and 2 percent hydroelectric.

## Nickel, Gold, and Other Resources in Overseas France

Mining contributes greatly to the economy of New Caledonia, a self-governing territory of France whose inhabitants are French citizens and vote in national elections. Between 2014 and 2019, New Caledonia, an island about 18,575 square kilometers located in the southwest Pacific Ocean, will decide by referendum whether or not to become independent. One-quarter of the world's nickel resources are located on the islands; New Caledonia is also rich in cobalt and chromium. Nearby regions of the Pacific Ocean also promise significant nodules of polymetallic resources yet to be exploited. In 2007, mineral and alloy exports, largely nickel ore and ferronickel, amounted to around $2 billion. However, open-pit mining has been heavily criticized as responsible for the loss of the unique natural heritage of the islands.

In French Guiana, an overseas department of France, gold deposits in jungle regions have attracted illegal mining, which poses a threat to ecologically sensitive areas and the indigenous Amerindian population. An estimated ten thousand illegal miners, known as *garimpeiros*, are destroying forest areas and polluting streams with mercury. The region also has petroleum, kaolin, niobium, tantalum, and clay.

## Soil and Agricultural Production

In France, agriculture has always figured prominently in economic development because of the country's temperate climate, good soils, and ample rainfall. In 2005, continental France had some 295,690 square kilometers devoted to agriculture, including crops and livestock, a total greater than any Western European nation and one that amounts to 54 percent of France's total land area. In 2000, the "World Soil Resources Report" of the Food and Agriculture Organization of the United Nations ranked France as having the fewest constraints on agriculture in Western Europe because of its soil quality, placing it fifteenth in the world in the agricultural potential of its soils (referred to by the French as "green oil"). Farms in France are much larger and fewer in number than in the past and have shifted increasingly to intensive, mechanized cultivation techniques. This has, in turn, provoked heated criticism from French food and agricultural activists. Around 5 percent of the French labor force is involved in agriculture, and in 2004, a notable 40 percent of all budget expenditures of the European Union's Common Agricultural Policy program went to French farm subsidies.

France is divided into vast cleared areas suitable for farming or animal husbandry that are separated by heaths, moors, and extensive forest areas. France is well known as a mosaic of different regional features arising in part from differences in geology, morphology, climate, soil, and vegetation as well as different human cultural responses to habitats. The agriculturally rich low plains of Beauce, Seine-et-Marne, and Picardy were created by limestone and clay sedimentation on the seabed during the Mesozoic era and Tertiary period. Fertile alluvial plains are also found along the Seine and Loire rivers. Southern France is distinguished by biennial rotation of crops, while northern France is characterized by triennial rotation, and cultivation also can be categorized into open or enclosed fields; the latter are typical in western France and are known as *bocage* (hedged farmland). France has the widest range of latitude of any European nation, enjoying some of the subtropical climate of the Mediterranean as well as the temperate climate of northwestern Europe. This allows for a wide variety of crops. France usually suffers from few of the extremes—cold or drought—that affect both northern and southern Europe. On average, almost the entire country receives at least 50 centimeters of precipitation as either rain or snow.

France ranks regularly in the top ten among countries in the global production of wheat and other cereals, sugar beets, potatoes, apples, apricots, and wine grapes. With 6.5 million metric tons of meat production, France ranked fourth globally and first in Europe in 2001. Producing 6.5 million metric tons of wheat per hectare, France ranked fourth in the world in wheat yield in 2004. In the same year, France cultivated 70.5 million metric tons of cereals, including 39.7 million metric tons of wheat, 11 million metric

tons of barley, 16.3 million metric tons of corn, 598,200 metric tons of oats, and 257,600 metric tons of sorghum. France also produces 7.25 million metric tons of potatoes, 30.5 million metric tons of sugar beets, 3.9 million metric tons of rapeseed, 2.1 million metric tons of pulses, 26.8 million metric tons of citrus fruit, 7.5 million metric tons of grapes, 808,000 metric tons of tomatoes, 2.2 million metric tons of oil crops, 2.2 million metric tons of apples, 90,700 metric tons of fiber crops, 15,000 metric tons of honey, 11 million metric tons of total fruit, and 8.8 million metric tons of vegetables. For centuries, France's wine production has ranked near the top among countries in quantity (and some would say quality), with 2 percent of its arable land used for wine grapes. In 2005, France produced 5.3 billion liters of wine, which was second only to Spain.

Although France is popularly known for its extensive cereal production, which includes its famous bread and pastry products, and its vineyards and wines, it produces large quantities of meat as well, some 6.53 million metric tons annually. In 2004, livestock production resulted in 6.3 million metric tons of total meat, including 1.6 metric tons of beef, 2.3 million metric tons of pork, 131,000 metric tons of lamb and goat meat, and 1.9 metric tons of poultry. France also produced 1 million metric tons of eggs, 150,000 metric tons of cattle hides, and 11,000 metric tons of horsemeat. France is also a producer of dairy products, notably milk, cheese, and butter. Winston Churchill declared famously upon the occasion of the German invasion of France in 1940, "A country producing almost 360 different types of cheese cannot die." Finally, it should be noted that France is the top European producer of oysters and among the top three in mussels, fishing, and aquaculture, which includes freshwater trout, bass, and bream from marine farms.

### FORESTS AND FOREST RESOURCES
Forests are France's richest natural resource, with one-quarter of the land covered by forest, amounting to 13.8 million hectares. One-quarter of this land is managed by the National Forests Office, whose efforts led to the doubling of forest areas during the twentieth century. Forest areas are concentrated in the east, south, and southwest, the largest of which is the Landes coastal region south of Bordeaux. France's forests are made up of 63 percent deciduous and 38 percent coniferous or mixed trees; another 8 percent are considered brushwood. France imports softwoods and pulp largely for paper production, but the

French are the largest producers of sawn hardwood in Europe, with about $7.1 billion in exports.

*Bland Addison*

## FURTHER READING

Chandler, Virginia. *The Changing Face of France*. Austin, Tex.: Raintree, 2003.

Cleary, Mark C. *Peasants, Politicians, and Producers: The Organisation of Agriculture in France Since 1918*. Reprint. New York: Cambridge University Press, 2007.

Dormois, Jean-Pierre. *The French Economy in the Twentieth Century*. New York: Cambridge University Press, 2004.

Fanet, Jacques. *Great Wine Terroirs*. Translated by Florence Brutton. Berkeley: University of California Press, 2004.

Hecht, Gabrielle. *The Radiance of France: Nuclear Power and National Identity After World War II*. Cambridge, Mass.: MIT Press, 1998.

Pinchemel, Philippe, et al. *France: A Geographical, Social, and Economic Survey*. Translated by Dorothy Elkins with T. H. Elkins. Reprint. Cambridge, England: Cambridge University Press, 2009.

## WEB SITES

THE GREENS-EFA GROUP, EUROPEAN PARLIAMENT
Nuclear Power in France Beyond the Myth
http://www.greens-efa.org/cms/topics/dokbin/ 258/258614.mythbuster@en.pdf

INVENTAIRE FORESTIER NATIONAL (ENGLISH LANGUAGE VERSION)
http://www.ifn.fr/spip/?lang=en

2006 MINERALS YEARBOOK
France
http://minerals.usgs.gov/minerals/pubs/country/ 2006/myb3-2006-fr.pdf

SEE ALSO: Agricultural products; Agriculture industry; Nuclear energy; Uranium.

# Freeze-drying of food

CATEGORY: Obtaining and using resources

*The first modern quick-freezing process was developed by Clarence Birdseye in 1925; he used refrigerated moving metal belts to quick-freeze fish.*

## DEFINITION

Freeze-drying, also called lyophilization, is a method of preserving substances for future use by removing water from them. Freeze-dried foods retain their nutrients almost intact. Their flavor characteristics are almost undiminished, and the process prevents the growth of microbes.

## OVERVIEW

Food was not dried in great volume in the United States until World War I (1914-1918), when dried food became important for feeding soldiers. During World War II (1939-1945), the need for dried foods for soldiers led to the development of such items as instant coffee and dried milk. Modern freeze-drying techniques began in the late 1960's.

Freeze-drying differs from other drying methods because the substance is frozen into a solid state (at a temperature of about −29° Celsius) before being dried. The substance is then placed on trays in a refrigerated vacuum chamber, and heat is carefully applied until the frozen moisture content is evaporated without melting. A technician controls the rate of heating so that the pressure inside the vacuum chamber never becomes great enough to melt the ice in the substance. The process of changing the ice directly from a solid to a vapor without its first becoming a liquid is known as sublimation.

As the ice vaporizes, the food maintains its shape but becomes a porous (full of tiny holes), spongelike, lightweight dry solid. Drying takes from four to twelve hours, depending on the type of substance, the particle size, and the drying system used, with more than 90 percent of the water being removed. Freeze-dried foods are usually packed in an inert gas, such as nitrogen, and then packaged in moisture-proof containers. Since freeze-drying prevents microbial growth and freeze-dried foods can regain a close approximation of their original shape, texture, and flavor when reconstituted with the addition of water, freeze-drying is an ideal method for storing food supplies.

Among the foods most commonly preserved by freeze-drying are soup mixes, strawberries, mushrooms, bamboo sprouts, shrimp, a variety of vegetables, and beverages, especially instant coffee, tea, and dried milk. Many other substances are also freeze-dried. Drug companies use the process to prepare many medicines, including medicines derived from plants, since the low temperature at which the process takes place allows serums and other drug solutions to retain their original characteristics. Biologists use the freeze-drying process to prepare animal specimens for displays in museums, or to prepare parts of organisms for microscopic studies. The process is also used to restore valuable papers damaged by water, and military personnel, hikers, and campers often carry freeze-dried foods because the products are light and compact. Although it has many diverse, practical applications, freeze-drying is not used extensively for food preservation because the difficulties in freeze-drying animal and plant cells make it relatively uneconomical.

*Alvin K. Benson*

SEE ALSO: Agricultural products; Agriculture industry; Biotechnology; Canning and refrigeration of food; Plants as a medical resource; Population growth; Water.

# Friends of the Earth International

CATEGORY: Organizations, agencies, and programs
DATE: Established 1969

*Friends of the Earth International (FOEI) is a federation of national environmental organizations focusing on global environmental problems, such as rain-forest destruction, ozone-layer depletion, marine pollution, and the hazardous-waste trade.*

## BACKGROUND
Friends of the Earth was founded in the United States by David Brower. Over the years, national groups were established in other countries. There are nearly eighty national member groups throughout the world. Each national group is an autonomous body with its own funding and strategy.

FOEI takes an active part in the international environmental policy process. It has had observer status at convention proceedings and consultative status at a number of United Nations organizations, such as United Nations Educational, Scientific and Cultural Organization and the United Nations Economic and Social Council. It has also participated in meetings of the International Atomic Energy Agency, the International Panel on Climate Change, and the Montreal Protocol.

The Rainforest Action Network and the Interna-

tional Rivers Network are affiliates of Friends of the Earth International, and FOEI is a member of the International Union for Conservation of Nature and the Environmental Liaison Center International.

## IMPACT ON RESOURCE USE
The organization's objectives include protecting the Earth from damage by humans; increased public participation in environmental protection; social, economic, and political justice; and the promotion of environmentally sustainable development. FOEI has been instrumental in coordinating the activities of networks of environmental, consumer, and human rights organizations.

*Marian A. L. Miller*

## WEB SITE

FRIENDS OF THE EARTH INTERNATIONAL
http://www.foei.org/

SEE ALSO: Conservation; Earth First!; Environmental movement; Montreal Protocol; Oceans; Ozone layer and ozone hole debate; Rain forests.

# Fuel cells

CATEGORY: Energy resources

*Fuel cells, which most often use hydrogen as their fuel, are an attractive idea for the generation of electric power because high efficiencies are possible. Research and development were spurred by the special needs of spacecraft in the 1960's. Commercial use will increase as designs and materials of construction improve.*

## BACKGROUND
The first fuel cell was demonstrated in 1839 by the English scientist Sir William Robert Grove. In 1889, Ludwig Mond and Carl Langer developed another version of the device and gave it the name "fuel cell," but not until 1932 was the first useful fuel cell designed by Francis Thomas Bacon at Cambridge University. Explosive growth in cell research followed in the 1960's, supported by the need for electric power aboard manned spacecraft. Units for the commercial generation of power followed roughly twenty years later.

## How Fuel Cells Work

A fuel cell consists of a pair of electrodes separated by an electrolyte. Although according to this description a battery could be considered a fuel cell, batteries are not classified as such because they consume chemicals that form part of their structure or are stored within the structure. With fuel cells, on the other hand, the reactants are supplied from outside the cell, and the cell continues to operate as long as the supplies of fuel and oxidant continue.

Most commonly, the fuels are gaseous and are supplied to porous electrodes impregnated with a catalyst. Reactions occur at each electrode, setting up a voltage between them. Thus the electrodes can be connected to a device such as a light or a motor. The electric circuit is completed within the cell itself through the electrolyte through which ions flow from one electrode to the other. Grove's cell used hydrogen as the fuel and oxygen as the oxidant, but various types of fuels, oxidants, and electrolytes can be used.

## Efficiency

In one of the more common methods for generating electric power from fossil fuels, combustion occurs and is used to generate steam. The steam, in turn, passes through a turbine that drives an electrical generator. Because of the constraints of the second law of thermodynamics, some of the energy of the combustion must be released into the surroundings—for example, into a river or a lake. As a result, the overall efficiency is usually between 30 and 40 percent. By contrast, a fuel cell converts the chemical energy of the fuel directly to electricity. Theoretically, the efficiency can approach 100 percent. In actual practice, an efficiency of about 75 percent can be achieved, roughly twice that of conventional power plants using steam.

## Uses of Fuel Cells

The first practical uses of fuel cells were in such exotic areas as manned exploration of space and the oceans. Costs and efficiencies were not critical items in the selection of fuel cells for these applications. Since these early uses, fuel cells have made inroads into the area of commercial power generation. Growth has been slow because the technology lags behind that of more advanced conventional power plants using gas and steam turbines. As might be expected, there is more development of fuel cell technology in countries and regions where the cost of fossil fuels is relatively high—for example, in Japan and Europe.

In the United States, there has been increased interest in distributed power generation, in which small power plants are located at the sites where the power is actually needed. In this case, power transmission lines from a central power station would not be needed. Fuel cells are well suited to this type of generation, because they are efficient, even in small sizes (such is not the case for conventional power plants).

The transportation industry, in particular the automobile industry, is interested in using fuel cells to generate electricity to power automobiles and other vehicles. The ongoing research into developing smaller fuel cells with higher performance could lead to a revolution in electric vehicles.

## Hydrogen as a Fuel

Hydrogen was the first fuel used in fuel cells and is an attractive fuel because there are enormous amounts of it on the Earth. However, most of the hydrogen is combined with oxygen in the form of water, and it would cost more to separate these components than any gain in efficiency that could be achieved in using them in a fuel cell. Nevertheless, Canada has used excess hydroelectric power to separate the hydrogen and oxygen. On the positive side, hydrogen can be produced from natural gas using steam in a process referred to as steam reforming. Refineries have gas streams that can be converted to hydrogen as well. Research is being carried out on the use of sunlight in photoelectrochemical and photobiological methods of separating the hydrogen and oxygen in water.

**Principal Parts of a Fuel Cell**

$H_2$ — + $O_2$

Electrolyte

Porous electrodes

Anode        Cathode

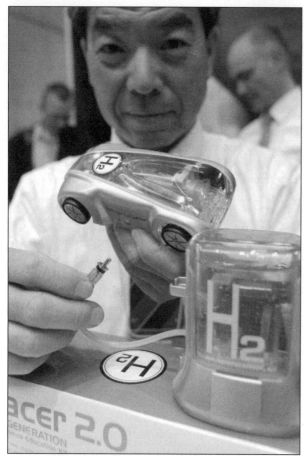

At the 2009 International Hydrogen and Fuel Cell Expo in Tokyo, Japan, a man holds a toy model that demonstrates the operation of a car powered by a fuel cell. (Kim Kyung-Hoon/Reuters/Landov)

There has been occasional political interest in promoting hydrogen as the "fuel of the future." Assuming that it were economical to produce, problems regarding storage, distribution, and safety would still exist. As long as the cost of producing hydrogen remains high, it will be used mostly for specialized needs such as fueling space rockets or running fuel cells on spacecraft. As might be expected, the future of fuel cells is tied to the availability of hydrogen.

### FUTURE OF FUEL CELLS

As noted earlier, fuel cells can have high efficiencies. The cell itself has no moving parts, so it operates quietly. There are no toxic or polluting exhaust emissions. When hydrogen and oxygen are used, the byproduct is water, which can be used for drinking and humidification of the air on a spacecraft. Fuel cells produce direct-current (DC) power, which is a significant advantage in some applications. Use of fuel cells has increased as their technology has advanced. When smaller fuel cells with higher performance are perfected, the increased use will cause costs to decline, removing any past disadvantage to their use.

*Thomas W. Weber*

FURTHER READING

Adamson, Kerry-Ann. *Stationary Fuel Cells: An Overview.* Boston: Elsevier, 2007.

Bagotsky, Vladimir S. *Fuel Cells: Problems and Solutions.* Hoboken, N.J.: John Wiley & Sons, 2009.

Barclay, Frederick J. *Fuel Cells, Engines, and Hydrogen: An Exergy Approach.* Hoboken, N.J.: John Wiley & Sons, 2006.

Busby, Rebecca L. *Hydrogen and Fuel Cells: A Comprehensive Guide.* Tulsa, Okla.: PennWell, 2005.

Goswami, D. Yogi, and Frank Kreith, eds. *Energy Conversion.* Boca Raton, Fla.: CRC Press, 2008.

Harper, Gavin D. J. *Fuel Cell Projects for the Evil Genius.* New York: McGraw-Hill, 2008.

Mench, Matthew M. *Fuel Cell Engines.* Hoboken, N.J.: John Wiley & Sons, 2008.

O'Hayre, Ryan, et al. *Fuel Cell Fundamentals.* 2d ed. Hoboken, N.J.: John Wiley & Sons, 2009.

Sorensen, Harry A. *Energy Conversion Systems.* New York: J. Wiley, 1983.

Weston, Kenneth C. *Energy Conversion.* St. Paul, Minn.: West, 1992.

WEB SITES

ALTERNATIVE FUELS AND ADVANCED VEHICLES DATA CENTER, U.S. DEPARTMENT OF ENERGY
Fuel Cell Vehicles
http://www.afdc.energy.gov/afdc/vehicles/ fuel_cell.html

BREAKTHROUGH TECHNOLOGIES INSTITUTE
Fuel Cells 2000: The Online Fuel Cell Information Resource
http://www.fuelcells.org

SEE ALSO: Electrical power; Hydroenergy; Hydrogen; Photovoltaic cells.

# G

## Gallium

CATEGORY: Mineral and other nonliving resources

### WHERE FOUND

Gallium is widely distributed in the Earth's crust in small amounts. It is found in ores of aluminum, zinc, and germanium. The richest concentration of gallium is found in germanium ores in South Africa.

### PRIMARY USES

The main use of gallium is in the production of semiconductors for use in the electronics industry. It is also used in research and development.

### TECHNICAL DEFINITION

Gallium (abbreviated Ga), atomic number 31, belongs to Group IIIA of the periodic table of the elements and resembles aluminum in its chemical and physical properties. It has two naturally occurring isotopes and an average atomic weight of 69.72. Pure gallium is a silvery-white, soft metal that takes on a bluish tinge when exposed to air. Its density is 5.9 grams per cubic centimeter; it has a melting point of 29.8° Celsius and a boiling point of 2,403° Celsius.

### DESCRIPTION, DISTRIBUTION, AND FORMS

Gallium is a rare but widely distributed element resembling aluminum. It occurs mostly as an oxide but may also occur as a sulfide. It is combined with antimony, arsenic, or phosphorus to create compounds useful in making semiconductors.

### HISTORY

Gallium was discovered in 1875 by the French chemist Paul-Émile Lecoq de Boisbaudran. Although it was seen to have unusual properties, including a large difference between its melting and boiling points, it was of little practical use until the middle of the twentieth century.

### OBTAINING GALLIUM

Although gallium is found in concentrations of up to 1 percent in South African germanium ores, this ore has been exhausted to the point where recovery is no longer practical. Instead, it is obtained from worldwide aluminum ores and from zinc ores in Missouri, Oklahoma, and Kansas. These ores contain about 1 percent gallium as the same amount of the South African germanium ores.

Gallium is obtained as a by-product of aluminum production by chemically removing leftover aluminum from the liquid remaining after most of the aluminum is obtained from the ore. The gallium is then removed from the liquid by electrolysis. Gallium is obtained as a by-product of zinc production by treating the ore with sulfuric acid and neutralizing it to remove iron, aluminum, and gallium. This solution is treated with a base and neutralized to remove the aluminum and gallium. The mixture is next treated with hydrochloric acid to remove the gallium and some aluminum. It is then treated with ether to remove the

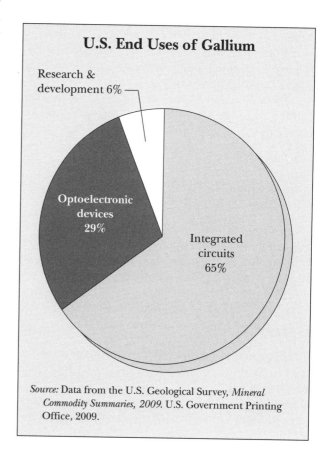

**U.S. End Uses of Gallium**

Research & development 6%

Optoelectronic devices 29%

Integrated circuits 65%

Source: Data from the U.S. Geological Survey, *Mineral Commodity Summaries, 2009*. U.S. Government Printing Office, 2009.

gallium, treated with a base to remove traces of iron, and electrolyzed to recover the gallium.

## USES OF GALLIUM

Gallium used for semiconductors must be very pure. Iron and organic impurities may be removed by treating the gallium with a base. Zinc and remaining iron may be removed by treating it with an acid. Other impurities may be removed by crystallizing the gallium.

In 1952, German chemists produced the first semiconductors using gallium compounds. Gallium antimonide, gallium arsenide, and gallium phosphide are the most useful for this purpose. These compounds are used in much the same way that silicon compounds and germanium compounds are used in electronic devices. In 2008, about 65 percent of gallium consumption in the United States was for integrated circuit manufacture.

Another and increasingly important use of gallium is in optoelectronic devices such as light-emitting diodes (LEDs), laser diodes, and solar cells for applications in consumer goods, aerospace medical equipment, industrial equipment, and telecommunications. Gallium phosphide and gallium indium arsenide can be used in these devices to convert nearly 41 percent of the light that strikes them into electricity. In 2008, U.S. consumption of gallium for such purposes comprised about 29 percent.

*Rose Secrest*

## WEB SITE

U.S. GEOLOGICAL SURVEY
Minerals Information: Gallium Statistics and
    Information
http://minerals.usgs.gov/minerals/pubs/
    commodity/gallium/

SEE ALSO: Aluminum; Germanium; Semiconductors; Silicon; Zinc.

# Garnet

CATEGORY: Mineral and other nonliving resources

## WHERE FOUND

Garnet occurs worldwide; it is common in many metamorphic and igneous rocks, especially gneisses and schists, and in garnet-rich sands that develop by ero-

sion of such rocks. Garnet is an important constituent of the Earth's mantle. Gem-quality garnets are notably found in Brazil, Sri Lanka, Tanzania, and the Ural Mountains. Industrial garnets are mined in the United States, India, China, and Australia.

## PRIMARY USES

Garnet is used primarily as an abrasive and secondarily as a semiprecious gemstone. The color is the principal factor in determining the value of gem-quality garnets.

## TECHNICAL DEFINITION

Garnet is a family name for a group of minerals that have a common internal structure but vary in their composition and physical properties. The color of garnet is usually red, sometimes yellow or brown, and rarely green. Garnet commonly forms equidimensional crystals that have from twelve to thirty-six faces. The hardness of garnet varies from 6.5 to 7.5 on the Mohs scale. Garnet is brittle and forms subconchoidal fractures when it breaks.

## DESCRIPTION, DISTRIBUTION, AND FORMS

There are about twenty minerals called garnet. Each has the same general formula, "A"$_3$ "B"$_2$Si$_3$O$_{12}$, where "A" is calcium, magnesium, iron, manganese, or a combination and "B" is aluminum, iron, vanadium, zirconium, titanium, chromium, or a combination. Most of the formal garnet names are based upon hypothetical pure compositions in which a single element occurs in the A and B sites. Such "pure" garnets are rarely found in nature; most natural garnets are mixtures. The most common mixture is called pyralspite, which is an acronym for a mixture of the pure garnets named pyrope (Mg$_3$Al$_2$Si$_3$O$_{12}$), almandine (Fe$_3$Al$_2$Si$_3$O$_{12}$), and spessarite (Mn$_3$Al$_2$Si$_3$O$_{12}$). The second most common mixture is called ugrandite, an acronym for a mix of uvarovite (Ca$_3$Cr$_2$Si$_3$O$_{12}$), grossularite (Ca$_3$Al$_2$Si$_3$O$_{12}$), and andradite (Ca$_3$Fe$_2$Si$_3$O$_{12}$).

The color of a garnet is controlled by its chemical composition. Garnets rich in iron are dark red to nearly black. Garnets containing mostly calcium and aluminum are yellow to cinnamon brown. Shades of green result when abundant chromium is present. Garnets grow as isometric crystals that commonly develop as dodecahedron or trapezohedron forms or as a combination of both.

Garnets grow in a variety of geological settings. Pyralspite forms during metamorphism of shale or ba-

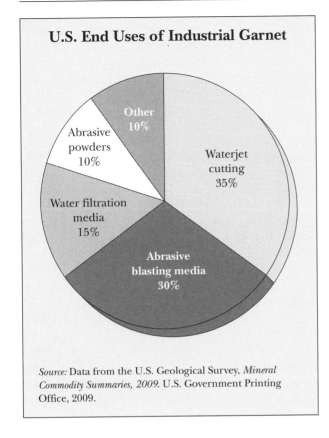

**U.S. End Uses of Industrial Garnet**

- Waterjet cutting 35%
- Abrasive blasting media 30%
- Water filtration media 15%
- Abrasive powders 10%
- Other 10%

*Source:* Data from the U.S. Geological Survey, *Mineral Commodity Summaries, 2009.* U.S. Government Printing Office, 2009.

salt at moderate temperatures and pressures, whereas ugrandite forms during metamorphism of limestone at moderate temperatures and low pressures. Semi-pure pyrope occurs in rocks of the lower mantle, and gem-quality almandine can be found in igneous pegmatites.

New York State has the largest known deposit of high-quality abrasive garnet. Bodies of ore can be found 30 to 120 meters wide, more than 30 meters thick, and approximately 1.5 kilometers long. Once the ore is mined and taken to the mill, the garnet is separated from other minerals by a combination of crushing and grinding, screening, tabling, flotation, magnetic separation, water sedimentation, and/or air separation. The maximum grain size of the garnet concentrate is less than one-half of a centimeter. Grains of differing grades are grouped into a variety of sizes depending on the requirements of the specific industrial use.

## HISTORY

Garnet has been prized as a gemstone for most of history. Some Bronze Age jewelry contained garnet. The Greeks and Egyptians also used garnet ornamentally. During the Middle Ages, garnet was used for medicinal purposes.

## OBTAINING GARNET

High-quality garnets are cut as semiprecious gemstones and made into jewelry. The transparent red almandine is the most common garnet gemstone, but the most valuable is the brilliant green-colored demantoid garnet.

## USES OF GARNET

The major use of garnet is as an abrasive. Its hardness and brittle fracturing allow garnet particles to undergo little chemical or structural change when crushed or ground into a powder. Abrasive uses include the finishing of wood furniture, the production of plastic, and the processing of sheet aluminum for the aircraft and shipbuilding industries. Garnet is also used in the petroleum industry, in filtration media, in ceramics and glass, and as an electronic component. The United States is one of the dominant producers and consumers of abrasive garnet. Industrial garnets are also used in waterjet cutting and water filtration media. Gem-quality garnets are used in jewelry.

*Dion C. Stewart*

## WEB SITE

U.S. GEOLOGICAL SURVEY
Minerals Information: Garnet Statistics and Information
http://minerals.usgs.gov/minerals/pubs/commodity/garnet/

SEE ALSO: Abrasives; Gems; Metamorphic processes, rocks, and mineral deposits; Pegmatites.

# Gases, inert or noble

CATEGORY: Mineral and other nonliving resources

## WHERE FOUND

The noble gases—neon, argon, krypton, helium, radon, and xenon—naturally compose a small part of the atmosphere. The gases are also found in hot-spring water. Argon has been found in certain igneous rocks with helium. Helium is addressed in its own entry and therefore is not covered here. Radon gas, which is ubiquitous, is an end product of uranium decay that is radioactive and emanates from soil, rocks, and hot springs in areas where uranium and thorium are found.

## PRIMARY USES
The primary uses of these gases are in arc welding, neon lights, fluorescent lights, and lasers. They are also used as Geiger counters and inert atmospheres.

## TECHNICAL DEFINITION
The inert or noble gases are Group VIIIA of the periodic table of the elements. They are colorless, tasteless, and odorless monoatomic gases.

## DESCRIPTION, DISTRIBUTION, AND FORMS
Neon (abbreviated Ne), atomic number 10, has three naturally occurring stable isotopes: neon 20 (90.51 percent), neon 21 (0.27 percent), and neon 22 (9.22 percent). The atomic weight is 20.183, with a boiling point of −246° Celsius and a melting point of −249° Celsius. Argon (Ar), atomic number 18, has three naturally occurring stable isotopes: argon 40 (99.600 percent), argon 38 (0.0632 percent), and argon 36 (0.3364 percent). The atomic weight is 39.944, with a boiling point of −186° Celsius and a melting point of −189° Celsius.

Krypton (Kr), atomic number 36, has six naturally occurring stable isotopes (78, 80, 82, 83, 84, and 86), of which 84 is the most abundant (57.0 percent). The atomic weight is 83.80, with a boiling point of −157° Celsius and a melting point of −153° Celsius. One isotope that has been studied, krypton 85, is mainly generated in uranium reprocessing plants but also in nuclear reactors and as a product of spontaneous fission. The study concluded that the concentration could grow to the point that krypton 85 could produce as much radiation exposure for humans as is the natural background radiation. The outcome of this could be an increase in skin cancer.

Xenon (Xe), atomic number 54, has nine naturally occurring stable isotopes. The atomic weight is 131.30, with a boiling point at −112° Celsius and a melting point of −107° Celsius.

Although argon has been found in certain igneous rocks with helium, and all the gases have been found in water from hot springs, the atmosphere is still the major source of the noble gases. Dry air contains 0.937 percent (9,370 parts per million) argon, 18 parts per million neon, 1.1 part per million krypton, and 0.086 part per million xenon. The higher concentration of argon is thought to be because radioactive potassium 40 decays to argon. The group has been called rare gases or inert gases, but since the atmosphere is almost 1 percent argon, and because krypton and xenon are not totally inert, the name "noble gases" has gained favor. The noble gases are always found as inert, monoatomic gases. Although compounds of xenon and krypton have been formed, they can be formed only under extreme conditions; no compounds occur naturally.

Radon (Rn), atomic number 86, is a decay product of radium and occurs in nature as a very dense, odorless, colorless, and highly radioactive gas. Its radioactivity, ubiquity, and tendency to accumulate in homes makes it a health hazard and a major contributor to lung cancer.

## HISTORY
In 1785, Henry Cavendish found that a very small portion (less than 1/120) of the air could not be reacted in the experiments that reacted oxygen and nitrogen. This clue was not followed, however, and it was 1882 before a noble gas was discovered by Lord Rayleigh and Sir William Ramsay. In experiments to measure the density of gases, Rayleigh found that the density of nitrogen from ammonia and that from air with the oxygen removed were not the same. Ramsay then studied atmospheric nitrogen. By reacting the nitrogen with red-hot magnesium, he isolated a small amount of much denser gas. When its spectrum was examined there were lines that did not match any known element. This new element was named argon, from the Greek word for idle or lazy, because of its inert nature.

Ramsay suspected that another element might exist between argon and helium (which had been discovered in the Sun in 1868), as their atomic weights of 40 and 4 were so different. In May of 1898, Ramsay and Morris William Travers allowed liquid air to boil away gradually until only a small amount was left. They removed the nitrogen and oxygen with red-hot copper and magnesium. When they examined the spectrum, there were new lines. This new element was named krypton, from the Greek word for hidden.

Krypton was a new element of the group, but it was not the one for which they had searched. In June, 1898, Ramsay and Travers liquefied and solidified an argon sample. Instead of keeping the last gas to boil away (which had led them to krypton), they kept the first fraction. When they examined the spectrum it produced, they found a blaze of crimson light unlike that of any other element. The new element was named neon, from the Greek word for new.

Ramsay and Travers continued their search for elements using a new liquid-air machine supplied by Ludwig Mond. By repeated fractionation of krypton, a still heavier gas was extracted in July, 1898. The spectrum identified it as a new element, which they called xenon, from the Greek for stranger. It has been known for some time that clathrates, organic hydroxy compounds with large cavities, would contain (but not bond to) the larger noble gases (argon, krypton, and xenon), but it was not until 1962 that compounds of the noble gases were first made by Neil Bartlett. Most of the compounds are xenon, but a few are krypton with fluorine or oxygen. No compounds of neon or argon have been prepared.

## OBTAINING THE NOBLE GASES

The noble gases are obtained as a by-product of the liquefaction and separation of air. Dry carbon-dioxide-free air is liquefied and distilled. The volatile fraction contains nitrogen, neon, and helium. The remaining liquid of oxygen, argon, krypton, and xenon is fractionated to yield argon contaminated with oxygen. The oxygen is removed by reaction with hot copper-copper oxide. Further separation of the gases is achieved by selective adsorption and desorption with charcoal. Some argon is obtained as a by-product in the production of ammonia ($NH_3$). The argon is an impurity in the nitrogen and hydrogen gases. About 635,000 metric tons of argon are obtained annually. Smaller amounts of the other gases are collected.

## USES OF NOBLE GASES

The main use of argon is as an inert atmosphere for high-temperature metallurgical work. It is also used to fill incandescent lamps. The inert atmosphere allows the filament to burn for a long period of time before it burns out. Argon is also used in lasers and Geiger counters (radiation counters). The naturally occurring presence of argon isotopes is used to date geological formations. There are two methods that use the amount of argon isotopes to date materials in the millions of years range. One method uses the argon 40 to argon 39 ratio; the other uses the argon 40 to potassium 40 ratio.

All the noble gases are used in discharge tubes (neon lights). Each gas produces a particular color—for example, red by neon and blue by xenon. Other colors can be produced by a combination of gases. The neon-light industry was started by Georges Claude in the early 1900's and grew into a large industry. Fluorescent tubes are also filled with the noble gases, but the color of the tube depends on the phosphor coat on the inside of the tube. The denser noble gases, especially argon, have been used to fill the space between layers of glass in thermal insulating windows. Neon is also used in fog lights, television tubes, lasers, and voltage detectors. Krypton is used in flashbulbs and ultraviolet lasers. The wavelength of one isotope of krypton is the standard for the metric system. Xenon is also used in ultraviolet lamps, sunlamps, paint testers, projection lamps, and electronic flashes. Radon has been used in radiation therapy to treat cancers but for the most part has been superseded by radionuclides. It also has some uses in research.

*C. Alton Hassell*

FURTHER READING

Greenwood, N. N., and A. Earnshaw. "The Noble Gases: Helium, Neon, Argon, Krypton, Xenon, and Radon." In *Chemistry of the Elements*. 2d ed. Boston: Butterworth-Heinemann, 1997.

Henderson, William. "The Group 18 (Noble Gas) Elements: Helium, Neon, Argon, Krypton, Xenon, and Radon." In *Main Group Chemistry*. Cambridge, England: Royal Society of Chemistry, 2000.

Israël, H., and G. W. Israël. *Trace Elements in the Atmosphere*. Ann Arbor, Mich.: Ann Arbor Science, 1974.

Krebs, Robert E. *The History and Use of Our Earth's Chemical Elements: A Reference Guide*. Illustrations by Rae Déjur. 2d ed. Westport, Conn.: Greenwood Press, 2006.

Ojima, Minoru, and Frank A. Podosek. *Noble Gas Geochemistry*. 2d ed. New York: Cambridge University Press, 2002.

Porcelli, Donald, Chris J. Ballentine, and Rainer Wieler, eds. *Noble Gases in Geochemistry and Cosmochemistry*. Columbus, Ohio: Geochemical Society, 2002.

Stern, Rudi. *The New Let There Be Neon*. Enlarged and updated ed. Cincinnati, Ohio: ST, 1996.

Weeks, Mary Elvira. *Discovery of the Elements*. 7th ed. New material added by Henry M. Leicester. Easton, Pa.: Journal of Chemical Education, 1968.

WEB SITES

UNIVERSAL INDUSTRIAL GASES, INC.
Argon (Ar) Properties, Uses, Applications: Argon
Gas and Liquid Argon
http://www.uigi.com/argon.html

UNIVERSAL INDUSTRIAL GASES, INC.
Properties, Applications and Uses of the "Rare
Gases": Neon, Krypton, and Xenon
http://www.uigi.com/rare_gases.html

SEE ALSO: American Gas Association; Atmosphere;
Haber-Bosch process; Helium; Hydrogen; Nitrogen
and ammonia; Oxygen.

# Gasoline and other petroleum fuels

CATEGORIES: Energy resources; products from
resources

*Gasoline is the most important product from petroleum
and is the dominant transportation fuel in the world.
Other petroleum products with important fuel uses include kerosene (usually refined to jet fuel), diesel oil for
railway locomotives and trucks, and heating oils.*

## BACKGROUND

Petroleum is the source of nearly all the world's transportation fuels: gasoline for automobiles, light trucks,
and light aircraft; jet fuel for airplanes; and diesel fuel
for locomotives, heavy trucks, and agricultural vehicles. Heating oils (also called fuel oils or furnace oils)
are used for domestic heating and industrial process
heat; they are also used in oil-fired electric generating
plants. Petroleum fuels are a vital component of the
energy economies of industrialized nations.

The first step in making all petroleum fuels is distillation of the petroleum or crude oil. Kerosene, diesel
oil, and heating oils require comparatively little refining thereafter to be ready for marketing. Considerable effort is put into gasoline production both to ensure adequate engine performance and to guarantee
that sufficient quantities will be available to meet market requirements.

## GASOLINE

The most important characteristic of gasoline is its
combustion performance. When gasoline is ignited

in the cylinder, the pressure rises as combustion proceeds. The pressure can, potentially, get so high that
the remaining unburned gasoline-air mixture deto-
nates rather than continuing to burn smoothly. The
explosion, which can readily be heard, is usually
called "engine knock." Engine knock puts undue mechanical stresses on the engine components, is wasteful of fuel (which the driver will experience as reduced mileage), and reduces engine performance,
such as acceleration. Several factors contribute to engine knock. One is the compression ratio of the engine—the ratio of volumes of the cylinder when the
piston is at the upward and downward limits of its
stroke. Generally, the higher the compression ratio,
the more powerful the engine and the greater the acceleration and top speed of the car. A higher compression ratio results in higher pressures inside the cylinder at the start of combustion. If the cylinder pressure
is higher to begin with, the engine is more likely to
knock.

A second characteristic affecting knocking tendency is the nature of the fuel. The dominant family
of chemical components of most gasolines is the paraffins. These compounds contain carbon atoms arranged in chains, either straight (the normal paraffins) or with branches (isoparaffins). Normal
paraffins have a great tendency to knock, whereas
branched paraffins do not. An octane rating scale
was established by assigning the normal paraffin hep-
tane the value 0 and the isoparaffin "iso-octane"
(2,2,4-trimethylpentane) the value 100. The octane
rating of a gasoline is found by comparing its knocking characteristics (in a carefully calibrated and standardized test engine) to the behavior of a heptane/
iso-octane blend. The percentage of iso-octane in a
blend having the same knocking behavior of the gasoline being tested is the octane number of the gasoline. Gasoline is sold in three grades, a regular gasoline with octane number 87, a premium gasoline of
about 93 octane, and a medium grade of about 89 octane.

Another important property of gasoline is its ability
to vaporize in the engine, measured by the vapor pressure of the gasoline. Gasoline with high vapor pressure contains a large number of components that vaporize easily. This is desirable for wintertime driving
in cold climates, since easy vaporization helps starting
when the engine is cold. It is not desirable for driving
in hot weather, because the gasoline could vaporize in
the fuel system before it gets to the engine, leading to

the problem of vapor lock, which temporarily shuts down the engine. Oil companies adjust the vapor pressure of their gasolines depending on the region of the country, the local climate, and the season of the year.

Many process streams within a refinery are blended to produce the gasolines that actually appear on the market. Gaseous molecules that would be by-products of refining can be recombined to produce gasoline in processes called alkylation or polymerization. Some gasoline, called straight-run gasoline, comes directly from distillation of the petroleum. Refinery streams of little value can be converted into high-octane gasoline by catalytic cracking. The octane numbers of straight-run gasoline, or a related product called straight-run naphtha, can be enhanced by catalytic reforming. Other refinery operations can also yield small amounts of material boiling in the gasoline range. Various of these streams are blended to make products of desired octane, vapor pressure, and other characteristics.

Environmental concerns about gasoline have centered on the emission of unburned hydrocarbons (including evaporation from fuel tanks), carbon monoxide and nitrogen oxide emissions from combustion, and the presence of aromatic compounds, some of which are suspected carcinogens and contribute to smoke or soot formation. These concerns have led to the development of reformulated gasolines. One aspect of production of reformulated gasoline is increased vapor pressure, which retards evaporation. A second is removal of aromatic compounds; removal actually complicates formulation because aromatics have desirably high octane numbers. A third step is the addition of oxygen-containing compounds, oxygenates, which serve several purposes: They reduce the flame temperature, for example, and change the combustion chemistry to reduce formation of carbon monoxide and nitrogen oxides. Oxygenates also have high octane numbers, so they can make up for the loss of aromatics. An example of an oxygenate useful in reformulated gasoline is methyl tertiary-butyl ether.

## JET FUEL

Jet fuel is produced by refining and purifying kerosene. Kerosene is a useful fuel, particularly for some agricultural vehicles, but the most important fuel use of kerosene today is for jet aircraft engines. Because many jet planes fly at high altitudes, where the outside air temperature is well below zero, the flow characteristics of the fuel at very low temperature are critical. When the fuel is cooled, large molecules of paraffins settle out from the fuel as a waxy deposit. The temperature at which the formation of this wax first begins, noticeable as a cloudy appearance, is called the cloud point. Eventually a fuel can be cooled to an extent where it cannot even flow, not even to pour from an open container. This characteristic temperature is the pour point.

Smoke emissions from jet engines are an environmental concern. The "smoke point" measures an important property of jet fuel combustion. Aromatics are the most likely compounds to produce smoke, while paraffins have the least tendency. A jet fuel with a low smoke point will have a high proportion of paraffins relative to aromatics. The sulfur content of jet fuel can be important, both to limit emissions of sulfur oxide to the atmosphere and because some sulfur compounds are corrosive. Both sulfur and aromatics contents of jet fuel can be reduced by treating with hydrogen in the presence of catalysts containing cobalt, or nickel, and molybdenum.

## DIESEL FUEL

A familiar automobile engine operates by igniting the gasoline-air mixture with a spark plug. Diesel engines operate differently: They have no spark plugs, but rely on compression heating of the air in the cylinder to ignite the fuel. A diesel engine has a much higher compression ratio than a comparable spark-ignition engine. In a crude sense, a diesel engine actually operates by knocking. The desirable composition for diesel fuel is essentially the inverse of that for gasoline: Normal paraffins are ideal components, while iso-paraffins and aromatics are not. The combustion behavior of a diesel fuel is measured by the cetane number, based on a blend of cetane (hexadecane), assigned a value of 100, and alpha-methylnaphthalene, assigned 0, as the test components. A typical diesel fuel for automobile and light truck engines would have a cetane rating of about 50.

Many of the physical property characteristics of jet fuel are also important for diesel fuel, including the cloud and pour points and the flow characteristics (viscosity) at low temperature. Sulfur and aromatic compounds are a concern. Aromatics are particularly undesirable because they are the precursors to the formation of soot. As environmental regulations continue to become more stringent, refiners will face additional challenges to reduce the levels of these components in diesel fuels.

## HEATING OILS

Heating oils, also called furnace oils or fuel oils, are often graded and sold on the basis of viscosity. The grades are based on a numerical classification from number 1 to number 6 (though there is no number 3 oil). As the number increases, so do the pour point, the sulfur content, and the viscosity. Number 1 oil is comparable to kerosene. Number 2 is an oil commonly used for domestic and industrial heating. Both have low pour points and sulfur contents and are produced from the distillation of petroleum. The other oils (numbers 4-6) are obtained by treating the residuum from the distillation process. They are sometimes called bunker oils because they have such high viscosities that they may have to be heated to have them flow up, from the storage tank, or bunker, and into the burners in the combustion equipment.

*Harold H. Schobert*

## FURTHER READING

Berger, Bill D., and Kenneth E. Anderson. *Modern Petroleum: A Basic Primer of the Industry.* 3d ed. Tulsa, Okla.: PennWell Books, 1992.

Black, Edwin. *Internal Combustion: How Corporations and Governments Addicted the World to Oil and Derailed the Alternatives.* New York: St. Martin's Press, 2006.

Conaway, Charles F. *The Petroleum Industry: A Nontechnical Guide.* Tulsa, Okla.: PennWell Books, 1999.

Kunstler, James Howard. *The Long Emergency: Surviving the Converging Catastrophes of the Twenty-first Century.* New York: Atlantic Monthly Press, 2005.

Middleton, Paul. *A Brief Guide to the End of Oil.* London: Constable and Robinson, 2007.

Mushrush, George W., and James G. Speight. *Petroleum Products: Instability and Incompatibility.* Washington, D.C.: Taylor & Francis, 1995.

Royal Dutch Shell, comp. *The Petroleum Handbook.* 6th ed. New York: Elsevier, 1983.

Speight, James G. *The Chemistry and Technology of Petroleum.* 4th ed. Boca Raton, Fla.: CRC Press/Taylor & Francis, 2007.

Yergin, Daniel. *The Prize: The Epic Quest for Oil, Money, and Power.* New ed. New York: The Free Press, 2008.

SEE ALSO: Oil and natural gas chemistry; Oil industry; Petroleum refining and processing; Propane; Transportation, energy use in.

# Gems

CATEGORY: Mineral and other nonliving resources

## WHERE FOUND

Mineral gems occur within the Earth's crust and are widely distributed on the planet. The most important source of the world's diamonds is the African continent. Emerald has been found primarily on the South American continent, particularly near Bogotá, Colombia. Because sapphire and ruby are color varieties of the same mineral, corundum, they frequently occur in the same regions. Historically, rubies and sapphires have been found in Sri Lanka, Burma (Myanmar), Thailand, and Cambodia.

## PRIMARY USES

All naturally occurring gems are primarily used for jewelry, ornamentation, or decorative purposes. The most beautiful, durable, and uncommon gems are frequently embedded in or dangle from works of gold, silver, or platinum. Historically, kings and queens, aristocrats, popes, and other important societal figures wore these ornaments. In modern society anyone who can afford to purchase the jewels may acquire them. Synthetic gems are used in electronics, drills, and cutting tools.

## TECHNICAL DEFINITION

A gemstone is a gem that has been cut, ground, or polished from a large rock. Attributes that impart magnificent beauty to a gem include flawless crystalline structure, uniformity and intensity of color (or uncommon color), hardness, durability, and extent of transparency and refractivity.

All minerals of the Earth, including gems, come from rock. The geological events that yield igneous rock produce all the precious gems and most semiprecious gems. Igneous rock is formed upon the cooling of hot molten lava (magma). During this cooling process, the liquid rock solidifies.

## DESCRIPTION, DISTRIBUTION, AND FORMS

Gems are minerals of beauty, rarity, and durability. Like all minerals, gems have a definite chemical composition in which the atoms are arranged in a specific pattern. Repetition of this pattern generates a crystalline shape that imparts a characteristic color, luster, hardness, and transparency to each gem. The traditional precious gems are diamond, emerald, ruby, and sapphire, but any gem may be considered precious if it is uncommonly beautiful.

Gems are subdivided into two categories: organic gems (such as pearls, amber, and coral) and mineral gems (from rock or of other geological origin). Organic gems are derived from living or once living organisms. Aside from the traditional precious stones—diamond, emerald, ruby, and sapphire—familiar mineral gems include aquamarine, garnet, jade, olivine, topaz, turquoise, and many forms of quartz. These "semiprecious" gems have a combination of beauty and affordability that makes them both desirable and marketable.

Diamond is found in ultrabasic rock and alluvial deposits. (Alluvial deposits are the deposits that remain after the physical wearing of rock.) Ultrabasic rock is igneous rock (volcanic) that is essentially made of silicate minerals or ferromagnesian minerals such as olivine, hornblende, augitite, and biotite (mica). Also found in igneous rock are corundum, the mineral of emerald, commonly in hexagonal, elongated, and broad crystals, as well as beryl, the mineral of ruby and sapphire, often shaped as bipyramids or barrel-shaped hexagons.

Diamonds are valued based upon the overall quality of the diamond, which is assessed by the "four C's": color, cut, carat, and clarity. Most gemologists agree that a colored diamond is the rarest gem of all. Transition metal ions, when present in trace amounts within the crystalline structure, impart a light color to an otherwise colorless diamond. Colored diamonds range from blue, blue-white, and blue-green to red and yellow. Because the cut of a gem is critical to maximizing both beauty and value, cutting must be done by experts who know exactly where and how to cut a stone to reveal the optimal brilliance (or "fire") of the crystal's refractive planes. The size of a diamond is expressed in carats, where one carat weighs 200 milligrams. In addition to color, "fire," and size, the degree of flawlessness and the hardness of a stone are important in determining its final market value. The other precious gems are assessed for market value in a manner similar to that of diamond.

Two of the semiprecious gems, garnet and olivine, are silicate minerals. Garnet stones are often rhombo-dodecahedral (twelve-sided) or hexaoctahedral shapes in nature; these intriguing crystals occur in colors of red, green, and black. Olivine crystals are perfect small cubes with colors of green to brown-green. Garnet occurs commonly in the Earth's crust in metamorphic rock (formed by the action of heat and pressure) rather than in igneous (volcanic) rock, the origin of most gems.

Colorless diamond is made exclusively of carbon atoms arranged in rigid tetrahedrons. Yet blue, yellow, and other colors of diamond also occur in nature. Chemists discovered that the trapping of certain transition metal ions in the crystal as it forms can result in coloration of the stone. The same fact holds for other precious gems. For example, the mineral corun-

## Properties of Gem Minerals

| Gem Material | Hardness | Specific Gravity | Refractive Index |
|---|---|---|---|
| Amber | 2-2½ | 1.05 | 1.54 |
| Beryl | 7½-8 | 2.67-2.85 | 1.57-1.58 |
| Chrysoberyl | 8½ | 3.73 | 1.746-1.755 |
| Corundum | 9 | 4.00 | 1.76-1.77 |
| Diamond | 10 | 3.52 | 2.42 |
| Feldspar | 6-6½ | 2.55-2.75 | 1.5-1.57 |
| Garnet* | 7 | 3.88 | 1.784 |
| Hematite | 5½-6½ | 5.20 | |
| Jade* | 6½ | 3.15 | 41.645 |
| Lapis lazuli | 5-6 | 2.4-3.05 | 1.50 |
| Malachite | 3½-4 | 3.34-3.95 | 1.66-1.91 |
| Opal | 5-6½ | 2.15 | 1.45 |
| Peridot | 6½-7 | 3.34 | 1.654-1.690 |
| Quartz* | 7 | 2.63 | 1.541 |
| Spinel | 8 | 3.60 | 1.72 |
| Spodumene | 6-7 | 3.18 | 1.66-1.676 |
| Topaz | 8 | 3.53 | 1.61-1.62 |
| Tourmaline | 7-7½ | 3.06 | 1.624-1.644 |
| Turquoise | 5-6 | 2.76 | 1.61-1.65 |
| Zircon* | 6½ | 4.35 | 1.88 |

*Average for a variety of types.

Source: Data are derived from Sybil P. Parker, ed., McGraw-Hill Concise Encyclopedia of Science and Technology, 2d ed., 1989.

dum ($Al_2O_3$) is an oxide of aluminum, a hard, white substance. The presence of transition metal impurities within the corundum crystal results in colorful gems. Specifically, ruby is corundum with chromium cations, which give the crystal a rich red color. Iron and titanium cations cause the brilliant blue of the sapphire, while iron cations give oriental topaz its yellow color. Finally, oriental amethyst acquires its violet color from chromium and titanium cations within the corundum lattice.

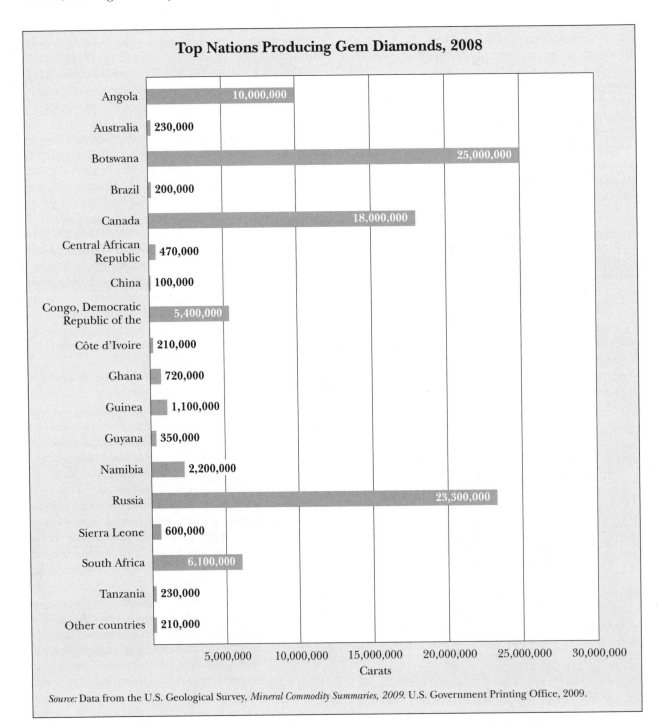

**Top Nations Producing Gem Diamonds, 2008**

| Nation | Carats |
| --- | --- |
| Angola | 10,000,000 |
| Australia | 230,000 |
| Botswana | 25,000,000 |
| Brazil | 200,000 |
| Canada | 18,000,000 |
| Central African Republic | 470,000 |
| China | 100,000 |
| Congo, Democratic Republic of the | 5,400,000 |
| Côte d'Ivoire | 210,000 |
| Ghana | 720,000 |
| Guinea | 1,100,000 |
| Guyana | 350,000 |
| Namibia | 2,200,000 |
| Russia | 23,300,000 |
| Sierra Leone | 600,000 |
| South Africa | 6,100,000 |
| Tanzania | 230,000 |
| Other countries | 210,000 |

*Source:* Data from the U.S. Geological Survey, *Mineral Commodity Summaries, 2009.* U.S. Government Printing Office, 2009.

Similarly, silicon dioxide ($SiO_2$), or quartz, is a clear, colorless crystal unless transition metal impurities are present. Then rose, purple, or smoke-gray colors may be produced. Another example is found in the simple arrangement of sulfate ($SiO_4$) tetrahedrons about a metal cation; when they are around a magnesium cation, olivine ($Mg_2SiO_4$) results, but when around a zirconium cation, zircon ($ZrSiO_4$) is formed.

Mineral gems are widely distributed on the Earth. Gems have been found on all continents except Antarctica. (Antarctic exploration for this purpose has not yet occurred.) A country that has yielded a great variety and abundance of gems is Sri Lanka. This small island has yielded more than a dozen different types of gemstones. Located just south of the tip of India, which itself is famous for its diamonds and emeralds, Sri Lanka has rich alluvial deposits.

The African continent has been the main source of all known diamonds. Aside from India, other minimally productive diamond sources have been Brazil and the Democratic Republic of the Congo. Within the United States, Arkansas has yielded the most diamonds, although the number is very low in comparison with the other regions mentioned. Even less productive mines have been found on the eastern slopes of the Appalachian Mountains.

Rubies are found in Sri Lanka, Burma, Thailand, and Cambodia; sapphires occur in the same regions as rubies, since both are color varieties of corundum. Both ruby and sapphire stones are found in Russia, China, Germany, India, and Australia as well as on the African continent. In the United States, a small number of rubies have been found in North Carolina, while Montana has provided a mining site for small but exceptionally brilliant blue sapphires.

Emerald has primarily been found on the South American continent near Bogotá, Colombia. Another important source of emeralds is Siberia; emeralds have also been mined in Brazil, Egypt, Austria, Zimbabwe, Mozambique, Tanzania, and South Africa. Within the United States pale, muted green emeralds with many flaws have been found in North Carolina. These crystals are poor-quality gems and have little value. Emerald is a color variety of the mineral beryl; another color variety of beryl is the semiprecious gem aquamarine. Aquamarine is more abundant in the Earth's crust than emerald and is plentiful in Northern Ireland, Italy, Russia, Namibia, and Brazil, where the largest (110.5 kilograms) aquamarine stone was found in 1910. Other semiprecious stones are as diverse in their distribution as the precious gems are, but most of these stones are more common.

Synthetic garnets are useful in industry. One synthetic gem, yttrium iron garnet, is used in microwave devices. Another, yttrium aluminum garnet (YAG), is used in lasers as a source of coherent light; it is also used as an artificial gemstone. On the molecular level, the crystals of synthetic gems are subtly different from those of natural stones. These differences, however, typically evade the untrained eye. For this reason, synthetic gemstones are used in jewelry but cannot be sold as fine jewels.

HISTORY

Since ancient times, gems have been used to adorn the human body and create artwork. Although no one knows when gems were first discovered, desired, or used, there is archaeological evidence that beads of garnet were worn by people of the Bronze Age five thousand years ago. The Old Testament refers to a variety of gems, including amethyst, diamond, emerald, malachite, and cinnabar. It is known that, in the first century B.C.E., emerald was the preferred stone of Cleopatra VII, the last queen of ancient Egypt.

Emeralds represented regeneration and spring in some ancient societies. The Incan civilization used the rich green stones to guard sacred temples. Emeralds and rubies are among the rarest of gems, and carat per carat their monetary value often exceeds that of most colorless diamonds. There is virtually no such thing as a truly flawless emerald, as internal fractures mar the interior of the crystals. True ruby (or "oriental ruby") is the only subclass of corundum to have a distinct category of its own. When asterism (the appearance of a six-rayed star) is found in a stone, it is coveted even more; legend has it that asterism conquers evil forces. Excluding red ruby, all corundum is classified as sapphire, which may range in color from clear yellow, green, and lavender to the traditional cornflower blue. Other corundum gems may also have asterism; the Star of India, a 563-carat, blue-gray stone, is the largest sapphire known.

Historically, diamond has been the most important of the precious stones. The word "diamond" is derived from *adamas*, a Greek term meaning "invincible" or "unconquerable." The earliest recorded reference to diamond comes from a civilization in India during the fourth century B.C.E. Until the eighteenth century, India was believed to be the only source of diamonds. Then, in the early 1800's, small, productive diamond mines were discovered in Brazil. In 1867, the first of the rich South African mines was found. India and Africa have produced the largest and most famous diamonds known, including the Hope, the Victoria-Transvaal, the Cullinan, and the Koh-i-Noor diamonds.

In 1902, Auguste Verneuil, a researcher in Paris, was able to grow red crystals of beryl in the laboratory. Thus, the first synthetic gem was a ruby. More recently, chemists have been able to synthesize diamonds for industrial use. The General Electric Company achieved laboratory synthesis of diamond in 1955. Because events in nature cannot be exactly mimicked in the laboratory, synthetic diamonds lack the aesthetic appeal of naturally occurring stones; therefore they are not used in fine jewelry making. A synthetic substance used to mimic diamond in jewelry is cubic zirconium (imitation diamond or faux diamond). This material can be synthesized in bulk and at a low cost. Although the durability, refractivity, and transparency of the stone resemble diamond, zirconium lacks its hardness and durability.

## Obtaining Gems

Traditional mining methods have been used to mine gems. Historically, mines were operated through the exploitation of imported slaves or local natives. Typically the laborers were used to dig pits deep into the Earth. The removed earth was pulverized and sifted through, either using water to flush away the gravel or using dry sifting methods. These techniques were used in the mines of Africa, Brazil, and Colombia during the eighteenth and nineteenth centuries. African mines have become more mechanized, using large drills and other equipment, but mining with manual labor continues in Colombia. As in the past, there are risks of mine collapse and suffocation.

Gems can also be collected by sifting through alluvial deposits along the edges of streams and rivers. The gems of India and Sri Lanka have mostly been collected by this method. Miners in Sri Lanka still use the bottoms of their feet to feel for gems within the stones under running river water. In Thailand miners continue to take their boats out in low tide to dredge the mud for gems.

## Uses of Gems

Aside from having aesthetic appeal, some gems are useful in industry and instrumentation. For example,

diamond, the hardest substance known, has been used as a cutting tool. In mining and exploratory geology, diamond drills are used to cut through stones and layers of rock. Additionally, finely powdered diamond is used to grind, shape, and polish large diamond stones as well as other gemstones. Synthetic diamond has replaced the natural gem for industrial tools, while synthetic ruby and sapphire are used to make lasers that emit coherent light and in microwave devices. Ranking just below diamond on the Mohs hardness scale, ruby and sapphire gems are also used in cutting, grinding, and drilling tools.

*Mary C. Fields*

FURTHER READING

Bonewitz, Ronald Louis. *Rock and Gem.* New York: DK, 2005.

Chatterjee, Kaulir Kisor. "Gemstones—Miscellaneous." In *Uses of Industrial Minerals, Rocks, and Freshwater.* New York: Nova Science, 2009.

Hall, Cally. *Gemstones.* 2d American ed. Photography by Harry Taylor. New York: Dorling Kindersley, 2002.

Maillard, Robert, Ronne Peltsman, and Neil Grant, eds. *Diamonds: Myth, Magic, and Reality.* New rev. ed. New York: Bonanza Books, 1984.

O'Donaghue, Michael. *Gems: Their Sources, Descriptions, and Identification.* 6th ed. Oxford, England: Butterworth-Heinemann, 2006.

Read, P. G. *Gemmology.* 3d ed. Boston: Elsevier/ Butterworth-Heinemann, 2005.

Schumann, Walter. *Gemstones of the World.* 3d rev. and expanded ed. New York: Sterling, 2007.

_____. *Handbook of Rocks, Minerals, and Gemstones.* Translated by R. Bradshaw and K. A. G. Mills. Boston: Houghton Mifflin, 1993.

White, John Sampson. *Minerals and Gems.* Special photography by Chip Clark. Washington, D.C.: Smithsonian Institution Press, 1991.

Zim, Herbert S., and Paul R. Shaffer. *Rocks, Gems, and Minerals: A Guide to Familiar Minerals, Gems, Ores, and Rocks.* Rev. and updated ed. Revised by Jonathan P. Latimer et al., illustrated by Raymond Perlman. New York: St. Martin's Press, 2001.

WEB SITES

U.S. GEOLOGICAL SURVEY
Gemstones: Statistics and Information
http://minerals.usgs.gov/minerals/pubs/ commodity/gemstones/index.html#mcs

U.S. GEOLOGICAL SURVEY
An Overview of Production of Specific U.S.
   Gemstones
http://minerals.usgs.gov/minerals/pubs/
   commodity/gemstones/sp14-95/contents.html

SEE ALSO: Abrasives; Aluminum; Beryllium; Crystals;
Diamond; Garnet; Geology; Igneous processes, rocks,
and mineral deposits; Magma crystallization; Metamorphic processes, rocks, and mineral deposits; Minerals, structure and physical properties of; Mohs hardness scale; Olivine; Oxides; Pegmatites; Zirconium.

# General Mining Law

CATEGORIES: Laws and conventions; government
   and resources
DATE: Signed May 10, 1872

*The General Mining Law of 1872 was one of several*
*pieces of legislation passed by Congress in the years fol-*
*lowing the Civil War. Its purpose was to combat eco-*
*nomic depression and unemployment by opening up*
*for development the vast federal lands in the West.*
*Amended many times over the years, this law continues*
*to govern the exploitation of "hard-rock" minerals in*
*the United States.*

## BACKGROUND
In its original form, the General Mining Law covered
all mineral resources on more than 405 million hectares of federal land. Later, it covered only "hard-rock"
minerals, those associated with igneous and metamorphic rocks. By the Mineral Leasing Act of 1920, the
fossil fuels and some minerals were "withdrawn" from
coverage under the law. The Common Varieties Mineral Act of 1955 withdrew sand, gravel, stone, and
other common rocks and minerals. In 1976, the last of
the national parks and monuments were withdrawn
from coverage, thus protecting them from mining. As
a result of these withdrawals, the total land covered
under the law was reduced to approximately four
hundred million hectares.

## PROVISIONS
The General Mining Law permits U.S. citizens to lay
claim to federal land. In exchange, the claimant has
only to pay a $100 fee and make minimal annual im-
provements ("assessments") to the land or pay a $100
annual assessment fee. Actual mining need not be
done. Claimants possess the right to any mineral deposits below ground; they also possess the right to the
exclusive use of the land surface. Claims can be of two
types: placer or lode. Placer claims are for 8-hectare
sites, whereas lode claims, those designed to exploit
localized veins of ore, are for tracts measuring 457 by
183 meters. For a fee of six dollars per hectare (placer
claim) or twelve dollars per hectare (lode claim), a
claim can be "patented," or converted to private ownership.

## IMPACT ON RESOURCE USE
Opponents of the law find fault with it in three areas.
First, the federal treasury receives no income from
minerals taken from lands that belong to the public.
Second, the law makes no provision for environmental concerns, which did not exist in 1872. Third,
abuses of the law abound, including the resale of
claims for thousands of times the original purchase
price.

Proponents of the law, primarily the major mining
companies, argue that while royalties are not paid,
mining provides thousands of jobs and significant tax
revenue. The mining industry must compete in a
global market against companies that exploit cheap
labor and are government-subsidized. Whereas the
original mining law took no cognizance of environmental concerns, any mining on federal lands is now
covered by the same environmental legislation that
governs all mining.

Proposed modifications to the law revolve around
three key issues: royalty payments, patenting, and environmental concerns. Suggested levels of royalty pay-
ment range from 2 percent on the net value (after
taxes and cost) to 8 percent on the gross value of the
minerals produced. Either patenting would be eliminated or claimants would be allowed to purchase the
mining patents for the fair market value of the land
surface. Environmental concerns would be addressed
by requiring restoration of the land and by using royalty payments to establish a fund for the cleanup of
abandoned mine properties.

*Donald J. Thompson*

SEE ALSO: Environmental degradation, resource exploitation and; Mineral Leasing Act; Mineral resource
ownership; Mining wastes and mine reclamation;
Public lands; United States.

# Genetic diversity

CATEGORY: Ecological resources

*Genetic diversity includes the inherited traits encoded in the deoxyribonucleic acid (DNA) of all living organisms and can be examined on four levels: among species, among populations, within populations, and within individuals. Populations with higher levels of diversity are better able to adapt to changes in the environment, are more resistant to the deleterious effects of inbreeding, and provide more opportunities for animal and plant breeders to cultivate types or varieties with qualities desired by humans.*

## BACKGROUND

Genetic diversity is the most fundamental level of biological diversity because genetic material is responsible for the variety of life. For new species to form, genetic material must change. Changes in the inherited properties of populations occur deterministically through gene flow (mating between individual organisms representing formerly separated populations) and through natural or artificial selection (which occurs when some types of individuals breed more successfully than others). Change can also occur randomly through mutations or genetic drift (when the relative proportions of genes change by chance in small populations). Populations with higher levels of diversity tend to do better—to have more survival options—as surroundings change than do populations (particularly smaller ones) with lower levels of genetic diversity.

## PRESERVATION EFFORTS

Conservation efforts directed at maintaining genetic diversity involve both germ plasm preservation (germ plasm kept in a steady state for periods of time) and germ plasm conservation (germ plasm kept in a natural, evolving state). The former usually involves ex situ laboratory techniques in which genetic resources are removed from their natural habitats. They include seminatural strategies such as botanical gardens, arboretums, nurseries, zoos, farms, aquariums, and captive fisheries as well as completely artificial methods such as seed reserves or "banks," microbial cultures (preserving bacteria, fungi, viruses, and other microorganisms), tissue cultures of parts of plants and animals (including sperm storage), and gene libraries (involving storage and replication of partial segments of plant or animal DNA).

Conservation areas are the preferred in situ (at the natural or original place) means of protecting genetic resources. Ideally these include preserving the number and relative proportions of species and the genetic diversity they represent, the physical features of the habitat, and all ecosystem processes. It is not always enough, however, to maintain the ecosystem which the threatened species inhabits. It is sometimes necessary to take an active interventionist position in order to save a species. Controversial strategies can include reintroduction of captive species into the wild, sometimes after they have been genetically manipulated. Direct management of the ecosystem may also be attempted either by lessening human exploitation and interference or by reducing the number of natural predators or competitors. However, management of a specific conservation area varies in terms of what is valued and how preservation is accomplished.

## CROP DIVERSITY

One area of keen interest that illustrates the issues involved with the preservation of any kind of genetic diversity is how to preserve crop germ plasm. Largely conserved in gene banks, crop germ plasm was historically protected by farmers who selected for success in differing environments and other useful traits. Traditionally cultivated varieties (landraces) diversified as people spread into new areas. Colonial expansion produced new varieties as farmers adapted to new conditions and previously separated plant species interbred; other species were lost when some societies declined and disappeared.

By the early 1900's, field botanists and agronomists were expressing concern about the rapidly escalating loss of traditionally cultivated varieties. This loss accelerated after the 1940's as high-yielding hybrids of cereal and vegetable crops replaced local landraces. Wild relatives of these landraces are also disappearing as their habitats are destroyed through human activity. Gene banks preserve both kinds of plants because, as argued by Nikolai Ivanovich Vavilov in 1926, crop plant improvement can best be accomplished by taking advantage of these preserved genetic stocks. Vavilov also noted that genetic variation for most cultivated species was concentrated in specific regions, his "centers of diversity," most of which are regions where crop species originated.

The vulnerability to parasites and climate of an agriculture that relies on one or a few varieties of crops necessitates the maintenance of adequate reserves of genetic material for breeding. In addition to the preservation of species known to be useful, many people advocate preservation of wild species for aesthetic reasons as well as for their unknown future potential.

*The Hawaiian monk seal is an endangered species partly because of its level of genetic diversity, which is the lowest among all animals studied. (©Henry Fu/Dreamstime.com)*

THE MAINTENANCE OF PRODUCTIVITY

Farmers in developed nations change crop varieties every four to ten years in order to maintain consistent levels of food production. This necessitates an ongoing search for new breeds with higher yields and an ability to withstand several environmental challenges, including resistance to multiple pests and drought. Over time, older varieties either mutate, become less popular at the marketplace, or are unable to adapt to new conditions. However, farmers from developing nations are not always able to take advantage of the new breeds or afford the expensive support systems, including chemical fertilizers. Moreover, not all types of crops have benefited equally from conservation efforts.

Another tension between the world's developing and developed nations concerns ownership of genetic diversity. The Convention on Biological Diversity, signed by 167 nations in 1992, states that genetic materials are under the sovereign control of the countries in which they are found. This policy is particularly controversial regarding medicinal plants, because "biodiversity prospecting" for new drugs has economically benefited either individuals or corporations based in the developed countries.

*Joan C. Stevenson*

FURTHER READING

Carroll, Scott P., and Charles W. Fox, eds. *Conservation Biology: Evolution in Action.* New York: Oxford University Press, 2008.

Frankham, Richard, Jonathan D. Ballou, and David A. Briscoe. *Introduction to Conservation Genetics.* Line drawings by Karina H. McInness. New York: Cambridge University Press, 2002.

_____. *A Primer of Conservation Genetics.* Line drawings by Karina H. McInness. New York: Cambridge University Press, 2004.

Hawkes, J. G. *The Diversity of Crop Plants.* Cambridge, Mass.: Harvard University Press, 1983.

Hunter, Malcolm L., Jr., and James P. Gibbs. *Fundamentals of Conservation Biology.* 3d ed. Malden, Mass.: Blackwell, 2007.

Lowe, Andrew, Stephen Harris, and Paul Ashton. *Ecological Genetics: Design, Analysis, and Application.* Malden, Mass.: Blackwell, 2004.

Orians, Gordon H., et al., eds. *The Preservation and Valuation of Biological Resources.* Seattle: University of Washington Press, 1990.

Plucknett, Donald L., et al. *Gene Banks and the World's Food.* Princeton, N.J.: Princeton University Press, 1987.

Van der Werf, Julius, Hans-Ulrich Graser, Richard Frankham, and Cedric Gondro, eds. *Adaptation and Fitness in Animal Populations: Evolutionary and Breeding Perspectives on Genetic Resource Management.* London: Springer, 2009.

SEE ALSO: Animal breeding; Biodiversity; Biological invasions; Biotechnology; Conservation; Conservation biology; Fisheries; Forest management; Genetic prospecting; Genetic resources; Monoculture agriculture; Plant domestication and breeding; Plants as a medical resource; Species loss; United Nations Convention on Biological Diversity.

## Genetic engineering. *See* Animal breeding; Biotechnology; Plant domestication and breeding

## Genetic prospecting

CATEGORIES: Obtaining and using resources; scientific disciplines

*As the world's population continues to grow, the search expands for plant and animal species whose genes can lead to new medicines, better crops, and products that make daily life easier. If not undertaken with great care, however, this twenty-first century "gold rush" has the potential to wreak havoc on many of the most fragile ecosystems of the world as well as on the indigenous populations that rely upon them.*

### DEFINITION

There is no universally agreed upon definition for the term "genetic prospecting" or the synonym "biological prospecting (bioprospecting)." However, the United Nations University Institute for Advanced Studies defines these terms as "the collection, research, and use of biological and/or genetic material for purposes of applying the knowledge derived there from for scientific and/or commercial purposes. Bioprospecting entails the search for economically valuable genetic and biochemical resources from nature."

### OVERVIEW

Estimates indicate that more than 80 percent of the world's population uses traditional medicines derived from local plants or animals for basic medical needs. In addition, at least 25 percent of prescription drugs used in the United States contain at least one active ingredient that has been derived from genetic prospecting. In fact, the creation of new medicinal and agricultural products from living materials is more than a $2-billion-per-year industry.

Much of the information about which plants or animals may yield genetic opportunities for medicine has come from indigenous knowledge of natural resources. In fact, most of the plants that have been prospected have come from the world's great rain forests, especially those of the Southern Hemisphere,

and have been identified by the indigenous peoples who inhabit these areas. It should be noted that the term "genetic prospecting" may also be used to describe the search for compounds of promise in plants or animals that have never been used for medicines or cures by indigenous cultures.

According to the report of the United Nations Convention on Biological Diversity (2004), many prospectors are now turning their attention to the world's remaining frontiers, including the Antarctic ice fields, hydrothermal vents deep in the world's oceans, and the deep seafloor. The unique genes of many extremophiles (organisms that live in extreme conditions) are expected to yield great opportunities for new medicines well into the second half of the twenty-first century.

A real concern that has been partially addressed by the United Nations in the landmark 1993 Convention on Biological Diversity is that of "biopiracy," "genetic piracy," or "biocolonialism." These terms refer to the appropriation of genetic materials without the express informed consent of the indigenous peoples, that landowners, or the appropriate government. For instance, making use of indigenous knowledge of the healing powers of a particular plant to find, replicate, and market a new drug without compensating those whose knowledge was the foundation of the work is a form of genetic piracy. For this reason, many countries in the tropical belt have written strict laws on genetic prospecting, including appropriate consent of, and compensation to, the host nation and its people.

*Kerry L. Cheesman*

SEE ALSO: Genetic resources; Plants as a medical resource; Resources as a medium of economic exchange; Resources as a source of international conflict; United Nations Convention on Biological Diversity.

## Genetic resources

CATEGORY: Plant and animal resources

*The raw material used in biotechnology is the genetic code found within the DNA of living organisms. While not viewed as a natural resource historically, genetic material has, with the advent of modern biotechnology, become a commodity that not only can be manipulated to improve agricultural yield but also can be used as a source by which to produce novel pharmaceutical or chemical products.*

## BACKGROUND

Biotechnology can be defined as the use of living organisms to achieve human goals; in this sense, humans have used biotechnology throughout history to provide themselves with such things as food, clothing, shelter, cosmetics, and medicine. Starting around 10,000 B.C.E., humans began to alter the genetic makeup of the plants and animals that they used by artificially selecting certain traits in the crops and livestock that they were breeding. Because farmers lived in different areas around the world with varying environmental conditions, the varieties of domesticated organism that eventually developed initially preserved what is known as "genetic diversity." Every organism on Earth has a particular genome, its entire set of DNA, which is specific to that particular living thing. Therefore, genetic diversity is at its greatest when the widest variety of organisms available are in existence in a particular area. The term "biodiversity" refers to the number of different species (or other taxonomical units) that inhabit a given ecosystem or geographical area.

## GENETIC EROSION OF PLANTS AND ANIMALS

A process known as "genetic erosion" decreases the biodiversity of cultivated areas. In this process, local species are lost from an area as they are replaced by less diverse, domesticated varieties. Human activities such as urbanization, the replacement of traditional agriculture with more modern techniques, and the introduction of high-yield varieties of crops have been blamed for such erosion of genetic resources. One example can be seen in the crops that are utilized for food in modern society. Among the 300,000 or so flowering plants that have been characterized to date, estimates indicate that humankind has used around 7,000 of these throughout history to satisfy basic human needs. However, only 30 of these account for 95 percent of the world's dietary calories, less than 10 account for 75 percent, and a mere 3 (corn, wheat, and rice) make up nearly 50 percent of the caloric intake of humankind. Not only has the number of different crops decreased over time, but also the variety of crop species has declined. Such a narrow genetic base of crops puts the food supply at risk from pests or diseases that affect a specific type of crop. Apparently, humans, in their eagerness to improve crop varieties, have somehow robbed the Earth of a portion of the genetic diversity that has taken millions of years to develop. Traditional subsistence agriculture, although it may have lacked the productivity of modern methods, actually increased the likelihood of a reasonable level of production by preserving the genetic diversity of the crops that were being grown.

This is not to say that using plants as a food source is their only economically viable use. Terrestrial plants have long been used as medicine or for other chemical applications. The recent loss of plant biodiversity is alarming for this reason also. Possibly, some undiscovered cure for a particular disease is at risk from disappearing permanently from the Earth, if it has not done so already. Of the remaining flowering plants on Earth, estimates indicate that one in four could become extinct by 2050. Compounding the problem, most of the world's biodiversity is located in geographically or politically unstable areas, namely in tropical or subtropical developing countries. A full two-thirds of all plant species known to humankind are located in the tropics; about 60,000 species are found in Latin America alone.

Animals have also served as an important source of food and medicine throughout history and have also been submitted to artificial genetic selection, along with accompanying genetic erosion. Marine invertebrates, in particular, have been investigated as a source of molecular compounds with medicinal properties. It has also been during more recent times that the importance of microorganisms in producing therapeutically relevant products has become known. While the full extent of microbial diversity remains unclear and bacterial diversity in particular appears to follow different biogeographical patterns from those found for plants and animals, it is evident that many natural habitats that may harbor medicinally relevant microbes are disappearing rapidly. The worldwide loss of biodiversity comprises all types of living organisms, including plants, animals, fungi, protists, and bacteria.

## PARADIGM SHIFT

In the 1990's, a significant shift occurred in the way that genetic resources were viewed as well as how their ownership was determined. Before this time, genetic resources were considered to be a common heritage of humankind and were to be treated so that they were

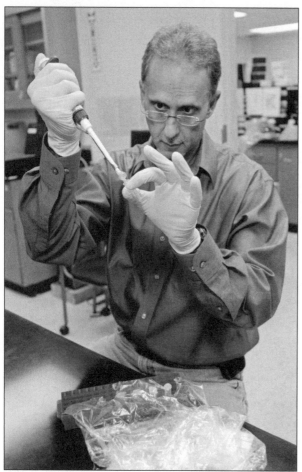

*A genetics professor at the Nova Southeastern University Oceanographic Center transfers fish samples into a test tube for purposes of genetic research.* (Joe Rimkus, Jr./MCT/Landov)

source of genetic innovation with a potential for practical application but also decreased the cost of working with genetic material to a level at which many more laboratories could afford to participate in genetic engineering efforts.

The United Nations Convention on Biological Diversity (CBD) was signed at a meeting in Rio de Janeiro, Brazil, in 1992 and went into effect the following year. The CBD affirmed the sovereign right of individual nations to their biodiversity and gave them a means by which to regulate access to their genetic resources, creating the stipulation that entities such as bioengineering firms secure informed written consent before collecting genetic material from any particular country. The export of a seed, microbe, or other plant- or animal-derived sample has been compared to exporting a very small chemical factory, complete with blueprints and its own source of venture capital. While most countries would not allow this to happen using conventional technology, prior to 1992 this had been the norm for biological goods.

Despite the establishment of the CBD, a number of potential problems concerning genetic resources remain. Developing countries are leery of corporations from developed nations that may, given the opportunity, engage in biopiracy. This includes taking advantage of indigenous knowledge and local technologies without providing adequate compensation. Genetic material is similar to electronic media in that it can be reproduced easily and relatively inexpensively, a fact that makes enforcing antipiracy legislation difficult. Conditions of contracts and changes in patent legislation must be followed closely by developing nations to ensure that undue control is not handed to foreign investors.

In addition, just because a country as a whole receives compensation for a particular genetic resource does not mean that a given region of that country will see any economic benefit. Two examples from the United States (which predate the CBD) include the cancer drug Taxol and Taq polymerase, an enzyme used in genetic engineering. These products were discovered respectively in Pacific yew bark from the Pacific Northwest and from hot springs in Yellowstone National Park. Despite the fact that both of these products have produced millions of dollars worth of profits, the regions of the country where they were first discovered ended up receiving little or no financial benefit. This somewhat flawed system of compensation and financial incentive is not expected to work

used to the benefit of all. The only problem with this notion is that it gave host countries little economic incentive for conservation. Another reason for this paradigm shift was a revolution in biology which had taken place in the decade that preceded the change. Biological tools that allowed for genetic engineering had been developed during this time, thereby expanding the number of organisms amenable to biotechnology. These included those that could be artificially selected for particular traits and bred with one another to any organism from which DNA could be extracted. This extracted DNA could then be introduced into a number of living vectors that may have been completely unrelated to the original source of genetic material. This new technology not only ensured that virtually any organism could be used as a much better in developing countries. Historically, even when indigenous knowledge was used to develop a specific product, indigenous peoples often received little or no benefit from sharing their knowledge.

## CONSERVATION EFFORTS

The same year the CBD was signed, an interdepartmental effort in the U.S. government created the International Conservation of Biodiversity Groups (ICBG) initiative. The objectives of the ICBG were to establish an inventory of species that have been used in traditional medicine, identify lead compounds for the treatment of human disease from this group, conduct economic assessments of species in the host country, establish study plots in developing countries to study changes in rain-forest ecology, and train local scientists in the principles of drug-development and biodiversity conservation. Conservation of genetic resources typically fits into one of two categories, in situ or ex situ: The former is Latin for "in the place," and the latter means "out of the place." In situ conservation takes place on farms, for agricultural crops, or in natural reserves, for wild plants. This type of conservation preserves the evolutionary dynamics of the species in question. Ex situ conservation usually involves storing samples, called accessions, of seeds or vegetative material for plants in what are known as gene banks. This type of conservation can also be applied to animals, where embryos or germ cells are stored frozen. This latter conservation technique has the disadvantage of being able to preserve only a small amount of the genetic diversity present in a given population but often plays a critical role in the preservation of many varieties of organisms, particularly those which are endangered or have already become extinct.

## SCREENING FOR COMPOUNDS

Biological organisms of interest to the pharmaceutical or chemical industries are typically those which produce small organic compounds known as secondary metabolites. Some hypothesize that these compounds serve either defensive or signaling roles in the cell: Plants and animals use these compounds to defend themselves from potential predators, and microbes use these to defend themselves from and signal to the other organisms that surround them. Overall, more than one-half of the best-selling pharmaceuticals in use are derived from such natural products.

Bioprospecting is the act of systematically searching through given genetic resources for compounds that may have a commercial application. Scientists are thus screening large numbers of extracts from plants, microbes, and marine organisms for secondary metabolites containing antifungal, antiviral, or antitumor activities.

There are a number of hurdles that must be overcome before a specific activity can be gleaned from a particular natural product. Because most natural products consist of mixtures of crude extracts, a certain degree of purification must take place before a lead compound can be tested for a desired application. "Time-to-lead" is a term that refers to the degree of purification and structural characterization that is necessary before a sample can be effectively assayed for a given activity. Another issue is the continued supply of a given natural product. In the past several decades, techniques for the extraction, fractionation, and chemical identification of secondary metabolites have become more routine and less expensive to perform. Before this was the case, it was often necessary to re-collect samples of particular natural products for use in large-scale purifications. Frequently, developers would then discover that it was impossible to reproduce the originally detected activity. Advances in genetic engineering as well as cell culture techniques have largely eliminated the need to re-collect an original sample. These advances actually make it more challenging for a supplier country to adequately charge for the use of a natural resource, because they can no longer rely on the need for re-collection of biological material to take place. This leaves two basic strategies for institutions seeking to benefit from international biotrade: becoming a low-cost supplier or becoming a value-added supplier.

This latter strategy relies on the fact that selection of natural products for testing purposes does not have to occur randomly: Both chemotaxonomic and ethnomedical techniques can be applied to create a value-added product. Chemotaxonomic strategies rely on the selection of organisms from a related taxonomic group that are expected to produce a similar chemical category of substances as the original sample. An example of this can be seen in the soil-derived filamentous fungi as well as in the Actinobacteria. Since the antibiotics penicillin and streptomycin were isolated from the former group in the 1930's and from the latter group a decade later, taxonomically related groups have been successfully screened for secondary metabolites. In contemporary society, such compounds are used to treat cancer, arteriosclerosis, and infectious disease and are even used as immuno-suppressive agents. In ethnomedical selection, knowledge of the use of a natural product in traditional medicine is expected to increase the chance of getting positive results with a particular extract. This approach involves sending experts into the field to conduct interviews with traditional healers. While this type of value-added product is more likely to generate a positive "hit," it is time-consuming and therefore often slow to generate high numbers of potential compounds. Another disadvantage of this type of approach is that it has proven difficult to select with efficacy for agents against complex diseases like cancer, because indigenous traditional healers may be unfamiliar with such maladies.

The most recent approach to the isolation of bioactive natural products eliminates the supply and subsequent screening of live organisms altogether. Because it is actually the genetic data that are of interest to most researchers and not the isolated organism, collecting DNA from environmental samples and directly cloning it into a host vector is becoming more commonplace. While the nature of the organism which contributed its genetic material to any meta-genome, the collection of a large number of genomes, may not be determined with any certainty, the end result of having a gene that produces a particular compound of interest has been achieved. This approach is especially adaptable to microorganisms that inhabit soil and water samples in high numbers, the DNA of which can be extracted with relative ease. This approach gained favor when it became evident that a minority of microbial diversity exists in those microbes amenable to being grown under laboratory conditions, and that vast amounts of biodiversity are present in the microorganisms, which resist culturing in the lab for some reason. While activity-based screening of cloned metagenomic libraries is, by definition, a random process, it is believed that new classes of useful compounds are bound to be discovered using this technique.

*James S. Godde*

FURTHER READING

Esquinas-Alcazar, José. "Protecting Crop Genetic Diversity for Food Security: Political, Ethical, and Technical Challenges." *Nature Reviews: Genetics* 6, no. 12 (December, 2005): 946-953.

Ferrer, Manuel, et al. "Metagenomics for Mining New Genetic Resources of Microbial Communities." *Journal of Molecular Microbiology and Biotechnology* 16, nos. 1/2 (2009): 109-123.

Reid, Walter V. "Gene Co-ops and the Biotrade: Translating Genetic Resource Rights into Sustainable Development." *Journal of Ethnopharmacology* 51, nos. 1-3 (April, 1996): 75-92.

Schuster, Brian G. "A New Integrated Program for Natural Product Development and the Value of an Ethnomedical Approach." *Journal of Alternative and Complementary Medicine* 7, no. 1 (2001): S61-S72.

Singh, Sheo B., and Fernando Pelaez. "Biodiversity, Chemical Diversity, and Drug Discovery." *Progress in Drug Research* 65, no. 141 (2008): 142-174.

SEE ALSO: Animal breeding; Biodiversity; Biotechnology; Genetic diversity; Genetic prospecting; Resources as a source of international conflict.

# Geochemical cycles

CATEGORY: Geological processes and formations

*Geochemical cycles refer to the movement, or cycling, of elements through the biosphere and/or ecosystems. Both biotic (living) and abiotic (nonliving) components make up such systems.*

BACKGROUND

Geochemical cycles are generally considered to be those involving nutrient elements utilized by organisms in various ecosystems. Cycling involves both biological and chemical processes. While nearly all natural elements are cycled through both abiotic and living systems, certain elements are most commonly described in such systems. These include carbon, nitrogen, phosphorus, and a variety of lesser elements (including iron, sulfur, and trace elements such as copper and mercury).

Although the cycling of elements is often thought of as occurring in a relatively rapid fashion, many of these elements spend long periods locked in abiotic systems. For example, carbon may be found in materials that require millions of years to cycle through ocean sediment back into the atmosphere. The fate of such elements depends on many factors, including their chemical properties and their ability to erode or return to the atmosphere. Some chemical elements, such as carbon, oxygen, and nitrogen, are incorporated into organisms from the atmosphere. Other elements, such as phosphorus, potassium, sulfur, and iron, are found mainly in rocks and sediments.

CARBON AND OXYGEN CYCLES

The carbon and oxygen cycles are greatly dependent on each other. Molecular oxygen, which represents approximately 20 percent of the atmosphere, is used by organisms through a metabolic process called

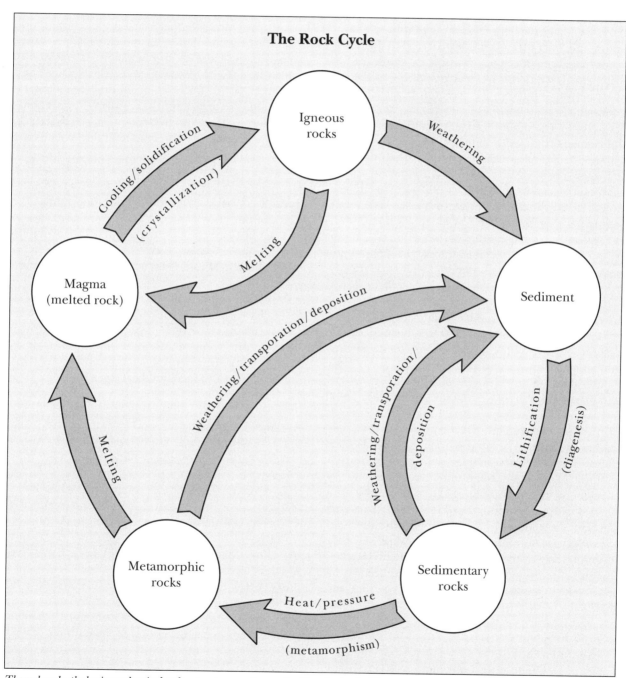

**The Rock Cycle**

*The rock cycle, the basic geochemical cycle, operates on a time scale of hundreds of millions to billions of years. It includes subcycles such as the oceanic cycle and the biological cycle, which could be called parts of the "atmospheric-hydrologic-biological-sedimentary" cycle.*

respiration. In these reactions, the oxygen reacts with reduced carbon compounds such as carbohydrates (sugars) and generates carbon dioxide ($CO_2$). Though carbon dioxide constitutes only a small proportion of the volume of the atmosphere (0.04 percent), it is in this form that it is used by primary producers such as plants. In the process of photosynthesis, utilizing sunlight as an energy source, plants and some microorganisms bind, or fix, the $CO_2$, converting the carbon again into carbohydrates, resulting in growth of the plant or replication of the microorganism. The complex carbohydrates that are generated in photosynthesis serve as the food source for consumers—organisms such as animals (including humans) that eat the plants. The carbohydrates are then broken down, regenerating carbon dioxide. In a sense, the combinations of respiration and photosynthesis represent the cycle of life. The concentration of carbon dioxide in the atmosphere is a factor in regulating the temperature of Earth. Consequently, the release of large quantities of the gas into the atmosphere through the burning of fossil fuels could potentially alter the Earth's climate.

### NITROGEN CYCLE

Nitrogen gas ($N_2$) represents 78 percent of the total volume of the atmosphere. However, because of the extreme stability of the bond between the two nitrogen atoms in the gas, plants and animals are unable to use atmospheric nitrogen directly as a nutrient. Nitrogen-fixing bacteria in the soil and in the roots of leguminous plants (peas, clover) are able to convert the gaseous nitrogen into nitrites and nitrates, chemical forms that can be used by plants. Animals then obtain nitrogen by consuming the plants. The decomposition of nitrogen compounds results in the accumulation of ammonium ($NH_4^+$) compounds in a process called ammonification. It is in this form that nitrogen is commonly found under conditions in which oxygen is limited. In this form, some of the nitrogen returns to the atmosphere. In the presence of oxygen, ammonium compounds are oxidized to nitrates (nitrification). Once the plant or animal has died, bacteria convert the nitrogen back into nitrogen gas, and it returns to the atmosphere.

### PHOSPHORUS CYCLE

Unlike carbon and nitrogen, which are found in the atmosphere, most of the phosphorus required for biotic nutrition is found in mineral form. Phosphorus is relatively water insoluble in this form; it is only gradually dissolved in water. Available phosphorus is therefore often growth-limiting in soils (it is second only to nitrogen as the scarcest of the soil nutrients). Ocean sediments may bring the mineral to the surface through uplifting of land, as along coastal areas, or by means of marine animals. Enzymatic breakdown of organic phosphate by bacteria and the consumption of marine organisms by seabirds cycle the phosphorus into forms available for use by plants. Deposition of guano (bird feces) along the American Pacific coast has long provided a fertilizer rich in phosphorus.

Bacteria also play significant roles in the geochemical cycling of many other elements. Iron, despite its abundance in the Earth's crust, is largely insoluble in water. Consequently, it is generally found in the form of precipitates of ferric ($Fe^{+3}$) compounds, seen as brown deposits in water. Acids are often formed as by-products in the formation of ferric compounds. The bacterial oxidation of pyrite ($FeS_2$) is a major factor in the leaching process of iron ores and in the formation of acid mine drainage. Likewise, much of the sulfur found in the Earth's crust is in the form of pyrite and gypsum ($CaSO_4$). Weathering processes return much of the sulfur to water-soluble forms; in the absence of air, the bacterial reduction of sulfate ($SO_4^{-2}$) to forms such as hydrogen sulfide ($H_2S$) allows its return to the atmosphere. Since sulfide compounds are highly toxic to many organisms, bacterial reduction of sulfates is of major biogeochemical significance.

*Richard Adler*

### FURTHER READING

Adriano, Domy C., ed. *Biogeochemistry of Trace Metals.* Boca Raton, Fla.: Lewis, 1992.

Arms, Karen, et al. *Biology: A Journey into Life.* 3d ed. Fort Worth, Tex.: Saunders College, 1994.

Bashkin, Vladimir N., and Robert W. Howarth. *Modern Biogeochemistry.* Boston: Kluwer Academic, 2002.

Heimann, Martin, ed. *The Global Carbon Cycle.* New York: Springer, 1993.

Libes, Susan. *Introduction to Marine Biogeochemistry.* 2d ed. Boston: Elsevier/Academic, 2009.

Madigan, Michael T., et al. *Brock Biology of Microorganisms.* 12th ed. San Francisco: Pearson/Benjamin Cummings, 2009.

Schlesinger, William H. *Biogeochemistry: An Analysis of Global Change.* 2d ed. San Diego, Calif.: Academic Press, 1997.

_____, ed. *Biogeochemistry.* Boston: Elsevier, 2005.

*Scientific American* 223 (September, 1970). Special issue on geochemical cycles.

SEE ALSO: Biosphere; Carbon cycle; Carbonate minerals; Guano; Hydrology and the hydrologic cycle; Leaching; Nitrogen and ammonia; Nitrogen cycle; Phosphorus cycle; Sulfur cycle.

# Geodes

CATEGORY: Mineral and other nonliving resources

*A host of different minerals may be found in the interior of some geodes, and when cut open a geode typically makes a beautiful display.*

### DEFINITION

Geodes are roughly spherically shaped bodies that are lined on the inside with inward-projecting small crystals surrounded by a layer of crystalline quartz. Geodes are most frequently found in limestone beds, but they may also occur in volcanic rocks and in some shales.

### OVERVIEW

Typically, a geode consists of a thin outer shell of dense chalcedonic silica (silicon dioxide) and an inner shell of crystals made of quartz or calcite. These crystals are often beautifully terminated, pointing toward the hollow interior. New crystal layers frequently grow on the terminations of old layers, sometimes nearly or even completely filling the geode. Many geodes are filled with water, while others that have been exposed at the surface for some time are dry.

Geodes typically range in size from less than 5 centimeters to more than 30 centimeters in diameter, but they can be much larger. Although the crystals are usually composed of quartz, they may also be composed of carbonate minerals, such as calcite, dolomite, and aragonite; of oxide minerals, such as hematite and magnetite; or of sulfide minerals, such as pyrite, calcopyrite, and sphalerite. In some geodes, there is an alternation of layers of silica and calcite, and almost all geodes show some kind of banding. When sulfide minerals are present, they are often the innermost crystals, whereas the carbonate minerals are typically next to the outermost layer of chalcedony (a fine-grained, fibrous variety of quartz). Some geodes are partially filled by mounds of banded chalcedony in which successive layers differ markedly in color and translucency. These layers form a colorful agate when stained.

The origin of geodes is somewhat similar to the formation of large limestone caves. Groundwater dissolves some of the limestone and forms a cavity in the rock, and the cavity is usually left filled with salty water. Silica-bearing waters then coagulate into a gel that surrounds the salt solution. The geode grows by expansion because of osmotic pressure between the salty water trapped inside the silica gel shell and fresh water on the outside of the gel. These pressures cause the geode to expand until equilibrium is reached. De-

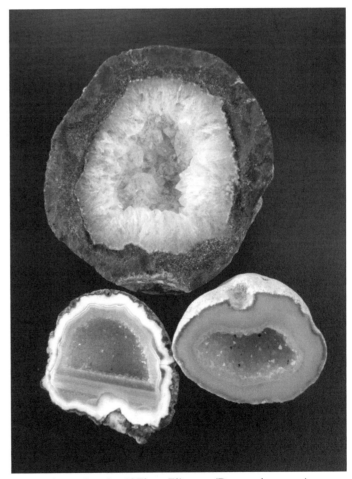

*Assorted geodes.* (©Elena Elisseeva/Dreamstime.com)

hydration of the gel and subsequent crystallization occur, along with shrinkage and cracking of the geode wall, allowing mineral-bearing waters to percolate into the geode and deposit crystals on the cavity wall. Subsequent periods of water circulation and crystallization may follow, forming the characteristic layers of crystals.

Geodes are found in many parts of the world. One well-known type found in Uruguay is called hydrolite, or water stone, because it contains quartz crystals left when water containing silica in solution evaporated. Many highly prized geodes that are filled with beautiful crystals and curved-banded colors of agate can be found at various collecting sites in the United States, such as near Dugway, Utah, and Keokuk, Iowa.

*Alvin K. Benson*

SEE ALSO: Groundwater; Hydrothermal solutions and mineralization; Limestone; Quartz; Sedimentary processes, rocks, and mineral deposits; Silicates.

# Geographic information systems

CATEGORY: Scientific disciplines

*Geographic information systems (GIS) originated primarily from efforts to manage natural resources and analyze environmental issues. In recent years, advances in computing technology and the development of large digital databases have made GIS a powerful tool for analyzing the natural environment. GIS is particularly suited to support multidisciplinary analyses of natural systems at a variety of scales.*

BACKGROUND

Although geographic information systems (GIS) scientists and practitioners may define GIS in broader terms, the initials are commonly used to refer to the computer software and peripheral technologies that are used to collect, manipulate, analyze, and visualize geographic information. While many of the concepts that underpin GIS have a long history in academic disciplines such as cartography, geography, and planning, GIS computer software largely originated in the 1960's with academic and government initiatives to study how computers could be used to make maps and manage geographic data. In academia, this included work by cartographers to develop computer

programs that replicated manual procedures for creating maps. It also included research by geographers, planners, and computer scientists to develop methods for conducting spatial analysis with computers. The pioneering work of researchers at the Harvard Laboratory for Computer Graphics and Spatial Analysis from the 1960's to the 1980's was an important factor in the development of early GIS.

The origins of GIS software also lie in government efforts to develop spatial information systems for military applications and to manage large demographic and environmental datasets. The U.S. military, for instance, was active in developing highly accurate digital maps and information systems to manage large databases of remotely sensed imagery. Starting in the 1970's the Department of Defense also developed the Global Positioning System (GPS), a satellite navigation system used for a number of applications—including in-car navigation systems and mobile devices—to determine location. In the late 1960's, the U.S. Census Bureau developed GIS resources to facilitate the collection, analysis, and dissemination of data collected in the census. Similar efforts were undertaken by environmental resource managers and organizations like the United States Geological Survey and the National Park Service to manage natural resources. One of the first GIS programs to be developed and used on a large scale was the Canada Geographic Information System (CGIS). CGIS was developed by the Canadian government to inventory natural resources, manage how resources were used, and structure decisions regarding the development and conservation of natural resources.

The widespread use of GIS by private companies and nonprofit organizations and at multiple levels of government began in the late 1980's with the development of the personal computer and "off-the-shelf" GIS software. These developments were significant to the field of natural resource management because they fostered broader efforts to develop and share environmental datasets. They also facilitated efforts by researchers from different disciplines to collaborate on environmental issues. Today, most GIS software is developed by private companies. Common packages include ArcGIS, Manifold Systems, MapInfo, Intergraph, and IDRISI. While most GIS programs are developed for a broad range of applications, some programs like IDRISI are designed specifically for natural resource management and planning and environmental modeling. Organizations such as Google,

Microsoft, and the National Aeronautics and Space Administration have also made significant investments in Web-based GIS resources, which have numerous applications in the environmental sciences.

GIS DESIGN

Three fundamental concepts that underlie the design of modern software are map overlay, vector and raster data models, and the relationship between spatial and attribute information. Map overlay refers to the manner in which different types of spatial data (for example, the locations of wells, rivers, and lakes or changes in elevation) are stored as individual thematic layers in the GIS. The GIS allows the user to superimpose the layers on top of one another to explore the relationships between them. In the GIS community, this technique is commonly attributed to landscape architect Ian McHarg, who, in the 1960's, used overlays of maps drawn on Mylar transparencies in environmental planning.

The data stored in the thematic layers are typically structured according to two data models, known as vector and raster. The vector data model represents entities as one of three simple geometric features: a point, line, or polygon. It is best suited to represent discrete entities as exemplified by a point layer, depicting the locations of water wells; a line layer, depicting the layout of a stream network; or a polygon layer, depicting the boundaries of large water bodies. The raster data model, in contrast, is better suited to represent phenomena that vary continuously across space, such as temperature or elevation. The raster data model partitions a data layer according to a uniform grid mesh. This is similar to the manner in which a digital photograph partitions space into uniform pixels that each store information on light characteristics. In this manner, the raster data model is particularly well suited to represent natural resource imagery collected from satellites and other forms of remote sensing.

Additionally, the vector and raster data models not only store information on where an entity is located but also store information on the characteristics of entities. Thus, a user can click on a map layer in a GIS and receive additional information about a feature or location. This is an important design characteristic because it enables GIS users to analyze the spatial characteristics of attributes that do not necessarily have a spatial component. For example, a natural resource manager could use GIS to analyze how water characteristics, such as pH or dissolved oxygen, vary along a stream network based on point samples collected at various locations throughout a watershed.

GIS APPLICATIONS

GIS can be applied to almost any task that has been traditionally evaluated using maps. In the social sciences, for example, GIS is used to map crimes, modify election districts, and model population migration. Business analysts use GIS to identify potential sites for businesses, identify consumer markets, and distribute products. The medical community uses GIS technology to track diseases and study environmental impacts on health. GIS software is used in schools to teach geography and promote spatial literacy. There are also numerous applications of GIS in the natural sciences. For one, GIS is used to observe and study natural systems. This includes efforts to monitor agricultural production, track endangered species, or study bird migration patterns. GIS is used to explore the relationships between different environmental systems to delineate wildlife habitats or study the impact of climate change on local ecosystems. It is also used to manage the use of natural resources, such as forests, water, and fossil fuels. It can also be used to model human-environment interactions, develop predictions, and structure debates regarding the conservation or development of natural resources. Finally, and perhaps most routinely, GIS can be used to visualize spatial data and disseminate information regarding environmental systems.

An example of how GIS is used to analyze environmental systems is illustrated in the following scenario of identifying an acceptable location for a wind farm. To begin, a power company could use a GIS to analyze wind-speed data to identify locations where the average wind speed is strong enough to generate wind power. Next, the company might compare the locations to a digital layer that shows high-power transmission lines to determine which sites will be easiest to connect to the existing energy grid. The company could then use GIS to explore the land-cover characteristics and the cost of developing access roads to prepare acceptable building sites for construction. GIS could also be used to identify property owners that would be impacted by the project or determine which municipalities the company will have to contact for legal and tax purposes. In a similar manner, GIS may be used to empower opponents of the wind farm. For example, opponents could use GIS to evaluate and debate the aesthetics of the proposed wind farm or the impacts it would have on culturally sensitive landscapes or wildlife.

## FUTURE OF GIS

GIS software and related technologies have become increasingly common in research, education, and people's daily lives. The development of Web-based GIS, mobile GPS devices, off-the-shelf software, and advances in remote sensing have fostered a broad interest in developing GIS data and resources in many different domains. For the natural sciences, these developments have resulted in greater access to high-quality digital datasets and improved ability to consider a broad range of factors in environmental analyses. The developments have also highlighted many of the limitations of existing GIS software packages regarding the analysis of environmental systems. The most noteworthy limitations draw on the fact that GIS is designed to represent space based on static, two-dimensional maps and is therefore poorly suited to represent three-dimensional, dynamic environmental entities such as weather phenomena or ocean circulation patterns. In recent years an academic discipline called GIScience has evolved to address research issues regarding the design and use of GIS.

*Jeffrey C. Brunskill*

## FURTHER READING

Bolstad, Paul. *GIS Fundamentals: A First Text on Geographic Information Systems.* 3d ed. White Bear Lake, Minn.: Eider Press, 2008.

Lang, Laura. *Managing Natural Resources with GIS.* Redlands, Calif.: Environmental Systems Research Institute Press, 1998.

Longley, Paul, et al. *Geographic Information Systems and Science.* 2d ed. New York: Wiley, 2005.

Randolph, John. *Environmental Land Use Planning and Management.* Washington, D.C.: Island Press, 2004.

Scally, Robert. *GIS for Environmental Management.* Redlands, Calif.: Environmental Systems Research Institute Press, 2006.

## WEB SITES

CLARK LABS IDRISI HOMEPAGE
http://www.clarklabs.org/

ENVIRONMENTAL SYSTEMS RESEARCH INSTITUTE
http://www.esri.com

SEE ALSO: Aerial photography; Environmental engineering; Forest management; Land-use planning; Landsat satellites and satellite technologies; Oceanography; Remote sensing.

# Geology

CATEGORY: Scientific disciplines

*The study of Earth and its geological processes is essential to the discovery, extraction, and management of natural resources, from minerals to energy resources.*

## BACKGROUND

Geology is the study of the planet Earth: its composition, origin, and history, and the environmental, biological, chemical, and physical forces outside and within it. As a science, geology grew from the nineteenth century study of natural features, stratigraphy, and fossils in rock outcroppings to a wide variety of scientific subspecialties covering myriad aspects of the planet. Since the early nineteenth century, geology has involved accurate mapping of the Earth's topography and discovery, study, and exploitation of major mineral deposits around the world.

A guiding principle in geology has been uniformitarianism: geological processes that are observed today are the same as those that occurred in the past and those that will occur in the future. Application of this concept on a planetary scale allows scientists to prospect for minerals using remote-sensing techniques.

Catastrophic events, including meteor impacts, have been deduced from geological deposits and have been credited with causing widespread mass extinctions observed in the fossil record. Identification of the large meteor impact responsible for forming Chesapeake Bay has provided an explanation for recent earthquakes in the region and for the presence of saltwater aquifers in Virginia. Some economic geologists have postulated that the platinum deposit at Sudbury, Ontario, is a meteor impact site from billions of years ago.

The United States Geological Survey (part of the Department of the Interior) is the governmental agency responsible for producing official maps and reports. Most other nations have similar agencies, including the Geological Survey of Canada, Servicio

Geológico Mexicano, the British Geological Survey, Geoscience Australia, the Geological Survey of Japan, and the South Africa Council for Geoscience, which all host informational Web sites.

Knowledge of geology is fundamental to the understanding of all inanimate resources on Earth. Geothermal energy can provide an inexpensive alternative to fossil and nuclear sources for generating electricity. Discovery of necessary mineral resources is a prerequisite to exploitation, while the mechanics of exploiting those resources also requires geological expertise. Environmental geologists are involved in mapping and investigating toxic contamination areas for possible mitigation. Search for permanent geological sites for radioactive materials is going on in countries around the world. Potential natural hazards—including unstable topography, earthquake fault lines, and volcanic activity—require geological monitoring to warn people of impending disasters.

EXPLORATION GEOLOGY

Exploration geologists focus on the discovery and exploitation of mineral and ore deposits and fossil fuels. Stone Age humans found outcroppings of flint and chert with which to make arrowheads and other tools. Eventually, humans moved on to easily worked metals such as copper, tin, silver, gold, and iron. Precious gems have been highly valued for millennia, and new sources for these ores and minerals continue to be found.

Modern industrialized society requires metals for basic construction and manufacturing. The increasing technological demand has moved geological exploration from the California gold rush era of the American West to the worldwide search for uranium for nuclear weapons to the search for rare earth elements for high-tech electronics and lithium deposits for batteries. Geologists in the twenty-first century rarely engage in time-consuming initial field exploration and prospecting, relying on remote sensing from aircraft and satel-

## Primary Rocks and Minerals in Earth's Crust

| ROCKS | % VOLUME OF CRUST | MINERALS | % VOLUME OF CRUST |
|---|---|---|---|
| **Sedimentary** | | Quartz | 12 |
| Sands | 1.7 | Alkali feldspar | 12 |
| Clays and shales | 4.2 | Plagioclase | 39 |
| Carbonates (including | | Micas | 5 |
| salt-bearing deposits) | 2.0 | Amphiboles | 5 |
| | | Pyroxenes | 11 |
| **Igneous** | | Olivines | 3 |
| Granites | 10.4 | Clay minerals (and | |
| Granodiorites, diorites | 11.2 | chlorites) | 4.6 |
| Syenites | 0.4 | Calcite (and aragonite) | 1.5 |
| Basalts, gabbros, | | Dolomite | 0.5 |
| amphibolites, eclogites | 42.5 | Magnetite (and | |
| Dunites, peridotites | 0.2 | titanomagnetite) | 1.5 |
| | | Others (garnets, kyanite, | |
| **Metamorphic** | | andalusite, sillimanite, | |
| Gneisses | 21.4 | apatite, etc.) | 4.9 |
| Schists | 5.1 | | |
| Marbles | 0.9 | **Totals** | |
| | | Quartz and feldspars | 63 |
| **Totals** | | Pyroxene and olivine | 14 |
| Sedimentary | 7.9 | Hydrated silicates | 14.6 |
| Igneous | 64.7 | Carbonates | 2.0 |
| Metamorphic | 27.4 | Others | 6.4 |

*Source:* Michael H. Carr et al., *The Geology of the Terrestrial Planets*, NASA SP-469, 1984. Data are from A. B. Ronov and A. A. Yaroshevsky, "Chemical Composition of the Earth's Crust," American Geophysical Union Monograph 13.

lites to determine where new mineral deposits might be found. Confirmation of mineral deposits and plans for exploitation require geological expertise.

The exploitation of coal, oil, and gas deposits around the world provides vital sources of energy to the billions of people on Earth. Most geologists are employed, usually by governments and private industry, in this aspect of geology.

Coal remains the most important fuel for electric power production worldwide, with reserves of anthracite ("hard") and bituminous ("soft") coal widespread in North America, Europe, and Asia. Large-scale underground coal mining is labor intensive and expensive. Many American coal companies have opted to use cheaper methods of obtaining coal, such as strip mining and mountaintop removal mining (MTR), in which coal deposits are located at or near surface level. MTR in areas like West Virginia and Kentucky is unpopular with the general public because of the widespread environmental degradation that occurs when entire mountains are leveled and overburden (soil and non-coal rock) materials are placed in adjacent valleys. Land use after MTR may be determined by geological studies; the areas are usually left unvegetated after mining activities end. Coal slurry impoundments are used to hold huge amounts of MTR coal waste, and if the impoundment fails, aquatic wildlife in the area's streams and rivers is eradicated. In March, 2009, the U.S. Environmental Protection Agency announced that permits for MTR of coal would be carefully scrutinized.

Oil deposits occur around the world, and geological exploration teams continue to find major discoveries. Exploration and development of new oil fields are often complicated by politics, on both national and international scales. Opening up the Alaskan National Wildlife Reserve (ANWR) to oil exploration and drilling is an example of such complications. Even though President George W. Bush and Vice President Dick Cheney both strongly favored drilling, Congress was unwilling to authorize oil leases in the eight years (2001-2009) of the Bush presidency. In the 2008 U.S. presidential election, ANWR became a major campaign issue when Alaskan governor Sarah Palin, who was the Republican vice presidential candidate, strongly endorsed drilling.

Discovery and commercial exploitation of heavy bitumen oil sands, which cannot be pumped out of the ground like petroleum deposits, have become major political issues because this fossil fuel leaves a large carbon footprint. Oil sands are strip-mined or hauled from massive open-pit mines. An estimated 780,000 barrels of oil are produced per day from Canadian oil sands in Alberta, and about 60 percent of this is exported to the United States. Oil sands in Alberta are estimated to contain more than one trillion barrels of oil, 80 percent of which is not accessible through present surface mining methods. Oil sand deposits also occur in Utah, Venezuela, and Russia.

## GEOLOGICAL MONITORING OF VOLCANOES AND EARTHQUAKES

The devastating Boxing Day tsunami of December 26, 2004, which engulfed Indian Ocean shorelines from Indonesia to East Africa and killed more than 225,000 people, followed an undersea event known as the Great Sumatra-Andaman earthquake. The countries most affected by the tsunami lacked geological monitoring stations. Such a seismological monitoring network could have provided many areas with several hours warning of the impending tsunami and lessened the death toll. The U.S. National Oceanic and Atmospheric Administration operates the Pacific Tsunami Warning System, which warns of potential problems for Hawaii, Alaska, and the Pacific coast of North America.

Volcano monitoring is necessary to warn people of impending eruptions. Erupting volcanoes emit clouds of ash that can be sucked into jet aircraft engines, where the ash liquefies and then deposits a solid glass coating to the rear of the jet turbine. This glass coating interferes with the jet enough to cause the aircraft to crash. Ash problems necessitate closure of airports within the reach of the erupting volcano, and aircraft must be diverted from routes that pass through the ash clouds.

## ENVIRONMENTAL GEOLOGY

Environmental geologists use a variety of geological, geochemical, microbiological, and hydrological techniques to identify and mitigate hazards resulting from urban sprawl, industrialization, and mining activities. The most common environmental problems include surface water and groundwater contamination, dumping of hazardous wastes in unprotected ground, and air pollution related to improper waste handling.

A permanent geological storage site for reactor waste in the United States has been a limiting factor in public support for the nuclear power industry. (Nuclear weapons waste is stored in Carlsbad, New Mexico.) Requirements for geological storage include the absence of groundwater and total lack of seismic activity in a solid bedrock formation. Many locations have been proposed. In 1987, Yucca Flat, Nevada, was selected, but the selection met with almost immediate opposition because of unanswered geological questions. In March, 2009, President Barack Obama announced that plans to use Yucca Flat had been abandoned. Stephen Chu, the secretary of energy for the Obama administration, indicated that the United States might build nuclear power reactors that could utilize nuclear waste, thus dramatically lessening (but not eliminating) the amount of radioactive waste requiring permanent storage. Other countries, including Sweden, have conducted rigorous nationwide geological surveys to identify potential nuclear waste storage sites and are moving closer to final site selection. Some nuclear industry experts believe that the United States will not select a site until 2030.

## COMMERCIAL POWER PRODUCTION FROM GEOTHERMAL ENERGY

Harnessing hot springs and geysers to produce electricity has been going on at Larderello, Italy, for more than a century and is well established in Iceland and the Philippines; the latter two countries produce about 20 percent of their electricity from geothermal energy. Iceland has a geothermal capacity of 1.3 terawatt-hours per year. There are twenty-seven electricity plants at The Geysers, in Northern California, producing 750 megawatts. Important geological concerns arise when harnessing geothermal sources. The major problem at generating locations like Wairakei, New Zealand, and The Geysers is local depletion of heat sources; heated zones are tapped too intensively for too long of a period to allow recharge of heat from deep within the Earth. Other problems include the need for drilling deep wells and for fracturing rock around the deep wells at geothermal locations. Although the technology for drilling deep wells exists, it is a costly process.

*Anita Baker-Blocker*

SEE ALSO: Department of Energy, U.S.; Earth's crust; Ecology; Igneous processes, rocks, and mineral deposits; Metamorphic processes, rocks, and mineral deposits; Minerals, structure and physical properties of; Oceanography; Sedimentary processes, rocks, and mineral deposits.

# Geothermal and hydrothermal energy

CATEGORIES: Geological processes and formations; energy resources; obtaining and using resources

*Geothermal energy is the energy associated with the heat in the interior of the Earth. The common usage of the term refers to the thermal energy relatively near the surface of the Earth that can be utilized by humans. Hydrothermal energy is the energy associated with hot water, whereas geothermal is a more general term. Geothermal energy has been exploited since early history. It is a source of energy with a low pollution potential that can be used for producing electricity as well as for heating and cooling and helping with a number of other needs.*

## BACKGROUND

A geothermal system is made up of three elements: a heat source, a reservoir, and a fluid that transfers the heat. The heat source can be a magmatic intrusion or the Earth's normal temperature, which increases with depth. The reservoir is a volume of hot permeable rock from which circulating fluids extract heat. Fluid convection transports the heat from the higher-temperature low regions to the upper regions, where it can be accessed and used.

## CAUSES OF GEOTHERMAL PHENOMENA

While individuals in early mining operations may have noted the general increase in temperature with depth, not until the eighteenth century were subsurface temperature measurements performed. The results often showed an increase in temperature with depth. The rate of increase varied from site to site. An average value that is often used today is a 2.5° to 3° Celsius increase per 100 meters increase in depth from the surface. The geothermal gradient suggested that the source of the Earth's heat was below the surface, but the exact cause of the heat was open to discussion for many years. It was not until the early part of the twentieth century that the decay of radioactive materials was identified as the primary cause of this heat. The thermal energy of the Earth is very large; however, only a small portion is available for capture and utilization. The available thermal energy is primarily limited to areas where water or steam carries heat from the deep hot regions to, or near, the surface. The water or steam is then available for capture and may be put to such uses as electricity generation and heating.

The interior of the Earth is often considered to be divided into three major sections, called the crust, mantle, and core. The crust extends from the surface down to about 35 kilometers beneath the land and about 6 kilometers beneath the ocean. Below the crust, the mantle extends to a depth of roughly 2,900 kilometers. Below, or inside, the mantle is the Earth's core. The crust is rich in radioactive materials, with a much lower density in the mantle and essentially none in the core. The radioactive decay of these materials produces heat. The Earth is also cooling down, however. The volume of the mantle is roughly forty times that of the crust. The combination of the heat generated from the decay of radioactive materials and the cooling of the Earth results in the flow of heat to the Earth's surface. The origin of the total heat flowing to the surface is roughly 20 percent from the crust and 80 percent from the mantle and core.

The outermost shell of the Earth, made up of the crust and upper mantle, is known as the lithosphere. According to the concept of plate tectonics, the surface of the Earth is composed of six large and several smaller lithospheric regions or plates. On some of the edges of these plates, hot molten material extends to the surface and causes the plates to spread apart. On other edges, one plate is driven beneath another. There are densely fractured zones in the crust around the plate edges. A great amount of seismic activity occurs in these regions, and they are where large numbers of volcanoes, geysers, and hot springs are located. High terrestrial heat flows occur near the edges of the plates, so the Earth's most important geothermal regions are found around the plate margins. A concentration of geothermal resources is often found in regions with a normal or elevated geothermal gradient as well as around the plate margins.

## HISTORY OF DEVELOPMENT

The ancient Romans used the water from hot springs for baths and for heating homes. China and Japan also used geothermal waters for bathing and washing. Similar uses are still found in various geothermal regions of the world. Other uses of thermal waters were not developed until the early part of the nineteenth century. An early example occurred in the Larderello area of Italy. In 1827, Francesco Larderel developed an evaporation process that used the heat from geothermal waters to evaporate the thermal waters found in the area, leaving boric acid. Heating the water by burning wood had been required in the past.

Also in the early nineteenth century, inventors began attempting to utilize the energy associated with geothermal steam for driving pumps and winches. Beginning in the early twentieth century, geothermal steam was used to generate electricity in the Larderello region. Several other countries tried to utilize their own geothermal resources. Geothermal wells were drilled in Beppu, Japan, in 1919, and at The Geysers, California, in 1921. In the late 1920's, Iceland began using geothermal waters for heating. Various locations in the western United States have used geothermal waters for heating homes and buildings in the twentieth century. Among these are Klamath Falls, Oregon, and Boise, Idaho.

After World War II, many countries became interested in geothermal energy; geothermal resources of some type exist in most countries. Geothermal energy was viewed as an energy source that did not have to be imported and that could be competitive with other sources of electricity generation. In 1958, New Zealand began using geothermal energy for electric power production. One of the first power plants in the United States began operation at The Geysers, California, in 1960. Mexico began operating its first geothermal power plant at Cerro Prieto, near the California border, in 1973.

By 2007, the United States was a leading country in electric power production from geothermal resources with 2,700 megawatts of installed electrical capacity. By 2004, Costa Rica, El Salvador, Iceland, Kenya, and the Philippines had significant geothermal energy outputs that accounted for at least 15 percent of each countries' energy production. Nonelectric uses of geothermal energy occur in most countries. In 2000, the leading nonelectric users of geothermal energy in terms of total usage were, in descending order, China, Japan, the United States, Iceland, Turkey, New Zealand, the Republic of Georgia, and Russia.

## CLASSIFICATION OF GEOTHERMAL RESOURCES

Geothermal resources are classified by the temperature of the water or steam that carries the heat from the depths to, or near, the surface. Geothermal resources are often divided into low temperature (less than 90° Celsius), moderate temperature (90° to 150° Celsius), and high temperature (greater than 150° Celsius). There are still various worldwide opinions on how best to divide and describe geothermal resources. The class or grouping characterizing the geothermal resource often dictates the use or uses that can be made of the resource.

A distinction that is often made in describing geothermal resources is whether there is wet or dry steam present. Wet steam has liquid water associated with it. Steam turbine electric generators can often use steam directly from dry steam wells, but separation is necessary for the use of steam from wet steam wells. In various applications the water needs to be removed from wet steam. This is achieved through the use of a separator, which separates the steam gas from liquid hot water. The hot water is then re-injected into the reservoir; used as input to other systems to recover some of its heat; or, if there are not appreciable levels of environmentally threatening chemicals present, discharged into the environment after suitable cooling.

## EXPLORATION

The search for geothermal resources has become easier in the twenty-first century than it was in the past because of the considerable amount of information and maps that have been assembled for many locations around the world and because of the availability of new instrumentation, techniques, and systems. The primary objectives in geothermal exploration are to identify geothermal phenomena, determine the size and type of the field, and identify the location of the productive zone. Further, researchers need to determine the heat content of the fluids that are to be discharged from the wells, the potential lifetime of the site, problems that may occur during operation of the site, and the environmental consequences of developing and operating the site. Geological and hydrological studies help to define the geothermal resource.

Geochemical surveys help to determine if the resource is vapor- or water-dominated as well as to estimate the minimum temperature expected at the resource's depth. Potential problems later in pipe scaling, corrosion, and environmental impact are also determined by this type of survey. Geophysical surveys help to define the shape, size, and depth of the resource. The drilling of exploration wells is the true test of the nature of the resource. Because drilling can be costly, use of previous surveys in selecting or siting each drill site is important.

## ELECTRICITY GENERATION

The generation of electrical energy from geothermal energy primarily occurs through the use of conventional steam turbines and through the use of binary plants. Conventional steam turbines operate on fluid temperatures of at least 150° Celsius. An atmospheric exhaust turbine is one from which the steam, after passing through the turbine, is exhausted to the atmosphere. Another form of turbine is one in which the exhaust steam is condensed. The steam consumption

*Geothermal steam is funneled through the pipes in the foreground from the geyser drilling station in the background at this Northern California location.* (Manny Crisostomo/MCT/Landov)

per kilowatt-hour produced for an atmospheric exhaust unit is about twice that for a condensing unit, but atmospheric exhaust units are simpler and cheaper.

The Geysers has one of the largest dry-steam geothermal fields in the world. Steam rises from more than forty wells. Pipes feed steam to the turbogenerators at a temperature of 175° Celsius. Some of the wells are drilled to depths as great as 2,700 meters. The geothermal field at Wairakei on North Island of New Zealand has been a source of electric power for several decades. The hot water (near 300° Celsius) rises from more than sixty deep wells. As the pressure falls, the hot water converts to steam. The flashing of hot water to steam is the major source of geothermal energy for electric power production.

Binary plants allow electricity to be generated from low- to medium-temperature geothermal resources as well as from the waste hot water coming from steam/water separators. Binary plants use a secondary working fluid. The geothermal fluid heats the secondary fluid, which is in a closed system. The working fluid is heated, vaporizes, drives a turbine, is cooled, condenses, and is ready to repeat the cycle. Binary plant technology is becoming the most cost-effective means to generate electricity from geothermal resources below 175° Celsius.

In cascaded systems, the output water from one system is used as the input heat source to another system. Such systems allow some of the heat in waste water from higher temperature systems to be recovered and used. They are often used in conjunction with electric generation facilities to help recover some of the heat in the wastewater or steam from a turbine.

### SPACE HEATING

Space heating by geothermal waters is one of the most common uses of geothermal resources. In some countries, such as Iceland, entire districts are heated using the resource. The nature of the geothermal water dictates whether that water is circulated directly in pipes to homes and other structures or (if the water is too corrosive) a heat exchanger is used to transfer the heat to a better fluid for circulation. Hot water in the range from 60° to 125° Celsius has been used for space heating with hot-water radiators. Water with as low a temperature as 35° to 40° Celsius has been used effectively for heating by means of radiant heating, in which pipes are embedded in the floor or ceiling. Another way of using geothermal energy for heating is

through the circulation of heated air from water-to-air heat exchangers. Heat pumps are also used with geothermal waters for both heating and cooling.

In district heating, the water to the customer is often in the 60° to 90° Celsius range and is returned at 35° to 50° Celsius. The distance of the customers from the geothermal resource is important. Transmission lines of up to 60 kilometers have been used, but shorter distances are more common and desirable. When designing a district heating system, the selection of the area to be supplied, building density, characteristics of the heat source, the transmission system, heat loss in transmission, and heat consumption by customers are all important factors.

There are more than 550 geothermal wells serving a variety of uses in Klamath Falls, Oregon. Utilization includes heating homes, schools, businesses, and swimming pools as well as snow-melting systems for sidewalks and a section of highway pavement. Most of the eastern side of the city is heated by geothermal energy. The principal heat extraction system is the closed-loop downhole heat exchanger utilizing city water in the heat exchangers. Hot water is delivered at approximately 82° Celsius and returns at 60° Celsius.

Hot water from springs is delivered through pipes to heat homes in Reykjavík, Iceland, and several outlying communities. This is the source of heating for 95 percent of the buildings in Reykjavík. Hot water is delivered to homes at 88° Celsius. The geothermal water is also used for heating schools, swimming pools, and greenhouses and is used for aquaculture.

### GREENHOUSE HEATING

Using geothermal resources to heat greenhouses is similar to using it to heat homes and other buildings. The objective in this case is to provide a thermal environment in the greenhouse so that vegetables, flowers, and fruits can be grown out of season. The greenhouse is supplied with heated water, and through the use of radiators, embedded pipes, aerial pipes, or surface pipes, the heat is transferred to the greenhouse environment. Forced air through heat exchangers is also used. The United States, Hungary, Italy, and France all have considerable numbers of geothermal greenhouses.

### AQUACULTURE

One of the major areas for the direct use of geothermal resources is in aquaculture. The main idea is to adjust the temperature of the water environment in a production pond so that freshwater or marine fish, shrimp, and plants have greater growth rates and thus reach harvest age more quickly. There are many schemes to regulate the temperature of the pond water. For supply wells where the geothermal water is near the required temperature, the water is introduced directly into the pond. For locations having a well-water temperature too high, the water is spread in a holding pool where evaporative cooling, radiation, and conductive heat loss to the ground can all be used to reduce the temperature to a level in which it can be added to the main production pond.

### INDUSTRIAL APPLICATIONS

The Tasman Pulp and Paper Company, located in Kawerau, New Zealand, is one of the largest industrial developments to utilize geothermal energy. Geothermal exploration started there in 1952; it was directed toward locating and developing a geothermal resource for a pulp and paper mill. In 1985, the company was using four wells to supply steam to the operations. The steam is used to operate log kickers directly, to dry timber, to generate clean steam, and to drive an electricity generator. Geothermal energy supplies about 30 percent of the total process steam and 4 percent of the electricity for the plant. Geothermal energy in the form of steam is used to dry diatomaceous earth in Námafjall, Iceland. The diatomaceous earth is dredged from the bottom of a lake and pumped 3 kilometers by pipeline to a plant where it is dried.

Numerous other industrial applications of geothermal resources exist in the world. These range from timber drying in Japan to salt production from evaporating seawater in the Philippines, vegetable drying in Nevada, alfalfa drying in New Zealand, and mushroom growing in Oregon.

### ENVIRONMENTAL IMPACT

The environmental impacts associated with the use or conversion of geothermal resources are typically much less than those associated with the use or conversion of other energy sources. The resource is often promoted as a clean technology without the potential radiation problems associated with nuclear energy facilities or the atmospheric emissions problems often associated with oil and coal electric plants. Nonetheless, although associated environmental problems are low, there are some present. In the exploration and development phases of large-scale geothermal devel-

opments, access roads and platforms for drill rigs must be built. The drilling of a well can result in possible mixing of drilling fluids with the aquifers intersected by the well if the well is not well-cased. Blowouts can also pollute the groundwater. The drilling fluids need to be stored and handled as wastes.

Geothermal fluids often contain dissolved gases such as carbon dioxide, hydrogen sulfide, and methane. Other chemicals, such as sodium chloride, boron, arsenic, and mercury, may also be associated with the geothermal water. The presence of these gases and chemicals must be determined, and appropriate means must be selected to prevent their release into the environment. In some cases this problem is reduced by the re-injection of wastewater into the geothermal reservoir.

The release of thermal water into a surface water body such as a stream, pond, or lake can cause severe ecosystem damage by changing the ambient water temperature, even if only by a few degrees. Any discharge of hot water from the geothermal site needs to involve a means of cooling the water to an acceptable level—one that will not cause environmental damage. This result is often achieved through the use of holding ponds or evaporative cooling. The removal of large volumes of geothermal fluid from the subsurface can cause land subsidence. This is irreversible and can cause major structural damage. Subsidence can be prevented by the re-injection of a volume of fluid equal to that removed.

Noise pollution is one of the potential problems with geothermal sites where electricity generation is conducted. Noise reduction can require costly measures. Because many geothermal electric generation sites are rural, however, this is often not a problem. The noise generated in direct heat applications is typically low.

### ECONOMICS

The initial cost of a geothermal plant is usually higher than the initial cost of a similar plant run on conventional fuel. On the other hand, the cost of the energy for operating a geothermal plant is much lower than the cost of conventional fuels. In order to be economically superior, the geothermal plant needs to operate long enough to at least make up for the difference in initial cost.

Cascaded systems can be used to optimize the recovery of heat from the geothermal water and steam and therefore to decrease the overall costs. Systems

## Top Consumers of Geothermal Energy, 2005

|  | MEGAWATT CAPACITY | GIGAWATT-HOURS PER YEAR |
|---|---|---|
| United States | 7,817 | 8,678 |
| Sweden | 4,200 | 12,000 |
| China | 3,687 | 12,605 |
| Iceland | 1,844 | 6,806 |
| Turkey | 1,495 | 6,900 |
| Japan | 822 | 2,862 |
| Hungary | 694 | 2,206 |
| Italy | 607 | 2,098 |
| New Zealand | 308 | 1,969 |

*Note:* Worldwide installed capacity for direct use increased from 8,604 megawatts in 1995 to 28,268 megawatts in 2005. Yearly direct use increased from 31,236 gigawatt-hours per year in 1995 to 75,943 gigawatt-hours per year in 2005.

can be cascaded such that the wastewater and heat from one is the input heat source to the next. An example is the cascading of systems used for electricity generation, fruit drying, and home heating. Finally, the distance between the geothermal source and the plant or user should be minimized, as there can be significant transmission losses in heat as well as high costs for pipe, pumps, valves, and maintenance.

### ELECTRICTITY: CURRENT AND FUTURE PROSPECTS

The United States leads the world in electrical generating capacity. The U.S. installed geothermal electrical generating capacity has moved from 2,228 megawatts in 2000 to 2,534 megawatts in 2005 to 2,958 megawatts as of 2008. This U.S. generating capacity is spread over seven states but is concentrated in California. As of 2008, California had 2,555 megawatts of generating capacity. The other states with geothermal electrical generating capacity are Alaska; Idaho, with one plant of 13-megawatt capacity; Hawaii, with one plant that delivers 25 to 35 megawatts, supplying about 20 percent of the island's electrical needs; New Mexico, with a 0.24-megawatt pilot project online and a 10-megawatt station that was expected to come online in 2009; Nevada, with seventeen geothermal power plants totaling 318 megawatts of capacity;

and Utah, with one plant with a capacity of 36 megawatts.

As of 2009, projects totaling 3,960 megawatts of additional generating capacity were at least at stage one of development; that is, they had secured rights to the resource and had begun initial exploratory drilling. Many of the projects were farther along than that, with some in the facility construction and production drilling stage. These projects are located in thirteen different states. Arizona, Colorado, Florida, Oregon, Washington, and Wyoming will be added to the list of states with geothermal electrical-generating facilities when these are all completed.

As of 2009, Alaska had four projects totaling 53 megawatts at least at stage one. Arizona had one project of 2-megawatt capacity under development. California continued to expand its capacity, with twenty projects totaling 928 megawatts under development. Colorado had a 10-megawatt plant at stage one of development. Florida had a plant of 0.2-megawatt capacity under development. Hawaii had an 8-megawatt expansion project under way. Idaho had six projects under development, which would increase its generating capacity by 251 megawatts. Nevada had forty-two projects under development, which would add 1,082 megawatts and more than quadruple its current generating capacity. New Mexico had a 10-megawatt plant under development. Oregon had eleven projects under way, totaling 297 megawatts of capacity. Utah planned to added 244 megawatts to its generating capacity with six geothermal electrical generating projects. Washington had one project of unspecified capacity under development. Finally, Wyoming, had a 0.2-megawatt project under way.

Total worldwide geothermal power generation (based on installed capacity) rose from 5,832 megawatts in 1990 to 8,933 megawatts in 2005, according to the Geothermal Resources Council. As of early 2005, the United States was the world's top generator, at 2,564 megawatts, followed by the Philippines (1,930 megawatts), Mexico (953 megawatts), Indonesia (797 megawatts), Italy (791 megawatts), Japan (535 megawatts), New Zealand (435 megawatts), and Iceland (202 megawatts), and fifteen more nations (producing fewer than 200 megawatts each).

### DIRECT USE: CURRENT AND FUTURE PROSPECTS

More geothermal energy is directly used as thermal energy than is used to generate electricity, both in the United States and worldwide. Direct use of geothermal energy includes space heating (both district heating and individual space heating), cooling, greenhouse heating, fish farming, agricultural drying, industrial process heat, snow melting, and swimming pool and spa heating.

In the United States, installed capacity for direct use of geothermal energy increased from 1,874 megawatts in 1995 to 7,817 megawatts in 2005. The U.S. yearly direct use increased from 3,859 gigawatt-hours per year in 1995 to 8,678 in 2005. The greatest direct use for geothermal energy in the United States, by a wide margin, is geothermal heat pumps. Of the 2005 direct-use figures, 7200 megawatts are for geothermal heat pumps. The 2005 U.S. capacities and yearly use rates for the other direct-use categories were as follows: individual space heating (146 megawatts, 371 gigawatt-hours per year); district heating (84 megawatts, 213 gigawatt hours per year); cooling (less than 1 megawatts, 4 gigawatt-hours per year); greenhouse heating (97 megawatts, 213 gigawatt-hours per year); fish farming (138 megawatts, 837 gigawatt-hours per year); agricultural drying (36 megawatts, 139 gigawatt-hours per year); industrial process heat (2 megawatts, 13 gigawatt-hours per year); snow melting (2 megawatts, 5 gigawatt-hours per year); and swimming pool and spa heating (112 megawatts, 706 gigawatt-hours per year).

Worldwide installed capacity for direct use increased from 8,604 megawatts in 1995 to 28,268 megawatts in 2005. Yearly direct use increased from 31,236 gigawatt-hours per year in 1995 to 75,943 gigawatt-hours per year in 2005. Countries with large direct use of geothermal energy, as of 2005, included the United States, Sweden, China, Iceland, Turkey, Japan, Hungary, Italy, and New Zealand. Eighty-nine percent of Iceland's space-heating needs were provided by geothermal energy in 2005, and projections indicated that 30 percent of Turkey's space heating would be geothermal by 2010.

Geothermal heat pumps are economical, energy efficient, and available in most places. They provide space heating and cooling and water heating. They have been shown to reduce energy consumption by 20 to 40 percent. Their use worldwide increased greatly between 2000 and 2005. In energy production from geothermal heat pumps the five-year increase was 272 percent for an average annual growth of 30 percent. As of 2005, there were approximately 1.7 million units installed in thirty-three countries, with the majority concentrated in the United States and Europe. In the United States, fifty to sixty thousand geothermal heat pump units are installed per year.

Enhanced geothermal systems constitute an emerging technology. Most current geothermal systems use steam or hot water that is extracted from a well drilled into a geothermal reservoir. Geothermal resources available for use can be expanded greatly, however, by using geothermal resources that do not produce hot water or steam directly but can be used to heat water to a sufficient temperature by injecting water into the hot underground region using injection wells and extracting it through production wells. The term "engineered geothermal system" is also used for this type of system. For this system, increasing the natural permeability of the rock may be necessary, so that adequate water flow in and out of the hot rock can be obtained. Estimates indicate that use of geothermal resources requiring enhanced geothermal systems would make more that 100,000 megawatts of economically usable generating capacity available in the United States. This is more than thirty times the 2009 U.S. geothermal generating capacity.

*William O. Rasmussen, updated by Harlan H. Bengtson*

FURTHER READING

Armstead, H. Christopher H. *Geothermal Energy: Its Past, Present, and Future Contributions to the Energy Needs of Man.* 2d ed. New York: E. & F. N. Spon, 1983.

Batchelor, Tony, and Robin Curtis. "Geothermal Energy." In *Energy: Beyond Oil,* edited by Fraser Armstrong and Katherine Blundell. New York: Oxford University Press, 2007.

Dickson, Mary H., and Mario Fanelli, eds. *Geothermal Energy: Utilization and Technology.* 1995. Reprint. Sterling, Va.: Earthscan, 2005.

DiPippo, Ronald. *Geothermal Power Plants: Principles, Application, Case Studies and Environmental Impact.* 2d ed. Boston: Butterworth-Heinemann, 2008.

Gupta, Harsh K., and Sukanta Roy. *Geothermal Energy: An Alternative Resource for the Twenty-first Century.* Boston: Elsevier, 2007.

Lee, Sunggyu, and H. Bryan Lanterman. "Geothermal Energy." In *Handbook of Alternative Fuel Technologies,* edited by Sunggyu Lee, James G. Speight, and Sudarshan K. Loyalka. Boca Raton, Fla.: Taylor & Francis, 2007.

Lienau, Paul J., et al. *Reference Book on Geothermal Direct Use.* Klamath Falls, Oreg.: Geo-Heat Center, Oregon Institute of Technology, 1994.

Lund, John W. "Characteristics, Development and Utilization of Geothermal Resources." *Geo-Heat Center Quarterly Bulletin* 28, no. 2 (2007).

Lund, John W., Derek H. Freeston, and Tonya Boyd. "World-Wide Direct Uses of Geothermal Energy 2005." *Proceedings of the World Geothermal Congress 2005* (April, 2005).

McCaffrey, Paul, ed. *U.S. National Debate Topic, 2008-2009: Alternative Energy.* New York: H. W. Wilson, 2008.

Rinehart, John S. *Geysers and Geothermal Energy.* New York: Springer, 1980.

Simon, Christopher A. "Geothermal Energy." In *Alternative Energy: Political, Economic, and Social Feasibility.* Lanham, Md.: Rowman & Littlefield, 2007.

Slack, Kara. *U.S. Geothermal Power Production and Development Update.* Washington, D.C.: Geothermal Energy Association, 2008.

WEB SITES

OREGON INSTITUTE OF TECHNOLOGY
Geo-Heat Center
http://geoheat.oit.edu
U.S. Department of Energy
Geothermal
http://www.energy.gov/energysources/geothermal.htm

U.S. GEOLOGICAL SURVEY
Geothermal Energy: Clean Power from the Earth's Heat
http://pubs.usgs.gov/circ/2004/c1249

SEE ALSO: Department of Energy, U.S.; Earth's crust; Energy economics; Energy politics; Geysers and hot springs; Ocean thermal energy conversion; Plate tectonics; Renewable and nonrenewable resources; Thermal pollution and thermal pollution control; Tidal energy; Water.

# Germanium

CATEGORY: Mineral and other nonliving resources

## WHERE FOUND
Germanium is the thirty-sixth most abundant element in the Earth's crust, with an average abundance of about 7 grams per metric ton. It occurs in small quantities in ores of silver, such as argyrodite, as well as in ores of copper and zinc, and is found most abundantly in Germany.

## PRIMARY USES
Germanium is of central importance in the manufacture of semiconductor materials and devices, especially transistors. It is also used in a variety of optical devices.

## TECHNICAL DEFINITION
Germanium, symbol Ge, is located in Group IVA of the periodic table, having atomic number 32 and an atomic weight of 72.59. It is a hard, brittle, grayish-white metal. Its melting point is 937.4° Celsius, its boiling point is 2,830° Celsius, and its specific gravity is 5.32.

## DESCRIPTION, DISTRIBUTION, AND FORMS
Germanium forms a diamond-like tetrahedral crystal lattice similar to that of silicon. On the Mohs hardness scale, its hardness is six (diamond is ten). Germanium exhibits valences of +2 and +4. The +2 state is both easily reduced to the element and also oxidized to +4 germanium. Finely divided germanium ignites in chlorine gas to form germanium tetrachloride, and germanium forms a tetrahydride with hydrogen, which is a gas under ordinary conditions.

At low temperatures, pure germanium is almost an insulator because its four valence electrons are localized in the bonds between neighboring atoms. At room temperature, sufficient electrons enter higher-energy levels, become mobile, and conduct a weak current. The conductivity of germanium can be improved by the addition (doping) of 1 part per million of a Group V element, such as arsenic, because it has one more electron than germanium, or by the addition of a Group III element, such as indium, which has one less valence electron than germanium.

## HISTORY
Germanium was discovered in 1886 by the German chemist Clemens Winkler and was named in honor of Germany. Ultrapure germanium is an intrinsic semiconductor, which accounts for its major use in solid-state electronics. Furthermore, it can be produced in near-crystalline perfection more easily than any other semiconductor. Thus the electronic properties of germanium have been widely studied. The earliest research on semiconductors was done with germanium,

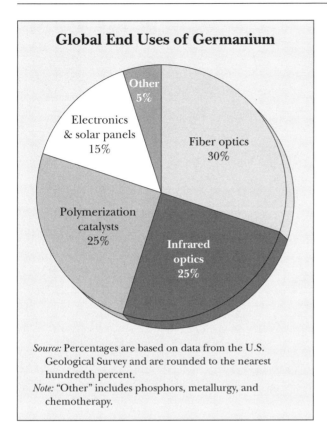

**Global End Uses of Germanium**

Other 5%

Electronics & solar panels 15%

Fiber optics 30%

Polymerization catalysts 25%

Infrared optics 25%

*Source:* Percentages are based on data from the U.S. Geological Survey and are rounded to the nearest hundredth percent.
*Note:* "Other" includes phosphors, metallurgy, and chemotherapy.

and William Shockley used it to make the first transistor in 1948.

OBTAINING GERMANIUM

Germanium is recovered by treating enriched wastes and residues from zinc sulfide ores, pyrometallic ores, and coal with hydrochloric acid to form a volatile liquid which is extracted with carbon tetrachloride and purified by distillation. The resulting germanium tetrachloride is treated with demineralized water to precipitate germanium dioxide, which is then reduced to germanium with hydrogen. The highly pure element, which contains impurities less than 1 part per million, is obtained by zone refining, a selective fusion-recrystallization process that concentrates impurities which can be removed from the melt.

USES OF GERMANIUM

The major use of germanium is in semiconductor devices, such as transistors, diodes, solar cells, and solar batteries. It is also used in infrared optical devices, such as lenses, prisms, and windows, and germanium dioxide is used to produce optical glasses of high re-

fractive index. Magnesium germanate is used in phosphors, and an alloy of germanium and gold is used in dental materials.

*Alvin K. Benson*

WEB SITE

U.S. GEOLOGICAL SURVEY
Minerals Information: Germanium Statistics and Information
http://minerals.usgs.gov/minerals/pubs/commodity/germanium/

SEE ALSO: Alloys; Arsenic; Copper; Indium; Silicon; Silver; Solar energy; Zinc.

# Germany

CATEGORIES: Countries; government and resources

*Germany lacks large amounts of natural resources with the exception of coal. The country has large deposits of anthracite and bituminous coal, also known as black or hard coal, located in the Ruhr and Saarland, and large deposits of lignite, or brown coal, located in Leipziger Bucht and Niederlausitz.*

THE COUNTRY

Germany is located in central Europe. It is bordered in the north by the North Sea, Denmark, and the Baltic Sea; in the west by the Netherlands, Belgium, France, and Luxembourg; in the south by Switzerland and Austria; and in the east by Poland, the Czech Republic, and Austria. Germany is primarily a country of basins, hills, and high and low plains except for the Harz Mountains in the central highlands and the Bavarian alps in the south. Germany has an abundance of rivers, including the Elbe, the Oder, and the Danube, which is the second largest river in Europe.

Germany has the largest economy in Europe and the third largest in the world. It ranked sixth in the world in purchasing power parity in 2008. Germany is one of the most technologically advanced countries in the world. Its economy is basically one of free enterprise, though government control exists in some sectors. Germany ranks among the world's largest producers of iron, steel, coal, and cement. Germany exports approximately one-third of its production. In 2008, Germany was ranked second in exports and

# Germany: Resources at a Glance

*Official name:* Federal Republic of Germany
*Government:* Federal republic
*Capital city:* Berlin
*Area:* 137, 857 mi²; 357,022 km²
*Population (2009 est.):* 82,329,758
*Language:* German
*Monetary unit:* euro (EUR)

## ECONOMIC SUMMARY:

*GDP composition by sector (2008 est.):* agriculture, 0.9%; industry, 30.1%; services, 69.1%
*Natural resources:* coal, lignite, natural gas, iron ore, copper, nickel, uranium, potash, salt, construction materials, timber, arable land, hydropower potential
*Land use (2005):* arable land, 33.13%; permanent crops, 0.6%; other, 66.27%
*Industries:* iron, steel, coal, cement, chemicals, machinery, vehicles, machine tools, electronics, food and beverages, shipbuilding, textiles
*Agricultural products:* potatoes, wheat, barley, sugar beets, fruit, cabbages, cattle, pigs, poultry
*Exports (2008 est.):* $1.498 trillion
*Commodities exported:* machinery, vehicles, chemicals, metals and manufactures, foodstuffs, textiles
*Imports (2008 est.):* $1.232 trillion
*Commodities imported:* machinery, vehicles, chemicals, foodstuffs, textiles, metals
*Labor force (2008 est.):* 43.6 million
*Labor force by occupation (2005):* agriculture, 2.4%; industry, 29.7%; services, 67.8%

## ENERGY RESOURCES:

*Electricity production (2007 est.):* 594.7 billion kWh
*Electricity consumption (2006 est.):* 549.1 billion kWh
*Electricity exports (2007 est.):* 62.31 billion kWh
*Electricity imports (2007 est.):* 42.87 billion kWh

*Natural gas production (2007 est.):* 17.96 billion m³
*Natural gas consumption (2007 est.):* 97.44 billion m³
*Natural gas exports (2007 est.):* 12.22 billion m³
*Natural gas imports (2007 est.):* 88.35 billion m³
*Natural gas proved reserves (Jan. 2008 est.):* 254.8 billion m³

*Oil production (2007 est.):* 148,100 bbl/day
*Oil imports (2005):* 3.026 million bbl/day
*Oil proved reserves (Jan. 2008 est.):* 367 million bbl

*Source:* Data from *The World Factbook 2009.* Washington, D.C.: Central Intelligence Agency, 2009.
*Notes:* Data are the most recent tracked by the CIA. Values are given in U.S. dollars. Abbreviations: bbl/day = barrels per day; GDP = gross domestic product; km² = square kilometers; kWh = kilowatt-hours; m³ = cubic meters; mi² = square miles.

third in imports in the world. Germany's main trading partners are European Union members, the United States, and China.

## HARD COAL

Coal is a fossil fuel containing carbon. Hard coal, also called black coal, is either bituminous or anthracite, depending on the percentage of carbon it contains. Bituminous coal contains 45 to 86 percent carbon; anthracite has a higher percentage of carbon, ranging from 86 to 97 percent.

In Germany, anthracite and bituminous are found in the Ruhr and in Saarland. In 2005, Germany had 152 million metric tons of anthracite and bituminous reserves. Both anthracite and bituminous require underground mining. In the 1950's, hard-coal mining in Germany was at its peak. The mines produced 136 million metric tons. Since that time, the amount of coal mined has decreased considerably. In 2005, 23.2 million metric tons were mined. The reduction in hard-coal mining has been because hard coal can be imported more cheaply than it can be mined domestically. The industry has had to be subsidized by the government in order to be profitable. However, in 2005, 20 percent of electricity in Germany was still generated by burning domestically mined black coal. In addition, the steel industry used 5.4 million metric tons of the 2005 production total. Also in 2005, Germany imported 40,898 metric tons of coal; in 2007, the amount of hard coal imported rose to 50,996 metric tons.

Environmental concerns and European Union policies and directives have caused problems for Germany's hard-coal mining industry. Land destruction and water pollution are the primary environmental concerns. The problem of greenhouse gases is also of great importance. When burned, coal emits considerable amounts of carbon dioxide, the major greenhouse gas, and significant amounts of sulfur, nitrous oxide, and mercury. Because of the pollutants created by both mining and burning the coal, Germany has attempted to replace coal as a major energy resource with cleaner fuels, such as natural gas or biogas or solar, wind, or hydropower. The government of Germany has set several goals for using renewable energy sources. In 2000, the German government established a goal to produce 4.5 percent of its primary energy consumption from renewable sources by 2010. The proposed goal for 2050 is that one-half of the energy will be provided by renewable sources. In 2007, the

German government made the decision to phase out the mining of hard coal starting in 2009. The plan is to be completed by 2018 but must be reviewed by the German parliament in 2012.

In January, 2007, when the government and the mining companies agreed to ceasing the production of coal, eight underground mines still produced hard coal. Seven of them were located in the Ruhr industrial region, and one was in Saarland. Coal mining has long been a significant industry in Germany, and opposition exists to the elimination of underground mining. In 2007, the underground mines provided employment for about 33,000 people. This creates unemployment and retirement-benefits problems. The underground mines and the companies involved in this type of mining also play an important role in the country's economy as a base for the mining equipment industry. Germany is a world leader in the manufacture and export of such equipment. The final complication is that phasing out the mines will make Germany totally dependent on imports for coal.

## LIGNITE

Lignite, also called brown coal, is a fossil fuel that requires considerable processing before it is suitable for burning. It has a high moisture content and crumbles easily. It has a much lower heating value than hard coal. Almost 5 metric tons of lignite are needed to produce as much energy as 1 metric ton of hard coal. However, lignite has played an important role in the German economy, especially in that of East Germany before the reunification of the country, and still provides a considerable number of jobs. There are 6.6 million metric tons of lignite reserves located in the Leipziger Bucht and Niederlausitz regions. Lignite is extracted by strip-mining, which causes extensive environmental damage. The processing of lignite produces large amounts of greenhouse gases. The intensive mining of lignite by East Germany caused severe damage to the forests, lakes, and rivers in the areas where mining occurred and damage, to a lesser degree, throughout Germany and neighboring countries. Beginning in 1990 there was a reduction in the use of lignite. Because of its detrimental effect upon the environment, lignite mining could be banned by Germany and the European Union. However, there are significant economic reasons for continuing to mine lignite. The cost of lignite is well below the world market price for other coals. It is less expensive to produce because it can be strip-mined, and the lignite industry provides a large number of jobs. Lignite provides an inexpensive domestic source of energy for Germany and provides 31 percent of Germany's electric power. Anthracite, bituminous, and lignite coal furnish 30 percent of Germany's energy needs.

## POTASH

Potash is used primarily in making fertilizers. It is produced from various potassium compounds in which the potassium is water soluble, including potassium carbonate and potassium oxide. Potash is produced from either underground mines, which are the most common, or solution mining. It is then milled and refined in processing plants, which separate the potassium chloride from the halite (salt) and process it into potash. Potash is found in the central part of western Germany and southern Germany. In the west, it is located in the Werra-Fulda district. In the Zechstein basin, there are six potash mines. All of the mines are under the ownership of K+S GmbH. In 2006, Germany ranked fourth among European Union countries in potash production. In 2007, Germany produced 7.4 million metric tons of potash. Traditionally, the world potash market has been one with a surplus of product; however, most believe that the demand will increase and raise the profitability of potash mining. This belief is based on the increasing world population; the increasing consumption of meat, requiring more animal feedstuffs; and the diminishing amount of land available for farming, which, in turn, must be fertilized more intensely for greater production.

## NATURAL GAS AND BIOGAS

Natural gas is a fossil fuel. It is a combustible mixture of hydrocarbon gases, primarily methane. When it is almost pure methane, it is referred to as dry gas. Natural gas is commonly found in the same areas as deposits of oil. It is clean burning and emits lower levels of pollutants into the air than other fossil fuels. Germany has 255 billion cubic meters of natural gas reserves, which is less than 1 percent of the total natural gas reserves in the world. In 2007, Germany produced nearly 18 billion cubic meters of natural gas but consumed more than 97 billion cubic meters. Thus, the country's production fell drastically short of providing for its natural gas needs. The 2008 numbers for production and consumption of natural gas were relatively the same. Germany imported 89.9 percent of the natural gas it used. Thus, Germany ranked second in the world in imports of natural gas. Of the natural

gas imported by Germany, 40 percent comes from Russia. Germany serves as the major hub of the pipeline system that brings natural gas from Russia into Europe.

Germany and other members of the European Union are concerned about their large dependency on imported natural gas to meet such a large portion of domestic energy needs. Consequently, the European Union is investigating the use of renewable resources. Germany is one of the leaders in the plan to replace imported natural gas with biogas generated by European Union countries. Biogas is a bio-based methane that is produced from three different sources: landfill gas, sewage sludge gas, and agricultural waste and similar matter. In Germany, biogas is the renewable energy resource that is receiving the greatest attention and development. Of the energy derived by Germany from renewable resources, 22 percent is from biogas; only wind outranks biogas as a renewable energy resource in Germany's energy production. In 2006, Germany accounted for 49 percent of the biogas produced in the European Union. The total amount of biogas produced by Germany was 1,932.2 kilotons of oil equivalent. The sources from which biogas was produced were landfill gas (approximately 37 percent), sewage sludge gas (approximately 13 percent), and agricultural waste and similar waste types (approximately 50 percent). Germany has proposed a goal to provide 10 percent of its total gas consumption from biogas by 2030.

## CRUDE OIL

Crude oil is a fossil fuel; the term "crude oil" refers to the oil before it is processed. In 2005, Germany ranked forty-seventh in production and seventh in consumption of oil among countries. Germany ranked fifth in imports and twenty-seventh in exports. In 2006, Germany imported the majority of its oil from Russia, Norway, and Libya. As of January, 2008, Germany had an estimated 367 million barrels of oil in proven reserves and ranked fifty-second in the world in proven reserves. The north and northeastern regions of Germany are the primary locations of these reserves. Oil accounts for 40 percent of the energy consumption in Germany. Domestic production provides only about 3 percent of the oil used in Germany. The amount of crude oil produced annually in Germany is approximately 2.7 million metric tons. Germany's largest crude oil deposit is at Mittelplate, off the German North Sea coast. This deposit furnishes approximately two-thirds of the crude oil produced in Germany each year. Germany also has oil fields located at Emlichheim in Lower Saxony and at Aitingen, south of Augsburg. The fields at Emlichheim produce approximately 127,000 metric tons per year; those at Aitingen produce about 32,700 metric tons. Although Germany does not have large crude oil deposits, it affords certain advantages in oil exploration. The price of crude oil is generally higher than elsewhere. Furthermore, the geological conditions present in the oil fields make them excellent places to develop new technologies and to solve problems of extracting oil. The German oil fields have been one of the major places where steam-flooding techniques and horizontal drilling have been used and perfected.

## HYDROPOWER

Hydropower uses the force of water to generate electricity. There are three types of hydropower stations: run-of-the-river, impoundment, and pump-storage plants. Run-of-the-river is the most common type. Pump-storage plants are the most efficient for controlling energy output and producing more electricity at peak periods of need, but impoundment and run-of-the river provide some storage electricity output. Germany has used hydropower as a source of energy for more than one hundred years. With Germany's lack of fossil fuels, concerns about greenhouse-gas emissions and the ever-increasing cost of fossil fuels, hydropower is and will remain an important source of electricity in Germany. However, much of the new hydropower capacity will probably be provided by mini-hydropower stations (below 1 megawatt) because of environmental concerns about both the damage done to wildlife and flora by the creation of dams and the impact of changing the flow of rivers. At the end of 2006, with 7,500 hydropower plants in operation, Germany had a total installed capacity of 4,700 megawatts. The 21.6 billion kilowatts of electricity generated by hydropower provided 3.5 percent of Germany's electricity demand. Germany's long history of using hydropower and of developing designs and technology for hydropower plants has made the country a major contributor to hydropower projects throughout the world.

## WIND POWER

Wind power harnesses the force of the wind through the use of windmills and turbines. Germany ranks first in the world in the use of energy derived from wind. In the past, the noise created by the turbines used in the wind stations limited the places where they could be located. With the development of quieter generators, the acceptability of wind stations has increased greatly. Thus, wind stations can be located in the most favorable areas for efficient production of wind energy. In 2007, Germany produced 1,677 megawatts from wind power. The tallest wind energy system in the world is located in Cottbus, Germany. It reaches a height of 205 meters and generated in excess of 5.6 million kilowatt-hours of electricity in 2005. The German wind systems, producing 6 megawatts, are the most powerful wind energy systems in the world. German scientists and engineers have built wind-operated generators with and without gears, and they have developed technologies which have enabled the use of wind power throughout the world. Although Germany's wind-power stations are land stations, German engineers and manufacturers are involved in developing systems placed offshore. There are projects in the seas near the coasts of Denmark, Sweden, and the Netherlands as well as Great Britain and Ireland.

## IRON ORE

Iron ore consists of iron, other minerals, and rock. It varies in color by its composition and may be light yellow, reddish brown, purple, or even gray. The ore is graded as high or low according to the amount of iron it contains. Any ore that contains less than 54 percent iron is assessed as low-grade ore. Germany's iron ore is almost entirely low-grade. The largest deposit of iron ore in Germany is southwest of Brunswick in the Harz Mountains. The ore is no longer mined. During the 1980's, Germany did considerable mining of iron ore. The output of iron ore reached its peak at 95,200 metric tons in 1989. Germany now imports the iron ore used in its thriving steel industry. Germany ranks third among the countries importing iron ore from South Africa. The iron ore exported to Germany accounts for almost 19 percent of the iron ore exported by South Africa.

## OTHER RESOURCES

Salt (NaCl) is an important resource in Germany. Salt for fertilizer and industrial uses is found in several areas in Germany, including Hesse, Thuringia, and Saxony, where the mining is often done at considerable depths (1,000 meters). Rock salt mined in limestone areas is used to produce table-grade salt. The Stetten Salt Mine near Haigerloch produces approximately

500,000 metric tons of salt annually. In 2006, Germany was the second largest producer of salt in the European Union.

Germany also ranked third among in the European Union in the production of kaolin, a fine clay used to manufacture porcelain and coated paper. Germany is also a leading producer of feldspar, which is used in both the glass and ceramic industries, and of crude gypsum, barite, and bentonite.

*Shawncey Webb*

FURTHER READING

Deublein, Dieter, and Angelika Steinhauser. *Biogas from Waste and Renewable Resources: An Introduction.* Weinheim, Germany: Wiley-VCH, 2008.

Førsund, Finn R. *Hydropower Economics.* New York: Springer, 2008.

Garrett, Donald E. *Potash: Deposits, Processing, Properties, and Uses.* New York: Chapman & Hall, 1996.

Gillis, Christopher. *Windpower.* Atglen, Pa.: Schiffer, 2008.

Master, Gilbert M. *Renewable and Efficient Electric Power Systems.* New York: John Wiley & Sons, 2004.

Williams, Alan, et al. *Combustion and Gasification of Coal.* New York: Taylor & Francis, 2000.

SEE ALSO: Coal; Hydroenergy; Oil and natural gas distribution; Oil industry; Potash; Wind energy.

companies at depressed prices, particularly that of Tide Water Oil, the nation's ninth largest oil company. As stocks rose, Getty became a multimillionaire.

IMPACT ON RESOURCE USE

After World War II, Getty expanded into the Middle East, challenging the powerful existing oil interests, the so-called Seven Sisters. He discovered oil in the neutral zone between Saudi Arabia and Kuwait in 1953. By 1957, he was the richest person in the United States, his wealth exceeding one billion dollars. Getty's fortune was invested in many businesses, but he personally held the controlling interests. He was a rugged individualist in an age of faceless corporations, a throwback to the likes of John D. Rockefeller and Andrew Carnegie. A trust fund had long been established for the Getty relatives. Getty's major bequest, $600 million, was to his art museum in Malibu, California (which later expanded and moved to the hills south of the Sepulveda Pass in Los Angeles), making it the best endowed in the world. After Getty Oil was sold to Texaco in 1984, the museum became Getty's lasting legacy.

*Eugene Larson*

SEE ALSO: Oil and natural gas exploration; Oil industry; Petroleum refining and processing; Rockefeller, John D.

# Getty, J. Paul

CATEGORY: People
BORN: December 15, 1892; Minneapolis, Minnesota
DIED: June 6, 1976; Sutton Place, Surrey, England

*Getty, an oil entrepreneur, was an exception in the mid-twentieth century world of anonymous corporations. He built his fortune through oil investments.*

BIOGRAPHICAL BACKGROUND

J. Paul Getty's father, George F. Getty, an insurance lawyer, became wealthy during the Oklahoma oil boom. Young Getty began his oil career in 1914, also in Oklahoma, and within three years, he was a millionaire. In the 1920's, father and son bought oil leases and drilled wells around Southern California. Getty's father died in 1930, and during the Great Depression, rather than drill wells, Getty bought oil stock in other

# Geysers and hot springs

CATEGORY: Geological processes and formations

*Hot springs are natural pools or springs of hot water occurring where water heated within the Earth reaches its surface. Geysers are essentially hot springs that erupt intermittently, throwing a stream of water, sometimes mixed with other materials, into the air.*

BACKGROUND

The heat that produces superheated water and the resulting geysers and hot springs originates in magma, molten rock beneath the Earth's crust. Such heat travels to the surface most easily through underground faults and fissures. Many areas with geysers and other geothermal features are tectonically active, subject to earthquakes and volcanoes. The geyser fields of Iceland and of North Island, New Zealand, show this connection. Magma may also rise through the Earth's crust and remain trapped and molten relatively near the Earth's surface. The Yellowstone geyser basin in the western United States is believed to lie atop such a heat source. Heat can be carried upward through porous rock layers to reservoirs of underground water; this process may account for some hot springs in areas that show no other geothermal features. Geysers and hot springs often exist in proximity to related geothermal phenomena such as fumaroles (steam vents) and bubbling mud pots.

Geysers are relatively rare, because they require the right combination of water channels, water pool, and heat cycle as well as an opening through which the hot water is ejected. Major geyser fields are found in the Yellowstone basin, Iceland, New Zealand, and Japan and on the Kamchatka Peninsula in Asiatic Russia. Smaller groups or isolated geysers occur in a few other regions, including Oregon, Nevada, and California in the United States. In contrast, there are more than five thousand known hot springs. They exist in almost every country and have been used by humanity since the beginning of history, and probably before.

### GEYSERS AND HOT SPRINGS AS AN ENERGY RESOURCE

Hot springs water was diverted for warm baths by the Etruscans and then the Romans, and subsequently by most societies which prized cleanliness. In New Zealand, the Maoris used hot springs directly for cooking and laundry purposes as well as bathing. In present-day Iceland, hot springs supply hot-water heating to most of Reykjavík's houses. Such heating is also used for Iceland's greenhouses, enabling fruits and vegetables to be grown in a generally cold, inhospitable climate. Russia has several towns whose buildings are heated by geothermal wells. Similar heating systems have been developed in such diverse locations as Hungary, Japan, and Klamath Falls, Oregon. Hot springs water is also used in agriculture for soil warming, in fish hatcheries, and for egg incubators.

The promise of cheap and relatively nonpolluting energy from geothermal sources was pursued beginning in the early 1900's. An electrical plant using

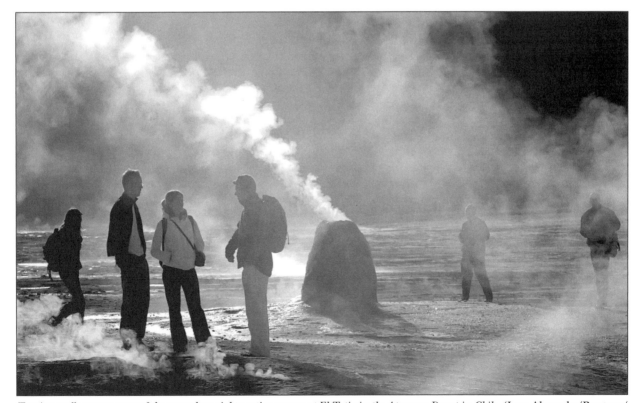

*Tourists walk among some of the more than eighty active geysers at El Tatio in the Atacama Desert in Chile.* (Ivan Alvarado/Reuters/Landov)

steam from steam vents to drive turbines was put into operation in Larderello, Italy, in 1913. Destroyed during World War II, it was later rebuilt as part of a larger power network. A large natural-steam plant was opened at The Geysers in Northern California in 1960, but its output later slowed because of over-drilling. Other geothermal power plants were built beginning in the late 1950's in various countries, including Mexico, Japan, New Zealand, and the former Soviet Union.

Large-scale exploitation of geyser fields, hot springs, and fumaroles to produce electricity presents two main problems. One is the threat of weakening the geothermal field through overuse. Geysers are fragile and complex, and many have already been destroyed through drilling or other human interference. The second problem involves the necessity to shield equipment against damage from mineral deposits. This damage can be lessened by filtering the steam or by employing binary systems using natural hot water to turn low-boiling-point fluids such as isobutane into steam.

SOCIAL AND HEALTH ASPECTS
Hot springs have been prized by many societies for their actual and presumed health benefits. Hot-springs bathing is relaxing; the heat and buoyancy also ease the pain and immobility of arthritis and other joint and muscle ailments. Drinking water from hot springs may act as a purgative or offer other benefits because of its dissolved minerals. For example, Tunbridge Wells in Kent was considered a miracle spring in eighteenth and nineteenth century England; one reason was that its high iron content cured anemia.

Bottled water from various hot springs is sold commercially. Hot springs have been nuclei for resorts and spas since ancient times. Among the best known in North America are Warm Springs, Georgia (made famous by the patronage of President Franklin D. Roosevelt); Hot Springs, Arkansas; and White Sulphur Springs, West Virginia. The spectacular geyser fields of Yellowstone National Park, Wyoming, and to a lesser extent those of Rotorua, New Zealand, attract a large tourist trade.

OTHER RESOURCES FROM HOT SPRINGS
    AND GEYSERS
Minerals extracted from hot springs water or taken from deposits at geyser sites include borax, sulfur, alum, and ammonium salts. Rivers that drain geothermally active areas pick up dissolved minerals that enrich soils or water supplies downstream. Neutral or alkaline hot springs support a variety of animal, plant, and bacterial life. During Yellowstone winters, elk and buffalo drink their water and browse the surrounding plant growth. A unique microbe from these springs is used in laboratory deoxyribonucleic acid (DNA) replication, and others have been studied for use as biodegradable solvents and as possible survivals of early life-forms.

*Emily Alward*

FURTHER READING
Armstead, H. Christopher H. *Geothermal Energy: Its Past, Present, and Future Contributions to the Energy Needs of Man.* 2d ed. New York: E. & F. N. Spon, 1983.
Bryan, T. Scott. *The Geysers of Yellowstone.* 4th ed. Boulder: University Press of Colorado, 2008.
_____. *Geysers: What They Are and How They Work.* 2d ed. Missoula, Mont.: Mountain Press, 2005.
Rinehart, John S. *Geysers and Geothermal Energy.* New York: Springer, 1980.

WEB SITES

GEYSER OBSERVATION AND STUDY ASSOCIATION
http://www.geyserstudy.org/default.asp

NATIONAL PARK SERVICE, U.S. DEPARTMENT OF THE
    INTERIOR
Geysers and How They Work
http://www.nps.gov/yell/naturescience/
    geysers.htm

SEE ALSO: Geothermal and hydrothermal energy; Hydrothermal solutions and mineralization; Marine vents; Plate tectonics; Steam and steam turbines.

# Glaciation

CATEGORY: Geological processes and formations

*Glaciation is the effect of glaciers on the Earth's surface, including erosion and the deposition of glaciated materials. Glaciers are related to a number of natural resources, helping to provide fresh water, rich soils, and deposits used for building materials.*

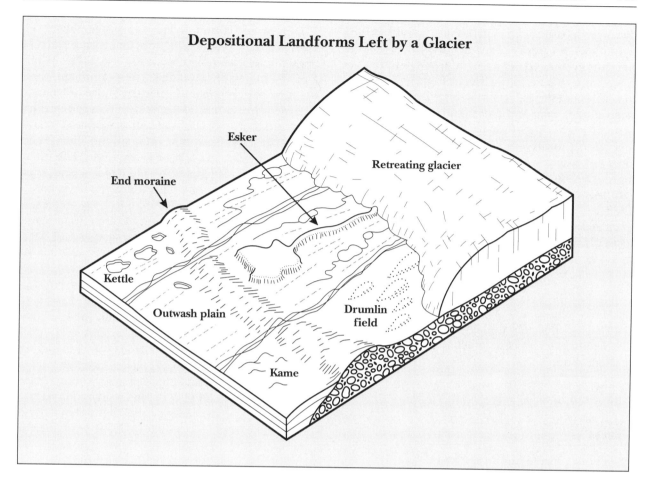

**Depositional Landforms Left by a Glacier**

## DEFINITION

The American Geological Institute's *Dictionary of Geological Terms* defines glaciation as the "alteration of the Earth's solid surface through erosion and deposition by glacier ice." As much as 75 percent of Earth's fresh water is tied up in the form of glaciers and ice caps. Glaciation has a profound effect on climate (as does climate on glaciation), and glaciers have important economic benefits. For example, water melted from glaciers is an important source of fresh water.

## OVERVIEW

Glaciers begin above the snow line. Snow becomes compacted into granules, and as additional snow is added, weight and pressure lead to recrystallization in the form of dense glacial ice. Once the ice reaches sufficient thickness, the internal strength of the crystals is overcome by the weight of the ice, and the ice begins to flow in the form of a glacier. Glaciers can flow by internal deformation only, or by deformation in

combination with basal sliding on a thin layer of meltwater. As glaciers flow, they erode the surface of the Earth, scouring it and plucking up boulders large and small. Glaciated valleys are distinctly U-shaped, as contrasted with the typical V shape of river valleys.

Glacial scouring can create a number of landforms. These include small, steep-sided valleys called cirques and sharp ridges called arêtes. Three or more cirque valleys can leave land in a recognizable horn shape, such as the famous Matterhorn in the Pennine Alps. Smaller glaciers feed larger glaciers much the same way that small rivers feed larger ones. Since the depth of scour is proportional to the mass of the glacier, smaller tributaries can leave forms known as hanging valleys isolated more than 100 meters above a steep-sided main valley.

Rock and boulders pushed or carried along by a glacier form moraines, drumlins, and glacial till. As glaciers retreat, they leave their burden of rock behind. Erratics, boulders that have been carried great distances and then left behind as glaciers retreat, have been used since prehistoric times as construction material for homes and stone fences. Meltwater from glaciers can sort transported sand and gravel, forming long sinuous eskers and landforms called kames. The finely graded sand and gravel is an important source of aggregate for the construction industry.

In some northern countries, meltwater from glaciers not only is used as a source of fresh water but also—where there is sufficient height and volume—can be used to generate hydroelectric power. Glaciation has other important economic benefits. The scouring effect of glaciers creates a fine dust-sized material called loess. Wind eventually transports and deposits the mineral-rich loess, helping to create some of the richest agricultural soils in the world.

*Raymond U. Roberts*

SEE ALSO: Agronomy; Climate and resources; Farmland; Hydroenergy; Hydrology and the hydrologic cycle; Sedimentary processes, rocks, and mineral deposits; Soil; Water.

# Glass

CATEGORY: Products from resources

*"Glass" commonly describes materials rich in silicon dioxide that are produced by solidification from the molten state without crystallizing. Glass's many valuable qualities have made it one of the most widely used materials in the world, with applications ranging from windows to optical instruments to electronics.*

## BACKGROUND

Glass, although it has been a commonplace material for centuries, is an exceptional substance: It is a solid that is technically considered a liquid. All other familiar solids are crystalline in structure. That is, they possess a definite, orderly internal geometric form that is a reflection of the arrangement of their constituent atoms. Their atoms are packed in repetitive forms called crystal networks or lattices. Liquids, in contrast, are termed amorphous in structure. They lack the rigid, repeating internal structure of solids. Glasses can be considered a borderline case between classic solids and liquids, and they have been called "amorphous solids."

Glasses are considered to be "supercooled" liquids—liquids chilled so rapidly that they never undergo the crystallization process of true solids. When a solid's molecules cool down from a molten state, the material undergoes a series of internal dynamic changes in response to the loss of heat. Molecules move in a more rigid fashion until reaching a point at which their patterns of movement and their interatomic bonds reach a state of discontinuity. This point of discontinuity is commonly called the freezing point of the solid; at this point it begins rapidly to lock into the pattern of crystallinity. Liquids, such as glasses, never actually reach this point of discontinuity and are considered to be in a "metastable" state. Glasses, besides possessing liquid structures, are typically also solutions; that is, they are composed of homogenous mixtures of substances possessing dissimilar molecular structures. The primary constituent of most common glass is silica, or silicon dioxide ($SiO_2$). Soda (sodium oxide), lime (calcium oxide), and small amounts of many other possible materials, including boron oxide, aluminum oxide, and magnesium oxide, are also used in the making of sand.

The properties of glass can be modified by industrial processes to suit various uses, but in general these properties include a generally excellent resistance to chemical corrosion; a high resistance to heat; an outstanding ability to insulate against electrical current, even at high voltages; high surface smoothness; good scratch resistance; a high ratio of weight to strength, coupled with a tendency toward brittleness; radiation absorbance and sensitivity; and a range of optical properties that include the ability to disperse, refract, or reflect light. All of the foregoing properties have made various forms of glass a preferred material for numerous applications.

## INGREDIENTS AND MANUFACTURE

Silica—in the form of sand that is processed and cleaned before use—is the primary ingredient in almost all glass. In addition, the common glass that is generally used in such items as bottles, drinking glasses, lightbulbs, and window glass (sheet glass) contains soda ($Na_2O$), which makes the glass easier to work with in manufacturing, and lime (CaO), which overcomes weaknesses introduced by the soda. A wide range of other materials may be used in small amounts, among them aluminum oxide and magnesium oxide. The three most common types of glass are soda-lime glass, borosilicate glass, and lead glass. Lead glass, used in optics and "crystal" tableware, is soda-lime glass to which lead oxide is added to provide exceptional clarity and refractivity. Boron oxide is added in the production of borosilicate glass, used in kitchenware (such as Pyrex) and laboratory ware because it resists breakage during rapid temperature changes.

Both window glass (sheet glass) and plate glass are soda-lime glass, but their manufacturing processes are different. Window glass, for example, is cooled, flattened into shape by rollers, then finished and cut into standard sizes. The manufacture of plate glass is more complex; the glass is strengthened by annealing, then ground smooth and polished. Plate glass is stronger and has less distortion than window glass. Safety glass, or laminated glass, as used in automobile windshields, generally contains a layer of plastic between two layers of glass to keep the glass from shattering completely upon impact.

## HISTORY

The production of synthetic glass has a long history. In fact, aside from metallurgy, glassmaking can be considered the oldest of industrial arts practiced by early civilizations. The use of natural high-silica minerals having glasslike properties, such as obsidian (produced by volcanic action and sometimes called volcanic glass), is even older. It can be traced many tens of thousands of years into prehistory back to the early Paleolithic era (the Old Stone Age). Early humans and even protohominids made tools and weapons by "flintknapping": shaping obsidian and obsidian-like rocks and minerals by percussion and pressure flaking. These materials were artfully manipulated; prehistoric artisans took advantage of the natural tendency of glasses to be brittle and to break at the surface into chonchoidal fractures (arcuate shapes). Blades, chisels, awls, gouges, and other implements could be produced in this way.

*An employee at a Russian factory cuts a large piece of glass.* (Lystseva Marina/ITAR-TASS/Landov)

The earliest artificial glass was produced at least three thousand years ago in Egypt for decorative purposes. Colored glazes were fired onto pottery or stone beads and other objects, originally in imitation of the surface colors and lusters of precious and semi-precious stones. Eventually, experimentation led to the development of freestanding, three-dimensional glass objects such as vials and bottles. This development is believed to have occurred in Egypt around 1500 B.C.E. during the New Kingdom period. Eventually, much higher transparency and ease of fabrication evolved with the discovery of the art of glassblowing, circa 50 B.C.E., in the area of Phoenicia (modern coastal Lebanon). Glassmaking and glassblowing spread rapidly throughout the Mediterranean world with the expansion of the Roman Empire but declined with the waning of the Roman civilization. Glassmaking centers survived in the Middle East and other areas. Eventually glassmaking experienced a resurgence in Europe beginning in the eleventh century, and new techniques and glass compositions were developed. Glass technology continued to improve gradually until the nineteenth century, when it experienced rapid improvements because of the increasing needs of science and the new industries spawned by the Industrial Revolution. Experimenters such as Michael Faraday contributed greatly to the understanding of the physics and chemistry of glass during the nineteenth century. A glassblowing machine had been developed by the 1890's, and automated machines were producing molded and blown glass items in the early twentieth century. The growing demands of science and industry in the twentieth century engendered the production of glasses of increasingly sophisticated composition and fabrication.

## USES OF GLASS

The earliest use of synthetic glass seems to have been in the form of decorative or artistic objects, including jewelry. Glass is still considered an artistic medium and an attractive material for decoration; it is used in sculpture, stained glass windows, vases, vials, jewelry, and mirrors. Particularly beginning with the Industrial Revolution, however, glass has been much more extensively used in the form of utilitarian objects and devices. Plate glass, sheet glass, and wired glass are found in virtually every modern building and vehicle, whether automobile, boat, or aircraft. Countless glass bottles and jars are used in every country to store and transport liquids of all sorts. Lighting fixtures in the form of incandescent and fluorescent lightbulbs and tubes are one of the most familiar of modern uses of glass, and they number in the billions. Hundreds of millions of glass cathode-ray tubes (CRTs) are found worldwide in the form of television sets and video display terminals (VDTs) for personal computers. Military and civilian applications of optical-quality glass elements in the form of magnifying lenses for microscopes, telescopes, binoculars, periscopes, prisms, and other eyepieces also number in the millions and are in use on land, at sea, and in the air. Structural insulation in the form of glass fiber mats is a common manufactured good produced from fine, woollike glass fibers.

Chemistry and physics laboratories use glass extensively in the form of piping, tubes, rods, storage vessels, vacuum flasks, and beakers. Some of the more sophisticated recent uses of glass are in the telecommunication industry. Optical fibers (or fiber optics) are very fine, flexible, high-quality glass strands designed to transmit signals in the form of light impulses.

*Frederick M. Surowiec*

FURTHER READING

Doremus, Robert H. *Glass Science*. 2d ed. New York: Wiley, 1994.

Frank, Susan. *Glass and Archaeology*. New York: Academic Press, 1982.

Macfarlane, Alan, and Gerry Martin. *Glass: A World History*. Chicago: University of Chicago Press, 2002.

Shackelford, James F., and Robert H. Doremus, eds. *Ceramic and Glass Materials: Structure, Properties, and Processing*. New York: Springer, 2008.

Shelby, James E. *Introduction to Glass Science and Technology*. 2d ed. Cambridge, England: Royal Society of Chemistry, 2005.

Sinton, Christopher W. *Raw Materials for Industrial Glass and Ceramics: Sources, Processes, and Quality Control*. Hoboken, N.J.: Wiley, 2006.

Zerwick, Chloe. *A Short History of Glass*. Redesigned and updated 2d ed. New York: H. N. Abrams in association with the Corning Museum of Glass, 1990.

WEB SITE

CORNING MUSEUM OF GLASS
A Resource on Glass
http://www.cmog.org/dynamic.aspx?id=264

SEE ALSO: Ceramics; Crystals; Fiberglass; Oxides; Oxygen; Potash; Quartz; Sand and gravel; Silicates; Silicon.

# Global Strategy for Plant Conservation

CATEGORIES: Laws and conventions; organizations, agencies, and programs

DATE: Adopted April 2002

*The Global Strategy for Plant Conservation (GSPC) aims to protect plant species from extinction. Estimates indicate that there are as many as 300,000 plant species in the world and that more than 9,000 of them are facing extinction. GSPC provides a framework for international and regional cooperation to protect plant diversity.*

## BACKGROUND

At the end of the twentieth century, scientists estimated that as much as 15 percent of the world's plant species were at risk of extinction. In 1999, at a meeting of the International Botanical Congress held in St. Louis, Missouri, an urgent call was made for an international effort to preserve plant diversity. In 2000, a smaller group of botanists from conservation organizations met in Grand Canary, Canary Islands, and drew up the Gran Canaria Declaration on Climate Change and Plant Conservation. In April, 2002, this declaration, in turn, was presented to and expanded by the 180 parties of the United Nations Convention on Biological Diversity, who unanimously called for a Global Strategy for Plant Conservation (GSPC). To help countries understand and address the specific targets of the GSPC, several international and American plant conservation organizations joined to form the Global Partnership for Plant Conservation in 2003. As of 2009, the United States had signed but not ratified the Convention on Biological Diversity.

## PROVISIONS

The strategy presents six broad tasks: conducting research and establishing databases to produce a clear record of existing plant diversity; conserving plant diversity, particularly those plants that are directly important to human survival; controlling the use and exchange of plant diversity to sustain diversity and to provide fair distribution of benefits; educating the public about the importance of plant diversity; training an expanded corps of conservation officers; and establishing networks and organizations to expand the capacity for conserving plant diversity. To accomplish these tasks, the strategy identified sixteen specific international targets to be reached by 2010. These targets included compiling a list of all of the known plant species, assuring that no endangered plant species were harmed through international trade, and ensuring the protection of 50 percent of the most important plant diversity areas. Each nation created its own internal targets, in collaboration with other nations.

## IMPACT ON RESOURCE USE

A 2008 progress report to the Conference of the Parties to the Convention on Biological Diversity reported substantial progress on eight of the sixteen specific targets and was generally optimistic about the chances for meeting several of the targets by 2010, thanks to enhanced national, regional, and international structures and strategies. Several countries, including Ireland, the United Kingdom, and South Africa, have drawn up aggressive plans to protect biodiversity, and in 2007, China announced a massive "National Strategy for Plant Conservation," hoping to save five thousand threatened species from extinction. By 2009, 189 countries had endorsed the GSPC.

*Cynthia A. Bily*

## WEB SITES

BOTANIC GARDENS CONSERVATION INTERNATIONAL
The Global Partnership for Plant Conservation
http://www.plants2010.org/

UNITED NATIONS ENVIRONMENT PROGRAMME (UNEP)
Global Strategy for Plant Conservation
http://www.cbd.int/gspc/

SEE ALSO: Biodiversity; Conservation; Conservation biology; Ecosystem services; Ecosystems; Ecozones and biogeographic realms; Endangered species; Endangered Species Act; Svalbard Global Seed Vault; United Nations Environment Programme.

# Global 200

CATEGORY: Ecological resources

*The Global 200 are ecoregions that have been designated for conservation in order to preserve the Earth's biological diversity. This group of ecoregions contains a diverse collection of plants, animals, and sea life.*

## DEFINITION

In 1961, a group of individuals became alarmed at the increasing rate of species extinction. The group formed the World Wildlife Fund (WWF) to work toward preservation of biological diversity (biodiversity) by fostering conservation methods. WWF is a nonprofit organization headquartered in Gland, Switzerland, that has become one of the largest environmental organizations in the world. The tropical rain forests contain half of the world's plant and animal species and are the focus of many conservation groups. However, WWF realized that the other half of the species also needed to be protected.

## OVERVIEW

The Global 200 is actually 238 ecoregions, containing most of the world's plant and animal species. An ecoregion is a large area of land or water that contains a distinct grouping of species that interact in the same environmental conditions. The 238 ecoregions were chosen from a total of 867 ecoregions. The 238 ecoregions comprise 142 terrestrial, 53 freshwater, and 43 marine ecoregions. The Global 200 were selected as the most critical ecoregions to be preserved if the world's biodiversity is to be saved.

The classification process divides the Earth's landmass into eight realms (kingdoms or ecozones) based on the grouping of animals and plants. The biome system divides the world into ecosystems based on climate and vegetation. Ecoregions are parts of biomes (major habitat types) that are distinct because of their plants, animals, or climate. The Global 200 were chosen to encompass the widest selection of the world's plants and animals. They contain all major habitat types, each of the different ecosystems, and species from every major habitat type.

WWF assigns a conservation status to each ecoregion in the Global 200. The three levels of status are critical (endangered), vulnerable, and stable. More than one-half of the Global 200 are rated as critical.

The WWF has more than thirteen hundred conservation projects in progress around the world and finds partners around the world to work on local projects. The partners include local leaders, nonprofit organizations, regional governments, and businesses. All are encouraged to protect and preserve the Global 200. WWF produces informational materials on conservation of species and habitats. The foundation also works with government leaders to initiate projects of conservation. One major research topic concerns invasive species and how their invasions can be stopped. WWF started the Living Planet Campaign in the late 1990's to encourage people, businesses, and governments to protect the Global 200 by reducing humankind's impact on natural habitats. As part of the campaign, the ship *Odyssey* has visited some of the Global 200.

*C. Alton Hassell*

## WEB SITE

WORLD WILDLIFE FUND
http://www.panda.org

SEE ALSO: Biodiversity; Conservation; Conservation biology; Earthwatch Institute; Ecology; Ecosystems; Ecozones and biogeographic realms; Endangered species; Endangered Species Act.

# Global warming. *See* Greenhouse gases and global climate change

# Gneiss

CATEGORY: Mineral and other nonliving resources

*The term "gneiss" is used loosely to encompass many different mineral combinations and a variety of structures. It includes a great many rocks of uncertain origins.*

## DEFINITION

In the narrowest meaning of "gneiss" (pronounced "nice"), it is defined as a coarse-grained, feldspar-rich, metamorphic rock with a parallel structure (foliation) that assumes the form of streaks and bands.

Gneiss is primarily identified by its structure rather than by its composition. It is a medium- to coarse-grained banded or coarsely foliated crystalline rock.

The rock is characterized by a preferred orientation of platy grains such as biotite, muscovite, or hornblende, or the segregation of minerals into bands or stripes. Unlike schist, gneiss is more often characterized by granular minerals than by platy minerals. Most gneisses are light to dark gray, pink, or red because of the high feldspar content.

## OVERVIEW

Gneiss is exposed in regions of uplift where erosion has stripped away surficial rocks (sediments and lower grade metamorphic rocks) to expose rocks that have been altered at depth. In North America, gneiss may be found in New England, in the central Atlantic states, the Rockies, the Cascades, and much of Canada.

Gneiss, with mineralogy similar to that of granite, has similar uses except that it is generally restricted by the presence of a higher percentage of ferromagnesium minerals and micas, which weather rapidly to weaken and discolor the finished stone. The major use is as riprap, aggregate, and dimension stone. Wavy foliation in polished slabs results in an especially decorative stone for monuments.

The most common gneisses are similar to granite in composition and resemble granite except for the foliation. The predominant minerals are equidimensional grains of quartz and potassium feldspar, usually microcline. Sodium plagioclase may also be present. Biotite, muscovite, and hornblende, alone or in combination, are the most common minerals that define the foliation. Other minerals, almost exclusively metamorphic in origin, that may be present in minor quantities include almandine garnet, andalusite, staurolite, and sillimanite.

True gneiss is a high-grade metamorphic rock formed by recrystallization and chemical reaction within existing rocks in response to high temperature and pressure at great depths in the Earth's crust. Often the precursor rock is a feldspar-rich sandstone, a clay-rich sediment such as shale, or granite. Gneissic fabric may be produced in some igneous rocks by flowage within a magma. Some gneisses are formed by intrusion of thin layers of granitic melt into adjacent schists, which produces lit-par-lit structure or injection gneiss.

The rock name is often modified by the addition of a term to indicate overall composition, unique mineral, or structure. Thus, granitic gneiss or gabbroic gneiss may distinguish between gneisses composed predominantly of quartz and feldspars and those composed of calcium-rich feldspar and ferromagnesian minerals such as pyroxene. In like manner, garnet gneiss or sillimanite gneiss may be used to flag the appearance of an important metamorphic mineral. The term "augen gneiss" (*Augen* being the German word for "eyes") is used to describe those rocks which have prominent almond-shaped lenses of feldspar or feldspar and quartz, which are produced by shearing during the formation of the rock.

*René A. De Hon*

SEE ALSO: Aggregates; Feldspars; Metamorphic processes, rocks, and mineral deposits; Quarrying.

# Gold

CATEGORY: Mineral and other nonliving resources

## WHERE FOUND

Although widely distributed in nature, gold is a rare element. It has been estimated that all of the Earth's gold could be gathered into a single cube measuring only 20 meters on each side. Because of its rarity, gold is considered a precious metal. The largest deposits of gold have been found in South Africa and the former Soviet Union (in the Urals and Siberia). Other large deposits have been found in the western United States and in Canada, Mexico, and Colombia.

## PRIMARY USES

Gold is used in jewelry, decorations, electroplating, and dental materials. Other uses include medicinal compounds for the treatment of arthritis and the use of the $Au^{198}$ isotope, with a half-life of 2.7 days, for treating some cancers. Since gold is an excellent heat and electrical conductor, and remains inert when exposed to air or moisture, it has also been used in precision scientific and electrical instruments. Specifically, gold has been used to coat space satellites, to transmit infrared signals, and to serve as the contact point for triggering the inflation of protective air bags in some automobiles. Few countries today use gold coinage systems; an exception is the Krugerrand coin of South Africa. Most nations use gold symbolically as a standard of their monetary systems rather than as actual coinage. Similarly, international monetary exchanges remain based on the world market value of gold, but actual exchanges of gold are uncommon.

## TECHNICAL DEFINITION

Gold is represented by the chemical symbol Au, derived from the Latin word *aurum,* meaning "shining dawn." The weighted mass average of these isotopes gives gold an atomic mass of 196.9665 atomic mass units. Pure gold is a soft, shiny, and ductile metal with a brilliant yellow luster. Changing from solid to liquid at 1,064° Celsius, gold has a high melting point. To vaporize gold requires an even higher temperature (2,808° Celsius). Highly purified gold has a specific gravity of 19.3 (at 20° Celsius).

## DESCRIPTION, DISTRIBUTION, AND FORMS

On the periodic table, gold (atomic number 79) is a member of Group IB of transition metals. This group, also known as the coinage metals, includes copper, silver, and gold. Chemically, gold behaves similarly to platinum, although the arrangement of its chemically reactive electrons is similar to that of copper and silver. Both gold and platinum are largely nonreactive metals. Elemental gold exists in eighteen isotopic forms in nature.

Gold is a rare and precious metal. As such, pure gold has been highly valued and coveted by societies over millennia. Because of its nonreactive nature, elemental gold maintains its brilliant yellow luster. Because of this luster, gold is widely considered the most beautiful and unique of all the metals, which typically display colors of gray, red, or white-silver. Gold does not air-oxidize (tarnish) or corrode upon exposure to moisture. Similarly, it does not readily react to common acids or bases. Nonetheless, gold does dissolve in a reagent known as aqua regia, which is a mixture of nitric acid and hydrochloric acid; alone, neither acid acts upon gold. Aqua regia is a Latin term meaning the "liquid" (*aqua*) that dissolves the "king" (*regia*) of all metals. This reagent is used to separate gold from its ores.

Although predominantly inert, gold can be oxidized to form compounds. When it oxidizes, gold atoms may lose either one, two, or three outer electrons to generate a +1, +2, or +3 charged metal cation, respectively. The most common oxidation state of gold is the +3 form.

Gold is the softest of all metals; thus, it is also the most ductile (capable of being drawn into thin wire) and most malleable (capable of being hammered into thin sheets, or foil). Gold can be hammered into foil sheets so thin that it would take 300,000 sheets, stacked on top of one another, to make a pile 2.5 centimeters high. It has been estimated that one gram of gold could be drawn into a wire that would span about 2.5 kilometers.

Jewelry and coins are rarely made of pure gold because the very soft nature of pure gold makes these items susceptible to loss of gold mass as well as loss of the intended artistic form. To prevent this problem, gold is alloyed with metals such as copper (into materials called red, pink, or yellow gold), palladium, nickel, or zinc (called white gold), and silver or platinum. The purity of gold that is "diluted" by another metal in an alloy is expressed in carats. Pure gold is 24 carats, meaning that 24 out of 24 parts are made of gold. In 18-carat gold, 18 out of 24 parts of the alloy are gold, and the other 6 parts are some other metal. Similarly, 10-carat gold means 10 of 24 parts are gold.

Gold is widely distributed across the world's continents. Approximately half of the world's gold has come from South Africa, including the region near Johannesburg. Other major gold deposits have been found in regions of the Urals and Siberia (Russia), Canada, the western United States, Mexico, and Colombia. Less significant deposits are found in Egypt, Australia, Asia, and Europe.

Two-thirds of all the gold produced in the United States originates in regions of South Dakota and Nevada. Locations of other important U.S. gold finds include California, made famous by the California gold rush of 1849; Alaska, popularized by the Klondike gold rush of 1896; and Colorado, with a ski resort town named Telluride because the gold-containing ore telluride is found in the region.

Through geological activity, the genesis of elemental gold is favored by postmagmatic processes occurring in the presence of medium-intensity hydrothermal energy. Such activity upon gold-bearing lavas produces primary deposits of gold, in which elemental gold remains in the site where it was formed. Postmagmatic processes also favor the formation of quartz, copper and iron pyrites, and other minerals containing the metals copper, gold, cobalt, and silver. As could be expected, these minerals and metals often occur together. Because copper and iron pyrites have a golden luster, although less brilliant than that of gold, their presence in primary gold deposits posed problems for miners. These pyrites are responsible for the term "fool's gold," and many a miner was betrayed by partners, bankers, or himself when mistaking chunks of cheap copper and lead pyrites for real gold.

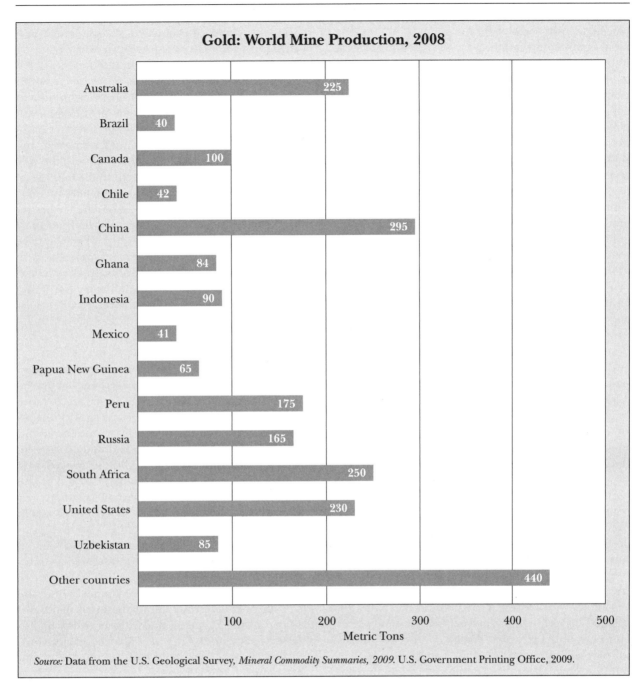

Gold: World Mine Production, 2008

| Country | Metric Tons |
|---|---|
| Australia | 225 |
| Brazil | 40 |
| Canada | 100 |
| Chile | 42 |
| China | 295 |
| Ghana | 84 |
| Indonesia | 90 |
| Mexico | 41 |
| Papua New Guinea | 65 |
| Peru | 175 |
| Russia | 165 |
| South Africa | 250 |
| United States | 230 |
| Uzbekistan | 85 |
| Other countries | 440 |

*Source:* Data from the U.S. Geological Survey, *Mineral Commodity Summaries, 2009.* U.S. Government Printing Office, 2009.

Gold can also be found in areas where mechanical processes acted upon sedimentary rock to yield secondary deposits of gold. Wind and water act to pulverize rock into sand and gravel. Through erosion, clastic and placer deposits of gold and platinum form. Since gold and platinum are inert, they remain unaltered by erosive forces. As rock erosion continues, the movement and accumulation of these metals along rivers occur. Since these metals are seven times denser than sand and gravel, they migrate downstream at a more sluggish rate. This sluggish movement, plus the heavy density of gold and platinum, encourages the metals to settle in riverbeds. Conglomerates, or large nuggets, of gold and platinum, can be found only in placer deposits formed in this manner. Among the more famous nuggets found are a 93-kilogram nugget found in Hill End, Australia, and a 153-kilogram nugget found in Chile. The spectacular classic placer deposits found in the Klondike, in the Yukon (Canada), and near Sacramento, California, explain the subsequent gold bonanzas and migration of prospectors, then settlers, into the American West. Secondary deposits have also yielded the abundant alluvial gold deposits found near Johannesburg. By far, most gold is found in placers of sedimentary origin. In areas of recent erosion, gold is usually found in small, shapeless grains, in small sheets, or as flakes. When fine-grain gold is found in alluvial deposits, "panning for gold" is performed to separate the precious metal from the sand.

Formed in primary deposits, crystals of elemental gold may occur as veins or as dendritic (arborescent) aggregates in association with quartz crystals. Dendritic aggregates look as though the metallic crystal developed with a fernlike growth on large, colorful and translucent quartz crystals. Gold veins are often natural alloys of gold and silver rather than pure gold. These naturally occurring gold-silver alloys are known as electrum, in which the silver content may range from 15 percent to 50 percent. Other natural alloys, as of gold and palladium (porpezite) or gold and rhodium (rhodite), are less frequently found. Gold also occurs in telluride ores, such as tetradymite, nagyagite, and sylvanite. These ores are primarily sulfide compounds of tellurium. In addition to tellurium (Te) and sulfur (S) atoms, tetradymite contains gold and lead. Similarly, sylvanite and nagyagite (black tellurium) contain gold and silver, but in different arrangements and ratios. Elemental gold can be extracted from these minerals via chemical reactions.

Gold is not an essential element for life, although trace amounts are found in humans and some plants concentrate the element. Trace amounts in humans may arise from ingestion of gold from certain alcoholic beverages, from gold dental amalgams, or from exposure to gold therapy for arthritis. Because gold is minimally absorbed by the digestive system, these trace amounts pose no toxic concern.

Most of the world's gold deposits have been well exploited and are therefore nearly devoid of the precious metal. In the South American continent, which was the least mined of all continents up to the 1980's, the environment has begun to suffer from the hunt for gold. Past methods of obtaining gold have yielded to the more dangerous practice of using liquid mercury to form a mercury-gold amalgam in the panning process. To recover even the tiniest amount of gold, a large quantity of mercury must be used. In South American rivers, gold occurs in brown, iron-stained sand. Some deposits have been profitable even though only a few dollars' worth of gold may be gathered per metric ton of sand panned and amalgamated. Whether or not gold is actually found, the leftover mercury is dumped directly into the rivers. Mercury, a neurotoxin, is lethal in high amounts. Reportedly, the dumping of untreated mercury has reduced populations of fish, has caused high levels of mercury in fish eaten by people, and is likely to have health impacts on children, pregnant women, and future generations. Some researchers suspect that neurological symptoms that suggest mercury poisoning can already be seen in some South American population areas.

HISTORY

The Group IB metals, or coinage metals, were the first metals used in primitive cultures. It is believed that elemental metals were easy to find in nature because their bright lusters shone in natural light. Precious metals have been in use since at least seven thousand years ago by civilizations of the Middle East and Afghanistan. Wealthy members of these groups possessed decorative jewels fashioned from gold. The metalworkers of these ancient societies manipulated the gold physically using hammers or other tools to carve or cut the soft metal.

Exploration of the tomb of King Tutankhamen, from the fourteenth century B.C.E., revealed an entry guarded by gold funerary masks inlaid with colorful glass. A gold sarcophagus and gold panel behind the king's throne were also found. Between 4000 and 3500 B.C.E., the Egyptians and Sumerians learned to smelt silver and gold. They were able to generate fires in furnaces that could achieve the extreme temperatures required to melt metals, to cast molten metal into molds, to forge metal, and to make alloys (by blending molten metals). The use of gold for dental fillings among wealthy Egyptians dates back to between 2680 and 2160 B.C.E.

In Mesopotamia, a region that is now part of Iraq, an ornate headdress of Queen Puabi, dated to 2700 B.C.E., was fashioned with gold-carved leaves to adorn her face. Trading and business deals of Mesopotamia involved the exchange of precious metals, although there was no system of standardized coins. Archaeological studies have also shown that the Incan civilization of pre-Columbian South America possessed considerable gold-working skill and achieved mastery of soldering and welding techniques.

The alchemists of the medieval period believed that gold was one of the most important keys to immortality. They also believed that base metals, which were abundant and cheap, could be converted into gold, which was rare and expensive. It was assumed that by simple manipulation in the presence of a spiritual agent—such as the Philosopher's Stone—an elixir could be formed that possessed all the ingredients required for immortality. Because of its inert behavior and timeless beauty, gold was believed to impart some qualities required to achieve worldly immortality. During medieval times it was widely thought that the emperors and kings who had the most gold would have the longest lives. If a king ruled for many years there could be long periods of economic stability, access to food, security of family, and safety from conquerors. Thus the pursuit of gold was serious business, and the king's magician, who was usually an alchemist, was highly regarded in the king's court. As a final historical note, gold amalgams, mixtures of mercury and gold, were described in the year 27 B.C.E. by a Roman architect, Vitruvius. Mercury and gold amalgamation is still in use today as a means of collecting gold from sand deposits of riverbeds.

### OBTAINING GOLD

Gold is separated from rocks, minerals, and alluvial deposits by panning or sluicing methods. The extraction of gold from telluride ores (tetradymite, nagyagite, and sylvanite) requires chemical reactions. The use of cyanide compounds, formation of amalgams, or smelting gold may be necessary to extract the gold from ores. The extracted gold is frequently refined by electrolysis (the use of an electric current). Electrolysis is particularly useful in separating mercury-gold amalgams back into their separate and purified metallic state.

In telluride ores (minerals), gold is not in the free, elemental state; rather, it is in a cationic form. As a metallic cation, each atom of gold carries a positive charge of either +1 or +3. A chemical reaction involving the addition of potassium cyanide to the crushed rocks (covered with water) makes a new compound of gold that dissolves in the water. This layer of water can be collected off the crushed rock, and through electrolysis the gold cations can be converted into gold crystals.

### USES OF GOLD

As described previously, jewelry and decorative ornaments fashioned from gold are marketed using carats to describe the quantity of gold present. Compounds of gold are used for decorating china or glass items. Gold chloro compounds, containing gold cations having a +3 charge, are mixed with sulfurized terpenes or resins to form a mixture known as "liquid gold," which can be applied directly to glass or china.

Compounds of gold with +1 cations are used in rheumatology as an anti-inflammatory agent for the treatment of active, refractory forms of juvenile and adult rheumatoid arthritis. These biologically active compounds are sodium gold thiomalate and sodium gold (or auro) thioglucose; aurothioglucose seems to be less painful when injected into a muscle near the joint. The gold therapy must be started before permanent changes have occurred in the afflicted joints if it is to benefit the patient. Some of the side effects of these therapies include skin, liver, and kidney changes or damage. Approximately 20 percent of patients who

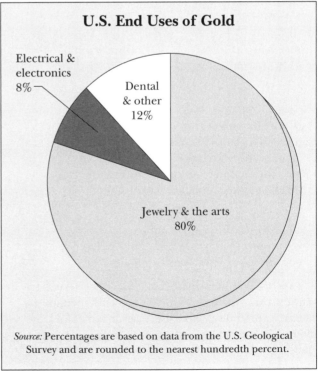

**U.S. End Uses of Gold**

Electrical & electronics 8%

Dental & other 12%

Jewelry & the arts 80%

*Source:* Percentages are based on data from the U.S. Geological Survey and are rounded to the nearest hundredth percent.

try gold therapy have to discontinue treatment because of these adverse reactions. However, newer anti-inflammatory agents have limited the number of patients who need to try gold therapy for relief.

Finally, gold has been used in an abstract manner as the basis or standard of valuation for currencies and monetary systems throughout the world. The origins of this ancient practice lie in Mesopotamian, Assyrian, and Lydian societies.

*Mary C. Fields*

FURTHER READING

Bernstein, Peter L. *The Power of Gold: The History of an Obsession.* New ed. New York: Wiley, 2004.

Boyle, Robert W. *Gold: History and Genesis of Deposits.* New York: Van Nostrand Reinhold, 1987.

Green, Timothy. *The New World of Gold: The Inside Story of the Mines, the Markets, the Politics, the Investors.* New York: Walker, 1981.

Greenwood, N. N., and A. Earnshaw. "Copper, Silver, and Gold." In *Chemistry of the Elements.* 2d ed. Boston: Butterworth-Heinemann, 1997.

Macdonald, Eoin H. *Handbook of Gold Exploration and Evaluation.* Boca Raton, Fla.: CRC Press, 2007.

Marx, Jenifer. *The Magic of Gold.* Garden City, N.Y.: Doubleday, 1978.

Pellant, Chris. *Rocks and Minerals.* 2d American ed. New York: Dorling Kindersley, 2002.

Schumann, Walter. *Handbook of Rocks, Minerals, and Gemstones.* Translated by R. Bradshaw and K. A. G. Mills. Boston: Houghton Mifflin, 1993.

WEB SITES

NATURAL RESOURCES CANADA
Canadian Minerals Yearbook, Mineral and Metal Commodity Reviews
http://www.nrcan-rncan.gc.ca/mms-smm/busi-indu/cmy-amc/com-eng.htm

U.S. GEOLOGICAL SURVEY
Gold: Statistics and Information
http://minerals.usgs.gov/minerals/pubs/commodity/gold/index.html#mcs

SEE ALSO: Alloys; Australia; Canada; Hydrothermal solutions and mineralization; Metals and metallurgy; Mexico; Mineral resource use, early history of; Native elements; Placer deposits; Russia; Sedimentary processes, rocks, and mineral deposits; South Africa; United States.

# Gore, Al

CATEGORY: People
BORN: March 31, 1948; Washington, D.C.

*As congressman, senator, and vice president of the United States, and as author of several best-selling books, Al Gore tried to alert the American government and public to environmental problems and their deleterious effects on world resources.*

BIOGRAPHICAL BACKGROUND
The son of a U.S. senator, Albert Arnold Gore, Jr., went to school in Washington, D.C., during the winter and spent summers working at the family farm in Tennessee. He first became aware of environmental problems when seeing topsoil washing into rivers during floods. A course at Harvard College taught by Roger Revelle, whose pioneering research brought the question of global warming to the attention of scientists, strongly impressed Gore.

After serving in the Army during the Vietnam War, Gore attended Vanderbilt Theological Seminary and Vanderbilt Law School. In 1976, he dropped out of law school and successfully ran for a seat in the United States House of Representatives, where he served until being elected to the Senate in 1984. In 1992, Gore was elected vice president of the United States. He lost the 2000 presidential contest despite winning a majority of the popular vote.

IMPACT ON RESOURCE USE
Gore believed the environment was the most fundamental global resource, whose degradation threatened the life and economy of the entire world. His major role in the environmental movement was as a publicist, bringing data on global warming and other forms of pollution to the attention of his government colleagues and the general public. While in the House of Representatives he was the subcommittee chairman presiding over hearings examining dumping of toxic chemicals in the Niagara Falls Love Canal area.

In the Senate, Gore called attention to the challenge of global warming and traveled the world collecting data on environmental problems affecting global resources, which informed his first book, *Earth in the Balance* (1992). The book described many threatening developments—destruction of rain forests, indiscriminate dumping of toxic residues, and

*Nobel Prize winner Al Gore discusses climate change at a 2009 summit in Mexico City.* (AP/Wide World Photos)

the growing danger posed by greenhouse gases—and called for action to control these activities before they caused irreparable damage. Published in the spring of 1992, the book became a best seller, informing a wide audience of possible perils to the globe.

As vice president Gore pushed, without great success, for government action to protect the environment. He helped facilitate the Kyoto Protocol on global warming, but the United States never adopted the pact.

Gore's most effective contribution to environmental awareness was his 2006 book *An Inconvenient Truth*, made into a powerful film the following year that won an Academy Award for Best Documentary. The movie dramatizes the statistics, graphs, and charts that Gore used in his lectures and in the book, stressing the evidence for global warming and refuting skeptics who question whether the threat to the globe is real. *The Assault on Reason* (2007) excoriates President George W. Bush's administration and others who weakened environmental security by ignoring the rational arguments of scientists regarding human con-

tributions to climate change. Gore's lifelong devotion to defending the environment won him many awards, climaxed by the 2007 Nobel Peace Prize, which he won jointly with the Intergovernmental Panel on Climate Change.

*Milton Berman*

SEE ALSO: Climate Change and Sustainable Energy Act; Environmental degradation, resource exploitation and; Environmental movement; Greenhouse gases and global climate change.

# Granite

CATEGORY: Mineral and other nonliving resources

*Granite is a medium- to coarse-grained igneous rock composed principally of interlocking grains of the light-colored silicate minerals—potassium feldspar, sodium-rich plagioclase, and quartz. The overall color may blend to reddish, pink, or white depending on which mineral predominates in the rock. Dark minerals may add a spotted appearance to the rock. Granite is an igneous rock formed at great depths in the Earth's crust.*

## DEFINITION

The three essential minerals in granite are quartz, which makes up 20 to 40 percent of the rock, and feldspars in which potassium feldspar is more abundant than plagioclase. Five to 10 percent ferromagnesian minerals, usually biotite or hornblende, or muscovite are common as accessory minerals. Garnet, tourmaline, corundum, or even pyroxene may be present in some granites.

## OVERVIEW

The continents are primarily granite, with a thin veneer of sedimentary rocks. Granite is found in the exposed core of linear mountain chains and regions of highly eroded continental shields associated with regional metamorphism. The Sierra Nevada mountain range consists of a composite granitic batholith that is 640 kilometers by 110 kilometers. Granites also form such notable sites as Mount Rushmore, South Dakota; Half Dome in Yosemite National Park, California; and Stone Mountain, Georgia.

Granite is used extensively as building stone. It is strong and weather resistant. Cut and polished slabs are used for internal and external facing, and polished or horned blocks are used for ornamental stones as tombstones and monuments. Large blocks are used in sea walls and jetties. Smaller blocks and crushed stone are used as rip-rap.

Variations in texture and composition give rise to distinctive varieties of granite. Pegmatite is an extremely coarse-grained rock of granite composition formed in the late, fluid-rich stage of magma crystallization. Individual crystals may reach several centimeters or tens of meters in length. Aplite is a fine-grained granite with a sugary texture. Graphic granite is conspicuous by its intergrowth of quartz within orthoclase crystals, which gives a pattern similar to cuneiform writing. Alaskite is a granite with no dark minerals. Charnockite is granite containing hypersthene as its chief ferromagnesian silicate.

Granite magma is formed by melting continental crustal rocks and thick prisms of sediments that form along the margins of convergent plates. The melt migrates upward in the crust through overlying rocks by assimilation of surrounding rocks and by forcefully pushing rocks out of the way. As the magma moves upward, blocks of overlying rocks are incorporated into the melt. If the melt is hot enough, the included rocks may be melted. If the magma has cooled sufficiently, the blocks are preserved as xenoliths (foreign rocks) within the magma. Granite magmas cool to form large intrusive bodies known as batholiths (*bathos* for deep, and *lithos* meaning rock) and smaller intrusions such as dikes and sills. As batholiths are emplaced fairly deep in the crust, the surrounding materials are usually high-grade metamorphic rocks such as schist and gneiss. Some granites may form by extreme metamorphism in which existing rocks are converted to granitic rock by recrystallization and chemical reaction with chemically active fluids.

*René A. De Hon*

SEE ALSO: Aggregates; Earth's crust; Feldspars; Igneous processes, rocks, and mineral deposits; Pegmatites; Plutonic rocks and mineral deposits; Quarrying.

# Graphite

CATEGORY: Mineral and other nonliving resources

## WHERE FOUND

Natural graphite is distributed widely in the world. Major deposits are found in Sri Lanka, North and South Korea, India, Austria, Germany, Norway, Canada, Mexico, China, Brazil, and Madagascar. The United States imports virtually all of the natural graphite it needs from the latter four countries. However, most of the graphite used in the United States is synthesized from a wide variety of carbon-containing materials—for example, anthracite coal and petroleum coke. Synthetic graphite is denser, purer, and more expensive than the natural form.

## PRIMARY USES

Graphite is used in "lead" pencils. To a lesser extent, it is also used in brake linings, steelmaking, and lubricants.

## TECHNICAL DEFINITION

Graphite is composed of parallel planes of fused hexagonal rings of carbon atoms. It exists in two forms, alpha (also called hexagonal) and beta (also called rhombohedral), which have apparently identical physical properties but differ in their crystal structure. In the alpha form, the carbon atoms in alternate layers are directly above each other, while in the beta form, the carbons do not line up again until every fourth layer. In both forms, the distance between neighboring carbon atoms within the layers is 142 picometers, which is intermediate between the length of typical single and double C—C bonds. The distance between the layers is 335 picometers. The larger distance between the layers reflects the weaker forces holding the planes together compared with the forces holding neighboring atoms together within the planes.

Because of graphite's weak interplanar forces, the planes can readily slip past each other, causing graphite to cleave easily and preferentially parallel to its planes. This process accounts for its flaky appearance and excellent lubricating ability even when dry. The planar structure also causes several of its physical properties to be highly anisotropic (exhibiting different properties when measured in different directions). For example, its thermal conductivity is several hundred times larger, and its electrical conductivity is several thousand times larger, when measured parallel to the planes than perpendicular to them.

The density of synthetic graphite is 2.26 grams per

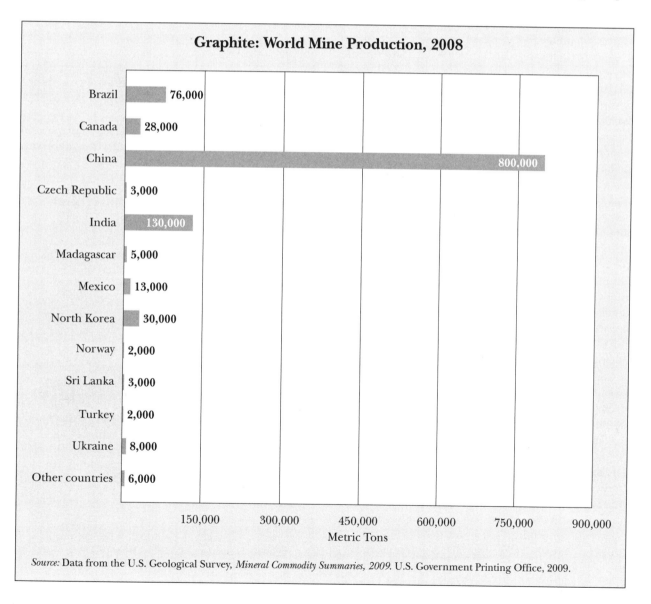

**Graphite: World Mine Production, 2008**

| Country | Metric Tons |
|---|---|
| Brazil | 76,000 |
| Canada | 28,000 |
| China | 800,000 |
| Czech Republic | 3,000 |
| India | 130,000 |
| Madagascar | 5,000 |
| Mexico | 13,000 |
| North Korea | 30,000 |
| Norway | 2,000 |
| Sri Lanka | 3,000 |
| Turkey | 2,000 |
| Ukraine | 8,000 |
| Other countries | 6,000 |

*Source:* Data from the U.S. Geological Survey, *Mineral Commodity Summaries, 2009.* U.S. Government Printing Office, 2009.

cubic centimeter, but that of natural graphite is usually lower, varying from 2.23 to 1.48 grams per cubic centimeter, due to the presence of pore spaces and impurities.

## DESCRIPTION, DISTRIBUTION, AND FORMS

Graphite and diamond are the two predominant forms in which free carbon is found in nature. Graphite is a greasy, opaque, highly reflective black or gray solid.

Although graphite can be found throughout the world, much of it is of little economic importance. Large crystals, called flake, occur in metamorphosed sedimentary silicate rocks such as quartz, schists, and gneisses and have an average crystal size of about four millimeters (ranging from fractions of a millimeter to about six millimeters). Deposits have also been found in the form of lenses up to 30 meters thick and stretching several kilometers, with average carbon content of 25 percent (reaching 60 percent in Madagascar). The graphite in these cases was probably formed from the carbon in organic materials. Deposits containing microcrystalline graphite (sometimes referred to as "amorphous carbon") can contain up to 95 percent carbon. In Mexico such amorphous carbon occurs in metamorphosed coal beds. The graphite deposit in New York occurs in a hydrothermal vein and was probably formed from carbon-bearing rocks during metamorphism in the region. Graphite occurs occasionally as an original constituent of igneous rocks (for example in India), and it has been observed in meteorites. Graphite has the unusual property that it is very soft at room temperature (with a hardness between 0.5 and 1 on the Mohs scale, which is similar to talc) but has increasing strength at high temperatures. At about 2,000° Celsius, its crushing strength is increased by 20 percent, and at about 3,000° Celsius, its tensile strength is increased by 50 to 100 percent. Other important properties of graphite that are exploited in its many uses listed previously are its stability at high temperatures and in the presence of corrosive and reactive chemicals.

## HISTORY

Carbon was known in prehistory in the forms of charcoal and soot, but it was not recognized as a chemical element until the second half of the eighteenth century. In 1779, graphite was shown to be carbon by Carl Wilhelm Scheele, a Swedish chemist; ten years later the name "graphite" was proposed by Abraham Gottlob Werner, a German geologist, and D. L. G.

Harsten, from the Greek *graphein* (to write). Commercially, "lead" pencils were first manufactured in about 1564 in England during Queen Elizabeth's reign, using Cumberland graphite. In 1896, Edward Goodrich Acheson, an American chemist, was granted a patent for his process whereby graphite is made from coke, and within one or two years, production began on a large scale. Diamond was first synthesized from graphite between 1953 and 1955.

## OBTAINING GRAPHITE

Graphite can be made to sublime directly to carbon vapor or to melt to liquid carbon at temperatures above approximately 3,500° Celsius, depending on the pressure and other conditions. It can also be transformed into diamond at extremely high pressures and temperatures (for example, 100,000 atmospheres and 1,000°-2,000° Celsius). The rate of conversion of diamond back to graphite at atmospheric pressure is not significant below temperatures of about 4,000° Celsius.

The mining and purification process of natural graphite includes flotation followed by treatment with

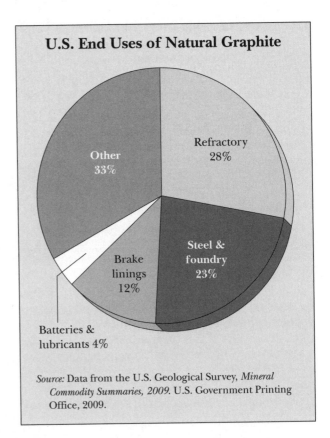

### U.S. End Uses of Natural Graphite

Other 33%

Refractory 28%

Steel & foundry 23%

Brake linings 12%

Batteries & lubricants 4%

*Source:* Data from the U.S. Geological Survey, *Mineral Commodity Summaries, 2009.* U.S. Government Printing Office, 2009.

acids and then heating in a vacuum to temperatures on the order of 1,500° Celsius.

## USES OF GRAPHITE

The most familiar use of graphite is in the manufacture of "lead" pencils, where it is mixed with clay and other materials and baked at high temperatures. The "lead" increases in softness as the ratio of graphite to clay increases. Graphite has much more extensive use in the manufacture of lubricants and oilless bearings; electrodes in batteries and industrial electrolysis; high-temperature rocket casings, chemical process equipment, furnaces, and crucibles for holding molten metals; tanks for holding corrosive chemicals; and strong and lightweight composite materials that are used, for example, in airplanes and high-quality sports equipment such as tennis rackets and golf clubs. Graphite is also a component in the cores of some nuclear reactors as the moderator to slow down the neutrons, and it is the major raw material for synthetic diamonds.

*Leslie J. Schwartz*

## FURTHER READING

Chatterjee, Kaulir Kisor. "Graphite." In *Uses of Industrial Minerals, Rocks, and Freshwater.* New York: Nova Science, 2009.

Delhaès, Pierre, ed. *Graphite and Precursors.* Boca Raton, Fla.: CRC Press, 2000.

Greenwood, N. N., and A. Earnshaw. "Carbon." In *Chemistry of the Elements.* 2d ed. Boston: Butterworth-Heinemann, 1997.

Inagaki, Michio. *New Carbons: Control of Structure and Functions.* New York: Elsevier Science, 2000.

Kogel, Jessica Elzea, et al., eds. "Graphite." In *Industrial Minerals and Rocks: Commodities, Markets, and Uses.* 7th ed. Littleton, Colo.: Society for Mining, Metallurgy, and Exploration, 2006.

Morgan, Peter. *Carbon Fibers and Their Composites.* Boca Raton, Fla.: Taylor & Francis, 2005.

Pellant, Chris. *Rocks and Minerals.* 2d American ed. New York: Dorling Kindersley, 2002.

Petrucci, Ralph H., William S. Harwood, Geoff E. Herring, and Jeffrey Madura. *General Chemistry: Principles and Modern Applications.* 9th ed. Upper Saddle River, N.J.: Pearson/Prentice Hall, 2007.

Pierson, Hugh O. *Handbook of Carbon, Graphite, Diamond, and Fullerenes: Properties, Processing, and Applications.* Park Ridge, N.J.: Noyes, 1993.

## WEB SITES

NATURAL RESOURCES CANADA
Canadian Minerals Yearbook, Mineral and Metal Commodity Reviews
http://www.nrcan-rncan.gc.ca/mms-smm/busi-indu/cmy-amc/com-eng.htm

U.S. GEOLOGICAL SURVEY
Graphite: Statistics and Information
http://minerals.usgs.gov/minerals/pubs/commodity/graphite/index.html#mcs

SEE ALSO: Austria; Brazil; Canada; Carbon; China; Crystals; Diamond; Germany; Gneiss; India; Metamorphic processes, rocks, and mineral deposits; Mexico; Minerals, structure and physical properties of; Mohs hardness scale; Native elements; South Korea; Talc; United States.

# Grasslands

CATEGORIES: Ecological resources; plant and animal resources

*Grassland ecosystems contain a great diversity of plant and animal life, and grasslands have supported human habitation for tens of thousands of years. Grasslands are crucial in the growing of crops and the grazing of livestock.*

## BACKGROUND

One way that botanists and ecologists classify regions of the Earth is according to their vegetation. Woodland, desert, tundra, and grassland are major classifications. All have their own types of climate, physical environment, soil, plants, and animals. Grasslands are so named because the dominant plant species are low plants, most notably various grass species. Throughout the world there are differing types of grasslands—some tropical, some temperate, some with a relatively moderate amount of rainfall, some with little rainfall that are subject to harsh droughts. Grasslands have many regional names, including shrub steppe, the prairie of North America, and the pampa of South America. A savanna, or parkland, is typically a mixed zone, often considered a transitional region between grassland and forest. A grassland itself may be bordered by desert, parkland, or forest. Humans have

*Sheep graze on a Tibetan grassland.* (Xinhua/Landov)

lived in grassland environments for thousands of years, and in parts of the world it is impossible to determine which aspects of a grassland ecosystem are natural and which have been changed by countless generations of human activity related to agriculture and the grazing of domesticated animals.

### CLIMATE AND FIRE

The defining characteristics of grassland climates are a marked seasonal variation between the wet and dry seasons and a dry season or overall climate that is too dry for forests to develop. A major distinction can be drawn between temperate and tropical grasslands, with tropical grasslands having higher temperatures and, generally, greater rainfall. In temperate grasslands annual rainfall is quite low, ranging from 25 to 75 centimeters. In tropical and subtropical grasslands, rainfall is in the range of 60 to 150 centimeters. With their distinct seasonal shifts, many grasslands are subject to monsoons in the rainy season and drought in the dry season. Drought periods may last from several weeks to several months.

Fire is a natural and prominent part of the grassland environment, and lightning fires are common. Fire can serve a number of purposes. As drought does, it can help maintain the grassland boundary, keeping forests from moving into the zone. Perhaps surprisingly, it also fosters the growth of grasses and grasslike plants by burning off old plant layers while leaving the growth zones of new plants, much of which are below the soil line, generally unharmed.

### SOIL, PLANTS, AND ANIMALS

Grassland and prairie soils are distinct from those of forest regions. Tropical grassland soils are often leached by periods of heavy rain and therefore tend to have relatively low nutrient levels. Temperate grassland soils retain many more of their nutrients and can be rich in humus (organic matter) as well, making them quite fertile. Therefore, they have long been used for crop production and grazing.

Both the plant and animal communities of grasslands are diverse, although grasses may compose up to 90 percent of grassland biomass. Grasses are well adapted to endure drought because of their root masses and because they can reproduce asexually if conditions make seed reproduction impossible. Some also go into a dormant state to survive the dry season. Perennial grasses and forbs are the most common plants, but there are also small shrubs, fungi, lichens, and mosses. In addition, some grasslands do have scattered trees, most often along stream channels. Small grassland animals include birds, reptiles, insects, worms, mice, and prairie dogs. Larger animals include large herbivores such as bison, elk, and wildebeest as well as the carnivores (wolves, the large cat species) that prey on them.

### GRASSLANDS AND HUMANS

Humans have lived on, and relied on the resources of, grasslands for at least tens of thousands of years. Hunter-gatherers roamed grasslands and savannas, and the first agriculture was almost certainly practiced in grassland regions. Throughout the world, grasslands have extensively been converted from their natural state to areas used for grazing and crop production. A huge percentage of the world's commercial grains—notably corn, wheat, and soybeans—is grown in temperate grassland regions.

Many ecologists believe that human-induced changes to grasslands can have both positive and negative effects, in some cases stabilizing grassland regions, in others abusing them and unintentionally causing desertification. Humans have introduced nonnative species of plants and animals, in some cases replacing native species. Cattle replaced the buffalo and elk that once roamed North America, for example. Grasslands can support a considerable amount of grazing activity, even by non-native animals, as long as overgrazing does not occur. Modern range management techniques are intended to ensure that animal numbers do not exceed a sustainable level. In order to protect their investments in livestock, humans have hunted, and in many areas virtually eliminated, the large grassland carnivores (wolves, bears, cats) that prey on grazing animals.

Human activities can also decrease or damage grassland habitats themselves; chief among these activities are suppressing the fires that are a natural part of grassland environment and draining prairie wetlands. Desertification is a significant problem. It is likely that some areas that have been inhabited by humans for thousands of years—such as lands around the Mediterranean Sea as well as in Asia Minor, Iran,

and India—that are now desertlike were once grasslands. More recently, desertification caused or exacerbated by human activity has been noted elsewhere—in central Africa, for example.

On the other hand, human activity can stabilize and help maintain grasslands, and in many cases grasslands seem to adapt well to human habitation. One possible positive aspect of livestock grazing is that range managers can potentially control animal numbers and density far more than wild animals can be controlled, providing a stabilizing effect. Finally, there are ongoing efforts to preserve some of the remaining small regions of relatively unaffected prairie in North America.

*McCrea Adams*

### FURTHER READING

Coupland, R. T., ed. *Grassland Ecosystems of the World: Analysis of Grasslands and Their Uses.* New York: Cambridge University Press, 1979.

Cushman, Ruth Carol, and Stephen R. Jones. *The Shortgrass Prairie.* Boulder, Colo.: Pruett, 1988.

Editors of Time-Life Books. *Grasslands and Tundra.* Alexandria, Va.: Author, 1985.

Fast, Dennis, and Barbara Huck. *The Land Where the Sky Begins: North America's Endangered Tall Grass Prairie and Aspen Parkland.* Winnipeg, Man.: Heartland Associates, 2007.

Gibson, David J. *Grasses and Grassland Ecology.* New York: Oxford University Press, 2009.

Licht, Daniel S. *Ecology and Economics of the Great Plains.* Lincoln: University of Nebraska Press, 1997.

Manning, Richard. *Grassland: The History, Biology, Politics, and Promise of the American Prairie.* New York: Penguin, 1995.

Price, Elizabeth A. C. *Lowland Grassland and Heathland Habitats.* Illustrations by Jo Wright. New York: Routledge, 2003.

Reynolds, S. J., and J. Frame, eds. *Grasslands: Developments, Opportunities, Perspectives.* Enfield, N.H.: Science Publishers, 2005.

Woodward, Susan L. *Grassland Biomes.* Westport, Conn.: Greenwood Press, 2008.

### WEB SITES

ENVIRONMENT CANADA
The Prairie Ecosystem
http://www.pnr-rpn.ec.gc.ca/nature/ecosystems/da00s01.en.html

U.S. GEOLOGICAL SURVEY
Grassland Ecosystems
http://www.usgs.gov/science/
　science.php?term=499

SEE ALSO: Agriculture industry; Desertification; Dust
Bowl; Farmland; Overgrazing; Rangeland; Soil management.

# Gravel. *See* Sand and gravel

# Greece

CATEGORIES: Countries; government and resources

*Greece leads the world in the production of perlite and
leads Europe in the production of bauxite and bentonite. It also produces important quantities of magnesite
and nickel. Greece exports about one-half of its extracted minerals, but its substantial production of lignite is consumed internally. The country has few reserves of petroleum, and it must import most of its oil
and natural gas.*

## THE COUNTRY

Greece is a small, mountainous country occupying
the southern portion of the Balkan Peninsula in southeastern Europe. It has a deeply indented coastline,
and its more than 1,400 islands and islets make up
about one-fifth of its area. Once very weak, Greece's
economy has expanded considerably since the middle of the twentieth century, thanks in large part to
economic aid from other countries, trade with the
rest of Europe and the Middle East, and a steadily increasing influx of tourists. The rapid industrialization
that the country has experienced since the 1970's has
encouraged a shift of population from rural areas to
cities and has created serious air and water pollution.

In 2008, Greece had an estimated gross domestic
product (GDP) in purchasing power parity of $343.6
billion, making it the thirty-third or thirty-fourth largest economy in the world and the eleventh largest in
Europe. Greece joined the European Union (EU) in
1981, and in 2008, its per capita GDP was estimated to
be thirty-two thousand dollars, which was fourteen
hundred dollars below the average of the European

Union. Manufacturing accounts for approximately
one-fifth of its GDP, with service industries accounting for most of the remainder. The value of the country's exports is only about one-third of the value of its
imports.

## BAUXITE, ALUMINA, AND ALUMINUM

Greece possesses Europe's largest known deposits of
bauxite, the mixture of minerals from which aluminum is indirectly refined. Bauxite is regarded as the
only naturally occurring material that the country exploits at full capacity. Greece is believed to have reserves of more than 100 million metric tons of bauxite, with most of the deposits concentrated along the
central mountain region of Parnassus-Giona-Helikon
and on the country's second largest island, Euboea, in
the western Aegean Sea. Both underground and open-
pit mines are operated.

Greece mined an estimated 2.16 million metric
tons of bauxite in 2007, while its output of alumina,
which represents an intermediate stage in the production of aluminum, reached an estimated 780,000 metric tons the same year. The combined value of its exports of bauxite, alumina, and related materials was
$152 million in 2007. Greece is the largest supplier of
bauxite in the European Union, although its increasing ability to produce its own aluminum has led to
greater domestic consumption of bauxite and alumina.

Bauxites Parnasse Mining Company pioneered the
extraction of bauxite in Greece in 1933. However, only
with the creation of Aluminum of Greece S.A. did the
nation's production of the metal itself begin. Aluminum of Greece—a combine headed by the French-
owned firm Pechiney and involving the American
company Reynolds Metals as well as public and private
Greek funding—began operations in the 1960's. The
firm S&B Industrial Minerals S.A. supplied the company with ore and went on to absorb Bauxites Parnasse in 1996, while Aluminum of Greece merged with
Mytilineos Holdings S.A. in 2007. As of 2009, most
Greek bauxite production was under the direction of
S&B and its subsidiary, Greek Helicon Bauxites S.A.

## PERLITE

According to published figures, Greece produces
more perlite than any other nation on earth, turning
out an estimated 1.65 million metric tons of the material in crude and screened forms in 2007. Perlite is a
volcanic glass whose particles expand to many times

# Greece: Resources at a Glance

*Official name:* Hellenic Republic
*Government:* Parliamentary republic
*Capital city:* Athens
*Area:* 50,953 mi²; 131,957 km²
*Population (2009 est.):* 10,737,428
*Language:* Greek
*Monetary unit:* euro (EUR)

## ECONOMIC SUMMARY:

*GDP composition by sector (2008 est.):* agriculture, 3.7%; industry, 20.6%; services, 75.7%
*Natural resources:* lignite, petroleum, iron ore, bauxite, lead, zinc, nickel, magnesite, huntite, marble, salt, hydropower potential, perlite, bentenite, kaolin, pumice
*Land use (2005):* arable land, 20.45%; permanent crops, 8.59%; other, 70.96%
*Industries:* tourism, food and tobacco processing, textiles, chemicals, metal products, mining, petroleum
*Agricultural products:* wheat, corn, barley, sugar beets, olives, tomatoes, wine, tobacco, potatoes, beef, dairy products
*Exports (2008 est.):* $29.14 billion
*Commodities exported:* food and beverages, manufactured goods, petroleum products, chemicals, textiles
*Imports (2008 est.):* $93.91 billion
*Commodities imported:* machinery, transport equipment, fuels, chemicals
*Labor force (2008 est.):* 4.96 million
*Labor force by occupation (2005 est.):* agriculture, 12.4%; industry, 22.4%; services, 65.1%

## ENERGY RESOURCES:

*Electricity production (2007 est.):* 59.33 billion kWh
*Electricity consumption (2006 est.):* 55.98 billion kWh
*Electricity exports (2007 est.):* 269 million kWh
*Electricity imports (2007 est.):* 5.894 billion kWh

*Natural gas production (2007 est.):* 24 million m³
*Natural gas consumption (2007 est.):* 4.069 billion m³
*Natural gas exports (2007 est.):* 0 m³
*Natural gas imports (2007 est.):* 4.1 billion m³
*Natural gas proved reserves (Jan. 2008 est.):* 1.982 billion m³

*Oil production (2007 est.):* 4,265 bbl/day
*Oil imports (2005):* 527,200 bbl/day
*Oil proved reserves (Jan. 2008 est.):* 10 million bbl

*Source:* Data from *The World Factbook 2009.* Washington, D.C.: Central Intelligence Agency, 2009.
*Notes:* Data are the most recent tracked by the CIA. Values are given in U.S. dollars. Abbreviations: bbl/day = barrels per day; GDP = gross domestic product; km² = square kilometers; kWh = kilowatt-hours; m³ = cubic meters; mi² = square miles.

their original sizes when heated and is used extensively in construction, horticulture, and industry. It has also proven useful in dispersing oil spills at sea. Perlite is found associated with sites of ancient volcanic activity in the northeastern region of Thrace and on several islands in the southern Aegean Sea, including Melos, Kos, and Gyali—the last of which is also a major source of pumice.

S&B is the country's (and the world's) largest miner of perlite. The company maintains several open-pit facilities on Melos, where it discovered deposits in 1954 and opened the continent's largest facility in 1975. It operates another mine on Kos. The company exports most of its production to Europe, North America (where Armstrong Industries is a major customer), and Asia. Smaller producers include S&B subsidiary Otavi Mines Hellas S.A., with operations on Melos, and Aegean Perlites S.A., on Gyali. Easy access to inexpensive transportation by ship has helped these companies maintain an international price advantage. Thanks to a project sponsored by the European Union, the expansion process necessary to perlite's commercial utilization has also been greatly enhanced in recent years, resulting in higher quality.

### Bentonite and Kaolin

Greece produces more bentonite than any other country in Europe and is second in world production only to the United States. Its total output (crude and processed) amounted to an estimated 952,500 metric tons in 2007, nearly 9 percent of the world's total. Bentonite is a clay utilized in iron ore pelletizing, in foundering, as a binding agent in cement and adhesives, and in pet litter. The material is usually formed from the weathering of volcanic ash, and deposits are found on Melos and, to a lesser extent, the island of Cimolus. It is mined from the surface in both locations.

As is the case with many of the country's other minerals, the bentonite market is dominated by S&B, which absorbed the second largest bentonite mining operation on Melos, Mykobar Mining Company S.A., in 1999. Mediterranean Bentonite S.A. also operates a small surface mine on Melos, but S&B accounts for about 85 percent of the country's production. Most is exported to other countries of the European Union and to North America.

Greece also possesses deposits of a second type of clay, kaolin, near Drama in the northeastern part of the country. The country produced an estimated 60,300 metric tons of kaolin in 2007, but because of its inferior nature, it was used only domestically in cement and ceramic glazes.

### Nickel

The common, industrially important element nickel is utilized primarily in the manufacture of stainless steel and other alloys. Greece mined an estimated 2.7 million metric tons of nickel ore in 2007, a level it had maintained more or less unchanged over the preceding several years. The country is thought to have nickel reserves of 250 million metric tons, with deposits concentrated on the Aegean island of Euboea, on the mainland near Larimna opposite Euboea, and in northwestern Greece near the Albanian border. Deposits in the first two regions are "transported," or secondary, meaning that they have been eroded and redeposited in new locations by natural forces—a situation that makes for easier extraction. The deposits of ore in the north evolved in place, and while they are more difficult to mine, they contain a higher content of nickel.

Greece's primary nickel producer (and one of the largest in the world) is the state-controlled General Mining and Metallurgical Company S.A. (LARCO), which was founded in 1963 and operates complexes of underground, open-pit, and closed-pit mines. Its oldest operation is at Agios Ioannis near Larimna, the ore from which it began smelting in 1966. The company's mines in Euboea went into operation three years later. Today LARCO is one of the world's largest producers of iron-nickel alloys and exports to a number of steel manufacturers in Western Europe.

### Magnesite and Huntite

Magnesite ore and its various processed forms— "dead burned" magnesia, calcined magnesite, and so on—have a variety of uses, including the manufacture of refractories (the linings of furnaces and the like) and synthetic rubber. The ore is also one of the sources of the important industrial metal magnesium. High-grade deposits of magnesite are found in the Chalcidice peninsula in the northern part of Greece as well as in Euboea, but the latter deposits were not exploited after 1999.

Greece produced more than 3 percent of the world supply of the material in 2007, an estimated 628,000 metric tons. Grecian Magnesite S.A. is the only active producer in Greece and the largest in the European Union. The company operates open-pit mines near Yerakina, where it also crushes and processes the magnesite into various application-specific grades, and exports virtually all its production to other European Union countries.

Deposits of the related mineral huntite are found in the Kozáni basin in the northern province of Macedonia (not to be confused with the Republic of Macedonia). It is used in paper coatings and sealants and as a component of flame retardants. Greece is virtually the only commercial source for huntite and produced an estimated 18,000 metric tons of the mineral in 2007, most of it for export. White Minerals S.A. and Microfine Hellas S.A. are the two producers.

### PUMICE AND RELATED MATERIALS

Greece is the second largest source of pumice in the world, producing an estimated 960,000 metric tons in 2007. The light, highly porous volcanic glass is used in horticulture and, particularly outside the United States, as aggregate in construction. Pumice is found on several Greek islands in the southern Aegean Sea. It was once mined on Thíra (also known as Santorini), but today the only extraction taking place is on the island of Gyali, where pumice was deposited approximately 200,000 years ago by a volcano on the nearby island of Nísiros. Lava Mining and Quarrying Company, a subsidiary of Heracles General Cement, is Greece's only pumice producer as well as the largest pumice exporter in the world. The company quarries the pumice without the use of explosives and loads ships by means of a complex series of conveyor belts.

Lava Mining also quarries and distributes other industrial materials associated with ancient volcanic activity. It extracts pozzolanic rock at Xylokeratia on Melos and gypsum at Altsi on the island of Crete, with the bulk of its production of both materials going into the domestic manufacture of cement. The microcrystalline quartz it quarries on Melos is used in glass and ceramics.

### LIGNITE

Lignite, or brown coal, is Greece's only important natural fuel source, and it accounts for about 60 percent of the country's power generation. The country is the second largest producer of the material in the European Union (after Germany) and the fourth largest in the world. Greece is thought to possess reserves of nearly 7 billion metric tons of lignite in more than forty widely scattered basins, the largest of which is in Macedonia. Lignite is an inferior grade of coal, and the deposits in the Megalópolis region in the Pelo-

ponnese Peninsula are of particularly poor quality. A large deposit in the Drama basin is also of poor quality and remains relatively unexploited. Greece produced an estimated 74 million metric tons of the material in 2007, most of it from open pits.

Virtually all Greek lignite is mined by Public Power Corporation (PPC) S.A., which was founded in 1951 to exploit the reserves in Aliveri on the island of Euboea. A second company, Ptolemais Lignite Mines (LIPTOL), undertook a larger operation to extract the material from the Ptolemais deposit in the Pindus Mountains of northern Greece, eventually leading to one of the most substantial lignite mining and processing operations in the world. PPC acquired 90 percent of LIPTOL in 1959, and the two merged in 1975. PPC owns rights to about 60 percent of Greece's known lignite reserves, using most of the material itself. The company, which is state-controlled, generates virtually all of Greece's electrical power.

Lignite's use as an energy source poses serious environmental problems, and Greece is under pressure from the European Union to modernize its operation to reduce carbon emissions. Although it continues to rely on lignite, PPC also generates small amounts of hydroelectric power from dams on rivers in the Pindus Mountains.

### OTHER RESOURCES

Greece possesses modest deposits of gold, silver, chromite, lead, barite, and zinc. S&B has been active in identifying further deposits of gold, and Thracean Gold Mines S.A. (of which S&B is a part-owner) discovered a substantial deposit in Thrace in 1998.

A small oil field in the northern Aegean Sea has been exploited since 1981. Discovered by the American firm Oceanic and developed by the North Aegean Petroleum Company (NAPC)—a consortium headed by Denison Mines of Canada—the field reached a maximum production of 30,000 barrels per day (bpd) in 1989. However, production has fallen, while the country's dependence on foreign petroleum has grown. In 2004, a larger field in the same area was identified west of the island of Thásos. Believed to contain approximately 227 million barrels, it is being developed by Kavala Oil S.A. and Energiaki S.A. and may reach production levels of 50,000 bpd.

Marble has been quarried throughout Greece for millennia, and the country produced an estimated 150,000 cubic meters of the stone in various sizes of cuts in 2007. The major suppliers are Aghia Marina

Marble Ltd., with quarries at Pallini, and Chris G. Karantanis & Sons Company at Corinth. Greece also produced about 60,000 metric tons of dolomite and 95,000 metric tons of flysch in 2007. Salt production yielded an estimated 195,000 metric tons the same year.

*Grove Koger*

FURTHER READING

Arvanitidis, Nikos. "Northern Greece's Industrial Minerals: Production and Environmental Technology Developments." *Journal of Geochemical Exploration* 62, nos. 1-3 (1998): 217-227.

Couloumbis, Theodore A., Theodore Kariotis, and Fotini Bellou, eds. *Greece in the Twentieth Century.* New York: Frank Cass, 2003.

Curtis, Glenn E., ed. *Greece: A Country Study.* 4th ed. Washington, D.C.: Federal Research Division, Library of Congress; Headquarters, Department of the Army, 1995.

Grossou-Valta, M., and F. Chalkiopoulou. "Industrial Minerals and Sustainable Development in Greece." In *Mineral Resource Base of the Southern Caucasus and Systems for Its Management in the Twenty-first Century,* edited by Alexander G. Tvalchrelidze and Georges Morizot. Boston: Kluwer Academic, 2002.

Hatzilazaridou, Kiki. "A Review of Greek Industrial Minerals." In *Industrial Minerals and Extractive Industry Geology,* edited by Peter W. Scott and Colin Malcolm Bristow. London: Geological Society, 2002.

Kavouridis, Konstantinos. "Lignite Industry in Greece Within a World Context: Mining, Energy Supply, and Environment." *Energy Policy* 36, no. 4 (2008): 1257-1272.

Kennedy, Bruce A. *Surface Mining.* Littleton, Colo.: Society for Mining, Metallurgy, and Exploration, 1990.

Kogel, Jessica Elzea, et al. *Industrial Minerals and Rocks: Commodities, Markets, and Uses.* 7th ed. Littleton, Colo.: Society for Mining, Metallurgy, and Exploration, 2006.

Konsolas, Nicholas, A. Papadaskalopoulos, and I. Plaskovitis. *Regional Development in Greece.* New York: Springer, 2002.

WEB SITES

GREEK INSTITUTE OF GEOLOGY AND MINERAL EXPLORATION
http://www.igme.gr/enmain.htm

HELLENIC REPUBLIC MINISTRY OF DEVELOPMENT
http://www.ypan.gr/index_uk_c_cms.htm

SEE ALSO: Aluminum; Marble; Perlite; Pumice.

# Green Revolution

CATEGORIES: Environment, conservation, and resource management; historical events and movements

*Impending famine in the 1960's in the underdeveloped countries of Asia, Africa, and Latin America was averted by the Green Revolution, which was made possible by the introduction of hybrid "miracle grains" of wheat and rice.*

BACKGROUND

From 1960 to 1965 a number of poor countries in the world could not produce enough food for their growing populations. The Earth's population had almost doubled to 3.7 billion people in fifty years, with more than 900 million people not getting adequate nourishment to lead productive lives. Famine had been avoided during the post-World War II period of history only because production was high for American farmers and surplus grains were shipped overseas as food aid.

In 1966 and 1967, the Indo-Pakistan subcontinent suffered two consecutive crop failures because of monsoons. The United States shipped one-fifth of its wheat reserves to India and sustained sixty million persons in India for a two-year period on American food shipments. It became obvious, as populations continued to grow, that the United States would not be able to continue to supply enough food to feed the world's growing population adequately. In the mid-1960's, American policy began to change from giving poor countries direct food aid to educating and helping them to increase their own food production.

The United States had, in the 1950's, responded to an ailing agricultural economy in Mexico by sending scientists from the Rockefeller Foundation to develop a new wheat that yielded twice as much grain as traditional varieties. The project was successful, and in 1962, the Rockefeller Foundation collaborated with the Ford Foundation to establish the International Rice Research Institute at Los Baños, in the Philippines. Two strains of rice, PETA from Indonesia and DGWG from China, were crossbred to produce a high-yield semidwarf variety of rice called IR-8.

Both the new rice and new wheat were developed to have short but strong and stiff stalks to support large heads of grain. Yields from the rice and wheat seeds were two to five times higher than traditional varieties as long as they were grown with large inputs of fertilizer, water, and pesticides.

Seeds were shipped to ailing countries. Asia expanded acreage planted in the new varieties from 81 hectares to 14 million hectares between 1965 and 1969. Pakistan's wheat harvest increased 60 percent between 1967 and 1969. India's production of wheat increased 50 percent, and the Philippines' production of rice was so successful that it stopped importing rice and became an exporter.

### POSITIVE ASPECTS

The new seeds were dependent on irrigation by tube wells (closed cylindrical shafts driven into the ground) and electrical pumps. Irrigation methods were installed in poor countries. This new availability of water made it feasible for farmers to grow crops year-round. The dry season, with its abundant sunlight, had previously been a time when crops could not be grown. With the advent of irrigation, the dry season became an especially productive growing season. Poor countries in tropical and subtropical regions were able to grow two, three, and sometimes four crops a year. Approximately 90 percent of the increase of the world's production of grain in the 1960's, 70 percent in the 1970's, and 80 percent in the 1980's was attributable to the Green Revolution.

The Green Revolution brought to politicians in developing countries the realization that they could not depend permanently on food aid from other nations. Whereas leaders and politicians in these countries had previously concentrated on developing industrial projects, the extreme pressure of overpopulation on their limited food and land supplies caused them to address agricultural problems and give emphasis to programs to encourage production of food supplies. Countries that were affected by, and benefited from, the Green Revolution include India, Pakistan, Sri

*In this 1970 photograph, Norman Borlaug, considered the father of the Green Revolution, studies grains that he helped develop.* (AP/Wide World Photos)

Lanka, the Philippines, Turkey, Burma (Myanmar), Malaysia, Indonesia, Vietnam, Kenya, the Ivory Coast, Tunisia, Morocco, Algeria, Libya, Brazil, and Paraguay.

### DRAWBACKS AND ENVIRONMENTAL IMPACT

Large-scale pesticide application not only is costly but also can have an adverse effect on the environment. Only a small percentage of insecticides used on crops actually reach the target organism. The rest affects the environment by endangering groundwater, aquatic systems, pollinators, various soil-dwelling insects, microbes, birds, and other animals in the food chain. In addition, large water inputs are needed for proper irrigation of crops. Of the farmers who can afford to irrigate in poor countries, many do not do so properly, and thereby cause salinization, alkalization, and waterlogging of soils, rendering them useless for growing crops.

Large-scale application of fertilizers is costly and reaches a point where further applications do not produce the expected increase in yield and begin to cost far more than they are worth. Crop yields also decrease because of increased soil erosion, loss of soil fertility, aquifer depletion, desertification, and pollution of groundwater or surface waters.

The Green Revolution exemplifies monoculture agriculture, the planting of large areas with a single type of seed. This use of monotypes can create multiple environmental problems. In many cases, the widespread use of genetically homogeneous seed caused old varieties with great genetic variability to be abandoned. Crops consisting entirely of genetically homogeneous rice and wheat are more vulnerable to disease and insects, requiring inputs of agrochemicals which can be harmful to both the environment and human health. Planting vast hectares of monotypes has the potential to result in massive crop failure due to destructive fungi or chemical-resistant insects.

Moreover, Green Revolution techniques rely heavily on fossil fuel to run machinery, to produce and apply inorganic fertilizers and pesticides, and to pump water for irrigation. Gasoline is costly and is often in short supply in many of the poor nations. Sociologically, the Green Revolution in poor countries favored wealthier farmers with the capital to pay the considerable costs of irrigation, seeds, fertilizers, pesticides, and fossil fuels. This fact has accentuated the financial gap between the big and small farmers.

## Outlook

The drawbacks of the Green Revolution have led farmers and scientists to seek safer and more diverse solutions to world food needs. Genetic engineers hope to be able to breed high-yield plant strains that have greater resistance to insects and disease, need less fertilizer, and are capable of making their own nitrogen fertilizer so as not to deplete the soil of nutrients. Proponents of integrated pest management continue to investigate combinations of crop rotation, time of planting, field sanitation, and the use of predators and parasites as ways to control insects without the use of harmful chemicals. Regardless of developments in food production and technology, however, in the long term the most important aspect of addressing world food needs is to control population growth.

*Dion C. Stewart*

FURTHER READING

Alauddin, Mohammad, and Clement Tisdell. *The "Green Revolution" and Economic Development: The Process and Its Impact in Bangladesh.* New York: St. Martin's Press, 1991.

Brown, Lester R. *Seeds of Change: The Green Revolution and Development in the 1970's.* New York: Published for the Overseas Development Council by Praeger, 1970.

Chiras, Daniel D., and John P. Reganold. *Natural Resource Conservation: Management for a Sustainable Future.* 10th ed. Upper Saddle River, N.J.: Pearson Prentice Hall, 2009.

Cotter, Joseph. *Troubled Harvest: Agronomy and Revolution in Mexico, 1880-2002.* Westport, Conn.: Praeger, 2003.

Miller, G. Tyler, Jr., and Scott Spoolman. *Environmental Science: Problems, Concepts, and Solutions.* 12th ed. Belmont, Calif.: Brooks Cole, 2008.

Perkins, John H. *Geopolitics and the Green Revolution: Wheat, Genes, and the Cold War.* New York: Oxford University Press, 1997.

Shiva, Vandana. *The Violence of the Green Revolution: Third World Agriculture, Ecology, and Politics.* London: Zed Books, 1991.

Singh, Himmat. *Green Revolutions Reconsidered: The Rural World of Contemporary Punjab.* New York: Oxford University Press, 2001.

Wu, Felicia, and William Butz. *The Future of Genetically Modified Crops: Lessons from the Green Revolution.* Santa Monica, Calif.: RAND Institute, 2004.

SEE ALSO: Fertilizers; Genetic diversity; Monoculture agriculture; Pesticides and pest control; Population growth; Rice; Wheat.

# Greenhouse gases and global climate change

CATEGORIES: Environment, conservation, and resource management; geological processes and formations; pollution and waste disposal

*The greenhouse effect protects Earth and all life on the planet from succumbing to extremes of temperature at the same time that it threatens to overheat the planet as the concentration of greenhouse gases increases.*

## BACKGROUND

The atmosphere is heated directly by carbon dioxide and water vapor absorbing heat or infrared energy from the Earth's surface. Without this natural process, called the greenhouse effect, the average atmospheric temperature would be around 16° Celsius lower than it is now—too cold to support life. The activities of human beings have increased natural concentrations of carbon dioxide and other gases, including chlorofluorocarbons (CFCs), fluorinated gases (HCFCs), methane ($CH_4$), nitrous oxide ($N_2O$), and, to some extent, ozone ($O_3$), all now labeled, along with water vapor, as greenhouse gases. The average temperature has increased as well. This concurrent rise in temperature and greenhouse gas concentra-tion is called global climate change or global warming.

The concern is not with the "greenhouse effect" itself, which in actuality is necessary for life on Earth. The cause for alarm is the intensification or enhancement of the greenhouse effect and the resulting changes in climate, weather patterns, and the oceans, and the effect of these on living organisms. Thus, the term global climate change is preferred over global warming because the effects are expected to extend to other aspects of climate beyond that of temperature.

The climate of the Earth is not stable; it has changed from natural causes throughout Earth's history, before human beings existed, and it will continue to change. However, increased concentrations of green-

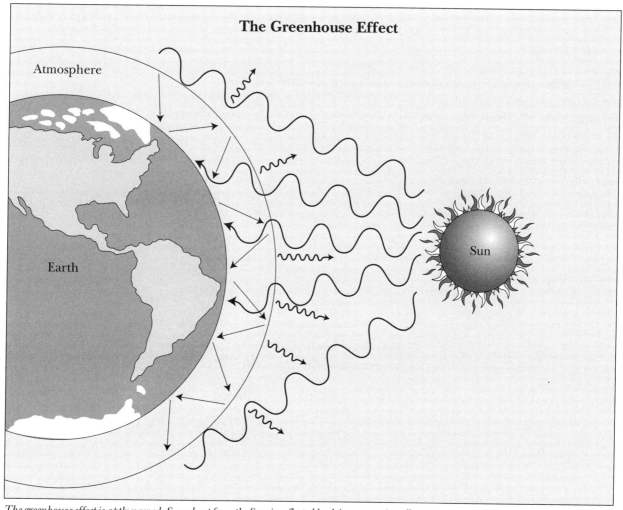

**The Greenhouse Effect**

Atmosphere

Earth

Sun

*The greenhouse effect is aptly named: Some heat from the Sun is reflected back into space (small squiggled arrows), but some becomes trapped by Earth's atmosphere and re-radiates toward Earth (straight arrows), heating the planet just as heat is trapped inside a greenhouse.*

house gases from human activities, particularly industrialization, are now recognized as having a warming effect on the Earth's atmosphere. The U.S. National Oceanic and Atmospheric Administration reported that measurements from land and oceans show that between 1850 and 2006 the global mean surface temperature increased between 0.56° and 0.92° Celsius, while from preindustrial times to 2006, the concentration of $CO_2$ grew from about 280 to about 380 parts per million (ppm). Much debate occurred in the late twentieth century about correlation or causality of temperature increase and the level of $CO_2$. Most respected scientists ascribed the increase to human causes. However, resistance to this assessment existed, including from the federal government of the United States. In 2007, the Intergovernmental Panel on Climate Change, created by the United Nations and the World Meteorological Organization, released a report based on solid research and analysis of data by respected scientists from many different countries. It stated, at a high confidence level, with 90 percent assurance statistically, that human activities were inducing climate change. Consequences—such as coastal flooding, loss of biodiversity, widespread drought, and extended heat waves—were more likely with continued increases of greenhouse gases. As a result, calls came for people and governments to act to reduce the chance of serious or even disastrous impacts.

GREENHOUSE GASES AND RESOURCE USE
Fossil fuels—petroleum, natural gas, and coal—have been identified as the main culprits in global climate change. The name fossil fuels reflects their origin from decomposed dead plants and animals over hundreds of millions of years. Industrialization has been literally fueled by the carbon in fossil fuels, providing heat energy for factories, electricity production, and transportation. Large amounts of carbon, which had been sitting in the Earth's crust in the form of fossil fuels, were burned and combined with oxygen, producing $CO_2$, which in the atmosphere absorbed heat from the Earth's surface, leading to documented increases in temperature.

Methane, a major component of natural gas, is produced naturally and by human activities, including livestock production and rice cultivation. Methane's concentration grew from preindustrial levels of about 715 parts per billion to about 1,774 ppb in 2005, a gain of about 148 percent. Fluorinated gases, replacements for CFCs (contributors to ozone depletion), have grown in concentration. They have a higher greenhouse impact than CFCs. Nitrous oxide, produced naturally by plants, also reaches the atmosphere largely as a result of fertilizer use and fossil-fuel combustion. Its concentration increased about 18 percent from preindustrial levels of about 270 ppb to 319 ppb in 2005.

Other actions contributing to increased greenhouse gases include removal of natural vegetation for urban and agricultural purposes. The elimination of green plants leads to reduced photosynthesis and therefore less carbon dioxide being removed and replaced by oxygen. Furthermore, economic problems can result from deforestation and desertification as land loses its productivity.

CLIMATE CHANGE AND RESOURCE USE
Sea levels have risen around 12.2 to 22.3 centimeters from partial melting of the Greenland and Antarctic ice sheets, augmented by the physical expansion of

## U.S. Greenhouse Gas Emissions
### (millions of metric tons)

|                 | 1990    | 2000    | 2002    | 2003    | 2004    | 2005    | 2006    |
|-----------------|---------|---------|---------|---------|---------|---------|---------|
| Carbon dioxide  | 5,017.5 | 5,890.5 | 5,875.9 | 5,940.4 | 6,019.9 | 6,045.0 | 5,934.4 |
| Methane gas     | 708.4   | 608.0   | 598.6   | 603.7   | 605.9   | 607.3   | 605.1   |
| Nitrous oxide   | 333.7   | 341.9   | 332.5   | 331.7   | 358.3   | 368.0   | 378.9   |
| High GWP gases  | 87.1    | 138.0   | 137.8   | 136.6   | 149.4   | 161.2   | 157.6   |

Source: U.S. Energy Information Administration, Emissions of Greenhouse Gases in the United States, 2006, 2006.
Note: High GWP (global warming potential) gases are hydrofluorocarbons, perfluorcarbons, and sulfur hexafluoride.

the warming ocean water. Coastal zones and small islands especially are in danger not only from flooding but also from effects of enhanced storms. Biodiversity of the oceans, including in the Great Barrier Reef, is threatened. In Europe, although the growing season is now warmer and crop yields and forest growth have increased, more intense heat waves and widespread flooding have caused health and safety problems. Melting of glaciers in the Himalayas and snowpacks in the mountains of the western United States and Canada is likely to cause floods and maybe avalanches. Because ice reflects sunlight, as Arctic ice melts, the rate of global warming may accelerate. Salinization and desertification are likely in currently productive agricultural lands in dry regions in South America. As the oceans have become warmer, levels of salinity and $CO_2$ have changed, probably altering ocean currents and their distribution of heat. The acidity of the oceans has changed as well, perhaps greatly disrupting fisheries, coral reefs, and marine ecosystems as a whole.

## POSSIBLE CHANGES IN RESOURCE USE

Calls and actions for reducing carbon emissions and lessening the output of other greenhouse gases have intensified around the world. Conservation is an important option, but some people are concerned that limiting the economic activities that produce $CO_2$ will hurt the economy. Yet conservation can build its own industries, as indicated by the number of "green" products being introduced.

*Margaret F. Boorstein*

FURTHER READING

Abrahmason, Dean Edwin, ed. *The Challenge of Global Warming.* Washington, D.C.: Island Press, 1989.

Archer, David. *Global Warming: Understanding the Forecast.* Malden, Mass.: Blackwell, 2007.

Firor, John. *The Changing Atmosphere: A Global Challenge.* New Haven, Conn.: Yale University Press, 1990.

Gore, Al. *An Inconvenient Truth: The Planetary Emergency of Global Warming and What We Can Do About It.* Emmaus, Pa.: Rodale Press, 2006.

Gribbin, John. *Hothouse Earth: The Greenhouse Effect and GAIA.* New York: Grove Weidenfeld, 1990.

Johansen, Bruce E. *Global Warming 101.* Westport, Conn.: Greenwood Press, 2008.

Kraljic, Matthew A., ed. *The Greenhouse Effect.* New York: H. W. Wilson, 1992.

Krupp, Fred, and Miriam Horn. *Earth, the Sequel: The Race to Reinvent Energy and Stop Global Warming.* New York: W. W. Norton, 2008.

Metz, Beth, ed. *Climate Change 2007: Mitigation of Climate Change—Contribution of Working Group Three to the Fourth Assessment of the Intergovernmental Panel on Climate Change.* New York: Cambridge University Press, 2007.

Rowlands, Ian H. *The Politics of Global Atmospheric Change.* New York: St. Martin's Press, 1995.

Schneider, Stephen H. *Global Warming: Are We Entering the Greenhouse Century?* San Francisco: Sierra Club Books, 1989.

Solomon, Susan, ed. *Climate Change 2007: The Physical Science Basis—Contribution of Working Group One to the Fourth Assessment Report of the Intergovernmental Panel on Climate Change.* New York: Cambridge University Press, 2007.

Somerville, Richard C. J. *The Forgiving Air: Understanding Environmental Change.* 2d ed. Boston: American Meteorological Society, 2008.

Svensson, Lisa. *Combating Climate Change: A Transatlantic Approach to Common Solutions.* Washington, D.C.: Center for Transatlantic Relations, Johns Hopkins University, 2008.

Tickell, Oliver. *Kyoto2: How to Manage the Global Greenhouse.* New York: Palgrave Macmillan, 2008.

WEB SITES

ENERGY INFORMATION ADMINISTRATION, U.S. DEPARTMENT OF ENERGY
Greenhouse Gases, Climate Change, and Energy
http://www.eia.doe.gov/bookshelf/brochures/greenhouse/Chapter1.htm

ENVIRONMENT CANADA
Greenhouse Gas Sources and Sinks
http://www.ec.gc.ca/pdb/ghg/ghg_home_e.cfm

NATIONAL OCEANIC AND ATMOSPHERIC ADMINISTRATION
Climate Program Office
http://www.climate.noaa.gov

U.S. ENVIRONMENTAL PROTECTION AGENCY
Greenhouse Gas Emissions
http://www.epa.gov/climatechange/emissions/index.html#ggo

SEE ALSO: Agenda 21; American Chemistry Council; Climate Change and Sustainable Energy Act; Earth

Summit; Environmental law in the United States; Gore, Al; Kyoto Protocol; United Nations climate change conferences; United Nations Convention on Long-Range Transboundary Air Pollution; United Nations Environment Programme.

# Greenpeace

CATEGORY: Organizations, agencies, and programs
DATE: Established 1969

*Greenpeace is an international environmental watchdog organization concerned with protecting the Earth's natural resources.*

## BACKGROUND

Greenpeace evolved from activists' concerns about nuclear testing near Alaska in the late 1960's. Fearing catastrophic environmental damage, the organization's founders relied on confrontational tactics to draw attention to their cause. Notably, Greenpeace members sought to "bear witness": Simply being present where a wrongdoing was committed symbolized one's objection to the act. This approach could entail such perilous and controversial tactics as sailing right up to a proposed nuclear test site and daring officials to set off devices with humans within the safety zone.

## IMPACT ON RESOURCE USE

The idea of "bearing witness" expanded to include several other campaigns intended to protect the Earth's natural resources and maintain biodiversity. Its activities on behalf of marine life, especially whales and seals, represented Greenpeace's fight to protect wildlife from human destruction. Through showdown encounters with whaling vessels and seal hunters, Greenpeace joined an international call for a decrease in—and ultimately the halting of—whale and seal hunting.

Other environmental issues soon moved the organization into new arenas. Campaigns emerged to arouse people's concern and educate the world to the environmental dangers associated with hazardous waste dumping, toxic chemical production, and global warming.

Greenpeace's techniques, although often controversial, brought international notice to its causes. The organization proved successful in raising public awareness of threats to the Earth's natural resources and calling for action to protect them.

*Jennifer Davis*

## WEB SITES

GREENPEACE
Greenpeace International
http://www.greenpeace.org/international/

GREENPEACE
Greenpeace USA
http://www.greenpeace.org/usa/

SEE ALSO: Earth First!; Environmental ethics; Environmental movement; Friends of the Earth International; Hazardous waste disposal; National Audubon Society; Nuclear energy; Sea Shepherd Conservation Society.

# Groundwater

CATEGORIES: Ecological resources; geological processes and formations; mineral and other nonliving resources

*Groundwater is that portion of the Earth's subsurface water that is contained within the zone of saturation. It accounts for a much larger fraction of the total volume of water in storage on the Earth than all of the combined fresh surface water.*

## BACKGROUND

Groundwater is one of the most valuable natural resources: It serves as the source of a significant percentage of the water used for all purposes. However, even though it is so widely used and so vital to the health and economy of all nations, the occurrence of groundwater is not only poorly understood but also subject to many misconceptions. For example, one common misconception is that groundwater flows in large underground rivers that resemble surface streams. Folklore has it that these streams can be detected by certain special individuals who practice "water dowsing." Such misconceptions have hindered the development and conservation of groundwater and have negatively affected the protection of water quality.

## INFILTRATION

Groundwater is a major component of the hydrologic cycle, which is the constant movement of water above, on, and below the Earth's surface. That fraction of precipitation that can infiltrate the Earth's surface can become part of the subsurface component of the hydrologic cycle. Infiltration rates vary enormously, depending upon the intensity and duration of precipitation, land use, and the physical characteristics and moisture content of the soil. For example, the infiltration rates can range from a high of 25 millimeters per hour in mature forests on sandy soils to only a few millimeters per hour in clayey and silty soils to zero in paved areas.

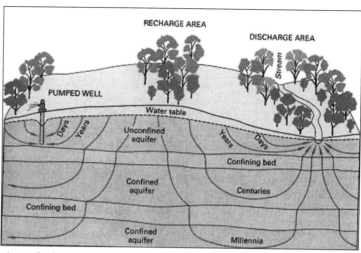

*A standard aquifer system, featuring the flow times of different paths.* (USGS)

## THE UNSATURATED ZONE

Subsurface water occurs in two distinct zones in the ground. The uppermost zone contains both water and air and is called the unsaturated zone. It is divided into three parts: a soil zone or soil-water belt, an intermediate zone, and the upper part of the capillary fringe. The soil-water belt extends from the top of the land surface to a maximum depth of about 1 to 2 meters. The porosity (the amount of openings in earth material) and the permeability (velocity of fluid flow within the Earth material) are higher in the soil-water belt than in the underlying intermediate zone. The capillary fringe is located in the lowest part of the unsaturated zone and results from the attraction between water and rocks. The thickness or depth of the unsaturated zone varies from zero in swamps to a few meters in humid regions to more than 300 meters in deserts.

## THE SATURATED ZONE

The zone below the unsaturated zone has all interconnected openings filled with water and is called the saturated zone. The top of the saturated zone is marked by the water table, which is the level at which the hydraulic pressure is equal to atmospheric pressure. Water in the saturated zone is the only subsurface water that supplies wells, springs, and base flow to streams and is the only water which is properly called groundwater.

## GROUNDWATER MOVEMENT

In sharp contrast to surface water, groundwater moves very slowly. For example, surface water can move tens of kilometers per day, whereas groundwater flow ranges approximately from 1.5 meters per day to as low as 1.5 meters per year. This slow movement means that any contaminant that gets into groundwater will be there for a long time.

As part of the hydrologic cycle, groundwater also furnishes the stream with base flow or dry-weather flow. This is why streams in humid areas have water flowing in the channel days after precipitation has occurred. In fact, a large portion of streamflow is derived from base flow which is groundwater.

## GROUNDWATER RECHARGE

The source of groundwater is precipitation in the recharge area that has percolated through the unsaturated zone and reached the water table. Once there, groundwater flows down the hydraulic gradient to discharge areas along floodplains and streams. Average annual recharge rates in the United States range from zero in desert areas to as much as 600 millimeters per year in rural areas in Long Island, New York, and similar places along the Atlantic coastal plain that are underlain by permeable sands. These high recharge rates account for as much as 50 percent of average annual precipitation.

The rate of groundwater movement from recharge areas to discharge areas depends upon the permeability and porosity of the Earth material. Shallow groundwater flow to discharge areas can be measured in days as compared with deep groundwater flow which can take decades, centuries, or even millennia to reach a discharge area.

## GROUNDWATER QUALITY AND GROUNDWATER POLLUTION

Water is often referred to as the universal solvent because of its ability to dissolve at least small amounts of almost all substances that it contacts. Since groundwater moves very slowly, it has plenty of time to dissolve earth materials. Thus, groundwater usually contains large amounts of dissolved solids.

Groundwater pollution refers to any degradation of water quality that results from anthropogenic activities. In urban and suburban areas, these activities include disposal of industrial and municipal wastes in unlined landfills, leaking sewers, and application of lawn fertilizers, herbicides, and pesticides. Groundwater can be polluted in rural areas by septic tanks, animal feedlots, and application of crop fertilizers, herbicides, and pesticides. Other sources of groundwater pollution include leaking gasoline and home-heating oil tanks, salt coming from unprotected stockpiles, and saltwater encroachment in coastal areas that have been overpumped. There have been numerous instances of groundwater pollution: Municipal wells on Long Island were forced to close because of a pre–World War II application of fertilizers to potato fields; public supply wells were closed in Massachusetts because of excessive road salt applications; and well fields were contaminated by saltwater encroachment in Dade County, Florida, and Southern California (Manhattan Beach).

*Robert M. Hordon*

FURTHER READING

Appelo, C. A. J., and D. Postma. *Geochemistry, Groundwater, and Pollution*. 2d ed. New York: Balkema, 2005.

Fetter, C. W. *Applied Hydrogeology*. 4th ed. Upper Saddle River, N.J.: Prentice Hall, 2001.

_____. *Contaminant Hydrogeology*. 2d ed. Upper Saddle River, N.J.: Prentice Hall, 1999.

Palmer, Christopher M. *Principles of Contaminant Hydrogeology*. 2d ed. Boca Raton, Fla.: CRC Lewis, 1996.

Price, Michael. *Introducing Groundwater*. 2d ed. New York: Chapman & Hall, 1996.

Todd, David Keith, and Larry W. Mays. *Groundwater Hydrology*. 3d ed. Hoboken, N.J.: Wiley, 2005.

Younger, Paul L. *Groundwater in the Environment: An Introduction*. Malden, Mass.: Blackwell, 2007.

Zektser, Igor S., and Lorne G. Everett, eds. *Ground Water Resources of the World and Their Use*. Paris: UNESCO, 2004. Reprint. Westerville, Ohio: National Ground Water Association Press, 2006.

WEB SITES

NATURAL RESOURCES CANADA
Groundwater
http://atlas.nrcan.gc.ca/site/english/maps/freshwater/distribution/groundwater/1

U.S. ENVIRONMENTAL PROTECTION AGENCY
Aquatic Biodiversity: Groundwater
http://www.epa.gov/bioiweb1/aquatic/ground-r.html

U.S. GEOLOGICAL SURVEY
USGS Groundwater Information Pages
http://water.usgs.gov/ogw

SEE ALSO: Aquifers; Glaciation; Hydrology and the hydrologic cycle; U.S. Geological Survey; Water; Water pollution and water pollution control; Water supply systems; Wetlands.

# Guano

CATEGORY: Plant and animal resources

*Accumulated bird excrement, rich in nitrogen, is known as guano and offers a renewable source of fertilizers.*

## DEFINITION

Guano is a renewable natural fertilizer. It is found in commercial quantities only on a few desert islands where millions of fish-eating sea birds roost undisturbed.

## OVERVIEW

There is archaeological evidence that guano was collected and used by prehistoric Peruvian farmers, who called it *huano*. Nineteenth century application of guano to the exhausted soils of Europe was first advocated by the German agronomist Georg Leibig after its introduction in the 1830's by the noted scientist and South American explorer Alexander von Humboldt. The dramatic increases it caused in wheat, corn, and cotton production created enormous demand for this product, which was soon being dug by hundreds of Chinese laborers forced to work on the Chincha Islands south of Lima, Peru.

These rain-free guano islands are populated by millions of cormorants, gannets, and pelicans that fly out to sea daily to eat anchovies and sardines. The fish themselves feed on plankton they find in the cold, north-flowing Chile-Peru (Humboldt) Current. When this current is occasionally displaced by a warm (El Niño) countercurrent, the entire ecosystem collapses, and many sea birds begin to die of starvation.

A guano boom began in 1851, when the U.S. Congress passed legislation allowing any American citizen to declare uninhabited guano islands as territory of the United States. Under the provisions of this little-known act, several Caribbean and South Pacific islands were so claimed. One of them, Navassa, located midway between Cuba and Haiti, remains an undisputed U.S. territorial possession to this day under jurisdiction of the U.S. Fish and Wildlife Service. Subfossil guano deposits found there are thought to be the excrement of a fish-eating bat.

Although the Peruvian government recognized guano as a strategic and highly valuable natural resource, little was done to protect the industry from foreign interests and political intrigue. In order to meet financial obligations and service debts, the government mortgaged its guano resources for quick cash loans from foreign business firms selling the increasingly valuable Chincha guano.

Failure to protect the guano-producing birds, as well as ignorance of the complex ecology of their habitat, eventually resulted in the decline of the industry in the face of overwhelming competition from Chilean sodium nitrate deposits discovered in the 1870's. Not until the 1910's was any progress made in reviving the resource. Based on the advice of foreign ichthyologists and the American ornithologist Robert Cushman Murphy, good conservation practices were begun by Francisco Ballen, director of the newly created Compañía Administradora del Guano.

*A massive guano-collecting structure juts from the guano-covered, rocky shoreline of the Ballestas Islands off the coast of Peru.* (©Jarnogz/Dreamstime.com)

The impact of several disastrous El Niño events beginning in 1925, together with severe overfishing of anchovy stocks, seriously retarded the buildup of new Peruvian guano deposits. No longer exported, Chincha guano is now used exclusively for the benefit of Peruvian agriculture.

Guano is also collected elsewhere in the world and used locally; farmers in Baja California, Mexico, and some regions of western Africa, for example, use it as fertilizer. Bat-guano deposits often occur in caves with sufficiently large bat populations. Seal excrement is also sometimes included in the definition of guano. Bird guano, however, has a higher concentration of fertilizing nutrients (notably nitrogen and phosphoric acid) than either bat or seal guano.

From the study of any deep undisturbed sequence of guano may come a valuable scientific record of environmental conditions that prevailed while it was accumulating. Identifying and dating ancient layers showing disturbed conditions can give statistical clues to hidden climatic cycles and the ability to predict future long-range changes in weather patterns.

*Alan K. Craig*

SEE ALSO: El Niño and La Niña; Fertilizers; Nitrogen and ammonia.

# Guggenheim family

CATEGORY: People

*The Guggenheims are an American family who dominated mining and refining operations worldwide in the first quarter of the twentieth century. Aggressively controlling and extracting metals and minerals in the United States and developing countries, the Guggenheims built one of the world's great fortunes, which they used for philanthropic enterprises in the latter half of the twentieth century.*

BIOGRAPHICAL BACKGROUND

The founder of the family business, Meyer Guggenheim (1828-1905), was a Jewish immigrant from a Switzerland ghetto. Accumulating capital from his Philadelphia store, he bought shares in Colorado mines in 1880. When the mines struck a silver bonanza, the Guggenheims' rise was launched on an empire of global resources. A partnership of Meyer and his seven sons, M. Guggenheim's Sons, bought mines and smelting operations in Mexico and throughout the world. (Smelting is the refining operation that extracts the valuable metal resources from the mined ore.) In 1899, Guggenheim and his sons started the Guggenheim Exploration Company (Guggenex) to consolidate and extend their interests.

In 1901, after an epic business battle, the Guggenheims took control of the American Smelting and Refining Company (ASARCO), a trust that dominated the mining industry. Second-oldest son Daniel (1856-1930) became president of ASARCO and aggressively expanded Guggenheim ventures into zinc and copper mining and to other continents. Daniel's son Harry Guggenheim (1890-1971) led a third generation of Guggenheims in additional entrepreneurial and philanthropic enterprises; his palatial Sands Point estate is preserved in Port Washington, New York. Peggy Guggenheim (1898-1979) was a prominent art collector and socialite.

IMPACT ON RESOURCE USE

The Guggenheims dominated the worldwide mining and smelting industry in the beginning of the twentieth century through their ASARCO trust. Their operations began with silver and lead mines and smelters in the western United States, and, in 1890, in Monterrey, Mexico. Contracting with autocratic Mexican president Porfirio Díaz and with low-wage Mexican workers, the Guggenheims became the leading industrialists of Mexico. Their ASARCO and Guggenex firms expanded into copper mines in Utah in 1905 and silver mines in Nevada and Ontario, Canada, in 1906. In 1910, they acquired extensive copper mines in Chile, adding the label "Copper Kings" to their sobriquet of "Silver Kings."

Pioneering large-scale mining operations throughout the globe, the Guggenheims mined for nitrates in Chile, tin in Bolivia, copper in Australia, diamonds in Africa, and gold in Peru and the Yukon. Their rubber plantations in the Congo were barely profitable and entangled the Guggenheims in the brutal colonial competition for African resources. In 1911, they were subjected to congressional scrutiny for their efforts to develop Alaskan resources. Their various firms were continually suspected of antitrust violations. The Guggenheims did not hesitate to use force against striking mineworkers but later attained a reputation for better treatment of their employees and for steps to reduce the pollutants spewing from their refineries.

After World War I, the extended Guggenheim clan sold many of their mining and smelting interests, increasing their vast liquid fortune and turning their attention to charitable and social matters. Among their many philanthropies were a foundation to provide dentistry for the poor, donations to the Mayo Clinic and Mount Sinai Hospital, and the support of various educational enterprises, most prominently the Guggenheim Fellowships. The Guggenheim Aeronautical Laboratory opened in 1926, and the magnificent Solomon Guggenheim Art Museum in Manhattan opened in 1959.

*Howard Bromberg*

SEE ALSO: Copper; Diamond; Silver; Tin.

# Gypsum

CATEGORY: Mineral and other nonliving resources

## WHERE FOUND
Gypsum is the most common sulfate mineral. It is widely distributed in sedimentary rocks, frequently occurring with limestones and shales. It is commonly associated with minerals such as rock salt, anhydrite, dolomite, calcite, sulfur, pyrite, galena, and quartz. Gypsum is mined extensively in many parts of the world.

## PRIMARY USES
Gypsum is used in the construction industry, especially for the manufacture of plasters, wallboard, and tiles. It is also used in cements, as a filler in paper and paints, and as a fertilizer and soil conditioner.

## TECHNICAL DEFINITION
Gypsum is a hydrated calcium sulfate ($CaSO_4 \cdot 2H_2O$). Its average molecular weight is 172.18, and its specific gravity is 2.32. This mineral forms white or colorless prismatic crystals; impurities may add a grayish, reddish, yellowish, bluish, or brownish tint. Its hardness on the Mohs scale is 1.5 to 2. Gypsum has a characteristic three-way cleavage; that is, it breaks along three different crystallographic planes. It is insoluble in water and soluble in acids. When heated to between 190° and 200° Celsius, gypsum loses three-quarters of its water of crystallization to become calcium sulfate hemihydrate ($2CaSO_4 \cdot H_2O$), also known as plaster of

paris. Heating to more than 600° Celsius drives off all water to produce anhydrous or dead-burned gypsum.

## DESCRIPTION, DISTRIBUTION, AND FORMS
Gypsum, a widely distributed sedimentary deposit, is a soft, colorless, or light-colored mineral that can be scratched with the fingernail. Its crystals often form arrowhead-shaped or swallowtail-shaped twins (two individual crystals joined along a plane). When heated to drive off much of its water of crystallization, gypsum is transformed into plaster of paris (so named because of the famous gypsum deposits of the Montmartre district of Paris, France). When reduced to a powder and mixed with water, plaster of paris forms a slurry that sets quickly and gradually re-forms again as tiny interlocking crystals of gypsum. Its properties as a natural plaster make gypsum an important resource for construction and other industries. In 2008, the United States produced about 12.7 million metric tons of gypsum, and total world production was about 151 million metric tons.

Gypsum, the most common sulfate mineral, is widely distributed in sedimentary rocks. It forms thick, extensive evaporite beds, especially in rocks of Permian and Triassic age. In the United States, gypsum is present in rocks of every geologic era except the Cambrian. Because gypsum is normally deposited before anhydrite and salt during the evaporation of seawater, it often underlies beds of these minerals. Other minerals with which gypsum is frequently associated include dolomite, calcite, sulfur, pyrite, galena, quartz, and petroleum source rocks. Massive layers of gypsum frequently occur interbedded with limestones and shales, and lens-shaped bodies or scattered crystals are found in clays and shales. Gypsum is common in volcanic regions, particularly where limestones have been acted upon by sulfur vapors. It is also found in association with sulfide ore bodies. Extensive gypsum deposits are found in many localities throughout the world, including the United States, Great Britain, Thailand, Iran, Canada, China, France, and Australia. In Arizona and New Mexico there are large deposits in the form of wind-blown sand.

Gypsum occurs in nature in five varieties: gypsum rock, a bedded aggregate consisting mostly of the mineral gypsum; gypsite, an impure, earthy variety that is found in association with gypsum-bearing strata in arid regions; alabaster, a massive, fine-grained form, white or delicately shaded and often translucent; satin spar, a white, translucent mineral with a fibrous struc-

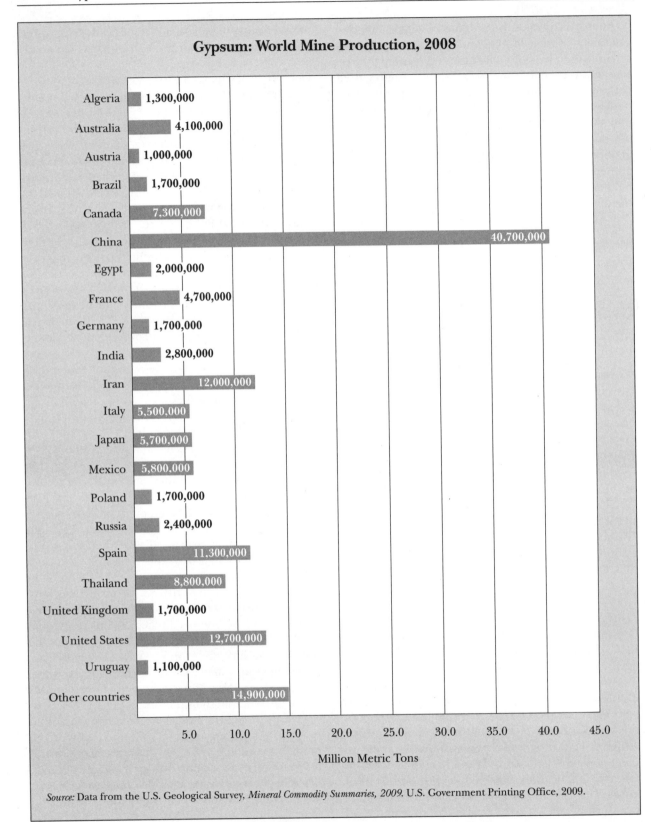

**Gypsum: World Mine Production, 2008**

| Country | Production |
|---|---|
| Algeria | 1,300,000 |
| Australia | 4,100,000 |
| Austria | 1,000,000 |
| Brazil | 1,700,000 |
| Canada | 7,300,000 |
| China | 40,700,000 |
| Egypt | 2,000,000 |
| France | 4,700,000 |
| Germany | 1,700,000 |
| India | 2,800,000 |
| Iran | 12,000,000 |
| Italy | 5,500,000 |
| Japan | 5,700,000 |
| Mexico | 5,800,000 |
| Poland | 1,700,000 |
| Russia | 2,400,000 |
| Spain | 11,300,000 |
| Thailand | 8,800,000 |
| United Kingdom | 1,700,000 |
| United States | 12,700,000 |
| Uruguay | 1,100,000 |
| Other countries | 14,900,000 |

Million Metric Tons

*Source:* Data from the U.S. Geological Survey, *Mineral Commodity Summaries, 2009.* U.S. Government Printing Office, 2009.

ture and a silky luster; and selenite, a transparent, colorless, crystalline variety.

Gypsum is rarely found in its pure form. Deposits may contain quartz, sulfide minerals, carbonates, and clayey and bituminous materials. Gypsum dehydrates readily in nature to form anhydrite ($CaSO_4$), a mineral with which it is often associated; bassanite ($2CaSO_4 \cdot H_2O$) forms much more rarely. High-temperature and low-humidity environments favor the formation of anhydrite. Anhydrite can also hydrate to form gypsum. Gypsum deposits formed by the alteration of anhydrite may show folding due to the increased volume of the mineral in its hydrated state.

## HISTORY

The Chinese, Assyrians, and Greeks made decorative carvings from gypsum. The Greek philosopher Theophrastus (371-287 B.C.E.) wrote of burning gypsum to create plaster. Gypsum's properties as a plaster were also known to the early Egyptians, who used a crude gypsum plaster in such building projects as the pyramids. Gypsum gained widespread use as a soil conditioner in eighteenth century Europe. The development of a commercial method for retarding the setting of gypsum plaster in 1885 made it possible to use gypsum for more construction applications.

## OBTAINING GYPSUM

Gypsum is generally obtained through open-pit mining, although some underground mining is performed where the material is of a high quality or is close to the consuming market. Gypsum may be crushed and ground for use in dihydrate form, heated to produce plaster of paris, or completely dehydrated to form anhydrous gypsum.

## USES OF GYPSUM

Unaltered gypsum is commonly used to slow the rate of setting in portland cement. Other major uses include the manufacture of wallboard, gypsum lath, and artificial marble products. Its sulfate contents make it useful for agriculture, where it serves as a soil conditioner and fertilizer. Gypsum is used as a white pigment, filler, or glaze in paints, enamels, pharmaceuticals, and paper. It is also used in making crayons, chalk, and insulating coverings for pipes and boilers. Other uses are as a filtration agent and a nutrient in yeast growing.

Plaster of paris is used for builder's plaster and the manufacture of plaster building materials such as moldings and panels. In medicine, plaster of paris is used for surgical casts, bandages, and supports and for taking dental and other impressions. The anhydrous form of gypsum is used in cement formulations; in metallurgy; in the manufacture of tiles, plate glass, pottery, and paints; and as a paper filler. Because of its water-absorbing nature, it is also used as a drying agent.

Alabaster, a form of gypsum that can be carved and polished with ease because of its softness, is fashioned into ornamental vessels, figures, and statuary. Satin spar is used in jewelry and other ornaments.

*Karen N. Kähler*

## FURTHER READING

Bates, Robert L. *Geology of the Industrial Rocks and Minerals.* New York: Dover, 1969.

Carr, Donald D., ed. *Industrial Minerals and Rocks.* 6th ed. Littleton, Colo.: Society for Mining, Metallurgy, and Exploration, 1994.

Chatterjee, Kaulir Kisor. "Gypsum." In *Uses of Industrial Minerals, Rocks, and Freshwater.* New York: Nova Science, 2009.

Kogel, Jessica Elzea, et al., eds. "Gypsum and Anhydrite." In *Industrial Minerals and Rocks: Commodities, Markets, and Uses.* 7th ed. Littleton, Colo.: Society for Mining, Metallurgy, and Exploration, 2006.

Myers, Richard L. *The One Hundred Most Important Chemical Compounds: A Reference Guide.* Westport, Conn.: Greenwood Press, 2007.

Pellant, Chris. *Rocks and Minerals.* 2d American ed. New York: Dorling Kindersley, 2002.

## WEB SITES

NATURAL RESOURCES CANADA
Canadian Minerals Yearbook, Mineral and Metal Commodity Reviews
http://www.nrcan-rncan.gc.ca/mms-smm/busi-indu/cmy-amc/com-eng.htm

U.S. GEOLOGICAL SURVEY
Gypsum: Statistics and Information
http://minerals.usgs.gov/minerals/pubs/commodity/gypsum

SEE ALSO: Australia; Canada; Cement and concrete; China; Evaporites; Fertilizers; France; Iran; Mexico; Mohs hardness scale; Sedimentary processes, rocks, and mineral deposits; Thailand.

# H

## Haber-Bosch process

CATEGORY: Obtaining and using resources

*The Haber-Bosch process, named for Fritz Haber (1868-1934) and Carl Bosch (1874-1940), two Nobel Prize-winning German chemists, was the first commercially successful process to overcome the chemical inertness of nitrogen gas and allow it to be transformed into ammonia, which can be utilized as a nitrogen fertilizer for plant growth.*

### DEFINITION

The Haber-Bosch process is a chemical process, developed in Germany in the early twentieth century, that enables nitrogen to be obtained from the atmosphere and transformed into ammonia. Afterward, it becomes usable in products such as chemicals, pharmaceuticals, and fertilizers.

### OVERVIEW

All living things need nitrogen. It is an essential component of compounds such as proteins and amino acids. However, although plants and animals live in a world surrounded by nitrogen gas (78 percent of the atmosphere is nitrogen gas, a relatively inert compound), little of it is available to them. The stability of nitrogen gas, because of the strength of the triple bond in the molecule, means that of all nutrients in the biosphere, nitrogen is one of the least available nutrients for plant and animal growth. Only a few specialized bacteria, in a process called biological nitrogen fixation, are able to utilize the nitrogen gas surrounding them.

Fritz Haber developed the process of extracting ammonia from nitrogen in his laboratory at Karlsruhe, Germany. Carl Bosch made its industrial application possible by scaling up the laboratory process for his employers at Badische Anilin und Soda Fabrik (BASF) in Ludwigshafen am Rhein, Germany.

The Haber-Bosch process mimics biological nitrogen fixation on an industrial scale. One molecule of nitrogen gas ($N_2$) and three molecules of hydrogen gas ($H_2$) are combined to yield two molecules of ammonia ($NH_3$):

$$N_2 + 3H_2 \leftrightarrow 2NH_3$$

The reaction is reversible, and there is no tendency for ammonia to form unless an enzyme catalyst is used (as in biological nitrogen fixation) or the reaction is conducted at an extremely high temperature (450° Celsius) and extremely high pressure (200 atmospheres or 20.2 million pascals) in the presence of an iron catalyst.

More than 90 million metric tons of nitrogen fertilizer are produced by the Haber-Bosch process each year. Much is used directly for fertilizer. Most, however, is used for other processes, such as production of nitrogen-containing chemicals, pharmaceuticals, and explosives. The Haber-Bosch process, which became a commercial reality when the first plant began operating in 1913, allowed Germany to continue making armaments and explosives despite a blockade of its ports by England in World War I.

The nitrogen in the Haber-Bosch process comes from air, but the hydrogen generally comes from the reaction of natural gas or methane with steam at high temperatures. Consequently, most of the cost associated with the process comes from the hydrocarbons used to heat the system and supply the hydrogen. As a result, the price of fertilizer nitrogen tends to fluctuate with the price of energy. The oil embargo instituted in 1973 by the Organization of Petroleum Exporting Countries (OPEC) had a trickle-down effect on agriculture, since it raised the cost of energy required for the Haber-Bosch process enormously. As a result, it had the unintended effect of stimulating research in biological nitrogen fixation as a cheaper alternative for improving the nitrogen fertility of soil.

*Mark S. Coyne*

SEE ALSO: Agriculture industry; Eutrophication; Fertilizers; Food shortages; Nitrogen and ammonia; Oil embargo and energy crises of 1973 and 1979; Organization of Petroleum Exporting Countries; Soil management.

# Halite. *See* Salt

# Hall, Charles Martin

CATEGORY: People
BORN: December 6, 1863; Thompson, Ohio
DIED: December 27, 1914; Daytona Beach, Florida

*Aluminum was well known by the middle of the nineteenth century, but it was expensive to obtain. Charles Martin Hall developed a method of reducing aluminum oxide cheaply by electrolysis of a molten salt mixture—essentially the same method used in the twenty-first century. World production of aluminum by the electrolytic process has risen into the range of billions of kilograms annually.*

## BIOGRAPHICAL BACKGROUND

In 1873, Charles Martin Hall's parents moved from Thompson to Oberlin, Ohio, where Hall studied at Oberlin College, graduating with a bachelor of arts degree in 1885. He became interested in the production of aluminum and started to do research in the college laboratory. After graduation, Hall continued his research in a woodshed behind the family home, assisted from time to time by his sister Julia. He constructed his own equipment, even the voltaic cells, for a source of electricity. A key discovery was the use of the mineral cryolite (sodium hexafluoroaluminate) as a solvent for aluminum oxide at an elevated temperature. By the summer of 1886, Hall had obtained his first samples of aluminum and submitted a patent application for his process. The electrolytic method was discovered virtually simultaneously by Paul Héroult (1863-1914) in France.

Hall went on to found an aluminum industry, first at the Pittsburgh Reduction Company and later at the Aluminum Company of America (ALCOA). He was awarded the Perkin Medal of the American Section of the Society of Chemical Industry in 1911.

## IMPACT ON RESOURCE USE

Aluminum compounds are abundant in the Earth's crust, firmly united with oxygen in minerals such as bauxite, clay, and feldspar. Bauxite is the only important ore. Freeing the metal from oxygen constitutes the essential problem for aluminum production. Electrolysis of water solutions of aluminum compounds

*Charles Martin Hall developed an inexpensive method of obtaining aluminum that is essentially the same method in use today. (Courtesy, Alcoa Inc.)*

failed to produce the metal. Early commercial processes involved electrolysis of sodium chloride to form sodium metal, which was then used to produce aluminum from its chloride, a relatively inefficient and costly arrangement.

Hall's discovery of the direct electrolytic process, and its refinements over the years of 1889 to 1914, made possible a dramatic reduction of the price of aluminum to about $0.08 per kilogram. The process operates at about 1,220 kelvins (947° Celsius) and involves passage of electric current between carbon electrodes through a molten electrolyte of aluminum oxide (alumina) dissolved in the mineral cryolite (sodium hexafluoroaluminate). The alumina used is made from bauxite by the Bayer process. Resistive heating is sufficient to keep the electrolyte liquid, and the aluminum metal is formed as a liquid at the cathode and tapped off periodically at the bottom of the electrolysis cell. Oxygen gas is formed at the anode and combines with the carbon of the electrode. The process is a heavy consumer of electric power and most economical where power is inexpensive.

*John R. Phillips*

SEE ALSO: Aluminum; Hall-Héroult process; Oxides; Oxygen; Silicates.

# Hall-Héroult process

CATEGORY: Obtaining and using resources

*Aluminum is second only to iron as the most used metal. Although aluminum is the most common metal in the Earth's surface, 8 percent by weight, it is almost always combined with other elements. Aluminum is difficult to separate from the common ores of aluminum such as oxides and silicates. The Hall-Héroult process separates aluminum from bauxite ore. The process is the only industrial source of aluminum.*

## DEFINITION

The Hall-Héroult process is the process by which aluminum is separated from alumina, $Al_2O_3$, through electrolysis. The alumina is made from bauxite ore. The alumina is dissolved in a carbon-lined bath of molten cryolite, $Na_3AlF_6$. Aluminum fluoride is added to reduce the melting point of cryolite. During electrolysis, liquid aluminum is deposited at the cathode.

## OVERVIEW

In 1886, Charles Martin Hall, an American, and Paul Héroult, a Frenchman, developed the process separately. The key ideas were that aluminum can be isolated by electrolysis and that a small amount of alumina could be dissolved in molten cryolite at a much lower temperature than the melting point of alumina. The energy saved allowed aluminum to be separated at an economical price. Carbon electrodes are used with a low voltage of 3 to 5 volts and a high amperage of up to 350,000 amps. Oxygen is produced at the anode and reacts with the electrode to produce carbon dioxide. The carbon dioxide is exhausted into the atmosphere after it is cleaned. Some hydrogen fluoride is also produced and is removed in a water bath before the carbon dioxide is exhausted. As the alumina is used up, new alumina is added by breaking through the solid crust that develops on the surface. The electrolytic cell is lined with carbon, but a layer of cryolite

forms on the carbon. The liquid aluminum falls to the bottom of the cell, where it is siphoned off by a vacuum system. Then it is transferred to a casting area where it is either poured into a mold to solidify or alloyed with other elements and cast. The aluminum produced by most smelters is about 99.7 percent pure.

There are two technologies for producing the carbon anodes: Söderberg and prebake. In the Söderberg method, petroleum coke and coal tar are added continuously to the anode. The heat from the electrolytic cell bakes the electrode to the form needed for electrolysis. In the prebake method, the electrodes are baked in large ovens before being placed in the electolytic cell.

The alumina used in the electrolytic cell is prepared by the Bayer method. Bauxite is dissolved in concentrated sodium hydroxide. The insoluble compounds in bauxite are filtered off. The alumina in the filtrate is precipitated, washed, dried, and ground into a fine white powder. The sodium hydroxide can be recycled for further use. About 3.6 metric tons of bauxite are required to form 1.8 metric tons of alumina, and 1.8 metric tons of alumina are required to form 0.9 metric ton of aluminum.

*C. Alton Hassell*

SEE ALSO: Aluminum; Carbon; Hall, Charles Martin; Oxides; Silicates.

# Hazardous waste disposal

CATEGORY: Pollution and waste disposal

*Hazardous waste disposal involves the care and remediation of solid or liquid wastes that have certain harmful effects on the environment or human health.*

## BACKGROUND

Hazardous wastes are largely the product of industrial society. Produced both by industry and by households, they pose hazards to human health and the environment. Remediation and cleanup of these wastes involves substantial economic cost. In the United States in the early twenty-first century, approximately 97 percent of all hazardous waste has been produced by 2 percent of the waste generators. In other industrial countries a larger percentage of waste generators produced hazardous waste, but the major producers still produced the largest volume of hazardous waste. Beginning in the 1970's the United States and other Western democracies tried to regulate hazardous waste disposal. Hazardous waste disposal is also a serious problem in the countries of the former Soviet Union and in Eastern European nations. In parts of Africa hazardous waste is often a product of military conflict, not industrialization, creating some dangerous situations. Improper disposal of hazardous waste causes numerous environmental and health problems. For example, wastes placed in unlined landfills or lagoons may leach into surrounding soil and water supplies over time, while wastes placed in metal drums can corrode the drums and leak.

### THE NATURE OF HAZARDOUS WASTE

Hazardous waste disposal can release chemicals into the air, surface water, groundwater, and soil. High-risk wastes are those known to contain significant concentrations of constituents that are highly toxic, persistent, mobile, and bioaccumulative. Examples include dioxin-based wastes, polychlorinated biphenyls (PCBs), and cyanide wastes. These wastes often enter the food chain, increasing the concentration as they move up the food chain. People who consume meat that comes from animals that have eaten grass that has accumulated a hazardous chemical may take on a significant chemical risk to their health. High-risk wastes can easily migrate from one location to another (by entering the water table, for example).

Intermediate-risk wastes may include metal hydroxide sludges, while low-level wastes are generally high-volume low-hazard materials. Radioactive waste is a special category of hazardous waste, often presenting extremely high risk. Even low-level wastes may pose significant contamination problems because of the volume of the material. Radioactive waste may be classified as low-level waste, including such items as nuclear medicine waste. High-level radioactive waste, such as spent reactor fuel rods, presents a significant level of health risks, often for extremely long periods of time.

*An employee at a German hazardous waste disposal site packs hazardous waste into barrels that will be stored for safety.* (Uwe Zucchi/dpa/Landov)

The Chernobyl nuclear site in Ukraine presents a case of widespread radioactive waste contamination. The meltdown of the Chernobyl reactors in 1986 produced an area immediately surrounding the reactors that was contaminated with high-level nuclear waste, while several hundred square kilometers of the surrounding countryside were also contaminated with radioactive material. Much of this contamination remains.

Military waste is a special category and a problem in parts of Africa and Asia that have undergone civil wars or other conflicts. Probably the most deadly military waste are land mines, although unexploded shells and bombs and leaking chemicals and gasoline also pose problems. In some cases, belligerents have made extensive use of defoliants, which also are hazardous to animal and human life, to kill vegetation. In some areas, such as a few islands in the South Pacific, nuclear weapons testing has left a legacy of radioactivity. Biological weapons testing has also left a hazardous legacy in some areas, especially in the former Soviet Union. In parts of the Democratic Republic of the Congo and some West African countries military waste poses a real danger to local populations.

Thus, hazardous waste presents varying degrees of health and environmental hazards. When combined, two relatively low-risk materials may pose a high risk. Particularly when improper disposal techniques are utilized, the risk of any sort of hazardous waste will increase.

Factors that affect the health risk of hazardous waste for individuals include dosage received, age, gender, body weight, and weather conditions. The health effects posed by hazardous waste include carcinogenesis (the ability to cause cancer), genetic defects, reproductive abnormalities, and negative effects on the central nervous system. Environmental degradation resulting from hazardous waste can potentially render various natural resources, such as cropland or forests, useless. Hazardous wastes may also harm animal life. Because the amount of waste in any period is based on the amount of natural resources used up, the generation of both hazardous and nonhazardous waste poses a threat to the sustainability of the economy.

## MEANS OF HANDLING HAZARDOUS WASTE

In the past, because there were no standards for what constituted a hazardous waste, these materials were often buried or simply stored in unattended drums or other containers. This situation created a threat to the environment and human health when the original containers began to leak or the material leached into the water supply.

The technology for dealing with hazardous solid and liquid waste continues to evolve. By the 1990's, there were two preferred solutions, and they both had a positive impact on reducing contamination of natural resources. The first approach is to reduce the volume of the waste material by generating less of it. The second is to recycle as much of the hazardous material as possible. A third means of dealing with hazardous waste is to treat it so as to render it less harmful and often to reduce its volume. The least-preferred solution is to store the waste in a landfill. Most industrial countries have instituted policies that put emphasis on the first two solutions, but the third and fourth are often followed, particularly in emerging industrializing countries, such as China, that do not want to deal with the costs of the first two alternatives.

Incineration has long been used to reduce the volume of hazardous waste and household trash. Incineration can create problems as the remaining waste is often highly toxic and may include heavy metals such as cadmium or arsenic as well as dioxin, which is one of the most toxic substances known. At times, industrial countries have shipped their waste ash to less-industrialized countries in Africa or Asia.

Exporting waste has become commonplace in several industrial countries such as the United States. Electronic wastes, such as used computer monitors, are shipped to India and China for recycling. Monitors contain several highly toxic heavy metals and pose problems for local workers and residents. The most notorious waste-exporting incident involved the ship *Khian Sea*, which dumped incinerator ash from Philadelphia in Haiti and the Indian Ocean in 1987.

Often hazardous waste is treated so as to reduce its toxicity. This can be accomplished by physical, chemical, or biological means. High-temperature incineration, for example, reduces such compounds as PCBs into safe products such as water and carbon dioxide. Incineration does not work for all liquids and solids, however, and it may produce highly toxic ash and sludge that will have to be landfilled. Technologies such as the use of extremely high-temperature (in the range of 10,000° Celsius) plasma torches have the potential to reduce some hazardous wastes to harmless gases.

Biotransformation is a process that simplifies a harmful compound into less harmful compounds, while mineralization is a complete breakdown of organic materials into water, carbon dioxide, cellular mass, and inert inorganic residuals. Some hazardous solids that cannot be treated are stored in specially designed hazardous waste landfills.

Various forms of bioremediation have been increasingly adopted in industrial countries. Bioremediation techniques are often low-cost, low-technology solutions that tend to have higher public acceptance than other techniques such as incineration. They do not work for all contaminants, such as chlorinated organic compounds, and often require long time periods. Nonetheless, bioremediation has been successful in dealing with PCBs that are residues from electric power transformers and electrical manufacturing, some pesticides, some heavy metals, and hydrocarbons. In particular, bioremediation has been used to deal with some oil spills, diesel-oil-contaminated soil at a ski resort in Austria, and heavy-metal contamination at mine tailings in Australia. The preferred approach is to engage in bioremediation on-site, but at times contaminated materials are transported elsewhere for treatment. In some off-site approaches the contaminated material is placed in a slurry or aqueous reactor in order to achieve the degradation of the contaminated material (often soil or sludge). Although bioreactors provide for a more rapid means of treatment than on-site methods, they are also more expensive to operate and incur substantial transportation costs.

A variant on bioremediation that has been used with petroleum-based contaminants is the application of microbe technology, phytoremediation. This vegetation-based remediation has the potential to accumulate, immobilize, and transform low-level, persistent contaminants such as oil. In essence, plants act as filters to metabolize material generated by nature. Particularly in areas with large surface contamination of low-level waste, phytoremediation has proved to be a cost-effective, environmentally sound solution.

THE STATUTORY AND REGULATORY FRAMEWORK
Most industrial countries have developed a legal framework to deal with hazardous wastes over a ten- to fifteen-year period. The process in the United States is similar to that of many other counties. The basic statutory and regulatory framework for dealing with hazardous waste in the United States comes from the 1976 amendments to the Solid Waste Disposal Act of 1965, which forms the basis for the Resource Conservation and Recovery Act of 1976 (RCRA). RCRA was

completely rewritten in 1984, and regulations resulting from it continued to be issued well into the 1990's. The Environmental Protection Agency (EPA) has published a list of more than five hundred chemical products and mixtures considered to be hazardous on prima facie grounds. EPA defines other substances to be hazardous based on four criteria: ignitability, corrosivity, reactivity, and toxicity. The EPA also established standards for responsibility and tracking of hazardous wastes, based on the principle that waste generators are responsible for their waste "from cradle to grave."

This principle has involved extensive record-keeping by waste generators and disposal sites as well as technical standards for disposal facilities, including landfills, incinerators, and storage tanks. Landfills must have liners, have collection systems above the liners to trap liquid wastes that might leak out, and adhere to inspection and post-closure standards. Facilities that incinerate hazardous wastes must achieve a 99.99 percent reduction of the principal organic hazardous constituents. Emission and reduction standards were also set for other constituents. All surface storage tanks must have containment systems to minimize leaks and spills.

Congress's 1984 RCRA revisions involved a thorough overhaul of the legislation. Previously, sources that generated between 100 and 1,000 kilograms of hazardous waste per month were exempt from the provisions of RCRA. The 1984 provisions brought them under RCRA. Congress further tried to force the EPA to adopt a bias against landfilling of hazardous waste with the provision, "[N]o land disposal unless proven safe." Congress also added underground storage tanks for gasoline, petroleum, pesticides, and solvents to the list of facilities to be regulated and remediated.

RCRA was designed to deal with present and future hazardous wastes; it did not deal with material that had already been disposed of in some way. Congress passed the Comprehensive Environmental Response, Compensation, and Liability Act of 1980 (CERCLA), better known as Superfund, to deal with existing hazardous waste sites. Superfund was further amended in 1986 by the Superfund Amendments and Reauthorization Act (SARA), as well as later amendments in the 1990's and 2000's. Superfund requires the EPA to regulate past hazardous waste disposal sites and to conduct the cleanup of such sites. The EPA was required to devise a plan for the identification of these sites, select appropriate remedies, determine who will pay for the cleanup, and clean up the site. The resulting National Priority List identified more than twelve hundred priority hazardous waste sites. Superfund legislation did not specify the degree of restoration required, although the original standards required that sites be returned to conditions comparable to the standards established under existing environmental legislation. Cleanup costs are often extremely high, yet full cleanup is often difficult, if not impossible, to obtain. The EPA has not been able to resolve the issue of how clean is clean enough for Superfund sites.

Not all hazardous waste falls under the RCRA rubric. When Congress drafted the RCRA, several categories of waste were purposefully omitted: radioactive waste, mining waste, biomedical waste, military waste, and household waste. Superfund deals with all categories of dormant sites except for radioactive waste. Several other statutes (and ensuing EPA regulations) deal with these aspects of the hazardous waste problem.

Most other industrial countries have their own hazardous waste legislation. In Germany, for example, the Waste Avoidance and Management Act governed hazardous wastes until it was superseded by the Recycling and Waste Management Act in 1996. During the 1990's the Canadian government passed several laws dealing with hazardous waste with an overall purpose of encouraging recycling. Cleanup efforts, however, vary dramatically from country to country. Numerous untreated hazardous waste sites, particularly in Eastern Europe and the former Soviet Union, exist that continue to pose environmental and health problems. Western European governments have made extensive efforts to require polluters to clean up hazardous waste sites or have done so themselves when the responsible parties cannot be found.

There are several international agreements that deal with the disposition of hazardous wastes. The Basel Convention on the Control of Transboundary Movements of Hazardous Wastes and Their Disposal (1989) placed limits on the movement of hazardous wastes across international borders, and the amendment of 1995 (the Basel Ban) limited the movement of hazardous waste from industrial to less industrialized countries; the latter amendment has been difficult to enforce. The Basel Convention expresses what has come to be the three-part strategy for dealing with hazardous waste, which has become the international standard. First, hazardous waste generation should be minimized. Second, wastes should be treated as close to the site as possible. Third, international movement of hazardous wastes should be minimized.

## WHERE WILL OUR HAZARDOUS WASTE GO?

The costs for the cleanup and remediation of hazardous waste are substantial and are likely to continue to grow. This situation is particularly true in Eastern Europe and the former Soviet Union, where the magnitude of past dumping of hazardous materials is slowly becoming apparent. In some places, such as that around the Aral Sea in Russia, large areas remain contaminated from chemical and industrial waste. Developing nations are largely ignoring the hazardous waste issue or trying to force industrial countries to help with cleanup, focusing instead on increasing productivity and the standard of living.

The waste-minimization philosophy expressed in RCRA, European statutes, and the Basel Convention is a sound long-range strategy for dealing with hazardous waste and is being followed by almost all industrialized countries. Even some industrializing nations, such as China, are trying to minimize the generation of hazardous waste. However, China remains quite polluted in some areas, as little money has been spent to deal with existing hazardous waste sites.

Some materials will continue to be deposited in landfills. Incineration offers a partial solution to reducing the volume of material, yet it poses an air-quality dilemma, as it can produce a highly toxic ash, often laden with heavy metals. Various forms of bioremediation are increasingly being utilized in several industrial nations. As some firms have found, minimizing their waste stream affords them economic benefits in addition to conserving natural resources. Household waste, which is not always regulated, often includes minute quantities of hazardous materials, such as pesticides, and most of this waste was landfilled in the mid-1990's. The cleanup of existing sites will continue to be a troubling problem, fraught with high cost and emotional controversies. The cleanup and disposal of radioactive civilian and military waste remains another major issue for the future.

*John M. Theilmann*

## FURTHER READING

Blackman, William C. *Basic Hazardous Waste Management.* 3d ed. Boca Raton, Fla.: Lewis, 2001.

Cabaniss, Amy D., ed. *Handbook on Household Hazardous Waste.* Lanham, Md.: Government Institute/Scarecrow Press, 2008.

Carroll, Chris. "High-Tech Trash: Toxic Components of Discarded Electronics are Ending up Overseas." *National Geographic* 213, no. 1 (January, 2008): 64-87.

Gerrard, Michael B. *Whose Backyard, Whose Risk: Fear and Fairness in Toxic and Nuclear Waste Siting.* Cambridge, Mass.: MIT Press, 1994.

Grisham, Joe W., ed. *Health Aspects of the Disposal of Waste Chemicals: A Report of the Executive Scientific Panel.* New York: Pergamon, 1986.

LaGrega, Michael D., Phillip L. Buckingham, Jeffrey C. Evans. *Hazardous Waste Management.* 2d ed. Boston: McGraw-Hill, 2001.

Moore, Emmett B. *An Introduction to the Management and Regulation of Hazardous Waste.* Columbus, Ohio: Battelle Press, 2000.

O'Neill, Kate. *Waste Trading Among Rich Nations: Building a New Theory of Environmental Regulation.* Cambridge, Mass.: MIT Press, 2000.

Pellow, David N. *Resisting Global Toxics: Transnational Movements for Environmental Justice.* Cambridge, Mass.: MIT Press, 2007.

Portney, Paul R., and Robert N. Stavins, eds. *Public Policies for Environmental Protection.* 2d ed. Washington, D.C.: Resources for the Future, 2000.

Probst, Katherine N., and Thomas C. Beierle. *The Evolution of Hazardous Waste Programs: Lessons from Eight Countries.* Washington, D.C.: Center for Risk Management, Resources for the Future, 1999.

Shah, Kanti L. *Basics of Solid and Hazardous Waste Management Technology.* Upper Saddle River, N.J.: Prentice Hall, 2000.

Winslow, Philip C. *Sowing the Dragon's Teeth: Land Mines and the Global Legacy of War.* Boston: Beacon Press, 1998.

### WEB SITES

ENVIRONMENT CANADA
Welcome to Environment Canada's Management of Toxic Substances Web Site!
http://www.ec.gc.ca/TOXICS/EN/index.cfm

U.S. ENVIRONMENTAL PROTECTION AGENCY
Wastes: Hazardous Wastes
http://www.epa.gov/osw/hazard/index.htm

SEE ALSO: Arsenic; Cadmium; Environmental Protection Agency; Incineration of wastes; Landfills; Mining wastes and mine reclamation; Nuclear waste and its disposal; Superfund legislation and cleanup activities; United Nations Convention on Long-Range Transboundary Air Pollution.

# Health, resource exploitation and

CATEGORIES: Social, economic, and political issues; pollution and waste disposal

*Pollution and other types of environmental degradation, unfortunate side effects of resource exploitation, affect human health. Workers who mine or process resources are particularly susceptible to adverse effects because of repeated exposures or exposures at high concentrations. When the obtaining, processing, or consuming of resources disseminates pollutants throughout air, soil, or water, public health is affected as well.*

### BACKGROUND

Human well-being is inextricably linked to the Earth's natural resources. These resources provide food, shelter, and warmth as well as transportation, medicine, and a host of other improvements, conveniences, and luxuries that enhance the quality of life. Ironically, however, the act of exploiting resources can so affect the environment that human health is affected. Resources that are toxic (such as mercury and lead) or radioactive (such as uranium) become pollutants when mining, processing, or consumption releases them into the air, the water, and the food chain. Other wastes generated through resource exploitation are also discharged into the environment, compromising its ability to sustain life. Through overuse and misuse, human populations deplete and degrade soil and water, essential resources upon which their survival depends. Increasing population size makes it harder for ecosystems to withstand the stresses imposed upon them so that they cannot simultaneously meet human demands for materials, absorb wastes, and act as a life-support system. The growing population is also exhausting its frontiers: As pristine and productive areas disappear, so does the option of simply moving away from polluted or damaged ecosystems.

Modern societies recognize that resource exploitation involves trade-offs. The needs and desires of the Earth's huge human population cannot be met without some disruption of the environment or some risk to workers and public health. Risk-management efforts such as regulation and environmental cleanup are intended to minimize such adverse effects, notably where human exposure to chemicals is involved. Risk management relies heavily on risk assessments—science-based estimates that combine information on exposure levels and toxicity to assess the type and magnitude of human health risk a particular substance poses. Such estimates may be expressed as a probability (for instance, one additional case of cancer per one thousand people) or a range of likely probabilities. Risk managers who determine acceptable exposure levels, impose restrictions on the use of toxic chemicals, and make other regulatory and policy decisions to protect human health base their decisions on risk-assessment results, economic considerations, legal constraints, and social concerns.

Laws, policies, and practices that pertain to resource exploitation and other activities that can degrade the environment have been influenced by an increasing public awareness of the associated health risks. Community opposition to the presence of dangerous or aesthetically offensive facilities in its vicinity—known as the "not in my back yard (NIMBY) syndrome"—often can keep an undesired operation out of a community. However, the NIMBY syndrome tends to push such facilities into minority and low-income communities that lack the financial and political clout to resist them. These areas generally experience more severe environmental contamination and are subjected to higher concentrations of harmful pollutants than their majority counterparts. Along the lower 137 kilometers of the Mississippi River, for instance, low-income residents share the area with approximately one hundred oil refineries and petrochemical plants; many experts attribute above-average incidences of cancers, massive tumors, and miscarriages among the residents to chemical pollution and have even dubbed the area "Cancer Alley."

The unequal societal distribution of environmental damage and health risk—known as "environmental injustice" or "environmental racism"—exists on a global scale as well. Developed nations often export environmentally controversial operations or products to developing countries. There, where unsafe water and inadequate sewage facilities are common, drinking and washing in water from tainted streams and wells can expose people to toxic pollutants. Economic considerations have led many mining and industrial operations to move from the United States to developing countries where regulations pertaining to environmental protection, labor, and the like are often less restrictive. Similarly, the manufacturers of dichloro-diphenyl-trichloroethane (DDT) and related pesticides—chemicals banned in the United States—continue to supply the pesticides to developing countries.

## OCCUPATIONAL HEALTH

Workers who obtain or process resources have the potential to be exposed to a set of harmful substances and conditions on a regular basis. Common workplace hazards include toxic chemicals, airborne dust, poor ventilation, noise, high humidity, and extremes of heat and cold. In the developed nations, efforts by labor organizations, management, and government to protect worker health have helped to track and control the incidence of work-related injuries and illnesses. Government agencies such as the United States' Occupational Safety and Health Administration (OSHA) and Mine Safety and Health Administration (MSHA) oversee and enforce regulations pertaining to such things as acceptable exposure levels, protective clothing, and health and safety training and notification of workers. Developing countries, however, often lack effective occupational health standards or enforcement. Workers there are also less likely to receive sufficient training or equipment to carry out their jobs safely.

In workers around the world, common occupational illnesses include hearing loss caused by excessive noise, skin disorders resulting from chemical exposures, lead poisoning, pesticide poisoning, and respiratory diseases resulting from particulate inhalation. Particulates are a problem in many industries: Wood, cotton, and mineral dusts, for instance, all can induce illness if inhaled. Particles measuring 0.5 to 5 micrometers in diameter settle in the lungs and, over time, can cause severe respiratory disease. The most well-publicized of the particulate-related illnesses are found among miners and mineral-processing workers. Coal miners are susceptible to black lung disease, a lung disorder caused by coal-dust inhalation. Silicosis, a fibrous lung disease brought on by silica dust, affects workers in quarries and limestone mines.

Perhaps the most notorious of the disease-causing particulates is asbestos. A useful fibrous mineral able to resist heat, friction, and chemical corrosion, asbestos was widely used through much of the twentieth century as an insulating and fireproofing material and as a strengthener in cement and plastics. Only after decades of use and dissemination throughout the urban environment was asbestos recognized as a health hazard. Inhaling asbestos fibers can cause asbestosis, a chronic lung inflammation whose symp-

*Coal miners—like these in the Wuda coal fields of Nei Monggol (Inner Mongolia), China—face numerous health risks.* (Getty Images)

toms may not appear until twenty to thirty years after exposure. More than 50 percent of asbestosis patients eventually die from lung cancer. Persons working directly with asbestos are most likely to be affected; however, extensive use of the mineral in public buildings, private residences, and consumer goods may place the general public at risk as well. (There has been considerable debate as to the seriousness of the asbestos danger to people not actively working with the material; some studies have indicated that the risk to the general population is actually quite small.)

In 1973, as part of the Clean Air Act, the United States Environmental Protection Agency (EPA) was charged with developing and enforcing regulations to protect the general public from asbestos exposure, notably during building demolition and renovation and asbestos-waste transport and disposal. In the 1980's, the EPA issued regulations controlling asbestos in schools and other public buildings. OSHA also promulgated standards that covered occupational ex-

posures. While asbestos is still in use, its consumption declined precipitously beginning in the 1970's because of regulatory and economic factors and the increased use of alternative materials.

EFFECTS OF AIR POLLUTION

Fuel consumption by motor vehicles is a major source of urban air pollution in many cities. Vehicles emit nitrogen oxides, which mix with water vapor to form acid precipitation. Nitrogen oxides may exacerbate some chronic lung ailments and reduce the body's natural immune response. Lead exposure is associated with neurological damage and motor-physical impairment in children. Blood-lead concentrations in the United States have decreased substantially since leaded fuels were phased out in the late 1970's.

Electric power plants that burn fossil fuels (oil, natural gas, and coal) are another source of nitrogen oxides. They also emit sulfur dioxide, particularly when high-sulfur coal is used. Like nitrogen oxide, sulfur dioxide produces acid precipitation. Normally, when inhaled, sulfur dioxide will react with moisture in the upper respiratory tract to produce sulfuric acid; however, if sulfur dioxide adheres to a respirable particle, it can travel deeper into the lungs and have a greater impact on health. The adsorption of sulfur dioxide onto coal particulates is believed to have been responsible for the severity of London's coal-smog disaster of 1952, which ultimately claimed around four thousand lives. In that year, heavy use of coal-fired home heaters during a chilly December produced a thick smog that blanketed the city for four days and exacerbated existing respiratory illnesses, particularly in children and the elderly.

In developing countries, smoky fuels (crop residues, wood, charcoal, and coal) used for cooking and heating in homes are a significant health hazard. Particulates from these fuels irritate the respiratory tract, contribute to chronic lung diseases such as bronchitis, emphysema, and asthma, and increase the risk of cancer. Women and children are most affected by smoky household fuels. In Beijing, the number of households that used these fuels was great enough that overall city air quality was affected.

### EFFECTS OF WATER POLLUTION

The Earth's streams, rivers, lakes, and oceans are multiple-use resources. They supply humankind with water and food, serve as a means for travel and transport, and provide recreation and scenic beauty. They also are widely employed for waste disposal, which frequently conflicts with their other uses. Industrial wastes introduce toxic organic chemicals and heavy metals into aquatic ecosystems, polluting the water and tainting the food chain. Industrial pollution of water was found to be responsible for an epidemic of organic mercury poisoning among the residents of Minamata, Japan, that was first identified during the 1950's. Mercury-containing wastes discharged into Minamata Bay by a plastics and petrochemical company contaminated fish and shellfish with methyl mercury. Residents who ate the seafood subsequently developed a profound central nervous system disorder. More than a thousand persons were ultimately identified as victims of Minamata disease.

Untreated or poorly treated human sewage is another hazardous pollutant of water. Aqueous discharge of this material introduces harmful bacteria and viruses that make water unsafe for human consumption, washing, or recreation. In developing countries, where sewage is often released into open waterways, this practice can contribute to the spread of potentially fatal illnesses such as diarrheal disease and cholera.

### EFFECTS OF AGROCHEMICALS

Pesticides are used extensively in agriculture as well as in forestry and rangeland management. Indiscriminate and excessive pesticide application has dire consequences for the environment and human health. Pesticides can enter the human body through inhalation, ingestion of drinking water or food, and, in some cases, absorbtion through the skin. Exposure at sufficiently high concentrations causes immediate pesticide poisoning. Where safety precautions are disregarded, the potential for overexposure is great. Exposure to lower concentrations has health implications as well. Environmentally persistent chemicals such as DDT, which do not readily break down after application, accumulate in body tissues and in the food chain. Many pesticides are immunotoxins, which even at low concentrations alter the human immune system and make a person more prone to contracting infectious disease. Children, the elderly, and persons whose health is already compromised are particularly susceptible. Pesticides may also weaken the immune system's ability to combat certain cancers, such as Hodgkin's disease, melanoma, and leukemia.

Synthetic fertilizers are another type of agrochemical whose indiscriminate use poses a health risk. Nitrate that is not absorbed by crops can infiltrate into groundwater and thus contaminate drinking water. In infants, nitrate induces methemoglobinemia, or "blue baby syndrome," a serious and often fatal blood disease. The nitrate is converted in the infant's intestines to nitrite, which inhibits the blood's ability to carry oxygen. Brain damage or death by suffocation may result. In the United States, numerous cases of methemoglobinemia have been reported in California, Illinois, Missouri, Minnesota, and Wisconsin.

### EFFECTS OF RADIOACTIVITY

Radioactive emissions occur when uranium is mined, milled, processed, and transported. Nuclear fission and breeder reactors also emit low levels of radiation; reprocessing plants that recover uranium 235 and plutonium from spent fuel rods emit more radiation than properly operating nuclear power plants. High-level radioactive wastes—which include spent fuel from reactors and radioactive water from nuclear power plants, reprocessing operations, and temporary spent-rod storage—require long-term storage in repositories capable of keeping the material safely isolated from the environment. While normal operations involve relatively low-level emissions, major accidents at nuclear power plants can introduce massive amounts of radioactivity into the environment.

Persons exposed to high radiation dosages (of 1,000 rads or more) die as a result of internal-organ damage and bone-marrow destruction. Humans may survive the symptoms of exposure to lower levels of radiation (100 to 1,000 rads)—radiation burns, vomiting, diarrhea, fever, hair loss, and internal bleeding—but may experience subsequent genetic effects in the form of cancer and damage to sperm and ova. According to the National Academy of Sciences, a continuous exposure of 0.1 rem per year throughout a lifetime would be expected to produce 5.6 cancers per 1,000 people. The average person in the United States receives an annual radiation dosage of 0.4 rem from natural sources, 0.053 rem from medical sources, and less than 0.001 rem from nuclear power.

The 1986 explosion and reactor fire at the Chernobyl nuclear power plant in the former Soviet Union released between 150 and 250 million curies of radiation. Radiation spread across twenty countries, contaminating livestock and crops and exposing human populations as far away as West Germany, Sweden, and the United Kingdom. In 1989, unsafe radiation levels (over 15 curies per square kilometer) were reportedly present in portions of Belarus (about 7,000 square kilometers), Russia (about 2,000 square kilometers), and Ukraine (about 1,500 square kilometers); twenty years later, areas of each of these countries still exhibited some contamination. It is unclear how many persons have died as a result of the Chernobyl disaster; reported deaths range all the way from 600 to 90,000. Health effects attributed to the Chernobyl incident included neuropsychological disorders and thyroid cancer among children. Amazingly, the last of the nuclear reactors at Chernobyl remained in operation until 2001, despite the fact that scientists estimated that the area would remain contaminated and uninhabitable for at least two centuries.

## EFFECTS OF ENVIRONMENTAL CHANGE

When resource exploitation imposes stresses on an ecosystem that cause it to change significantly, human health is frequently affected. Environmental change can deprive a community of food or fuel, make it more susceptible to diseases, or have other adverse effects. If environmental degradation is so severe as to force a community to evacuate or relocate, its people may be subjected to unhealthful conditions—such as crowding, poor sanitation, or psychological stress—that they did not experience previously.

Desertification, the transformation of once-productive land to a desertlike environment, is a side effect of imprudent resource use. Poor agricultural, forestry, and rangeland management practices encourage soil erosion. In semiarid climates, extreme devegetation, soil nutrient depletion, and erosion lead to desertification. Human health is impaired through the loss of productive land. In sub-Saharan Africa, desertification has resulted largely from overgrazing and excessive harvesting of wood for fuel. The region's rapidly expanding population has exceeded the production capabilities of its agricultural land, and widespread malnourishment has resulted.

The consumption of fossil fuels, the burning of wood, deforestation, and other factors have contributed to a buildup of carbon dioxide in the atmosphere. Many scientists believe that the accumulation of carbon dioxide and other "greenhouse gases" is responsible for a global warming trend. Scientists considering the health implications of the "greenhouse effect" anticipate increased mortality due to heat stress, increased incidence of chronic and infectious respiratory diseases, more allergic reactions, and altered geographic ranges for insect-borne and parasitic diseases.

*Karen N. Kähler*

FURTHER READING

Ayres, Jon, Robert Maynard, and Roy Richards, eds. *Air Pollution and Health.* London: Imperial College Press, 2006.

Brown, Phil, ed. *Health and the Environment.* Thousand Oaks, Calif.: Sage, 2002.

Campbell-Lendrum, Diarmid, and Rosalie Woodruff. *Climate Change: Quantifying the Health Impact at National and Local Levels.* Edited by Annette Prüss-Üstün and Carlos Corvalán. Geneva, Switzerland: World Health Organization, 2007.

Chivian, Eric, and Andrew Bernstein. *Sustaining Life: How Human Health Depends on Biodiversity.* New York: Oxford University Press, 2008.

Colfer, Carol J. Pierce, ed. *Human Health and Forests: A Global Overview of Issues, Practice, and Policy.* Sterling, Va.: Earthscan, 2008.

Kabat, Geoffrey C. *Hyping Health Risks: Environmental Hazards in Daily Life and the Science of Epidemiology.* New York: Columbia University Press, 2008.

Lippmann, Morton, ed. *Environmental Toxicants: Human Exposures and Their Health Effects.* 3d ed. Hoboken, N.J.: John Wiley & Sons, 2009.

Rodricks, Joseph V. *Calculated Risks: The Toxicity and Human Health Risks of Chemicals in Our Environment.* 2d ed. New York: Cambridge University Press, 2007.

Sala, Osvaldo E., Laura A. Meyerson, and Camille Parmesan, eds. *Biodiversity Change and Human Health: From Ecosystem Services to Spread of Disease.* Washington, D.C.: Island Press, 2009.

Skjei, Eric, and M. Donald Whorton. *Of Mice and Molecules: Technology and Human Survival.* New York: Dial Press, 1983.

WEB SITE

WORLD HEALTH ORGANIZATION
Environmental Health
http://www.who.int/topics/environmental_
    health/en

SEE ALSO: Air pollution and air pollution control; Asbestos; Environmental degradation, resource exploitation and; Greenhouse gases and global climate change; Mining safety and health issues; Nuclear waste and its disposal; Pesticides and pest control; Population growth; United Nations Convention on Long-Range Transboundary Air Pollution; Water pollution and water pollution control.

# Helium

CATEGORY: Mineral and other nonliving resources

## WHERE FOUND

Helium is concentrated in some natural gas wells, particularly in Texas, Oklahoma, and Kansas. Helium is also found in the Earth's atmosphere.

## PRIMARY USES

The most important use of helium is as a cryogenic coolant, since it permits cooling to temperatures lower than any other substance. Helium is also used as a lifting gas for airships, as a replacement for nitrogen in the breathing gas for deep-sea divers, and as an inert atmosphere for welding.

## TECHNICAL DEFINITION

Helium (abbreviated He), atomic number 2, belongs to the last column of the periodic table of the elements. It has two naturally occurring isotopes and an average molecular weight of 4.003. Helium is a gas, having a density of 0.1637 gram/liter at 25° Celsius and 1 atmosphere of pressure. Helium boils at −268.9° Celsius. It is the most chemically inert element in the periodic table.

## DESCRIPTION, DISTRIBUTION, AND FORMS

Helium does not form any chemical compounds. It is the lightest of the noble gases, so light that it quickly escapes into space from the Earth's atmosphere. Thus, much of the helium now found on the Earth was produced by radioactive decay. In excess of 130 million cubic meters of helium is produced annually in the United States. A majority of this helium is used by government agencies, including the Department of Energy and the National Aeronautics and Space Administration (NASA).

Small quantities of helium, pure helium 4, are produced by the radioactive decay of uranium or thorium in the Earth. In locations where uranium or thorium concentrations are high, helium collects in the same cavities as natural gas. The largest concentrations of helium are found in some natural gas wells in New Mexico, Texas, Oklahoma, Utah, and Kansas in the United States; in Saskatchewan and Alberta, Canada; in South Africa; and in Russia.

Helium is also present in the Earth's atmosphere. Some of this helium was produced by radioactive decay in the Earth and subsequently escaped into the air. However, high-energy cosmic rays hitting the Earth's atmosphere also produce helium by spallation, a process in which a heavier nucleus breaks into two or more lighter nuclei when it is hit by a high-energy particle. Radioactive decay produces only helium 4, while spallation produces both helium 3 and helium 4. Thus, atmospheric helium has a much higher content of helium 3 than the helium obtained from natural gas wells.

## HISTORY

Helium was discovered in 1868. A French astronomer, Pierre Janssen, observed the emission spectrum of the Sun's chromosphere during the August 18 solar eclipse. He saw a yellow-orange emission line that did not correspond to that of any known element. Later that year, both Janssen and an English astronomer,

Sir Norman Joseph Lockyer, observed this emission again. Lockyer named this new element helium, for the Sun (*helios* in Greek).

In 1889, William Hildebrand, an American mineral chemist, extracted a gas from a uranium-bearing mineral, uranite. Sir William Ramsay, an English chemist, performed a similar extraction on cleveite, another uranium-bearing mineral. Ramsey sent the gas to Lockyer, who showed in 1895 that it had the same emission lines he previously observed in the Sun, providing the first identification of helium on Earth.

## OBTAINING HELIUM

The U.S. Bureau of Mines, which established three experimental plants to extract helium from the Petrolia natural gas field in Clay County, Texas, had produced about 6,000 cubic meters of helium by 1920. Helium-bearing well gas, typically about 80 percent methane, is compressed and then treated to remove carbon dioxide, hydrogen sulfide, and water vapor. The remaining gas is cooled to a temperature of about −150° Celsius, which liquefies almost all the hydrocarbons, leaving nitrogen and helium in the gas phase. This gas is compressed again, then cooled to −196° Celsius, at which point the nitrogen liquefies, leaving almost pure helium in the gas phase.

## USES OF HELIUM

Helium has a much lower density than air; thus a helium-filled balloon will rise. The first practical application of helium was as a lifting gas for lighter-than-air craft. Although hydrogen has an even lower density, making it a more efficient lifting gas than helium, the extreme flammability of hydrogen makes its use dangerous. The U.S. Navy experimented with rigid airships, called dirigibles, during the 1920's and 1930's. In the modern era, the Goodyear Aircraft Corporation built a series of nonrigid airships, called blimps, which have been used as platforms for aerial photography. Helium-filled balloons are also used for scientific research in the upper atmosphere.

In 1908, Heike Kamerlingh Onnes, a physicist at the University of Leiden, in Holland, liquefied helium by compressing it to a high pressure, cooling it, then allowing the helium to expand through a small opening. Expansion causes a gas to cool, and some of the helium liquefied.

Since the boiling point of helium under 1 at-

mosphere of pressure is −268.9° Celsius, material brought into contact with liquid helium cools rapidly. In 1911, Kamerlingh Onnes demonstrated that the electrical resistance of mercury vanishes at liquid helium temperature. He had discovered superconductivity.

Helium is used to dilute oxygen in the breathing gas used by deep-sea divers. Divers must breath an atmosphere at the same pressure as the surrounding water. At ocean depths the pressure is high, and both oxygen and nitrogen dissolve in body fluids. The oxygen is consumed, but the nitrogen remains in the fluids. If divers return suddenly to the surface, they can suffer the "bends," which results when the nitrogen expands rapidly. The substitution of helium, the least soluble gas known, for nitrogen allows divers to operate at depth and then return to the surface more quickly.

*George J. Flynn*

## FURTHER READING

Cook, Gerhard A. *Argon, Helium, and the Rare Gases: The Elements of the Helium Group.* 2 vols. New York: Interscience, 1961.

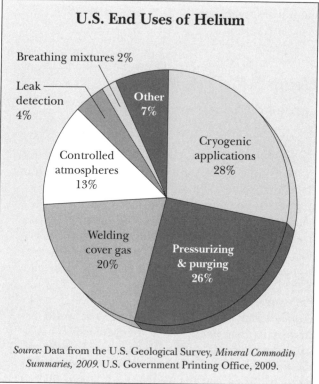

**U.S. End Uses of Helium**

Breathing mixtures 2%
Leak detection 4%
Other 7%
Controlled atmospheres 13%
Cryogenic applications 28%
Welding cover gas 20%
Pressurizing & purging 26%

*Source:* Data from the U.S. Geological Survey, *Mineral Commodity Summaries, 2009.* U.S. Government Printing Office, 2009.

Greenwood, N. N., and A. Earnshaw. "The Noble Gases: Helium, Neon, Argon, Krypton, Xenon, and Radon." In *Chemistry of the Elements*. 2d ed. Boston: Butterworth-Heinemann, 1997.

Henderson, William. "The Group 18 (Noble Gas) Elements: Helium, Neon, Argon, Krypton, Xenon, and Radon." In *Main Group Chemistry*. Cambridge, England: Royal Society of Chemistry, 2000.

Krebs, Robert E. *The History and Use of Our Earth's Chemical Elements: A Reference Guide*. Illustrations by Rae Déjur. 2d ed. Westport, Conn.: Greenwood Press, 2006.

Ojima, Minoru, and Frank A. Podosek. *Noble Gas Geochemistry*. 2d ed. New York: Cambridge University Press, 2002.

Simpson, Charles H. *Chemicals from the Atmosphere*. Garden City, N.Y.: Doubleday, 1969.

WEB SITE

U.S. GEOLOGICAL SURVEY
Helium: Statistics and Information
http://minerals.usgs.gov/minerals/pubs/
   commodity/helium

SEE ALSO: Atmosphere; Gases, inert or noble; Hydrogen; Oil and natural gas drilling and wells; Oil and natural gas reservoirs.

# Hemp

CATEGORY: Plant and animal resources

## WHERE FOUND

Hemp, *Cannabis sativa*, is indigenous to temperate regions in Asia. All major industrialized countries but the United States cultivate hemp for its fibers and oil-rich seeds. The former Soviet Union was the world's leading producer until the 1980's. Ukraine and Russia are the two major producers, followed by China, Canada, Austria, Australia, Great Britain, North Korea, Hungary, Romania, Poland, France, Italy, and Spain.

## PRIMARY USES

*Cannabis* was initially spread around the world because of its fiber, not its intoxicant chemicals or its nutritious oil seeds. It is one of the oldest sources of textile fiber, whose use for cloth can be traced to 8000 B.C.E. in China and the Middle East. Hemp fiber is also used for the manufacture of cordage, sail cloth, and fish nets. Oil extracted from seeds is used in paints, medicines, and foods.

## TECHNICAL DEFINITION

*Cannabis sativa* is a multipurpose plant that has long been cultivated for its (bast) fiber in the stem, versatile oil in the seeds, and a resin secreted by its leaves that contains a compound, tetrahydrocannabinol (THC), known to have psychotropic effects. The somewhat confusing common names hemp and marijuana have been applied loosely to all three forms of *Cannabis sativa*. However, this essay focuses primarily on its fiber and seed uses. The plants are dioecious annual herbs that produce fibers of the best quality when cultivated under temperate and warm conditions. Hemp produces the longest bast fiber among plants. Seeds are rich in oil, which is extracted and used in a variety of products.

## DESCRIPTION, DISTRIBUTION, AND FORMS

*Cannabis* is the generic name for hemp, a highly adaptive and successful species cultivated throughout temperate and tropical regions across the globe. The classification of *Cannabis* has been a source of much controversy for a long time. It was first thought a relative of the nettle and later considered a member of the Moraceae family. Finally, *Cannabis* was classified into its own family, Cannabaceae, in which the genus *Cannabis* and *Humulus lupulus* (hops) are included. It was first named in 1753 by Carolus Linnaeus as *Cannabis sativa*, which means "useful hemp" in Latin.

More confusion concerning the taxonomy of *Cannabis* resulted from the naming of two other closely related "species," *Cannabis indica*, by Jean-Baptiste Lamarck, for hemp plants in India, and *Cannabis ruderalis*, by a Russian botanist, for wild *Cannabis* plants he observed in western Siberia and central Asia. Even today, some still doubt that *Cannabis sativa* and *Cannabis indica* are two different species.

Nevertheless, *Cannabis sativa* is the most widespread among the three. It is a tall, thin annual that grows from 1.5 to 4.5 meters, with most leaves concentrated at the top. The leaves are dark green in color, and each consists of five to nine serrated tapering leaflets with sharp ends and measures at 5 to 13 centimeters long and 0.76 to 2 centimeters wide. The stem is angular, hollow, branched on top, and covered by fine hairs. Plants can grow in both loamy soil and poor sandy soil. They can grow in altitudes as high as 2,500 meters. *Cannabis* requires plenty of light and is less tolerant to low temperatures. Male plants are generally taller than female ones. Male flowers also bloom two to four weeks earlier than female flowers and are small, with colors ranging from pale green, yellow, and brown to purple-red. Female flowers are bundled tightly together into clusters.

The cultivation of *Cannabis sativa* is easy. Seeds are planted 15 to 20 centimeters apart. Plants grow quickly, up to 15 centimeters a day, with an average daily growth of 2 to 5 centimeters in height. Fruits (achenes) mature 10 to 35 days after fertilization, each containing one seed. The entire life cycle can be completed within 70-110 days. *Cannabis sativa* can grow in almost any soil, requiring little fertilizer, and is resistant to pests and tolerant to weeds. Hemp cultivation and processing was one of the world's most significant industries until the mid-1800's. The labor-intensive work of harvesting and extracting fibers from the stalk, combined with the emergence of more easily extracted fiber sources such as cotton and jute, doomed hemp's status as the top fiber crop.

## HISTORY

*Cannabis* is generally believed to have originated from the temperate regions of central Asia, near the Irtysh River, along the edge of the Gobi Desert, or the Taklimakan Desert in China's Xinjiang Uygur Province, north of Tibet. Hemp cultivation and use date back to prehistoric times in the Middle East and China, where the fiber was used for textiles, the seeds for food, and the oil for various products. Hemp fiber imprints found in pottery shards in Taiwan were more than 10,000 years old. The ancient Asian societies used hemp fibers to make clothes, shoes, ropes, and a primitive form of paper. Evidence for such uses was uncovered in the Great Wall of China and dates back to as early as 10,200 years ago.

Hemp was introduced to western Asia and Egypt and, subsequently, to Europe between 1000 and 2000 B.C.E. Extensive hemp cultivation in Europe began around 500 B.C.E. From 1500 to 1700 C.E., hemp (along with flax) was the major fiber crop in Russia and Europe. In 1545, the Spanish brought hemp to South America (Chile). The earliest cultivation of hemp in North America took place in 1606, by French botanist Louis Hébert in Port Royal, Acadia (now in Nova Scotia). Hemp was first grown in New England by Puritans in 1645. By 1850, hemp was the third largest crop in the United States.

## OBTAINING HEMP

Hemp is raised and harvested in temperate regions. Upon harvest, seeds are separated from the stalks, whose leaves had been stripped off. The stalks are then processed to extract fibers through retting, pounding, and scutching. Retting begins with submerging the flax stems in water and ends with bacteria rotting away cellular tissues and gummy substances, leaving the outer fibers intact. Following retting, the stalk is pounded and broken up into short bits, leaving the fiber unharmed. The scutching acts to comb nonfiber residues out of the fiber.

Following these steps, the well-processed hemp fiber appears creamy white and soft and has a silky sheen. Hemp fiber so extracted was used by Levi Strauss to make the original set of jeans. However, most hemp fiber is extracted as quickly and inexpensively as possible. As a result, hemp is mostly used for cordage, rope, canvas, and sailcloth. Fibers for human cloth, including jeans, are obtained primarily from cotton.

## USES OF HEMP

All parts of *Cannabis* plants are useful. For centuries, *Cannabis* has been the source of a versatile natural fiber and oil-rich seeds. Major uses of industrial hemp include, but are not limited to, body care products, construction, essential oils, food, livestock bedding and feed, medicines, molded plastics, nutritional supplements, paper products, and textiles.

Hemp oil contains omega-3, -6, and -9 fatty acids, which nourish skin and thus can be included in many cosmetic products, such as baby moisturizer, facial cream, shaving cream, shampoo, and conditioner. The mineral oil typically used in these products has been derived from fossil fuel, the use of which is not sustainable or environmentally friendly. For construction, hemp plants can be used to make caulking, cement, fiberboard, flooring, insulation, paneling, plaster, plywood, and roofing. Hemp oil can be used to produce nontoxic paint, varnish, and detergent. The essential oil is used as emulsion in medicines and is a key ingredient in nutritional supplements. More important, hemp seeds contain high levels of proteins and essential fatty acids, which make hemp a premier food source.

The plant residues that remain after harvest and processing are an excellent source of animal bedding. Meal after oil extraction from seeds contains 30 percent proteins, carbohydrates, and mineral nutrients and is often used as feed for livestock. Because of its high biomass in a wide range of habitats, hemp has an unmatched potential to be a source of biofuel, either ethanol or biodiesel.

Above all, however, is the versatility of hemp fiber. Hemp fiber has been valued for three characteristics: length, strength, and durability. The primary bast fibers in the bark can reach up to 40 millimeters long, making it a great raw material for papers, clothing, and textiles. The use of hemp fibers in cloth was more common than that of linen until the fourteenth century. Hemp paper is bleached with hydrogen peroxide, a much more environmentally friendly chemical than chlorine bleach, which is required by tree-based paper mills and pollutes water sources heavily. By the

1820's, hemp fibers were used to make 90 percent of the canvas sails, caulk, fish nets, and rigging for ships because of their strength and resistance to decay and salt water. Hemp was considered to provide the very best of canvas for painting. Estimates indicate that five thousand textile products and as many as twenty-five thousand other products could be produced using hemp. Because hemp is adaptable to a wide range of habitats, has an extremely high biomass, and can be used in a variety of products, legalizing its cultivation may be inevitable in the near future.

*Ming Y. Zheng*

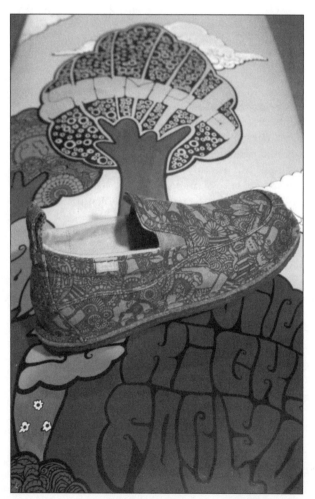

*Numerous products are derived from hemp, including this shoe from the company Simple, featuring a design by a California teenager. (Mike Blake/Reuters/Landov)*

FURTHER READING

Bócsa, Iván, and Michael Koras. *The Cultivation of Hemp: Botany, Varieties, Cultivation, and Harvesting.* Translated by Chris Filben. Sebastopol, Calif.: Hemptech, 1998.

Brown, L. R., et al. *State of the World, 1998: Worldwatch Institute Report on Progress Toward a Sustainable Society.* New York: W. W. Norton, 1998.

Conrad, C. *Hemp: Lifeline to the Future—The Unexpected Answer for Our Environmental and Economic Recovery.* Los Angeles: Creative Expressions, 1994.

Leizer, C., et al. "The Composition of Hemp Seed Oil and Its Potential as an Important Source of Nutrition." *Journal of Nutraceuticals Functional and Medical Foods* 2, no. 4 (2000): 35-54.

Roulac, John W. *Hemp Horizon: The Comeback of the World's Most Promising Plant.* White River Junction, Vt.: Chelsea Green, 2006.

Small, E., and D. Marcus. "Hemp: A New Crop with New Uses for North America." In *Trends in New Crops and New Uses,* edited by Jules Janick and Anna Whipkey. Alexandria, Va.: ASHS Press, 2002.

WEB SITES

HEMP INDUSTRIES ASSOCIATION
http://thehia.org/

NORTH AMERICAN INDUSTRIAL HEMP COUNCIL, INC.
Hemp Facts
http://www.naihc.org/hemp_information/
hemp_facts.html

SEE ALSO: Agricultural products; American Forest and Paper Association; Biodiversity; Biofuels; Cotton; Flax; Hydroponics; Paper; Paper, alternative sources of; Plant fibers; Plants as a medical resource; Renewable and nonrenewable resources; Textiles and fabrics.

# Herbicides

CATEGORIES: Environment, conservation, and
resource management; pollution and waste
disposal

*Herbicides are a class of pesticide used to kill or other-
wise control unwanted vegetation. They are frequently
employed in agriculture and forestry.*

## BACKGROUND

Herbicides are used for the control of grasses, weeds,
and other plant pests. These chemical compounds
kill plants or inhibit their normal growth. In general,
herbicides work by interfering with photosynthesis, so
that a plant dies from lack of energy, or by a combination of defoliation (leaf removal) and systemic herbicidal action.

Herbicides are used to clear rights-of-way beneath
power lines and along railways and roads. In agriculture and forest management, they are used to control
weeds or to remove the leaves from some crop plants
to facilitate harvesting. While herbicides may be employed in lieu of tillage, their use is more often in conjunction with tillage and other agronomic practices.
During wartime, defoliants and other herbicides have
been used to destroy plants that an enemy uses for
cover during battle or for food.

## TYPES OF HERBICIDES

Herbicides may be selective or nonselective. Selective
herbicides, such as amitrole, atrazine, monuron, pyr-
idine, 2,4-dichlorophenoxyacetic acid (2,4-D), and
2,4,5-trichlorophenoxyacetic acid (2,4,5-T), target a
particular plant pest and will kill or stunt weeds among
crop plants without injuring the crop. For example,
2,4-D targets soft-stemmed plants, while 2,4,5-T is effective against woody plants. Cereals are crops particularly suited for treatment with 2,4-D, since the compound does not harm narrow-leafed plants but kills
broad-leaved weeds. Selective toxicity minimizes the
environmental impact of an herbicide. Nonselective
herbicides (also called broad-spectrum or general-
usage herbicides) are toxic to all plants. Examples include dinoseb, diquat, paraquat, and arsenic trioxide.
Nonselective compounds are best suited for areas
where all plant growth is to be suppressed, such as
along railroad rights-of-way.

Some compounds, known as contact herbicides,
kill only those plant parts to which they are directly
applied. Others, called systemic herbicides, are absorbed through the plant's foliage or roots and carried to other parts of the plant. When mixed with the
soil, some herbicides kill germinating seeds and small
seedlings.

Popular inorganic herbicides include ammonium
sulfate, sodium chlorate, sulfuric acid solutions, and
borate formulations. Among the organic herbicides
are the organic arsenicals, substituted amides and
ureas, nitrogen heterocyclic acids, and phenol derivatives. Phenoxyaliphatic acids and their derivatives, a
major group of organic herbicides, are selective poi-
sons that readily travel from one part of a plant to another.

## HISTORY

Agricultural societies have used simple chemical herbicides such as ashes and common salts for centuries.
In 1896, a fungicidal compound known as Bordeaux
mixture (a combination of copper sulfate, lime, and
water) was found also to be effective against some
weeds. Subsequently, copper sulfate was employed as
a selective weed killer in cereal crops. By the early
1900's, sodium arsenate solutions and other selective
inorganic herbicidal mixtures had been developed.
In 1932, dinitrophenol compounds were introduced.

In the early 1940's, a new generation of herbicidal
compound emerged. In an attempt to mimic natural
plant hormones, the defoliant 2,4-D was created. At
low concentrations 2,4-D promotes retention of fruit
and leaves; at higher concentrations, it overstimulates
plant metabolism, causing the leaves to drop off. A related chemical, 2,4,5-T, came into general use in 1948.
The years after World War II saw the first large-scale
application of herbicides in agriculture and other
areas. The new defoliants rapidly gained acceptance
because of their effectiveness against broad-leaved
weeds in corn, sorghum, small grains, and grass pastures.

A few years after their development, these defoliants were employed as chemical weapons. During its
conflict with Communist guerrillas in Malaya during
the late 1940's and early 1950's, Britain sprayed 2,4,5-
T on crops and jungle foliage to deprive the guerrillas
of food and cover. The United States conducted a similar antifood and antifoliage campaign in South Vietnam during the 1960's. In this campaign, dubbed
"Operation Ranch Hand," massive quantities of herbicidal mixtures were sprayed from aircraft onto Viet-

*A plane is used to spray herbicide on a rice field in Arkansas.* (Robert Cohen/The Commercial Appeal/Landov)

cong food plantations, infiltration routes, staging areas, and bases. The quantity and frequency of the spraying greatly exceeded recommended levels; in addition, mechanical problems or military need often forced aircraft to dump their herbicide loads all at once, drenching the jungle below. Soldiers, civilians, and the environment were subjected to unusually high concentrations of defoliants. One of the herbicides used in this campaign was Agent Orange, a mixture that included 2,4-D and 2,4,5-T. Commercial preparations of 2,4,5-T contain varying amount of dioxin, a highly toxic contaminant. Agent Orange has been implicated in the increased incidence of still births and birth defects among the Vietnamese living in the areas sprayed, in the cancers and other illnesses suffered by American and Australian soldiers who were involved in the operation, and in birth defects among the children of these veterans. In 1970, the United States placed severe restrictions on domestic and agricultural use of 2,4,5-T, at about the same time the defoliation campaign was halted.

## U.S. REGULATION OF HERBICIDES

In 1947, the Federal Insecticide, Fungicide, and Rodenticide Act (FIFRA) authorized the United States Department of Agriculture (USDA) to oversee registration of herbicides and other pesticides and to determine their safety and effectiveness. In December, 1970, the newly formed United States Environmental Protection Agency (EPA) assumed statutory authority from the USDA over pesticide regulations. Under the Federal Environmental Pesticide Control Act of 1972, an amendment to FIFRA, manufacturers must register all marketed pesticides with the EPA before the product is released. Before registration, the chemicals must undergo exhaustive trials to assess their potential impact on the environment and human health. The EPA's decision to grant registration is based on the determination that unreasonable adverse effects on human health or the environment are not anticipated within the constraints of approved usage. Beginning in October, 1977, the EPA classified all pesticides to which it has granted registration as either a restricted-usage (to be applied only by certified pest control operators) or unclassified (general-usage) pesticide.

*Karen N. Kähler*

FURTHER READING

Clark, J. Marshall, and Hideo Ohkawa, eds. *Environmental Fate and Safety Management of Agrochemicals.* Washington, D.C.: American Chemical Society, 2005.

_____. *New Discoveries in Agrochemicals.* Washington, D.C.: American Chemical Society, 2005.

Crone, Hugh D. *Chemicals and Society: A Guide to the New Chemical Age.* New York: Cambridge University Press, 1986.

Monaco, Thomas J., Stephen C. Weller, and Floyd M. Ashton. *Weed Science: Principles and Practices.* 4th ed. New York: Wiley, 2002.

Vencill, William K., et al., eds. *Herbicide Handbook.* 8th ed. Lawrence, Kans.: Weed Science Society of America, 2002.

Ware, George W. *Complete Guide to Pest Control: With and Without Chemicals.* 4th ed. Willoughby, Ohio: MeisterPro Information Resources, 2005.

_____. *Fundamentals of Pesticides: A Self-Instruction Guide.* 2d ed. Fresno, Calif.: Thomson, 1986.

Zimdahl, Robert L. *Fundamentals of Weed Science.* Boston: Elsevier/Academic Press, 2007.

### WEB SITES

AGRICULTURE AND AGRI-FOOD CANADA
Manure, Fertilizer, and Pesticide Management in Canada
http://www4.agr.gc.ca/AAFC-AAC/display-afficher.do?id=1178825328101&lang=eng

HEALTH CANADA
Pesticides and Pest Management
http://www.hc-sc.gc.ca/cps-spc/pest/index-eng.php

U.S. ENVIRONMENTAL PROTECTION AGENCY
Pesticides
http://www.epa.gov/pesticides/index.htm

SEE ALSO: Agriculture industry; Environmental Protection Agency; Food chain; Monoculture agriculture; Pesticides and pest control.

# Hill, James Jerome

CATEGORY: People
BORN: September 16, 1838; Rockwood, Upper Canada (now in Ontario, Canada)
DIED: May 29, 1916; St. Paul, Minnesota

*James Jerome Hill was a railroad entrepreneur who contributed greatly to American economic growth. He was also a conservationist and proponent of natural science. He wrote books, gave lectures, and financially endorsed advanced scientific farming methods for optimum agricultural land management.*

### BIOGRAPHICAL BACKGROUND

James Jerome Hill had nine years of formal schooling, leaving upon the death of his father in 1852. He studied math and land surveying, then learned bookkeeping and later worked for wholesalers, dealing with freight and fuel shipping and supply. Within a decade, Hill had begun his own freight transportation business, soon owning both steamboat and coal businesses. Hill also entered banking and began buying up bankrupt companies, remaking and selling them for a great profit. When the St. Paul and Pacific Railroad went bankrupt during the Panic of 1873, Hill went into financial collaboration with four others and bought the line. As general manager, Hill bargained for trackage rights, upgraded the Great Northern, and built rails through the upper Midwest, the Great Plains, and the Pacific Northwest, from Minnesota to Montana.

As Hill came upon areas where industry was weak, he bought and placed companies along the railroad

*James Jerome Hill was a railroad executive cum conservationist who was a proponent of agricultural land management. (Hulton Archive/Getty Images)*

lines. He also promoted European immigration, paying travel and settlement expenses for incoming immigrants. Knowing the railroad business and the changes occurring in it, Hill bargained for better rates. Knowing grain and other markets, Hill stayed keen to the fluctuations in agricultural management. Acknowledging that his rail business shipped mostly agricultural products, Hill came to be concerned about water and land use, misuse, and what would become known as sustainable resource management.

### IMPACT ON RESOURCE USE

A savvy entrepreneur and a staunch conservationist, Hill took interest in both high-yield agriculture and sustainable resources. With concern for how farming practices degraded the soil, he began to experiment with crop rotation, hybridizing Russian wheat in the Dakotas and developing superior livestock—using the manure to yield superior crops and to conserve soil quality. He toured the country-fair circuit, speaking to farmers on the subject of sustainable farming and conservation, the topic of several books he wrote to further the cause. He created his own lab and hired agronomists to analyze soil and train farmers, whom he paid to practice the contemporary techniques. He also purchased livestock for farmers, extracting from them only the promise to make the prize hogs, rams, and bulls available for breeding.

Hill's work was so impressive that President Theodore Roosevelt was prompted to hold a White House conference on conservation in 1908—despite Hill's contention that natural resource control should stay at state and local levels. Hill not only was keen on agricultural management but also was a financial expert. Together these traits made the economic concerns of conservative land management Hill's number-one focus.

*Roxanne McDonald*

### WEB SITES

HISTORYLINK.ORG
Spokane Neighborhoods: Hillyard
Http://www.historylink.org/
index.cfm?DisplayPage=output.cfm&File_
Id=7294

RAIL SERVE
James J. Hill
http://www.railserve.com

SEE ALSO: Agriculture industry; Agronomy; Animal breeding; Conservation; Conservation biology; Soil management.

# Horticulture

CATEGORIES: Scientific disciplines; environment, conservation, and resource management

*Horticulture is the branch of agriculture that is connected with the production of plants that are directly used by humans for food, medicine, and aesthetic purposes.*

### BACKGROUND

The ability to produce crops, particularly those crops associated with food and fiber, is a major economic and natural resource. Horticulture, a multibillion-dollar-per-year industry, is a multidisciplinary science that encompasses all aspects of production, for fun or profit, of intensively cultivated plants to be utilized by humans for food, medicinal purposes, or aesthetic satisfaction. Crop production is largely determined by a variety of environmental conditions, including soil, water, light, temperature, and atmosphere. Therefore, horticulture science is primarily concerned with the study of how to manipulate the plants or these environmental factors to achieve maximum yield. Since there is tremendous diversity in horticultural plants, the field is subdivided into pomology, the growth and production of fruit crops; olericulture, the growth and production of vegetable crops; landscape horticulture, the growth and production of trees and shrubs; and floriculture, the growth and production of flower and foliage plants. Each of these subdivisions is based on a fundamental knowledge of plant-soil interactions, soil science, plant physiology, and plant morphology.

### PROPAGATION

Horticulture science is concerned with all aspects of crop production, from the collection and germination of seed to the final marketing of the products. Plant propagation, protection, and harvesting are three areas of particular interest to horticulturists. Generally, propagation from seed is the most common and least expensive way of propagating plants. In order to prevent cross-pollination from undesirable

*The Chinese floral industry has vigorously expanded since the year 2000.* (Xinhua/Landov)

varieties, plants to be used for seed production are grown in genetic isolation from other, similar plants. At maturity, the seed is collected and is usually stored at low temperatures and under 50 to 65 percent relative humidity to maintain full viability. The seed is often tested for viability prior to planting to determine the percentage of seed that should germinate. At the appropriate time, the seed is usually treated with a fungicide to ensure an adequate crop stand and planted under proper temperature, water, and light conditions. For most crops, the seed is germinated in small containers, and the seedlings are then transplanted to the field or greenhouse.

For many horticultural crops it is not feasible to produce plants from seed. For some, the growth from seed may require too much time to be economically practical. In other cases, the parent plants may produce too little or no viable seed, and in still others, there may be a desire to avoid hybridization in order to maintain a pure strain. For some plants, almost any part of the root, stem, or leaf can be vegetatively prop-

agated, but chemical treatment of the detached portion to ensure regeneration of the missing tissue is often required.

For other plants, a variety of specific vegetative plant tissues, including the roots, bulbs, corms, rhizomes, tubers, and runners, must be used for propagation. Individual runners are used for propagation purposes, but a number of cuttings can be propagated from one rhizome. Tubers are propagated by slicing the organ into several pieces, each of which must contain an "eye" or bud. Corms and bulbs are propagated by planting the entire structure. A relatively new process of generating plants from cell cultures grown in the laboratory, called tissue culture, is a method often used to propagate pure lines of crops with a high economic value. Grafting, a specialized form of vegetative propagation, is particularly useful in tree farming. The shoot from one plant with a particularly desirable fruit quality can be grafted onto the root stock of another, more vigorous plant with a less desirable fruit quality.

## PEST CONTROL

Since plants are besieged by a panoply of biological agents that utilize plant tissues as a food source, plant protection from pests is a major concern in the horticulture industry. Microbial organisms, nematodes, insects, and weeds are the major plant pests. Weeds are defined as unwanted plants and are considered to be pests because they compete with crop plants for water, sunlight, and nutrients. If left unchecked, weeds will drastically reduce crop yields because they tend to produce a large amount of seed and grow rapidly. Weed control is generally accomplished either by removing the weed physically or by use of a variety of herbicides that have been developed to chemically control weeds. Herbicides are selected on the basis of their ability to control weeds and, at the same time, cause little or no damage to the desired plant.

Plant protection from microbes, nematodes, and insects generally involves either preventing or restricting pest invasion of the plant, developing plant varieties that will resist or at least tolerate the invasion, or a combination of both methods. The application of chemicals, utilization of biological agents, isolation of an infected crop by quarantine, and cultural practices that routinely remove infected plants or plant tissues are examples of the different types of control methods. A large number of different bactericides, fungicides, nematocides, and insecticides have been developed in recent years, and the use of these pesticides has been particularly useful in plant protection. Since many of these chemicals are harmful to other animals, including humans, the use of pesticides, and insecticides in particular, requires extreme caution. There is an increasing interest in the use of biological control methods because many of the chemical pesticides pose a threat to the environment. The development and use of pest-resistant crop varieties and the introduction of natural enemies that will not only reduce the pest population but also live harmoniously in the existing environment are two of the more promising biological measures employed.

## HARVEST

A crop must be harvested once it has grown to maturity. Harvesting is one of the most expensive aspects of crop production because it is usually extremely labor intensive. For almost all crops, there is a narrow window between the time the plants are ready to harvest and the time when the plants are too ripe to be of economic value. Hence, the process requires considerable planning to ensure that the appropriate equipment and an adequate labor supply are available when the crop is ready to be harvested. Predicting the harvest date is of paramount importance in the planning process. The length of the harvest window, the length of the growing season that is necessary for a given plant to mature under normal environmental conditions at a given geographic location, and the influence of unexpected weather changes on the growing season all have to be considered in the planning process. Since nature is unpredictable, even the best planning schedules sometimes have to be readjusted in midseason.

Some crops are picked from the plant by hand and then mechanically conveyed from the field, while other crops are harvested entirely by hand. New mechanical harvesting equipment is continually being developed by agricultural engineers, and crops that lend themselves to mechanical harvesting are growing in importance as the manual labor force continues to shrink. After harvest, most crops are generally stored for varying lengths of time, from a few days to several months. Since postharvest storage can affect both the quality and appearance of the product, considerable care is given as to how the crop is stored. Sometimes storage improves the quality and appearance, while in other cases, it causes them to deteriorate. The ideal storage conditions are those that maintain the product as close to harvest condition as possible.

## FUTURE OF THE RESOURCE

In order for horticulture to remain a viable resource in the future, advances in horticulture technology have to continue to keep pace with the needs of an ever-increasing population. However, horticulturists also have to be mindful of the fragile nature of the environment. New technologies must be developed with the environment in mind, and much of this new technology will center on advances in genetic engineering. New crop varieties that will both provide higher yields and reduce the dependency on chemical pesticides by exhibiting greater resistance to a variety of pests will have to be developed. The future development of higher-yielding crops that can be harvested mechanically and the production of new types of equipment to facilitate the harvesting process will also be important improvements in the horticulture industry.

*D. R. Gossett*

FURTHER READING

Acquaah, George. *Horticulture: Principles and Practices.* 4th ed. Upper Saddle River, N.J.: Pearson Prentice Hall, 2009.

Adams, C. R., K. M. Bamford, and M. P. Early. *Principles of Horticulture.* 5th ed. Boston: Butterworth-Heinemann, 2008.

Bailey, L. H. *The Standard Cyclopedia of Horticulture.* 2d ed. 3 vols. New York: Macmillan, 1963.

Hartmann, Hudson T., et al. *Hartmann and Kester's Plant Propagation: Principles and Practices.* 7th ed. Upper Saddle River, N.J.: Prentice Hall, 2002.

Janick, Jules. *Horticultural Science.* 4th ed. New York: W. H. Freeman, 1986.

Reiley, H. Edward, and Carroll L. Shry, Jr. *Introductory Horticulture.* 7th ed. Clifton Park, N.Y.: Thomson Delmar Learning, 2007.

Rice, Laura Williams, and Robert P. Rice, Jr. *Practical Horticulture.* 6th ed. Upper Saddle River, N.J.: Pearson Prentice Hall, 2006.

Ward, Janet D., and Larry T. Ward. *Principles of Food Science.* Tinley Park, Ill.: Goodheart-Willcox, 2002.

WEB SITES

AGRICULTURE AND AGRI-FOOD CANADA
Horticulture
http://www4.agr.gc.ca/AAFC-AAC/display-afficher.do?id=1204824463519&lang=eng

U.S. DEPARTMENT OF AGRICULTURE
Horticulture
http://www.csrees.usda.gov/horticulture.cfm

SEE ALSO: Agricultural products; Agriculture industry; Biotechnology; Hydroponics; Monoculture agriculture; Plant domestication and breeding.

# Hot springs. *See* Geysers and hot springs

# Hydroenergy

CATEGORY: Energy resources

*The first recorded uses of hydroenergy, or water power, occurred during the first century B.C.E. Water eventually drove mills for grinding grain, powered machine tools in factories, and, finally, in the twentieth century, became an important source of energy for generating electricity.*

## BACKGROUND

Although devices for moving water have existed since prehistoric times, apparently no one realized that water could be used to power mills or other equipment until approximately two thousand years ago. Farmers throughout the ancient Middle East used primitive waterwheels, known as noria, to transfer water from one level to another, as from a flowing river to an irrigation canal. Similar devices, which consist of jars or buckets attached to a wheel that is turned by the pressure of water flowing against it, can still be seen in use in Egypt and Iraq. Sometime around 100 B.C.E. an unknown inventor harnessed the power of the moving water to a mill for grinding grain.

## THE ROMAN EMPIRE THROUGH THE NINETEENTH CENTURY

Following the invention of the waterwheel, its use for moving millstones spread throughout the Roman Empire. The water-powered mill made possible a dramatic increase in the production of flour. Sixteen to twenty man-hours were required to grind sixty kilograms of grain. Even a primitive waterwheel, one with the equivalent of perhaps three horsepower in motive power, could produce two and one half times that amount in only one hour.

Waterwheels and milling techniques remained relatively unchanged until the Middle Ages. Between the years 800 C.E. and 1200 C.E., innovations in waterwheel technology exploded across Europe. Millwrights refined waterwheels for greater efficiency and adapted wheels for use in a wide variety of applications. In addition to milling grain, waterwheels drove fulling hammers for processing wool in manufacturing felt and softened hides at tanneries. Towns grew up around milling complexes in European cities. Millers constructed dams to regulate the flow of water, while landowners became wealthy through the lease fees collected for choice mill sites on rivers and streams. A narrow stream might be dammed to provide water for one wheel, while wider rivers, such as the Seine in France, were spanned by a series of waterwheels and mills all constructed side by side. Artisans devised varied types of waterwheels and gearing to use with different levels of available water, such as undershot, overshot, and breast wheels, and they built ingenious systems of stone dams and timber crib weirs to exploit every conceivable source of moving water, from tidal flows to the smallest freshwater streams.

Waterwheels were also built in the Middle East, India, and China, but these never reached the level of complexity common in Europe even before the Renaissance. In the 1600's, European colonists brought waterwheel technologies with them to the New World, and, not surprising, patterns of settlement followed streams and rivers inland from the ocean. Although the eighteenth century invention of the steam engine and its contribution to the Industrial Revolution changed patterns of industrial development in Europe and elsewhere, the steam engine did not eliminate the importance of water power to manufacturing. While steam engines quickly found applications

in the mining industry, it took many years for steam power to displace water power elsewhere. Steam engines eventually allowed industry to develop factory sites located away from sources of moving water, but did not reduce the importance of water power to many factories already in place. In fact, the rapid expansion of the textile industry in the United States relied far more on water power than it did on steam, even though steam engines were commonplace by the 1820's.

Textile factories, such as those located in Lowell, Massachusetts, used water power by developing elaborate systems of drive belts that extended through factories that were several stories high and hundreds of meters long. Dams on the river above the town diverted water into multiple canals, allowing factory construction well back from the original banks of the river. The development of the water-powered Lowell

*Hydroenergy has been used for centuries. The power station above, in Vienna, Austria, is a modern example of how hydroenergy is produced.* (©Richard Kittenberger/Dreamstime.com)

sites began in the early years of the nineteenth century and continued for almost one hundred years. It was not until the twentieth century, following the invention of the electric motor and the widespread distribution of electrical power, that factories began to abandon water power as a motive source. Even then, only the presence of other factors, such as the buildup of silt in mill ponds and the movement of industry from the New England states to the South, may have pushed factory owners to implement changes in sources of motive power.

## TWENTIETH CENTURY DEVELOPMENTS

At the beginning of the twentieth century, industry moved away from direct exploitation of hydroenergy through the use of waterwheels and began instead to use electricity generated from hydroelectric power plants. Hydroelectric power plants generate electricity by converting the motive power of the water into electrical current. The water enters the plant through a power tunnel or penstock that directs the water into a casing. The casing, which looks like a gigantic snail, narrows as it spirals in and directs the water toward the blades of a turbine that turns the shaft an electric generator. Early hydroelectric plants utilized designs that converted the force of the water striking the waterwheel directly into electrical energy, but engineers and scientists quickly developed more efficient turbines to take advantage of available water resources.

The amount of energy potential in a water power site depends on two factors. First is the effective head, or the height difference between the level of the water standing behind the dam (before the water enters the power tunnel) and where it will exit at the tailrace on the downstream side of the turbine. Second is the volume of water. A large volume of water can compensate for a low effective head, just as an extremely high head can compensate for a low volume of water. High-head, low-volume hydroelectric plants generally rely on impulse wheels. Water enters the casing around the wheel under tremendous pressure and strikes the wheel buckets with incredible force. As the wheel spins in response to the force of the water striking it, it turns the shaft of a generator to convert kinetic energy to electricity. Impulse wheels have a fairly low efficiency rating, but they are often the only practical turbines for use in situations where water is in short supply. These impulse wheels, also known as Pelton wheels, are vertical water wheels that to the observer share an obvious ancestry with the old-fashioned wa-

terwheels seen in bucolic illustrations of gristmills and ponds. Impulse wheels were once widely used throughout the western United States, where effective heads of several hundred meters are common.

Most large modern hydroelectric plants use a different type of turbine, a reaction turbine, that exploits the pressure differential between the water entering the turbine casing and the tailrace below. Engineers such as James B. Francis turned the vertical waterwheel on its side. In the process, Francis designed a turbine that creates a partial vacuum in the space between the turbine and the tailrace. The Francis turbine and other reaction turbines work, in effect, by sucking the water through the turbine casing, causing the water to flow faster and to increase the overall efficiency of the system. Reaction turbines can be used in settings that have extremely low heads if a sufficient volume of water exists to create an effective pressure differential. Reaction turbines are especially well suited for applications in run-of-the-river power plants in which the dam diverting the water into the turbine may be only a couple of meters high.

## THE EARLY PROMISE OF HYDROENERGY

Noted conservationists of the early twentieth century, such as Gifford Pinchot, unabashedly pushed for the widespread exploitation of hydroelectric sites. Pinchot and others in the conservation movement encouraged the U.S. government to take a more active role in the development of hydroelectricity. The alternative to hydroelectricity was electricity generated by steam turbines, and steam required a fuel source such as coal or oil. Even before World War I first created shortages of fossil fuels, conservationists advocated greater use of renewable resources, such as hydroelectricity. Because hydroelectricity does not permanently remove water from a watershed—it merely diverts the flow to pass it through a powerhouse and then returns the water to the system—conservationists argued that hydroelectric sites should be exploited in order to conserve nonrenewable energy sources, such as coal. Conservationists devoted almost twenty years to lobbying for a water power bill, finally succeeding in 1920 with the passage of the Federal Water Power Act, which created the Federal Power Commission.

Not surprisingly, the following decades witnessed an explosion of hydropower development. The size of early hydro development had been limited by the available technology, but engineers quickly solved problems that had restricted turbine and generator size. Construction journals and the popular press alike regularly reported on new dams and power plants that would be the largest in the world, with each gigantic project quickly supplanted by a newer, bigger project. In the United States, this fascination with ever bigger hydroelectric projects became a physical reality with the construction of Hoover Dam on the Colorado River and the Bonneville Power Project along the Columbia. The arrival of the Great Depression in 1929 did not slow the construction boom. If anything, it may have accelerated it. In a time when millions of Americans were unemployed, massive construction projects such as Bonneville in the Pacific Northwest or the Tennessee Valley Authority dams in the South provided meaningful work.

### Reassessing Hydro

By the 1950's, the enthusiasm for large hydroelectric projects had abated. Conservationists who had once advocated hydroelectricity because it was clean and renewable began to realize that it nonetheless posed significant environmental problems. Construction of a high dam such as Ross Dam on Washington's Skagit River or Glen Canyon on the Colorado inevitably required that hundreds of square kilometers of land be permanently covered with water. Deserts, forests, farmland, and entire towns were all lost forever as reservoirs filled.

Nor were hydroelectric plants neutral in affecting aquatic life. The percentage of dissolved oxygen present in water changes as it passes through turbines, as does the water temperature. Water downstream from a hydroelectric plant may flow faster than before, vary widely in volume depending on power demands, and be warmer than it would be naturally. Some species of fish may disappear or be displaced by other species that find the changed conditions more favorable than the original native fish do. Upstream from the dam, the water on the surface of the reservoir will be both calmer and warmer than prior to construction, while the water at the bottom will be colder. Again, these changed conditions affect which fish will thrive and which fish will gradually disappear. Construction of a hydroelectric plant can change a stretch of a river from a trout stream into a bass lake.

The dam and power plant themselves present a physical barrier to spawning fish, a barrier that technical solutions such as fish ladders only partially solve. Fish may make it past the dam going upstream via a fish ladder, for example, but then be killed by pressure changes as they inadvertently pass through the turbines as they swim downstream.

In addition, twentieth century dam builders had to relearn what the mill owners of the Middle Ages and the early Industrial Revolution knew: Dams stop sediment as well as water. Mill owners in past centuries had learned to drain mill ponds periodically to remove accumulated silt, but such a procedure is impractical for a mammoth hydroelectric power plant. The effective life of dams has also begun to be examined: If a 90-meter dam was designed and built in 1920 to last for fifty years, what happens when it is time to replace it? About six hundred dams have been decommissioned in the United States.

### The Promise of Hydroenergy

Despite the problems inherent in hydroelectricity, many environmentalists and advocates for sustainable development believe that the creation of small-scale hydroelectric power plants could significantly reduce reliance on nonrenewable fossil fuels. A typical small-scale hydroelectric plant might have a turbine rated at only 3,000 horsepower, as opposed to the 60,000 horsepower capacity of a large plant. On the other hand, where a large hydroelectric development, such as Glen Canyon, may cost millions of dollars, take many years to complete, and have a devastating environmental impact, small-scale hydro can be easily and cheaply implemented. Diversion dams for small-scale hydro need not even block the entire flow of a stream. That is, if a stream or river has a steady flow of water, a diversion dam to steer water into the power tunnel or penstock can be constructed that extends only partway across the streambed, allowing the water and aquatic life to continue their normal passage almost free from restriction. Such small dams can utilize indigenous materials, such as timber or rocks available on the site, making construction in underdeveloped regions easy and affordable.

In the United States, development of small-scale hydroelectric power plants has been explored by independent power producers. Changes in federal energy regulations require public utilities to purchase electricity produced by independent power producers, which can be companies that generate excess electricity as part of their normal manufacturing process as well as firms that have chosen to develop alternative energy sources rather than using fossil fuels. Small hydroelectric plants once existed in many small towns throughout the nation but were abandoned as economies of scale pushed public utilities to invest in larger plants or steam turbines. Exploiting these sites suited for small-scale run-of-the-river hydroelectric power is both possible and desirable. Hydroenergy harnessed by a 200-meter-high dam can be an environmental disaster, but hydroenergy behind a 2-meter dam has few negative side effects.

*Nancy Farm Männikkö*

## FURTHER READING

Alternative Energy Institute, and Kimberly K. Smith. "Hydropower." In *Powering Our Future: An Energy Sourcebook for Sustainable Living.* New York: iUniverse, 2005.

Boyle, Godfrey, ed. *Renewable Energy.* 2d ed. New York: Oxford University Press in association with the Open University, 2004.

Craddock, David. *Renewable Energy Made Easy: Free Energy from Solar, Wind, Hydropower, and Other Alternative Energy Sources.* Ocala, Fla.: Atlantic, 2008.

Gimpel, Jean. *The Medieval Machine: The Industrial Revolution of the Middle Ages.* 2d ed. London: Pimlico, 1993.

Gordon, Robert B., and Patrick M. Malone. *The Texture of Industry: An Archaeological View of the Industrialization of North America.* New York: Oxford University Press, 1994.

Raphals, Philip. *Restructured Rivers: Hydropower in the Era of Competitive Markets, a Report.* Montreal: Helios Centre, 2001.

Reynolds, Terry S. *Stronger than a Hundred Men: A History of the Vertical Water Wheel.* Baltimore: Johns Hopkins University Press, 1983.

Twidell, John, and Tony Weir. "Hydro-Power." In *Renewable Energy Resources.* 2d ed. New York: Taylor & Francis, 2006.

U.S. Bureau of Reclamation. *Hydropower 2002: Reclamation's Energy Initiative.* Denver, Colo.: U.S. Dept. of the Interior, Bureau of Reclamation, 1991.

## WEB SITE

U.S. GEOLOGICAL SURVEY
Water Science for Schools: Hydroelectric Power Water Use
http://ga.water.usgs.gov/edu/wuhy.html

SEE ALSO: Dams; Electrical power; Energy storage; Federal Energy Regulatory Commission; Streams and rivers; Tidal energy; Water rights.

# Hydrogen

CATEGORY: Mineral and other nonliving resources

## WHERE FOUND

Hydrogen is the most abundant substance in the universe and is the principal constituent of stars such as the Sun. Because of its low molecular weight, gaseous hydrogen is not retained in the Earth's atmosphere, and it must be produced by the decomposition of its chemical compounds. The principal source of hydrogen is water, from which the hydrogen must be extracted by chemical reaction or electrolysis.

## PRIMARY USES

Hydrogen is useful both as a chemical reactant and as a source of energy. Hydrogen is used in the commercially important Haber-Bosch process for the production of ammonia. It is added to oils and fats to raise their melting points. It is also used as a fuel in certain engines and in fuel cells. The production of energy by the controlled fusion of hydrogen nuclei has been explored as an alternative to fossil and nuclear (fission) energy sources.

## TECHNICAL DEFINITION

Hydrogen (chemical symbol H), atomic number 1, is the simplest chemical element, existing under normal conditions as a diatomic gas or in chemical combination with other elements. It has three isotopes. The lightest isotope, atomic mass 1.00797, is sometimes referred to as protium to distinguish it from the much rarer deuterium, or heavy hydrogen, with atomic mass 2.014. The third isotope, tritium, with atomic mass 3.016 and a half-life of 12.26 years, is produced in trace amounts by cosmic rays bombarding the atmosphere. Hydrogen has a melting point of $-259.14°$ Celsius and a boiling point of $-252.87°$ Celsius.

## DESCRIPTION, DISTRIBUTION, AND FORMS

Nearly all the hydrogen that exists on Earth is found in chemical combination with other elements. Since the vast majority of chemical compounds involve hydrogen, there is little point in trying to identify a separate chemistry of hydrogen. As the supply of hydrogen available is inexhaustible for all practical purposes, the main reason for including it in a discussion of natural resources is the effect of hydrogen-based technologies on the use of more limited resources.

## HISTORY

Credit for the discovery of hydrogen is generally awarded to the English scientist Henry Cavendish, who collected the flammable gas released when iron and other metals reacted with acid and reported its properties in 1766. Later, English surgeon Anthony Carlisle and English chemist William Nicholson made use of the newly developed voltaic pile to produce hydrogen through the electrolysis of water. Because of its inherently low density, hydrogen was used to provide buoyancy for balloons and other lighter-than-air craft, a practice that ended with the destruction by fire of the zeppelin *Hindenburg* in 1937. Helium replaced hydrogen for buoyancy applications.

Much research in the later third of the twentieth century was directed toward achieving hydrogen fusion under controlled conditions on Earth. The principal engineering challenge has been the containment of the extremely hot plasma necessary for sustained nuclear fusion, but at least partial success has been obtained with the tokamak, a device that uses strong magnetic fields to confine the plasma. Considerable excitement was generated within the scientific community in 1989 when two electrochemists at the University of Utah announced that they had achieved deuterium fusion by electrochemical means in a table-top apparatus. Numerous attempts were made to repeat their experiment, with disappointing results. Within a few years most scientists had come to consider the evidence for "cold fusion" to be inconclusive at best.

## OBTAINING HYDROGEN

Hydrogen gas may be produced by the action of an acid on a reactive metal, by the electrolysis of water, or by the reaction of water with carbon or hydrocarbons at high temperature. Because of its small size, hydrogen can enter the lattice structure of many metallic elements. This creates a problem in steels, particularly in oil-drilling equipment, in which hydrogen embrittlement can cause mechanical failure. On the other hand, a number of transition metals, notably palladium, can absorb large quantities—up to one hydrogen atom per metal atom—of hydrogen and release it under controlled conditions, thus offering the potential for safe and compact storage of this high-energy fuel.

## USES OF HYDROGEN

Hydrogen is a very dense energy source in the sense that the combustion of a few grams of hydrogen in air releases a great deal of heat energy. The usefulness of hydrogen as a fuel is somewhat limited by its low boiling point and the fact that it readily forms an explosive mixture with oxygen from the air. Hydrogen tends to be used as a fuel only in situations in which weight is an overriding concern. Thus it is used to provide electrical power in spacecraft. There is some interest in using hydrogen as a fuel for motor vehicles, because the only combustion product is the environmentally acceptable water. Use of hydrogen in the load leveling of power-generating systems has also been proposed. In this case it would be produced by electrolysis when demand for electrical energy is low and used to power fuel cells during peak demand periods. Hydrogen can be produced from solar energy either by using photovoltaic cells to electrolyze water or directly by a photogalvanic process in which light energy absorbed by a semiconducting material is used to split the hydrogen-oxygen bond in water. Steam reacts with coal to form synthesis gas, a mixture of hydrogen, carbon monoxide, carbon dioxide, and methane that can be burned as a fuel or exposed to a catalyst to form further hydrocarbons.

*Donald R. Franceschetti*

## FURTHER READING

Eubanks, Lucy Pryde, et al. *Chemistry in Context: Applying Chemistry to Society.* 6th ed. New York: McGraw-Hill Higher Education, 2009.

Greenwood, N. N., and A. Earnshaw. "Hydrogen." In *Chemistry of the Elements.* 2d ed. Boston: Butterworth-Heinemann, 1997.

Gupta, Ram B., ed. *Hydrogen Fuel: Production, Transport, and Storage.* Boca Raton, Fla.: CRC Press, 2009.

Henderson, William. "The Chemistry of Hydrogen." In *Main Group Chemistry.* Cambridge, England: Royal Society of Chemistry, 2000.

Holland, Geoffrey B., and James J. Provenzano. *The Hydrogen Age: Empowering a Clean-Energy Future.* Salt Lake City, Utah: Gibbs Smith, 2007.

Hordeski, Michael Frank. *Alternative Fuels: The Future of Hydrogen.* 2d ed. Boca Raton, Fla.: CRC Press, 2008.

_____. *Hydrogen and Fuel Cells: Advances in Transportation and Power.* Boca Raton, Fla.: CRC Press, 2009.

Rifkin, Jeremy. *The Hydrogen Economy: The Creation of the Worldwide Energy Web and the Redistribution of Power on Earth.* New York: J. P. Tarcher/Putnam, 2002.

Rigden, John S. *Hydrogen: The Essential Element.* Cambridge, Mass.: Harvard University Press, 2002.

Romm, Joseph J. *The Hype About Hydrogen: Fact and Fiction in the Race to Save the Climate.* Washington, D.C.: Island Press, 2004.

WEB SITES

UNIVERSAL INDUSTRIAL GASES, INC.
Hydrogen (H₂) Properties, Uses, Applications: Hydrogen Gas and Liquid Hydrogen
http://www.uigi.com/hydrogen.html

U.S. DEPARTMENT OF ENERGY
Hydrogen
http://www.energy.gov/energysources/hydrogen.htm

U.S. DEPARTMENT OF ENERGY, ALTERNATIVE FUELS AND ADVANCED VEHICLES DATA CENTER
Hydrogen
http://www.afdc.energy.gov/afdc/fuels/hydrogen.html

SEE ALSO: Coal gasification and liquefaction; Fuel cells; Haber-Bosch process; Nuclear energy; Solar energy.

# Hydrology and the hydrologic cycle

CATEGORIES: Geological processes and formations; scientific disciplines

*Hydrology is the study of the Earth's water. It involves a number of scientific disciplines related to its acquisition, planning, and management. The hydrologic cycle is the cycle that water passes through as it is transformed from seawater to atmospheric moisture to precipitation on land surfaces and its eventually to water vapor or the sea.*

## BACKGROUND

Unlike any other planet in our solar system, the Earth has a vast abundance of water. More than 70 percent of the Earth's surface is covered by water. Therefore, the life that has evolved on the Earth is extremely dependent on water for continued survival. The American Geologic Institute's *Dictionary of Geological Terms* defines hydrology as "the science that relates to the water of the Earth." It can also be described as the study of the Earth's water in all its forms and areas of occurrence. This study includes an array of scientific disciplines, such as civil engineering, geology, oceanography, chemistry, geography, and ecology, to name only a few.

## IMPORTANCE OF WATER AS A RESOURCE

On a casual appraisal, that water would be considered an important natural resource seems unlikely given its abundance on the Earth. However, as Benjamin Franklin observed, "When the well's dry, we know the worth of water." Despite the vast volumes of water on our planet, fresh water is in fact one of our most important natural resources. Without it, much terrestrial life, including humans, could not exist. Water fit for human consumption is an absolute necessity, and much of the Earth's water is too salty to be consumable by humans.

Although desalinization is used in some areas, it is often not economically feasible on a large scale. Although not readily consumable by humans, the water in the oceans is of unquestionable importance as a resource. It supports the biodiversity of the oceans, and all creatures of the Earth are either directly or indirectly dependent on it for survival. Water of acceptable quality is necessary for irrigation and livestock operations. Huge quantities of water are necessary for certain industrial processes and as a coolant for various industrial processes.

## FORMS OF WATER

Although estimates vary, more than 97 percent of the Earth's water exists in the form of the seawater found in the oceans. Of the remaining percentage, much is tied up in ice caps, glaciers, saline lakes, and soil moisture. Freshwater lakes, rivers, and streams account for a surprisingly small percentage of the total of the Earth's water, about 0.01 percent.

Fresh groundwater accounts for roughly 0.76 percent of the overall total. It can be seen by this comparison that fresh groundwater sources far outweigh surface water sources. In reality, only a small portion of the Earth's water is readily available in the form of fresh water. Although the amounts of fresh groundwater and surface water are comparatively small, much of the study of hydrology involves these two forms because of their crucial importance. The search for new sources of groundwater is primarily accomplished by exploratory drilling coupled with a knowledge of hydrologic and geologic processes. Artificial lakes and reservoirs increase the supply of water by lengthening the residence time of surface water.

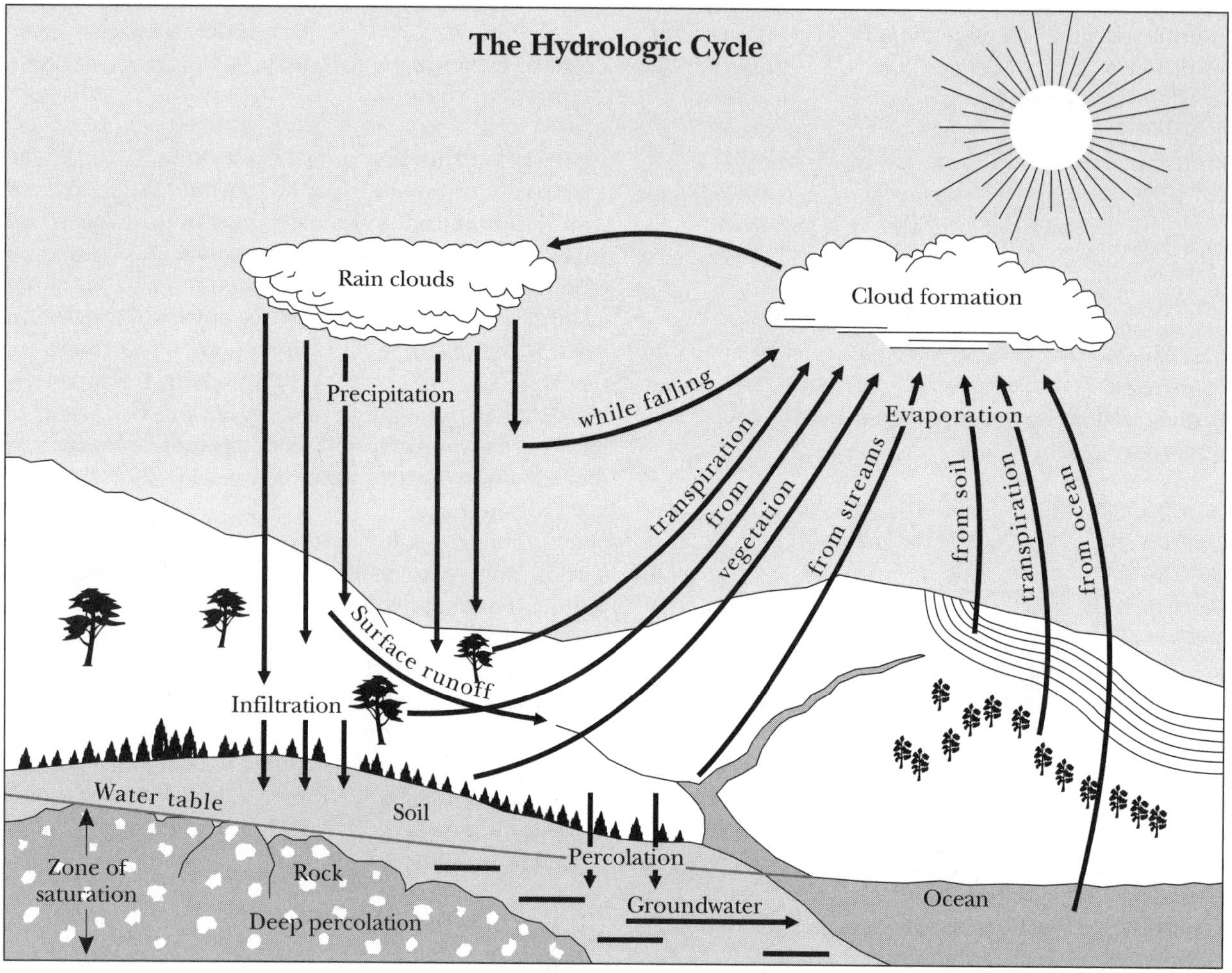

## The Hydrologic Cycle

Rain clouds

Cloud formation

Precipitation

while falling

Evaporation

transpiration from vegetation

from streams

from soil

transpiration

from ocean

Surface runoff

Infiltration

Water table

Soil

Percolation

Ocean

Zone of saturation

Rock

Deep percolation

Groundwater

*Source:* U.S. Department of Agriculture, *Yearbook of Agriculture* (Washington, D.C.: Government Printing Office, 1955).

## IMPORTANCE OF WATER

Since World War II, agricultural, residential, and industrial demands on water supplies have increased dramatically. In areas such as California and Idaho, where groundwater is used extensively for irrigation, some sources of fresh water appear to be dwindling rapidly. Although its full extent is not known, human pollution of water resources is also a major concern. The U.S. Environmental Protection Agency has indicated that roughly 40 percent of assessed rivers and lakes and more than 30 percent of assessed estuaries were not suitable for fishing, swimming, or other uses. Civil engineers, geologists, chemists, and others work in concert with cities and other governmental agencies to expand water supplies, to provide better planning for future water use, and to protect remaining sources of water.

## THE HYDROLOGIC CYCLE

Although there is no true beginning or end to the hydrologic cycle, descriptions often begin with the oceans. Solar radiation provides the energy for the cycle. It not only transforms some of the Earth's liquid waters to water vapor but also leads to a planetary heat imbalance. In general the Northern Hemisphere has a net heat loss to space, and equatorial areas have a net heat gain. To counteract this imbalance, heat is transferred in the form of ocean currents and atmospheric currents.

As water evaporates from the oceans, it leaves behind many of its impurities, including salts. As water vapor collects in clouds it is carried along by atmospheric currents. When conditions are right, atmospheric water vapor precipitates as rain, snow, sleet, and so on. Some of this precipitation falls back on the oceans to begin the cycle again, but some falls on land surfaces.

Of the precipitation that falls on land surfaces, much becomes locked up in ice caps and glaciers, but some falls in the form of rain (or snow that melts when temperatures rise). The majority of the precipitation that falls on land surfaces runs off in the form of surface flow, referred to as overland flow. This flow is observed in the complex surface drainage systems of streams, creeks, rivers, and lakes. The residence time of surface water can be as short as a few days or weeks. Surface water is a major area of study. Evaporation from surface water adds to atmospheric moisture, as does water vapor that transpires from the leaves of trees and other plants.

Although the majority of precipitation takes the form of overland flow, in areas where surface soil or rock is porous and permeable, water can move downward into the ground by the process of infiltration. This water of infiltration becomes groundwater. Groundwater flows through void spaces in soil or rock; therefore its flow is restricted by the porosity and permeability of the material it enters. The residence time of groundwater can be on the order of months, centuries, or even thousands of years. In essence the water is stored for a time. The soil zone or rock stratum in which the water is stored is called an aquifer. Aquifers are further categorized as major or minor and as confined or unconfined. An unconfined aquifer, also called a water table aquifer, is said to have a water table. A confined aquifer has a potentiometric surface, or level to which water will rise, rather than a water table.

Since precipitation and infiltration have seasonal variability, the height of the water table in an unconfined aquifer also has seasonal variability. There is complex interaction between groundwater and surface water, based on gravity and the height of the water column, expressed as hydrostatic head. An axiom is that water moves from high head to low head. Another way to view this is by picturing a lake. Water tries to move from high elevation to low elevation; the ultimate level is sea level. The same is true for groundwater.

In the absence of geologic complexity, the water table in an unconfined aquifer tends roughly to follow the topographic surface. This creates areas of higher hydrostatic head and areas of lower hydrostatic head, providing a gravitation impetus for groundwater flow, expressed numerically as the gradient. As groundwater flows from higher elevations to lower elevations, it encounters incised streambeds that may have a base

level lower than the level of the water table. In this instance, groundwater will discharge to the streambed, creating the base flow of the stream. In this situation, the stream is considered a gaining stream. If the incised bed of the stream has a higher elevation than the groundwater, the stream can lose surface water to groundwater by the process of infiltration; in this instance the stream would be considered a losing stream. Because of the seasonal variation in the water table, streams can change seasonally from gaining to losing and vice versa.

Because of geologic processes, many beds of rock, or strata, are not flat. As the strata composing an aquifer dip away, groundwater can become confined under a less permeable layer such as a shale. In this type of aquifer the recharge area of the strata exposed at the surface is at a higher elevation than down-dip portions of the strata under the confining bed. The water table at higher elevations exerts hydrostatic pressure on the confined portion of the aquifer at lower elevations. A well penetrating the confined portion of an aquifer is said to be artesian because the hydrostatic pressure causes the water column in the well to rise above the confining layer, and, in many cases, water from confined aquifers will flow to the surface.

*Raymond U. Roberts*

FURTHER READING

Brutsaert, Wilfried. *Hydrology: An Introduction.* New York: Cambridge University Press, 2005.

Davie, Tim. *Fundamentals of Hydrology.* London: Routledge, 2003.

Dingman, S. Lawrence. *Physical Hydrology.* 2d ed. Upper Saddle River, N.J.: Prentice Hall, 2002.

Fetter, C. W. *Applied Hydrogeology.* 4th ed. Upper Saddle River, N.J.: Prentice Hall, 2001.

Freeze, R. Allan, and John A. Cherry. *Groundwater.* Englewood Cliffs, N.J.: Prentice-Hall, 1979.

Manning, John C. *Applied Principles of Hydrology.* Illustrated by Natalie J. Weiskal. 3d ed. Upper Saddle River, N.J.: Prentice Hall, 1997.

Ward, Andrew D., and Stanley W. Trimble. *Environmental Hydrology.* 2d ed. Boca Raton, Fla.: Lewis, 2004.

WEB SITES

U.S. GEOLOGICAL SURVEY
Water Science for Schools: The Water Cycle
http://ga.water.usgs.gov/edu/watercycle.html

U.S. GEOLOGICAL SURVEY
Water Science for Schools: What Is Hydrology and
    What Do Hydrologists Do?
http://ga.water.usgs.gov/edu/hydrology.html

SEE ALSO: Aquifers; Atmosphere; Biodiversity; Geochemical cycles; Glaciation; Groundwater; Lakes;
Oceans; Streams and rivers; Water pollution and water
pollution control; Water rights.

# Hydroponics

CATEGORIES: Scientific disciplines; environment,
conservation, and resource management

*The term "hydroponics" literally means water culture
and originally referred to the growth of plants in a liquid medium. It later applied to all systems used to grow
plants in nutrient solutions with or without the addition of inert material (synthetic soil) for mechanical
support.*

## BACKGROUND

The ability to produce food and fiber for an ever-
growing population is the most fundamental of all resources, and hydroponics has become an important
method of crop production. The increase in the number of commercial greenhouse operations has resulted in a tremendous increase in the use of hydroponic systems. Greenhouses are utilized in the
production of a wide array of bedding plants, flowers,
trees, and shrubs for commercial as well as for home
and garden use. Cash receipts from greenhouse and
nursery crops total billions of dollars annually. In
some arid regions, the vast majority of vegetable crops
are produced in greenhouses.

## TYPES OF HYDROPONIC SYSTEMS

The four most commonly used hydroponic systems
are sand-culture systems, aggregate systems, nutrient
film techniques, and floating systems. While these systems are similar in their use of nutrient solutions, they
vary in both the presence and type of supporting medium and in the frequency of nutrient application. In
sand culture, coarse sand is used in containers or
spread over an entire greenhouse floor or bed on top
of a recirculating drain system. A drip irrigation system is used to apply nutrient solution periodically,
and a drainage system is used to collect the excess
solution as it drains through the sand. In an aggregate open system, plants are transplanted into plastic
troughs filled with an inert supporting material, and
nutrient solution is supplied via drip irrigation. The
aggregate and sand culture systems are open systems
because the nutrient solution is not recycled. In the
nutrient film technique, there is an absence of supporting material. Seedlings are transplanted into troughs
through which the nutrient solution is channeled,
and the plants are in direct contact with the nutrient
solution. In this closed system, the nutrient solution is
channeled past the plant, collected, and reused. The
floating hydroponic system involves the floating of
plants over a pool of nutrient solution.

While the nutrient film technique and floating hydroponic systems are primarily used in research applications, the sand culture and aggregate systems
are commonly used in commercial plant production.
These two systems require the use of a nutrient solution and synthetic soil for mechanical support. Although a variety of nutrient solutions have been formulated, one of the earliest was developed in 1950,
and this solution and slight modifications of it remain
popular. Beginning in 1950, other nutrient solutions
with different concentrations of chemical salts were
developed, but the elemental ratios remained similar
to the original solution.

## MATERIALS USED FOR MECHANICAL SUPPORT

A large variety of both organic and inorganic materials have been used to formulate the synthetic soils
used for mechanical support in hydroponic systems.
Commonly used organic materials include sphagnum
moss, peat, manures, wood, and other plant residues.
Sphagnum moss, the shredded, dehydrated remains
of several species of moss in the genus *Sphagnum*, is
specifically harvested for the purpose of producing
synthetic soil. "Peat" is a term normally used to describe partially decomposed remains of wetlands vegetation that has been preserved under water. Moss
peat is the only type of peat suitable for synthetic soil
mixes. Moss peat is harvested from peat bogs, dried,
compressed into bales, and sold. Animal manures are
almost never used in commercial synthetic soil mixtures because they require costly handling and steril-
ization procedures. Wood residues such as tree bark,
wood chips, shavings, and sawdust are generally produced as by-products of the timber industry. A variety
of other plant residues, including corn cobs, sugar-

*A hydroponic farmer displays a head of lettuce grown in an Illinois greenhouse.* (AP/Wide World Photos)

cane stems, straw, and peanut and rice hulls, have been substituted for peat in synthetic soil mixtures in localities where there is sufficient supply of these materials.

Commonly used inorganic materials include vermiculite, sand, pumice, perlite, cinders, and calcined clay. Vermiculite is a very lightweight material produced by heating mica to temperatures above 1,090° Celsius. Sand is one of the most preferred materials for formulating synthetic soils because it is both inert and inexpensive, but it is heavier than other commonly used materials. Pumice, a natural glasslike material produced by volcanic action, provides a good inert supporting material when ground into small particles. Perlite, a porous material that will hold three to four times its weight in water, is produced by heating lava at temperatures above 760° Celsius. Cinders are derived from coal residues that have been thoroughly rinsed to remove harmful sulfates. Calcined clay is derived from the mineral montmorillonite baked at temperatures above 100° Celsius.

### FUTURE USE OF HYDROPONICS

The use of hydroponics will increase in the future as the population continues to grow and as more and more farmland is converted to urban use. Modern greenhouses can be constructed almost anywhere— on land that is unsuitable for agriculture and wildlife and on the tops of buildings in metropolitan areas. Improved technology will result in the development of better hydroponic systems as well as an increase in the economic feasibility of greenhouse production.

*D. R. Gossett*

### FURTHER READING

Brady, Nyle C., and Ray R. Weil. *The Nature and Properties of Soils.* 14th ed. Upper Saddle River, N.J.: Prentice Hall, 2008.

Bridgewood, Les. *Hydroponics: Soilless Gardening Explained.* Marlborough, England: Crowood Press, 2003.

Janick, Jules. *Horticultural Science.* 4th ed. New York: W. H. Freeman, 1986.

Jones, J. Benton, Jr. *A Guide for the Hydroponic and Soilless Culture Grower.* Portland, Oreg.: Timber Press, 1983.

_____. *Hydroponics: A Practical Guide for the Soilless Grower.* 2d ed. Boca Raton, Fla.: CRC Press, 2005.

Resh, Howard M. *Hydroponic Food Production: A Definitive Guidebook of Soilless Food-Growing Methods, for the Professional and Commercial Grower and the Advanced Home Hydroponics Gardener.* 6th ed. Santa Barbara, Calif.: Woodbridge Press, 2001.

WEB SITE

U.S. DEPARTMENT OF AGRICULTURE
Perlite and Hydroponics: Possible Substitute for Methyl Bromide?
http://www.ars.usda.gov/is/np/mba/apr99/perlite.htm

SEE ALSO: Horticulture; Monoculture agriculture; Plant domestication and breeding; Soil.

# Hydrothermal energy. *See* Geothermal and hydrothermal energy

# Hydrothermal solutions and mineralization

CATEGORIES: Geological processes and formations; mineral and other nonliving resources

*Hydrothermal solutions are "hot-water" solutions rich in base metals and other ions that create deposits of minerals. Most hydrothermal solutions are exhalations from magmas, but some hydrothermal deposits have no identifiable magma source. Hydrothermal processes are responsible for the major part of the world's base metals upon which modern society is so dependent. They have given rise to many of the great mining districts of the world.*

BACKGROUND
Essential conditions for the formation of hydrothermal mineral deposits include metal-bearing mineralizing solutions, openings in rocks through which the solutions are channeled, sites for deposition, and

chemical reaction resulting in deposition. The term "ore" is used for any assemblage of minerals that can be mined for a profit. "Gangue" is the nonvaluable mineral that occurs with the ore.

During the crystallization of igneous rocks, water and other volatile fluids concentrate in the upper part of the magma. These volatiles carry with them varying amounts of the ions from the melt, including high concentrations of ions that are not readily incorporated into silicate rock-forming minerals. If the vapor pressure in the magma exceeds the confining pressure of the enclosing rocks, the fluids are expelled to migrate though surrounding country rock. These solutions travel along natural pathways in the rock such as faults, fissures, or bedding planes in stratified rocks. As the solutions migrate away from their source region, they lose their mineral content through deposition in natural openings in the host rock (forming open space-filling deposits) or by chemical reaction with the host rock (forming metasomatic replacement deposits). A part of these solutions may make it to the surface to form fumaroles (gas emanations) or hot springs. In addition, some hydrothermal solutions may be derived from water trapped in ancient sediments or by dehydration of water-bearing minerals during metamorphism.

The observed volatiles from magmas, as seen during volcanic eruptions and at fumaroles, are 80 percent water. Carbon dioxide, hydrogen sulfide, sulfur, and sulfur dioxide are also abundant. Nitrogen, chlorine, fluorine, boron, and other elements are present in smaller amounts. In addition, metal ions are carried in this residual fluid. Especially abundant are the base metals—iron, tungsten, copper, lead, zinc, molybdenum, silver, and gold. Quartz is the most common nonore, or gangue, mineral deposited. Calcite, fluorite, and barite are also common as gangue minerals. Base metals combined with sulfur as sulfide minerals, with arsenic as arsenides, or with tellurium as tellurides form the most common ore minerals. Gold often occurs as a native mineral.

NATURE OF OPEN SPACES
Hydrothermal solutions find ready-made escape routes through the surrounding country rock in the form of faults and fissures. Ore and gangue minerals of cavity-filling deposits are found in faults or fissures (veins), in open spaces in fault breccias, in solution openings of soluble rocks, in pore spaces between the grain of sedimentary rocks, in vesicles of buried lava

flows, and along permeable bedding planes of sedimentary strata. The shape of the mineral deposit is controlled by the configuration of structures controlling porosity and permeability. Fracture patterns, and therefore veins, may take on a wide variety of geometric patterns, ranging from tabular to rod-shaped or blanketlike deposits.

Some deposits are characterized by ore minerals that are widely disseminated in small amounts throughout a large body of rock such as an igneous stock. These igneous bodies undergo intense fracturing during the late stage of consolidation, and residual fluids permeate the fractured rock to produce massive deposits of low-grade ores. In such deposits, the entire rock is extracted in mining operations. The famous porphyry copper deposits of the southwestern United States—including those of Santa Rita, New Mexico; Morence, Arizona; and Bingham, Utah—are of this type, as are the molybdenum deposits of Climax, Colorado.

## METASOMATIC REPLACEMENT

Some hydrothermal deposits are emplaced by reaction of the fluids with chemically susceptible rocks such as limestone or dolostone. Metasomatic replacement is defined as simultaneous capillary solution and deposition by which the host is replaced by ore and gangue minerals. These massive deposits or lodes take on the shape and the original textures of the host. Replacement is especially important in deep-seated deposits where open spaces are scarce. Replacement deposits of lead-zinc are common in limestones surrounding the porphyry copper of Santa Rita, New Mexico, and at Pioche, Nevada.

## CLASSIFICATION BY TEMPERATURE AND DEPTH

Veins are zoned, with higher-temperature minerals deposited near the source and lower-temperature minerals farther away. Hypothermal or high-temperature and high-pressure mineral assemblages include the minerals cassiterite (tin), scheelite and wolframite (tungsten), millerite (nickel), and molybdenite (molybdenum), associated with gangue minerals quartz, tourmaline, topaz, and other silicates. The mineral deposits of Broken Hill, Australia, the tin deposits of Cornwall, England, and Potosí, Bolivia, and the gold of the Homestake Mine, South Dakota, are hypothermal.

Mesothermal, or moderate-temperature and moderate-pressure deposits consist of pyrite (iron sulfide),

bornite, chalocite, chalcopyrite and enargite (copper), galena (lead), sphalerite (zinc), and cobaltite or smaltite (cobalt). Gangue minerals include calcite, quartz, siderite, and rhodochrosite. The zinc-lead-silver replacement deposits of Leadville, Park City, and Aspen, Colorado, and the Coeur d'Alene, Idaho, lead veins are mesothermal.

Epithermal or low-temperature, near-surface deposits are often associated with regions of recent volcanism. The ore is characterized by stibnite (antimony), cinnabar (mercury), native silver and silver sulfides, gold telluride, native gold, sphalerite, and galena. Gangue minerals include barite, fluorite, chalcedony, opal, calcite, and aragonite. The extensive silver-gold mineralization of the San Juan Mountains of Colorado, including Cripple Creek, Ouray, and Creede, are epithermal deposits.

Telethermal deposits are formed by hydrothermal solutions that have cooled to approximately the same temperature as the near-surface rocks. These solutions may originate as mobilized connate and deeply circulating meteoric waters rather than fluids expelled from magma. The principal ore minerals are sphalerite and galena, with gangue minerals marcasite, fluorite, calcite, and chalcopyrite. The Mississippi Valley-type deposits of the tristate district of Missouri, Kansas, and Oklahoma exemplify this low-temperature mineralization.

*René A. De Hon*

## FURTHER READING

Barnes, Hubert Lloyd. "Energetics of Hydrothermal Ore Deposition." In *Frontiers in Geochemistry: Organic, Solution, and Ore Deposit Geochemistry*, edited by W. G. Ernst. Columbia, Md.: Bellwether for the Geological Society of America, 2002.

_____, ed. *Geochemistry of Hydrothermal Ore Deposits*. 3d ed. New York: John Wiley & Sons, 1997.

Guilbert, John M., and Charles F. Park, Jr. *The Geology of Ore Deposits*. Long Grove, Ill.: Waveland Press, 2007.

Pirajno, Franco. *Hydrothermal Processes and Mineral Systems*. London: Springer/Geological Survey of Western Australia, 2009.

Thompson, J. F. H., ed. *Magmas, Fluids, and Ore Deposits*. Nepean, Ont.: Mineralogical Association of Canada, 1995.

SEE ALSO: Magma crystallization; Open-pit mining; Pegmatites; Secondary enrichment of mineral deposits; Underground mining.

# I

## Ickes, Harold

CATEGORY: People
BORN: March 15, 1874; Frankstown Township,
Pennsylvania
DIED: February 3, 1952; Washington, D.C.

*Ickes, U.S. secretary of the interior from 1933 to 1946,
expanded the responsibilities and powers of the Department of the Interior in the areas of conservation and
preservation of the nation's natural resources.*

### BIOGRAPHICAL BACKGROUND
Harold L. Ickes was a lawyer, journalist, and municipal
reformer in Chicago before his appointment as secretary of the interior. His selection was political; President Franklin D. Roosevelt, a Democrat, was eager
to gain the support of progressive Republicans and
chose Ickes, who quickly became one of the most powerful figures in the nation. Always contentious and
ready to battle for his beliefs, Ickes's enemies and ad-
mirers were legion.

### IMPACT ON RESOURCE USE
As interior secretary, Ickes administered the Biological
Survey, the Bureau of Fisheries, and the Grazing Division. Particularly committed to the wilderness ideal, he
added several parks and monuments to the National
Park System and opposed their overdevelopment. He
fought to have the Forest Service transferred to the
Department of the Interior but lost; he also failed to
obtain his ultimate dream: to turn the Department of
the Interior into the Department of Conservation.

   In the enduring struggle within the conservation
movement between preservationists and utilitarian
conservationists, Ickes personified both strains but
leaned toward the former. Nevertheless, as head of
the Works Progress Administration (WPA), one of the
New Deal agencies, he supported the building of
dams and other massive public works projects that re-
made the land and provided jobs during the Depression. Still, like few others in American government,
Ickes exemplified the importance of the wilderness to
the human spirit.

*Eugene Larson*

SEE ALSO: Conservation; Department of the Interior,
U.S.; National Park Service; Roosevelt, Franklin D.;
Roosevelt, Theodore; Taylor Grazing Act.

## Igneous processes, rocks, and mineral deposits

CATEGORIES: Geological processes and formations;
mineral and other nonliving resources

*Igneous rocks and mineral deposits, created by the crys-
tallization and solidification of magma, are found all
over the world. Many of the world's most economically
important mineral deposits result, directly or indirectly, from igneous activity.*

### BACKGROUND
Igneous rocks are created by the crystallization and
solidification of hot, molten silicate magma. Magma
consists of silicate liquid (the major component is the
silica molecule $SiO_4^{-4}$), solid crystals, rock fragments,
dissolved gases such as carbon dioxide, water, and various sulfurous oxides. Familiar examples of igneous
rocks are granite (an "intrusive" or "plutonic" rock
that is crystallized at depth) and basalt (as in dark "extrusive" lava flows, such as those in Hawaii). Igneous
rocks are found worldwide on all continents, on oceanic islands, and on the ocean floors. They are particularly common in mountain ranges or other areas
where the Earth has undergone tectonic activity. Oceanic islands, such as Hawaii and Iceland, are nearly exclusively igneous in origin, and the world's oceans are
floored by basalt lava flows.

   Metallic ores produced by igneous activity may be
mined directly from the igneous rocks or obtained
through the injection of hydrothermal (hot water) veins
into adjacent rocks. Some of the most important commodities obtained from igneous sources include copper, nickel, gold, silver, platinum, iron, titanium, tungsten, and tin. Nonmetallic products include crushed
stone, construction stones for buildings and monuments, and some precious and semiprecious gemstones.

## Typical Ore Minerals Associated with Igneous Rocks

| ROCK TYPE | MINERAL | METAL OR OTHER COMMODITY OBTAINED |
|---|---|---|
| **Felsic—Intermediate** | | |
| Granite | Feldspar | Porcelain, scouring powder |
| | Native gold | Gold |
| Pegmatite | Cassiterite | Tin |
| | Beryl | Beryllium, gemstones (emerald; aquamarine) |
| | Tourmaline | Gemstone |
| | Spodumene | Lithium |
| | Lepidolite | Lithium |
| | Scheelite | Tungsten |
| | Rutile | Titanium |
| | Apatite | Phosphorus |
| | Samarskite | Uranium, niobium, tantalium, rare-earth elements |
| | Columbite, Tantalite | Niobium, tantalium, used in electronics |
| | Thorianite | Uranium, thorium |
| | Uraninite | Uranium |
| | Amazonite (microcline feldspar) | Gemstone |
| | Rose quartz | Gemstone |
| | Topaz | Gemstone |
| | Sphene (titanite) | Titanium, gemstone |
| | Muscovite mica | Electrical insulation |
| | Zircon | Zirconium |
| Rhyolite | Chalcopyrite | Cooper |
| | Molybdenite | Molybdenum |
| **Mafic—Ultramafic** | | |
| Gabbro and Anorthosite | Ilmenite | Titanium |
| | Labradorite (plagioclase feldspar) | Gemstone |
| | Chalcopyrite | Copper |
| | Bornite | Copper |
| | Pentlandite | Nickel |
| Peridotite | Chromite | Chromium |
| | Native platinum | Platinum |
| | Sperrylite | Platinum |
| | Serpentine | Nickel (from weathered soils) |

Igneous (from the Latin word *ignis*, meaning fire) rocks form by the crystallization of hot, molten magma produced by the heat of the Earth's interior. Surface exposures of igneous rock bodies are widespread throughout the globe. On continents they mostly occur in mountainous areas or ancient "Precambrian shield" areas where billions of years of erosion reveal the roots of old mountain ranges. In the oceans, igneous rocks cover the floors of ocean basins below a thin layer of sediment. Most oceanic islands owe their very existence to ocean floor volcanic eruptions that produce volcanoes of sufficient stature to project above the waves. Familiar examples are the Hawaiian chain, the Galápagos Islands, and Iceland.

TYPES OF IGNEOUS ROCKS

Igneous rocks are divided into two major categories defined by their mode of emplacement in or on the Earth's crust. If molten magma cools and solidifies below the surface, the rocks are called "intrusive" or "plutonic." Because these rocks generally take a long time to cool and solidify (a process called "crystallization"), their component minerals grow large enough to see with the naked eye (coarse-grained rocks). On the other hand, if magma flows out onto the Earth's surface, it forms "extrusive" or "volcanic" rock. These rocks lose heat rapidly to air or water, and the resulting rapid crystallization produces tiny, nearly invisible crystals (fine-grained rocks). Some volcanic rocks cool so quickly that few crystals have time to form; these are glassy rocks such as obsidian. Two kinds of volcanic rock exist: lava flows and "pyroclastic" deposits formed by explosive volcanism. Pyroclastic materials (volcanic ash) are deposited as layers of particles that have been violently ejected into the air.

Igneous rocks are also classified according to chemical composition. At one extreme are the light-colored "felsic" rocks that contain high concentrations of silica (up to about 75 percent silicon dioxide, $SiO_2$) and relatively little iron, magnesium, and calcium. Examples of felsic rocks are granite, a plutonic rock, and its volcanic equivalent, rhyolite (obsidian glass is rapidly cooled rhyolite).

At the other extreme are the dark "mafic" rocks with relatively low silica (as low as about 46 percent $SiO_2$) but with higher concentrations of iron, magnesium, and calcium. Examples of mafic rocks are gabbro (plutonic) and its volcanic equivalent, basalt. Rocks of intermediate composition also exist, for example plutonic diorite and its volcanic equivalent, andesite. It is andesite (and a more silicic variety called "dacite") that is expelled from the potentially explosive volcanoes of the Cascade range in the American Pacific Northwest (Mount St. Helens, Mount Rainier, Mount Hood, and others).

INTRUSIVE (PLUTONIC) STRUCTURES

Intrusive igneous rock bodies come in many shapes and sizes. The term "pluton" applies to all intrusive bodies but mainly to granitic rocks (granites, diorites, and related rocks). Specific terms applied to plutons mostly describe the size of the body. "Stocks" are exposed over areas less than 100 square kilometers, whereas "batholiths" are giant, commonly lens-shaped, bodies that exceed 100 square kilometers in exposed area. The Sierra Nevada range in eastern California is a good example of a batholith.

Some specialized pluton varieties are "laccoliths," commonly mountainous areas (for example, the Henry and La Salle mountains in Utah) in which in-

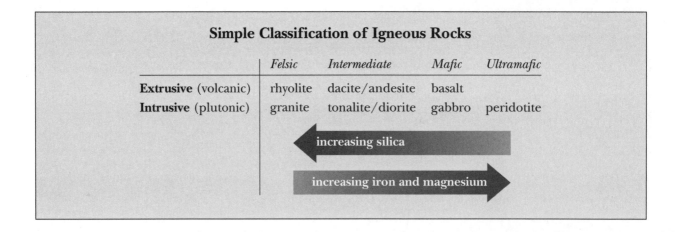

**Simple Classification of Igneous Rocks**

| | Felsic | Intermediate | Mafic | Ultramafic |
|---|---|---|---|---|
| **Extrusive** (volcanic) | rhyolite | dacite/andesite | basalt | |
| **Intrusive** (plutonic) | granite | tonalite/diorite | gabbro | peridotite |

← increasing silica

increasing iron and magnesium →

trusive granitic magma has invaded horizontal sedimentary layers and has bowed them up into a broad arch. A "phacolith" is similar to a laccolith only the magma has invaded folded sedimentary rocks so that the pluton itself appears to have been folded.

Minor intrusive bodies include "sills," tabular bodies intruded parallel to rock layers (a laccolith can be considered a "fat sill"), and "dikes," tabular bodies that cut across rock layers. Sills and dikes are common features around the margins of plutons where they contact "country rock" (older, pre-intrusion materials).

Another intrusive body, mostly produced by mafic (gabbroic) magmas, is the "lopolith." Lopoliths are relatively large funnel-shaped bodies (on the order of large stocks or small batholiths) in some cases created where magma fills the down-warped part (syncline) of a fold structure. An excellent example is the Muskox intrusion of northern Canada; another possible one (one limb is unexposed under Lake Superior) is the Duluth gabbro intrusion of northeastern Minnesota.

### Extrusive (Volcanic) Structures

The nature of volcanoes and volcanic rock deposits in general is greatly influenced by the composition of their parent magmas. Basalt magma is a low-viscosity liquid (it is thin and flows easily) and thus produces topographically low, broad volcanic features. Typical of these are the "fissure flows" (also known as plateau basalts) in which basalt lava issues from fractures in the Earth and spreads out almost like water in all directions. Examples are the Columbia River basalt plateau in Oregon and Washington, the Deccan plateau in India, and the Piraná basalt plateau in Brazil. The basalt flows that floor the oceans are underwater versions of fissure flows.

Basaltic volcanoes tend to have low profiles but laterally extensive bases typified by the "shield" volcanoes of Hawaii and other areas. These volcanoes resemble giant ancient shields lying on the ground. Pyroclastic eruptions of basalt, powered mostly by the violent release of dissolved carbon dioxide, produce cinder-cone volcanoes, otherwise known as "Strombolian" volcanoes, after the Italian volcano Stromboli.

In contrast to mafic magmas, the more silica-rich felsic and intermediate magmas are more viscous, and thus flow less readily. This magma tends to pile up in one place, producing towering volcanoes of mountainous proportions. Because felsic-intermediate magmas also tend to contain significant dissolved water,

steam trapped during eruption may explode violently, producing thick blankets of volcanic ash near the volcano. The best North American example of these potentially violent volcanoes, called "stratovolcanoes" or "composite" volcanoes, is the Cascade Range in the Pacific Northwest. The terms for these volcanoes reflect their tendency to have layers of mud and lava flows (generally andesite or dacite) that alternate with pyroclastic ash deposits. Stratovolcanoes occur worldwide, particularly at continental margins and in the oceans near continents where "lithospheric plates" (thick horizontal slabs of crust and upper mantle) collide, with one plate moving under the other (subduction zones). Volcanism associated with subduction zones has produced the Andes of South America as well as islands such as Japan, the Philippines, New Zealand, the Aleutian islands of Alaska, and the islands of Indonesia.

Another important volcanic feature is the "rhyolite complex," or "caldera complex," exemplified by Yellowstone National Park in Wyoming and the Valles Caldera (Jemez Mountains), New Mexico. When fully active, these areas produce violently explosive volcanism and rhyolite lava flows that blanket many square kilometers. The most violent activity occurs when the roof of a large underground magma chamber collapses into the shallow void created by expulsion of magma during previous eruptions. The crater formed during this process is called a caldera. Roof collapse during caldera formation has the effect of ramming a large piston into the heart of the magma body, violently expelling gas-charged, sticky rhyolite into the atmosphere, from which it may cascade along the surface as a *nuée ardente* (French for "glowing cloud"). These roiling infernos of hot noxious gases, bubbling lava fragments, and mineral crystals are capable of speeds in excess of 300 kilometers per hour and temperatures in excess of 400° Celsius. They deposit ash blankets (welded ashflow tuffs) over wide regions, as in the case of Yellowstone. Stratovolcanoes (described above) can also form calderas and ashflow deposits, as exemplified at Crater Lake, Oregon.

### Ore Deposits of Felsic-intermediate Rock

Granite and related rocks are the source of many metals and other products that are the foundation of an industrial society. Quartz veins intruding granite may contain gold and other precious metals, as in the "mother lode" areas of the Sierra Nevada Range in California. These veins originate as hydrothermal deposits, minerals precipitated from hot-water fluids flowing through fractures in cooling granitic bodies. Felsic and intermediate composition igneous rocks contain significant dissolved water in their magmas (called "juvenile" water), which is finally expelled as hydrothermal fluids in the late stages of plutonic crystallization. Hydrothermal veins occur in the parent granite itself or are injected into the surrounding rocks. Many important metallic ore bodies formed as hydrothermal deposits.

So-called porphyry copper deposits such as those of the American southwest (Arizona, New Mexico, Colorado, and Utah) are low-grade deposits of widely scattered small grains of chalcopyrite ($CuFeS_2$) and other copper minerals in felsic plutonic and volcanic rocks, mostly residing in a multitude of extremely thin hydrothermal veins. Some porphyry copper deposits also have considerable deposits of molybdenite (in the sulfide molybdenite, used in high-temperature alloys), especially at the Questa mine in New Mexico and at Climax, Colorado.

By far the greatest concentration of valuable minerals associated with granitic rocks comes from pegmatite deposits. Like hydrothermal deposits, pegmatites form in the late stages of granite crystallization after most of the other rock-forming minerals have already crystallized. Another similarity to hydrothermal fluids is their high volatile content—materials that tend to melt or form gases at relatively low temperatures, such as water, carbon dioxide, and the halogens fluorine and chlorine. Elements with large atomic sizes (ionic radii) and valence charges also tend to concentrate in pegmatitic fluids because the majority of minerals in granites (mostly quartz and feldspars) cannot accommodate these giant atoms in their mineral structures. Thus, pegmatite deposits may contain relatively high concentrations of uranium, thorium, lithium, beryllium, boron, niobium, tin, tantalum, and other rare metals. The high water content of pegmatite fluids, some of it occurring as vapor, allows minerals such as quartz, feldspar, and mica to grow to enormous sizes, the largest of which are on the order of railway boxcars. Pegmatites are generally fairly small bodies; some deposits are no larger than a small house. They may also occur as veins or dikes. Excellent North American examples containing rare and exotic minerals are located in the Black Hills of South Dakota, Maine, New Hampshire, North Carolina, the Adirondacks of New York state, Pala and Ramona in California, and Bancroft and Wilberforce, Canada. Notable

international occurrences are in Brazil (Minas Gerais), Russia (the Urals and Siberia), Greenland, Italy, Australia, Germany (Saxony), Madagascar, and Sri Lanka.

### ORE DEPOSITS IN MAFIC AND RELATED ROCK

Owing to their low viscosity, mafic magmas produce some unique mineral deposits compared with thicker felsic magmas. In plutonic settings formed early, heavy mineral crystals can easily sink through the magma to form crystal-rich layers on the bottom of the magma chamber. These gravitationally deposited layers are called "cumulates" (from the word accumulate) and, depending on their mineralogical makeup, may constitute important ore bodies. Because cumulates are generally enriched in iron and depleted in silica compared with their mafic parent magma, they are termed "ultramafic," the common rock type being "peridotite," a rock rich in olivine [$(Fe,Mg)_2SiO_4$]. Most of the world's chromium that is used in high-temperature, corrosion-resistant alloys comes from cumulate layers of the mineral chromite ($FeCr_2O_4$), mostly mined in South Africa. The other major commodities recovered from cumulates are the precious metals platinum and palladium, mined in South Africa and Russia.

Intrusive mafic magmas may also form layers of sulfide-rich minerals called "late-stage immiscible segregations" that constitute some of the richest copper and nickel ore bodies in the world. As some mafic magmas cool and change chemically, sulfur and metal-rich fluids may separate from the silicate liquid, just as oil would from water. These "immiscible" (incapable of mixing) sulfide droplets then sink through the lower density silicate magma to form thick layers of "massive sulfide" deposits on the magma chamber floor. The major minerals in massive sulfide copper-nickel mines are chalcopyrite, bornite ($Cu_5FeS_4$), pyrrhotite ($Fe_{1-x}S$), and pentlandite [$(Fe,Ni)_9S_8$]. Platinum, gold, and silver, among minerals, are commonly recovered as by-products. Major magmatic segregation sulfide mines are located in South Africa (Messina and Bushveld districts, Transvaal) and Norway, and at Sudbury, Ontario, Canada, which has ore rich in nickel.

Titanium and iron ores may also form as magmatic segregations. Massive titanium ores, mostly the oxide ilmenite ($FeTiO_3$), are mined from anorthosite rock, a plagioclase [$(Ca,Na)AlSi_3O_8$] feldspar-rich variation of gabbro. Typical examples of these deposits occur in the titanium mines in the Adirondacks of New York state and at Allard Lake, Quebec. Iron deposits of this type, mostly the mineral magnetite ($Fe_3O_4$), are located at Kiruna, Sweden; the Ozarks of Missouri; Durango, Mexico; and Algarrobo, Chile.

## OTHER IMPORTANT IGNEOUS COMMODITIES

Some valuable mineral commodities are recovered from igneous rocks that do not lend themselves to simple classification. For example, diamonds occur in deposits called "kimberlites," a type of general deposit called "diatremes," explosively injected mixtures of mantle (mostly serpentine) and crustal materials that in rare localities contain diamonds. The diamonds form deep in the upper mantle, where pressures are sufficiently high to produce them by the reduction (removal of oxygen) of carbon dioxide. They are then injected into more shallow crustal levels upon the carbon dioxide-powered eruption of kimberlite. Diamonds are mostly mined in South Africa, Ghana, the Democratic Republic of the Congo, Russia, Brazil, India, and the United States (Murfreesboro, Arkansas).

Two other deposits with chemical affinities to kimberlites are "nepheline syenites" and "carbonatites." Like kimberlites, these bodies are rare, and their magmas probably originate deep in the Earth's mantle. Nepheline syenites contain mostly the mineral nepheline ($NaAlSiO_4$) and are sources of apatite (phosphate mineral) and corundum ($Al_2O_3$), used as an abrasive. Nepheline itself is used to make ceramics. Carbonatites are unusual igneous deposits in that they are composed mostly of the carbonate mineral calcite ($CaCO_3$). They have become increasingly important as sources of the rare elements niobium and tantalum, used in the electronics industry.

*John L. Berkley*

## FURTHER READING

Best, Myron G. *Igneous and Metamorphic Petrology.* 2d ed. Malden, Mass.: Blackwell, 2003.

Best, Myron G., and Eric H. Christiansen. *Igneous Petrology.* Malden, Mass.: Blackwell Science, 2001.

Blatt, Harvey, Robert J. Tracy, and Brent E. Owens. *Petrology: Igneous, Sedimentary, and Metamorphic.* 3d ed. New York: W. H. Freeman, 2006.

Hutchison, Charles S. *Economic Deposits and Their Tectonic Setting.* New York: J. Wiley, 1983.

Jensen, Mead L., and Alan M. Bateman. *Economic Mineral Deposits.* 3d ed. New York: Wiley, 1979.

Philpotts, Anthony R., and Jay J. Ague. *Principles of Igneous and Metamorphic Petrology.* 2d ed. New York: Cambridge University Press, 2009.

Winter, John D. *An Introduction to Igneous and Metamorphic Petrology.* 2d ed. New York: Prentice Hall, 2010.

Young, Davis A. *Mind over Magma: The Story of Igneous Petrology.* Princeton, N.J.: Princeton University Press, 2003.

## WEB SITE

U.S. GEOLOGICAL SURVEY
Igneous Rocks
http://vulcan.wr.usgs.gov/LivingWith/
VolcanicPast/Notes/igneous_rocks.html

SEE ALSO: Beryllium; Boron; Chromium; Copper; Feldspars; Geology; Gold; Granite; Lithium; Magma crystallization; Molybdenum; Nickel; Pegmatites; Plate tectonics; Plutonic rocks and mineral deposits; Pumice; Quartz; Tantalum; Tin; Titanium; Tungsten; Uranium; Volcanoes; Zirconium.

# Incineration of wastes

CATEGORY: Pollution and waste disposal

*The incineration of wastes provides a means for reducing the volume of various sorts of waste by destroying the organic components of waste.*

## BACKGROUND

The incineration of household and hazardous waste material can help to reduce its volume and can provide the potential for electric power generation. The incineration of waste material is not a preferred strategy, however, because it does not stop the depletion of natural resources, and it may cause further environmental problems such as air pollution.

Thermal methods have been developed for dealing with solid, liquid, and the in-between slurry types of waste. Household trash has long been incinerated, often in backyard settings, but many governments now regulate this method except in rural areas. Some cities have built large incinerators for burning solid household waste; these are designed to reduce the waste stream as well as to provide for energy generation. Several types of incinerators have also been developed to deal with hazardous liquid and solid wastes in carefully regulated circumstances. Some of these

*A garbage incinerator in Amsterdam, the Netherlands, belches smoke into the atmosphere.* (AFP/Getty Images)

incinerators have been used for energy production, although not on a large scale.

### HOUSEHOLD WASTE AND "TRASH-TO-ENERGY" PROGRAMS

The large volume of household waste is becoming an increasing problem for many localities in the United States. Landfill space is at a premium in some areas, and incineration offers a means of reducing the waste stream through the destruction of organic material. Open burning is prohibited by the Clean Air Act as well as by many municipal ordinances. However, incineration in grate-type furnaces or kilns can reduce toxic releases to the air, and well-designed facilities can capture the ash for landfilling. This approach involves extensive sorting so that primarily organic material will be incinerated.

Because waste incineration requires high temperatures, a possibility exists for the generation of electrical energy as a by-product of the process. In the late 1970's and early 1980's, "trash-to-energy" processes appeared to have a promising future in several U.S. metropolitan

areas. Several local governments intended to use incinerators to generate electrical energy, either on their own or in tandem with an electric utility. However, a number of factors hampered the adoption of this approach. There were significant costs involved in sorting waste, and there was public reluctance to accept waste incineration. Landfill fees proved to be cheaper than incineration, and low-cost electric power continued to be available from other sources. Charlotte, North Carolina, for example, adopted a trash-to-energy program in the 1980's but abandoned it in the early 1990's as energy costs remained low and the costs of operating the incineration facility continued to increase. According to the Environmental Protection Agency, by the end of 2008, the United States had nearly five hundred landfill-gas-to-energy sites.

### HAZARDOUS WASTE INCINERATION

Thermal methods have been a commercial success in dealing with many types of hazardous industrial wastes as well as in cleaning contaminated Superfund sites. The Resource Conservation and Recovery Act regulates the incineration of both liquid and solid hazardous wastes in the United States. Although some municipal incinerators were intended to provide electrical energy as well as reduce the volume of waste, hazardous waste incineration is intended primarily to reduce the waste stream. In only a few cases is energy generation a product of the process, and they usually involve specialized thermal methods such as firing cement kilns with certain types of liquid hazardous waste.

Liquid injection incinerators are the most common type of thermal method for dealing with hazardous waste. As the name implies, this method deals almost exclusively with pumpable liquid wastes. The waste material is injected into the burner or combustion zone of an incinerator through atomizing nozzles. When waste with a low heating value, such as aqueous-organic material, is being incinerated, secondary burners must be used. These incinerators operate at temperature levels from 1,000° to 1,700° Celsius. Residence time for the combustion products ranges from milliseconds to 2.5 seconds. Liquid injection incinerators are carefully regulated as to the type of waste they can burn, the release of gaseous products, and the disposition of the ash.

Three major types of solid waste incinerators exist: grate-type incinerators, hearth-type incinerators, and fluidized bed incinerators. Grate-type incinerators are generally not suitable for hazardous waste incineration because the high temperatures necessary for the decomposition of many hazardous compounds can destroy the grates. There are several types of hearth-type incinerators; the most common are rotary kilns, controlled-air (two-chamber fixed hearth) systems, and multiple-hearth incinerators. The nonslagging type of rotary kiln, often used in the United States, does not require close monitoring, but it also does not have the feed flexibility that a slagging system does. Both types are viable and produce significant energy that can be used to burn additional waste. Multiple-hearth systems were originally designed to handle sewage sludge, but they have been adapted to other circumstances. Fluidized bed technology utilizes a sand or alumina bed sitting on a porous surface. An air flow from below with a carefully controlled velocity places the bed of sand in suspension. Some rotary kilns and fluidized bed systems are portable and have been used to incinerate contaminated soil at Superfund sites and soil contaminated by underground fuel tanks.

## ISSUES OF CONCERN

In the United States, there is a high level of suspicion regarding thermal methods for handling waste materials. This suspicion applies particularly to hazardous waste incinerators, but municipal incinerators are often opposed as well. The public's worries about safety have helped to curtail the adoption of municipal trash-to-energy facilities in the United States. They have also led to citizen protests regarding local hazardous waste incinerators. Yet the incineration of liquid and solid hazardous organic materials can reduce substantially the amount of hazardous material that needs to be landfilled. Before trash-to-energy incinerators can become fully viable, citizen opposition needs to be reduced, and the costs of operation need to be controlled. Hazardous waste incineration does produce highly toxic ash that requires careful handling, often in specially designed landfills. It is thus not a panacea for curtailing the use of natural resources; rather, it is simply a means of reducing the volume of waste.

*John M. Theilmann*

## FURTHER READING

Blumberg, Louis, and Robert Gottlieb. *War on Waste: Can America Win Its Battle with Garbage?* Washington, D.C.: Island Press, 1989.

Cheremisinoff, Nicholas P. "Incineration of Municipal Sludge." In *Handbook of Solid Waste Management and Waste Minimization Technologies.* Boston: Butterworth-Heinemann, 2003.

Gandy, Matthew. *Recycling and the Politics of Urban Waste.* New York: St. Martin's Press, 1994.

Hester, R. E., and R. M. Harrison, eds. *Waste Incineration and the Environment.* Cambridge, England: Royal Society of Chemistry, 1994.

LaGrega, Michael D., Phillip L. Buckingham, and Jeffrey C. Evans. *Hazardous Waste Management.* 2d ed. Boston: McGraw-Hill, 2001.

National Research Council. *Waste Incineration and Public Health.* Washington, D.C.: National Academy Press, 2000.

Neal, Homer A., and J. R. Schubel. *Solid Waste Management and the Environment: The Mounting Garbage and Trash Crisis.* Englewood Cliffs, N.J.: Prentice-Hall, 1987.

Santoleri, Joseph J., Joseph Reynolds, and Louis Theodore. *Introduction to Hazardous Waste Incineration.* New York: John Wiley, 2000.

Tammemagi, Hans. *The Waste Crisis: Landfills, Incinera-*

tors, and the Search for a Sustainable Future. New York: Oxford University Press, 1999.

WEB SITE

U.S. ENVIRONMENTAL PROTECTION AGENCY
Wastes—Hazardous Waste—Treatment and
    Disposal—Combustion
http://www.epa.gov/epawaste/hazard/tsd/td/
    combustion.htm

SEE ALSO: Air pollution and air pollution control; Landfills; Solid waste management; Superfund legislation and cleanup activities; Waste management and sewage disposal.

# India

CATEGORIES: Countries; government and resources

*As of 2009, India was the world's twelfth largest economy based on currency exchange rates and the fourth largest based on purchasing power parity. India's global trade rose by 72 percent from 2004 to 2007. India has been a source of cheap natural resources for much of the past 250 years, but it may be transitioning into a supplier of finished goods and technology services as technology industries outpace agriculture and raw materials in the gross domestic product (GDP).*

THE COUNTRY
Located between 7.5° and 36° north latitude and 65° to 97.5° east longitude, India borders the regions of Tibet, Nepal, Bhutan, Pakistan, Bangladesh, and Myanmar (Burma), with Sri Lanka, Afghanistan, China's Xinjiang Province, and Tajikistan in close proximity. India includes the Andaman-Nicobar Islands in the Bay of Bengal and the Lakshadweep archipelago in the Arabian Sea. With a warm, humid climate and plentiful rivers, this region has seen continuous human habitation for more than ten thousand years and is home to a very diverse population of more than one billion people. Himalayan peaks in the northern part of the country rise well above 8,000 meters and slope down to the fertile northern Indus-Ganga-Brahmaputra plain. The Deccan plateau in south-central India is bordered by the Eastern and Western Ghats mountain ranges along the respective coasts, the Vindhya-Satpuras to the north, and the

Nilgiris in the South. Key resources in addition to ones already listed include aluminum, titanium, petroleum, natural gas, diamonds, limestone, and small reserves of uranium. Agriculture and dairy farming employ more than 60 percent of the workforce.

SUNSHINE
India receives an average of three hundred days of annual sunshine, giving a theoretical solar power reception of 5 quadrillion kilowatt-hours per year. Dense population in most of India means that a good percentage of incident solar power can be captured at the point of use. The western Thar Desert and the dry Deccan plateau of central India are suited to large solar plants. India plans to use solar power to eliminate more than 60 million metric tons of carbon dioxide emissions a year by 2020.

COASTAL RESOURCES
India has a total of more than 7,000 kilometers of coastline, including the Andaman-Nicobar and Lakshadweep Islands. Fishing and salt extraction employ more than six million people. The backwaters of Kerala on the southwest coast and the river deltas in the Rann of Kachchh and the Sunderbans in Bengal are unique ecosystems, enabling special rice crops and fishing. These resources sustain a large seafood industry that also specializes in prawns and shrimp. India produces 9.4 million metric tons of coconuts a year, putting the country in third place behind the Philippines and Indonesia. Coconut and other palm-based industries are major employers in the coastal states.

HYDROELECTRIC POTENTIAL
The Deccan plateau is relatively dry, while the coasts and northern plains receive heavy rains from the southwest monsoon (June to August) and the northeast monsoon (November to December), and the northern plains receive Himalayan snowmelt through spring and summer. In 2007, nearly 25 percent of Indian electricity came from hydroelectric projects, and India ranked fifth in the world in hydroelectric potential. Viable potential is estimated at 84 gigawatts at 60 percent load factor, corresponding to 149 gigawatts installed capacity. This is distributed as follows: the Indus basin in the northwest, 34 gigawatts; the Brahmaputra basin in the northeast, 66 gigawatts; the Ganga basin in the north, 21 gigawatts; the Central Indian River system, 4 gigawatts; the west-flowing rivers

# India: Resources at a Glance

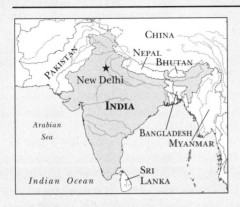

*Official name:* Republic of India
*Government:* Federal republic
*Capital city:* New Delhi
*Area:* 1,269,312 mi²; 3,287,263 km²
*Population (2009 est.):* 1,166,079,217
*Languages:* English, Hindi, Bengali, Telugu, Marathi, Tamil, Urdu, Gujarati, Malayalam, Kannada, Oriya, Punjabi, Assamese, Kashmiri, Sindhi, and Sanskrit
*Monetary unit:* Indian rupee (INR)

## ECONOMIC SUMMARY:

*GDP composition by sector (2008 est.):* agriculture, 17.6%; industry, 29%; services, 53.4%
*Natural resources:* coal (fourth largest reserves in the world), iron ore, manganese, mica, bauxite, titanium ore, chromite, natural gas, diamonds, petroleum, limestone, arable land, hydropower potential, thorium
*Land use (2005):* arable land, 48.83%; permanent crops, 2.8%; other, 48.37%
*Industries:* textiles, chemicals, food processing, steel, transportation equipment, cement, mining, petroleum, machinery, software
*Agricultural products:* rice, wheat, oilseed, cotton, jute, tea, sugarcane, potatoes, onions, dairy products, sheep, goats, poultry, fish
*Exports (2008 est.):* $176.4 billion
*Commodities exported:* petroleum products, textile goods, gems and jewelry, engineering goods, chemicals, leather manufactures
*Imports (2008 est.):* $305.5 billion
*Commodities imported:* crude oil, machinery, gems, fertilizer, chemicals
*Labor force (2008 est.):* 523.5 million
*Labor force by occupation (2003):* agriculture, 60%; industry, 12%; services, 28%

## ENERGY RESOURCES:

*Electricity production (2007 est.):* 665.3 billion kWh
*Electricity consumption (2006 est.):* 517.2 billion kWh
*Electricity exports (2006 est.):* 378 million kWh
*Electricity imports (2006 est.):* 3.189 billion kWh

*Natural gas production (2007 est.):* 31.7 billion m³
*Natural gas consumption (2007 est.):* 41.7 billion m³
*Natural gas exports (2007 est.):* 0 m³
*Natural gas imports (2007 est.):* 10 billion m³
*Natural gas proved reserves (Jan. 2008 est.):* 1.075 trillion m³

*Oil production (2007 est.):* 880,500 bbl/day
*Oil imports (2005 est.):* 2.159 million bbl/day
*Oil proved reserves (Jan. 2008 est.):* 5.7 billion bbl

*Source:* Data from *The World Factbook 2009.* Washington, D.C.: Central Intelligence Agency, 2009.
*Notes:* Data are the most recent tracked by the CIA. Values are given in U.S. dollars. Abbreviations: bbl/day = barrels per day; GDP = gross domestic product; km² = square kilometers; kWh = kilowatt-hours; m³ = cubic meters; mi² = square miles.

of southern India, 9 gigawatts; and the east-flowing rivers of southern India, 15 gigawatts.

Major hydroelectric projects are the Damodar Project, serving Jharkhand and West Bengal; Bhakra Nangal Dam on the Sutlej River, serving Punjab, Haryana, and Rajasthan; Hirakud Dam on the Mahanadi River in Orissa; on the Kosi River in Bihar; on the Chambal River, serving Madhya Pradesh and Rajasthan; Thungabhadra Dam, serving Karnataka and Andhra Pradesh; Nagarjuna Sagar Dam on the Krishna River in Andhra Pradesh; Narmada Dam, serving Madhya Pradesh, Gujarat, and Rajasthan; Indira Gandhi Canal, connecting the Beas and Sutlej rivers and serving Punjab, Haryana, and Rajasthan; Krishnaraja Sagar Dam in Karnataka; and Idukki Dam in Kerala. Another 7 gigawatts are viable from microhydel plants, suitable for distributed generation in ar-

eas that are hard to reach for the main power grid, with some estimates of up to 15 gigawatts. Of the total, less than 20 percent had been exploited by 2009. Large dam projects encounter extreme political opposition in India, stemming from public concern over the displacement of the generally poor people in the fertile catchment areas and the potential for earthquakes in a seismically active region.

## ARABLE LAND AND AGRICULTURE

The northern Gangetic Plain, spanning Uttar Pradesh, Haryana, and Punjab, and the eastern and western coastal strips of India have rich alluvial soil suitable for cultivation. The large Maharashtra-Gujarat region has black soil, suitable for cultivation of cotton and other crops that do not demand as much water as rice. Tropical rain forests and deciduous forests occur in the coastal and northeastern regions and in the Andaman-Nicobar Islands. Temperate forests and grasslands are found in the foothills of the Himalayas between 1,000 and 3,000 meters, rising to alpine and tundra regions above 3,600 meters. Terraced cultivation is practiced extensively in the mountains.

As of 2009, India was second in the world in agricultural output. In 2007, the share of agriculture in the Indian GDP was less than 17 percent, having fallen from its 30 percent share in the mid-1990's. However, the industry still employed more than 60 percent of the total Indian workforce. India is the world's leading producer of coconuts, tea, black pepper, turmeric, ginger, and cashew nuts. With the world's largest number (more than 280 million) of cattle, it is also the leading producer of dairy milk, though per-unit productivity is low. India is the second largest producer of wheat, rice, sugar, peanuts (called "groundnuts" in India), and freshwater fish and the third largest producer of tobacco. India produces 10 percent of the world's fruit, led by bananas and kiwifruit.

Farms are generally fragmented, averaging less than 20,000 square meters. Therefore, farming depends heavily on human labor. Exceptions are the larger wheat fields in the Punjab, where modern machinery enables efficiencies of scale. Tea, coffee, and rubber are major products from plantations

*India's economy is dependent on the country's agriculture industry. In this photo, a woman sorts dried corn.* (AFP/Getty Images)

in the hilly regions of Assam, West Bengal, and Tamil Nadu/Kerala/Karnataka.

Since ancient times, the growing of crops in India was tied to the monsoon rains and northern snowmelt flooding cycles, with limited establishment of artificial irrigation. Indian crop cycles are classified into three seasonal names: kharif (or monsoon) crops, sowed in June and harvested in November, which include rice, maize, cotton, millets, jute, sugarcane, and groundnut; rabi (or winter) crops, sowed in November and harvested in March, which include wheat, tobacco, mustard, pulses, and linseed; and zaid (or hot season) crops, sowed in March and harvested in June, which include fruits and vegetables. Although an extensive network of dams and canals has been established for flood control, irrigation, drinking water, and hydroelectric power since Indian independence in 1947, irrigation reaches less than 55 percent of the agricultural land; therefore the dependence on monsoon timing and intensity remains strong. Wells are used in most microfarms, and these again depend on the groundwater table through the year. Rainwater harvesting was practiced in some regions in ancient times and has been reestablished in the twenty-first century through home building codes and public education, with mandated rooftop collection on new homes and drilling of groundwater replenishment holes to compensate for tube wells. While these activities alleviate the monsoon dependence, the monsoons are such massive water deliverers that even a delay of a few days and variations in intensity still have large effects on national crop yield.

Given fragmented farms and a distributed marketing system dependent on cattle-drawn carts and unpaved roads to deliver produce, agricultural output grew more slowly than population in the impoverished colonial and postcolonial years, and India was known as a nation in which monsoon failures resulted in mass famine in several parts. In the 1960's, modern agricultural practices were adopted through national-level planning. High-yielding strains of rice and wheat from American and Indian agricultural research were introduced in the larger farms of north and east India. Japanese intensive cultivation techniques suitable for microfarms were adopted in other parts. From the 1950's to 1990, food grain output rose from 46.07 million metric tons to 159.6 million metric tons, a 246 percent increase, outpacing the 175 percent population growth. By 2000, India was a net exporter of food. Wheat production rose by a factor of eight in forty

*Textiles, such as those produced from silk, the material in use above, are a key component of India's industrial economy.* (AFP/Getty Images)

years, and rice grew by more than 350 percent. In the twenty-first century, there is rising concern that agricultural output is not increasing fast enough to meet demand, as rising urban wealth and population accelerate demand.

TEXTILE FIBERS
Textiles from natural fibers have been one of India's largest industries for both the domestic market and exports for many centuries. The black soil of the Deccan plateau is suited to cotton cultivation. The silk industry employs more than 6 million people in Andhra, Tamil Nadu, Karnataka, Jammu and Kashmir, Himachal Pradesh, Chhattisgarh, Jharkhand, and West Bengal. Silk output is almost 16,000 metric tons per year and is tied into a village industry and urban marketing system that achieves superlative levels of artistry, craftsmanship, and quality, highly attuned to changing fashions and customer preferences.

COAL
India has the world's fourth largest coal reserves (197 billion metric tons, or 7 percent of the world total), of

which 102 billion are believed to be recoverable, but produces the third largest amount. Production is 403 million metric tons per year. Open-cast methods are used to mine the 64 billion metric tons located within a depth of 300 meters. Coal generates 67 percent of India's total primary energy consumption. Noncoking coal constitutes 85 percent of reserves, and coking coal the rest. High ash content of 15 to 45 percent means low calorific value for Indian coal. Coal deposits are spread over the states of Chhattisgarh, Orissa, Madhya Pradesh, West Bengal, Assam, and Meghalaya. Lignite (60 percent carbon) resources are present in Jammu and Kashmir, Rajasthan, Gujarat, and Tamil Nadu.

## IRON ORE

Iron-ore deposits of 22 billion metric tons, amounting to 20 percent of the world total, are estimated to be in India. These are found in the states of Orissa, Jharkhand, Andhra, Karnataka, West Bengal, Bihar, and Madhya Pradesh and in two locations each in Rajasthan, Gujarat, and Tamil Nadu. India produced nearly 47 million metric tons of finished steels and 4.4 million metric tons of pig iron in 2008, putting the country in seventh place among steel-producing nations. However, roughly two-thirds of iron ore is used for export, primarily to China, South Korea, and Japan. This is a controversial issue in India as domestic demand and the Indian steel industry expand.

## THORIUM

The black sands of southern Kerala beaches contain large deposits of thorium, which is a low-grade nuclear fuel. This deposit has been known since Germany tried to ship out large quantities of black sand for its nuclear weapon program prior to World War II. India is estimated to have the world's third largest reserves of thorium. With the civilian nuclear deal with the United States and Nuclear Suppliers Group, uranium imports are projected to enable India to irradiate the thorium and set up a "third-stage thorium cycle" in which thorium becomes a primary energy source for electric power reactors, making India self-sufficient in nuclear energy and eliminating the need for uranium imports. Because thorium is much more abundant than uranium worldwide, the Indian thorium reactor approach is watched with great interest as a possible breakthrough technology for nuclear power.

## OIL AND NATURAL GAS

As of 2007, India had 5.6 billion barrels of proven oil reserves, second to China in the Asia-Pacific region. New resources have been identified in the Bay of Bengal and in the Rajasthan desert. Production in 2007 was 810,000 to 850,000 barrels per day. Thus, more than 70 percent of oil demand must be met by imports, mainly from the Middle East. Petroleum dependence has had a primary destructive effect on Indian economic growth, with "oil shocks" in the 1970's and 1980's draining foreign exchange revenues and forcing steep loss of value of the Indian rupee by as much as 90 percent between 1972 and 2000.

Domestic production of natural gas is 52 billion cubic meters per year, a sudden growth in production from 30,000 cubic meters per year because of new fields in the Krishna-Godavari basin. According to the *Oil and Gas Journal*, India had 1 trillion cubic meters of confirmed natural gas reserves as of 2007.

## OTHER RESOURCES

India contributes 60 percent of the world supply of mica, used as a nonconductor in electrical switchgear manufacturing. Major mica-producing regions are Jharkhand, Bihar, Andhra, and Rajasthan. Bauxite and other aluminum-ore reserves are estimated at more than 2 billion metric tons, out of a global estimate of 75 billion metric tons. India produced more than 700,000 metric tons of aluminum (spelled as aluminium in India) in 2001. India is known to have more than 16 percent of the world's ilmenite reserves, but production of titanium is very low. The catastrophic tsunami of December, 2004, exposed substantial offshore deposits along the Tamil Nadu coast. Sitting on approximately 20 percent of the world's resources, India is the world's fifth largest producer of manganese. Deposits are found in Karnataka, Maharashtra, Gujarat, Jharkhand, Orissa, Chhattisgarh, Madhya Pradesh, and Tamil Nadu.

Medicinal herbs are a major natural resource for India. Empirical experience over thousands of years has been codified through the ayurveda medicinal knowledge base. As modern diagnostics open up genetic engineering and nanoscience, the importance of these various natural resources is beginning to be understood.

Finally, the fauna of India serve as natural attractions to a growing tourism industry, complementing geographic attractions such as the Himalayas, the Sunderbans river delta, the Nilgiri and Kerala mountains, and the ocean beaches. Several unique animal species, including the Indian elephant, lion, tiger, rhinoceros, peacock, pheasant, and black deer, are found in the forests and animal sanctuaries of India.

*Narayanan M. Komerath and Padma P. Komerath*

FURTHER READING

Abdul Kalam, A. P. J., with Y. S. Rajan. *India 2020: A Vision for the New Millennium.* New York: Viking, 1998.

Ali, N. *Natural Resource Management and Sustainable Development in North-East India.* New Delhi: Mittal, 2007.

Mukhopahdyay, Durgadas. "Indigenous Knowledge and Sustainable Natural Resource Management in the Indian Desert." In *The Future of Drylands: International Scientific Conference on Desertification and Dryland Research,* edited by Cathy Lee and Thomas Schaaf. Dordrecht, the Netherlands: Springer, 2008.

Parikh, Kirit S. *Natural Resource Accounting: A Framework for India.* Mumbai: Indira Gandhi Institute of Development Research, 1993.

Pearce, Fred. *When the Rivers Run Dry: Water—The Defining Crisis of the Twenty-first Century.* Boston: Beacon Press, 2006.

Rao, R. Rama. *India and the Atom.* New Delhi: Allied, 1982.

Sachs, Jeffrey D. *The End of Poverty: Economic Possibilities for Our Time.* New York: Penguin, 2005.

Singh, Amrik. *The Green Revolution: A Symposium.* New Delhi: Harman, 1990.

Sur, A. K. *Natural Resources of India.* Vadodara: Padmaja, 1947.

Varma, C. V. J., and B. L. Jatana. *A Century of Hydro Power Development in India.* New Delhi: Central Board of Irrigation and Power, 1997.

SEE ALSO: Agricultural products; Agriculture industry; Aluminum; Coal; Hydroenergy; Iron; Mica; Textiles and fabrics; Thorium.

# Indium

CATEGORY: Mineral and other nonliving resources

## WHERE FOUND

Indium is widely distributed in the Earth's crust in small amounts. It is fairly rare and is about as common as silver. Indium is never found as a free metal but only in combination with other elements. It is found as a trace component in many minerals, particularly in ores of zinc, copper, lead, and tin. The richest concentrations of indium are found in Colorado, Argentina, the United Kingdom, and Canada.

## PRIMARY USES

Indium is used for a variety of purposes in the electronics industry, including liquid-crystal displays and transistors. It is also used in batteries, solders, coatings for glass, sealants, and alloys that melt at low temperatures.

## TECHNICAL DEFINITION

Indium (abbreviated In), atomic number 49, belongs to Group IIIA of the periodic table of the elements and resembles aluminum in its chemical and physical properties. It has two naturally occurring isotopes and an average atomic weight of 114.82. Pure indium is a soft, white metal. Its density is 7.31 grams per cubic centimeter; it has a melting point of 156.61° Celsius and a boiling point of 2,080° Celsius.

## DESCRIPTION, DISTRIBUTION, AND FORMS

Indium, a fairly uncommon element, occurs in the Earth's crust with an average concentration of about one part in ten million. It is most commonly found in ores that are rich in zinc, particularly those which contain sphalerite (zinc sulfide). It is also found in ores of copper, lead, and tin.

## HISTORY

Indium was discovered in 1863 by Ferdinand Reich and Hieronymous Theodor Richter. It was not produced in large amounts until 1940. Its first major industrial use was in the production of automobile and aircraft engine bearings, where it added strength, hardness, resistance to corrosion, and ability to retain a coating of oil. In the 1960's, it was first used in transistors.

## OBTAINING INDIUM

Indium is usually obtained as a by-product of zinc production. A variety of methods exist for obtaining indium from the residue left over after most of the zinc is removed from the ore. One method involves treating the residue with dilute sulfuric acid to dissolve the remaining zinc. The undissolved material left behind is then treated with stronger acid to dissolve the in-

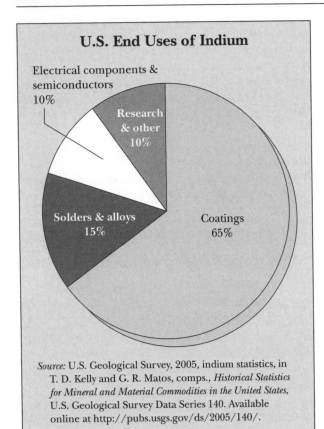

## U.S. End Uses of Indium

Electrical components & semiconductors 10%

Research & other 10%

Solders & alloys 15%

Coatings 65%

*Source:* U.S. Geological Survey, 2005, indium statistics, in T. D. Kelly and G. R. Matos, comps., *Historical Statistics for Mineral and Material Commodities in the United States,* U.S. Geological Survey Data Series 140. Available online at http://pubs.usgs.gov/ds/2005/140/.

dium. The indium is treated with zinc oxide to obtain indium hydroxide or with sodium sulfite or sodium bisulfite to obtain indium sulfite. Pure indium metal is then obtained by subjecting these compounds to electrolysis.

### USES OF INDIUM

Indium is often combined with other metals such as bismuth, cadmium, lead, and tin to form alloys with a low melting point; production of indium tin oxide was the most common end use worldwide as of 2008. These alloys are used in fuses and heat-detecting sprinkler systems. It has also been mixed with lead to form solders that remain flexible over a wide range of temperatures. Molten indium has the unusual property of clinging to glass and other smooth surfaces and is often used to form seals and coatings. High-purity indium is used in combination with germanium to form transistors. The electronics industry also uses indium in liquid-crystal displays, infrared detectors, and solar cells.

*Rose Secrest*

### WEB SITES

NATURAL RESOURCES CANADA
Canadian Minerals Yearbook: Indium
http://www.nrcan-rncan.gc.ca/mms-smm/busi-indu/cmy-amc/content/2005/31.pdf

U.S. GEOLOGICAL SURVEY
Minerals Information: Indium Statistics and Information
http://minerals.usgs.gov/minerals/pubs/commodity/indium/

SEE ALSO: Alloys; Aluminum; Metals and metallurgy; Zinc.

# Indonesia

CATEGORIES: Countries; government and resources

*Analysis of Indonesia's natural resource potential is complicated by several factors. After Indonesia's long heritage as a Dutch colony (and a source for cheap raw materials), its more attractive resources gradually took on global importance. Both massive supplies of rare hardwoods and important mineral deposits have made the country a key, but extremely vulnerable, participant in the global economy. Although all sections of the archipelago have some form of economically attractive resources, development is inevitably confronted with two obstacles: the high cost of necessary infrastructural improvements and the high cost of shipping over long distances to markets beyond Southeast or East Asia.*

### THE COUNTRY

Indonesia is an archipelago of more than seventeen thousand islands, extending from the southeastern boundaries of the Indian Ocean in an arc leading to the South China Sea. Most of these islands are small and economically insignificant. In such cases local populations depend on mainly subsistence agriculture and animal husbandry. The country's main islands, especially Sumatra, Java, Sulawesi (formerly Celebes), and Kalimantan (formerly Borneo), are characterized by volcanic peaks, generally rugged terrain broken by stretches of arable land, and extensive tropical forests. Each of the main islands possesses one or more major maritime ports linking it to the rest of the archipelago and to international ship-

## Indonesia: Resources at a Glance

*Official name:* Republic of Indonesia
*Government:* Republic
*Capital city:* Jakarta
*Area:* 735,412 mi²; 1,904,569 km²
*Population (2009 est.):* 240,271,522
*Language:* Bahasa Indonesia
*Monetary unit:* Indonesian rupiah (IDR)

### ECONOMIC SUMMARY:

*GDP composition by sector (2008 est.):* agriculture, 14.4%; industry, 48.1%; services, 37.5%
*Natural resources:* petroleum, tin, natural gas, nickel, timber, bauxite, copper, fertile soils, coal, gold, silver, gypsum
*Land use (2005):* arable land, 11.03%; permanent crops, 7.04%; other, 81.93%
*Industries:* petroleum and natural gas, textiles, apparel, footwear, mining, cement, chemical fertilizers, plywood, rubber, food, tourism
*Agricultural products:* rice, cassava (tapioca), peanuts, rubber, cocoa, coffee, palm oil, copra, poultry, beef, pork, eggs
*Exports (2008 est.):* $139.3 billion
*Commodities exported:* oil and gas, electrical appliances, plywood, textiles, rubber
*Imports (2008 est.):* $116 billion
*Commodities imported:* machinery and equipment, chemicals, fuels, foodstuffs
*Labor force (2008 est.):* 112 million
*Labor force by occupation (2006 est.):* agriculture, 42.1%; industry, 18.6%; services, 39.3%

### ENERGY RESOURCES:

*Electricity production (2007 est.):* 142.4 billion kWh
*Electricity consumption (2007 est.):* 121.2 billion kWh
*Electricity exports (2007 est.):* 0 kWh
*Electricity imports (2007 est.):* 0 kWh

*Natural gas production (2007 est.):* 56 billion m³
*Natural gas consumption (2007 est.):* 23.4 billion m³
*Natural gas exports (2007 est.):* 32.6 billion m³
*Natural gas imports (2007 est.):* 0 m³
*Natural gas proved reserves (Jan. 2008 est.):* 2.659 trillion m³

*Oil production (2008 est.):* 977,000 bbl/day
*Oil imports (2008 est.):* 672,000 bbl/day
*Oil proved reserves (Jan. 2008 est.):* 3.8 billion bbl

*Source:* Data from *The World Factbook 2009.* Washington, D.C.: Central Intelligence Agency, 2009.
*Notes:* Data are the most recent tracked by the CIA. Values are given in U.S. dollars. Abbreviations: bbl/day = barrels per day; GDP = gross domestic product; km² = square kilometers; kWh = kilowatt-hours; m³ = cubic meters; mi² = square miles.

ping—a necessity for the development of Indonesia's export markets.

## PETROLEUM

Before Indonesia's independence after World War II, Royal Dutch Shell dominated oil production in the country, with concessions on the three main islands of Java, Sumatra, and Kalimantan (then Borneo). Initial involvement of other foreign firms (most notably Caltex and Texaco) led to discovery of the Duri and Minas fields in Riau Province in Sumatra just before World War II. These fields became the most active areas of oil production in Indonesia in the postcolonial era, representing nearly one-half of the total production by the early 1960's.

By the late 1960's, the Indonesian government had begun exercising stringent control over concessions, undertaking production and marketing of Indonesian oil. The National Oil and Natural Gas Mining Company—also known as Pertamina, whose official name and bylaws would be altered several times into the twenty-first century—brought two earlier governmental entities under one roof and introduced profit-sharing arrangements with foreign contractors that were advantageous for Indonesian interests. Pertamina's operations came to involve processing and marketing of a variety of petroleum products, including various petrochemicals. Boom conditions in the 1970's, combined with peak production of more than 600 million barrels in 1977, seemed to promise continuation of these advantages. Prices reached thirty-five dollars per barrel and brought in about $15 billion annually by 1981.

However, changing conditions after the 1980's had negative effects on Indonesia's oil sector. Price drops (to as low as ten dollars per barrel) followed by partial recoveries seem to have induced Pertamina to push for maximum (some say wasteful) production—keeping output near 500 million barrels, even though total revenue intake fell to one-half of earlier figures. Attempts to keep the oil sector healthy seem to have only partially succeeded. Loosening contractual terms with foreign companies (a field of about twenty firms, mainly U.S. registered) had the aim of encouraging investment to expand production to new areas (because only slightly more than one-half of sixty likely basins had been explored).

Even though estimates indicate that Indonesia probably has reserves of between 5 and 10 billion barrels, the country's place among oil producers has dropped considerably. Government policies after 2000, which included closing down marginally productive oil wells, did not lead to real improvement in the oil sector. Indonesia's act of resorting to domestic subsidies of billions of dollars a year to keep gasoline and kerosene (for home heating and cooking fuel) prices down for Indonesian consumers has been criticized widely as an economic anomaly.

## TIMBER AND FOREST PRODUCTS

The harvesting of timber from Indonesia's extensive forests, many of which are classified as rain forests, represents the country's second most important resource after oil. In the 1960's, estimates indicated that more than 80 percent of the land surface of the archipelago was forested. Extensive harvesting of timber for export has reduced that surface considerably—some say to 50 percent. As a side effect, given the high rainfall in this tropical zone, serious soil erosion has become widespread.

At various times in the second half of the twentieth century concessions were granted by the Indonesian government to ten private companies for the right to log more than 50 million hectares of forest (out of an estimated total surface of more than 120 million hectares). The giant island of Kalimantan (formerly Borneo) relies almost entirely on timber harvesting as the basis of its economy. Sumatra's forests rank as the second most intense zone. Other potentially productive areas, such as the westernmost island of Irian Jaya (for many decades relatively immune to heavy logging), have been affected by the expanding logging industry.

Numerous controversies have arisen and continue to be debated, concerning not only questionable political favoritism in timber concession granting but also forest conservation programs that have been initiated (with funding from timber concession royalties) to save Indonesia's forests from depletion. Various measures are included in these programs, ranging from mandatory reforestation to "police" investigations of widespread instances of illegal logging. There is also a major ecological issue of widespread fires, many of which are caused by traditional tribal slash-and-burn methods of agriculture that have gotten out of control, but some of which are assumed to be illegal policies carried out by logging firms. Some ecologists suggest that the massive reduction of Indonesia's forested area has already had the result of lowering the overall levels of humidity that are necessary to sustain certain species of tropical vegetation. However, reforestation projects are not without potential controversy. After some progress in controlling levels of deforestation from the late 1980's to 1997, figures rose alarmingly (to more than 3.5 million hectares per year in the last three years of the twentieth century). Critics claim that, instead of replacing extremely valuable hardwood trees with the same species, some companies plant fast-growing softwood trees on arbitrarily chosen "nonproductive" land.

Indonesia derives a number of commercially valuable products from its forests. "Raw" logs for sawmill treatment constitute the largest category in terms of cubic meters processed. Between 2001 and 2006 processing of raw timber (qualities of which ranged from valuable hardwoods through more common varieties) more than doubled, from slightly more than 10 million cubic meters to nearly 25 million cubic meters. A number of other categories of commercially valuable processed wood products count almost as heavily, most notably high-quality plywood and composite (wood chip) building materials.

Despite this movement toward diversification of production in Indonesia's timber industry, the world's attention has been increasingly directed at issues relating to the country's tropical rain-forest area and a number of endangered species—both animal and vegetal—whose future depends on Indonesian timber industry policy makers. Severe criticism has been leveled not only against the logging industry but also against what is viewed as an excessive consumer demand in developed countries for rare hardwoods, natural supplies of which are rapidly diminishing.

## COPPER

Indonesia is the world's third largest producer of copper (after Chile and the United States). However, this position is not a guaranteed source of economic potential. A lesson was learned when the price for copper reached a sixty-year low point in 1999, coming at a time when Indonesia was already in the midst of a major region-wide economic crisis (affecting mainly, but not only, Indonesia, Malaysia, and Thailand). The 1999 price of only $0.27 per kilogram recovered to $1.70 by 2006. However, between 2006 and 2009, considerable fluctuation occurred, and available stockpiles during the onset of the global financial and economic crisis suggested that decreasing demand would push prices below $0.68, or even lower.

Despite such trends, Indonesia may be able to capitalize on combining different sectors of its mining potential. For example, copper can be alloyed with nickel (another, less developed resource of Indonesia) to produce cupronickel (or commercial name Monel), which is highly resistant to corrosion and, thus, important for the modern shipbuilding industry.

Meanwhile, there is worldwide concern that, despite what sometimes looks like a copper "surplus" (especially when demand lessens, pushing prices down), the sudden reappearance of demand, and therefore expansion of mining efforts, could result in early depletion of reserves in countries like Indonesia.

## TIN

Indonesia ranks high among the ten countries producing tin for the world market. While its proven reserves are not as substantial as those of China, Malaysia, or Brazil, Indonesia fills almost as important a role as China and even more of a role than Malaysia as a producer of tin. However, new worldwide developments may affect Indonesia: High-grade tin reserves in the Democratic Republic of the Congo and Colombia may attract importers away from Asian producers.

As of 2009, the global market for tin was dominated by ten major mining companies, the two largest of which, Yunnan Tin and the Malay Company in China, both produced more than 54,000 metric tons in 2007. The third largest producer was the Indonesia-based company PT Timah, which produced approximately 53,000 metric tons in the same year. PT Timah's shares are divided between the Indonesian government (holding 65 percent) and local and international private investors (holding the remaining 35 percent). PT Timah produces several varieties of tin, the most highly refined (99.9 percent pure) carrying the label "Banka Four Nines." Meanwhile, like aluminum, global consumption of tin may be affected over time by growing efforts to recycle scrap metals.

## NICKEL

The most important areas for the production of nickel are in the Sudbury region of Ontario, Canada, several zones of Australia, and the Siberian region of Russia. Together these areas have reserves amounting to about 70 percent of the world's nickel. Indonesia, whose yearly production follows that of Canada and Australia, continues to hold an important share of the world market. Nickel is highly resistant to corrosion and, therefore, has been used for generations either for nickel plating or as an alloy in the manufacture of steel. Technological advances—a factor that may change the nature of demand and therefore global prices—have produced a particularly refined product, called nickel superalloy, used in the manufacture of jet-engine turbines and some spacecraft parts. Therefore, Indonesia has several reasons to be careful when considering its nickel industry. This need to calculate carefully was particularly clear following an apparent boom period in 2006-2007, when nickel's price reached more than $50,000 per metric ton and then dropped dramatically by early 2009 to $10,800 per metric ton. Indonesia has an interest, therefore, in calculating whether it should concentrate on producing high quantities of "ordinary" nickel (mainly for export to China) or experimenting with higher-priced alloys.

### BAUXITE

Although Indonesia has significant quantities of bauxite ore, it does not figure among the world's ten most important suppliers. This fact might result from its proximity to Australia, the world's main producer of bauxite. In terms of relative costs of production, bauxite may offer attractive advantages to less technically developed countries like Indonesia, because the mineral is typically strip-mined close to the surface or under a ferruginous surface layer. However, the costly process involved in extracting aluminum from ore means that, unless Indonesia could some day reach the bulk volume of exports supplied by the top five world suppliers, it would have difficulty matching the economies of scale enjoyed by its competitors.

Another factor of increasing importance has to do with the success of aluminum recycling processes that have been adopted throughout the world. Although recycling does not hold out the prospect of reducing the price of aluminum itself, it can have the effect of reducing demand for bauxite, making Indonesia's global position even more vulnerable.

### OTHER RESOURCES

In the first two years of the twenty-first century, Indonesia produced significant quantities of iron ore, a necessary component for producing another of its potentially significant exports: raw steel. In 2001, Indonesia produced more than 450 million metric tons of iron ore. The next year production dropped off nearly 20 percent, and by 2005 the decrease appeared drastic, going as low as 19 million metric tons. Significantly, production of steel, which began to slump in

2003, did not follow iron ore's drop, possibly because of continued emphasis on steel production for the construction industry.

Indonesia does not rank among major producers of gypsum, in part because of its geographical uniqueness as an island country. The main producers for the global market are found in Spain and North America. Gypsum is a basic crystalline mineral used to make plasterboard, or drywall, and other basic construction materials. Thus, Indonesia's rather stable annual production (about 6,000 metric tons) is mainly important as an import substitution resource.

Considerably rarer than ordinary gypsum is the more complex molecular crystal form known as alabaster. Indonesia is attempting to produce sufficient quantities of alabaster to complement its list of "luxury" exports.

*Byron D. Cannon*

### FURTHER READING

Carlson, Sevinc. *Indonesia's Oil.* Boulder, Colo.: Westview Press, 1977.

Lewis, Peter M. *Growing Apart: Oil, Politics, and Change in Indonesia and Nigeria.* Ann Arbor: University of Michigan Press, 2007.

Rosser, Andrew. *Why Did Indonesia Overcome the Resource Curse?* Brighton, Sussex, England: University of Sussex Institute of Development Studies, 2004.

World Bank. *Spending for Development: Making the Most of Indonesia's New Opportunities—Indonesia Public Expenditure Review.* Washington, D.C.: Author, 2008.

SEE ALSO: Aluminum; Copper; Forest fires; Forestry; Forests; Nickel; Oil and natural gas distribution; Timber industry; Tin.

# Industrial Revolution and industrialization

CATEGORY: Historical events and movements

*The term "Industrial Revolution" describes the historical period in which the exploitation of new energy technologies led to industrialization—the centralization of production with a reorganization of human living patterns and increased consumption of a broad range of natural resources.*

## BACKGROUND

The Industrial Revolution is generally considered to have begun in England in the eighteenth century and to have spread to North America, northern Europe, and then further throughout the world. It is still under way in emerging nations of Asia, Africa, and Latin America. Industrialization is characterized by increased consumption of energy and material resources, centralization of production, the growth of urban populations, and the evolution of extensive transportation and energy distribution infrastructures.

The production of nonagricultural goods has followed a common historical pattern in many parts of the world. At first, families (or somewhat larger tribal units) make enough for their own needs. Then a type of trade develops in which individuals specialize in the production of a limited number of goods, and a market economy—allowing the accumulation of money or capital—is established. The buying and selling then increasingly come under the control of merchants who buy from the producers and arrange transport to the buyers. At first, domestic manufacture prevails; in other words, production occurs within or near the home. Eventually, an industrial stage is achieved: Labor is centralized so that investment can be made in the means of production and economies of scale can be realized.

## PRECONDITIONS

In order for factory production to supplant domestic production in a nation or region, there must be adequate supplies of human power, mechanical energy, and capital. A transportation infrastructure must be in place. Further, some rudimentary knowledge of science and engineering is required, as are adequate materials with which to build machinery. Cultural assumptions are also important. Industrialization will not occur unless improvements in material wealth are considered both possible and desirable by those in positions of political and economic power.

The Industrial Revolution could not have occurred before an agricultural revolution made it possible for a smaller proportion of the population to be directly involved in food production, thereby freeing individuals to move to cities. Historians view the agricultural revolution as beginning with the transition in Western Europe, about the year 1600, from open fields to enclosed individual farms and the subsequent introduction of new crops (particularly feed for livestock), new tools for plowing and planting, and improvements in livestock. With the increased availability of animal muscle power and fertilizer from animal waste, farms became more productive, but they were also more expensive to run. Rural populations stratified into farm owners, tenants, and paid workers. The latter, having no direct tie to the land, were free to move to the city in search of work, and they formed the first pool of industrial workers.

Because building a factory requires capital and entrepreneurs who can afford to wait a period of time to realize a return on their investment, the Industrial Revolution also had to await the accumulation of wealth by merchants and the founding of banks with sufficient funds to finance industrial construction. Further, the centralization of production could only be effective with the availability of dependable transport of raw materials to, and finished goods from, the factories. Perhaps the most characteristically "industrial" feature of the revolution, and certainly the one with the greatest direct impact on natural resources, was the development of easily controlled mechanical power, essential to both production and the infrastructure upon which mechanized production depends.

## THE STEAM ENGINE

Prior to the eighteenth century the only available sources of mechanical energy were muscle, wind, and flowing or falling water. The latter had been widely exploited in milling and other industries. The development of the steam engine appears to have been a by-product of the metal- and coal-mining industries. A major problem in mining was water that seeped into mine shafts, and, in 1698, English inventor Thomas Savery introduced a water-lifting device based on steam pressure.

By 1713 an English craftsman named Thomas Newcomen had produced the first steam engine that could function at atmospheric pressure. The basic Newcomen design was improved by James Watt, a Scottish instrument maker, in the period between 1765 and 1790. By 1820 some sixty steam engines were at work in Birmingham, England, generating a total of about 1,000 horsepower. A scant eighteen years later there were more than three thousand steam engines in the United States—on steamboats, in railroad locomotives, and in manufacturing use.

The steam engine converts heat energy into mechanical energy. Its development meant that mechanical power could be available wherever there was an

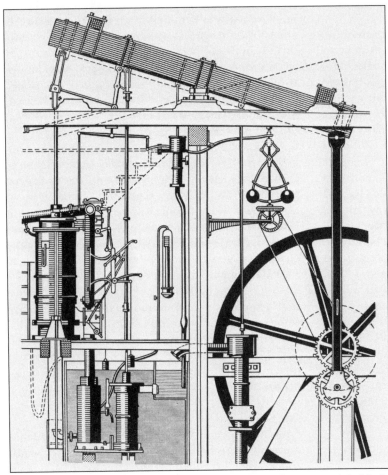

*Watt's steam engine, shown here in one of its earliest versions, became a symbol of the Industrial Revolution.* (The Granger Collection, New York)

adequate supply of fuel. The burning of coal, which had already begun to replace wood for home heating, became the principal source of power for the Industrial Revolution, with the early steam engines providing a means both of pumping water from mine shafts and of cutting the coal from deposits. With the extensive use of coal came the first industrial air pollution, because soot and sulfur oxides were released into the air.

### INDUSTRIALIZATION OF THE TEXTILE INDUSTRY

The textile production industry of fiber and cloth was the first manufacturing process to be industrialized, and cotton proved to be the fiber most amenable to the mechanized processing. Cotton is converted into cloth by the processes of carding, spinning, and weaving, in which the fibers are separated from one an-other, wound into thread or yarn, and then woven into fabric. The first spinning machine was put into production in London in 1740, with a carding machine developed about a decade later. Improvements in both these technologies were achieved by the English inventor James Hargreaves, who patented the "spinning jenny" in 1770 and a carding engine in 1775. The power loom was introduced by Edmund Cartwright, an English clergyman turned industrialist, in 1785. The number of power looms in England and Scotland grew from about fourteen thousand in 1820 to one hundred thousand in 1833.

The explosive growth of the textile industry had important implications for land use and for world politics. The British government sought to prevent the designs for textile machinery from leaving England so as to maintain a monopoly on textile production. The American textile industry began in 1790 when an English immigrant named Samuel Slater built successful water-powered spinning machines in Pawtucket, Rhode Island. Following the invention of the cotton gin (which separates cotton fiber from the seed) by the American Eli Whitney in 1793, cotton became a principal crop in the southern United States. After the industrialization of the American textile industry, the need for sources of raw cotton and markets for finished textiles became a major determinant of British colonial policy in the Middle East and India.

### TRANSPORTATION

With industrialization came the need for more efficient transportation of raw materials to manufacturing centers and of finished goods to consumers. The first steamboat, in which a steam engine produced the motive power for a paddlewheel, was demonstrated in 1787 by John Fitch, an American inventor. Regular steamboat service was not established until twenty years later, when American engineer Robert Fulton introduced regular service on New York's Hudson River. The first propeller-driven steamships were introduced in 1836, and in 1845, a propeller-driven ship crossed the Atlantic, inaugurating a new era in worldwide shipping.

The second major vehicle for the transport of goods and services was the railroad. The first designs that were called "railroads" consisted of short lengths of wooden rail on which horses moved coal for short distances. In 1804, an English inventor named Richard Trevithick mounted a steam engine on a four-wheeled carriage and used his invention to pull an 8-metric-ton load of coal over 14 kilometers of track. The first public railroad began operation in England in 1825. By that time railroad-building had already spread to the United States. With government support, the railroads expanded rapidly across North America, fueling the westward migration of farmers and cattlemen and resulting in the conversion of vast areas of wilderness to agricultural use.

## THE CHEMICAL INDUSTRY

The chemical industry is somewhat unusual in that most of its products are meant for use in other industries. It also is probably the industry with the greatest impact on natural resources other than energy. Sulfuric acid, used in the bleaching of textiles and the cleaning of metals, was perhaps the first major "chemical" to be used. At the end of the eighteenth century, new sources of alkali were sought to meet the demands of glassmaking and soapmaking. The depletion of the forests of Europe to produce charcoal had led to a scarcity of potash (potassium carbonate), traditionally obtained from wood ash. In 1780, Nicolas Leblanc developed a process whereby soda ash (sodium carbonate) could be produced from salt, chalk, and sulfuric acid. The modern chemical industry began about 1840 when chemists discovered that numerous organic chemicals could be extracted from coal tar, a by-product of the use of coke in blast furnaces. In addition to aromatic hydrocarbons such as benzene and toluene, then thought of mainly as solvents, the nitrogen-containing compound aniline and an entire family of aniline dyes were obtained. A great number of new chemical compounds and industrial by-products were thus released into industrial wastewater.

## THE INTERNAL COMBUSTION ENGINE

While the steam engine was the original workhorse of the Industrial Revolution, it had many inefficient features. Heat energy, provided by burning wood or coal,

was used to heat water, creating the steam that provided the moving force for a piston, which in turn produced the actual mechanical motion. Much of the generated heat energy escaped in the process. The strategy of using the fuel as the working material—thereby eliminating the middle steps in the production of motion—was realized in the internal combustion engine, developed in the years 1863 to 1866 by a German traveling salesman, Nikolaus August Otto.

The compactness of the internal combustion engine made it an extremely attractive power source for self-powered vehicles, including the automobile and the truck. The automobile became a major product of industry in the United States. The motor truck provided the capability to deliver goods wherever there was a road. Possibly no single aspect of industrialized society has had as much effect on land use and air quality as the automobile. In 1908, Henry Ford introduced the Model T, the first automobile to be affordable to many Americans. Within twenty years more than half of all American families owned motorcars. Petroleum refining and road construction became major industries. Unfortunately, the combustion of gasoline in the automobile engine was not complete, so carbon monoxide and volatile hydrocarbons were released into the air. To keep the engines running smoothly, tetraethyl lead was added to gasoline, resulting in the release of lead in automobile exhausts. Eventually improvements in engine design and the introduction of the catalytic converter were able to reduce the amount of polluting material released per kilometer traveled.

## ELECTRICITY

Italian physicist Alessandro Volta invented the electric battery in 1800, opening a new energy source to development. After the invention of the electromagnet by William Sturgeon in 1825, a number of inventors strove to perfect the electromagnetic telegraph, by which messages could be sent over wires almost instantaneously. Exploitation of the telegraph required the stringing of telegraph lines between major cities. Much of the development of electrical technology was driven by the potential for long-distance communication. The discovery of the electric motor and generator marked a new freedom in the generation of mechanical energy. Electrical energy could be produced wherever convenient and transmitted at low cost to wherever it might be needed. In particular, electricity could be generated by the energy of falling water, either at a natural waterfall, such as at Niagara Falls, or by damming the flow of rivers.

An explosion in energy consumption was heralded by Thomas Edison's invention of the incandescent electric light in the late nineteenth century. In order for profits to be generated by this innovation networks of generators, transmission lines, and transformers for the distribution of electrical energy had to be established. These networks could be powered by falling water (hydroenergy); by the burning of coal, oil, or natural gas; or, following World War II, by the energy released by nuclear fission. Each of these sources carried its own environmental price. The burning of fossil fuels produced air pollution, and nuclear energy plants produced nuclear waste as well as excessive quantities of heat, leading to the thermal pollution of streams and lakes. Even hydroelectric power, widely considered a "clean" and renewable energy source, alters local ecosystems and interferes with scenery; moreover, dams have a limited life cycle because they are eventually filled in with sediment.

IMPACT ON NATURAL RESOURCES

The course of industrialization in Western Europe and the United States demonstrates dramatically the interconnections between technological change, social and economic conditions, and the utilization of natural resources. Overall, industrialization is accompanied by an increased use of natural resources, punctuated by innovations and discoveries that may shift consumption from one resource to another. While industrialization has historically resulted in varying degrees of environmental degradation—ranging from deforestation to damage from huge strip mines to air and water pollution—advances in technology frequently allow a more efficient use of resources, moderating the demand for individual scarce resources and limiting environmental impact. The evolution of automobiles over the last forty years of the twentieth century, for instance, saw a reduction in metal usage, greatly increased fuel economy, the elimination of lead released to the environment, and a reduction in other pollutants.

There has been considerable debate over the question of whether continuing worldwide industrialization, coupled with population growth, will deplete crucial resources such as oil and certain mineral resources in the near future. On the one hand, reserves of materials such as oil are finite. On the other hand, a number of factors seem to be mitigating the problem.

Automation and computers are employed in industry to use resources more efficiently and minimize waste, reducing the drain on resources. Improvements in renewable energy resources such as solar and wind power, together with recycling technologies for key materials, offer at least the possibility of continued industrialization without the exhaustion of essential resources in the immediate future. However, with the accelerating industrialization of the economies of China, India and other formerly developing nations, resource sustainability is becoming a greater imperative.

*Donald R. Franceschetti*

FURTHER READING

Bronowski, Jacob. *The Ascent of Man.* Boston: Little, Brown, 1973.

Josephson, Paul R. *Industrialized Nature: Brute Force Technology and the Transformation of the Natural World.* Washington, D.C.: Island Press/Shearwater Books, 2002.

Kranzberg, Melvin, and Carroll W. Pursell, Jr., eds. *Technology in Western Civilization.* 2 vols. New York: Oxford University Press, 1967.

McPherson, Natalie. *Machines and Economic Growth: The Implications for Growth Theory of the History of the Industrial Revolution.* Westport, Conn.: Greenwood Press, 1994.

Marcus, Alan I., and Howard P. Segal. *Technology in America: A Brief History.* 2d ed. Fort Worth, Tex.: Harcourt Brace College, 1999.

Park, Se Hark, and Walter C. Labys. *Industrial Development and Environmental Degradation: A Source Book on the Origins of Global Pollution.* Northampton, Mass.: Edward Elgar, 1998.

Pursell, Carroll W., Jr., ed. *Technology in America: A History of Individuals and Ideas.* 2d ed. Cambridge, Mass.: MIT Press, 1990.

Singer, Charles, et al., eds. *The Industrial Revolution, c. 1750 to c. 1850.* Vol. 4 in *A History of Technology.* Oxford, England: Clarendon Press, 1954-1984.

Smith, Toby M. *The Myth of Green Marketing: Tending Our Goats at the Edge of Apocalypse.* Toronto: University of Toronto Press, 1998.

Stearns, Peter N. *The Industrial Revolution in World History.* 3d ed. Boulder, Colo.: Westview Press, 2007.

SEE ALSO: Air pollution and air pollution control; Capitalism and resource exploitation; Coal; Developing countries; Environmental degradation, resource exploitation and; Internal combustion engine; Iron; Manufacturing, energy use in; Oil industry; Steam engine; Steel industry; Transportation, energy use in; Watt, James.

# Integrated Ocean Drilling Program

CATEGORY: Organizations, agencies, and programs
DATE: Established October 1, 2003

*The Integrated Ocean Drilling Program (IODP) is an international research program that supports drilling into the Earth's crust below the oceans. Hundreds of scientists from around the world participate in proposing, conducting, and analyzing research and in disseminating results to enhance understanding of the Earth, its structure, and its history.*

## BACKGROUND

In 1961, the first sample of the Earth's crust at the bottom of the ocean was obtained through drilling off the coast of Guadalupe, Mexico. The value of such core samples was immediately apparent, and in 1966, the Deep Sea Drilling Project began, followed in 1985 by the Ocean Drilling Program (ODP). These international programs yielded thousands of core samples, helping scientists trace the history of the planet, confirming the movement of tectonic plates and the impact of an asteroid 65 million years ago, revealing the existence of salt domes, and suggesting the potential for drilling for oil under the ocean floor.

As new information led to scientific questions, and as the technology for exploration improved, a new model for cooperative funding and research was needed. In 2003, the U.S. National Science Foundation and the Japanese Ministry of Education, Culture, Sports, Science and Technology formed the Integrated Ocean Drilling Program (IODP). These two "lead agencies" shared responsibility and funding, and other countries in Europe and Asia soon joined as members.

## IMPACT ON RESOURCE USE

IODP provides a mechanism for scientists to share information, technology, and funding as an international community. The activities of IODP are informed by the Initial Science Plan, titled "Earth, Oceans and Life: Scientific Investigations of the Earth

System Using Multiple Drilling Platforms and New Technologies," formulated by an international multidisciplinary group of scientists as a blueprint for the first ten years of research. The plan identifies four major areas of inquiry: the deep biosphere and the subseafloor ocean; environmental changes; Earth effects and processes; and solid Earth geodynamics and cyclical activity. IODP has a complex organization, guided by a memorandum of understanding that defines how much money each member should contribute and how many of its scientists will participate in drilling cruises and in meetings. The program also has provisions for sharing information with scientists and the general public free of charge through conferences, papers, journals, magazines, Web sites, and teacher-at-sea programs. Undersea drilling has helped scientists expand their knowledge about the environments on and below the seafloor to reformulate understandings about how the Earth has changed both over the long term and in recent times and has enhanced understanding of global climate change.

*Cynthia A. Bily*

## WEB SITES

INTEGRATED OCEAN DRILLING PROGRAM—UNITED STATES IMPLEMENTING ORGANIZATION
http://www.oceandrilling.org/

INTEGRATED OCEAN DRILLING PROGRAM
http://www.iodp.org/

SEE ALSO: Coast and Geodetic Survey, U.S.; Deep drilling projects; Earth's crust; Oceanography; Oceans.

# Intergovernmental Panel on Climate Change

CATEGORY: Organizations, agencies, and programs
DATE: Established 1988

*The Intergovernmental Panel on Climate Change (IPCC) gathers, reviews, and reports scientific, technical, and socioeconomic information on climate change as directed by the Conference of Parties to the United Nations Conventions. IPCC task forces also prepare papers and special reports pertaining to the effect of climate change.*

## BACKGROUND

Concerns regarding the effect of greenhouse gases on Earth's climate prompted the World Meteorological Organization Executive Council to establish the Intergovernmental Panel on Climate Change following authorization by the United Nations Environment Programme. The IPCC reports and papers culminate from the efforts of thousands of experts from developed and developing countries working under a rigorous review, adoption, and approval process. The IPCC consists of the secretariat in Geneva, three working groups, and several special committees that prepare assessment reports on scientific, technological, and socioeconomic information related to climate change.

## IMPACT ON RESOURCE USE

In 1990, the IPCC adopted its First Assessment Report, which reported that emissions from human activities were substantially increasing the atmospheric concentration of greenhouse gases, the result of which would be additional warming of the Earth's surface. Furthermore, the report noted that adverse impacts on forestry and water resources would be most pronounced in developing countries. It also addressed mitigation and adaptation measures to protect food, water, land, and biological resources. This report spurred the establishment of the United Nations Framework Convention on Climate Change (1992) to address global warming.

The Second Assessment Report (1995) noted that the balance of evidence suggested a discernible human influence on global climate and that climate changes were projected to result in significant adverse impacts on food supply and water resources. This was key to the 1997 adoption of the Kyoto Protocol, which established binding targets to limit greenhouse-gas emissions for developed countries. IPCC responded to a request for a special report and published *Land Use, Land-Use Change, and Forestry* in 2000, which described carbon sequestration strategies involving land and forests. Sequestration of carbon dioxide in forests is one mechanism to offset greenhouse-gas emission limits.

The Third Assessment Report (2001) stated that most of the warming over the previous fifty years was attributable to human activities. It concluded that global temperature increases in the ensuing one hundred years could be significantly larger than previously thought. In 2002, IPCC published a technical paper, *Climate Change and Biodiversity*, requested by the United Nations Convention on Biological Diversity, which noted that humans will continue to cause a loss in biodiversity through climate change.

The Fourth Assessment Report (2007) noted that human-induced climate change could lead to some impacts that are abrupt or irreversible. In 2007, the IPCC, with Al Gore, received the Nobel Peace Prize for efforts to disseminate knowledge about climate change and mitigation measures. In 2008, IPCC published a technical paper, *Climate Change and Water*, which predicted that freshwater sources were vulnerable to climate change because of changes in temperature, precipitation variability, and glacial melting and predicted that water pollution would increase because of increases in sediments, nutrients, pesticides, and temperature. The IPCC scheduled its Fifth Assessment Report for 2014.

*Kathryn L. Rowberg*

## WEB SITE

INTERGOVERNMENTAL PANEL ON CLIMATE CHANGE
http://www.ipcc.ch/

*Following a 2009 meeting between the European Union and the Intergovernmental Panel on Climate Change (IPCC), European Commission president José Manuel Barroso speaks with the press. He is flanked on the right by Rajendra Kumar Pachauri of the IPCC and on the left by environmentalist Nicholas Stern. (AFP/Getty Images)*

SEE ALSO: Climate Change and Sustainable Energy Act; Gore, Al; Greenhouse gases and global climate change; Kyoto Protocol; United Nations climate change conferences; United Nations Framework Convention on Climate Change.


# Internal combustion engine

CATEGORIES: Obtaining and using resources; pollution and waste disposal

*Along with the electric motor, the internal combustion engine became the most widely used source of motive power in twentieth century technology. Its advantages of speed and intermittent operation made it a popular power source for transportation. Widespread use depended on a steady source of liquid fuel, so a huge demand for petroleum products was created.*

## BACKGROUND

The internal combustion engine uses the principle that an explosive mixture of air and fuel contained in a space will expand when ignited. Three basic types of engines developed from that principle: atmospheric, which used the pressure of the atmosphere to move a piston after an explosion created a vacuum; noncompression, which exploded a mixture of air and fuel in a chamber; and precompression, which compressed a mixture of air and fuel before ignition. Designers used either a reciprocal or turbine action as the basic motion in the devices.

As early as the seventeenth century, gunpowder-fueled cannons demonstrated the power generated by internal combustion. This knowledge led Christiaan Huygens to produce the first such gunpowder-powered device in 1673; it had little practical success. Although several people experimented with internal combustion designs for more than a century and a half after Huygens's pioneering efforts, no successful efforts emerged until William Murdoch produced a reliable source of coal gas as fuel for these engines in 1790. From that date until the 1850's, several inventors experimented with a variety of devices used to produce motive or stationary power. None was practical, and none saw commercial success, yet these efforts were important in the development of internal combustion power.

Jean-Joseph-Étienne Lenoir produced the first commercially viable internal combustion engine in 1859; it used town coal gas for fuel. Lenoir's noncompression engine generated as much as three horsepower and sold widely in the 1860's. However, its high fuel consumption, size, rough operation, and extensive maintenance demands kept it from developing into a major power source. The creation of a practical engine depended on the ingenuity of German engineers and on the ready availability of petroleum-based fuels.

Nineteenth century German inventor Nikolaus August Otto sensed that the Lenoir engine would have a greater potential if powered by a portable liquid fuel. That awareness motivated Otto to begin a long process of improving the Lenoir engine and creating his own design, which became the standard for decades. This process was typical of much innovation in technology: An inventor and a developer/financier formed a team to improve an existing design. In Otto's case, he was fortunate to work with Eugen Langen, who provided both technical and financial assistance in the development of an atmospheric engine.

By 1876, Otto had learned the importance of precompression and devised his famous "silent Otto engine": a four-stroke cycle engine using intake of fuel, compression, ignition, and expansion and exhaust phases. Using this Otto method of power generation in a four-cylinder engine, Gottlieb Daimler, in 1885, used an early form of gasoline to power the engine and created the prototype for the widely used automobile engines of the twentieth century. The use of petroleum fuel increased the mobility and convenience of the automobile and created a growing demand for both gasoline and the Otto-type engine. The practical motorcar also depended on further improvements to the Otto engine, such as Wilhelm Maybach's carburetor (1892) and an electric spark ignition system that was developed by 1900. These features made the car powered by an internal combustion engine a new and popular transportation device in the early years of the twentieth century.

## APPLICATIONS

The internal combustion engine also powered airplanes, marine vehicles, trucks, and factory machines. By the early 1900's, Rudolf Diesel's self-ignition engines, relying on fuel oil, saw use in heavy-duty applications. Frank Whittle's development work in Britain on a gasoline-powered turbine engine in the 1920's and 1930's led to jet aircraft toward the end of World War II. These engines became widespread in aviation

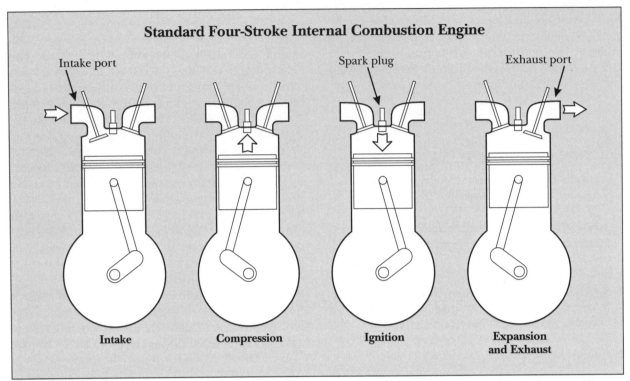

**Standard Four-Stroke Internal Combustion Engine**

Intake port          Spark plug          Exhaust port

Intake          Compression          Ignition          Expansion and Exhaust

*A generalized depiction of the four-stroke internal combustion engine. Intake: Air enters the cylinder and mixes with gasoline vapor. Compression: The cylinder is sealed, and the piston moves upward to compress the air-fuel mixture. Ignition: The spark plug ignites the mixture, creating pressure that drives the piston downward. Expansion (exhaust): The burned gases exit the cylinder.*

in the postwar era and added to the demand for petroleum fuels. These diverse uses of the internal combustion engine and its dependability made this design a favorite in the marketplace for more than one century despite its inefficiency and the fact that it polluted the environment.

RESOURCE USE

The demand and consumption of petroleum as a fuel grew with the increased uses of the internal combustion engine in the twentieth and early twenty-first centuries. For example, in the United States gasoline use increased more than tenfold from 1910 to 1950 as Americans embraced the car culture, and it tripled between 1950 and 2000, an era of suburban growth and multiple-car families. Gasoline consumption far outpaced domestic petroleum production, and the United States tripled the amount of oil it imported in the short time period from 1967 to 1973. As of 2010, the United States continued to import more than 60 percent of the petroleum it consumed each year. Although the internal combustion engine was the pre-

eminent mobile power source of the late twentieth and early twenty-first centuries, its use of nonrenewable energy resources and the pollutants it released generated a growing interest in finding alternative sources of reliable mobile power.

*H. J. Eisenman*

FURTHER READING

Black, Edwin. *Internal Combustion: How Corporations and Governments Addicted the World to Oil and Derailed the Alternatives.* New York: St. Martin's Press, 2006.

Cummins, C. Lyle, Jr. *Internal Fire.* Rev. ed. Warrendale, Pa.: Society of Automotive Engineers, 1989.

Josephson, Paul R. *Motorized Obsessions: Life, Liberty, and the Small-Bore Engine.* Baltimore: Johns Hopkins University Press, 2007.

Lay, M. G. *Ways of the World: A History of the World's Roads and of the Vehicles That Used Them.* New Brunswick, N.J.: Rutgers University Press, 1992.

Pulkrabek, Willard W. *Engineering Fundamentals of the Internal Combustion Engine.* 2d ed. Upper Saddle River, N.J.: Pearson/Prentice Hall, 2004.

Sher, Eran, ed. *Handbook of Air Pollution from Internal Combustion Engines: Pollutant Formation and Control.* Boston: Academic Press, 1998.

Stone, Richard. *Introduction to Internal Combustion Engines.* 3d ed. Warrendale, Pa.: Society of Automotive Engineers, 1999.

### WEB SITE

HOW STUFF WORKS
How Car Engines Work: Internal Combustion
http://auto.howstuffworks.com/engine1.htm

SEE ALSO: Air pollution and air pollution control; Clean Air Act; Gasoline and other petroleum fuels; Oil and natural gas distribution; Oil embargo and energy crises of 1973 and 1979; Oil industry; Petroleum refining and processing; Transportation, energy use in.

# International Association for Impact Assessment

CATEGORY: Organizations, agencies, and programs
DATE: Established 1980

*The International Association for Impact Assessment brings together researchers in the sciences and social sciences, policy makers, academics, and others to analyze the possible and probable consequences for development policies that have an impact on the environmental, social, economic, and cultural health of human societies around the world.*

### BACKGROUND

The International Association for Impact Assessment (IAIA) is a nongovernmental organization dedicated to the protection of biodiversity and the promotion of sustainable development on a local to global scale. IAIA supports free and open access to all its environmental impact assessment projects, which use the most current, comprehensive, and unbiased research findings available. IAIA consists of more than twenty-five hundred members in more than one hundred countries. All IAIA research projects aim to protect both the natural environment and human rights, while developing increasingly sophisticated environmental impact assessments.

### IMPACT ON RESOURCE USE

IAIA divides members' research projects into a number of departments. The agriculture, forestry, and fisheries department collects data to develop numerous and widely available sustainable practices. The biodiversity and ecology department provides information to help establish environmentally significant and sensitive locations and develop ways to protect them. The disaster and conflict department collects information on the environmental impact of natural disasters, including the negative impact on biodiversity in affected areas. This helps develop environmentally and human-sensitive policy responses. The corporate stewardship department assists corporations in designing environmentally positive decisions in their manufacturing, marketing, and distribution processes. Trade-related projects focus on environmentally benign international and transnational trade development.

IAIA includes a department dedicated specifically to assessing the impact of development policies on indigenous peoples and how best to preserve traditional forms of knowledge. The health impact department collects and disseminates information related to the connections between human health and environmental development and/or preservation. IAIA also tracks environmental impact legislation around the globe via its impact assessment law department.

All IAIA departments include options for public participation in environmental impact assessments and the provision of information helpful in constructing legislation in line with IAIA mission of environmentally aware development. IAIA publishes research findings, including requisite estimated cost-benefit analyses, in its professional journal, *Impact Assessment and Project Appraisal.* The journal also includes a best practices section, book reviews, and updates on global environmental projects and legislation. Additionally IAIA publishes numerous books on assessment methodologies in order to ensure that research findings are reported in the most credible and functional way for later use in drafting legislation or supporting policy decisions. These methodology texts include volumes on what to assess for biodiversity impact, how research samples must be constructed for social impact assessments, and options for developing corporate stewardship decisions. IAIA uses its publications to contribute to global sustainable development projects in line with the goals of the Ramsar Convention, the Convention on Biological Diversity, the World

Water Forum, the Espoo Convention, and the Convention on Migratory Species.

*Victoria Erhart*

SEE ALSO: Biodiversity; Ecology; Environmental ethics; Environmental impact statement; Ramsar Convention; Sustainable development; United Nations Convention on Biological Diversity.

# International Atomic Energy Agency

CATEGORY: Organizations, agencies, and programs
DATE: Established 1957

*The primary function of the International Atomic Energy Agency (IAEA) is to stimulate and support research, development, and practical implementation of atomic energy for peaceful, safe, and secure uses throughout the world. The organization plays a vital role in verifying that all member governments comply with their commitments made to the peaceful use of nuclear technology.*

## BACKGROUND
Impetus for the establishment of the IAEA was initiated by President Dwight D. Eisenhower in 1953 when he presented his "Atoms for Peace" speech before the United Nations General Assembly. The agency was launched on July 29, 1957, to regulate the global use of atomic energy.

## IMPACT ON RESOURCE USE
The IAEA is a center for the dissemination of information on peaceful applications of nuclear energy and technology worldwide. Although it is an independent organization, the IAEA reports its activities to the General Assembly and the Security Council of the United Nations. The organization—headquartered in Vienna, Austria—runs education programs to help train and direct young people from all over the world with career development in scientific endeavors that promote the peaceful uses of atomic energy and protect the global environment and safety of people.

In addition to promoting the peaceful use of atomic energy, the IAEA monitors relevant activities and applies safeguards that help ensure that atomic energy is not used for military purposes. The agency helps to enforce the Nuclear Non-Proliferation Treaty and other international treaties dealing with the use of atomic energy. IAEA inspectors visit nuclear facilities periodically to verify the locations and amounts of nuclear materials used by member countries and to check on instruments and surveillance equipment that have been installed by the IAEA. After an earthquake rocked the Niigata and Nagano districts of Japan in July, 2007, IAEA personnel investigated and confirmed the safe performance of the Kashiwazaki-Kariwa nuclear power plant.

The IAEA is actively involved in the development and utilization of uranium resources for use in the safe production of nuclear energy. Through its education programs, the IAEA helps those involved in the uranium industry share the best known practices so that people and the environment are protected. The agency monitors uranium mining projects that boost the world's uranium production capacity and add to the global uranium resource base.

The IAEA is committed to protecting global water resources and assuring an adequate supply of groundwater worldwide. The agency works jointly with UN-Water to ensure that nuclear technology is employed in strategic planning and development of water resources. It uses isotope hydrology and ground penetrating radar to help countries monitor and manage their water resources.

In February, 2009, in Monaco, members of the Marine Environment Laboratory of the IAEA met with 150 experts and discussed actions that need to be taken to halt increasing levels of acidity in the oceans worldwide. The main culprit is increasing levels of carbon dioxide that combine with water to form carbonic acid. The IAEA encourages alternative forms of energy production that will help reduce carbon dioxide emissions.

*Alvin K. Benson*

SEE ALSO: Atomic Energy Acts; Atomic Energy Commission; Energy politics; Nuclear energy; Nuclear Energy Institute; Renewable and nonrenewable resources; Uranium.

# International Union for Conservation of Nature

CATEGORY: Organizations, agencies, and programs

DATE: Established 1948

*The International Union for Conservation of Nature, also known as the World Conservation Union, plays a major role in developing and implementing conservation treaties, conventions, and agreements.*

## BACKGROUND

The founding of the International Union for Conservation of Nature (IUCN), a nongovernmental organization, was an integral aspect of the postwar evolution of international environmental politics. IUCN was established as the International Union for the Protection of Nature (IUPN). The IUCN has a federative structure with four categories of membership: states, governmental agencies, and national and international nongovernmental organizations. There are also nonvoting affiliates as well as nonvoting individual and organizational supporters. The IUCN does its work through a number of specialized commissions and committees. The union is headquartered in Gland, Switzerland. In addition, the IUCN has regional offices in Africa, Central America, Asia, and the Middle East. IUCN reports on its activities in the *IUCN Bulletin*, and it publishes reports and books on conservation issues. The organization is popularly known as the World Conservation Union.

## IMPACT ON RESOURCE USE

The IUPN's intended focus was the preservation of wildlife and the natural environment; education; scientific research; legislation; and the collection, analysis, and dissemination of data and information. Over several years, the IUPN's agenda broadened from a focus on wildlife protection to include the protection of renewable resources. This larger scope was reflected in its name change.

*Marian A. L. Miller*

## WEB SITE

INTERNATIONAL UNION FOR CONSERVATION OF NATURE
http://www.iucn.org/

SEE ALSO: Conservation; Environmental movement; Natural Resources Defense Council; Renewable and nonrenewable resources; United Nations Environment Programme; Wildlife.

# Iodine

CATEGORY: Mineral and other nonliving resources

## WHERE FOUND

Iodine is widely distributed at a low concentration. However, only in brines and caliche ores is the concentration sufficient to make separation practical. The largest producers of iodine are Chile, followed by Japan, China, Turkmenistan, Russia, Azerbaijan, Indonesia, and Uzbekistan.

## PRIMARY USES

Iodine is used primarily in animal feed supplements, catalysts, inks, colorants, photographic equipment, and disinfectants. An important use is in iodized salt, which prevents goiter.

## TECHNICAL DEFINITION

Iodine (abbreviated I), atomic number 53, belongs to Group VII (the halogens) of the periodic table of the elements and resembles chlorine in its chemical properties. One stable isotope exists with an atomic weight of 126.9045. At room temperature, iodine is a purple-black color with a metallic sheen. Its elemental form is diatomic (two atoms of iodine bonded together). The solid has a density of 4.942 grams per cubic centimeter and sublimes easily. The melting point of iodine is 113.7° Celsius, and the boiling point is 184.5° Celsius.

## DESCRIPTION, DISTRIBUTION, AND FORMS

Iodine is the sixtieth element in order of abundance, at 0.46 part per million in the Earth's crust. Commercial deposits are usually iodates such as lautarite $Ca(IO_3)_2$ and dietzeite $7Ca(IO_3)_2 \cdot 8CaCrO_4$. Some brines in Louisiana, California, and Michigan contain 30 to 40 parts per million iodide ion, while some Japanese brines contain 100 parts per million. Iodine is only 0.05 part per million in seawater, but some sea plants concentrate iodine up to 0.45 percent (4,500 parts per million) of their dry weight.

Iodine is a necessary trace element in animals. An iodine deficiency may cause a range of problems, including goiter, mental retardation, increased still-births and miscarriages, and the severe mental and physical handicaps of cretinism. Common table salt ("iodized" salt) contains iodine at a 0.01 percent level, which is enough to safely prevent these ailments. Iodine is used in the body to produce the growth-regulating hormone thyroxine. An excess of iodine may lead to thyroid cancer or interfere with hormone production. Although throughout history, iodine shortage has normally been the problem, the use of iodine in animal feed, sanitizers, and food processing causes Americans to consume many times the recommended daily allowance of iodine. The effects of this are not truly known, but it may prove to be unhealthy. Iodine is highly toxic to plants and does not appear to be necessary for plant life.

## HISTORY

In 1811, Bernard Courtois, the son of a saltpeter manufacturer, first noticed iodine while extracting compounds from the ash of algae gathered along the seashore. He observed a cloud of violet vapor and an irritating odor. Courtois tested the dark crystals that formed on cold objects as well as he could in his simple laboratory. Because he suspected that this was a new element, he provided samples to two of his friends, Charles-Bernard Desormes and Nicolas Clément at the Conservatoire des Arts et des Métiers. With better equipment, they continued the investigation of this new substance and announced the discovery of iodine in 1813. The name comes from the Greek word *iodes,* for "violetlike." The first iodine-containing mineral was found in Mexico in 1825. The discovery of iodate as a contaminant of the Chile saltpeter beds was an even more important discovery.

## OBTAINING IODINE

The method of iodine production depends on the source of the iodine. From the Chilean saltpeter beds, the sodium iodate is dissolved by an alkaline solution, converted to iodide ion by reaction with sodium hydrogen sulfite, and iodine is then precipitated by adding iodate solution. From brines, the iodide ion is converted to iodine by reaction with chlorine. Air blowing through the solution collects the iodine, which then precipitates. Purification is by resublimation. In an alternate method the iodide ion is precipitated with silver ion, reacted with iron to make iron iodide, and

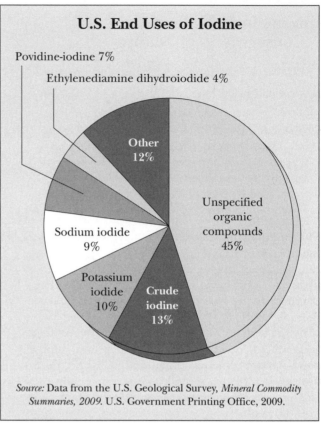

**U.S. End Uses of Iodine**

Povidine-iodine 7%
Ethylenediamine dihydroiodide 4%
Other 12%
Unspecified organic compounds 45%
Sodium iodide 9%
Potassium iodide 10%
Crude iodine 13%

*Source:* Data from the U.S. Geological Survey, *Mineral Commodity Summaries, 2009.* U.S. Government Printing Office, 2009.

reacted with chlorine to produce iodine. Another method uses an ion-exchange resin to collect the iodine after it has reacted with chlorine. The annual production of iodine is about 25,000 metric tons.

## USES OF IODINE

Iodine has a multitude of small-percentage usages. It is difficult to track percentages of iodine devoted to specific consumer end uses, because many intermediate iodine compounds—such as ethyl and methyl iodide, crude iodine, potassium iodide, sodium iodide, povidine-iodine, and ethylenediamine dihydroiodide—are marketed to manufacturers before end-use patterns can be established.

Iodine is used in catalysts for synthetic rubber manufacture, stabilizers, dyestuffs, pigments, sanitizers, pharmaceuticals, lithium-iodine batteries, high-purity metals, motor fuels, lubricants, and photographic chemicals for high-speed negatives (a declining use with the advent of digital cameras and other digital-imaging systems). An alcohol solution of iodine called tincture of iodine is a well-known antiseptic. A possible use may be in trifluoromethyl iodide ($CF_3I$) as a replacement for chlorofluorocarbons (CFCs) as refrigerants. The trifluoromethyl iodide does not cause the damage to the ozone layer that the CFCs do.

Radioactive iodine, either I-123 or I-131, can be used to treat thyroid disease, including cancer, or as a contrast agent in generating medical images, particularly of the thyroid. Iodine can also be used as a contrast agent in producing X rays of soft tissue such as the gallbladder. Uses of iodine will continue to develop, as it is a reactive element that forms compounds with every group of elements except the noble gases.

Global consumption for health and sanitation—to combat diseases caused by iodine deficiencies and to treat water, for example—is on the rise, as is the use of iodine in compounds designed to take the place of ozone-depleting CFCs.

*C. Alton Hassell*

FURTHER READING

Fernandez, Renate Lellep. *A Simple Matter of Salt: An Ethnography of Nutritional Deficiency in Spain.* Berkeley: University of California Press, 1990.

Greenwood, N. N., and A. Earnshaw. "The Halogens: Fluorine, Chlorine, Bromine, Iodine, and Astatine." In *Chemistry of the Elements.* 2d ed. Boston: Butterworth-Heinemann, 1997.

Hetzel, Basil S. *The Story of Iodine Deficiency: An International Challenge in Nutrition.* New York: Oxford University Press, 1989.

Kogel, Jessica Elzea, et al., eds. "Iodine." In *Industrial Minerals and Rocks: Commodities, Markets, and Uses.* 7th ed. Littleton, Colo.: Society for Mining, Metallurgy, and Exploration, 2006.

Massey, A. G. "Group 17: The Halogens: Fluorine, Chlorine, Bromine, Iodine, and Astatine." In *Main Group Chemistry.* 2d ed. New York: Wiley, 2000.

Mertz, Walter, ed. *Trace Elements in Human and Animal Nutrition.* 5th ed. 2 vols. Orlando, Fla.: Academic Press, 1986-1987.

WEB SITE

U.S. GEOLOGICAL SURVEY
Iodine: Statistics and Information
http://minerals.usgs.gov/minerals/pubs/
    commodity/iodine

SEE ALSO: Agricultural products; Lithium; Ozone layer and ozone hole debate; Rubber, synthetic.

# Iran

CATEGORIES: Countries; government and resources

*In 2007, Iran produced more than 4 million barrels per day (bbl/d) of crude oil (about 5.4 percent of global output) and 1.0 percent of the world's output of cement and fluorspar. Iran was also the fourth largest producer of natural gas in the world. The country exported 2.4 million bbl/d of oil, making it the world's fourth largest exporter of oil after Saudi Arabia, Russia, and Norway. In 2003, steel, aluminum, and refined copper were minor but noteworthy exports for Iran. In 2007, 2.9 million metric tons of agricultural products were exported.*

THE COUNTRY

Slightly larger than the state of Alaska, Iran is a theocratic Islamic republic located in the Middle East. It is bordered by the Gulf of Oman, the Persian Gulf, the Caspian Sea, and the nations of Afghanistan, Armenia, Azerbaijan, Iraq, Pakistan, Turkey, and Turkmenistan. Iran's terrain comprises a rugged, mountainous rim; a high, central basin with deserts; and small coastal plains. Iran had a gross domestic product (GDP) of $8.4 billion in 2008. Its economy was ranked seventeenth in the world by the International Monetary Fund in 2008, with a projected growth of 6.2 percent for 2009. The Central Bank of Iran (CBI) reported that for Iranian fiscal year 2007, industry contributed 45.3 percent and services contributed 43.7 percent to Iran's GDP.

Politically, the 2009 presidential elections in Iran pointed to the social turmoil in that nation, as thousands demonstrated against a perception of corruption in the vote count. Iran is home to a population dominated by younger persons, many of whom did not experience prerevolutionary secular society under Mohammad Reza Shah Pahlavi, who was ousted in 1979. A study in contrasts—with an autocratic, oligarchic, fundamentalist government ruling over a sophisticated, talented populace, many of whose younger members (through access to cell phones, the Internet, and higher education) are more globally oriented than their parents and whose women are beginning to militate against social repression—Iranian society is in flux, and its economy and resources could be expected to come under the influence of these conditions.

# Iran: Resources at a Glance

*Official name:* Islamic Republic of Iran
*Government:* Theocratic republic
*Capital city:* Tehran
*Area:* 636,418 mi$^2$; 1,648,195 km$^2$
*Population (2009 est.):* 66,429,284
*Language:* Persian
*Monetary unit:* Iranian rial (IRR)

## ECONOMIC SUMMARY:

*GDP composition by sector (2008 est.):* agriculture, 10.2%; industry, 41.9%; services, 47.8%
*Natural resources:* petroleum, natural gas, coal, chromium, copper, iron ore, lead, manganese, zinc, sulfur, fluorspar
*Land use (2005):* arable land, 9.78%; permanent crops, 1.29%; other, 88.93%
*Industries:* petroleum, petrochemicals, fertilizers, caustic soda, textiles, cement and other construction materials, food processing (particularly sugar refining and vegetable oil production), ferrous and nonferrous metal fabrication, armaments
*Agricultural products:* wheat, rice, other grains, sugar beets, sugarcane, fruits, nuts, cotton, dairy products, wool, caviar
*Exports (2008 est.):* $95.09 billion
*Commodities exported:* petroleum 80%, chemical and petrochemical products, fruits and nuts, carpets
*Imports (2008 est.):* $67.25 billion
*Commodities imported:* industrial raw materials and intermediate goods, capital goods, foodstuffs and other consumer goods, technical services
*Labor force (2008 est.):* 24.35 million (shortage of skilled labor)
*Labor force by occupation (2007):* agriculture, 25%; industry, 31%; services, 45%

## ENERGY RESOURCES:

*Electricity production (2006 est.):* 193 billion kWh
*Electricity consumption (2006 est.):* 145 billion kWh
*Electricity exports (2006 est.):* 2.775 billion kWh
*Electricity imports (2006 est.):* 2.54 billion kWh

*Natural gas production (2007 est.):* 111.9 billion m$^3$
*Natural gas consumption (2007 est.):* 111.8 billion m$^3$
*Natural gas exports (2007 est.):* 6.2 billion m$^3$
*Natural gas imports (2007 est.):* 6.1 billion m$^3$
*Natural gas proved reserves (Jan. 2008 est.):* 26.85 trillion m$^3$

*Oil production (2007 est.):* 4.7 million bbl/day
*Oil imports (2007):* 210,000 bbl/day
*Oil proved reserves (Jan. 2008 est.):* 136.2 billion bbl (based on Iranian claims)

*Source:* Data from *The World Factbook 2009.* Washington, D.C.: Central Intelligence Agency, 2009.
*Notes:* Data are the most recent tracked by the CIA. Values are given in U.S. dollars. Abbreviations: bbl/day = barrels per day; GDP = gross domestic product; km$^2$ = square kilometers; kWh = kilowatt-hours; m$^3$ = cubic meters; mi$^2$ = square miles.

## HYDROCARBONS

Oil, natural gas, and coal are composed of compounds containing both carbon and hydrogen—hence the term "hydrocarbons." Iran's hydrocarbon sector is overseen by its ministry of petroleum; the state-owned National Iranian Oil Company (NIOC) is responsible for oil and natural gas production and exploration. In 2007, hydrocarbons accounted for 82 percent of Iran's total exports, valued at $72.7 billion, an increase of more than 25 percent over 2006. Crude oil exports accounted for most of the hydrocarbon exports, and natural gas and refined petroleum made up the remainder. For most of 2008, Iran produced approximately 3.8 million bbl/d of crude oil. In March, 2009, Iran, along with other members of the Organization of Petroleum Exporting Countries (OPEC), cut its oil production quotas to bolster falling oil prices on the world market; Iran's production quota was lowered to 3.6 million bbl/d. Iran is OPEC's second largest producer and exporter of oil after Saudi Arabia. More than 60 percent of Iranian oil was exported in 2007.

Production and distribution of natural gas and oil, and the refining of crude oil, accounted for 10 percent of Iran's GDP. Of the hydrocarbon liquids produced by Iran, one-half of the crude oil was exported to China, India, and Japan; the remainder was consumed domestically. Most hydrocarbon-sector producers are required by Iranian law to satisfy domestic demand before exporting their output. As of 2009, Iran held proven oil reserves totaling 136.2 billion barrels and natural gas reserves of nearly 29 trillion cubic meters, the third and second largest proven stocks in the world, respectively. In 2007, Iran's production of natural gas totaled more than 111 trillion cubic meters, which equaled its domestic consumption.

Production of coal in Iran equaled domestic consumption, and there were no exports of coal in 2007-2008, although Iran planned to increase production of coal to 4.5 million metric tons in 2012 (up from 1.8 million metric tons in 2008). In 2006, primary energy production for Iran totaled 13.1 quadrillion British thermal units (Btu), while consumption totaled 7.7 quadrillion Btu, the latter comprising natural gas (53 percent), oil (44 percent), hydroelectric (2 percent), and coal (1 percent). Natural gas accounts for one-half of Iran's total domestic energy consumption; the other half is oil. Domestic demand for electricity was expected to grow by 7-9 percent.

Domestic demand for crude oil and natural gas is expected to increase, which may necessitate that Iran limit its hydrocarbon exports in order to meet domestic demand. Development of identified natural gas and oil resources was expected to continue, as was construction and renovation of oil refineries. These changes were subject to funding constraints and limitations imposed by the U.S. embargo on Iranian hydrocarbon goods and services because of Iran's nuclear development program. According to the U.S. Department of the Treasury's Office of Foreign Assets Control (OFAC), Americans may not trade, finance, or facilitate any goods, services, or technology to or from Iran that might benefit the Iranian oil industry. In 2009, U.S. president Barack Obama extended the U.S. sanctions against Iran for an additional year.

CRUDE OIL. While Iran produced 6 million bbl/d of crude oil in 1974, it has not been able to attain that level of production since the Islamic Revolution of 1979. The Iraq-Iran War (1980-1988), lack of foreign investors, economic sanctions, and the natural decline of mature oil fields have resulted in a production deficit of 400,000-700,000 bbl/d. According to the National Academy of Sciences, if this rate of decline continues, Iran's exports of oil could approach zero by 2015 unless measures are taken to restore the oil-producing infrastructure. Moreover, Iran has hoped to increase oil production to 5 million bbl/d provided it can secure foreign investments. In the past, Iran partnered with Venezuela and Russia. In 2007, Iran's oil exports reached 2.4 million bbl/d, with export revenues of $57 billion, accounting for one-third of the country's total revenues and 85 percent of its total earnings from exports. As of January, 2009, Iran had 10 percent of the world's total proven petroleum reserves, with the majority of crude oil reserves located in Khūzestān near the Iraqi border. In addition, Iran has an extensive domestic oil network, including five pipelines with many international projects under way. It has invested in its import capacity at the Caspian Sea port to handle increased product shipments from Russia and Azerbaijan and to enable crude oil swaps with its northern neighbors, Turkmenistan and Kazakhstan. Oil from the Caspian Sea in the north is consumed domestically, and an equal amount is produced for export through the Persian Gulf in the south. Iran has the largest oil tanker fleet in the Middle East.

GASOLINE. In 2007, Iran consumed 1.7 million bbl/d of oil and 400,000 bbl/d of gasoline. Because

Iran's production of refined oil products is sparse, it has to import most of its gasoline and spends $6 million a year on imports. In 2008, gasoline rationing decreased the need for imports by 40 percent. However, the National Iranian Oil Refining and Distribution Company (NIORDC) aims to raise production levels at Iran's oil refineries, while reducing the sulfur content of its diesel fuel. Iran's crude oil is of "medium" sulfur content; "high" sulfur content produces high levels of greenhouse-gas emissions, while "low" sulfur content is associated with lower emissions. The International Energy Agency (IEA) predicted a 5.3 percent growth in Iranian domestic demand for gasoline in 2009, with demand for other refined oil products

*A fuel-manufacturing plant in central Iran.* (AFP/Getty Images)

decreasing. The majority of Iran's motorists are permitted rations of 121 liters of gasoline per month, and gasoline costs about $1.44 per liter. However, the elimination of gasoline subsidies and the fruition of government-sponsored projects to increase production might transform Iran into a gasoline exporter.

NATURAL GAS. Colorless and odorless, natural gas is a typical mix of hydrocarbon gases, 70-90 percent methane ($CH_4$). Unlike other fossil fuels, natural gas burns "clean," emitting lower levels of greenhouse gases. Iran's extensive system of pipelines transports refined natural gas to domestic and international destinations. In 2007, 30 percent of Iran's natural gas output was used to enhance oil recovery through gas reinjection. Domestic production of natural gas equals domestic consumption, and both have rapidly increased: In 2007, production of natural gas totaled nearly 112 billion cubic meters. Domestic consumption of natural gas is heavily subsidized by the government. Despite Iran's plans to expand production of its most important energy project, the offshore South Pars natural gas field in the Persian Gulf, increasing domestic demand keeps natural gas exports at a minimum. Therefore, most of the South Pars output will be used to meet domestic needs and for production of liquefied natural gas (LNG), which is easier to transport and store than regular natural gas. Iran's LNG projects are second only to those of neighboring Qatar, with exports possibly reaching 1,462 billion cubic feet (Bcf). Even with the threat of economic sanctions by the United Nations, Iran had three LNG plants and gas pipelines to Armenia, Europe, Kuwait, and the United Arab Emirates either in the planning stage or under construction.

MINING AND METALS

Iran's Ministry of Industries and Mines oversees all mining, smelting, and refining industries, excepting the oil and gas sectors. In the 1970's, the Iran Geological Society began surveys to assess the value of Iranian mineral deposits and uncovered substantial reserves of iron ore, deposits of uranium, and other minerals in 1986. While most of Iran's active mines are privately owned, the government controls many of the larger commodity enterprises, especially those that produce aluminum, ammonia, coal, iron, and steel. In 2007, the Iranian government privatized a considerable percentage of its equity interests in enterprises that produce copper, steel, and aluminum. However, international funding for development of such projects was put aside because of the threat of U.N. sanctions related to Iran's nuclear development program, including the nuclear-fueled, electricity-generating reactor at Būshehr in western Iran.

In 2009, Iranian president Mahmoud Ahmadinejad inaugurated Iran's first nuclear fuel plan, while iterating the country's stance that its nuclear endeavors were solely for civilian purposes. That same year, Iran launched a rocket with a capability of reaching nearby countries. Iran has ample supplies of both uranium and fluorspar. Also in 2009, the International Atomic Energy Agency (IAEA) reported that Iran had increased its production of low-grade enriched uranium, raising its stockpile to 1,339 kilograms.

Copper (Cu), atomic number 29, is found mostly as ores of oxygen (O), iron (Fe), and sulfur (S). Copper's physical properties, abundance, and availability through low-cost bulk mining make the mineral a valued Iranian commodity. However, while Iranian copper deposits are among the world's largest, with reserves in Kermān Province in southeastern Iran, Iran is not one of the world's leading producers. Prior to the Iranian Revolution of 1979, Iran had planned to develop the copper industry in order to replace oil as a source of foreign exchange. However, the Iraq-Iran War and slumping copper prices discouraged development of the sector. Nonetheless, the Iranian government continued to promote private sector investment, which may have added to Iran's copper output in the 1980's. Iranian production of copper concentrate grew by 62.5 percent from 2002 to 2007. In 2007, the Iranian Mines and Mining Industries Development and Renovation Organization (IMIDRO) announced that Iran's copper mining industry had been mostly privatized, with output for the year standing at 200,000 metric tons. Iran expected to produce 250,000 metric tons of copper in the fiscal year ending in March, 2009, and to boost annual output by 64 percent through 2012.

Iron (Fe), atomic number 26, is a highly reactive, metallic element that oxidizes readily. Principle iron ores include hematite (70 percent iron), magnetite (72 percent iron), and taconite, which contains both magnetite and hematite. Chromite (ferrous chromic oxide, $FeCr_2O_4$), which also contains iron, is the only known ore of chromium, atomic number 24. Both iron ore and chromite are plentiful global resources. Iran has total chromite reserves of 18 to 27 million metric tons. From 2002 to 2007, chromite output in Iran decreased by 56 percent.

In 2007, IMIDRO reported that Iranian iron ore reserves and resources—mainly found at Chadormalu, near Gol-e-Gohar, and Sangan—totaled 1.2 billion metric tons. Iron ore production grew in Iran by about 37.5 percent from 2002 to 2007. Iranian iron ore and chromite are used mainly in the production of steel; from 2002 to 2006, Iranian production of steel, pig iron, ingots, and castings grew by 25 percent. By 2012, the predicted addition of 29 million metric tons per year of new crude steel capacity would increase Iran's total capacity fourfold to about 40 million metric tons per year. Because most of these crude steel "capacity" projects are to use electric arc furnaces, Iran's industrial demand for electricity is expected to increase.

AGRICULTURE

Beginning in 1979 commercial farming replaced subsistence farming as the major source of agricultural production. In 1997, the gross value of products in Iran's agricultural industry was an estimated $25 billion, and in 2003, almost 25 percent of Iran's exports (excluding oil and petrochemicals) were related to agricultural products and services. According to the CBI, Iran's exports of agricultural products had a total value of $3.2 billion in 2007. About 20 percent of Iran's land is arable, and one-third of Iran's arable land is irrigated via reservoirs and dams alongside rivers in the Alborz and Zagros mountains.

As of 2009, there were twenty-two thousand Iranian "food industries units." Iran's main food-producing areas are found near the Caspian Sea and the valleys of northwest Iran. Major agricultural exports include fruits (fresh and dried), spices, nuts, and processed food; fruits and nuts accounted for 2 percent of Iran's exports in 2008. Iran is the world's largest producer of saffron and pistachio nuts. Iran's livestock products include lamb, goat meat, beef, poultry and eggs, and dairy as well as wool and leather.

According to the CBI, Iran's agriculture sector (excluding wheat) greatly improved in 2008. Agricultural production totaled 98 million metric tons, 20 percent higher than in 2007, employing 33.3 percent of the labor force. Over a three-year period ending in 2007, the agricultural, horticultural, and livestock-processing sectors showed increasingly positive gains despite a severe drought in Iran throughout 2007. The value added in the agriculture sector increased to 6.2 percent, 1.5 percent higher than in 2006. During the same period, total agricultural and horticultural production reached 81.6 million metric tons, a 3.6 percent rise, while livestock, poultry, and dairy output increased by 7 percent. Livestock production increased to 10.2 million metric tons during 2007. While agricultural programs aimed at modernization have raised the production levels, problems remain; these include poor weather conditions, outdated equipment and farming techniques, and shortages of viable seed and water. Moreover, the combined burdens of government subsidies and price controls in the food sector remain burdensome to Iran's economy.

Wheat, Iran's most important crop, is grown mainly in the western and northwestern regions of the country. From 1999 to 2004, wheat imports in the Middle East began to contract, especially in Iran. In 2007, Iran was self-sufficient in wheat production and became a net exporter of wheat for the first time. However, this gain was short-lived after poor weather conditions in the second half of 2008 damaged Iran's wheat crop, resulting in the need to import a minimum of 1.8 million metric tons of wheat, increasing Iran's budget deficit. Acording to the U.N. Food and Agriculture Organization (FAO), Iran had to lower its wheat production forecasts from (13.6 to 11) metric tons and significantly reduce its wheat exports. In the past, Kazakhstan was able to meet Iran's demand for wheat, but it too had problems with its wheat crop in 2008, and Iran had to rely on wheat exporters such as the European Union, Canada, Australia, and the United States. Despite U.S. trade sanctions, in early 2009, Iran spent $96 million on imports from the United States—including wheat, soybeans, and medical supplies. Previously, rice, the major crop cultivated in the Caspian Sea region, did not meet domestic needs and resulted in substantial imports. In 2008, Iran imported 19 percent of its foodstuffs and other consumer goods.

*Cynthia F. Racer*

FURTHER READING

Axworthy, Michael. *A History of Iran: Empire of the Mind.* New York: Basic Books, 2008.

Hyne, Norman J. *Nontechnical Guide to Petroleum Geology, Exploration, Drilling, and Production.* 2d ed. Tulsa, Okla.: PennWell Books, 2001.

Louër, L. *Transnational Shia Politics: Religious and Political Networks in the Gulf.* New York: Columbia University Press, 2008.

Sagar, Abbuj D. "Wealth, Responsibility, and Equity: Exploring an Allocation Framework for Global GHG Emissions." *Climatic Change* 45, nos. 3/4 (June, 2000): 511-527.

SEE ALSO: Agricultural products; Agriculture industry; Copper; Iron; Nuclear energy; Oil and natural gas reservoirs; Organization of Arab Petroleum Exporting Countries; Steel.

# Iron

CATEGORY: Mineral and other nonliving resources

WHERE FOUND

Iron is one of the most abundant metals in the world, constituting 35 percent of the entire planet and 5 percent of the Earth's crust. It combines with other elements in hundreds of minerals, the most important of which are hematite and magnetite. Australia, Brazil, China, India, and Russia have been the top five producers of iron ore.

PRIMARY USES

Iron and its principal alloy, steel, are widely used in tools, machines, and structures. Historically, discoveries and inventions involving the many uses of iron have been crucially important. Iron is also essential to biological metabolism.

TECHNICAL DEFINITION

Iron is a chemical element (symbol Fe, from the Latin *ferrum*) and a metal of the transition Group VIII on the periodic table. Its atomic number is 26 and its atomic weight 55.487. Iron's melting point is 1,535° Celsius, its boiling point 3,000° Celsius, and its density 7.86 grams per cubic centimeter.

DESCRIPTION, DISTRIBUTION, AND FORMS

Iron is the cheapest and most widely used metal in the world. It is used in three main products: wrought iron, steel, and cast iron. Although each is approximately 95 percent iron and is produced with the same fuel, each has vastly different properties, arising from different production methods. Wrought iron, containing negligible amounts of carbon, has a melting point so high that it was not achieved by humans until the nineteenth century. When hot, wrought iron can be forged and welded, and even when it is cold it is ductile—capable of being shaped and hammered. Steel contains 0.25 to 1.25 percent carbon, with a lower melting point than wrought iron. It can be forged when hot and is extremely hard when quenched (cooled quickly by plunging into water or another cooling medium). Cast iron, with approximately 2 to 4.5 percent carbon, is easily melted and poured into molds. When cool it is soft and easily machined, but it is brittle and does not withstand tension forces well.

The principal iron ores are hematite, magnetite, limonite, pyrite, siderite, and taconite. Hematite and magnetite are the richest and most common ores. They are known as iron oxides because they are compounds of iron and oxygen.

Hematite ($Fe_2O_3$) can contain as much as 70 percent iron but usually contains closer to 25 percent. Significant deposits are found near Lake Superior, and in Alabama, Australia, Belgium, and Sweden. It may appear in colors ranging from black to dark red and may occur as shiny crystals, grains of rock, or loose particles.

Magnetite ($Fe_3O_4$) is a black magnetic material often called black sand. Limonite ($2Fe_2O_3 3H_2O$), or brown hematite, is a hydrated variety of hematite; it is also called bog-iron ore. It can contain as much as 60 percent iron ore and is yellowish to brown in color. It is found in Australia, France, Germany, the former Soviet Union, Spain, and the United States.

Pyrite ($FeS_2$), also called fool's gold because of its shiny yellowish surface, is about half sulfur. Siderite ($FeCO_3$) is a gray-brown carbonate ore that was once found in large deposits in Great Britain and Germany. Taconite is a hard rock that contains specks or bands of either hematite or magnetite.

## HISTORY

Iron was probably discovered accidentally in the late Bronze Age when it was found in the ashes of fires that had been built on top of red iron ore. Artifacts of iron weapons and tools have been found in Egypt (including the Great Pyramid of Giza) dating to 2900 B.C.E. Iron has probably been made on a regular basis since at least 1000 B.C.E. The Chinese had independently developed their own furnaces and techniques for producing cast iron by the sixth century B.C.E. The Romans acquired ironworking technology from the Greeks and spread it throughout northern Europe. Because iron ore was readily available throughout the Near East and Europe, iron was less expensive than copper and bronze, the "metals of aristocracy." As a result, it was used to make many everyday tools and utensils, earning its later nickname, "the democratic metal."

Through the Middle Ages, the common method of producing iron was the bloomery method. A bloomery may have been as simple as a circular hollow in the ground, several meters deep and several meters across. The iron ore was heated in a bed of burning charcoal within this hollow, often with the use of bellows to increase the fire's temperature. As the heat reached about 800° Celsius (normally the highest temperature attainable in early bloomeries), the oxygen in the ore separated from the iron and combined with carbon to form slag. The iron changed to a pasty mass called the "bloom." The operator removed the bloom when he judged it was ready and alternately hammered and reheated it to remove the slag and to consolidate the iron. The final product was wrought iron, produced at temperatures below iron's melting point, a process referred to as the "direct" method. Sometimes the iron would accidentally melt in the bloomery; this was undesirable, because prolonged exposure allowed the iron to absorb carbon from the charcoal, creating cast iron. Because of its lack of ductility and low resistance to abrasion, cast iron was unsuitable for working into tools and weapons and was therefore considered worthless.

### Iron and Steel: World Production, 2008

| NATION | PIG IRON | RAW STEEL |
|---|---|---|
| Brazil | 37,000,000 | 36,000,000 |
| China | 478,000,000 | 513,000,000 |
| France | 12,000,000 | 19,000,000 |
| Germany | 30,000,000 | 48,000,000 |
| Italy | 11,000,000 | 32,000,000 |
| Japan | 88,000,000 | 123,000,000 |
| Russia | 52,000,000 | 74,000,000 |
| South Korea | 31,000,000 | 55,000,000 |
| Ukraine | 34,000,000 | 40,000,000 |
| United Kingdom | 11,000,000 | 14,000,000 |
| United States | 36,000,000 | 94,000,000 |
| Other countries | 138,000,000 | 312,000,000 |

Source: Data from the U.S. Geological Survey, Mineral Commodity Summaries, 2009. U.S. Government Printing Office, 2009.

The major limitation of the bloomery was its low volume of output per unit of labor. Even when bloomery technology had fully matured, a large bloom might weigh only 90 kilograms, and the annual output of that bloomery would probably have been less than 20 metric tons of wrought iron. In an effort to increase output, the blast furnace was developed (by building up the walls of the bloomery, according to some sources). This new technology was so successful that by the middle of the sixteenth century the blast furnace had replaced the bloomery as the prevalent method of iron production.

Early blast furnaces stood about 4.5 meters high, later reaching 10 meters or more. (The use of coke—made by heating coal in an airtight container to drive out gases and tar—as a fuel, beginning in the early 1700's, allowed taller furnaces, since it did not crush as easily as charcoal and could be stacked higher.) The interior cavity widened as it descended from the top opening for about two-thirds of the furnace's height. At that point the cavity began to narrow, culminating in a chamber at the very bottom of the furnace, called the crucible.

The structure of the furnace created a chimney effect, drafting air through it to accelerate combustion; waterwheel-powered bellows usually supplemented the draft. The ore, charcoal, and limestone (a flux) were dumped into the blast furnace from above. As the ore melted and the level of raw materials dropped, more would be added on top of them. In this way, it was possible to keep a furnace in continuous operation for months at a time. As the ore slowly worked its way toward the crucible, it was exposed for a prolonged period to heat, which melted it (at about 1,400° Celsius), and carbon, which it absorbed. The molten iron collected in the crucible, and the slag, floating on top of the iron, was pulled off through side openings. The end product was a large volume of molten iron with a high carbon content—cast iron.

The molten iron could be tapped directly from the crucible. Some of it would be poured into oblong molds pressed into damp sand. These molds were usually laid out with several smaller molds attached at right angles to the largest mold, reminding the ironworkers of a sow and suckling pigs—hence the term "pig iron." The pig iron would later be converted to wrought iron at a forge. The molten iron might also have been cast directly into molds for stove and fireplace parts, pots and pans, cannons, cannon balls, and many other products. In the nineteenth century,

cast iron was also used for machine parts, railroad tracks, and structural elements. By that time cast iron had found many uses, and the demand for iron products increased dramatically.

A blast furnace could produce, typically, 180 metric tons of iron per year—a tenfold increase over the bloomeries. In producing a larger output for less labor, however, a trade-off was necessary: the addition of another step in the process. To create wrought iron—the most desirable iron product until the late nineteenth century—from the cast iron coming from the blast furnace, the carbon had to be removed. This was done in a refinery hearth in which the bloom was heated indirectly without coming in contact with the fuel. In this way, the carbon already present burned off, and no additional carbon was absorbed from the fuel. Despite this added step, the blast furnace produced a much larger volume of iron, and for less labor, than previous methods had. As a result, the development of the blast furnace was the key to making iron products much more common beginning in the fifteenth century.

Even with the blast furnace, the production of good wrought iron was limited by the use of coke. Coke introduced more impurities to the cast iron than charcoal had, making it more difficult to produce high-quality wrought iron. In 1784, an Englishman, Henry Cort, devised a new process to address this problem. Known as the "puddling process," it began by heating the pig iron in a coke-fired reverberatory furnace (one in which the heat was reflected off the roof of the furnace in order to keep the iron from coming in contact with the coke). Workers stirred the molten metal to expose more of it to the air, thus burning off carbon. As the carbon content decreased, the melting temperature increased, and the metal gradually stiffened, separating it from the more liquid slag. When the process was complete, workers gathered the low-carbon iron in a "puddle ball" and shaped it in a rolling mill. Thanks to Cort's puddling process, wrought iron became an important factor in the Industrial Revolution. Its dominance of the iron market lasted until the 1860's, when steel production began on a large scale via the Bessemer process.

OBTAINING IRON ORE

An ore's quality for commercial purposes depends on several factors. While a pure ore may contain as much as 70 percent iron, ores are seldom found in their pure state. It is more realistic to expect a 50 to 60 per-

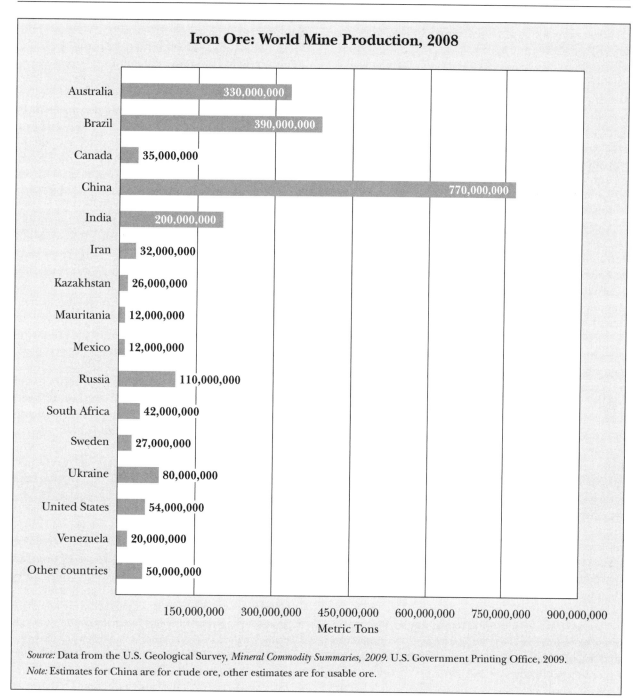

**Iron Ore: World Mine Production, 2008**

| Country | Metric Tons |
|---|---|
| Australia | 330,000,000 |
| Brazil | 390,000,000 |
| Canada | 35,000,000 |
| China | 770,000,000 |
| India | 200,000,000 |
| Iran | 32,000,000 |
| Kazakhstan | 26,000,000 |
| Mauritania | 12,000,000 |
| Mexico | 12,000,000 |
| Russia | 110,000,000 |
| South Africa | 42,000,000 |
| Sweden | 27,000,000 |
| Ukraine | 80,000,000 |
| United States | 54,000,000 |
| Venezuela | 20,000,000 |
| Other countries | 50,000,000 |

*Source:* Data from the U.S. Geological Survey, *Mineral Commodity Summaries, 2009.* U.S. Government Printing Office, 2009.
*Note:* Estimates for China are for crude ore, other estimates are for usable ore.

cent iron content. At less than 30 percent, an ore is probably uneconomical. Other factors in determining an ore's quality include the amount of constituents such as silicon and phosphorus in the ore, the geographical location of the ore, and the ease with which it can be extracted and processed.

In prehistoric times iron ore was probably gathered from meteorites, high-grade outcroppings, and other sources that required little or no work to extract. As the demand increased and those sources were exhausted, mining techniques had to be developed to extract iron ore from the Earth.

Most iron ore is obtained either by the open-pit mining process or by hard-rock shaft mining. Open-pit mining is employed when the ore is lying near the surface. Large machinery removes the overlying soil and rocks (called overburden) to expose the ore. It is then broken up with explosives and loaded onto a transportation system (usually large earth-moving trucks) by huge power shovels. As the process continues, the equipment digs deep into the Earth, creating a large pit often several square kilometers in area and 150 meters or more deep. Most of the world's iron ore is mined in this way.

Ore that lies deep below the surface is removed via the more traditional hard-rock shaft mining. A shaft is sunk near the deposit from which tunnels and additional shafts branch out into the deposit. Shaft mining is much more expensive and dangerous than open-pit mining and is normally used only for very high-grade ore that cannot be reached in any other way.

All ores must be processed before being sent to the blast furnace; the ore's quality and iron content determine the degree and type of processing needed. At a minimum, ore must be crushed, screened, and washed prior to reducing in a blast furnace.

In the screening process, ore is separated into lumps that are large enough to be put into the blast furnace (7 to 25 millimeters across) and smaller particles called fines. Fines are not suitable for use in a blast furnace because the particles will pack together and hinder the efficient flow of hot gases. To correct this, a process called sintering is used to make larger particles out of the fines. Sintering begins by moistening the fines to make particles stick together. Coke is then added to the mixture. After passing under burners, the coke ignites, heating the fines until they fuse into larger particles suitable for use in the blast furnace.

As the best ore deposits become exhausted (or become uneconomical to mine because of their inaccessibility), methods of upgrading low-quality ore become necessary. Collectively, these processes are known as beneficiation. The first step in beneficiation is to concentrate the ore by one of several techniques. The general objective is to concentrate the iron and remove the silica. Most techniques rely on the difference between the density of iron and that of the surrounding rock to separate the two materials. Ore might be leached and dried, pulverized and floated in a mixture of oil, agglomerated into larger particles, or separated magnetically. Concentrating the ore by these

techniques reduces both the shipping costs and the amount of waste at the blast furnace plant.

After beneficiation, the concentrated ore is a very fine powder that would not work properly in a blast furnace. Since the concentrate is too small even for sintering, the pelletizing process is used. In pelletizing, the concentrate is moistened and tumbled in a drum or on an inclined disk, and the resulting balls of ore are fired to a temperature of about 1,300° Celsius to dry and harden them. These pellets are usually about 10 to 15 millimeters across and are then ready for the blast furnace.

Although the exact chemical processes have been fully understood beginning only during the twentieth century, the goal of iron making has always been to release oxygen from its chemical bond with iron. The blast furnace is the most efficient and common way to do this. Modern blast furnaces work on the same principles as those developed in the fifteenth century, but they are larger and have benefited from centuries of refinement to the design, materials, and process. A modern blast furnace may be as much as 30 meters tall and 10 meters in diameter. Because of improvements in materials, a blast furnace may stay in continuous operation for two years, requiring maintenance only when its brick lining wears out. Some of the most important advances involve the use of mathematical modeling and supercomputers to provide more accurate and timely control over the process. The output of a modern furnace may exceed 10 million kilograms per day.

A modern blast furnace has five readily identifiable sections; from the top down they are: throat, stack, barrel, bosh, and hearth (or crucible). The ore, coke, and limestone (collectively called the charge) enter the furnace through the throat. The distribution and timing of the charge is carefully monitored at all times to ensure proper operation. The throat opens onto the stack, which resembles a cone with the top cut off. The stack widens as it descends because the temperature of the charge increases as it works its way down the furnace, causing the charge to expand. The next section, the barrel, is a short, straight section that connects the stack to the bosh, a shorter, upside-down version of the stack. The bosh narrows as it descends because the iron is beginning to liquefy and compact by the time the charge reaches the bosh. At the bottom of the bosh are nozzles called tuyeres through which blast air is blown into the furnace. The air coming through the tuyeres has been preheated to about 1,000° Celsius or higher, and oxygen is sometimes added to it. This hot air causes the coke in the charge to burn. The oxygen in the air combines with carbon from the coke to create carbon monoxide gas, which in turn removes the oxygen from the ore. The burning coke also produces temperatures up to 3,000° Celsius to melt the iron. The liquid metal collects in the bottom section, called the hearth or crucible. Just as in earlier furnaces, the slag floats on the molten iron, and workers periodically pull it off through openings in the side of the furnace.

Several direct reduction processes (in which the temperature never exceeds iron's melting point) were developed in the twentieth century but are used only in special circumstances. The basic process relies on hot gases to reduce the iron ore in a way roughly analogous to the process of the earlier bloomeries. Since the iron is never completely melted, slag never forms, and the final product contains impurities that must be removed during the steelmaking process. Direct reduction furnaces can be built more quickly and cheaply than blast furnaces, and they produce less pollution. The disadvantages are that they require a supply of cheap natural gas and the iron ore must be processed to a very high grade.

USES OF IRON ORE

The vast majority of iron produced in blast furnaces is converted to steel. The remainder is cast as pig iron and later converted to either cast iron or wrought iron. At a foundry, the pig iron is melted to a liquid state in a cupola (a small version of a blast furnace) and then cast in molds (some of them are still made with damp sand) to make machine parts, pipes, engine blocks, and thousands of other items. Wrought iron is now made in limited quantities. Its production begins by melting pig iron and removing impurities. The molten iron is then poured over a silicate slag and formed into blooms which can then be shaped into products.

Iron is used in a vast range of special-purpose alloys developed for commercial applications. The major classifications of these alloys are discussed below only in broad outline; within each grouping there remains an enormous variety because of the wide range of special needs.

Magnetic alloys are either retentive (hard) or nonretentive (soft) of magnetism. The hard alloys remain magnetized after the application of a magnetic field, thus creating a permanent mag-

net. One family of hard alloys contains cobalt and molybdenum (less than 20 percent of each), while another contains aluminum, nickel, cobalt, copper, and titanium. Once magnetized they are used in such applications as speaker magnets, electrical meters, and switchboard instruments because of the constancy of their magnetic field and their resistance to demagnetization. The soft alloys also fall into two families: those with nickel and those with aluminum. The nickel alloys are used in communications and electric power equipment, while those containing aluminum are used to carry alternating current.

High-temperature alloys, used in high-temperature environments such as turbine blades in gas turbines and superchargers, are generally referred to as either iron-based, cobalt-based, or nickel-based. They are formulated to retain their chemical identity, physical identity, and the strength required to perform their intended function, all at extreme, high temperatures.

The most common electrical-resistance alloys are best known as heating elements in toasters, radiant

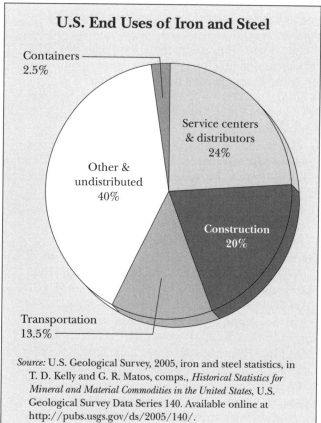

**U.S. End Uses of Iron and Steel**

Containers 2.5%

Service centers & distributors 24%

Other & undistributed 40%

Construction 20%

Transportation 13.5%

*Source:* U.S. Geological Survey, 2005, iron and steel statistics, in T. D. Kelly and G. R. Matos, comps., *Historical Statistics for Mineral and Material Commodities in the United States*, U.S. Geological Survey Data Series 140. Available online at http://pubs.usgs.gov/ds/2005/140/.

heaters, water heaters, and so on. They usually contain nickel (as much as 60 percent), chromium (approximately 20 percent), and sometimes aluminum (approximately 5 percent). Alloys without the nickel have higher resistivity and lower density and are used in potentiometers, rheostats, and similar applications.

Corrosion-resistant alloys are designed to resist corrosion from liquids and gases other than air or oxygen and usually contain varying amounts of nickel and chromium along with combinations of molybdenum, copper, cobalt, tungsten, and silicon. No one alloy is capable of resisting the effects of all corrosive agents, so each is tailored to its intended purpose.

The powdered iron technique employs iron that has been finely ground and mixed with metals or nonmetals to form the desired alloys. After a binder is added, the mixture is pressed to the desired shape in a mold. This process has the advantages of precise control over the makeup of the alloy and the ability to form iron pieces to precise dimensions with little or no working required afterward.

Iron is important to almost every organism and is used in a variety of ways. It is involved in oxygen transport, electron transfer, oxidation reactions, and reduction reactions. Iron is a constituent of human blood. Some iron compounds have medical uses, such as stimulating the appetite, treating anemia, coagulating blood, and stimulating healing.

*Brian J. Nichelson*

FURTHER READING

Dennis, W. H. *Foundations of Iron and Steel Metallurgy.* New York: Elsevier, 1967.

Gordon, Robert B. *American Iron, 1607-1900.* Baltimore: Johns Hopkins University Press, 1996.

Greenwood, N. N., and A. Earnshaw. "Iron, Ruthenium, and Osmium." In *Chemistry of the Elements.* 2d ed. Boston: Butterworth-Heinemann, 1997.

Harris, J. R. *The British Iron Industry, 1700-1850.* Basingstoke, England: Macmillan Education, 1988.

Hillstrom, Kevin, and Laurie Collier Hillstrom, eds. *Iron and Steel.* Vol. 1 in *The Industrial Revolution in America.* Santa Barbara, Calif.: ABC-CLIO, 2005.

Krebs, Robert E. *The History and Use of Our Earth's Chemical Elements: A Reference Guide.* Illustrations by Rae Déjur. 2d ed. Westport, Conn.: Greenwood Press, 2006.

Lewis, W. David. *Sloss Furnaces and the Rise of the Birmingham District: An Industrial Epic.* Tuscaloosa: University of Alabama Press, 1994.

Moniz, B. J. *Metallurgy.* 4th ed. Homewood, Ill.: American Technical Publishers, 2007.

WEB SITES

NATURAL RESOURCES CANADA
Canadian Minerals Yearbook, Mineral and Metal Commodity Reviews
http://www.nrcan-rncan.gc.ca/mms-smm/busi-indu/cmy-amc/com-eng.htm

U.S. GEOLOGICAL SURVEY
Iron and Steel: Statistics and Information
http://minerals.usgs.gov/minerals/pubs/commodity/iron_&_steel

U.S. GEOLOGICAL SURVEY
Iron and Steel Scrap: Statistics and Information
http://minerals.usgs.gov/minerals/pubs/commodity/iron_&_steel_scrap

U.S. GEOLOGICAL SURVEY
Iron and Steel Slag: Statistics and Information
http://minerals.usgs.gov/minerals/pubs/commodity/iron_&_steel_slag/index.html#mcs

U.S. GEOLOGICAL SURVEY
Iron Ore: Statistics and Information
http://minerals.usgs.gov/minerals/pubs/commodity/iron_ore

SEE ALSO: Alloys; Australia; Belgium; Bessemer process; Brazil; China; Coal; France; Germany; India; Industrial Revolution and industrialization; Metals and metallurgy; Mineral resource use, early history of; Open-pit mining; Russia; Steel; Steel industry; United States.

# Irrigation

CATEGORY: Obtaining and using resources

*Because agriculture is basic to human existence, irrigation has been practiced since prehistoric times. Essentially, irrigation is the application of water to soil to overcome soil moisture deficiency so that crops can have adequate water supply for optimal food production. Irrigation is essential to sustained large-scale food production.*

*An example of a field irrigation machine.* (©Edward Homan/Dreamstime.com)

## BACKGROUND

Irrigation systems were important to many ancient civilizations. They were the basis of life in the ancient civilizations of Egypt, India, China, and Mesopotamia (modern day Iraq). Some irrigation works in the Nile Valley that date back to around 3000 B.C.E. still play an important role in Egyptian agriculture. In the United States, the first irrigation systems were developed by American Indians, and traces of ancient water distribution systems, made up of canals, were still visible at the beginning of the twenty-first century.

## SCOPE AND LAND REQUIREMENTS

In 1977, the Food and Agriculture Organization (FAO) of the United Nations estimated that the total global land area under irrigation was 223 million hectares. By 2000, about 270 million hectares were irrigated worldwide. In the United States, more than 20 million hectares are irrigated for crop production. Some form of irrigation is practiced in every country in the world. Although irrigation results in increased food production, it is extremely water intensive. For example, to grow 1 metric ton of grain (adequate for 50 percent of an average person's supply for five years

and six months) requires as much as 1,700 cubic kilometers of water per person per year. In the United States, 40 percent of total freshwater withdrawals is for irrigation. The value of irrigation is that it greatly increases agricultural productivity. For example, in 1979, the FAO reported that although irrigated agriculture represented only about 13 percent of global arable land (agricultural land that, when properly prepared for agriculture, will produce enough crops to be economically efficient), the value of crop production from irrigated land was 34 percent of the global total production.

For irrigation to be economically viable, the land in consideration must be able to produce enough crops to justify the investment in irrigation works. The land must be arable and irrigable; that is, sufficient water for irrigation must exist. Soil suitable for irrigation farming has the following attributes. The soil must have a reasonably high water-holding capacity and be readily penetrable by water; the rate of infiltration (percolation) should be low enough to avoid excessive loss of water through deep percolation beyond the root zone of the crops. The soil must also be deep enough to allow root development and permit drainage of the soil, and it must be free of harmful (toxic) salts and chemicals—especially those that tend to bond to soil and reach dangerously high concentrations. Finally, it must have an adequate supply of plant nutrients.

Land slopes should permit irrigation without excessive runoff accompanied by high erosion rates. The land should be located in an area where irrigation is feasible without excessive pumping or conveyance costs. Generally, the land should permit the planting of more than one type of crop so that the investment in irrigation works can be utilized year-round, and ideally should allow the flexibility of planting more economically viable crop types should economic conditions dictate such changes.

## TYPES OF IRRIGATION SYSTEMS

Generally, irrigation systems can be classified as non-pressurized systems (also known as gravity or surface systems) and pressurized systems. Historically, non-pressurized systems, in which water was flooded onto the soil surface via open channels, were the first to be constructed. In fact, nonpressurized systems preceded pressurized ones by thousands of years. Nonpressurized systems include canals, open channels, and pipes that are not flowing full. Pressurized systems include all types of sprinkler systems and low-pressure nozzle systems.

There are five basic methods of implementing irrigation systems: flooding, furrow irrigation, subirrigation, trickle irrigation, and sprinkling. Several subcategories exist within these five basic categories. Flooding systems include wild flooding, controlled flooding, check flooding, and basin flooding applications. In all cases the irrigated area is flooded with water. The degree to which flooding is controlled or administered differentiates the types of flooding. For example, in wild flooding there is not much control or preparation of the irrigated land. In contrast, check flooding is accomplished by admitting water into relatively level plots surrounded by levees. In check flooding the check (area surrounded by levees) is filled with water at a fairly rapid rate and the water is allowed to infiltrate into the soil.

Furrow irrigation is used for row crops—hence the name (a furrow is a narrow ditch between rows of plants). In this method evaporation losses are minimized and only about 20 to 50 percent of the area is wetted during irrigation, in contrast to flooding irrigation. In sprinkler application water is sprinkled on the irrigated land. The sprinkling is possible because the water is delivered under pressure. Sprinkler systems provide a means for irrigation in areas where the topography does not permit irrigation by surface methods.

Subirrigation methods are useful in areas where there is permeable soil in the root zone and a high water table. In this method irrigation water is applied below the ground surface to keep the water table high enough so that water from the capillary fringe is available to crops. Subirrigation has the advantages of minimizing evaporation loss and requiring minimal field preparation. In trickle (or drip) irrigation a plastic pipe with perforations is laid along the ground at the base of a row of crops. The water issuing from the perforations is designed to trickle. Excellent control is achieved, and evaporation and deep percolation are minimized.

*Emmanuel U. Nzewi*

FURTHER READING

Albiac, Jose, and Ariel Dinar, eds. *The Management of Water Quality and Irrigation Technologies.* Sterling, Va.: Earthscan, 2009.

Cuenca, Richard H. *Irrigation System Design: An Engineering Approach.* Englewood Cliffs, N.J.: Prentice Hall, 1989.

Heng, L. K., P. Moutonnet, and M. Smith. *Review of World Water Resources by Country.* Rome: Food and Agriculture Organization of the United Nations, 2003.

Linsley, Ray K., et al. *Water Resources Engineering.* 4th ed. New York: McGraw-Hill, 1992.

Morgan, Robert M. *Water and the Land: A History of American Irrigation.* Fairfax, Va.: The Irrigation Association, 1993.

Postel, Sandra. *Pillar of Sand: Can the Irrigation Miracle Last?* New York: W. W. Norton, 1999.

Shortle, James S., and Ronald C. Griffin, eds. *Irrigated Agriculture and the Environment.* Northampton, Mass.: Edward Elgar, 2001.

Zimmerman, Josef D. *Irrigation.* New York: Wiley, 1966.

WEB SITE

U.S. GEOLOGICAL SURVEY
Irrigation Water Use
http://ga.water.usgs.gov/edu/wuir.html

SEE ALSO: Dams; Hydrology and the hydrologic cycle; Streams and rivers; Water; Water rights; Water supply systems.

# Isotopes, radioactive

CATEGORY: Mineral and other nonliving resources

## WHERE FOUND

All the known elements have at least one radioactive isotope, either natural or artificially produced. Therefore, the radionuclides are found in the Earth's crust, in its surface waters, and in the atmosphere.

## PRIMARY USES

Radioisotopes are used in many areas of science and industry as tracers or as radiation sources. They provide fuel for the nuclear generation of electricity and have found both diagnostic and therapeutic uses in medicine.

## TECHNICAL DEFINITION

Radioactive isotopes are unstable nuclides that decay ultimately to stable nuclides by emission of alpha, beta, gamma, or proton radiation, by K capture, or by nuclear fission.

## DESCRIPTION, DISTRIBUTION, AND FORMS

Alpha, beta, and gamma radiation are the three types of naturally occurring radioactivity; they result in the transmutation of one chemical nucleus to another. Alpha decay is the ejection from the nucleus of a particle equivalent in size to a helium nucleus. The daughter nucleus has an atomic number (Z) two less than that of the parent and a mass number (A) four less than the parent. The equation below represents the emission of an alpha particle from a polonium nucleus to produce an isotope of lead (a gamma ray is also emitted in rare cases).

$$ {}^{210}_{84}\text{Po} \rightarrow {}^{206}_{82}\text{Pb} + {}^{4}_{2}\text{He} + \gamma $$

Beta decay results from the change within the nucleus of a neutron into a proton. Z increases by one, while A is unchanged. The equation below illustrates beta emission by phosphorus to become sulfur.

$$ {}^{32}_{15}\text{P} \rightarrow \beta^- + {}^{32}_{16}\text{S} $$

In gamma decay, electromagnetic radiation is emitted as a nucleus drops to lower states from excited states. It is the nuclear equivalent of atomic line spectra that show wavelengths of visible light emitted by atoms when electrons drop from higher to lower energy levels. Nuclear fission is an extremely important process by which isotopes of the heavy elements such as uranium 235 capture a neutron and then split into fragments.

$$ {}^{235}_{92}\text{U} + {}^{1}\text{n} \rightarrow {}^{140}_{56}\text{Ba} + {}^{94}_{36}\text{Kr} + 2 \text{ neutrons} $$

The neutrons produced are captured by other nuclei, which in turn fission, producing a chain reaction. This is the process that resulted in the first atomic bomb and is now used in nuclear plants to produce electric power.

## HISTORY

The story of radioactivity begins with Wilhelm Conrad Röntgen's work with cathode-ray tubes. Roentgen allowed cathode rays to impinge on various metal surfaces and observed that highly penetrating radiations, which he called X rays, were produced. He noted similarities between the X rays and sunlight in that both could expose a photographic plate and could cause certain metals and salts to fluoresce.

This fluorescence was of interest to Antoine-Henri Becquerel, who discovered by accident that crystals of uranium salt left on a photographic plate in a drawer produced an intense silhouette of the crystals. Although his understanding of the phenomenon was limited at the time, what Becquerel had observed was the effect of uranium radioactivity.

Marie and Pierre Curie pursued the study of this phenomenon with other minerals. They worked to isolate and characterize the substances responsible and were able to isolate and purify samples of polonium and radium. Other scientists worked at the same time to characterize the radiations emitted. In 1903, Ernest Rutherford and Frederick Soddy proposed that the radiations were associated with the chemical changes that radiation produced, and they characterized three types of radiation: alpha ($\alpha$), beta ($\beta$), and gamma ($\gamma$) rays.

## OBTAINING RADIOISOTOPES

The use of nuclear fission to produce energy is based on a principle formulated by Albert Einstein, $E = mc^2$. $E$ is energy, $m$ refers to mass, and $c$ is a constant equal to $3.0 \times 10^8$ $m/c$. The complete conversion of one gram of matter per second would produce energy at the rate of nine trillion watts.

The main particles contained in the nucleus of an atom are protons and neutrons. The mass of a given nucleus is less than the sum of the masses of the constituent protons and neutrons. This mass defect has been converted, according to the equation above, to energy (binding energy) in the process of forming the nucleus. The separation of the nucleus into its constituent particles would require replacement of this energy. The binding energy per nucleon is a measure of the stability of a particular nucleus. Those nuclei having mass numbers between 60 and 80 have the highest binding energy per nucleon and are therefore the most stable. A large nucleus such as uranium can split into fragments with sizes in the 60 to 80 mass range. When this happens, the excess binding energy is released.

## USES OF RADIOISOTOPES

Radioisotopes are used in a number of ways in the fields of chemistry and biology. Radioimmunoassay (RIA) is a type of isotopic dilution study in which labeled and unlabeled analytes compete for limited amounts of a molecule that binds the analyte very specifically. RIA is used worldwide in the determination of hormones, drugs, and viruses. The technique is so specific that concentrations in the picomolar region can be measured. Another major use of radioisotopes is as tracers that determine metabolic pathways, transport processes, and reaction mechanisms. A compound labeled with a radioactive isotope is introduced into the process, and the radioactivity allows the compound to be followed through the mechanism.

Pharmacokinetics is the study of the rates of movement and biotransformation of a drug and its metabolites in the body. Many kinetic parameters, such as a drug's half-life in the body, can be determined by using radiolabeled drugs and measuring radioactivity after some type of chromatographic separation of the parent drug from its metabolites.

Radiopharmaceuticals are substances labeled with radionuclides that are used in the visualization of organs, the location of tumors, and the imaging of biochemical processes. This usage is based on the fact that a substance that is found in a healthy cell at a certain concentration has a different concentration in damaged cells. The particular isotope used depends on the organ or biochemical process under study.

Radioisotopes are used in many ways in industry. Gamma rays from cobalt 60 are used to examine objects for cracks and other defects. Radioisotopes can be used to measure thickness of all types of rolled materials and as tracers in locating leaks in pipes carrying liquids or gases. The fill level of closed containers is monitored by absorption or scattering of radiation.

In the chemical industry radioisotopes are used to indicate the completeness of a precipitation reaction. A radioisotope of the element to be precipitated is added to the solution to be precipitated. When the filtrate is free of radioactivity, precipitation is complete.

Radioisotopes are used in dating ancient rocks and fossils. Carbon is used in dating fossils. All living organisms are assumed to be in equilibrium with their environment, taking in carbon in food and expelling it through respiration and other processes. A living organism is assumed, when it dies, to have a certain percentage of carbon 14, radioactive carbon. As the fossil

ages the carbon 14 decays by beta emission, and its percentage is reduced. Since the decay rate is known, a reasonable age estimate can be obtained by measuring the rate of radioactive emission (proportional to percentage carbon 14) from the fossil. Uranium is used in a similar way to date rock samples that contain a mixture of uranium and lead, which is at the end of its decay chain.

*Grace A. Banks*

### Half-Lives of Some Unstable Isotopes Used in Dating

| PARENT ISOTOPE | DAUGHTER PRODUCT | HALF-LIFE VALUE |
|---|---|---|
| Uranium 238 | Lead 206 | 4.5 billion years |
| Uranium 235 | Lead 207 | 704 million years |
| Thorium 232 | Lead 208 | 14.0 billion years |
| Rubidium 87 | Strontium 87 | 48.8 billion years |
| Potassium 40 | Argon 40 | 1.25 billion years |
| Samarium 147 | Neodymium 143 | 106 billion years |

*Source:* U.S. Geological Survey.

FURTHER READING

Billington, D., G. G. Jayson, and P. J. Maltby. *Radioisotopes*. Oxford, England: BIOS Scientific Publishers in association with the Biochemical Society, 1992.

Choppin, Gregory R., Jan-Olov Liljenzin, and Jan Rydberg. *Radiochemistry and Nuclear Chemistry*. 3d ed. Boston: Butterworth-Heinemann, 2002.

Draganić, Ivan G., Zorica D. Draganić, and Jean-Pierre Adloff. *Radiation and Radioactivity on Earth and Beyond*. 2d ed. Boca Raton, Fla.: CRC Press, 1993.

Ehmann, William D., and Diane E. Vance. *Radiochemistry and Nuclear Methods of Analysis*. New York: Wiley, 1991.

Faure, Gunter, and Teresa M. Mensing. *Isotopes: Principles and Applications*. 3d ed. Hoboken, N.J.: Wiley, 2005.

Henriksen, Thormod. *Radiation and Health*. New York: Taylor & Francis, 2003.

Serway, Raymond A., Chris Vuille, and Jerry S. Faughn. *College Physics*. 8th ed. Belmont, Calif.: Brooks/Cole Cengage Learning, 2009.

Thornburn, C. C. *Isotopes and Radiation in Biology*. New York: Halstead Press Division, Wiley, 1972.

Tykva, Richard, and Dieter Berg, eds. *Man-Made and*

*Natural Radioactivity in Environmental Pollution and Radiochronology.* Boston: Kluwer Academic, 2004.

Umland, Jean B., and Jon M. Bellama. *General Chemistry.* 3d ed. Belmont, Calif.: Thomson/Brooks Cole, 1999.

WEB SITES

WORLD NUCLEAR ASSOCIATION
Radioisotopes in Industry
http://www.world-nuclear.org/info/
    default.aspx?id=548&terms=radioisotopes

WORLD NUCLEAR ASSOCIATION
Radioisotopes in Medicine
http://www.world-nuclear.org/info/
    default.aspx?id=546&terms=radioisotopes

SEE ALSO: Atomic Energy Commission; Isotopes, stable; Manhattan Project; Nuclear energy; Nuclear Regulatory Commission; Plutonium; Radium; Thorium; Uranium.

# Isotopes, stable

CATEGORY: Mineral and other nonliving resources

## WHERE FOUND

Stable isotopes comprise the bulk of the material universe. Some elements are found in only a single form, while others have several isotopes. For study and application, it is necessary to separate the various isotopes from one another. A number of methods have been developed to accomplish isotope separation.

## PRIMARY USES

Analysis of stable isotopes and isotopic composition is used extensively in a wide variety of fields. These include soil and water analysis, plant tissue analysis, determination of metabolic pathways in plants and animals (including humans), archaeology, forensics, the geosciences, and medicine.

## TECHNICAL DEFINITION

An isotope is one of two or more species of atom that have the same atomic number (number of protons) but different mass numbers (number of protons plus neutrons). Stable isotopes are those which are not radioactive. Because the chemical properties of an element are almost exclusively determined by atomic number, different isotopes of the same element will exhibit nearly identical behavior in chemical reactions. Subtle differences in the physical properties of isotopes are attributable to their differing masses.

## DESCRIPTION, DISTRIBUTION, AND FORMS

There are approximately 260 stable isotopes. While most of the eighty-one stable elements that occur in nature consist of a mixture of two or more isotopes, twenty occur in only a single form. Among these are sodium, aluminum, phosphorus, and gold. At the other extreme, the element tin exhibits ten isotopic forms. Two elements with atomic numbers less than 84, technetium and promethium, have no stable isotopes. The atomic weight of an element is the weighted average of its isotope masses as found in their natural distribution. For example, boron has two stable isotopes: boron 10 (an isotope with mass number 10), which accounts for 20 percent of naturally occurring boron, and boron 11, which accounts for 80 percent. The atomic weight of boron is therefore $(0.2) \times (10) + (0.8) \times (11) = 10.8$. In those elements that have naturally occurring isotopes, the relative abundance of the various isotopes is found to be remarkably constant, independent of the source of the material. There are cases in which the abundances are found to vary, and these are of practical interest.

## HISTORY

In the early part of the twentieth century, the discovery of radioactivity, radioactive elements, and the many distinctly different products of radioactive decays showed that there were far more atomic species than could be fit into the periodic table. Although possessing different physical properties, many of these species were chemically indistinguishable.

In 1912, Joseph John Thomson, discoverer of the electron, found that when a beam of ionized neon gas was passed through a properly configured electromagnetic field and allowed to fall on a photographic plate, two spots of unequal size were exposed. The size and location of the spots were those that would be expected if the original neon consisted of two components—about 90 percent neon 20 and 10 percent neon 22. Later Francis William Aston improved the experimental apparatus so that each isotope was focused to a point rather than smeared out. The device he developed, known as a mass spectrograph, allows much greater precision in the determination of isotope mass and abundance.

## OBTAINING ISOTOPES

All methods for separating stable isotopes are based on mass difference or on some isotopic property that derives from it. The difficulty of isotope separation depends inversely upon the relative mass difference between the isotopes. For example, the two most abundant isotopes of hydrogen are ordinary hydrogen (hydrogen 1) and deuterium (hydrogen 2). These isotopes have a relative mass difference of $(2-1)/1 = 1$, or 100 percent. The mass difference between chlorine 35 and chlorine 37, by contrast, is only $(37-35)/35 = 0.057$, or 5.7 percent.

There are two types of separation methods. The only single-step method is electromagnetic separation, which operates on the principle that the curvature of the path of a charged particle in a magnetic field is dependent on the particle mass. This is the same principle on which the mass spectrograph is based. Though it is a single-step technique, the amount of material that can be separated in this way is extremely small. All other processes result in a separation of the original material into two fractions, one slightly enriched in the heavier isotope. To obtain significant enrichment the process must be repeated a number of times by cascading identical stages. Such multistage methods include gaseous centrifugation, aerodynamic separation nozzles, fractional distillation, thermal diffusion, gaseous diffusion, electrolysis, and laser photochemical separation. For example, in centrifugation a vapor of the material to be separated flows downward in the outer part of a rotating cylinder and upward in the center. Because of the mass difference, the heavier isotope will be concentrated in the outer region and can be removed to be enriched again in the next stage.

## USES OF STABLE ISOTOPES

Most stable isotope applications are based on two facts. First, isotopes of a given element behave nearly identically in chemical reactions. Second, the relative abundances of isotopes for a given element are nearly constant. The three principal types of applications are those in which deviations from the standard abundances are used to infer something about the environment and/or history of the sample, those in which the isotopic ratio of a substance is altered so that the substance may be traced through a system or process, and those in which small differences in the physical properties of isotopes are used to understand process dynamics.

As an example of the first type of application, consider that the precise isotopic composition of water varies with place and time as it makes its way through the Earth's complex hydrologic cycle. Knowledge of this variation allows for the study of storm behavior, identification of changes in global climatic patterns, and investigation of past climatic conditions through the study of water locked in glaciers, tree rings, and pack ice. The cycling of nitrogen in crop plants provides an example of stable isotope tracer methods. Fertilizer tagged by enriching (or depleting) with nitrogen-15 is applied to a crop planting. Subsequent analysis makes it possible to trace the quantities of fertilizer taken up by the plants, remaining in the soil, lost to the atmosphere by denitrification, and leached into runoff water.

*Michael K. Rulison*

## FURTHER READING

Asimov, Isaac. *The History of Physics.* New York: Walker, 1984.

Bransden, B. H., and C. J. Joachain. *Physics of Atoms and Molecules.* 2d ed. New York: Prentice Hall, 2003.

Clayton, Donald D. *Handbook of Isotopes in the Cosmos: Hydrogen to Gallium.* New York: Cambridge University Press, 2003.

Ehleringer, James R., and Thure E. Cerling. "Stable Isotopes." In *The Earth System: Biological and Ecological Dimensions of Global Environmental Change,* edited by Harold A. Mooney and Joseph G. Canadell. Vol. 2 in *Encyclopedia of Global Environmental Change.* New York: Wiley, 2002.

Fry, Brian. *Stable Isotope Ecology.* New York: Springer, 2006.

Hobson, Keith A., and Leonard I. Wassenaar, eds. *Tracking Animal Migration with Stable Isotopes.* Amsterdam: Academic Press, 2008.

National Research Council. *Separated Isotopes: Vital Tools for Science and Medicine.* Washington, D.C.: National Academy Press, available from Office of Chemistry and Chemical Technology, National Research Council, 1982.

## WEB SITE

NORTHERN ARIZONA UNIVERSITY, COLORADO PLATEAU STABLE ISOTOPE LABORATORY
What Are Stable Isotopes?
http://www.mpcer.nau.edu/isotopelab/ isotope.html

SEE ALSO: Biotechnology; Hydrology and the hydrologic cycle; Isotopes, radioactive; Nitrogen cycle; Nuclear energy; Soil testing and analysis.

# Italy

CATEGORIES: Countries; government and resources

*Italy is one of the world's leading producers of wine, olive oil, and cheese. Olive trees and vineyards can be found throughout the country. The town of Carrara is world famous for the quality of its marble deposits.*

## THE COUNTRY

A founding member of the European Union, Italy became a nation-state in 1861 and a republic in 1946. Italy is a peninsula that extends into the Mediterranean Sea in southern Europe. The country comprises a boot-shaped mainland, the islands of Sicily and Sardinia, and several smaller islands. Italy shares borders with Austria, Switzerland, France, San Marino, and Slovenia. Natural threats to the nation include earthquakes, volcanic eruptions, mudslides, and avalanches, along with land subsidence in Venice. Three-quarters of the country is mountainous; the Alps stretch across the northern region, and the Apennines run southward along the peninsula. The southern area of the country has four active volcanoes, including Mount Vesuvius and Mount Etna. In 2008, Italy's economy was the fourth largest in Europe and seventh worldwide. The country is known for its cuisine, wine, cheese, olive oil, and marble. Italy has played a large role in European and global history. Home to Etruscans and later the Romans, Italy has been influential in the fields of architecture, literature, painting, sculpture, science, education, government, philosophy, music, and fashion.

## OLIVE OIL

Italy is one of the top-two leading producers of olive oil in the world. Fossils of olive trees have been found in Italy dating back 20 million years. The culture of producing olive oil, however, did not emerge in the area until much later. The spread of the Greek empire brought olives to southern Italy in the eighth century B.C.E. The Romans planted olive trees throughout the Mediterranean region. Ancient historians wrote about Italian olive oil as being reasonably priced and the best in the Mediterranean. Olive oil was a main ingredient in various ointments and was believed to increase strength and youthfulness. Leading producers of extra virgin olive oil are the regions of Liguria, Tuscany, Umbria, and Apulia. One-third of Italy's olive oil trees are in the Apulia region. The taste and quality of the oil is affected by the type of olives, climate and conditions where they are grown, the method of harvest, and the production process.

The Italian government strictly controls the extra virgin olive oil industry; in order to earn the distinction of extra virgin the oil must have an acidity level of less than 1 percent. In 1998, the United States imported 131 million liters of olive oil from Italy. Olive oil from Italy is among the highest priced and most in demand. This has led companies to mix lower quality oil with Italian oil in order to produce a cheaper product. The oil is then labeled as being imported from Italy. In March, 2008, the Italian government arrested twenty-three people and shut down eighty-five farms involved in schemes to sell counterfeit Italian olive oil. The following month, the government arrested forty people who were adding chlorophyll to sunflower and soybean oils. The oil was then sold throughout Italy and around the world as extra virgin olive oil. Twenty-five thousand liters of the counterfeit oil were confiscated before it could be exported.

## MARBLE

Carrara, located in the Apuan Alps in northwestern Tuscany, is the marble capital of Italy. It produces one-third of all the marble quarried in Italy. The area was first mined by the Romans, who used slaves and convicts to extract the rock. They would insert damp wooden wedges into existing cracking in the rock face; the wood would then expand, loosening the marble. In 1570, gunpowder was first used in Carrara to extract marble from the mountainside. Explosives drastically changed the landscape of the area as more quarries opened and larger chunks of marble were extracted. A hydroelectric plant was built nearby in 1910, which allowed the quarries to use electricity for the first time. This technology is used in the nearly three hundred active marble quarries in Carrara.

Several varieties of marble are mined in the area, including the uncommonly white, flawless marble for which the town is famous. The port of Marina di Carrara is one of the most famous in Italy and is known worldwide for loading and unloading marble and granite. During the early sixteenth century, sculptor

# Italy: Resources at a Glance

*Official name:* Italian Republic
*Government:* Republic
*Capital city:* Rome
*Area:* 116,314 mi²; 301,340 km²
*Population (2009 est.):* 58,126,212
*Language:* Italian
*Monetary unit:* euro (EUR)

## ECONOMIC SUMMARY:

*GDP composition by sector (2008 est.):* agriculture, 2%; industry, 27%; services, 71%
*Natural resources:* coal, mercury, zinc, potash, marble, barite, asbestos, pumice, fluorspar, feldspar, pyrite (sulfur), natural gas and crude oil reserves, fish, arable land
*Land use (2005):* arable land, 26.41%; permanent crops, 9.09%; other, 64.5%
*Industries:* tourism, machinery, iron and steel, chemicals, food processing, textiles, motor vehicles, clothing, footwear, ceramics
*Agricultural products:* fruits, vegetables, grapes, potatoes, sugar beets, soybeans, grain, olives, beef, dairy products, fish
*Exports (2008 est.):* $546.9 billion
*Commodities exported:* engineering products, textiles and clothing, production machinery, motor vehicles, transport equipment, chemicals, food, beverages and tobacco, minerals and nonferrous metals
*Imports (2008 est.):* $546.9 billion
*Commodities imported:* engineering products, chemicals, transport equipment, energy products, minerals and nonferrous metals, textiles and clothing, food, beverages, and tobacco
*Labor force (2008 est.):* 25.11 million
*Labor force by occupation (2005):* agriculture, 4.2%; industry, 30.7%; services, 65.1%

## ENERGY RESOURCES:

*Electricity production (2007 est.):* 292.1 billion kWh
*Electricity consumption (2006 est.):* 316.3 billion kWh
*Electricity exports (2007 est.):* 1.916 billion kWh
*Electricity imports (2007 est.):* 34.56 billion kWh

*Natural gas production (2007 est.):* 9.706 billion m³
*Natural gas consumption (2007 est.):* 84.89 billion m³
*Natural gas exports (2007 est.):* 68 million m³
*Natural gas imports (2007 est.):* 73.95 billion m³
*Natural gas proved reserves (Jan. 2008 est.):* 94.15 billion m³

*Oil production (2007 est.):* 166,600 bbl/day
*Oil imports (2005):* 2.223 million bbl/day
*Oil proved reserves (Jan. 2008 est.):* 406.5 million bbl

*Source:* Data from *The World Factbook 2009.* Washington, D.C.: Central Intelligence Agency, 2009.
*Notes:* Data are the most recent tracked by the CIA. Values are given in U.S. dollars. Abbreviations: bbl/day = barrels per day; GDP = gross domestic product; km² = square kilometers; kWh = kilowatt-hours; m³ = cubic meters; mi² = square miles.

Michelangelo (1475-1564) traveled often to the quarries to pick out marble for his projects, including *David*. Carrara marble was used to build the Pantheon, Trajan's Column in Rome, the Marble Arch in London, and the Cathedral of Siena. The stone is also used as a facade for buildings worldwide. Carrara is home to many fairs that celebrate marble and quarrying. In 1982, the town opened the Marble Museum of Carrara to preserve the history of marble and the marble industry in the area. The museum has several sections, including archaeological relics, drawings, photographs, plaster casts, sculptures, and industrial artwork. It also tells the history of marble quarrying and has machinery, technical diagrams, and photographs. The gallery contains more than three hundred samples of marble, granite, and rock from Italy and elsewhere.

## Feldspar

Feldspar is a group of minerals that compose up to 60 percent of the Earth's crust. The mineral can be found as crystals in granite or other igneous rock, in sedimentary rocks, in metamorphic rocks, or in veins. Feldspars are often pink, white, gray, or brown. The color varies with the chemical composition of the mineral. Feldspars are used in glassmaking, tile, ceramics, abrasive cleaners, and many other products. Italy was the leading feldspar producer throughout the 1990's, vastly outmining the rest of the world. By 1998, Italy was producing almost 2.1 million metric tons of feldspar. At that time, Italy's tile industry was among the top in the world, and the ceramics industry was among the leaders in Europe.

The Maffei Sarda company began mining feldspar in northern Sardinia in 1989. In the late 1990's, the company began producing a soda-potash feldspar that is unusually white in color and has been used to make bone china. At the time, another mining company developed a process to extract feldspar from granite that it recovered from a mining dump in Italy's Lake Maggiore region. Italy's yearly production of feldspar continues to increase; in 2008, the country mined 4.2 million metric tons. In 2008, Italy continued to be the top producer of feldspar, followed by Turkey, China, and Thailand. That year, Italian feldspar accounted for almost one-quarter of the total world production.

## Metal and Mineral Resources

Italy mines a variety of metals, including copper, lead, zinc, gold, and mercury. The majority of mining companies and mines are government controlled. Some privatization of the industry began during the 1990's. During the 1970's, Italy was a leading producer of pyrites, fluorite, salt, and asbestos. The country also mined enough zinc, sulfur, lead, and aluminum to meet its own demand. However, less than two decades later, Italy had drastically depleted these resources and was no longer self-sufficient.

One-half of the country's iron production is from Elba Island. The last iron cave was closed there in 1981. The island is also home to the Mining Museum. The museum has more than one thousand rocks and minerals on display and allows visitors to tour a mine. The majority of Italy's metals are found on its islands; the decline of mining and depletion of the deposits have severely impacted their economies.

The world's second largest mercury mine is located in Idrija, Slovenia. The region has been controlled by a number of different European nations; it was controlled by Italy between World Wars I and II. The Idrija mine was in operation by the time Christopher Columbus set sail for the West Indies in 1492. Mercury was first exported through Venice, followed by Amsterdam in 1659. After more than five hundred years in operation, the mine was shut down because of declining mercury ore prices. Mercury is still found in the Lake Maggiore region of Italy.

## Coal

The island of Sardinia has a long history of coal mining. During the fascist period, a large number of the island's swamplands were drained to produce farmable land. Several agrarian communities began to form in these areas. At this time, the city of Carbonia was also established, which became the mining center of Sardinia. Tourism increased on the island by the early 1950's, which led to a decrease in coal mining. By 2007, the Miniera Monte Sinni mine, located in the Sulcis basin in southwestern Sardinia, was the only active underground coal mine in Italy. It produced on average only 90,000 metric tons of coal each year. Italy, however, has large coal reserves: an estimated 544 million metric tons, of which 30.8 million metric tons are minable, according to a 2007 study. A 2003 estimate placed the country's reserves at more than 900 million metric tons. The study also estimated that the Sulcis basin had produced 72.6 million metric tons of coal. Production of lignite from Italy's only lignite mine declined drastically between 1998 (141,500 metric tons) and 2002 (9,000 metric tons). The Tuscan mine was shut down in 2003.

Italy was fourth among energy consumption in European countries. This growing demand for power sources has increased Italy's dependence on coal. The use of coal has met some political opposition but is aided by advances in the "clean coal" industry. In 2008, Italy's largest power company, Enel, converted a large power plant from oil to coal. The plant is located northwest of Rome, in Civitavecchia. The company defends this move as a means to lower costs; fuel costs have risen 151 percent since 1996. Italy has the highest electricity prices in Europe. The country plans to produce 33 percent of its power from coal, more than double the 14 percent it produced prior to 2008.

## WINE

The Etruscans, who were located in what is now northern Italy, and the Greek colonists to the south began Italy's long history with winemaking. After taking control of the area, the Romans started their own vineyards. Winemaking in the Roman Empire was a large enterprise and pioneered mass production storage methods like barrel making and bottling. The Romans operated several vineyard plantations manned with slave labor on much of the coastal area of the region. The plantations were so extensive that in 92 C.E. the emperor had to shut down a number of them in order to use the land for food production.

Today, Italy is one of the two leading wine producers in the world. In 2005, Italian wine accounted for 20 percent of the world's wine. The United States imported nearly one-third of the total from Italy (36 percent by dollar value). Italy produces wines of many flavors, colors, and styles. There are approximately one million vineyards throughout modern Italy. The country has twenty wine regions, which are also its political districts. The economy of the Apulia region is based primarily on wine, with 106,712 hectares of grapes and a yearly output of approximately 723.7 million liters of wine. The islands of Sardinia and Sicily are also major wine producers. Tuscany is famous for its red wines. About 70 percent of the 216 million liters produced there each year are red wines. The region has more than 63,537 hectares of vineyards. Starting in 1968, winemakers began producing "super Tuscans," wines that are not mixed according to the traditional blending laws of the area. During the 1970's, Tignanello became one of the first super Tuscans by eliminating the white grapes from a recipe for chianti. Piero Antinori replaced them with red Bordeaux grapes in order to produce a richer wine. The

new wines do not fit into any of the four traditional categories in which Italian wine is classified. However, winemakers throughout the country continue to experiment and create new wines.

## FISH

Even though the majority of fish and seafood consumed in Italy is imported, fish production in the country has risen since the 1960's. During the mid-1980's the European Union passed the Common Fisheries Policy. The policy is designed to eliminate overfishing and maintain a competitive fish and seafood industry within Europe. In 2002, a European Union commission reduced the catch limits on the number of cod and other species of fish that had dwindling numbers. In 2004, subsidies for fisherman to help procure new vessels were eliminated. Because of this, the number of Italian fishing ships has decreased, leaving mostly small-scale fishing operations. In 2003, Italian fishermen caught 26 percent less fish than the previous year. The northern region of Italy houses 62 percent of the country's fish farms; 22 percent are found in central Italy, and 16 percent in the southern region. These fisheries produced $405 million worth of fish in 2003. Canada is a large importer of fish to Italy, but retailers face a tough obstacle: Italian consumers are used to purchasing fresh goods, not canned or frozen. These companies may be added by the growing demand for value and the convenience of ready-made food.

## OTHER RESOURCES

In addition to olives and grapes, Italy is famous worldwide for its cheeses. The country produces more than four hundred different varieties of cheese. In 2008, the government purchased 200,000 wheels of cheese (29.9 kilograms each) to help feed the poor, as food lines and the number of needy grew in the major cities. Italy is also a major exporter of rice and tomatoes. During the late twentieth century, tomato farms doubled in size, and production quadrupled. Northern Italy grows three times the amount of wheat as the southern regions, which is used to make pizza crusts and pasta. The country consumes a large portion of the agricultural products that it produces. Eighty percent of Italy's citrus fruit is grown in Sicily. Italy is also a leading producer of apples, oranges, lemons, pears, and other fruits as well as flowers and vegetables.

Potash can be various chemical compounds, mostly potassium carbonate. Potassium oxide potash is used in fertilizer. The town of Agrigento in southern Sicily has an economy that is largely based on potash and sulfur mining. The nearby harbor is Italy's principal sulfur port.

*Jennifer L. Campbell*

## FURTHER READING

Clark, Martin. *Modern Italy: 1871 to the Present*. New York: Pearson Longman, 2008.

Davis, John Anthony. *Italy in the Nineteenth Century, 1796-1900*. New York: Oxford University Press, 2001.

Duggan, Christopher. *A Concise History of Italy*. Updated ed. New York: Cambridge University Press, 2006.

Knickerbocker, Peggy. *Olive Oil: From Tree to Table*. San Francisco: Chronicle Books, 2007.

Leivick, Joel. *Carrara: The Marble Quarries of Tuscany*. Palo Alto, Calif.: Stanford University Press, 1999.

Lintner, Valerio. *A Traveler's History of Italy*. 8th ed. Northampton, Mass.: Interlink, 2008.

Romaneili, Leonardo. *Olive Oil: An Italian Pantry*. San Francisco: Wine Appreciation Guild, 2003.

Scigliano, Eric. *Michelangelo's Mountain: The Quest for Perfection in the Marble Quarries of Carrara*. New York: Free Press, 2005.

SEE ALSO: Agricultural products; Agriculture industry; Coal; Feldspars; Fisheries; Marble; Potash; Wheat.

# Ivory

CATEGORY: Plant and animal resources

## WHERE FOUND

Ivory is obtained from the large teeth and tusks of several mammals, including the elephant, hippopotamus, walrus, extinct wooly mammoth, and narwhal. In these animals, an upper incisor grows throughout life into a large tusk. In elephants, for example, the average tusk weighs 7 kilograms, but in large males the weight might be much more. A major factor endangering the continued existence of these extant mammals has been the value of their ivory.

## PRIMARY USES

Ivory has been used by humans for thousands of years, often as a medium for carving. The art of scrimshaw makes use of ivory, and many other ornamental objects are carved from ivory. In the past, most ivory was used in the manufacture of piano keys, but billiard balls, bagpipes, flatware handles, and furniture inlays were other products made from ivory. Today, most ivory is used for the Chinese, Japanese, and Korean seals known as *hankos*; these small seals are used on official business documents.

## TECHNICAL DEFINITION

Ivory is the hardened dentine of the teeth and tusks of certain large mammals. In both male and female elephants, one incisor on each side of the upper jaw grows throughout life. In females, growth of the tusks tends to slow after age thirty, but in males both the length and bulk of the tusks increase through the life span, thus making old male elephants prime targets for ivory poachers. In walruses, the tusks form from upper canines and grow throughout life in both sexes. Narwhals have only two teeth, both in the upper jaw; these lengthen to become long, straight tusks, usually only one in males and sometimes two in females. Hippopotamuses have tusks of ivory that do not yellow with age, as elephant tusks tend to do.

## DESCRIPTION, DISTRIBUTION, AND FORMS

Both the Asiatic elephant, *Elephas maximus*, and the African elephant, *Loxodonta africana*, have been extensively exploited for the ivory in their tusks. Asiatic elephants are now restricted in range to southern Asia, although historically they had a much larger distribution, from Syria to northern China and south to Sri Lanka, Sumatra, and perhaps Java. According to 2008 population estimates, only 34,000 to 54,000 wild Asiatic elephants remain throughout the present range of the species. Approximately 17,000 to 23,000 are found on the Indian subcontinent, 11,000 to 20,000 in continental Southeast Asia, and 6,000 to 11,000 in Sri Lanka, Sumatra, and Borneo.

The African elephant includes two major kinds, which some experts consider subspecies: the forest elephant, *Loxodonta africana cyclotis*, of west and central Africa, and the savanna or bush elephant, *Loxodonta africana africana*, of the savanna areas of sub-Saharan Africa. Intense pressure from both legal and illegal ivory hunters caused the entire African elephant population to fall from around 1.3 million in 1979 to 625,000 in 1989. More recent estimates place the population throughout Africa to be no more than 500,000. In 1990, the United Nations Convention on

Trade in Endangered Species of Wild Fauna and Flora (CITES) put a ban on the international trade of ivory, and this slowed to some extent the killing of elephants.

A now-extinct relative of the elephant, the woolly mammoth, *Mammuthus primigenius*, once ranged throughout the cold, northern areas of Asia and portions of North America. Global climate change has exposed the bodies of many mammoths and their tusks have been gathered, mostly by Russian workers, as a source of ivory.

The walrus, *Odobenus rosmarus*, occurs in coastal areas of the Arctic Ocean and adjoining seas. This species has been heavily exploited for the ivory of its large upper canines, which may be more than 100 centimeters long in males and about 80 centimeters in females. Biologists are concerned that with the decline of the African elephant population as a source of ivory, poachers will turn to the killing of walruses.

Narwhals, *Monodon monoceros*, are found in the Arctic Ocean and nearby seas, primarily between 70° and 80° north latitude. Their normal range is entirely above the Arctic Circle. Narwhals have two upper-jaw teeth; in males, one of these remains embedded while the other erupts and grows in a spiral pattern to form a long, straight tusk. This tusk may be about one-third to one-half of the animal's total body length, sometimes becoming as long as 300 centimeters with a weight of 10 kilograms. Occasionally, one or two tusks are grown by a female narwhal. Most researchers believe that the narwhal uses the tusk as a defensive weapon, because extensive scarring is often found on the heads of males.

The hippopotamus, *Hippopotamus amphibius*, occurs throughout Africa in suitable waterways south of the Sahara Desert and also in the Nile River to its delta. It has disappeared throughout most of western and southern Africa, partially because it is killed for its ivory tusks. Some of the lower canine tusks of male hippos are just as large as many elephant tusks entering the ivory market, causing the hippo to be a target for illegal trafficking in ivory.

HISTORY

The trade in ivory is thought to date to the time of Cro-Magnon man, approximately thirty-five thousand years ago. The Asiatic elephant has been exploited for ivory for at least four thousand years; upper classes in both Asia and the Middle East greatly desired items made of ivory. Ivory demand in Europe in the 1600's drove the killing of many thousands of elephants around the Cape of Good Hope. From 1860 to 1930, 25,000 to 100,000 elephants were killed each year for the ivory trade, mostly to obtain material for piano key manufacture. By the early nineteenth century, the ivory-carving industry in India was being supported by imported African elephant tusks, as the Asiatic elephants had already been seriously depleted. The overall number of elephants in Africa in the early 1900's was still several million and remained so until after World War II.

The mid-twentieth century had a lag in commercial ivory hunting, but in the 1970's hunting resumed in earnest as the raw ivory price increased from five to one hundred dollars per kilogram. The African elephant was placed on appendix 2 of CITES in 1979, listed as vulnerable by the International Union for Conservation of Nature, and listed as threatened by the United States Department of the Interior. However, these listings did little to

*This Asian elephant displays tusks of ivory that are 2.5 meters long. The illicit ivory trade is an endangerment to elephants.* (©iStockphoto.com)

prevent poaching, and the African elephant population plummeted to 600,000 by 1997. In 1990, CITES banned the international trade of ivory, but in 1997, the convention approved the sale of more than 54 metric tons of ivory from Botswana, Namibia, and Zimbabwe. This stockpiled ivory was sold to Japan. CITES reinstated a trade ban again in 2000, then once more allowed an exception in 2002 for Botswana, Namibia, and South Africa. In 2004, Namibia's proposal to allow tourist trade in ivory carvings was approved; many conservationists believe that CITES' imposing and then temporarily lifting ivory bans has encouraged poaching in the African countries where larger populations of elephants still exist. In 2007, in response to public pressure on the ivory trade issue, eBay banned all international sales of elephant ivory products and in 2009 disallowed any sales of ivory by users of its Web site.

China's growing economy has driven illegal trade in ivory as well as attracted organized crime related to its sale. A kilogram of ivory brings about $750. Estimated illegal shipments to China total approximately 218 metric tons, an amount that would cause the deaths of at least 23,000 elephants.

One tool available to conservation law enforcement is DNA testing. A genetic test developed by Samuel Wasser of the University of Washington helps to track illegal shipments to their source. For example, an extremely large illegal shipment of 532 tusks and 42,000 *hankos* was seized in Singapore in 2002. Genetic testing traced this ivory to Zambia, and the tusks in the shipment weighed approximately 11 kilograms each, indicating that they came from old elephants.

## Obtaining Ivory

Generally, ivory is obtained by the killing of the animals that possess ivory teeth and tusks. As mentioned above, these include elephants, hippopotamuses, narwhals, and walruses.

Mammoth ivory is obtained primarily in Russia by those who find recently thawed mammoth carcasses. Because of global climate change, this has become a more common occurrence. Mammoth ivory has been used by Russian merchants in the manufacture of items to sell to Asia. About 90 percent of mammoth ivory exported to Asia is used to make *hankos* for Chinese, Japanese, and Korean markets. This ivory, because it comes from an extinct mammal, can be legally imported into the United States. More than 46 metric tons were imported in 2007. Dealers in Moscow report that they can sell mammoth ivory for three hundred to four hundred dollars per kilogram in Russia; in western markets it sells for up to sixteen hundred dollars per kilogram.

Native subsistence hunting of walruses, by harpooning or clubbing, has been occurring for thousands of years and probably had little negative impact on populations of the species. However, with the hunting of walruses by Europeans for ivory, hides, and oil, beginning in the sixteenth century, numbers of the animals on both sides of the North Atlantic declined dramatically. The last large populations in the Canadian Arctic were gone by the 1930's, and only about 25,000 of the Atlantic population remain. Recent surveys of the Pacific population indicate that some 200,000 walruses are present, but there is considerable concern among biologists that ivory demand in Asia will drive poaching of the remaining animals.

Hippopotamuses have been extensively killed for hundreds of years for meat, hides, and ivory. As populations of African elephants have steadily declined, there has been increased pressure on hippos for their ivory. The lower canine tusks of males are often as large as elephant tusks now entering the illegal market, and a sharp rise in the export of hippo ivory coincided with the placing of the African elephant under the more protective listing of appendix 1 of CITES.

The Vikings were probably the first culture to exploit the narwhal extensively for its tusk, which sold for high prices as early as the tenth century. The tusks were also in great demand in Asia, where they were used for carving and as medicine. During the late 1900's, narwhal tusks were sold for as much as forty-five hundred dollars. The annual kill of narwhals in Canadian waters is estimated to be approximately one thousand. The species has received little firm protection from any conservation law.

## Uses of Ivory

For many years, the use of ivory centered around decorative items, such as carved figurines and various gewgaws, primarily for customers in Europe, Asia, and the United States. The manufacture of ivory piano keys and billiard balls was a major factor in the demise of both Asiatic and African elephants. Estimates indicated that consumption of ivory—for the making of piano keys—in Great Britain in 1831 accounted for the deaths of four thousand elephants. More modern uses of ivory have been for flatware, jewelry, and furniture inlays, but by far the greatest recent use of ivory has been for *hankos*. These small ivory seals are used as a means of signing official documents in China, Japan, and Korea. A vegetable ivory from the ivory nut palm could be used in place of animal ivory, but, so far, the vegetable ivory has not been accepted by Asians as a suitable substitute.

*Lenela Glass-Godwin*

FURTHER READING

Feldhake, Glenn. *Hippos.* Stillwater, Minn.: Voyageur Press, 2005.

Harland, David. *Killing Game: International Law and the African Elephant.* New York: Praeger, 1994.

Nowak, Ronald M. *Walker's Mammals of the World.* 6th ed. Baltimore: Johns Hopkins University Press, 1999.

Ray, G. Carleton, and Jerry McCormick-Ray, eds. *Coastal Marine Conservation: Science and Policy.* Malden, Mass.: Blackwell, 2004.

Sukumar, Raman. *The Living Elephants: Evolutionary Ecology, Behavior, and Conservation.* New York: Oxford University Press, 2004.

WEB SITE

NATIONAL OCEANIC AND ATMOSPHERIC ADMINISTRATION
National Marine Fisheries Service
http://www.nmfs.noaa.gov

SEE ALSO: Endangered species; Endangered Species Act; International Union for Conservation of Nature; Resources as a source of international conflict; United Nations Convention on International Trade in Endangered Species of Wild Fauna and Flora.

# Izaak Walton League of America

CATEGORY: Organizations, agencies, and programs
DATE: Established 1922

*Members of the Izaak Walton League of America pledge to strive for the purity of water, the clarity of air, and the wise stewardship of the land and its resources. They seek to understand nature and the value of wildlife, woodlands, and open space.*

BACKGROUND
Founded in Chicago by fifty-four fishermen to protect fish habitat, the Izaak Walton League of America (IWLA) has grown into a national organization of almost three hundred local chapters encompassing all conservation activities. With a diverse membership of fishers, hunters, urban environmentalists, and conservationists in general, the IWLA is a respected voice of commitment and moderation throughout the environmental community. The league is organized as a bottom-up democracy. All policies are developed by local chapters and, after passing through state divisions, become official policy after action by a national convention of delegates from each chapter.

IMPACT ON RESOURCE USE
The IWLA has been instrumental in obtaining wilderness status for parts of the Boundary Waters Canoe Area in Minnesota, establishing the National Elk Refuge in Wyoming, cleaning up Chesapeake Bay, and maintaining a strong conservation reserve program in farm bill authorizations. Permanent projects include the league's well-respected, and often copied, Save-Our-Streams Program, in which local chapters and other groups "adopt" a stream. Using techniques developed by national staff, members monitor stream quality, identify pollution sources, and work to clean up problems. A Midwest office of the IWLA is an important watchdog that observes the power industry, monitoring environmental degradation of the Mississippi River basin and supporting alternative energy sources.

*John R. Dickel*

WEB SITE

IZAAK WALTON LEAGUE OF AMERICA
http://www.iwla.org/

SEE ALSO: Conservation; Environmental movement; Streams and rivers; Water pollution and water pollution control; Wilderness; wildlife.

# J

## Jackson, Wes

CATEGORY: People
BORN: June 15, 1936; near Topeka, Kansas

*Jackson, a plant geneticist by training, became one of the leading critics of modern industrialized agriculture. Cofounder of the Land Institute, he envisioned a radically different approach to farming based on ecological models and on polycultures rather than monocultures.*

### BIOGRAPHICAL BACKGROUND

Wes Jackson, president of the Land Institute at Salina, Kansas, was born in 1936 near Topeka, Kansas, where he grew up on a 16-hectare farm. He received a B.A. in biology at Kansas Wesleyan University in 1958, an M.S. at the University of Kansas in 1967, and a Ph.D. in plant genetics at North Carolina State University in 1967. He taught at Kansas Wesleyan and at California State University, Sacramento, where he established an environmental studies program. Becoming involved in the growing environmental movement, he and his wife, Dana, left California to found the Land Institute in 1976. Jackson developed strategies for using nature as the model for achieving a more sustainable approach to agriculture.

The author of several books, including *New Roots for Agriculture* (1980) and *Altars of Unhewn Stone: Science*

*Wes Jackson stands in the Wauhob prairie in Kansas near the Land Institute, which he founded.* (AP/Wide World Photos)

*and the Earth* (1987), and numerous articles, Jackson was honored as a Pew Scholar in 1990 and a MacArthur Fellow in 1992. In 2000, he received the Right Livelihood Award, established in 1980 for those "working on practical and exemplary solutions to the most urgent challenges facing the world today."

IMPACT ON RESOURCE USE

Jackson became one of a number of critics of mainstream American agriculture; others include Wendell Berry, Gary Paul Nabhan, and Robert Rodale. Jackson characterized mainstream agriculture as "extractive" in that it uses, or extracts, considerable amounts of resources—including soil, water, and petroleum—to grow food; furthermore, it is capital intensive, and its chemicals pollute streams and groundwater. Jackson and the Land Institute have had their share of criticism, with some calling their efforts impractical and doomed to failure. Nonetheless, they also have staunch supporters and have been influential in expanding modern views of agriculture by examining the sociocultural aspects of how a society decides to produce its food and through the growth of interdisciplinary approaches such as agroecology.

*Thomas A. Eddy*

SEE ALSO: Agriculture industry; Agronomy; Erosion and erosion control; Land Institute; Monoculture agriculture; Soil management.

# Japan

CATEGORIES: Countries; government and resources

*For a prime industrialized nation, Japan is surprisingly poor in natural resources and has to import most of its fuel and other resources for its manufacturing and food industry. Japan imports more fish, its key natural resource, than it exports and is only self-sufficient with select industrial mineral resources such as limestone.*

THE COUNTRY

Japan is an island nation in East Asia. To the east, it faces the North Pacific, and to the west, the Sea of Japan, across which lies the Korean Peninsula and Siberia. Japan is the world's tenth most populous nation, and 98.5 percent of its more than 127 million inhabi-

tants are ethnic Japanese. In 2008, Japan had the world's second largest gross domestic product ($4.84 trillion), behind the United States. Japan ran the world's third largest economy, if measured by its purchasing power parity of $4.4 trillion, falling just behind the United States and China. However, because of its large population, Japan ranked only twenty-fourth with its per-capita annual income of thirty-eight thousand dollars in 2008.

Japan comprises more than three thousand individual islands. The most important are, from north to south, the four main islands of Hokkaidō, Honshū, Shikoku, and Kyūshū. The four main islands have steep, inaccessible, forested mountains, including Mount Fuji near Tokyo, which is Japan's landmark. Earthquakes are common. Agriculture is generally limited to three narrow coastal plains around Tokyo and Ōsaka, with only about 15 percent of the land usable for agriculture. Japan's key natural resources are fish and a few industrial minerals. Thus, the resource-poor but industrialized country is a huge net importer of natural resources.

FISH

Fish is Japan's key natural resource. Fish, together with rice, has sustained the population of Japan for centuries, losing its importance only in the early twenty-first century as the Japanese have changed their diets. Consequently, the volume of fish and shellfish caught by coastal, offshore, and inland Japanese fisheries as well as produced by Japanese marine aquaculture declined by nearly one-half to about 5 billion metric tons by 2006, down from a peak of 11.5 billion metric tons in 1985.

Mackerel, Japanese anchovy, skipjack, scallops, and saury are key fish and shellfish species caught along the coast of Japan and within the roughly 450 nautical square kilometers of Japan's maritime exclusive economic zone (EEZ) established by the United Nations in 1995. These species accounted for about 1.9 billion metric tons caught in 2006. Bonito, Japanese common squid, salmon, and trout are also caught in significant numbers.

In addition to catching domestic Japanese fish resources, Japan sustains a long-distance fishing fleet. This fishing fleet operates by treaty in the maritime EEZs of other nations. The catch from the neighboring EEZs of South Korea, Russia, and China, are counted among Japan's domestic catch, slightly overestimating domestic fish haul. However, the prime tar-

# Japan: Resources at a Glance

*Official name:* Japan
*Government:* Parliamentary government with a constitutional monarchy
*Capital city:* Tokyo
*Area:* 145,924 mi²; 377,915 km²
*Population (2009 est.):* 127,078,679
*Language:* Japanese
*Monetary unit:* yen (JPY)

## ECONOMIC SUMMARY:

*GDP composition by sector (2008 est.):* agriculture, 1.5%; industry, 26.3%; services, 72.3%
*Natural resources:* negligible mineral resources, fish (largest importer of coal and liquefied natural gas; second largest importer of oil), limestone, silica sand and stone
*Land use (2005):* arable land, 11.64%; permanent crops, 0.9%; other, 87.46%
*Industries:* motor vehicles, electronic equipment, machine tools, steel and nonferrous metals, ships, chemicals, textiles, processed foods
*Agricultural products:* rice, sugar beets, vegetables, fruit, pork, poultry, dairy products, eggs, fish
*Exports (2008 est.):* $746.5 billion
*Commodities exported:* transport equipment, motor vehicles, semiconductors, electrical machinery, chemicals
*Imports (2008 est.):* $708.3 billion
*Commodities imported:* machinery and equipment, fuels, foodstuffs, chemicals, textiles, raw materials
*Labor force (2008 est.):* 66.5 million
*Labor force by occupation (2005):* agriculture, 4.4%; industry, 27.9%; services, 66.4%

## ENERGY RESOURCES:

*Electricity production (2007 est.):* 1.195 trillion kWh
*Electricity consumption (2006 est.):* 1.08 trillion kWh
*Electricity exports (2007 est.):* 0 kWh
*Electricity imports (2007 est.):* 0 kWh

*Natural gas production (2007 est.):* 3.729 billion m³
*Natural gas consumption (2007 est.):* 100.3 billion m³
*Natural gas exports (2007 est.):* 0 m³
*Natural gas imports (2007 est.):* 95.62 billion m³
*Natural gas proved reserves (Jan. 2008 est.):* 20.9 billion m³

*Oil production (2007):* 132,400 bbl/day
*Oil imports (2007):* 5.032 million bbl/day
*Oil proved reserves (Jan. 2008 est.):* 44.12 million bbl

*Source:* Data from *The World Factbook 2009.* Washington, D.C.: Central Intelligence Agency, 2009.
*Notes:* Data are the most recent tracked by the CIA. Values are given in U.S. dollars. Abbreviations: bbl/day = barrels per day; GDP = gross domestic product; km² = square kilometers; kWh = kilowatt-hours; m³ = cubic meters; mi² = square miles.

*Hirotaka Akamatsu (left), Japan's farm and fisheries minister, visits the Tsukiji fish market in Tokyo. The fishing industry is an important part of the Japanese economy.* (AP/Wide World Photos)

gets of the long-distance fleet are EEZs of Pacific Ocean countries farther away than Asia, as well as high seas. Here, the target is high-value predatory fish, particularly tuna. The contribution to Japan's overall catch by the distance fleet has declined from accounting for as much as 20 percent in 1985, when it added 2.1 billion metric tons, to just under 10 percent in 2005, when it contributed 544 million metric tons. Statistics often use the total number for all fish caught and harvested by Japanese fisheries, including those from foreign and open seas. For 2006, technically speaking, fish from the waters of Japan (Japan's own natural resources) accounted for about only 90 percent of the total.

By 2006, fish and shellfish caught by the Japanese in their own waters accounted for about 6.2 percent of the world's supply of fishery products for human consumption. Even though Japan used 85 percent of the fish and shellfish it caught in its waters for this purpose, and only 15 percent for fertilizer and animal feed, this could not satisfy the demand of Japanese consumers. Consequently, Japan imported one-half of its fishery products for domestic human consumption from other countries. Reflecting the Japanese trend to import low-value fish products and export high-value fish, rather than using all of its catch at home first before adding imports, some 16 percent of Japanese fish used for human food was exported and the resulting lack made up by cheaper imports.

Reflecting Japan's primary use of its fish for human food, the country imported more than 80 percent of fish products used for feed and fertilizer. Of the 15 percent of its own catch Japan used in this secondary category, only 10 percent was exported.

Aware of problems haunting its fishing industry, such as depletion of resources, marine environmental degradation, aging fish industry population, and commercial challenges to the small-scale operators constituting the bulk of the Japanese fishing enterprises, Japan passed the Fishery Master Plan of March, 2007. The plan envisioned promotion of resource recovery and sustainable management of marine resources, global competitiveness of the Japanese fishing industry, and support for fishing villages and their infrastructure.

LUMBER

Even though 66 percent of Japan is covered by forests for a total of about 250 million square kilometers, the importance of lumber as a natural resource has declined significantly. Key reasons have been the difficulty of accessing much of the forested terrain; the use of forests to conserve headwater and prevent soil runoff; the implementation of strict and growing environmental protection; and an underdeveloped, mostly part-time and small-scale lumber industry.

While the total forested area of Japan remained remarkably constant between 1980 and 2010, its use as a source of lumber shifted considerably. Protected forest area rose steadily from 80,000 square kilometers in 1985 to 113,000 square kilometers in 2005. This was done primarily to increase the area used for headwater conservation and soil runoff prevention, which are serious environmental problems in Japan that interfere with the use of forests as lumber sources. Massive reforestation, or artificial forest regeneration, was undertaken in the 1980's, peaking with the planting of 1,600 square kilometers in 1980; this number decreased to 284 square kilometers by 2004, as the plan's goals were within sight. As a result, by 2000, nearly 80 percent of the then existing, once heavily harvested needle-leaved tree forests of Japan were the result of reforestation, compared to 98 percent of broad-leaved trees still growing in natural forests.

Production of logs fell by approximately one-half from 33 million cubic meters in 1985 to 16 million cubic meters in 2005. Correspondingly, the final annual cutting area for lumber in Japan fell from 2,900 square kilometers in 1985 to just 295 square kilometers in 2004. Nevertheless, this indicated a more efficient yield of lumber per harvested area.

In 2004, the majority of logs came from the softwood needle-leaved trees of Japanese cedar, yielding 7.5 million cubic meters; Japanese cypress, yielding 2 million cubic meters; and Japanese larch, white fir, and Yezo spruce, accounting for a combined yield of 2.7 million cubic meters. The once heavily harvested Japanese red and black pines accounted for only 800,000 cubic meters, down from 3.8 million cubic meters in 1985. Hardwood from a variety of broad-leaved trees yielded 2.5 million cubic meters, or 16 percent of the total log yield of 15.6 million cubic meters for 2004. Of this lumber, the vast majority, 11.6 million cubic meters, was used for saw logs, with just 3.7 million cubic meters turned into wood chips and a negligible 860,000 cubic meters used for veneer sheets and plywood. This reflected the trend toward high-end products by the Japanese lumber industry.

Given the declining and limited domestic yields of lumber, Japan imported lumber in great quantities, making up for the domestic limits of this much-used natural resource. In 2006, Japan produced forestry products worth about $1.8 billion, while importing forestry products worth about $12 billion and exporting forestry products of about $77 million. Clearly, Japan was a large net importer of lumber, with its domestic production falling far behind its domestic demand.

### LIMESTONE

In the early twenty-first century, Japan was one of the world's leading producers of limestone, an industrial commodity essential for the construction industry. Limestone's key ingredient is the mineral calcite, chemically defined as calcium carbonate, $CaCO_3$. As the calcite in limestone comes primarily from calcified marine organisms, Japan benefits from its island nature, leading to rich calcite deposits.

In 2006, Japan's limestone production was 166.6 million metric tons. Almost all of Japan's limestone was used domestically, accounting for 157.2 million metric tons. Of this amount, Japanese industries used 42 percent for cement manufacturing, 22 percent for concrete aggregate, 15 percent in iron and steel manufacturing, 5 percent for road construction, and 7 percent for soda and glass manufacturing, with the remaining 15 percent accounting for all other uses.

Unlike the situation with other natural resources in Japan, because of the high volume of limestone production, there were eight industrial-size companies involved by 2006. That year the leading Japanese limestone producer was Taiheiyo Cement Company Limited. With 41.7 million metric tons of limestone extracted per year, Taiheiyo Cement produces about one-quarter of Japan's limestone, operating in seven prefectures on all four main islands of the nation.

Japan's substantial limestone production gave the country a rare self-sufficiency for a natural resource by 2009. Japan's proven exploitable reserves of 36.6 billion metric tons of limestone meant that its self-sufficiency for this natural resource would remain intact for the foreseeable future.

### SILICA SAND AND STONE

By 2006, Japan was one of the key producers of silica sand and stone in Asia and along the western Pacific rim. Chemically defined as silicon dioxide, or $SiO_2$, silica has been abundantly mined and quarried in Japan. From 2002 to 2006, the annual yield of silica sand was about 5.8 million metric tons. In the same years, silica stone and quartzite was produced in a quantity ranging from 12.8 to 12.9 million metric tons each year. Silica was the second most important of Japan's industrial minerals.

With its high domestic production, Japan was able to cover all its domestic demand for silica sand. In 2006, 25 percent of Japan's silica sand went toward domestic soda and glass manufacturing. Thirteen percent was used for casting and refractories, 9 percent for concrete aggregate, 2 percent for iron and steel manufacturing, and the remaining 50 percent for domestic cement manufacturing, road construction, and other, often highly specialized uses.

By 2006, Japan had exploitable resources of about 73.6 million metric tons of silica sand and some 462 million metric tons of white silica stone. There would be no shortage of this industrial mineral resource in the foreseeable future in Japan.

## GOLD

Japan once was self-sufficient in supplying gold for its industrial, craft, and monetary demands. However, by 2006, Japan's gold mining industry had shrunk to just one gold mine, down from fifteen major mines in 1986. The reason for this decline was primarily a depletion of ore reserves in old mines and the high cost of domestic gold mining and exploration compared to cheaper imports of gold ingots and gold powder for refining in Japan.

Thus, in 2006, all of Japan's gold mining took place at the Hishikari Mine of Sumitomo Metal Mining Company, located in Kagoshima Prefecture at the southern tip of Japan's southernmost main island of Kyūshū. There, a staff of 210 produced about 8,900 kilograms of gold each year.

Japan used about 200,000 kilograms of gold in 2006, one-half of it for electrical, electronic, and communication applications. This meant that domestic gold mining provided only 5 percent of the gold resources needed to fulfill this annual demand, with the rest having to be imported, either as ingots or as gold ore powder; almost one-half of it comes from Australia. Even though Japan still had exploitable reserves of gold ore, with an estimated pure gold content of 159,000 kilograms, extracting these reserves was considered more costly than importing gold ore. To facilitate gold imports, Japanese companies also formed joint ventures at foreign gold mines, securing supply of the resource.

## OTHER RESOURCES

Surprisingly for a major industrialized nation, Japan has very limited natural resources in general and even less indigenous mineral resources. Most of those other resources the country possesses are industrial minerals such as feldspar and related materials, iodine, and pyrophyllite, which is a talc-related material. Correspondingly, the mining sector contributed only a minuscule 0.11 percent to Japan's gross domestic product in 2005.

Indicative of the decline of Japan's metal mining industry was the March, 2006, closing of the Toyoha Mine on the northern main island of Hokkaidō. Until its closing for ore depletion, the Toyoha Mine was the primary source for Japan's lead, zinc, and silver. Even though small deposits of these resources remain, their extraction in Japan is considered cost prohibitive, as imports are much cheaper.

As a result of its own resource poverty, Japan was one of the largest importers of minerals and intermediate mineral products, including crude oil, to sustain its impressive chemical, ferrous, and nonferrous metals-manufacturing and power-generating industries. Securing the natural resources the country needs for its advanced manufacturing base and satisfying the changing food demands of its population remained key concerns of Japanese natural resource policies.

Japanese agriculture, limited to about 15 percent of the country's land because of the general hostility of the terrain, is of remarkable intensity and obtains one of the highest yields from the soil in the world. Nevertheless, together with a shift from rice and vegetables toward a more meat-oriented national diet, Japan became a heavy importer of foodstuffs beginning in the final decades of the twentieth century.

*R. C. Lutz*

## FURTHER READING

Bunker, Stephen G., and Paul S. Ciccantell. *East Asia and the Global Economy: Japan's Ascent, with Implications for China's Future.* Baltimore: Johns Hopkins University Press, 2007.

Cruz, Wilfrido, et al., eds. *Protecting the Global Environment: Initiatives by Japanese Business.* Washington, D.C.: World Bank, 2002.

Flath, David. *The Japanese Economy.* 2d ed. New York: Oxford University Press, 2005.

Pyle, Kenneth B. *Japan Rising: The Resurgence of Japanese Power and Purpose.* New York: Public Affairs, 2007.

Samuels, Richard J. *Securing Japan: Tokyo's Grand Strategy and the Future of East Asia.* Ithaca, N.Y.: Cornell University Press, 2007.

SEE ALSO: Fisheries; Limestone; Oceans; Rice; Timber industry.

# K

## Kaiser, Henry J.

CATEGORY: People
BORN: May 9, 1882; Sprout Brook, New York
DIED: August 24, 1967; Honolulu, Hawaii

*Henry J. Kaiser was an engineer involved in building roads, dams, bridges, ships, and even cars. He worked in the United States, Canada, and Cuba. The infrastructure he built was to improve the lives of people over many years.*

### BIOGRAPHICAL BACKGROUND

The early career of Henry John Kaiser did not give any indication of the achievements to come. Kaiser had virtually no formal education and worked early in his career in the dry goods, photography, and hardware businesses. By 1914, putting early business failures behind him and in an attempt to prove himself to win a bride, he moved to British Columbia, Canada, and began a company that paved roads. This work continued into the early 1930's. During this time, as business waxed and waned in British Columbia and Washington State, Kaiser completed a number of jobs outside the United States, including a series of roads and dams in Cuba. He also moved his business slowly south out of Canada, taking jobs in Washington, Oregon, and California before settling his business in Oakland, California. Kaiser shifted his business emphasis to dams and bridges. He contributed to a number of bridges in the San Francisco Bay Area as well as dams at Hoover, Bonneville, and Grand Coulee.

With the outbreak of World War II, Kaiser shifted again, this time to building ships. After the war and a short period in the automobile and aviation businesses, Kaiser moved to the then U.S. territory of Hawaii, where he remained until his death.

### IMPACT ON RESOURCE USE

Kaiser was an individual who, throughout his professional life, was in the business of making resources available to people. The roads his company built in the northwestern United States and British Columbia gave access to vast resources of timber and minerals in these areas. The dams he worked on at Hoover, Bonneville, and Grand Coulee gave hydroelectric power to large areas of the western United States. The flood control and irrigation from these dams also made the resources available. As Kaiser moved from roads and dams to bridges, ships, and cars, he was continuing to develop systems that allowed goods, people, and resources to move. Even when building piers in San Francisco Bay, he was facilitating the movement of resources through trade.

One of the statements consistently made about Kaiser was that, whether he was working with tar, concrete, steel, or aluminum, he always found the most efficient method of completing a project. He never depended on human strength to complete a task that a machine, vehicle, or processor could complete. This approach allowed his companies to bid successfully on many jobs, even when few workers were available. Over the years, Kaiser's treatment of his workers was outstanding; he provided them with health care, transportation, housing, and day care for their children. The crown jewel of the Kaiser empire was a prepaid health care system, Kaiser Permanente, which was one of the earliest and grew into one of the best of the managed health care systems.

*Robert J. Stewart*

SEE ALSO: Health, resource exploitation and; Hydroenergy; Timber industry; Transportation, energy use in.

## Kazakhstan

CATEGORIES: Countries; government and resources

*Kazakhstan, with a modest population and relatively undiversified industrial sector, is an important contributor to global resources because of its supply of raw materials, not because it is an important market.*

### THE COUNTRY

Kazakhstan, formerly a republic of the Soviet Union, is located in central Asia, positioned just south of Russia between the Caspian Sea and China. In 2007, in terms of total economic output, Kazakhstan's economy ranked fifty-fifth in the world, below Peru and above Morocco. Though Kazakhstan does not have a large population relative to its land size and is not considered a military or industrial power, it remains important to the world economy because of its impressive endowment of a diverse and abundant mix of raw-material natural resources. In fact, each of the naturally occurring elements in the periodic table can be found in Kazakhstan. The ninth largest country in the world in terms of area, Kazakhstan exhibits a wide climatic and physiographic variability. Its disparate climatic and landform regions include the Caspian Sea and surrounding deserts in the west; the vast arid and semiarid steppe, extending through central portions of the country; and the mountainous peaks and glaciers in the Alti Mountains of the northeast, the Tian Shan in the east, and the Ala Tau in the southeast. The enormous size of the country and the landform variation within conspire to improve natural resource potential, and Kazakhstan has become a world leader in production and reserves of many important energy and mineral resources. While most current press accounts focus on Kazakhstan's substantial oil and natural gas deposits, the country ranks in the top ten among countries in the production or reserves of at least thirteen different mineral resources, including chromium, uranium, zinc, coal, magnesium, cadmium, lead, titanium, iron ore, molybdenum, sulfur, silicon, and bauxite.

PETROLEUM

The extraction of crude oil and the revenue generated by its exportation form the dominant sector of Kazakhstan's economy. Oil production accounts for 30 percent of the country's gross domestic product (GDP) and 53 percent of export revenue. Revenue generated from the export of oil (combined with relatively successful privatization and economic reform efforts) contributed greatly to high rates of economic growth in the first decade of the twenty-first century, particularly during periods of high oil prices. The impact of Kazakhstan's oil resources on the global economy is substantial and is expected to increase for decades. In 2007, Kazakhstan produced approximately 1.45 million barrels of oil per day (1.7 percent of the world total), ranking it nineteenth in the world between the United Kingdom and Qatar. Of this total, 1,236,000 barrels per day are exported, ranking Kazakhstan seventeenth in the world, between Singa-

pore and Angola, in oil exports. While current production and export totals are significant, Kazakhstan's primary influence on the global economy may revolve around its expected production in the future. In terms of proved reserves (those deposits that can be recovered given current technological and market conditions) Kazakhstan is estimated to be home to 30 billion barrels of oil (2.2 percent of world total). This quantity places Kazakhstan eleventh among countries globally, between Nigeria and the United States. Kazakhstan's strategic importance in this regard (particularly for the United States) stems from its location outside the volatile Middle East.

Kazakhstan's economy is influenced by oil in many areas other than GDP and high rates of economic growth. It is a stimulant for foreign direct investment, a major source of employment and income, a source of revenue for public services, and a reason for the visible boom in urban office and residential building construction. The National Oil Fund of Kazakhstan (valued at more than $20 billion) is designed to insulate the economy from such sharp drops in crude oil prices as were experienced between summer, 2008, and winter, 2009 ($145 per barrel to $36 per barrel). While oil is an obvious asset to Kazakhstan's economy, its impacts have not been entirely positive. Such drawbacks include high levels of perceived corruption, high rates of inflation (around 18 percent), and possible Dutch disease-style diversion of economic resources from the manufacturing sector. (Dutch disease is an economic concept designed to relate the exploitation of natural resources to a decline in the manufacturing sector combined with moral decay.)

Initial global exuberance over Kazakhstan's oil reserves seems to have been tempered somewhat by unforeseen challenges, best exemplified by the experience with the large Kashagan oil field. This oil field, located deep below the northern Caspian Sea, is the world's largest oil field outside the Middle East and the fifth largest deposit in the world. Extraction of oil from the Kashagan field was first planned to begin in 2005, though production was delayed until at least 2014. Difficulties confronting the consortium of six foreign oil companies and Kazakhstan's national oil company include the deposit's high sulfur content and extreme geological pressure, heightened extraction challenges faced by the harsh physical environment, and the Kazakhstan government's levying of high tax rates and insistence on renegotiating contracts with foreign firms. Despite such difficulties,

# Kazakhstan: Resources at a Glance

*Official name:* Republic of Kazakhstan
*Government:* Republic under authoritarian
    presidential rule
*Capital city:* Astana
*Area:* 1,052,166 mi²; 2,724,900 km²
*Population (2009 est.):* 15,399,437
*Languages:* Kazakh and Russian
*Monetary unit:* tenge (KZT)

## ECONOMIC SUMMARY:

*GDP composition by sector (2008 est.):* agriculture, 5.3%; industry, 40.9%; services, 53.8%
*Natural resources:* major deposits of petroleum, natural gas, coal, iron ore, manganese, chrome ore, nickel, cobalt,
    copper, molybdenum, lead, zinc, bauxite, gold, uranium
*Land use (2005):* arable land, 8.28%; permanent crops, 0.05%; other, 91.67%
*Industries:* oil, coal, iron ore, manganese, chromite, lead, zinc, copper, titanium, bauxite, gold, silver, phosphates,
    sulfur, iron and steel, tractors and other agricultural machinery, electric motors, construction materials
*Agricultural products:* grain (mostly spring wheat), cotton, livestock
*Exports (2008 est.):* $71.97 billion
*Commodities exported (2001):* oil and oil products 59%, ferrous metals 19%, chemicals 5%, machinery 3%, grain,
    wool, meat, coal
*Imports (2008 est.):* $38.45 billion
*Commodities imported:* machinery and equipment, metal products, foodstuffs
*Labor force (2008 est.):* 8.412 million
*Labor force by occupation (2006):* agriculture, 31.5%; industry, 18.4%; services, 50%

## ENERGY RESOURCES:

*Electricity production (2007 est.):* 74.93 billion kWh
*Electricity consumption (2006 est.):* 61.81 billion kWh
*Electricity exports (2007 est.):* 3.528 billion kWh
*Electricity imports (2007 est.):* 3.665 billion kWh

*Natural gas production (2007 est.):* 27.88 billion m³
*Natural gas consumption (2007 est.):* 30.58 billion m³
*Natural gas exports (2007 est.):* 8.1 billion m³
*Natural gas imports (2007 est.):* 10.8 billion m³
*Natural gas proved reserves (Jan. 2008 est.):* 2.832 trillion m³

*Oil production (2007 est.):* 1.445 million bbl/day
*Oil imports (2005):* 127,600 bbl/day
*Oil proved reserves (Jan. 2008 est.):* 30 billion bbl

*Source:* Data from *The World Factbook 2009.* Washington, D.C.: Central Intelligence Agency, 2009.
*Notes:* Data are the most recent tracked by the CIA. Values are given in U.S. dollars. Abbreviations: bbl/day = barrels per day;
    GDP = gross domestic product; km² = square kilometers; kWh = kilowatt-hours; m³ = cubic meters; mi² = square miles.

Kazakhstan will continue to be a major player in the global oil market. Perhaps the crowning illustration of oil's significance to the Kazakh economy is President Nursultan Nazarbayev's ambitious "Kazakhstan 2030" campaign. This directive seeks to vault Kazakhstan into the world's fifty most economically developed counties. Perhaps not coincidentally, Kazakhstan's oil production is expected to peak in 2030.

## NATURAL GAS

While not nearly as significant to Kazakhstan's global resources as its oil deposits, natural gas is also an important resource, particularly in satisfying local demand. Kazakhstan's production of natural gas (nearly 28 trillion cubic meters in 2007) pales in comparison to neighboring Russia (654 trillion cubic meters), Turkmenistan (69 trillion cubic meters), and Uzbekistan (65 trillion cubic meters). Production is significant, however, placing Kazakhstan twenty-fifth among natural-gas-producing countries, between Pakistan and Venezuela. While much of the natural gas production fulfills domestic consumption, Kazakhstan does export more than 8 trillion cubic meters, ranking it twenty-third in the world between Brunei and the United Arab Emirates. Kazakhstan's importance to the global economy with respect to natural gas, however, stems from its substantial anticipated future production. Its natural gas reserves, in 2008, estimated to be 2.8 trillion cubic meters (1.6 percent of the world total), rank Kazakhstan eleventh in the world. Because Kazakhstan consumes slightly more natural gas than it produces (and also exports large amounts), it imports nearly 11 billion cubic meters from neighboring Uzbekistan. Kazakhstan's large area and inadequate internal natural gas transport infrastructure necessitate this import from Uzbekistan to serve the southern industrial and urban centers of Shymkent and Alma-Ata. Plans have been introduced to construct a gas pipeline linking Kazakhstan's gas fields with China's western province of Xinjiang.

## COAL

Kazakhstan is a major producer of coal and possesses large coal reserves. Kazakhstan ranks as the world's tenth largest coal producer. Estimates indicate that its coal reserves rank Kazakhstan eighth in the world. While domestic coal consumption of 78 short tons (in 2006) makes Kazakhstan a major consumer, the remaining 28 tons of coal it produces are exported. Kazakhstan was an important coal producer for the Soviet Union, though production declined after the country gained independence. However, production has risen from its 1999 low. More than one-half of Kazakhstan's Soviet-era subsurface coal mines have closed, falling victim to restructuring difficulties, numerous fatal mine accidents, and difficulty in attracting foreign investment. Coal is an important energy source within Kazakhstan, as coal-powered plants produce 80 percent of the country's electricity. The country's coalfields, located primarily in the central Qaraghandy region, are somewhat unique in the amount of coal-bed methane emitted. In fact, Kazakhstan is one of the only countries that actively harness this gas for energy purposes.

## URANIUM

Kazakhstan's uranium-related history includes its primacy as a source of the mineral for the Soviet Union and as the home of the Soviet nuclear weapons testing ground at the Polygon site near the northeastern city of Semey. Given the global concern over the burning of fossil fuels, greenhouse-gas emissions, and contributions to climate change and global warming, uranium is poised to become an increasingly important energy source in future decades, particularly as global electricity consumption is expected to double. Furthermore, more than thirty nuclear reactors are being built around the world, with an additional several hundred in advanced planning stages. As a result, Kazakhstan is well placed to capitalize on current and future demand, as it is the world's third largest uranium producer, behind Canada and Australia, and is home to the world's second largest uranium reserves, behind only Australia. Estimates put Kazakhstan's uranium endowment at 17 percent of the world's total. Kazakhstan's proximate location to the world's two most populous countries is also seen as an important aspect of its future uranium production and export. Increases in nuclear power in China and India are viewed as important markets for Kazakhstan's uranium. Unique features of Kazakhstan's uranium stocks include accessibility, high quality, and ease of extraction. By using the in situ leaching method, in which water and sulfuric acid free the mineral from surrounding rock, Kazakhstan is able to extract uranium at a relatively low cost. The arrest of Mukhtar Dzhakishev, former chief executive officer of the national uranium company Kazatomprom, is widely believed to be politically motivated. This arrest, and others like it, illustrates one aspect of the risky envi-

*Workers stand behind vessels containing uranium, one of Kazakhstan's main natural resources.* (Getty Images)

ronment associated with foreign investment in Kazakhstan's mining sector.

### CHROMIUM

Taking into account both current production and estimated reserves, Kazakhstan may be the global economy's most important source of chromium. Alternatively referred to as chrome ore or chromite, the mineral has a unique blend of corrosion resistance, hardness, and bright finish, which make it an indispensable input for jet-engine turbine blades, fuel-efficient engine, and, most important for the global economy, stainless steel. Kazakhstan produces 17 percent of the world's chromium, second only to South Africa. Regarding future production, Kazakhstan has the largest reserves of chromium in the world (26 percent of the world total), far outpacing South Africa (15 percent of world total) and India (3 percent of world total). Global demand for chromium largely mirrors that for stainless steel, the most important end use of chromium. In fact, there is not a substitute for chromium in the production of stainless steel, a fact that solidifies Kazakhstan's importance in the global chromium market. Kazkhrom, a chromium extraction company, nearly one-third of which is owned by the Kazakhstan government, is the world's second-largest chromium producer. About one-half of production is exported; the other half is used in Kazakhstan's sizable steel industry. Quantifying chromium's contribution to the Kazakhstan economy is difficult as the mineral is not an openly traded commodity and exchange details are not made public. Global shortages of chromium have, however, resulted from demand greatly outstripping supply. As a result, commodity prices were estimated to have doubled between 2007 and 2008. China—the world's largest steel producer and experiencing increases in construction, industrialization, and overall economic growth—is seen as an important current and future market for Kazakhstan's chromium.

### OTHER RESOURCES

Kazakhstan, ranked eighth in the world in production of manganese, is estimated to be home to the world's second largest manganese reserves. As of 2009, production was at only 20 percent capacity, and all manganese mining operations within Kazakhstan were foreign owned.

Kazakhstan is the eleventh largest producer among countries of lead and has the fourth largest lead reserves. Some estimates claim that global lead resources will be exhausted by 2050, so Kazakhstan may become a leading producer in coming decades. Much of the lead used now, however, is produced by recycled materials.

Home to the world's eleventh largest copper reserves, Kazakhstan is also the world's eleventh largest producer. Kazakhmys, the largest copper producer in Kazakhstan, exports 85 percent of its final product to China. Kazakhmys also produces silver, gold, and zinc.

Kazakhstan is the world's seventh largest producer of zinc and is home to the world's fifth largest reserves. While zinc is an important input in the galvanization of steel and the production of brass, its prices have fallen steadily as global demand has dropped precipitously. The Kazakhstan metals company Kazakhmys, in response to poor market conditions, announced in June, 2009, that it was suspending operations at its Balkhash zinc production facility.

Kazakhstan is the eleventh largest producer of iron ore in the world and is home to the world's seventh largest reserves. Production has been declining in recent years, however, and much of the country's deposits are considered of low-grade quality.

Kazakhstan's other resources include important animal and plant resources. The Caspian Sea, for example, is home to the endangered beluga sturgeon, noted for its production of world-class caviar. Apples appear to have originated in Kazakhstan, where forests of wild apples offer a vast genetic "library" for this valuable plant. Agricultural researchers have collected seeds from Kazakhstan's apple forests in an attempt to conserve the biodiversity of apples in case the monoculture varieties that dominate world markets should face catastrophic disease from pests, fungus, or viruses.

*Kristopher D. White*

FURTHER READING

Fergus, Michael, and Janar Jandosova. *Kazakhstan: Coming of Age.* London: Stacey International, 2004.
Koven, Peter. "Kazakhstan Unrest Dims Uranium Ore Shares Forty Percent." *Financial Post,* May 28, 2009.
Kramer, Andrew E. "Capitalizing on Oil's Rise, Ka-

zakhstan Expands Stake in Huge Offshore Project." *The New York Times,* January 15, 2008.
Lustgarten, Abrahm. "Nuclear Power's White-Hot Metal." *Fortune* 157, no. 6 (March 31, 2008).
Papp, John F. "Chromium." In *2006 Minerals Yearbook.* Denver, Colo.: U.S. Geological Survey, 2008.
Peck, Anne E. *Economic Development in Kazakhstan: The Role of Large Enterprises and Foreign Investment.* New York: Routledge, 2004.
Pomfret, Richard. "Kazakhstan's Economy Since Independence: Does the Oil Boom Offer a Second Chance for Sustainable Development?" *Europe-Asia Studies* 57, no. 6 (2005): 859-876.
Serafin, Tatiana. "Emerging Market Gold Mine." *Forbes* 177, no. 6 (March 27, 2006).
Timmons, Heather. "Kazakhstan: Oil Majors Agree to Develop Field." *The New York Times,* February 26, 2006.

SEE ALSO: Chromium; Coal; Nuclear energy; Oil and natural gas reservoirs; Strategic resources; Uranium.

# Kyanite

CATEGORY: Mineral and other nonliving resources

WHERE FOUND

Because metamorphosed high-alumina shales are common in the mountain belts of the world, kyanite group minerals are widely distributed. However, concentrations of the minerals in reasonably large crystal size are required for economic production. Major kyanite ore reserves are found in the southern Appalachian Piedmont and in India. Sillimanite has been mined in India, Australia, and South Africa. Large deposits of commercial-grade andalusite occur in France, South Africa, and North Carolina.

PRIMARY USES

Kyanite minerals are used in high-temperature metallurgical processes. They are also used in high-strength porcelain manufacture.

TECHNICAL DEFINITION

Kyanite is an aluminum silicate mineral, $Al_2SiO_5$, also written $Al_2O_3 \cdot SiO_2$. Two other minerals, sillimanite and andalusite, have identical composition but crystallize in different forms determined by the temperature and pressure at the time of crystallization. The three minerals are polymorphs (different forms) of $Al_2SiO_5$ and constitute the kyanite, or sillimanite, group of minerals.

### DESCRIPTION, DISTRIBUTION, AND FORMS
Kyanite crystallizes as blade-shaped crystals with vitreous luster and white to blue color. Sillimanite is most commonly finely fibrous and brown in color. Andalusite occurs as elongate, cigar-shaped crystals in a variety of colors. Kyanite-group minerals occur most commonly in metamorphosed high-alumina shales. Relatively high pressures and temperatures produce kyanite, intermediate pressures and high temperatures produce sillimanite, and low temperatures and pressures produce andalusite.

### HISTORY
Kyanite has been mined in many parts of the world. In the past, it was treasured for its blue color. Some traditions indicate kyanite has healing powers.

### OBTAINING KYANITE
Kyanite minerals require varying amounts of preparation before use. Massive aggregates of kyanite and sillimanite that occur in India have been sawed or carved to desired shapes, but kyanite group mineral resources in Europe and North America normally require separation of the minerals from associated quartz, micas, and other minerals, resulting in a granular product. The granules, which do not adhere to one another, are mixed with various materials, usually including fireclay and water, to produce a moldable product that can be used as mortar between refractory bricks or molded into bricks or other useful shapes.

As a high-temperature furnace lined with "green" (unfired) superduty refractory bricks is heated, the kyanite group minerals in the green brick and mortar convert to mullite. Uniquely, the volume of mullite and silica glass resulting from the conversion of kyanite to mullite is about 18 percent greater than the original volume of kyanite. The volume increase occurs at about the same temperature that other materials are shrinking in volume, and this phenomenon tends to mechanically stabilize the furnace lining. Therefore, there is a significant advantage to including raw kyanite in the green products.

### USES OF KYANITE
The kyanite group minerals are used as superduty refractories in high-temperature metallurgical processes, especially steel production, and in high-strength porcelain products, typically automobile spark plug insulators. On heating to about 1,400° Celsius, the kyanite group minerals alter to mullite ($3Al_2O_3 \cdot 2SiO_2$) plus silica glass. Mullite remains stable and strong to 1,810° Celsius. The kyanite group minerals are therefore very desirable as refractories in steel and glass furnace linings and as materials for kiln furniture (product supports) in high-temperature ceramic manufacture.

Kyanite group minerals compete economically with synthetic mullite refractories. Synthetic mullite is produced by heating or fusing an appropriate mixture of high alumina and siliceous materials. Near Americus, Georgia, naturally occurring mixtures of

*Kyanite is used in metallurgical processes and can range in color from white to blue.* (©John Carter/Dreamstime.com)

bauxite and kaolin—and at Niagara, New York, alumina and glass-grade silica sand—are used to produce synthetic mullite.

*Robert E. Carver*

WEB SITE

U.S. GEOLOGICAL SURVEY
Kyanite
http://minerals.usgs.gov/minerals/pubs/
    commodity/kyanite/index.html#myb

SEE ALSO: Ceramics; Clays; Metamorphic processes, rocks, and mineral deposits; Minerals, structure and physical properties of; Orthosilicate minerals.

# Kyoto Protocol

CATEGORY: Laws and conventions
DATE: Produced in June, 1992; adopted for use on December 11, 1997; entered into force February 16, 2005

*The Kyoto Protocol is an environmental treaty created to stabilize greenhouse gases (GHGs) in the atmosphere. It is a protocol to the United Nations Framework Convention on Climate Change, which was produced at the United Nations Conference on Environment and Development in Brazil from June 3 to 14, 1992.*

## BACKGROUND
In 1987, the Montreal Protocol was established, creating a treaty to phase out production of a major group of industrial gases, including chlorofluorocarbons, that deplete the ozone layer. The Kyoto Protocol was established to enhance energy efficiency in areas not covered in the Montreal Protocol. It encourages research and reform, reducing emissions of GHGs and methane, as well as facilitation of measures to address climate change. The protocol includes twenty-eight articles addressing climate change in transport, energy, and industry sectors and stresses the need for research, publications, and periodic review of the protocol.

## PROVISIONS
The Kyoto Protocol establishes legally binding commitments for the reduction of carbon dioxide ($CO_2$), methane ($CH_4$), nitrous oxide ($N_2O$), and sulfur hexafluoride ($SF_6$) for developed countries for the post-2000 period and control of hydrofluorocarbons (HFCs) and perfluorocarbons (PFCs), produced by Annex I (industrialized) nations. Cuts in these gases are measured against a baseline (from either 1990 or 1995).

As of 2008, 183 parties had ratified the Kyoto Protocol with specific goals of quantified emissions limitation or reduction commitments of 5.2 percent in comparison to 1990, collectively. The developed countries committed to reducing emissions of the six key GHGs through cuts of as much as 8 percent. For some countries, stabilization of emissions was the goal. By 2005, progress had to be demonstrated in all countries, and targets were to be achieved between 2008 and 2012.

## IMPACT ON RESOURCE USE
In order for the impact of the protocol to be evaluated, countries were required to submit information on their climate change programs and promote public awareness, education, and training. Monitoring and compliance procedures were designed to determine whether parties were fulfilling their obligations.

*Upon the adoption of the Kyoto Protocol, chairman Raul Estrada Oyuela shakes hands with a delegate, while other diplomats celebrate with applause. (AP/Wide World Photos)*

A national system for estimating the GHG emissions was also required. The protocol called for an expert team to review the inventories and manage their GHG portfolios, which all nations in Annex I and most of the non-Annex I countries established.

Ultimately, the protocol has forced countries to address their overuse of fuels responsible for global warming and gave them sufficient reason to reduce local and regional air pollution. Compliance was expected to reduce petroleum dependence and inefficiencies in energy production and use. Further, the economic burden of implementing the policies were expected to be worth the investment, especially when considering the socioenvironmental costs of not abiding by the protocol.

Germany, for example, reduced its GHG emissions by 22.4 percent between 1990 and 2008, and in 2004, France shut down its last coal mine to decrease its $CO_2$ emissions. Overall, the Kyoto Protocol demonstrated that the world could produce the same amount of energy with less coal, more gas, and the use of more renewable sources of energy.

*Gina M. Robertiello*

SEE ALSO: Agenda 21; Climate Change and Sustainable Energy Act; Edison Electric Institute; Greenhouse gases and global climate change; Intergovernmental Panel on Climate Change; Montreal Protocol; United Nations climate change conferences; United Nations Framework Convention on Climate Change.

# L

La Niña. *See* El Niño and La Niña

## Lakes

CATEGORY: Ecological resources

*Lakes are inland bodies of water that fill depressions in the Earth's surface. They are generally too deep to allow vegetation to cover the entire surface and may be fresh or saline.*

### BACKGROUND

Lakes are standing bodies of water that occupy hollows or depressions on the surface of the Earth. Small, shallow lakes are usually called ponds, but there is no specific size and depth that are used to distinguish ponds from lakes. The scientific study of the physical, chemical, climatological, biological, and ecological aspects of lakes is known as limnology.

Precipitation is the primary source of water for lakes, in the form of either direct runoff by streams that drain into a depression or groundwater that slowly seeps into a lake by passing through subsurface earth materials. Although lakes are generally thought of as freshwater bodies, many lakes in arid regions become very salty because of the high evaporation rate, which concentrates inflowing salts. The Caspian Sea, the Great Salt Lake, and the Dead Sea are classic examples of saline lakes.

Although freshwater and saline lakes account for a minute fraction of the world's water—almost all of it is in the oceans and in glaciers—they are an extremely valuable resource. In terms of ecosystems, lakes are divided into a pelagial (open-water) zone and a littoral (shore) zone where macrovegetation grows. Sediments free of vegetation that occur below the pelagial zone are in the profundal zone.

The renewal time for freshwater lakes ranges from one to one hundred years. The length of time varies directly with lake volume and average depth, and indirectly with a lake's rate of discharge. The rate of renewal, or turnover time, for lakes is much less than that of oceans and glacial ice, which is measured in thousands of years.

Lake size varies enormously. Lake sizes range from small depressions of a hectare or less to that of the Caspian Sea, the largest in the world, which covers 371,000 square kilometers. This one body of saline water is larger than all of Germany. The Great Lakes of North America (Lakes Superior, Huron, Michigan, Erie, and Ontario) make up the largest continuous mass of fresh water on the planet, with a combined area of more than 245,000 square kilometers—larger than the total area of Great Britain. The largest single freshwater lake in the world is Lake Superior, with a surface area of more than 82,000 square kilometers—nearly the size of Ireland. Other major freshwater lakes include Lake Victoria in Africa, Lake Huron, and Lake Michigan, with approximate areas of 69,000, 60,000, and 58,000 square kilometers, respectively.

Lake Baikal in Russia not only is the deepest lake in the world (1,620 meters) but also contains the largest amount of fresh water (23,600 cubic kilometers). This one lake alone contains approximately 20 percent of all of the fresh water in the world. The combined volume, 22,810 cubic kilometers, of all of the five Great Lakes is still less than Lake Baikal. However, Lake Baikal and the Great Lakes account for more than 40 percent of the total amount of fresh water in the world. The second and third largest freshwater lakes in the world in terms of volume are Lake Tanganyika in Africa and Lake Superior, with 18,900 and 12,100 cubic kilometers, respectively. Lake Tanganyika is also the second deepest lake in the world (1,433 meters). Lake Titicaca in the Andes Mountains of Peru and Bolivia is the highest lake in the world at 3,800 meters elevation, while the Dead Sea in Israel and Jordan is the lowest, at an elevation of 422 meters below sea level.

### ORIGINS OF LAKES

Lakes are unevenly distributed on the Earth's surface. Nearly half of the world's lakes are in Canada, and Minnesota is proud of its reputed count of ten thousand lakes. Both Canada and Minnesota were deeply affected by continental glaciation during the various stages of the Pleistocene epoch, or Ice Age, which lasted for approximately two million years. In fact, most of the world's lakes were formed as a consequence of the movement of continental ice sheets during the Pleistocene. For example, the Great Lakes were formed by advancing ice sheets that carved out large basins in the bedrock. In many other instances, existing valleys were eroded and deepened by glacial advance, resulting in the formation of large lakes such as Great Bear Lake and Great Slave Lake in central Canada (31,153 and 27,200 square kilometers, respectively). In some instances, long, narrow valleys were oriented parallel to the movement of the ice sheet. When the ends of these valleys became blocked by glacial debris,

*Aerial view of Lake Huron, one of North America's five Great Lakes.*

the basins filled up with water to form long, narrow lakes. The Finger Lakes of western New York State provide an excellent example of this process. Numerous small lakes and ponds were formed in kettles, which are small depressions found in glacial deposits called moraines. Blocks of stagnant ice that became trapped in the morainal deposits melted and formed kettle lakes. Minnesota and many other areas in the upper Midwest and central Canada have numerous kettle lakes with this type of origin.

Tectonic activity in the crust of the Earth formed lake basins in a number of ways. For example, faulting results in rift valleys that can fill with water. The downfaulted block is referred to as a graben and accounts for the deepest lakes in the world, Lakes Baikal and Tanganyika. These lakes are also unusual in that they contain a large number of relict endemic species of plants and animals. More than 80 percent of the plant and animal species in Lake Baikal are endemic only to this lake. Examples of graben lakes in the United States include Lake Tahoe, in the Sierra Mountains of California and Nevada, and Pyramid Lake, north of Reno in Nevada. The Truckee River flows from Lake Tahoe into Pyramid Lake.

Several large, isolated lake basins have resulted from tectonic movements that caused a moderate uplift of the marine seabed. The Caspian Sea and the Aral Sea in central Asia were separated by uplifted mountain ranges in the Miocene epoch (from 5 to 24 million

years ago). Lake Okeechobee in central Florida, which is the second largest freshwater lake in the coterminous United States (Lake Michigan is the largest), with an area of 1,890 square kilometers, was a shallow depression in the seafloor when it was uplifted during the Pliocene epoch some 2 to 5 million years ago as part of the formation of the Floridian peninsula.

The third major natural cause of lakes is volcanic activity. Lava flows can block stream valleys and form lake basins, and collapsing volcanic craters form large basins called calderas. Crater Lake in Oregon, with an area of 64 square kilometers and a depth of 608 meters (making it the ninth deepest in the world), is a well-known example of a caldera lake. The fourth type of natural origin occurs in humid regions underlain by limestone. This type of rock is susceptible to dissolution by percolating water. In time, the limestone goes into solution, and the result is a conical and circular sinkhole. These sinkhole lakes are very common in limestone areas of the Balkans and the midwestern United States and in central Florida. Oxbow lakes develop in meandering stream channels of gently sloping alluvial floodplains that have been abandoned by lateral shifts of the river. These are common in the floodplain of the lower Mississippi River.

Lakes, whatever the nature of their origin, are ephemeral features on the Earth's surface. In contrast to many other landforms on the Earth, such as mountains and valleys, lakes are transient. Drier climatic conditions, erosion of an outlet, natural and human-induced sedimentation, water diversion, and nutrient inflow inexorably result in a short life span of hundreds to thousands of years. On a geological time-scale, this longevity is extremely short.

LAKE STRATIFICATION

Solar heating of a lake results in thermal stratification, which is a major factor in lake structure. This process is the most important physical event in the annual cycle of a lake. Thermal stratification is common in many midlatitude lakes that are deeper than approximately 10 meters. During the high Sun or summer months, an epilimnion—a warm, lighter, circulating, and relatively turbulent layer—develops in the surface waters; it has a range of thickness of about 2 to 20 meters. A lower level of denser, cooler, and relatively quiet water develops below the epilimnion. The vertical extent of this hypolimnion level can be large or small, depending on the depth of the lake. The thermocline, or metalimnion, forms a zone of transition between the two layers where the temperature changes abruptly. It is generally several meters in thickness. The stratification is not caused by the temperature change but rather by the difference in the densities of the water in the epilimnion (lighter) and the hypolimnion (heavier). As the fall season approaches, heat loss from the surface exceeds heat inputs, and the epilimnion cools, becomes denser, and mixes with the deeper layers. Eventually, all of the water in the lake is included in the circulation as the fall turnover begins. Most lakes experience a seasonal cycle of stratification and mixing that is a key component of their ecology.

RESERVOIRS

Reservoirs are artificial lakes; they range from small farm or fish ponds of less than a hectare in size to massive impoundments. The three largest reservoirs in terms of capacity are Lake Kariba on the Zambezi River, which forms the boundary between Zimbabwe and Zambia in Africa; Bratsk on the Angara River in Siberia; and Lake Nasser on the Nile in Egypt. The largest reservoirs in the United States are Lake Mead and Lake Powell on the Colorado River. Reservoirs are built for hydropower, flood control, navigation, water supply, low flow maintenance for water quality purposes, recreation, or any combination thereof. Reservoir management is a specialized field, since water releases and storage requirements must fit in with the operating schedule for each system and watershed.

Although dams and reservoirs have brought many benefits to society, they are associated with several environmental problems. For example, the dams on the Columbia River in the Pacific Northwest inhibit the ability of salmon to return upstream where they spawn. Fish ladders have provided only a partial solution to this problem. Large impoundments such as Lake Mead (behind Hoover Dam on the Colorado River) can store so much water that the additional weight on the Earth's crust has been linked to small to moderate earthquakes in parts of Nevada hundreds of kilometers away. Reservoirs, by design, regulate the flow of water downstream. In the process of doing so, they deny the river its normal seasonal flush of water in the spring, which is necessary for a healthy aquatic ecosystem. As a means of addressing this flushing problem on the Grand Canyon portion of the Colorado River, a large amount of water was released from Lake Powell, which is upstream from the Grand Canyon, in a short period of time so as to replicate the spring flood. Considerable hydropower revenues were lost in this experiment, but there were many benefits to the ecology of the river.

EUTROPHICATION

The aging of a lake by biological enrichment is known as eutrophication. The water in young lakes is cold and clear, with minimal amounts of plant and animal life. The lake is then in the oligotrophic state. As time goes on, streams that flow into the lake bring in nutrients such as nitrates and phosphates, which encourage aquatic plant growth. As the fertility in the lake increases, the plant and animal life increases, and organic remains start accumulating on the bottom. The lake is in the process of becoming eutrophic. Silt and organic debris continue to accumulate over time, slowly making the lake shallower. Marsh plants that thrive in shallow water start expanding and gradually fill in the original lake basin. Eventually the lake becomes a bog and then dry land.

This natural aging of a lake can take thousands of years, depending upon the size of the lake, the local climate, and other factors. However, human activities can substantially accelerate the eutrophication process. Among the problems caused by humans are the pollution of lakes by nutrients from agricultural runoff and poorly treated wastewater from municipalities and industries. The nutrients encourage algal growth, which clogs the lake and removes dissolved oxygen from the water. The oxygen is needed for other forms of aquatic

life. The lake enters a hypereutrophic state as declining levels of dissolved oxygen result in incomplete oxidation of plant remains, a situation that eventually causes the death of the lake as a functioning aquatic ecosystem. In a real sense, the lake chokes itself to death.

## CLIMATIC EFFECTS

Lakes moderate local climates. Since the specific heat of water is five times that of dry land, lakes ameliorate cold-air-mass intrusions in midlatitude regions. The resultant extension of the frost-free period can be extremely beneficial to agriculture. The successful vineyards on the shores of the Finger Lakes in New York and the fruit-tree belts in upper New York just south of Lake Ontario are a well-known example of this benefit. Even in Florida, the presence of Lake Okeechobee helps the agricultural areas on the southern and southeastern shores; cold air from the northwest is warmed as it passes over the lake.

The Great Lakes are associated with a "lake effect" that results in additional snow falling in those areas where cold Canadian air masses pass over the lakes from the northwest in the winter, pick up moisture from the relatively warmer water, and then precipitate the snow on the southern and eastern shores of the lakes. The amounts of snow deposited during these routine occurrences can be substantial.

*Robert M. Hordon*

## FURTHER READING

Brönmark, Christer, and Lars-Anders Hansson. *The Biology of Lakes and Ponds.* 2d ed. Oxford, England: Oxford University Press, 2005.

Burgis, Mary, and Pat Morris. *The Natural History of Lakes.* Illustrations by Guy Troughton. New York: Cambridge University Press, 1987.

Cole, Gerald A. *Textbook of Limnology.* 4th ed. Prospect Heights, Ill.: Waveland Press, 1994.

Dempsey, Dave. *On the Brink: The Great Lakes in the Twenty-first Century.* East Lansing: Michigan State University Press, 2004.

Dodson, Stanley I. *Introduction to Limnology.* New York: McGraw-Hill, 2005.

Håkanson, Lars, and M. Jansson. *Principles of Lake Sedimentology.* New York: Springer, 1983.

Margalef, R., ed. *Limnology Now: A Paradigm of Planetary Problems.* New York: Elsevier, 1994.

Thornton, Kent W., Bruce L. Kimmel, and Forrest E. Payne, eds. *Reservoir Limnology: Ecological Perspectives.* New York: Wiley, 1990.

Thorson, Robert M. *Beyond Walden: The Hidden History of America's Kettle Lakes and Ponds.* New York: Walker, 2009.

Wetzel, Robert G. *Limnology: Lake and River Ecosystems.* 3d ed. San Diego, Calif.: Academic Press, 2001.

## WEB SITES

U.S. ENVIRONMENTAL PROTECTION AGENCY
Aquatic Biodiversity: Lakes, Ponds, and Reservoirs
http://www.epa.gov/bioiweb1/aquatic/lake-r.html

U.S. ENVIRONMENTAL PROTECTION AGENCY
Clean Lakes
http://www.epa.gov/owow/lakes

SEE ALSO: Dams; Ecosystems; Eutrophication; Glaciation; Groundwater; Hydrology and the hydrologic cycle; Streams and rivers; Water supply systems; Wetlands.

# Land ethic

CATEGORIES: Environment, conservation, and resource management; social, economic, and political issues

*Land ethic is a nonanthropocentric ethical perspective on the relationship between human beings and the natural environment.*

## DEFINITION

Land ethic is a nonanthropocentric perspective of ethics, in which *Homo sapiens* is seen as simply a member of the ecosystem and not as the master of the Earth. It is also the title of one of Aldo Leopold's essays, included in *A Sand County Almanac* (1949), one of the most influential books ever published on the ethics of modern nature conservation and one of the founding texts of environmental ethics. From this perspective, other nonhuman entities have in their own right a place on the planet, a concept which imposes on humans the duty to respect and preserve the integrity and stability of the natural environment for present and future generations of all living beings.

## OVERVIEW

The relevant moral community or the entities to whom a particular set of moral duties and obligations applies have three dimensions: biological, temporal, and geographical. In the anthropocentric perspective of ethics, the relevant moral community includes only *Homo sapiens*, while in the nonanthropocentric perspective (biocentrism, ecocentrism, ecofeminism, and deep ecology) the moral community is holistic and includes other nonhuman entities. This means that the moral community also includes, as Leopold said, soil, water, plants, and animals—or, in a single word, the entire Land. Therefore, all forms of life have an intrinsic value and deserve moral concern independently of their utilitarian value for humans. However, whether this means only sentient forms of life or also nonsentient forms, and whether this is a responsibility toward individuals or groups of individuals such as species, ecosystems, or ecological communities, remains open for debate. This enlarged and holistic responsibility to other forms of life extends also to future generations and to other geographic areas—in fact, to the entire Earth ecosystem. From a nonanthropocentric point of view, only those actions that tend to preserve the integrity and stability of the ecosystems at a local and global scale can be considered correct.

Since Leopold first enunciated the basic principles of his land ethic in the 1940's, nonanthropocentric perspectives gained gradual acceptance in society and in political discourses. Though the 1972 U.N. Stockholm Declaration on the Environment may be within the anthropocentric ethical paradigm, documents and policies adopted by the United Nations in relation to the environment in the 1980's and afterward reflected increasingly nonanthropocentric and nonconsequentialist perspectives. That was the case of the U.N. World Charter for Nature (1982), which stated the principle that human needs should be fulfilled with full respect for the essential natural processes; the creation, in 1983, of the U.N. World Commission on Environment and Development, which produced the landmark report *Our Common Future*, also known as the Brundtland Report; the subsequent developments associated with the Earth Summit of 1992 in Rio de Janeiro, Brazil; and conventions on other environmental issues.

*Carlos Nunes Silva*

FURTHER READING
Beatley, Timothy. *Ethical Land Use: Principles of Policy and Planning*. Baltimore: Johns Hopkins University Press, 1994.

Leopold, Aldo. *A Sand County Almanac*. Updated ed. Topeka, Kans.: Topeka Bindery, 2000.
Silva, Carlos Nunes. "Urban Planning and Ethics." In *Encyclopedia of Public Administration and Public Policy*, edited by Jack Rabin. New York: Marcel Dekker, 2005.

SEE ALSO: Agenda 21; Deep ecology; Earth Summit; Ecology; Ecozones and biogeographic realms; International Union for Conservation of Nature; United Nations climate change conferences; United Nations Framework Convention on Climate Change.

# Land Institute

CATEGORY: Organizations, agencies, and programs
DATE: Established 1976

*Through its Natural Systems Agriculture, the Land Institute seeks to make conservation a consequence of agricultural production by returning to natural and diverse perennial grain crops, as opposed to single species annual crops. Its mission is to improve food and fiber security, lessen soil erosion, reduce dependency on and pollution caused by fossil fuels and toxic chemicals, and enhance sustainable agriculture based on ecosystems that existed before industrialized agriculture.*

BACKGROUND
Globally, the demand for and production of food continue to increase, and major grain crops, such as wheat and corn, make up more than two-thirds of the human caloric intake. Plant geneticist Wes Jackson believed that the best agricultural practices are not being used to produce these grains. As a result, current methods of agricultural production may not be sustainable in the future because of their negative impact on global ecology. Among these practices are overreliance on nonrenewable resources such as fossil fuels. In addition, growing single-species annual crops, especially in areas that are not suitable for their production, causes serious soil erosion and depletion of nutrients from the soil because of tilling. This loss in soil and nutrients ultimately results in reduced production. Moreover, toxins, chemical fertilizers, and pesticides necessary to sustain nonnative, annual, single-species crops are increasingly being found in human tissues.

In 1976, Jackson left a tenured teaching position at California State University, Sacramento, to create the Land Institute, which has become a globally recognized model of sustainable agriculture. With his wife, Dana, Jackson founded the Land Institute for the purpose of performing sustainable agriculture research and breeding plants that would have the ecological stability of native, perennial prairie plants but would yield grain in amounts comparable to annuals.

Extremely critical of industrialized agriculture, Jackson sought to explore the possibilities of "perennial polyculture" as an alternative to the growing and harvesting of annual grains. One of his primary concerns was to halt the soil erosion that he believed was exacerbated by monoculture or single-species agriculture techniques and that he believed would eventually lead to a crisis in American agriculture.

The Jacksons established the Land Institute in Salina, Kansas, on a minimal budget, constructing the institute's building themselves. Although sustainable agriculture was the main purpose of the facility, early experiments involved testing wind power and using hay bales to construct houses. In 1980, Jackson published a book entitled *New Roots of Agriculture* that argued against agricultural practices that have been ongoing for more than ten thousand years, because of his belief that they are not sustainable. Jackson proposed a new form of agriculture based on natural ecosystems, which became known as Natural Systems Agriculture. Natural Systems Agriculture, as practiced on the Kansas prairie, involves the growing of diverse perennial plants to prevent depletion and erosion of the soil and destruction of the ecosystem.

The Land Institute consists of a 111-acre nonprofit research and education facility for a small number of students. The Land Institute utilizes the natural, surrounding prairie land for ecology and agronomy research and observation. The main research facility at the Land Institute is a large greenhouse. In-house scientists, including breeders and agroecologists, work with ten to twelve graduate students who receive fellowships to participate in the institute's research programs. The students also work on the institute's farm while completing an intensive, alternative education program. These students develop into informed multidisciplinary leaders who are dedicated to building a sustainable agriculture and integrating it into a sustainable society.

The research that takes place at the Land Institute involves breeding prototype plants from native edible perennial grains. Scientifically, the Land Institute has shown that producing perennial, edible grain crops is feasible. The goal of the institute is to one day make these grain crops commercially feasible.

Although sustainable perennial agriculture may not be available until 2030 or later, the Land Institute has made great strides in developing some of the following crops: perennial wheat varieties, drought-hardy grain sorghum, the prairie legume known as Illinois bundleflower, and a perennial species of sunflower. In the future, the Land Institute hopes to breed additional perennial grain species from crops such as rice, flax, maize, and chickpeas. The Land Institute has collaborated with many public institutions to carry out its Natural Systems Agriculture research in locations other than the Land Institute facility. The institute shares its research willingly and distributes perennial parent seeds freely, with the objective of supporting scientists conducting related research worldwide.

IMPACT ON RESOURCE USE

Jackson, through his agricultural practices at the Land Institute, seeks to develop what he refers to as an ecological agriculture, or a marriage between ecology and agriculture. This ecological agriculture involves the production of multiple plant species rather than just one and the planting of perennial rather than annual grain crops. Significant challenges include breeding perennials with increased seed yields and with heads of grain that resist shattering, as wild grains typically release their seeds if knocked. The Land Institute supports research mainly in two areas: perennial grain crop production, through breeding and nurturing of new major grain crops and domestication of wild perennials, and diversification of grain crops to achieve more efficient use of nutrients and water, enhance pest and disease control, and increase productivity.

The Land Institute has several programs that seek to develop sustainable agriculture and prosperous, enduring human communities. These programs include Perennial Grain Cropping Research, the Climate Energy Project, and Sunshine Farm Research. In addition, the Land Institute offers short courses to scientists and nonfarmers and conducts seasonal festivals for the purpose of educating others about its Natural Systems Agriculture. The Land Institute's "Land Report" and numerous other educational outreach projects, such as its Prairie Writer's Circle, help promote the institute's mission, demonstrate the resilience and sustainability of natural systems, and explain how natural ecosystems apply to agriculture and human communities.

The purpose of the Perennial Grain Cropping Research program is to breed and nurture perennial prototypes of annual grain crops that do not require tilling, chemicals, or pesticides. This program's dual goals are to supply humanity's food needs while conserving resources and eliminating toxins. Both plant breeders and agroecologists work in this program.

The Climate Energy Project (CEP) came about after a serious drought in Salina, during which the local river went dry. The CEP, now located in Lawrence, Kansas, has many purposes, including public outreach and education about climate and energy conservation. The CEP is also involved in climate change and renewable energy research. The CEP maintains a website that provides educational materials.

The Sunshine Farm Research Program seeks to respond to the fundamental and underlying question concerning the Land Institute's Natural Systems Agriculture: Can this new form of agricultural production based on a perennial polyculture be profitable for the small farmer? One purpose of this ten-year program has been to model a farm based on Natural Systems Agriculture. The model farm uses renewable energy including Sun power, wind power, photoelectric cells, and other natural sources that can be generated on the farm rather than using fossil fuel. Further reductions in fossil-fuel use are achieved by using refined soybean oil rather than diesel fuel in farm equipment and returning to draft horses for some of the farm work. In addition, soil erosion is reduced by raising hybrid perennial crops rather than annuals, and toxic chemical use is mitigated through planting of genetically diverse grain crops that are pest resistant. The Sunshine Farm Research Program also involves comparison of energy, materials, and labor data from a 20.2 hectare farm raising conventional crops with the same data from a 40.5 hectare perennial grain pasture for cattle grazing. The data will assist in the affordability and sustainability analyses of the new farming techniques.

The potential for sustainable agriculture is important. The Land Institute plans to continue research into such diverse areas as biofuel and ethanol production and how they may impact future food production, the use of crop biomass for synthetic organics, community-scale farmer cooperatives, alternative energy strategies, and perennial grain breeding. The

Land Institute also had proposed to study ecological community development, as opposed to conventional economic development, in Matfield Green, Kansas. However, the institute sold its properties in Matfield Green. People may visit the Salina facility, which includes prairie flora and herb gardens and an area of virgin tall-grass prairie, containing more than two hundred naturally growing species. Other displays at the Salina facility concern alternative energy and environmental strategies.

*Thomas A. Eddy, updated by Carol A. Rolf*

FURTHER READING

Jackson, Wes. *New Roots for Agriculture.* Lincoln: University of Nebraska Press, 1985.

_____. "The Next Forty-nine Years." *Public Library Quarterly* 27, no. 2 (2008): 167-173.

Richards, Donald. "Economics and 'Nature's Standard': Wes Jackson and the Land Institute." *Review of Radical Political Economics* 41, no. 2 (2009): 186-195.

WEB SITE

THE LAND INSTITUTE
http://www.landinstitute.org

SEE ALSO: Agriculture industry; Agronomy; Erosion and erosion control; Jackson, Wes; Land management; Monoculture agriculture; Soil management.

# Land management

CATEGORY: Environment, conservation, and resource management

*Efforts put toward using land to its best advantage are collectively called land management. Land management decisions affect both public and private lands, and they entail such issues as what use or uses—agriculture, forestry, mining, industry, residential development, and ecological preservation—should be encouraged or discouraged in a given area. Appropriate land management has become increasingly important as concerns about pollution and the environment have grown.*

BACKGROUND

"Land management" is a term that describes decisions and practices regarding the uses of land. Land management may emphasize any one of a variety of different land uses. Farmers, for example, may manage their land to obtain the most efficient crop production, while city planners seek to ensure that land within their boundaries is used to benefit the community as a whole. The land that comprises the fifty United States covers about 9.06 million square kilometers, and to some extent laws govern the management of every centimeter, public or private. The intent of much of this legislation is to prevent practices that pollute or harm the environment in other ways. Whether landowners wish to harvest timber, graze livestock, or operate ski areas, legislation sets clean air and water requirements. Permits are also required for any activity that disturbs stream beds or changes the channel of a water course.

As population increases, public land administrators are under greater pressure to resolve conflicts over land use while protecting the land from abuse. Myriad questions may be raised. How much timberland should be cut for forest products, and how much preserved for watershed and wildlife? Should New York City, for example, restrict economic development in the Hudson River watershed to reduce pollution caused by storm-water runoff?

### PUBLIC LAND MANAGEMENT

In 1960, Congress passed the Multiple-Use Sustained-Yield Act. In many respects it simply codified practices (particularly regarding forest management) that had been followed informally since the early twentieth century. Under a multiple-use approach, land is managed so as to support more than one use (such as forestry and recreation) simultaneously. Sustained yield refers to management (again, particularly forest management) that fosters continuous production without depleting the resource.

A few years later, in 1964, the Public Land Law Review Commission was chartered to study federal land policies. Its report, released in 1970, was criticized for its recommendation that there be designated areas on public lands that would produce income for private companies, such as mining and ranching interests. Termed "dominant use," the concept was not new. In 1878, John Wesley Powell, an explorer and member of a commission to study public lands, had proposed

*The Lost Coast of California is one of the National Conservation Areas controlled by the U.S. Bureau of Land Management.* (©James Bossert/Dreamstime.com)

that public lands be classified according to whether the land's most appropriate use was irrigated farming, livestock grazing, timber harvesting, or other uses. Critics of dominant use argued that a variety of activities should be allowed in any given area of public land.

Congress formed separate management systems requiring different management approaches for national forests, parks, wildlife refuges, and grasslands. In 1964, the Wilderness Act created another form of land management, one that recognized and emphasized recreation. The result was more hiking and biking trails, ski areas, and campgrounds as well as improved access to these recreational opportunities. In areas where primary uses overlap, such as a forest-covered mountain, a multiple-use approach permits different activities on or near the same site, such as logging alongside a ski area boundary.

A flurry of legislation in the 1970's, including the Federal Land Policy and Management Act and the National Forest Management Act, both enacted in 1976, had important consequences for public lands. For the first time, public comment was invited, and input from many diverse groups made setting common goals for public land management nearly impossible. Gridlock developed among those with various private rights to public lands (such as ranchers with grazing rights, outfitters and guides with hunting rights, and forest products companies with timber-cutting rights) and wilderness supporters with recreational-use rights.

WATER, MINING, RIGHTS-OF-WAY, AND WILDLIFE
Water rights are extremely important in the arid West. Land managers may register water rights and can then withdraw water if it is available. When allocation is restricted, those with the earliest dates of water use receive their allocations first. Such is not the case in the East, where water rights are not an issue. City dwellers can expect a rush of water when they turn a faucet and are not faced with negotiating their individual water rights.

The greatest source of income from U.S. public lands is royalties from oil, gas, and coal. Ninety percent of federal lands were once open to mining, but with passage of the Wilderness Act (1964), many public lands became off-limits to mining. A variety of legislation covers mining on federal land, the central act being the General Mining Act of 1872. It has provisions allowing citizens to lay claim to a specific tract of federal land for an annual fee. The claimant then has

mining and surface rights. This law remains in effect but has been limited through the years. In 1920, oil and coal were removed from coverage under the act and covered by separate legislation; in 1955, common rocks and minerals were withdrawn; and in 1976, all national parks were withdrawn.

Both public and private land managers routinely exchange right-of-way agreements to allow passage of livestock or access to timber sales. Private landowners of vast tracts of forest or rangeland often permit public access for recreational use. Wildlife on public and private land is subject to state and federal regulations, and game harvests are regulated. In many states private landowners with farmland damaged by game animals can apply for a depredation hunt, but they cannot legally trap or harvest the animals without state permission. Similarly, hunting seasons for waterfowl and migratory game birds are set by the federal government, and these seasons must be followed by all land managers, public and private.

FEDERAL, STATE, AND PRIVATE MANAGEMENT
There has been considerable debate concerning the effectiveness of private versus public management, and of federal versus state or local management. Private landowners have a strong financial incentive to take care of their land and use it wisely, or at least profitably. Public managers do not have the same motivation. Some advocates propose returning federal public lands to state and local ownership or control, thereby letting those people paying the bills—the local taxpayers—see that the lands are managed wisely. Opponents of this proposal argue that state managers could not manage the land as effectively as federal managers and fear that eventually the land would be acquired by private owners. There are existing state public lands; most are small and scattered parcels, many of which were gained from education land grants. Although land exchanges have consolidated some tracts, these small parcels are difficult to manage effectively. Proponents of the transfer of federal lands to state control claim that bigger parcels would result in improved land management by state administrators.

*Jill A. Cooper*

FURTHER READING
Babbitt, Bruce E. *Cities in the Wilderness: A New Vision of Land Use in America.* Washington, D.C.: Island Press/Shearwater Books, 2005.

Cawley, R. McGreggor. *Federal Land, Western Anger: The Sagebrush Rebellion and Environmental Politics.* Lawrence: University Press of Kansas, 1993.

Dale, Virginia H., and Richard A. Haeuber, eds. *Applying Ecological Principles to Land Management.* New York: Springer, 2001.

Fairfax, Sally K., et al. *Buying Nature: The Limits of Land Acquisition as a Conservation Strategy, 1780-2004.* Cambridge: Massachusetts Institute of Technology Press, 2005.

Francis, John G., and Leslie Pickering Francis. *Land Wars: The Politics of Property and Community.* Boulder, Colo.: Lynne Rienner, 2003.

Fretwell, Holly Lippke. *Who Is Minding the Federal Estate? Political Management of America's Public Lands.* Lanham, Md.: Lexington Books, 2009.

Nelson, Robert H. *Public Lands and Private Rights: The Failure of Scientific Management.* Lanham, Md.: Rowman & Littlefield, 1995.

Prescott, Samuel T. *Federal Land Management: Current Issues and Background.* New York: Nova Science, 2003.

Randolph, John. *Environmental Land Use Planning and Management.* Washington, D.C.: Island Press, 2004.

Skillen, James. *The Nation's Largest Landlord: The Bureau of Land Management in the American West.* Lawrence: University Press of Kansas, 2009.

WEB SITE

U.S. DEPARTMENT OF THE INTERIOR
U.S. Bureau of Land Management
http://www.blm.gov/wo/st/en.html

SEE ALSO: Bureau of Land Management, U.S.; Department of the Interior, U.S.; Forest management; General Mining Law; Land-use planning; Multiple-use approach; National parks and nature reserves; Public lands; Sagebrush Rebellion.

# Land-use planning

CATEGORY: Environment, conservation, and resource management

*Land-use planning is a management technique used to protect the environment while fostering responsible and compatible economic development. The basic philosophy of land-use planning is to mediate and avoid conflicts between land uses and users, avoid hazards, conserve natural resources, and generally protect the environment through the use of sound ecological and economic principles.*

## BACKGROUND

Some form of planning is involved in most decisions about land use, but the term "land-use planning" usually refers to a scale of decision making greater than that of an individual land unit. Land-use planning usually involves government at one level or another in the decision-making process and is usually concerned with reconciling the goals and objectives of individuals and groups that may be in conflict concerning prospective land uses.

The purpose of land-use planning is to make the most sensible, practical, safe, and efficient use of parcels of land. Much of the motivation for land-use planning arises from the current reality that a large and growing population occupies a fixed expanse of real estate and that some land is unstable and unsuitable for certain types of usage. Because land-use decisions are based, in part, on scientific and engineering considerations, land-use planning involves a great deal of interdisciplinary team work. Planners must weigh and consider decisions about the potential economic or practical benefits from a given use of the land and the possible negative environmental or aesthetic impacts. As a result, land-use planning often takes the form of assessing the suitability of a particular parcel of land for a particular purpose and proceeds somewhat like an environmental impact assessment.

## CONFLICTING VALUES AND OBJECTIVES

Land-use planning is conducted to reflect differences in goals between individual land users and the public as a whole or among broad interest groups within the general population. Individual land users may be concerned with selling or utilizing land to maximize its profitability, while government or concerned portions of the public may perceive greater utility in retaining the land as is, or for an alternate purpose. Similarly, individual land users may be content to manage their land in a fashion that does not maximize output, while the government may seek to use the land in such a way as to increase the resource's output. It is the goal of land-use planning to aid in resolving these conflicting societal values concerning land resources.

At one level, land-use planning is concerned with reconciling conflicting objectives. At another level,

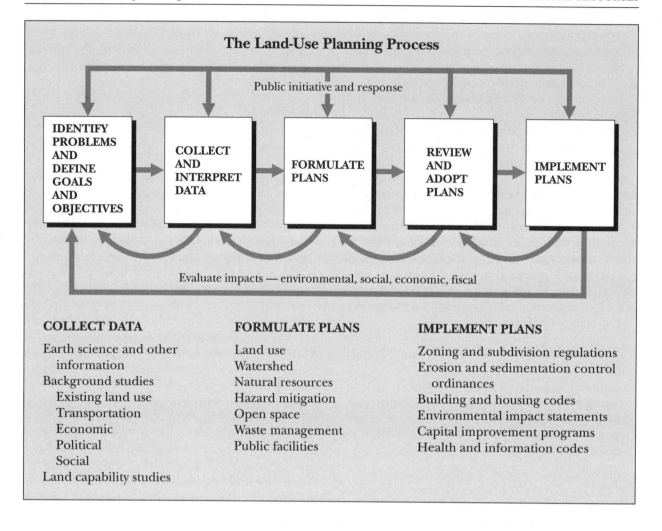

## The Land-Use Planning Process

Public initiative and response

IDENTIFY PROBLEMS AND DEFINE GOALS AND OBJECTIVES → COLLECT AND INTERPRET DATA → FORMULATE PLANS → REVIEW AND ADOPT PLANS → IMPLEMENT PLANS

Evaluate impacts — environmental, social, economic, fiscal

**COLLECT DATA**

Earth science and other
    information
Background studies
    Existing land use
    Transportation
    Economic
    Political
    Social
Land capability studies

**FORMULATE PLANS**

Land use
Watershed
Natural resources
Hazard mitigation
Open space
Waste management
Public facilities

**IMPLEMENT PLANS**

Zoning and subdivision regulations
Erosion and sedimentation control
    ordinances
Building and housing codes
Environmental impact statements
Capital improvement programs
Health and information codes

planning seeks to mediate or adjudicate between the objectives of interest groups and work to establish compromise in goal setting for the management of public lands so as to balance broad policies among land-exploiting sectors of the population. As a result, few environmental topics are as controversial as land-use planning. The controversy involves several factors. First, unlike concerns over environmental pollution, which can be measured, evaluated, and possibly corrected, it is difficult to determine the "best use" of the natural environment as opposed to the "most profitable use." Second, landowners often fear that planning will take away their right to decide what to do with their property. A frequent problem in land-use planning is that individual judgments about the relative importance or value of different land considerations are involved, and these judgments often differ sharply. For example, an old-growth forest may appeal

to a lumber company as a source of valuable timber, whereas campers may prefer it to remain pristine and unlogged. As a result, land-use planning has become an important political and environmental issue.

POLITICS AND THE PLANNING PROCESS

In the end, sound land-use planning depends on how political power is distributed and exercised. Land-use planning is not value free. Professional planners contribute the means of planning, but the ends and objectives are highly subjective and political in nature. They depend on how land is perceived by society, on whether land use should be dictated by market forces and the pursuit of profit by its owner, or whether land should be regarded as a common-property resource like air or water, and on whether land is seen as an inheritance to which an obligation of stewardship is owed to future generations.

Land-use planners, like land users, often have multiple goals, and the methods and techniques of planning are highly diverse and usually include a variety of steps. In any land-use planning project the first and most essential step is to identify and define issues, goals, and objectives concerning the lands in question. This step is usually accomplished through a combination of public input and scientifically based research and assessment. Data on the lands, including a complete inventory of resources and hazards, must be collected, analyzed, and interpreted. A series of land-use alternatives can be developed and tested based on the collected data; the results of this process can be used to formulate a potential land-use plan. After review, the plan can be adopted or revised prior to implementation. The key to the entire planning process is to match the natural capability of a land unit to specific potential uses.

*Randall L. Milstein*

FURTHER READING

Berke, Philip R., et al. *Urban Land Use Planning*. 5th ed. Urbana: University of Illinois Press, 2006.

Butterfield, Jody, Sam Bingham, and Allan Savory. *Holistic Management Handbook: Healthy Land, Healthy Profits*. Rev. ed. Washington, D.C.: Island Press, 2006.

Dale, Virginia H., and Richard A. Haeuber, eds. *Applying Ecological Principles to Land Management*. New York: Springer, 2001.

Dramstad, Wenche E., James D. Olson, and Richard T. T. Forman. *Landscape Ecology Principles in Landscape Architecture and Land-Use Planning*. Cambridge, Mass.: Harvard University Graduate School of Design, 1996.

Fabos, Julius Gy. *Land-Use Planning: From Global to Local Challenge*. New York: Chapman and Hall, 1985.

Mannion, A. M. *Dynamic World: Land-Cover and Land-Use Change*. New York: Arnold/Oxford University Press, 2002.

Meyer, William B., and B. L. Turner II, eds. *Changes in Land Use and Land Cover: A Global Perspective*. New York: Cambridge University Press, 1994.

Randolph, John. *Environmental Land Use Planning and Management*. Washington, D.C.: Island Press, 2004.

Savory, Allan, and Jody Butterfield. *Holistic Management: A New Framework for Decision Making*. 2d ed. Washington, D.C.: Island Press, 1999.

Steiner, Frederick. *The Living Landscape: An Ecological Approach to Landscape Planning*. 2d ed. Washington, D.C.: Island Press, 2008.

SEE ALSO: Bureau of Land Management, U.S.; Land management; Mineral resource ownership; Multiple-use approach; Population growth; Public lands; Soil management.

# Land-use regulation and control

CATEGORIES: Government and resources; social, economic, and political issues

*Government regulation and control of land use represents the point at which land management and land-use planning considerations become official policy that is enforced by law. Such government regulation is frequently controversial.*

## BACKGROUND

Land-use regulation and control represent the sets of rules established by governing entities in a particular area that permit or prohibit certain activities on a parcel of land. Numerous activities can have significant impacts on land, so a specific set of guidelines must be in place regarding the land uses that are considered to be of greatest importance. Subdivision controls were originally designed to obtain accurate land records as land was described, sold, and legally recorded. Later, these controls were better described as development controls, because subdivision laws resulted in standards for design and construction work. Zoning is the most well-known means of land-use control used by local governing bodies: A geographic area is divided into sectors or zones based on the specific land-use controls established for these areas. The most general land-use classes include agricultural, commercial, industrial, and residential, since these classes occur even in small towns and may occur in larger urban areas. Zoning ordinances contain a map which indicates the zones for the regulated areas and a text or narrative which explains the legal or allowed activities that may occur in each zone.

## TYPES OF REGULATION AND CONTROL

Various levels of government use specific types of land-use controls to allow, encourage, discourage, or forbid resource exploitation in given areas. One example is regulations concerning the development of floodplains or other potentially high-risk areas. A floodplain can be an excellent site for development as long as a carefully designed land-use plan incorporates a detailed cost-versus-benefit analysis of the advantages and disadvantages of building in this ecologically sensitive zone. Attempts to determine the true cost of developing the floodplain must consider the benefits of floodwater storage, aesthetic beauty, linear parkland, and opportunities for viewing animal or plant communities. Decisions on these kinds of complex and controversial development proposals should consider the full range of environmental, social, political, and legal issues that will affect the area. Scenic areas are valuable because of their aesthetic beauty. However, they are also attractive building sites because of that beauty.

Government entities have used land-use controls to foster conservation and preservation efforts in areas that are recognized as environmentally significant. Determination of environmental significance may be based on the limited land area of the resource or on the presence of endangered or threatened species within the boundary area. A growing emphasis on ecosystem-level (large-scale) approaches to conservation and management of terrestrial and aquatic areas has caused local governments to reconsider some of the adverse affects of their localized, community-based development plans. Since ecosystems can encompass a regional area, a wider view must be taken by the regional planning organization to mesh environmental preservation issues with environmental planning goals. Land-use regulation must be based on an understanding of the balance between environmental science and the discipline of urban planning.

LAND MANAGEMENT AND LAND-USE PLANNING
The regulation of land use is based on, and linked to, the processes of land management and land-use planning. Land management focuses on the proper maintenance of the land's condition and quality to maintain the property in the most efficient manner. Management should consider the land as a natural resource to be preserved and maintained as a valuable commodity. Land management can be regulated and controlled by governing entities through the use of subdivision and zoning laws. In rural areas, regional planning organizations can exert a strong influence on major land-management decisions if a proactive view has already focused on mid- to long-term development issues. Regional organizations generally have less policy enforcement strength than the local governing board. A properly conducted management plan comprises a number of steps that focus on the various parts of the selected environment; these must be accurately inventoried before a land-management plan is implemented.

Land-use planning focuses on the systematic definition and thoughtful design of the methods to be used to effect the present and future uses of land. The plan must be developed through intensive examination of the site conditions and project alternatives that may affect the implementation of the project. The site conditions inventory must include data collected from the soils, vegetation (plant cover), hydrology, and climatic conditions, which will be analyzed and reported as part of a summary of the plan. In addition, data acquired by remote sensing may be incorporated into the overall plan, because such data is significant on a large scale.

*Floodplains, like this one off the Nenana River in the Yukon region of Alaska, are examples of areas affected by land-use regulation.* (USGS)

## Trends in Planning and Control

Trends in land-use planning and control include increased public and institutional interest and participation, development of new land-use planning tools, and a larger role for environmental considerations. "New" land-use planning tools may be better thought of as creative combinations of older methods to achieve the desired outcome. Environmental and natural resource issues have caused citizens and planning organizations to consider further the benefits of including surrounding natural habitats as an enhanced part of the overall plan. Land-use regulation has begun to focus more intensely on the education of the public, because this is often the group that will make the final decision about whether a plan is accepted or declined.

*Richard Wayne Griffin*

## Further Reading

Arnold, Craig Anthony, ed. *Wet Growth: Should Water Law Control Land Use?* Washington, D.C.: Environmental Law Institute, 2005.

Elliott, Donald L. *A Better Way to Zone: Ten Principles to Create More Liveable Cities.* Washington, D.C.: Island Press, 2008.

Epstein, Richard A. *Supreme Neglect: How to Revive Constitutional Protection for Private Property.* New York: Oxford University Press, 2008.

Hoch, Charles J., Linda C. Dalton, and Frank S. So, eds. *The Practice of Local Government Planning.* 3d ed. Washington, D.C.: International City/County Management Association in cooperation with the American Planning Association for the ICMA University, 2000.

Juergensmeyer, Julian Conrad, and Thomas E. Roberts. *Land Use Planning and Development Regulation Law.* 2d ed. St. Paul, Minn.: Thomson/West, 2007.

Levy, John M. *Contemporary Urban Planning.* 8th ed. Upper Saddle River, N.J.: Pearson/Prentice Hall, 2009.

Nolon, John R., and Dan Rodriguez, eds. *Losing Ground: A Nation on Edge.* Washington, D.C.: Environmental Law Institute, 2007.

Nolon, John R., and Patricia E. Salkin. *Land Use in a Nutshell.* 5th ed. St. Paul, Minn.: Thomson/West, 2006.

Platt, Rutherford H. *Land Use and Society: Geography, Law, and Public Policy.* Rev. ed. Washington, D.C.: Island Press, 2004.

See also: Land management; Land-use planning; Public lands; Rangeland; Sagebrush Rebellion.

# Landfills

Category: Pollution and waste disposal

*Landfills, repositories for general municipal waste, have the potential for contaminating resources, most notably water resources.*

## Background

Landfills are naturally occurring depressions or artificial excavations that serve as repositories for municipal waste or general refuse. The waste is usually buried under successive layers of clay or other earth materials as the debris gradually accumulates. Generally, municipal wastes consist mostly of paper products (greater than 50 percent), with significant foodstuffs, glass, metals, minor garden and lawn debris, plastics, and wood scrap. Some special facilities are authorized to receive toxic waste such as industrial chemicals and contaminated soil. Carla W. Montgomery, in *Environmental Geology* (2006), states that a municipal sanitary landfill requires a land commitment of 1 hectare per year for each 10,000 people if the facility is filled to a depth of about 7.4 meters.

## Types and Site Selection

There are two types of repositories: area landfills and depression landfills. Area landfills are large open areas generally situated on low-lying, relatively flat terrain. Extensive excavation is involved, and the excavation is generally filled in sections. Depression landfills, characterized by individual cells, are usually located in places with irregular topography. The cells are long rectangular cuts that usually range from 100 meters to 150 meters long, up to 50 meters wide, and from 8 to 10 meters deep.

The location of a sanitary landfill is usually based on the following criteria. The primary consideration is the presence of a suitable host rock such as shale or marl with a minimum site thickness of 15 meters. If not structurally disturbed, these argillaceous rocks provide a nearly impervious container for long-term storage of waste material. The facility should also be sited in an area of low to moderate relief where the base of the landfill will be well above the groundwater table during all seasons of the year. The site should be within a moderate haul distance from the communities served and have an all-weather road network available. Geologic faults, both small and large, should be avoided.

## Schematic of a Municipal Landfill

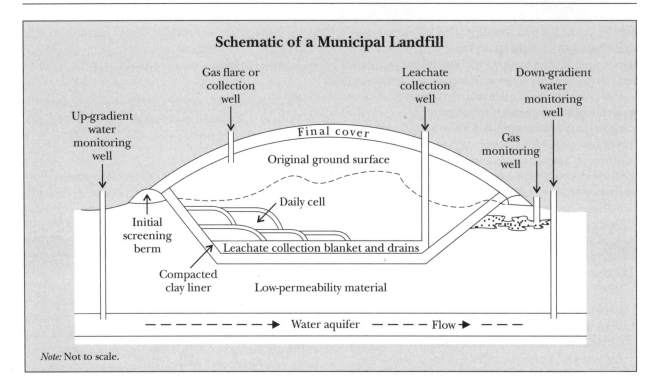

*Note:* Not to scale.

If present, these features could provide avenues for the downward or lateral migration of mineralized fluids generated in the landfill. The site should also not be near an airport because of the possibility of birds attracted to the site encountering aircraft in flight.

### DESIGN AND PROCEDURE

Most landfills employ a multiple-barrier approach to contain the materials placed at the site, The base and sides of the excavation are generally covered by an impervious synthetic (plastic) sheet and/or a compacted clay liner. The landfill is topped by a clay cap that is more than a meter thick. A clay dike is sometimes constructed within the Earthen cavity to separate the main trash collection area from a leachate collection basin. Dry wells surrounding the landfill monitor the vadose zone. This zone is a band above the water table where some water droplets suspended within the layer migrate downward toward the water table or move laterally to a discharge point. Deep wells on the fringe of the site penetrate the water table and monitor the quality of water stored there.

### POTENTIAL HAZARDS AND PROBLEMS

There are numerous potential health-related problems associated with the storage of municipal waste.

Joel B. Goldsteen, in *Danger All Around: Waste Storage Crisis on the Texas and Louisiana Gulf Coast* (1993), points out some of the major concerns about waste storage on the Texas and Louisiana Gulf Coast. Among the possible hazards are fluid (leachate) generation, gas generation, air and noise pollution, flooding, land subsidence, and fire.

Leachate is an undesirable fluid produced in most landfills as solid waste comes in contact with downward-percolating water within the vadose zone or migrating groundwater. Generally the fluid is acidic, with a high iron concentration (up to 5,000 parts per million). In rare cases the leachate produces a "bathtub effect" and overflows the confines of the landfill. This overflow may lead to contamination of surface waters. The leachate can also "burn" through the synthetic liner and escape through porous and permeable strata. The leachate may dissolve channelways in carbonate bedrock and result in groundwater pollution.

Anaerobic decomposition of compacted organic matter initially produces $CO_2$ and $SO_2$ that yields such gases as methane ($CH_4$) and hydrogen sulfide ($H_2S$). The methane that is generated may be sold locally, used in the landfill operation, or flared. However, the sulfurous gases are generally not recovered and may produce a strong, undesirable odor similar to rotten eggs. Brooks Ellwood and Burke Burkart, in "The Sanitary Landfill as a Laboratory" found in *Hydrocarbon Migration and Its Near-Surface Expression* (1996), note that upward-fluxing methane gas can produce authigenic magnetic minerals (primarily maghemite) in the capping soils of some landfills.

Small-size particle matter and noise from trucks traveling to and from the landfill site can disturb residents in the area. This is particularly a problem if the truck route passes near residences or schools. Liquid hazardous chemicals placed in the landfill may crystallize and form airborne particles that can be inhaled by local residents or settle in the surrounding area.

If the landfill is poorly located, such as on or near the floodplain of a drainage course, there is the potential for flooding. Floodwaters could erode the landfill and release hazardous fluids from the site. More than five thousand cities and small communities in the United States are located totally or in part on floodplains.

During operation of the landfill and after abandonment of the facility, materials within the landfill continue to adjust to changing physical conditions within the accumulation. These adjustments usually result in surface cracking and settlement.

Spontaneous combustion of flammable materials in a landfill can result in localized fires. Shredded rubber tire chips are sometimes placed at the base of the clay-lined landfills to help funnel fluids generated in the landfill to a collecting basin; it is a particular problem if these begin to burn. These fires are difficult to extinguish and may burn for days. The plume of smoke from the fires is usually considered dangerous because of substances added to the rubber during manufacturing.

Other problems include aesthetic considerations. Erosion sometimes produces short, narrow gullies that expose layered trash in the landfill. These areas are eyesores characterized by the exposed garbage, blowing trash, and circling birds. Vermin (rabbits, mice, rats) as well as various insects (ants, beetles, flies, and roaches) are common residents or visitors.

### MONITORING AND LEGISLATION

Landfills are usually monitored by visual inspection and through the use of recorded data from test wells that measure water quality within and around the site. Deep wells are bored below the undisturbed bedrock surface and sealed with a primary casing that is ce-

mented in place. The casing minimizes infiltration from fluids within the landfill.

Legislative requirements usually restrict landfills from certain areas such as airports, active fault zones, floodplains, wetlands, and unstable land. The design of landfills must include liners and a leachate collection system. Operators of landfills are required to monitor groundwater for specific toxic chemicals; they must also provide financial assurance criteria (usually bonds) to ensure that monitoring of the facility will continue for at least thirty years after closing.

*Donald F. Reaser*

### FURTHER READING

Cheremisinoff, Nicholas P. "Landfill Operations and Gas Energy Recovery." In *Handbook of Solid Waste Management and Waste Minimization Technologies*. Boston: Butterworth-Heinemann, 2003.

Coch, Nicholas K. *Geohazards: Natural and Human.* Englewood Cliffs, N.J.: Prentice Hall, 1995.

Goldsteen, Joel B. *Danger All Around: Waste Storage Crisis on the Texas and Louisiana Coast.* Austin: University of Texas Press, 1993.

Keller, Edward A. *Environmental Geology.* 8th ed. Upper Saddle River, N.J.: Prentice Hall, 2000.

Montgomery, Carla W. *Environmental Geology.* 7th ed. New York: McGraw-Hill, 2006.

O'Leary, Philip R., and George Tchobanoglous. "Landfilling." In *Handbook of Solid Waste Management,* edited by Tchobanoglous and Frank Kreith. New York: McGraw-Hill, 2002.

Qasim, Syed R., and Walter Chiang. *Sanitary Landfill Leachate: Generation, Control, and Treatment.* Lancaster, Pa.: Technomic, 1994.

Senior, Eric, ed. *Microbiology of Landfill Sites.* 2d ed. Boca Raton, Fla.: Lewis, 1995.

Sharma, Hari D., and Krishna R. Reddy. *Geoenvironmental Engineering: Site Remediation, Waste Containment, and Emerging Waste Management Technologies.* Hoboken, N.J.: Wiley, 2004.

Tammemagi, Hans. *The Waste Crisis: Landfills, Incinerators, and the Search for a Sustainable Future.* New York: Oxford University Press, 1999.

### WEB SITE

U.S. ENVIRONMENTAL PROTECTION AGENCY
Landfills
http://www.epa.gov/osw/nonhaz/municipal/
    landfill.htm

SEE ALSO: Air pollution and air pollution control; Groundwater; Hazardous waste disposal; Solid waste management; Superfund legislation and cleanup activities; Waste management and sewage disposal; Water pollution and water pollution control.

# Landsat satellites and satellite technologies

CATEGORIES: Government and resources; obtaining and using resources

*In 1972, a series of Earth resources satellites called Landsat began collecting images of Earth. They gather information about various surface or near-surface phenomena, including weather, landforms, and land-use patterns. Satellites are used for crop forecasting, mineral and energy resource exploration, navigation and survey applications, and the compilation of resource inventories.*

## BACKGROUND

Landsat satellites and similar satellite technologies designed for collecting information about Earth use a process known as remote sensing. Remote sensing is the collection of data concerning an object or area without being near or in physical contact with it. Landsat satellites occupy various orbits above Earth. Some orbit from pole to pole, some circle around the equator, and others remain fixed above a specific geography.

The first remotely sensed images may have been acquired in 1858 by Gaspard-Félix Tournachon, who mounted a camera to a balloon and raised it 80 meters above Bièvre, France, thereby taking the first aerial photograph. The first attempt at remote sensing from rockets was made by Ludwig Rahrmann, who was granted a patent in 1891 for "obtaining bird's eye photographic views." Rahrmann's rocket-launched camera, recovered by parachute, rarely exceeded 400 meters in height. The first cameras carried by modern rockets were mounted on captured German V-2 rockets launched by the U.S. Army over White Sands, New Mexico, shortly after World War II.

Comprehensive imaging of Earth's surface from a platform in space began with the development of a series of meteorological satellites in 1960. These first efforts, crude by later standards, were exciting at the time. However, scientists wanted to see more than cloud patterns. Later, during the manned space program, Gemini IV took a series of photographs of northern Mexico and the American southwest that guided geologists to new discoveries. The success of these and other attempts at space photography led to a program to develop satellites that could provide systematic repetitive coverage of any spot on Earth.

## EARLY LANDSAT SATELLITES

In 1967, the National Aeronautics and Space Administration (NASA) began to plan a series of Earth Resources Technology Satellites (ERTS). The first, ERTS-1, was launched on July 23, 1972. ERTS-1 was a joint mission of NASA and the U.S. Geological Survey (USGS), was the first satellite dedicated to systematic remote sensing of Earth's surface, and used a variety of medium-resolution scanners. Perhaps most important, all images collected were treated according to an "open skies" policy; that is, the images were accessible to anyone. This policy created some concern in the government because of the Cold War tensions of the time. However, scientists realized that the advantages of worldwide use and evaluation of remotely sensed data far outweighed any concerns of disclosure. The project was judged to be a tremendous success by researchers worldwide.

A second ERTS satellite, launched on January 22, 1975, was named Landsat, for "land imaging satellite," to distinguish it from Seasat, an oceanographic satellite mission then in the planning stages. Therefore, ERTS-1 was retroactively renamed Landsat 1, the 1975 satellite was designated Landsat 2, and the next satellite in the series, launched on March 5, 1978, was named Landsat 3.

The early Landsat satellites orbited Earth, north to south, about every 103 minutes at an approximate altitude of 920 kilometers. Orbiting in near-polar, sun-synchronous orbits, they crossed each latitude at the same time each day. This rendered every image with the same Sun angle (shadows) as recorded in previous orbits. The onboard scanners recorded a track 185 kilometers wide and returned to an adjacent western track twenty-four hours later. For example, if the satellite's target was the state of Iowa, eastern Iowa would be scanned on Monday, central Iowa on Tuesday, and the western part of the state on Wednesday. This cycle of images could then be repeated every eighteen days, or about twenty times per year. The early Landsat satellites carried two imaging systems, each designed to record different parts of the electromagnetic spectrum: a return beam vidicom (RBV) system and a multispectral scanner system (MSS). The satellites' data were sent back to Earth in a manner similar to television transmission.

The RBV system for Landsats 1 and 2 involved three television-type cameras aimed at the same ground area, while Landsat 3's RBV system used two side-by-side panchromatic cameras (that is, cameras sensitive to the broad visible wavelength range) with a spatial resolution higher than that of RBV systems aboard the earlier Landsat platforms. Each camera recorded its image in a different frequency of light. Data obtained via the RBV were in the form of images similar to those of a television.

The MSS, which collected its multispectral data in digital form, proved to be more versatile. An MSS is a collection of scanning sensors, each of which gather data from a different portion of the spectrum. In Landsats 1 and 2, two cameras collected images in the visible spectrum: green light and red light; the other two collected in the near infrared. Landsat 3 added a fifth camera, which recorded thermal infrared wavelengths; however, it failed shortly after launch.

Each MSS image covers an area of about 185-by-185 kilometers. This renders a scale of 1:1,000,000 and an area of 34,000 square kilometers per frame. The resolution of the scanners was largely dependent on the atmospheric conditions and the contrast of the target, but under ideal conditions, they could resolve an area about 80 square meters. Therefore, any objects "seen" by the scanner had to be the size of a football field or larger. In the early to mid-1970's, this was considered medium-resolution capability. It was sufficient to resolve various natural phenomena but not detailed enough to compromise security-sensitive areas and activities such as military bases and operations.

Once transmitted to Earth, MSS data were retained in digital format and/or scanned onto photographic film. On film, they became black-and-white images that could be optically registered to create a single image. Then a color image could be created by passing red, blue, and green light through each negative. This color was not intended to re-create the natural scene but rather to enhance the contrast between various features recorded in different wavelengths.

The early Landsat satellites all continued to operate past their minimum design life of one year. Landsat 1 ended its mission on January 6, 1978, Landsat 2 on February 25, 1982, and Landsat 3 on March 31, 1983. By the time Landsat 3 stopped transmitting data, a new generation of Landsat satellite had taken to the skies.

## LATER LANDSAT MISSIONS

Like their predecessors, the later Landsat satellites follow a near-polar, Sun-synchronous orbit to acquire data from a 56-meter-wide swath, but at a lower altitude of approximately 705 kilometers. These satellites orbit Earth about every 99 minutes, so that their repeat cycle is every sixteen days.

With Landsat 4, the National Oceanic and Atmospheric Administration (NOAA) and the private Earth Observation Satellite Company (EOSAT) joined NASA and the USGS as mission participants. Launched on July 16, 1982, Landsat 4 employed a four-band MSS like the ones aboard Landsats 1 and 2 but replaced the RBV (which had experienced a number of technical problems) with the more sophisticated thematic mapper (TM). The TM system, a multispectral imaging sensor similar to the MSS, added improved spatial resolution and midrange infrared to the data; three of its seven bands were dedicated to visible wavelengths, two to near-infrared, one to thermal infrared, and one to midinfrared. Landsat 4 ended its mission on December 14, 1993, with the failure of its last remaining science data downlink capability. Landsat 5 launched on March 1, 1984, with the same type of MSS and TM sensors used on Landsat 4. Like Landsat 4, it was a joint mission of NASA, the USGS, NOAA, and EOSAT. Although its MSS was powered off in August, 1995, as of 2009, Landsat 5 continued to collect and transmit data using only its TM system.

EOSAT's participation in Landsats 4 and 5 was a result of the Land Remote Sensing Commercialization Act of 1984, legislation that opened up Landsat program management to the private sector. EOSAT began managing the program in 1985; however, within a few years it was apparent that the market for Landsat images could not offset operational costs. The Land Remote Sensing Policy Act of 1992 ended privatization and restored program management of future Landsat missions to the federal government. In 2001, operational responsibility for Landsats 4 and 5 returned to the government, along with rights to the data these satellites collected. As of 2009, the USGS Landsat data archive was available via the Internet at no cost to users.

Landsat 6, launched on October 5, 1993, failed; it

did not achieve orbit. With Landsat 7, a joint mission of NASA, the USGS, and NOAA, a new generation of sensor began to gather data. Landsat 7 was launched on April 15, 1999, equipped with an Enhanced Thematic Mapper Plus (ETM+). This sensor, the only one carried aboard the satellite, uses an oscillating mirror and detector arrays to make east-west and west-east scans as the satellite descends over Earth's sunlit side. Of the sensor's eight bands, three are devoted to visible wavelengths, one to near-infrared, two to shortwave infrared, and one to thermal infrared. The remaining band is panchromatic.

Both Landsats 5 and 7 have exceeded their life expectancies by several years. NASA and the USGS planned to launch the next satellite in the series, the Landsat Data Continuity Mission (LDCM), in late 2012.

*Landsat 7 was launched in 1999 and was expected to last five years but exceeded its useful lifetime by more than a decade.* (NASA)

## USES AND BENEFITS

Generally, TM images can be used for a wider range of applications than MSS images can. The reason is that the TM records through more spectral bands with a greater spatial resolution. The MSS images are most useful describing and delineating large-scale phenomena such as geologic structures and land cover. The TM is perhaps more beneficial for land-use description and planning.

The ability of Landsat images to contrast target phenomena to the background or "noise" is what makes this research tool so powerful. Once the target has been delineated, a computer can inventory and/ or map the target phenomena. The usefulness of Landsat images has been demonstrated in many fields, among them agriculture and forestry, geology and geography, and land-use planning. The World Bank uses these images for economic geography studies. A distinct advantage of this database is the "big picture" perspective afforded by the format: A single Landsat image can replace more than sixteen hundred aerial photographs of 1:20,000 scale. However, with the increase of aerial coverage comes a decrease in resolution. Therefore, these images may best be used as a complementary or confirming database to be used with other aerial imagery and ground surveys. Identifying the appropriate season for viewing a phenomenon or target is critical. For geographic features, the low Sun angle and "leaf-down" conditions of winter are an advantage. For biological phenomena, wet-dry seasons and time of year are critical. A riverbed or lake can disappear in dry conditions or be misinterpreted as a pasture if covered with green moss or algae. Therefore, matching the target to time of year and seasonal conditions must be a consideration when selecting a time window for observation.

The power of this perspective is revealed when satellite images are used to examine regional or area formations, structures, and trends. The extent of many geologic structures has been delineated with satellite imagery. For example, Landsat imagery has clearly identified impact craters, such as the Manicouagan ring in east-central Quebec, Canada, and fault systems, such as those of California's San Andreas fault and Georgia's Brevard fault zone. These systems extend hundreds of kilometers and are difficult, if not impossible, to perceive from the ground.

Additionally, satellite imagery has suggested areas for fossil fuel and mineral exploration by decoding rock structure, potential oil and gas traps, and fault lines. Many of the areas involved are relatively inaccessible, and remote sensing has provided a map base and assisted in decoding the structures. Examples include the complex sedimentary structures on the east side of the Andes, ranging from Brazil to Argentina, and a number of structures in countries of the former Soviet Union: the Caspian Sea states of Azerbaijan, Kazakhstan, and Turkmenistan; northern Russia's tundra; the Timan-Pechora region near the Barents Sea; and western Siberia's Priobskoye region. Satellite imaging is assisting the exploration of these remote areas, for which reliable topographic and geologic maps are scarce or nonexistent.

The usefulness of remote sensing is by no means restricted to energy exploration. The imagery has been used to inventory agriculture cropland and crop yields and to monitor irrigation and treatment programs. Therefore, it aids in commodities analysis. It also aids in environmental monitoring. Different plants reflect different spectral energies, and sensors can differentiate these wavelengths. In this way, the distribution and health of forests and wetlands can be mapped. Extreme environmental impacts can be assessed as well: The effects of disasters such as volcanic eruptions, earthquakes, droughts, forest fires, floods, hurricanes, cyclones, and oil spills can be mapped and inventoried via the satellite platform. Technological advances in data processing, integration, and dissemination have allowed the Landsat program to become a valuable source of real-time data, so that, in the wake of disasters, satellite imagery can support cleanup and relief efforts and hazard assessments.

As the longest-running program for remote sensing of Earth's surface from orbit, Landsat provides an unparalleled view of the planet over time. Satellite images have proven to be an outstanding tool for observing changes to vegetation, coastal areas, and the land surface brought on by natural processes and human activity. They can be used to study everything from seasonal variations in vegetative cover to long-term trends in urban growth, wetlands loss, glacier movement and melting, and desert encroachment.

## OTHER SATELLITE PROGRAMS

Landsat 7 is part of the Earth Observing System (EOS), a program involving a series of polar-orbiting satellites and related interdisciplinary investigations looking into global change. As of 2009, other EOS missions in operation included the Quik Scatterometer, or QuikSCAT (launched June 19, 1999), which collects data on near-surface wind directions and speeds over Earth's oceans; Terra (launched December 18, 1999), the first satellite designed to look at Earth's air, oceans, land, ice, and life as a global system; the Active Cavity Radiometer Irradiance Monitor Satellite, or ACRIMSAT (launched December 20, 1999), which measures how much of the Sun's energy reaches Earth's atmosphere, oceans, and land surface; Jason-1 (launched December 7, 2001), a joint U.S.-French mission for studying global ocean circulation; Aqua (launched May 4, 2002), which gathers data on clouds, precipitation, atmospheric moisture and temperature, terrestrial snow, sea-ice and sea-surface temperature; the Ice, Cloud, and land Elevation Satellite, or ICESat (launched January 12, 2003), which monitors the elevations of ice sheets, clouds, and the land surface; the Solar Radiation and Climate Experiment, or SORCE (launched January 25, 2003), which measures irradiance from the Sun; Aura (launched July 15, 2004), which investigates atmospheric dynamics and chemistry; and the Ocean Surface Topography Mission, or OSTM (launched June 20, 2008), which measures ocean surface topography.

In 1986, the French government, with Sweden and Belgium as partners, launched the first of a series of Système Probatoire d'Observation de la Terre (SPOT) satellites. This commercial system, designed to compete with the American Landsat program, featured 10-meter resolution for its black-and-white imagery and 20-meter resolution for color imagery. SPOT had the further advantageous ability to create stereoscopic images. As of 2009, three of the five satellites launched in the SPOT series remained operational; the most recent, SPOT 5 (launched on May 4, 2002), boasts a 2.5-meter resolution.

Other satellite systems are also scanning the surface of Earth. For example, there are meteorological satellites serving the needs of the U.S. National Oceanographic and Atmospheric Administration (NOAA). Another large-scale satellite endeavor is the Geostationary Operational Environmental Satellite (GOES) series. A geostationary satellite is one that can remain stationary over a specific point above Earth and observe it twenty-four hours a day. A third class of meteorological satellite is the U.S. Defense Meteorological Satellite Program (DMPS). Another satellite program, Seasat, monitors the oceans. These satellites scan in the microwave wavelengths and have proven to be reliable in mapping temperatures and detecting chlorophyll and suspended solids.

While not revealing any information about Earth itself, a class of navigation satellite known as the Navstar Global Positioning System (GPS) assists in resource development in a different way. This system began in March, 1994, and is funded by the U.S. Department of Defense (DOD) and managed by the United States Air Force Fiftieth Space Wing. The GPS system consists of twenty-four to thirty-two satellites spaced so that between five and eight are visible from any point on Earth. By triangulation of a radio signal broadcast from each satellite, users equipped with a receiver may accurately locate their position on the ground in three dimensions. When the military first introduced global positioning via satellite, it intentionally degraded the signal so that civilian users could be accurate to only 100 meters or so, while DOD users could locate a position to within 20 meters for military operations. In 2000, after the military had demonstrated that regional signal degradation could provide sufficient protection for security-sensitive locations, civilian and commercial access to the higher-resolution data was enabled. GPS initially gained popularity among nonmilitary users as a valuable tool for people working in areas where maps were of poor scale or nonexistent—for instance, in remote oil or mineral exploration operations or environmental surveys or mapping efforts in the wild. Afterward, and particularly after the improvement of signal accuracy in 2000, GPS has found many commercial applications; civilians can access GPS signals from their cell phones, smart phones, car computers, and other wireless devices.

Remote sensing from near-space orbital platforms has revolutionized how humans see Earth and contributed greatly to the disciplines of agriculture, cartography, environmental monitoring, forestry, geology and geography, land-use planning, meteorology, and oceanography. Its impact has been not only scientific but also political and sociological. As other countries launch satellites, information concerning Earth becomes more democratic, and political boundaries become more artificial. Remote sensing has become an invaluable tool for scientific investigation, but its

data must be used and interpreted appropriately and in conjunction with other research tools and databases.

*Richard C. Jones, updated by Karen N. Kähler*

FURTHER READING

Campbell, James B. *Introduction to Remote Sensing*. 4th ed. New York: Guildford Press, 2007.

Cracknell, Arthur P., and Ladson Hayes. *Introduction to Remote Sensing*. 2d ed. Boca Raton, Fla.: CRC Press, 2007.

Drury, S. A. *Images of the Earth: A Guide to Remote Sensing*. 2d ed. New York: Oxford University Press, 1998.

Gupta, Ravi P. *Remote Sensing Geology*. 2d ed. New York: Springer, 2003.

Johnston, Andrew K. *Earth from Space: Smithsonian National Air and Space Museum*. 2d ed. Buffalo, N.Y.: Firefly Books, 2007.

Parkinson, Claire L. *Earth from Above: Using Color-Coded Satellite Images to Examine the Global Environment*. Sausalito, Calif.: University Science Books, 1997.

Strain, Priscilla, and Frederick Engle. *Looking at Earth*. Atlanta: Turner, 1992.

WEB SITES

NASA GODDARD SPACE FLIGHT CENTER
The Landsat Program
http://landsat.gsfc.nasa.gov

NASA GODDARD SPACE FLIGHT CENTER
Landsat 7 Science Data Users Handbook
http://landsathandbook.gsfc.nasa.gov/handbook/handbook_toc.html

NATIONAL AERONAUTICS AND SPACE ADMINISTRATION
Dr. Nicholas Short's Remote Sensing Tutorial
http://rst.gsfc.nasa.gov

U.S. GEOLOGICAL SURVEY
Land Remote Sensing Program
http://remotesensing.usgs.gov

U.S. GEOLOGICAL SURVEY
Landsat Missions
http://landsat.usgs.gov

SEE ALSO: Aerial photography; Geographic information systems; Land-use planning; National Oceanic and Atmospheric Administration; Oceanography; Remote sensing.

# Law of the sea

CATEGORY: Government and resources

*The Law of the Sea Treaty of 1982 was designed to help ensure and maintain the peaceful use of the seas for all nations. Its signatories hoped to accomplish this goal by standardizing and regulating areas of potential conflict between nations. Some important areas covered by this treaty include ship safety, mineral exploration and exploitation, and environmental protection.*

## BACKGROUND

The phrase "law of the sea" implies that activities at sea, like those on land, are subject to the rule of law and that compliance with the law is mandatory and enforced. In fact, the law of the sea is not a law but an agreement among nations. The Law of the Sea Treaty, signed December 10, 1982, and implemented November 24, 1994, set standards and regulations on all activities at sea and established clear lines of national jurisdiction. Compliance to the treaty is voluntary, and there is no provision in the agreement for its enforcement. Despite the apparent weaknesses of such an agreement, most nations have complied because the law of the sea is based on a fundamental principle on which all nations can agree: the freedom of the seas.

## EARLY CONCEPTS

As long as there have been ships, there has been some concept of freedom of the seas. While there were no written rules, a spirit of cooperation among mariners existed during times of peace. By the seventeenth century, the Dutch had begun global maritime trade, and their economy was dependent on free access to the seas. In 1609, Hugo Grotius, a Dutch lawyer, was asked to codify the concept of freedom of the seas. Grotius produced a large treatise on the law of the seas entitled *Mare Liberum* (1609). This work established the "freedom of the seas" as a concept based on law. Grotius concluded that all nations could use the oceans provided they did not interfere with one another's use. This first attempt at a law of the sea recognized three divisions of the seas: internal waters, territorial seas, and the high seas. Grotius maintained that a nation had sovereignty over internal and territorial seas but that the high seas were open to all. This concept of the law of the sea survived into the twentieth century.

## THE TRUMAN PROCLAMATION

In 1947, U.S. geologists advised President Harry S. Truman about the potential of large oil reserves on the continental shelf. To protect these resources, Truman declared that all resources of the continental shelf belonged exclusively to the United States. This became known as the Truman Proclamation. The decree had broad international implications, with many nations issuing similar edicts regarding the continental shelf.

## THE GENEVA CONFERENCES

Because of increased economic and military activity at sea, some formal agreement regarding the use of the oceans was needed to ensure peace. In 1958 and again in 1960, conferences on the law of the sea were convened in Geneva. The representatives drafted and ratified a treaty that included many basic issues on which there was wide agreement. Two points included in the treaty were particularly important. The depth limit of the continental shelf was limited by treaty to 200 meters. This depth limit included an "exploitability clause," however, whereby a nation could exploit ocean resources below 200 meters on adjacent seafloor if it had the technology to do so. Such a concept was favorable to the industrial nations and placed developing nations at a disadvantage.

After 1960, many formerly colonial countries received independence; these were primarily nonindustrial states. They feared that the ocean's resources would be exploited by the industrial nations. So great was the fear that, in 1967, the nation of Malta proposed to the United Nations that a treaty be developed to reserve the economic resources of the seafloor. The Maltese ambassador, Arvid Pardo, further declared that the ocean floor should be reserved for peaceful uses alone and that the ocean resources were the "common heritage of all mankind."

## THE THIRD LAW OF THE SEA CONFERENCE

The Third Law of the Sea Conference convened in 1973 and continued to meet until 1982. The major result of this conference was the Law of the Sea Treaty dealing with boundary issues, economic rights of nations, rights of passage through straits, the freedom of scientific research, and the exploitation of ocean-floor resources.

The Law of the Sea Treaty established the width of the territorial sea at 12 nautical miles. This could be modified to allow passage of ships through narrow straits critical to international commerce. Territorial sea fell under the direct jurisdiction of the adjacent nation, and that nation could enforce its laws and regulate the passage of ships through the territory. Beyond the territorial limit, a coastal nation or any inhabitable land could also declare an exclusive economic zone (EEZ) of 200 nautical miles. The EEZ is open to ships of all nations, but the resources within it can be exploited only by the nation declaring the EEZ.

## DEEP SEA MINING AND RESOURCE USE

The Law of the Sea Treaty established regulations on scientific research in the oceans. While the freedom of scientific research in the open ocean is universally recognized, investigations in a nation's territorial seas and EEZ require the permission of that nation. The treaty also governs the mining of deep sea mineral resources. In certain locations on the deep seafloor, there are nodules of manganese, cobalt, nickel, and copper. Exploitation of these resources requires a highly advanced and expensive technology. Such requirements place developing nations at a disadvantage. The Law of the Sea Treaty attempts to address this problem. Any group wishing to mine the deep seafloor must declare its intent to do so and state the geographic location of the mining operation. Then, an international authority grants permission to mine. All revenues from a successful mining operation on the deep seafloor must be shared among the nations of the world. Further, the technology used to mine the deep seafloor must be shared with all nations.

The Law of the Sea Treaty leaves many issues unresolved and others open to multiple interpretations. Despite areas of disagreement, however, most maritime nations adhere to the majority of the provisions of the Law of the Sea Treaty.

*Richard H. Fluegeman, Jr.*

FURTHER READING

Freestone, David, Richard Barnes, and David M. Ong, eds. *The Law of the Sea: Progress and Prospects.* New York: Oxford University Press, 2006.

Haward, Marcus, and Joanna Vince. *Oceans Governance in the Twenty-first Century: Managing the Blue Planet.* Northampton, Mass.: Edward Elgar, 2008.

Paulsen, Majorie B., ed. *Law of the Sea.* New York: Nova Science, 2007.

Ross, David A. *Introduction to Oceanography.* New York: HarperCollinsCollege, 1995.

*United Nations Convention on the Law of the Sea.* New York: Nova Science, 2009.

WEB SITE

UNITED NATIONS, DIVISION FOR OCEAN AFFAIRS AND THE LAW OF THE SEA
Oceans and Law of the Sea
http://www.un.org/Depts/los/convention_agreements/convention_overview_convention.htm

SEE ALSO: Exclusive economic zones; Fisheries; Manganese; Marine mining; Oceanography; Oceans; United Nations Convention on the Law of the Sea.

# Leaching

CATEGORIES: Geological processes and formations; obtaining and using resources

*Leaching is the removal of insoluble minerals or metals found in various ores, generally by means of microbial solubilization. Leaching is significant as an artificial process for recovering certain minerals, as an environmental hazard, notably as a result of acid mine drainage, and as a natural geochemical process.*

## BACKGROUND

Leaching is among the processes that concentrate or disperse minerals among layers of soil. Leaching is a natural phenomenon, but it has been adapted and applied to industrial processes for obtaining certain minerals. The recovery of important resource metals such as copper, uranium, and gold is of significant economic benefit. However, if the metal is insoluble or is present in low concentration, recovery through conventional chemical methods may be too costly to warrant the necessary investment. Bioassisted leaching, often referred to as microbial leaching or simply bioleaching, is often practiced under such circumstances. The principle behind such biotechnology is the ability of certain microorganisms to render the metal into a water-soluble form.

## BIOLEACHING OF COPPER ORE

The production of copper ore is particularly illustrative of the leaching process. Low-grade ore containing relatively small concentrations of the metal is put into a leach dump, a large pile of ore intermixed with bacteria such as *Thiobacillus ferrooxidans.* Such bacteria are able to oxidize the copper ore rapidly under acidic conditions, rendering it water soluble. Pipes are used to distribute a dilute sulfuric acid solution over the surface of the dump. As the acid percolates through the pile, the copper is solubilized in the solution and is collected in an effluent at the bottom of the pile. Two forms of the copper are generally found in the crude ore: chalcocite, $Cu_2S$, in which the copper is largely insoluble, and covellite, $CuS$, in which the copper is in a more soluble form. The primary function of the *Thiobacillus* lies in the ability of the bacteria to oxidize the copper in chalcocite to the more soluble form.

A variation of this method utilizes the ability of ferric iron, $Fe^{+3}$, to oxidize copper ore. Reduced iron ($Fe^{+2}$) in the form of pyrite ($FeS_2$) is already present in most copper ore. In the presence of oxygen and sulfuric acid from the leaching process, the *Thiobacillus* will oxidize the ferrous iron to the ferric form. The ferric form oxidizes the copper ore, rendering it water soluble, but becomes reduced in the process. The process is maintained through continued reoxidation of the iron by the bacteria. Since the process requires oxygen, the size of the leach dump may prove inhibitory to the process. For this reason, large quantities of scrap iron containing ferric iron are generally added to the leach solution. In this manner, sufficient oxidizing power is maintained.

Generally speaking, those minerals that readily undergo oxidation can more easily be mined with the aid of microbial leaching. As illustrated in the foregoing examples, both iron and copper ores lend themselves readily to such a process. Other minerals, such as lead and molybdenum, are not as readily oxidized and are consequently less easily adapted to the process of microbial leaching.

## LEACHING OF GOLD

The extraction of gold from crude ore has historically involved a cyanide leaching process in which the gold is rendered soluble through mixing with a cyanide solution. However, the process is both expensive and environmentally unsound, owing to the highly toxic nature of the cyanide. In an alternative approach that uses bioleaching as a first stage, crushed gold ore is mixed with bacteria in a large holding tank. Oxidation by the bacteria produces a partially pure gold ore; the gold can then be more easily recovered by a smaller scale cyanide leaching. The process was first applied on a large scale in Nevada; a single plant there can produce 50,000 troy ounces (1.6 million grams) of gold each year.

## ACID MINE DRAINAGE

The spontaneous oxidation of pyrite in the air contributes to a major environmental problem associated with some mining operations: acid mine drainage. When pyrite is exposed to the air and water, large amounts of sulfuric acid are produced. Drainage of the acid can kill aquatic life and render water undrinkable. Some of the iron itself also leaches away into both groundwater and nearby streams.

## NATURAL LEACHING AND GEOCHEMICAL CYCLING

The leaching of soluble minerals from soil contributes to geochemical cycling. Elements such as nitrogen, phosphorus, and calcium are all found in mineral form at some stages of the geochemical cycles that are constantly operating on the Earth. Many of these minerals are necessary for plant (and ultimately, human) growth. For example, proper concentrations of calcium and phosphorus are critical for cell maintenance. When decomposition of dead material occurs, these minerals enter into a soluble "pool" within the soil. Loss of these minerals through leaching occurs when soil water and runoff remove them from the pool. Both calcium and phosphorus end up in reservoirs such as those in deep-ocean sediments, where they may remain for extended periods of time.

Percolation of water downward through soil may also result in the leaching of soluble nitrogen ions. Both nitrites ($NO_2-$) and nitrates ($NO_3-$) are intermediates in the nitrogen cycle, converted into such forms usable by plants by the action of bacteria on ammonium compounds. Nitrate ions in particular are readily absorbed by the roots of plants. The leaching of nitrites and nitrates through movement of soil water may result in depletion of nitrogen.

In addition to the loss of nitrogen for plants, leaching can lead to significant environmental damage. Since both nitrite and nitrate ions are negatively charged, they are repelled by the negatively charged clay particles in soil, particularly lending themselves to leaching as water percolates through soil. High concentrations of nitrates in groundwater may contaminate drinking water, posing a threat to human health.

*Richard Adler*

FURTHER READING

Atlas, Ronald M., and Richard Bartha. *Microbial Ecology: Fundamentals and Applications.* 4th ed. Menlo Park, Calif.: Benjamin/Cummings, 1998.

Burkin, A. R. "Chemistry of Leaching Processes." In *Chemical Hydrometallurgy: Theory and Principles.* London: ICP, 2001.

Keller, Edward A. *Environmental Geology.* 8th ed. Upper Saddle River, N.J.: Prentice Hall, 2000.

Killham, Ken. *Soil Ecology.* New York: Cambridge University Press, 1994.

Madigan, Michael T., John M. Martinko, Paul V. Dunlap, and David P. Clark. *Brock Biology of Microorganisms.* San Francisco: Pearson/Benjamin Cummings, 2009.

Marsden, John, and C. Iain House. "Leaching." In *The Chemistry of Gold Extraction.* 2d ed. Littleton, Colo.: Society for Mining, Metallurgy, and Exploration, 2006.

Robertson, G. P., and P. M. Groffman. "Nitrogen Transformations." In *Soil Microbiology, Ecology, and Biochemistry,* edited by Eldor A. Paul. 3d ed. Boston: Academic Press, 2007.

SEE ALSO: Biotechnology; Igneous processes, rocks, and mineral deposits; Mining wastes and mine reclamation; Secondary enrichment of mineral deposits; Sedimentary processes, rocks, and mineral deposits; Soil degradation.

# Lead

CATEGORY: Mineral and other nonliving resources

## WHERE FOUND

Lead is widely distributed in the Earth's crust; it has an estimated percentage of the crustal weight of 0.0013, making it more common than silver or gold but less common then copper or zinc; these are the four minerals with which lead is most commonly found in ore deposits. All five may occur together in a deposit, or only two or three may occur in concentrations sufficiently rich to be economically attractive to miners.

## PRIMARY USES

The major use of lead in the United States is in the lead-acid batteries used in automotive vehicles. Because lead is so toxic, a fact that has been known since ancient times, many of its former uses have been curtailed or discontinued. While it is still used in cables, ammunition, solders, shielding of radiation, and electrical parts, its use as an antiknock additive in gasoline was phased out during the 1970's and 1980's. Nevertheless, lead production has been maintained at about the same level as before the phase out. Should a suitable substitute ever be developed for lead-acid batteries, the use of lead will decline to very low levels.

## TECHNICAL DEFINITION

Lead (abbreviated Pb), atomic number 82, belongs to Group IV of the periodic table of the elements. It is a mixture of four stable isotopes and has twenty-seven other isotopes, all radioactive, resulting from the fact that lead is the end product of three series of radioactive elements: the uranium series, actinium series, and thorium series. It has an average atomic weight of 207.2 and a density of 11.35 grams per cubic centimeter; it has a melting point of 327.5° Celsius and a boiling point of 1,740° Celsius.

## DESCRIPTION, DISTRIBUTION, AND FORMS

Lead is soft, malleable, and ductile, and is second only to tin in possessing the lowest melting point among the common metals. It may well have been the first metal smelted by humans, although it was probably not the first metal used—an honor claimed by gold, silver, or copper, which occur naturally in their metallic states. The fact that the principal ore of lead, galena (lead sulfide), frequently resembles the metal itself in its gray-black metallic color probably encouraged early humans to experiment with crude smelting. Inorganic lead also occurs as a carbonate (cerrusite), sulfate (anglesite), and oxides. Organic compounds of lead exist; these were used for many years in automobile gasoline as antiknock additives (tetraethyl and tetramethyl lead). Lead is widely distributed in the environment, but except in bedrock, concentrations are largely a consequence of human activity. Clair Patterson demonstrated that dramatic human-related increases in lead concentrations exist in the oceans, in polar ice sheets, and in the atmosphere. Before the human use of lead, the global flux into the oceans was only one-tenth to one-hundredth what it is today; lead in the atmosphere has increased a hundredfold globally and a thousandfold in urban areas.

Considering that only an estimated 0.0013 percent of the Earth's crust is lead, it is surprisingly widely dis-

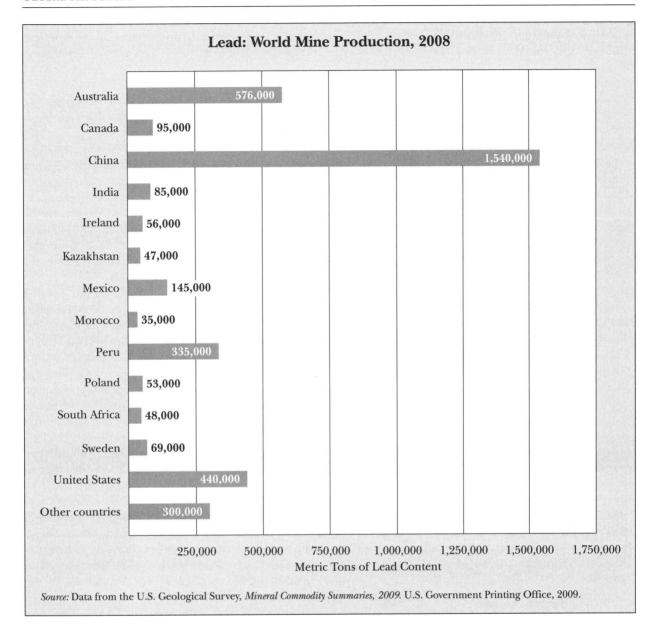

**Lead: World Mine Production, 2008**

| Country | Metric Tons of Lead Content |
|---|---|
| Australia | 576,000 |
| Canada | 95,000 |
| China | 1,540,000 |
| India | 85,000 |
| Ireland | 56,000 |
| Kazakhstan | 47,000 |
| Mexico | 145,000 |
| Morocco | 35,000 |
| Peru | 335,000 |
| Poland | 53,000 |
| South Africa | 48,000 |
| Sweden | 69,000 |
| United States | 440,000 |
| Other countries | 300,000 |

*Source:* Data from the U.S. Geological Survey, *Mineral Commodity Summaries, 2009.* U.S. Government Printing Office, 2009.

tributed in the environment. Lead is found in both crystalline (igneous and metamorphic) and sedimentary rocks. Because it is the stable end product of radioactive disintegration of minerals that form in igneous rocks (it is the rate of this disintegration that is employed to determine the age of the rock), virtually all older crystalline rocks contain at least tiny amounts of lead. As sedimentary rocks are derived from the weathering, erosion, and sedimentation of fragments from existing rocks, it follows that lead compounds will be among those that are sedimented. The higher

concentrations of lead—those that pose toxicity problems or are valuable to miners—depend upon quite different processes. Some toxic concentrations of lead are transported by water and then sedimented or absorbed by rock particles, depending on the salinity or acidity levels of the solution. Most toxic concentrations of lead, however, are transported as dust by the atmosphere.

Deposits of lead ore exist at far higher concentrations than those levels that pose problems in water, dust, or soil. They are the result of natural geologic processes, including igneous intrusions, mountain building, and the flow of hot and cold solutions through bedrock over millions of years. The richest lead ores may contain 20 to 25 percent lead, usually with substantial fractions of zinc and minor quantities of silver. Copper and gold are also frequently associated with lead deposits, or vice versa (minor amounts of lead are usually found in copper ore).

Lead affects the environment in two major ways: through mining and processing, and because many of its uses, particularly in the past, have exposed the general public to its toxicity. Lead mining has environmental impacts similar to those of the mining of any mineral. Surface mining destroys the local ecosystem and disrupts the use of land for other purposes; reclamation rarely prepares the land for as valuable a use as it enjoyed before mining. The majority of lead is mined underground, where surface disruption is not as great unless subsidence over the mined areas is a problem. In both surface and underground mining, water is generally contaminated, mine wastes must be stored (waste dumps frequently occupy more space than the mine itself), and the transportation of mine products and waste serves as a source of dust, noise, and disruption to the surrounding population. The milling, smelting, and refining of lead pose further problems. First, lead itself escapes and pollutes the atmosphere with toxic substances. Second, most lead is derived from sulfides, which upon heating in the smelting and refining processes form sulfur dioxide. Sulfur dioxide combines with water in the atmosphere to create sulfuric acid, which devastates and denudes the vegetation cover in the immediate vicinity and contributes to acid rain fallout generally.

Humans may come into contact with lead and its toxic effects in the air, dust, and water, and by direct contamination of food, drink, or cosmetics. The effects of lead on human health are diverse and severe, with their greatest impact on children. The effects are exacerbated by the fact that lead accumulates in the body, and damage is often irreversible—especially damage to the brain. Lead damages blood biochemistry, the renal and endocrine system, liver functions, and the central nervous system, and it contributes to osteoporosis, high blood pressure, and reproductive abnormalities. The Environmental Protection Agency and the Occupational Safety and Health Administration set standards of acceptable levels of lead in air, dust, soil, and water; the standards are updated frequently based on new research, and they are quite complex, depending on the duration and nature of exposure.

HISTORY

While lead apparently was not the first or second metal to attract early humans, because it did not occur in a metallic state, it was exploited relatively early and may have been smelted in Anatolia (modern day Turkey) as early as 7000-6500 B.C.E. The softness and malleability of lead proved to be both attractive and undesirable to people in antiquity. Most early lead mining was carried on to recover the associated silver, and the lead remaining from the process was piled in waste heaps. Lead may be strengthened by alloying with other metals, but this process was carried out only to a limited degree in lead's earliest usage.

While lead may not have proved attractive for uses requiring strength and hardness, its malleability caused the Romans, in particular, to put it to widespread use in piping, roofing, and vessels. In addition, lead compounds were used in paints, cosmetics, and as additives to wine and food. Lead poisoning was therefore widespread. The problem was recognized possibly as early as 370 B.C.E. by Hippocrates and certainly was known by Nikander in the second century B.C.E. The Romans nevertheless continued to press lead into a variety of services until the fall of their empire. Some authorities believe that lead poisoning was central to this fall, and many more believe that it at least contributed (especially to the disorganization of Roman leaders). Others maintain that the critical lead-related factor in the decline of Rome was the exhaustion of the richer silver-bearing ores. Exhaustion of mines or ores at any period in history is usually a function of the technology and economics of the time; many of these ores were particularly rich by modern standards. Silver was critical to maintenance of the Roman financial system, and the decline in its availability brought economic chaos.

Medieval production of lead declined dramatically in Europe following the fall of the Roman Empire, although recurring cases of lead poisoning during this period serve as a reminder that lead was still utilized widely in storage vessels. The Industrial Revolution, beginning with its earliest stages, revived the production level of lead, both for itself and as a by-product of silver mining. The expansion of European exploration into the Western Hemisphere and of European colonization worldwide from the fifteenth century onward undoubtedly contributed to the rise in lead production. Gold and silver were sought avidly in these expansions of domain, and lead mining frequently serves as the final use or "mop-up" stage in the life history of a mining district. Also, industrial uses and mining technology became increasingly sophisticated, leading to a new demand for lead and zinc, its frequent associate, especially beginning in the nineteenth century. The production curve of lead and zinc goes exponentially upward through history, with far greater production today than in earlier centuries.

## OBTAINING LEAD

The largest lead deposits in the United States and Europe are of the Mississippi Valley type: lead sulfide (galena) deposits of uncertain origin in limestone or dolomite rocks. Many large mines throughout the world are found in crystalline rocks, where they are usually associated with igneous intrusions. Some lead is recovered as a by-product of the mining of copper or other associated minerals from large open-pit mines developed in low-grade ores, called porphyries. This type of recovery is a triumph of modern technology and engineering, because the ores frequently contain less than 0.5 percent copper, with even smaller fractions of lead. Most lead is recovered from underground mines that are exploiting much smaller concentrations in veins or disseminated beds of lead-zinc, zinc-lead, or lead-silver ores.

From 2003 to 2007, the average U.S. primary lead production (lead from mines) was 162,000 metric tons per year, while production of secondary lead (recycled from scrap, chiefly automotive batteries) during the same time period was 1.2 million metric tons per year. World mine production was somewhat less than lead from secondary sources: about 3.5 million metric tons from mines compared to 3.8 million metric tons from secondary sources. Recycling should prove even more important in the future as the richest deposits—those in which the lead content of the ore ranges between 5 and 10 percent—are depleted. This type of "exhaustion" of a deposit is a function of the prevailing technology and economics. In the first half of the twentieth century, the tristate lead-zinc mining district of Missouri, Oklahoma, and Kansas was the world's greatest. Production there essentially ceased in the 1950's, not because the lead and zinc were literally exhausted but because the concentrations available dropped below the level at which mining could be done profitably.

Technology is continuously improving, however, and the history of mining is filled with examples (particularly concerning the five associated metals gold, silver, copper, lead, and zinc) in which improvements in technology, combined with changing economic conditions, have made it possible to reopen or rework older and less attractive deposits. Some mine tailings or waste dumps have been reworked several times under these circumstances.

## USES OF LEAD

More than most metals, the uses to which lead and lead compounds have been put have changed considerably throughout history. One reason is that new opportunities have presented themselves, such as automotive lead-acid batteries, the shielding of dangerous radiation, and antiknock additives for gasoline—all twentieth century phenomena. Largely, however, this has occurred because people have become increasingly cognizant of the dangers posed by lead's toxicity. While the dangers of exposure to lead have been known since Greek and Roman times, in few cases has this led to regulation of uses. Not until the 1960's, 1970's, and 1980's were specific controls or regulations imposed restricting the use of lead in paint pigments, as an additive to gasoline, and in construction.

---

### U.S. End Uses of Lead

| PERCENTAGE | USES |
|---|---|
| 88 | Lead-acid batteries |
| 10 | Ammunition, casting material, pipes, radiation shields, traps, extruded products, building construction, cable covers, caulking, solder, oxides (for ceramics, chemicals, glass, pigments) |
| 2 | Ballast, counterweights, brass, bronze, foil, terne metal, type metal, wire, other |

*Source:* Data from the U.S. Geological Survey, *Mineral Commodity Summaries, 2009.* U.S. Government Printing Office, 2009.

Lead piping is still found in structures built in the 1970's; the use of lead in storage vessels for food or drink has been regulated even more recently. Lead foil was used in capping wine bottles into the early 1990's, and many people are still unaware that storage of wine or other liquids in fine leaded-glass decanters permits leaching of the lead content into the fluid over time.

The post-World War II era saw the elimination or substantial reduction of the following uses of lead: water pipes, solder in food cans, paint pigments, gasoline additives, and fishing sinkers. The major remaining uses include storage batteries, ammunition, paint pigments (for nonresidential use), glass and ceramics, sheet lead (largely for shielding against radiation), cable coverings, and solder.

*Neil E. Salisbury*

FURTHER READING

Adriano, Domy C. "Lead." In *Trace Elements in Terrestrial Environments: Biogeochemistry, Bioavailability, and Risks of Metals.* 2d ed. New York: Springer, 2001.

Casas, José S., and José Sordo, eds. *Lead: Chemistry, Analytical Aspects, Environmental Impact, and Health Effects.* Boston: Elsevier, 2006.

Cheremisinoff, Paul N., and Nicholas P. Cheremisinoff. *Lead: A Guidebook to Hazard Detection, Remediation, and Control.* Englewood Cliffs, N.J.: PTR Prentice Hall, 1993.

English, Peter C. *Old Paint: A Medical History of Childhood Lead-Paint Poisoning in the United States to 1980.* New Brunswick, N.J.: Rutgers University Press, 2001.

Greenwood, N. N., and A. Earnshaw. "Germanium, Tin, and Lead." In *Chemistry of the Elements.* 2d ed. Boston: Butterworth-Heinemann, 1997.

Guilbert, John M., and Charles F. Park, Jr. *The Geology of Ore Deposits.* Long Grove, Ill.: Waveland Press, 2007.

Massey, A. G. "Group 14: Carbon, Silicon, Germanium, Tin, and Lead." In *Main Group Chemistry.* 2d ed. New York: Wiley, 2000.

National Research Council. *Lead in the Human Environment: A Report.* Washington, D.C.: National Academy of Sciences, 1980.

Nriagu, Jerome O. *Lead and Lead Poisoning in Antiquity.* New York: Wiley, 1983.

Warren, Christian. *Brush with Death: A Social History of Lead Poisoning.* Baltimore: Johns Hopkins University Press, 2000.

WEB SITES

NATURAL RESOURCES CANADA
Canadian Minerals Yearbook, Mineral and Metal Commodity Reviews
http://www.nrcan-rncan.gc.ca/mms-smm/busi-indu/cmy-amc/com-eng.htm

U.S. GEOLOGICAL SURVEY
Lead: Statistics and Information
http://minerals.usgs.gov/minerals/pubs/commodity/lead

SEE ALSO: Air pollution and air pollution control; Metals and metallurgy; Mineral resource use, early history of; Recycling; Silver; United States; Zinc.

# Leopold, Aldo

CATEGORY: People
BORN: January 11, 1887; Burlington, Iowa
DIED: April 21, 1948; near Baraboo, Sauk County, Wisconsin

*In his years of government service and private work, Leopold was active in game management and wildlife preservation. His* Sand County Almanac *was influential with succeeding generations of conservationists.*

BIOGRAPHICAL BACKGROUND
Aldo Leopold, born in Burlington, Iowa, graduated from the Yale Forest School (now the Yale School of Forestry and Environmental Studies) in 1906. In 1909, after completing his master's degree, he joined the U.S. Forest Service and fostered the ecological policies of Gifford Pinchot and Theodore Roosevelt. Stationed in the southwestern United States, he advocated game conservation to avoid the erosion of sport hunting. He also helped establish a 200,000-hectare roadless wilderness in the Gila National Forest. While pursuing wolf eradication to ensure deer viability, he realized the importance of ecological interactions.

IMPACT ON RESOURCE USE
Leopold moved to Wisconsin in 1924, joined the U.S. Forest Products Laboratory, and developed the policy of wildlife management. He published *Game Management,* subsequently retitled *Wildlife Management,* in 1933. In the same year, he joined the University of Wis-

*Aldo Leopold's seminal* Sand County Almanac *(1949) has influenced generations of conservationists.* (AP/Wide World Photos)

consin at Madison Department of Agricultural Economics. He assisted Robert Marshall in creating the Wilderness Society in 1935, and he established a one-man Department of Wildlife Management in 1939.

Leopold advocated integration of local concerns with universities, government agencies, and the private sector to balance farming, forestry, wildlife, and recreation. He escaped on the weekends to his sand farm in Wisconsin, where he wrote prolifically. His *Sand County Almanac*, published posthumously in 1949, represents a lifetime of observations concerning ecology, ethics, and aesthetics and concludes that a policy is right when it tends to preserve the integrity, stability, and beauty of the biotic community; any other policy, according to Leopold, is wrong.

*Aaron S. Pollak and Oliver B. Pollak*

SEE ALSO: Conservation; Pinchot, Gifford; Roosevelt, Theodore; Wilderness; Wilderness Society.

# Lime

CATEGORY: Mineral and other nonliving resources

## WHERE FOUND

Lime is a manufactured product not found in nature. It is usually derived from the common sedimentary rocks limestone, dolomitic limestone, and dolostone, although it can also be produced from other high-calcium materials such as marble, aragonite, chalk, shell, and coral.

## PRIMARY USES

An essential industrial chemical, lime is used in the manufacture of steel, pulp and paper, glass and porcelain, and chemicals. It is a component of construction materials such as plaster, mortar, stucco, and whitewash. It is also used in conditioning acidic soils, softening water, and treating wastewater and smokestack emissions.

## TECHNICAL DEFINITION

Lime (also known as quicklime, caustic lime, or calcia) is a common term for the chemical compound calcium oxide ($CaO$). The name is often applied to several related compounds, including hydrated or slaked lime (calcium hydroxide, $Ca(OH)_2$); dolomitic quicklime ($CaO{\cdot}MgO$); type N ($Ca(OH)_2{\cdot}MgO$) and type S ($Ca(OH)_2{\cdot}Mg(OH)_2$) dolomitic hydrates; and refractory lime, also called dead-burned or hard-burned lime. When pure, lime occurs as colorless, cubic crystals or in a white microcrystalline form; often impurities such as iron and oxides of silicon, aluminum, and magnesium are present. Lime has a specific gravity of 3.34, a melting point of 2,570° Celsius, and a boiling point of 2,850° Celsius.

## DESCRIPTION, DISTRIBUTION, AND FORMS

A highly reactive compound, lime combines with water to produce the more stable hydrated lime. This reaction, known as slaking, produces heat and causes the solid almost to double in volume. At temperatures around 1,650° Celsius, lime recrystallizes into the coarser, denser, and less reactive refractory lime. When heated to approximately 2,500° Celsius, lime is incandescent.

Lime is a highly reactive manufactured compound that is an essential part of many industrial processes. An alkali, it dissolves in water to produce a caustic, basic solution. Lime is typically obtained from limestone, although other natural substances that are high in calcium are also used as raw materials for lime manufacture. Total world production of lime approaches 300 million metric tons, about 20 million metric tons of which are produced in the United States (including Puerto Rico). From 2003 to 2007, the United States was second to China in lime production.

## History

Use of lime in construction dates back at least to the ancient Egyptians, who, between 4000 and 2000 B.C.E., employed it as a mortar and plaster. The Greeks, Romans, and Chinese used it in construction, agriculture, textile bleaching, and hide tanning. One of the oldest industries in the United States, lime manufacture began in colonial times. While the use of lime increased with the Industrial Revolution, it remained largely a construction material until the early twentieth century, when it became a crucial resource for the rapidly growing chemical industry.

## Obtaining Lime

Lime may be prepared from a variety of naturally occurring materials with a high calcium content. While lime is commonly obtained from limestone, a sedimentary rock composed chiefly of calcite (calcium carbonate, $CaCO_3$), it can also be derived from dolostone, a similar sedimentary rock that is predominantly dolomite ($CaMg(CO_3)_2$), or from rock with an intermediate composition (dolomitic limestone). Lime is also produced from marble, aragonite, chalk, shell, and coral (all mostly calcium carbonate). Because the raw materials for lime manufacture are plentiful and widespread, lime is produced all over the world, with production facilities generally located near the sources for the raw materials.

When calcium carbonate is heated in a masonry furnace to about 1,100° Celsius, it breaks down into lime and carbon dioxide. Heating dolomite in this fashion produces dolomitic quicklime and carbon dioxide. Approximately 100 metric tons of pure limestone yields 56 metric tons of lime. Adding water to stabilize lime or dolomitic quicklime yields the hydrated (slaked) form. Dolomite is typically used to make refractory (dead-burned) lime, which involves heating the materials to temperatures around 1,650° Celsius.

## Uses of Lime

A fundamental industrial chemical, lime is used in the manufacture of porcelain and glass, pigments, pulp and paper, varnish, and baking powder. It is employed in the preparation of calcium carbide, calcium cyanamide, calcium carbonate, and other chemicals; in the refining of salt and the purification of sugar; in treating industrial wastewater, sewage, and smokestack effluent; and in softening water. In metallurgy it is used in smelting and in concentrating ores. Lime and other calcium compounds are used in liming, a method for treating acidic soils. The application of lime to soil neutralizes acidity, improves soil texture and stability, and enriches the soil's nitrogen content by increasing the activity of soil microorganisms that secure nitrogen from the air. Lime's incandescing properties are employed in the Drummond Light, or limelight, in which a cylinder of lime is heated with the flame of an oxyhydrogen torch to produce a brilliant white light. Mixed with sand and water, lime serves as a mortar or plaster. The lime hydrates in

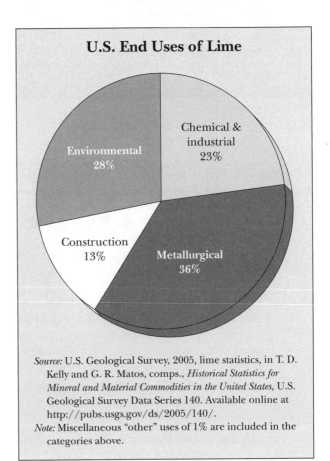

**U.S. End Uses of Lime**

Chemical & industrial 23%

Environmental 28%

Construction 13%

Metallurgical 36%

*Source:* U.S. Geological Survey, 2005, lime statistics, in T. D. Kelly and G. R. Matos, comps., *Historical Statistics for Mineral and Material Commodities in the United States,* U.S. Geological Survey Data Series 140. Available online at http://pubs.usgs.gov/ds/2005/140/.

*Note:* Miscellaneous "other" uses of 1% are included in the categories above.

combination with water; the mortar hardens quickly as the hydrated lime reacts with carbon dioxide in the air to form calcium carbonate. Dolomitic quicklime is used to produce a hard, strong, and elastic stucco.

Uses of hydrated lime include soil liming, sugar refining, and chemical preparation. In leather tanning, hydrated lime is used to remove hair from hides. In construction, it is used to increase the durability of mortar, plaster, and stucco. Hydrated lime in a highly dilute solution is whitewash. Filtering whitewash yields lime water, used in medicine as a burn treatment and as an antacid, and in chemistry as a reagent. Dolomitic hydrates are used as a flux in the manufacture of glass.

Dead-burned lime is a refractory material, able to withstand contact with often corrosive substances at elevated temperatures. Refractory lime is a component in tar-bonded refractory brick, which is used in the construction of the basic oxygen furnaces employed in steelmaking.

*Karen N. Kähler*

## FURTHER READING

Boggs, Sam. "Limestones." In *Petrology of Sedimentary Rocks.* 2d ed. Cambridge, England: Cambridge University Press, 2009.

Boynton, Robert S. *Chemistry and Technology of Lime and Limestone.* 2d ed. New York: Wiley, 1980.

Jensen, Mead L., and Alan M. Bateman. *Economic Mineral Deposits.* 3d ed. New York: Wiley, 1979.

Kogel, Jessica Elzea, et al., eds. "Lime." In *Industrial Minerals and Rocks: Commodities, Markets, and Uses.* 7th ed. Littleton, Colo.: Society for Mining, Metallurgy, and Exploration, 2006.

Oates, J. A. H. *Lime and Limestone: Chemistry and Technology, Production and Uses.* New York: Wiley-VCH, 1998.

## WEB SITES

NATURAL RESOURCES CANADA
Canadian Minerals Yearbook, Mineral and Metal Commodity Reviews
http://www.nrcan-rncan.gc.ca/mms-smm/busi-indu/cmy-amc/com-eng.htm

U.S. GEOLOGICAL SURVEY
Lime: Statistics and Information
http://minerals.usgs.gov/minerals/pubs/commodity/lime

SEE ALSO: Calcium compounds; China; Glass; Limestone; Metals and metallurgy; Oxides.

# Limestone

CATEGORY: Mineral and other nonliving resources

*Limestone is one of the most widely used rock materials. It is used as road metal, as aggregate for macadam and concrete, and as a building stone.*

## DEFINITION

Limestone is a widespread marine sedimentary rock found wherever shallow seas once encroached onto continents. Limestone accounts for 10 to 15 percent of all sedimentary rocks. Some limestones are formed in lakes, around springs, at geysers, and in caves. The term "limestone" encompasses many rocks of diverse appearance that have calcite as their essential component. They differ considerably in texture, color, structure, and origin.

## OVERVIEW

Although limestones may form by inorganic precipitation of calcite in lakes, springs, or caves, the most widespread limestones are of marine origin. Most limestones are formed by organic processes and consist largely of the shells and shell fragments of marine invertebrates. Because calcite is susceptible to solution and recrystallization, diagenetic processes may completely alter the texture of the original rock.

Limestone is a sedimentary rock composed largely of the mineral calcite (calcium carbonate). This relatively soft stone in its pure form is white, but it may be buff, pink, red, gray, or black, depending upon minor materials present. The texture ranges from fine- to coarse-grained and from highly porous to highly compact. Many limestones contain abundant fossils. Dolostone is a closely related rock composed primarily of dolomite (calcium-magnesium carbonate).

Coquina is a limestone of comparatively recent formation consisting of loosely cemented shell fragments. Compact rocks with abundant shell material are known as fossiliferous limestone. They may be described more specifically by adding the dominant fossil genera to the rock name. Chalk is a fine-grained, porous, white rock made up of minute tests of foraminifera. Lithographic limestone is a compact, fine-

*Lower magnesian limestone in Dane County, Wisconsin.* (USGS)

grained rock that is used in the printing process from which it derives its name. Travertine is an inorganic deposit usually formed in caves as coarse, crystalline dripstone. Tufa is a porous, spongy material deposited around springs and geysers. Oolitic limestone is composed of small, spherical bodies of concentrically layered calcite formed in shallow water with moderate agitation. Coarse crystalline limestone forms by recrystallization of primary, fine-grained limestones.

Limestone and other soluble rocks in warm, humid regions are susceptible to solution by meteoric water at the surface and in the subsurface. The resulting landscapes, characterized by abundant sinkholes and caverns, are known as karst topography. Because water moves rapidly into the subsurface in karst regions, rapid spreading of contamination in groundwater is of special concern.

Some limestones that take a good polish are marketed as marble. Limestone is used as a flux in open-hearth iron smelters. It is a basic raw material in the manufacture of portland cement. It is also used as an inert ingredient in pharmaceutical preparations. Limestone is the chief source of chemical and agricultural lime. It is also ground and pressed to make blackboard chalk. Limestone serves as a significant aquifer, and it constitutes about 50 percent of reservoir rocks for oil and gas. Prior to the introduction of electric lighting, carved chunks of limestone were fed into a gas flame to produce a fairly bright light used as stage lighting—hence the term "limelight."

*René A. De Hon*

FURTHER READING

Boggs, Sam. "Limestones." In *Petrology of Sedimentary Rocks*. 2d ed. Cambridge, England: Cambridge University Press, 2009.

Boynton, Robert S. *Chemistry and Technology of Lime and Limestone*. 2d ed. New York: Wiley, 1980.

Kogel, Jessica Elzea, et al., eds. "Lime." In *Industrial Minerals and Rocks: Commodities, Markets, and Uses*.

7th ed. Littleton, Colo.: Society for Mining, Metallurgy, and Exploration, 2006.

Oates, J. A. H. *Lime and Limestone: Chemistry and Technology, Production and Uses.* New York: Wiley-VCH, 1998.

### WEB SITES

NATURAL RESOURCES CANADA
Canadian Minerals Yearbook, Mineral and Metal Commodity Reviews
http://www.nrcan-rncan.gc.ca/mms-smm/busi-indu/cmy-amc/com-eng.htm

U.S. GEOLOGICAL SURVEY
Lime: Statistics and Information
http://minerals.usgs.gov/minerals/pubs/commodity/lime

SEE ALSO: Aggregates; Carbonate minerals; Cement and concrete; Groundwater; Marble; Oil and natural gas reservoirs; Quarrying.

# Lithium

CATEGORY: Mineral and other nonliving resources

### WHERE FOUND

Lithium makes up about 0.006 percent of the Earth's crust and is found as a trace element in most rocks. The most important lithium ore is spodumene, with extensive deposits in North Carolina, Canada (Quebec), Brazil, Argentina, Spain, and the Democratic Republic of the Congo. Another important commercial source of lithium is lepidolite.

### PRIMARY USES

In combination with other metals, lithium is used as a heat exchanger in nuclear reactors as well as a radiation shield around reactors. Lithium is used as an anode in high-voltage batteries, and lithium compounds are used in the manufacture of rubber products, ceramic products, enamels, dyes, glass, and high-temperature lubricants.

### TECHNICAL DEFINITION

Lithium, symbol Li, is located in Group IA of the periodic table. It has an atomic number of 3 and an atomic weight of 6.941. It is a soft, silvery-white metal and is the lightest known metal. It has a melting point of 180.54° Celsius, a boiling point of 1,347° Celsius, a specific gravity of 0.534, and a specific heat of 0.79 calorie per gram per degree Celsius.

### DESCRIPTION, DISTRIBUTION, AND FORMS

Lithium quickly becomes covered with a gray oxidation layer when it is exposed to air, and because it combines so easily with other elements, lithium is always found chemically bonded in nature. Although a highly reactive element, lithium is less reactive than the other alkali metals. Like the other alkali metals, it easily gives up an electron to form monovalent positive ions.

### HISTORY

Lithium was discovered by Swedish industrialist Johan August Arfwedson in 1817. The element was first isolated in 1818 by Sir Humphry Davy through electrolytic reduction of the lithium ion.

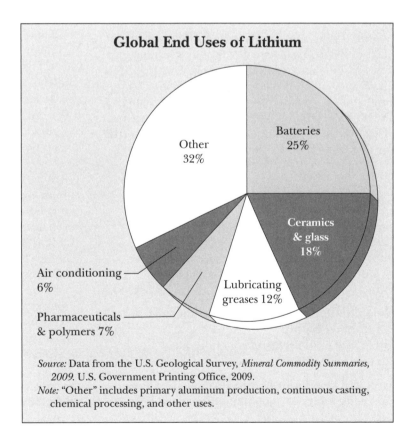

**Global End Uses of Lithium**

Other 32%
Batteries 25%
Ceramics & glass 18%
Lubricating greases 12%
Air conditioning 6%
Pharmaceuticals & polymers 7%

*Source:* Data from the U.S. Geological Survey, *Mineral Commodity Summaries, 2009.* U.S. Government Printing Office, 2009.
*Note:* "Other" includes primary aluminum production, continuous casting, chemical processing, and other uses.

## OBTAINING LITHIUM

Lithium chloride is obtained by treating either lithium hydroxide or lithium carbonate with hydrochloric acid. Chemists obtain pure metallic lithium by passing electricity through molten lithium chloride or through solutions of lithium chloride in ethanol or acetone in low-carbon steel cells having graphite anodes.

## USES OF LITHIUM

Lithium is used to make batteries found in electric meters, cameras, and other electronic equipment, and lithium compounds have numerous practical applications. Lithium carbonate and lithium borate are used in the ceramic industry as glaze constituents, while lithium perchlorate is a powerful oxidizing agent used in solid fuel for rockets. Lithium hydride, a powerful reducing agent, is used in fuel cells, as a shielding material for thermal neutrons emitted from nuclear reactors, and to inflate lifeboats and air balloons. Lithium fluoride is used in infrared spectrometers and as a flux in ceramics, brazing, and welding. Lithium chloride, the most common lithium salt, is used to increase the conductivity of electrolytes in low-temperature dry-cell batteries, as a dehumidifying agent in air-conditioners, and in metallurgical applications. Lithium is combined with aluminum and magnesium to produce structural alloys; lithium-magnesium alloys have the highest strength-to-weight ratio of all structural materials. In medicine, lithium amide is important in the synthesis of antihistamines, and lithium carbonate is used as a drug to treat a form of mental illness known as bipolar affective disorder (or manic-depressive disorder).

*Alvin K. Benson*

## WEB SITES

NATURAL RESOURCES CANADA
Canadian Minerals Yearbook, 2005: Lithium
http://www.nrcan-rncan.gc.ca/mms-smm/busi-indu/cmy-amc/content/2005/35.pdf

U.S. GEOLOGICAL SURVEY
Minerals Information: Lithium Statistics and Information
http://minerals.usgs.gov/minerals/pubs/commodity/lithium/

SEE ALSO: Aluminum; Carbonate minerals; Ceramics; Fuel cells; Glass; Magnesium; Nuclear energy; Rubber, natural.

# Lithosphere

CATEGORY: Geological processes and formations

*The usable mineral resources of the Earth are all within the lithosphere, and knowledge of its properties is particularly important in the search for gas and oil.*

## DEFINITION

The lithosphere ("stone sphere," from Greek *lithos*) consists of the outer, brittle portions of the Earth, including the upper mantle and crust.

## OVERVIEW

The interior of the Earth has a number of layers, or concentric spheres. At the center of the Earth is the inner core. Then, moving outward, come the outer core, the lower mantle, the upper mantle, and the Earth's crust. Scientists subdivide the upper mantle into the asthenosphere, a partially molten zone, and, above that, the lithosphere. The lithosphere, then, is the rigid (or brittle) outer shell of the Earth, which extends to a depth of between 70 and 100 kilometers and rests on the asthenoshere. It includes the Earth's crust and part of the upper mantle.

The upper mantle is approximately 700 kilometers thick. The asthenosphere begins at a depth of approximately 70 to 100 kilometers and shows a rapid increase in density and a temperature in excess of 1,000° Celsius. The asthenosphere is partially molten ultramafic material. Because of its partially molten properties, the asthenosphere probably exhibits plastic flow. Above the asthenoshere, the upper brittle portion of the upper mantle that is part of the lithosphere is a dense ultramafic material that directly underlies the Earth's crust. The lithosphere comprises seven to ten major lithospheric "plates" that move slowly as they rest on the asthenosphere. Plate tectonics refers to the movement of these plates and the land and ocean forms that are created as a result.

Within the lithosphere, the boundary between the upper mantle and the crust is called the Mohorovičić discontinuity, or Moho, which marks a compositional change in the rock. The earth's crust contains two basic types of crustal material, oceanic and continental, with an average density of 2.9 and 2.6, respectively. Oceanic crust ranges from 5 to 10 kilometers thick and is thinnest over seafloor-spreading areas. Oceanic crust is primarily composed of dense basaltic rock

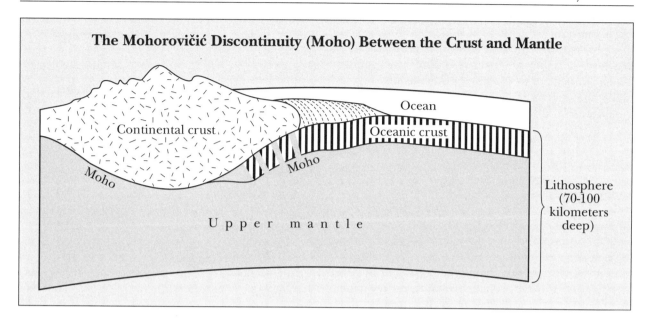

### The Mohorovičić Discontinuity (Moho) Between the Crust and Mantle

with a thin veneer of silt and carbonate precipitates; however, a variety of minerals have been observed at seafloor vents. Continental crust is primarily composed of felsic granitic rock, which is less dense than oceanic crust; however, continental crust also includes sedimentary and metamorphic rock and even uplifted oceanic basalt. A variety of minerals of varying economic importance occur in the continental crust. The continental crust averages 30 to 40 kilometers in thickness, but it may be more than 70 kilometers thick in some mountain areas.

Oceanic crust is less dense than the parent mantle material. This is probably attributable to partial melting and crystal fractionation. Felsic minerals have a lower melting temperature than mafic minerals, and mafic minerals are the first to crystallize out of a melt. As oceanic crust subducts below continental crust, the subducting plate eventually melts, and its upwelling liquid fraction produces less mafic intermediates.

The lithosphere is highly variable, according to regional studies. In parts of the middle United States and in the Gulf of Mexico region, for example, the crust has thick sedimentary layers. Oil companies were able to measure the seismic wave patterns generated by many controlled explosions and discover petroleum and natural gas within these layers. The later discovery of oil in northern Alaska was prompted by the similarity of the crust there to the crust of these regions. As the study of the characteristics of the lithosphere—including plate tectonics—continues, scientists will increasingly be able to use their knowledge to discover sites of mineral resources.

*Raymond U. Roberts*

SEE ALSO: Earth's crust; Igneous processes, rocks, and mineral deposits; Magma crystallization; Marine vents; Metamorphic processes, rocks, and mineral deposits; Plate tectonics; Plutonic rocks and mineral deposits; Seafloor spreading; Sedimentary processes, rocks, and mineral deposits; Volcanoes.

## Livestock and animal husbandry

CATEGORY: Plant and animal resources

*Animal husbandry refers to the management of domesticated animals such as beef or dairy cattle, sheep, goats, pigs, and chickens: livestock. Such animals constitute a renewable resource providing humans with food, fiber, fuel, power, implements, and other benefits.*

### BACKGROUND

Effective animal husbandry requires an affinity for the animals being managed, skill in handling them, and knowledge of them and their environment. Respect for animals is important to good management, as is skill in handling to minimize injuries and stress to both animal and handler. Knowledge is needed of their nutrition, reproduction, and behavior as well as the physical, biological, cultural, and economic context in which they are managed. While some inputs (such as aberrant weather and governmental regulations) are beyond the control of the producer, good management will ensure the most efficient productivity from the available inputs.

## INTENSIVE AND EXTENSIVE MANAGEMENT

Intensive and extensive management are the two main options for animal husbandry. Intensive management refers to confinement-type operations that provide animals with shelter, food, and water. It has been called "landless" because it requires very little property. Examples include beef feedlots, concentrate-based dairy farms, and confinement swine or poultry operations. In extensive systems, on the other hand, the animals are provided with an area in which they fend for themselves, finding their own food, water, and shelter. Examples are rangeland beef operations, pasture-based dairying, and free-range poultry farms. In practice, animal husbandry often includes both intensive and extensive management.

In the early twenty-first century, the U.S. beef industry generally involved extensive operations for at least the first year of life and an intensive phase just prior to market; availability and prices of feed grains may determine the extent to which intensive management is practiced. Dairy operations around the world range from intensive to extensive—from no to exclusive pasture, respectively. Seasonal variation of pasture may dictate when it is available and used. Because dairy cows must be milked two or three times a day, dairy operations are never as extensive as some beef operations, where the producer may have contact with the animals no more than once a year.

Intensive animal management generally requires more management expertise, more capital investment, and more energy utilization. Since the animal is totally under control of the producer, all needs of the animal must be provided. The inevitably greater concentration of animals requires closer attention to their housing and health. The larger capital investment is attributable to facilities and equipment. More energy utilization is needed to maintain temperature and ventilation as well as to operate equipment. Intensive management also places greater emphasis on maximizing animal performance. Because more capital and energy are used, effort is made to extend animal performance by genetics, nutrition, and other

| Meat: Leading Producers, 2006 | METRIC TONS |
|---|---|
| **World total** | **212,776,000** |
| **Beef and veal** | |
| United States | 11,981,000 |
| Brazil | 9,020,000 |
| European Union | 8,060,000 |
| China | 7,492,000 |
| Argentina | 3,100,000 |
| India | 2,375,000 |
| Australia | 2,183,000 |
| Mexico | 2,175,000 |
| Russia | 1,430,000 |
| Canada | 1,391,000 |
| **Pork** | |
| China | 51,972,000 |
| European Union | 21,677,000 |
| United States | 9,559,000 |
| Brazil | 2,830,000 |
| Canada | 1,898,000 |
| Russia | 1,805,000 |
| Vietnam | 1,713,000 |
| Japan | 1,247,000 |
| Philippines | 1,215,000 |
| Mexico | 1,200,000 |
| **Poultry** | |
| United States | 16,043,000 |
| China | 10,350,000 |
| Brazil | 9,355,000 |
| European Union | 7,803,000 |
| Mexico | 2,592,000 |
| India | 2,000,000 |
| Japan | 1,227,000 |
| Argentina | 1,200,000 |
| Russia | 1,180,000 |
| Thailand | 1,100,000 |

*Source:* U.S. Department of Agriculture, National Agricultural Statistics Service, *Agricultural Statistics*, 2007.

management tools. Intensive managment also requires more dependence on others for feed. While some intensive livestock producers raise their own feedstuff, many do not. They may depend on crop farmers within the region or half a world away. Contemporary swine operations in Japan and Korea require corn and soybeans from the U.S. Midwest.

Extensive animal management demands more land and more dependence on the animals' abilities than intensive management. The larger land requirement is a primary feature of this system. The greater dependence on the animals' abilities follows from less direct provision by the producer for their needs. Survival and growth may depend on their locating food, water, and shelter as well as avoiding danger. Reproduction may be left to natural service, easy birthing, and good mothering. Extensive management involves more tolerance for decreased animal performance. When weather conditions do not provide sufficient food, the animals will have less than maximal growth and fertility. Neonatal losses attributed to weather, predators, or terrain are tolerated. Indeed, human intervention may not be a realistic option when animals are widely dispersed. An important parameter is the "stocking rate," the number of animals per land area. Too few animals will not fully use the vegetation, as many grasses are most nutritious at an early stage of development and become less nutritious and coarser if not eaten then. Too many animals will overgraze, impairing regrowth of the vegetation. Optimum "stocking rate" corresponds closely to the ecological concept "carrying capacity," the number of animals that an area can sustain over an extended period of time. Extensive systems can demand substantial management expertise. For instance, pasture-based dairying in New Zealand requires considerable knowledge to optimize pasture growth and utilization.

### Biological and Nonbiological Parameters

Any animal management system must take into account numerous biological parameters pertinent to the animal under management. These include nutritional requirements, biological time lag (time from conception to market), reproduction (gestation length and number of newborn, newborn survival), efficiency of feed conversion, nature of weight gain, genetic selection, and susceptibility to disease. Decisions are made about using natural service or artificial insemination. The extent to which agricultural by-products, crop residues, and/or production enhancers are used depends on their efficacy, availability, and price.

Any animal management system also involves a number of nonbiological parameters. The available climate, water supply, and land are physical attributes that bear upon the husbandry options. Two other facets of the land affecting management are its tenure, whether owned, leased, or occupied, and its use, whether restricted or not. Husbandry is also affected by the availability and skill level of labor. Another factor is the infrastructure—the dependability of transportation providing access to markets, postfarm processing, and communication systems. Profitability, the difference between receipts and cost of inputs, as well as any subsidies, determines whether one can engage in any agricultural activity for long. Personal values, including lifestyle and risk management, also impact involvement in animal agriculture. Finally, historical and societal values, particularly those directly touching on the use of animals and natural resources, influence the extent and nature of animal husbandry.

### Issues

Three issues of contemporary interest relative to livestock and animal husbandry concern the need for animal agriculture, its sustainability, and its increasing corporate nature. The willingness of people to purchase and consume products of animal origin will always determine the need for animal agriculture. If the price people must pay for such products is too high, demand will decline. As the general affluence of a country increases, the demand for foods of animal origin increases.

The sustainability of contemporary agriculture has been called into question because of its heavy dependence on fossil fuels for energy and its adverse effects on the environment. Properly managed, animals have a role to play in sustainable agriculture. They can help dispose of some agribusiness by-products—crop residues and crops not suitable for human consumption—and generate waste that can be used to fertilize crops.

Animal agriculture is increasingly conducted by corporations rather than by family-owned farms or ranches. Once farming moves away from subsistence farming and generates excess over what the farm family needs, it becomes a business. The pressure for efficiency, as well as for high and consistent product quality, is driving animal agriculture toward increasingly specialized and integrated enterprises. While this tendency appears to be inevitable, serious concerns arise concerning the oligopolies, if not monopolies, that may control the production of animal products and the management of domestic animals, a valued renewable resource.

*James L. Robinson*

FURTHER READING

Campbell, John R., M. Douglas Kenealy, and Karen L. Campbell. *Animal Sciences: The Biology, Care, and Production of Domestic Animals.* 4th ed. Boston: McGraw-Hill, 2003.

Campbell, Karen L., and John R. Campbell. *Companion Animals: Their Biology, Care, Health, and Management.* 2d ed. Upper Saddle River, N.J.: Pearson Prentice Hall, 2009.

Cheeke, Peter R. *Contemporary Issues in Animal Agriculture.* 2d ed. Danville, Ill.: Interstate, 1999.

Ensminger, M. Eugene. *The Stockman's Handbook.* 7th ed. Danville, Ill.: Interstate, 1992.

Field, Thomas G., and Robert E. Taylor. *Scientific Farm Animal Production: An Introduction to Animal Science.* 9th ed. Upper Saddle River, N.J.: Prentice Hall, 2008.

Gillespie, James R., and Frank Flanders. *Modern Livestock and Poultry Production.* 8th ed. Clifton Park, N.Y.: Delmar Cengage Learning, 2009.

Shapiro, Leland. *Introduction to Animal Science.* Upper Saddle River, N.J.: Prentice Hall, 2001.

WEB SITE

U.S. DEPARTMENT OF AGRICULTURE
Animal Production
http://www.usda.gov/wps/portal/!ut/p/_s.7_0_A/
7_0_1OB?navid=ANIMAL_PRODUCTION&parentnav=AGRICULTURE&navtype=RT

SEE ALSO: Animal breeding; Animal domestication; Animal power; Farmland; Overgrazing; Rangeland.

# Logging. *See* Clear-cutting; Timber industry; Wood and timber

# Los Angeles Aqueduct

CATEGORIES: Historical events and movements; obtaining and using resources

*Construction of the Los Angeles Aqueduct generated considerable controversy; ultimately the aqueduct enabled Los Angeles to expand by taking water from sources in central California.*

## DEFINITION

The Los Angeles Aqueduct is a 544-kilometer-long system that transports water from the Owens Valley and Mono Basin east of the Sierra Nevada south to the Los Angeles metropolitan area. The original aqueduct was proposed in the early 1900's as a means of supplying the growing Los Angeles region with an enlarged and reliable water source for the twentieth century. The original aqueduct was completed in 1913 and its extension was completed in 1941. A second aqueduct was completed in 1970.

## OVERVIEW

Los Angeles' Department of Water and Power, under the leadership of William Mulholland and with the help of former Los Angeles mayor Fred Eaton, obtained the water rights to the Owens River by purchasing more than 97,000 hectares of land in Inyo County. Much of the population of the prosperous Owens Valley bitterly opposed the aqueduct but could not stop the construction once the water rights had been bought by the Los Angeles Department of Water and Power.

The city sold bonds worth more than $24 million to fund the construction of the aqueduct down the Owens Valley, across part of the Mojave Desert, and into the Los Angeles basin. Mulholland directed the construction of the mammoth project, which began in 1907 and took five years to complete. The entire 375 kilometers of the original aqueduct transports water by gravity flow and consists of more than 274 kilometers of open ditch, 19 kilometers of steel siphons, and 142 tunnels that totaled 85 kilometers. In addition, the project required the construction of more than 800 kilometers of trails and roads, 190 kilometers of railroad tracks, and 272 kilometers of transmission lines. The project was one of the greatest engineering accomplishments of the early twentieth century.

In 1930, Los Angeles approved another $38 million to extend the aqueduct northward into the Mono Basin in order to tap rivers and streams that feed into Mono Lake. The extension was completed in 1941, and waters were diverted into the aqueduct 544 kilometers north of the city. The diversion of water from Mono Lake eventually caused the lake level to drop 14 meters and the salinity of the lake to rise. Environmental groups went to court to halt the diversion of water, and lengthy litigation ensued. As Los Angeles continued to grow, the city saw the expanded need for more water from the eastern Sierra Nevada, and in 1963, it appropriated more money to build another aqueduct from the Owens Valley. This second aqueduct was completed in 1970 and increased the total amount of water that could be transported by about 50 percent to a total average capacity of 19 cubic meters per second. Much of the water for the second aqueduct was to be groundwater pumped from the Owens Valley. However, the Los Angeles Department of Water and Power has been restricted in their appropriations by litigation brought by local residents and environmental groups.

*Jay R. Yett*

SEE ALSO: Irrigation; Water rights; Water supply systems.

# M

## Maathai, Wangari

CATEGORY: People

BORN: April 1, 1940; Ihithe village, Nyeri District, Kenya

*An environmental and social activist, Maathai established the far-reaching Green Belt movement, a grassroots organization whose members have planted more than thirty million trees since the group's founding in 1977. Maathai received the Nobel Peace Prize in 2004 and helped launch the Billion Tree Campaign in 2006.*

### BIOGRAPHICAL BACKGROUND

Wangari Muta Maathai was born Wangari Muta on April 1, 1940, in the village of Ihithe, Nyeri District of Kenya, the daughter of subsistence farmers. With the help of scholarships, she was able to study in the United States, where she earned bachelor's and master's degrees in biological science. She then returned to Kenya to study anatomy at the University of Nairobi. According to her memoir, *Unbowed* (2006), in 1971, she became the first woman in east and central Africa to earn a Ph.D. However, her progressive views spurred criticism from male colleagues and government officials. These pressures strained her marriage to Mwangi Mathai, with whom she had three children; he eventually sued for divorce and demanded that she change her surname. In her memoir, Maathai explains that she chose instead to insert an extra "a," thus signifying her right to identify herself. In 2004, Maathai became the first African woman to win the Nobel Peace Prize.

### IMPACT ON RESOURCE USE

Maathai's inspiration had two sources: deforestation and poverty. Upon her return to Kenya from the United States, she realized how much of her country's landscape had changed, as farmers were forced to cut down increasingly more trees. Maathai also was determined to help her husband keep his campaign promises to create jobs. She created a business called Envirocare, which hired people to raise tree seedlings in nurseries for eventual planting throughout Kenya.

The program faced many obstacles, but in 1977, Maathai gained the support of Kenya's National Council of Women and renamed the endeavor the Green Belt movement. In *The Green Belt Movement: Sharing the Approach and the Experience* (1988, revised 2003), Maathai states that the organization's "one person, one tree" motto dictated its goal of planting fifteen million trees, one for each person in Kenya. By the early 2000's, Maathai and other members of the movement had planted more than twice that number.

Maathai simultaneously continued to build her influence in the environmental movement, campaigning vigorously against a planned skyscraper in Nairobi's Uhuru Park. Although the government evicted the Green Belt movement from its offices in response to the protest, the project was ultimately stopped.

*Wangari Maathai, winner of the 2004 Nobel Peace Prize, at the 2009 NAACP Image Awards.* (Getty Images)

Maathai similarly opposed the government's attempts to sell off valuable forestland to developers, shaming prospective financiers into withdrawing their support. In retaliation, Maathai was imprisoned several times, but her growing stature in the international community made detaining her without cause increasingly difficult for the authorities.

In 2002, Maathai won a seat in Kenya's parliament and was appointed as the assistant minister of the Environment, Natural Resources, and Wildlife the following year. After winning the Nobel Peace Prize in 2004, she helped the United Nations Environment Programme launch the Billion Tree Campaign. The group's target was reached more quickly than expected, and a new goal of planting seven billion trees by the end of 2009 was established. Although many individuals and organizations have contributed significantly to reforestation efforts, Maathai has had a profound influence on this issue.

*Amy Sisson*

SEE ALSO: Forests; Greenhouse gases and global climate change; Nobel, Alfred; Reforestation.

*Cyrus Hall McCormick invented the crop reaper that bears his name.* (Library of Congress)

# McCormick, Cyrus Hall

CATEGORY: People
BORN: February 15, 1809; Rockbridge County, Virginia
DIED: May 13, 1884; Chicago, Illinois

*As inventor of the mechanical reaper, McCormick transformed agriculture in the mid-nineteenth century by streamlining the process of harvesting grain, resulting in dramatic increases in grain production and the fueling of westward expansion.*

### BIOGRAPHICAL BACKGROUND

Cyrus Hall McCormick, the son of a prosperous Virginia farmer, developed the first successful mechanical grain reaper in 1831 by improving upon a design conceived by his father. Sales of the reaper—which was capable of cutting, threshing, and bundling up to 5 hectares of grain per day—grew slowly at first despite successful early demonstrations of its ability. Westward expansion and the resultant demand for greater grain yields increased interest in the mechanical reaper during the late 1830's. In 1839, McCormick formed a business partnership with his brothers and began mass-producing mechanical reapers in Chicago, the trade hub of the Midwest and western frontier. With the aid of innovative marketing techniques and an increasing availability of railroad lines for shipping, McCormick sold large numbers of mechanical reapers, particularly in grain-producing Midwestern states and territories, during the 1840's and 1850's.

### IMPACT ON RESOURCE USE

The McCormick reaper exerted an immediate and dramatic impact upon American agriculture, commerce, and society during the mid-nineteenth century. The reaper greatly decreased the cost of grain farming and increased grain yields per hectare, prompting farmers to produce more grain. The increase in production helped meet the growing demand for foodstuffs resulting from population expansion in the eastern United States and transformed the United States into a major exporter of grain. The reaper also contributed to American urbanization and industrialization by reducing demand for agricultural labor in rural areas, encouraging rural farm workers to migrate to cities, and providing a growing labor pool to meet the increased demand for industrial workers in urban areas. The production and marketing of foodstuffs thus assumed a larger role in business and industry as the number of food consumers grew and the ranks of food producers diminished.

Increasing urbanization prompted a growing emphasis upon transportation in the United States: Fewer Americans produced their own food and their proximity to food sources decreased, which fueled the growth of railroads, roads, turnpikes, and trails connecting consumers to local and regional commercial centers. By increasing demand for farmland in Midwestern states, the McCormick reaper became a driving force for westward expansion, producing changes in the American social and political landscape that affected numerous issues surrounding resource use, including conflicts with indigenous peoples over land and resources, conflicts between livestock owners over the use of grazing lands, and the escalating debate over utilization of slave labor in the American South.

The McCormick reaper was the first of a number of agricultural machines that collectively transformed agriculture, commerce, and daily living during the late nineteenth and early twentieth centuries. The mechanization of farming influenced a number of social and economic trends in the United States and worldwide, including the development of highways, the emergence of the petrochemical and agribusiness industries, and mass migrations of farm laborers from rural areas to cities. These trends resulted in dramatic changes in the production, delivery, utilization, and allocation of resources.

*Michael H. Burchett*

SEE ALSO: Agricultural products; Agriculture industry; Mineral resource use, early history of; Population growth; Transportation, energy use in; Wheat.

# Magma crystallization

CATEGORY: Geological processes and formations

*Magma crystallization is a geologic process in which molten magma in the Earth's interior cools and subsequently crystallizes to form an igneous rock. The crystallization process produces many different types of minerals, some of which are valuable natural resources.*

## BACKGROUND

Magma is molten rock material consisting of liquid, gas, and early-formed crystals. It is hot (900° to 1,200° Celsius), mobile, and capable of penetrating into or through the Earth's crust from the mantle, deep in the Earth's interior. Most magma cools in the Earth's crust; in a process similar to ice crystallizing from water as the temperature drops below the freezing point, minerals crystallize from molten magma to form a type of rock called igneous rock. Once completely crystallized, the body of igneous rock is called an intrusion. Some magma, however, works its way to the surface and is extruded as lava from volcanoes.

## MINERAL GROWTH

Magma that remains below the surface cools at a slow rate. Ions have time to collect and organize themselves into orderly, crystalline structures to form minerals. These minerals grow larger with time and, if the cooling rate is slow enough, may grow to several centimeters in diameter or larger. Igneous rocks with minerals of this size are said to have a phaneritic texture. Magma that reaches the surface, on the other hand, cools very rapidly and forms rocks that consist of extremely fine-grained minerals or quenched glass. These rocks have an aphanitic or glassy texture. Consequently, it is those minerals which grow beneath the surface that reach sizes large enough to be considered economically feasible resources.

## CONCENTRATION OF VALUABLE ELEMENTS

Minerals do not crystallize from magma all at once. Instead, they follow a sequence of crystallization as the temperature decreases. In general, silicate minerals (substances with silicon-oxygen compounds) with high contents of calcium, iron, and magnesium crystallize early, followed by silicate minerals with high contents of aluminum, potassium, and sodium. Excess silica crystallizes last as the mineral quartz. Bonding factors such as ionic size and charge prevent some elements from incorporation into early crystallizing minerals. Thus they are more highly concentrated in the residual magma and become incorporated into the last minerals to crystallize, forming rocks called granites and pegmatites. These rocks may contain minerals such as beryl, spodumene, lepido-lite, and uraninite, which include important elements such as beryllium, lithium, and uranium. Granites and pegmatites are also important sources for feldspar and sheet mica.

## DIAMONDS AND KIMBERLITES

Perhaps the best-known magmatic minerals are diamonds. Formed deep in the mantle at extremely high temperatures and pressures, diamonds are carried by a certain type of magma as it violently intrudes upward through the crust, sometimes reaching the surface. Upon cooling and crystallizing, this magma forms a pipe-shaped igneous rock known as kimberlite. It is in kimberlites that most diamonds are found. Most kimberlite pipes are less than one square kilometer in horizontal area, and they are often grouped in clusters. Most of the known diamond-bearing kimberlite pipes are found in southern Africa, western Australia, Siberia, and Canada.

## MAGMATIC SULFIDE DEPOSITS

Most major metals used in industry (copper, iron, lead, nickel, zinc, and platinum) are found in sulfide minerals, which are substances that contain metal-sulfur compounds. When magma is in the early stages of cooling and crystallizing underground, certain

processes can cause droplets of liquid sulfide to form within it. These sulfide droplets attract metallic cations and concentrate them by factors ranging from 100 to 100,000 over their normal levels in the host magma. The droplets eventually cool and solidify to form sulfide minerals such as pyrite ("fool's gold"), galena (lead sulfide), and sphalerite (zinc sulfide). Sulfide minerals such as these become important targets for mining because of their high concentration of metals.

## LAYERED MAGMATIC INTRUSIONS

Some magmas give rise to layered intrusions in which a specific sequence of minerals is repeated many times from bottom to top in a process called gravity layering (also called rhythmic layering). Dark-colored, heavier minerals such as pyroxene, olivine, and chromite concentrate near the base of each layer, grading to predominantly light-colored minerals such as plagioclase at the top. Each mineral sequence is a separate layer, averaging several meters thick and ranging from less than 2 centimeters to more than 30 meters. It has been suggested that the origin of gravity layering involves multiple injections of fresh magma into a crystallizing magma chamber, effectively replenishing the magma and allowing the same minerals to crystallize repeatedly.

The Bushveld intrusion in South Africa, one of the largest layered intrusions, contains multiple gravity layers and is more than 7,000 meters in total thickness. Layered intrusions contain the Earth's main reserves for chromium and platinum. In the Bushveld intrusion, chromium occurs in the mineral chromite, and platinum in platinum-iron alloys, braggite, and other platinum-metal compounds. The main source for platinum minerals in the Bushveld intrusion, and the source for approximately half the Earth's supply of platinum, is the Merensky Reef, a layer of chromite and platinum minerals 1 meter thick and more than 200 kilometers long. Also present in the Bushveld intrusion is the mineral magnetite, which yields important elements used in steel manufacturing such as iron and vanadium.

*This example of igneous rock, the end result of magma crystallization, is found in Garrizo Mountain in Arizona. (USGS)*

The Bushveld intrusion accounts for almost 50 percent of the world's production of vanadium.

*Stephen C. Hildreth, Jr.*

FURTHER READING

Best, Myron G. *Igneous and Metamorphic Petrology.* 2d ed. Malden, Mass.: Blackwell, 2003.

Brown, Michael, and Tracy Rushmer, eds. *Evolution and Differentiation of the Continental Crust.* New York: Cambridge University Press, 2006.

Evans, Anthony M. *Ore Geology and Industrial Minerals: An Introduction.* 3d ed. Boston: Blackwell Scientific Publications, 1993.

Naldrett, Anthony J. *Magmatics Sulfide Deposits: Geology, Geochemistry, and Exploration.* Berlin: Springer, 2004.

Schmincke, Hans-Ulrich. "Magma." In *Volcanism.* New York: Springer, 2004.

Young, Davis A. *Mind over Magma: The Story of Igneous Petrology.* Princeton, N.J.: Princeton University Press, 2003.

WEB SITE

U.S. GEOLOGICAL SURVEY
Magma, Lava, Lava Flows, Lave Lakes
http://vulcan.wr.usgs.gov/Glossary/LavaFlows/
    description_lava_flows.html

SEE ALSO: Earth's crust; Igneous processes, rocks, and mineral deposits; Ophiolites; Pegmatites; Plutonic rocks and mineral deposits; Vanadium; Volcanoes.

# Magnesium

CATEGORY: Mineral and other nonliving resources

WHERE FOUND

Magnesium is a widespread and abundant element. Magnesium chloride and magnesium sulfate are present in dissolved form in seawater and underground brines—these sources accounted for 43 percent of U.S. magnesium compound production in 2008. Magnesium is also found in many minerals, notably magnesite ($MgCO_3$), dolomite (CaMg ($CO_3$)$_2$), and brucite ($Mg(OH)_2$). China, Russia, Israel, Kazakhstan, Canada, and Brazil are among the main producers. For a number of years, the United States has withheld its magnesium production statistics to avoid disclosure of companies' proprietary data.

PRIMARY USES

Magnesium is used principally in alloys, refractory materials (60 percent of U.S. use), paper, fertilizer, chemicals, and pyrotechnics. As a compound, it can be used as an additive to food, in medicine, and as a sedative.

TECHNICAL DEFINITION

Magnesium (abbreviated Mg), atomic number 12, belongs to Group IIA of the periodic table of the elements (alkaline-earth metals). It has three stable isotopes and an average molecular weight of 24.312. Pure magnesium is a silver-white, ductile metal that is malleable when heated. A chemically active element, magnesium is a potent reducing agent. Its specific gravity is 1.738 at 20° Celsius, its melting point is 651° Celsius, and its boiling point is 1,100° Celsius.

DESCRIPTION, DISTRIBUTION, AND FORMS

Magnesium in the form of powder or ribbons readily ignites when heated, burning with an intense white light and releasing large amounts of heat while forming magnesia (magnesium oxide, MgO). Magnesium reacts with organic halides to produce Grignard reagents, an important class of chemical compounds used in the laboratory.

Magnesium is an alkaline-earth metal, a class of hard, heavy metals that are strongly electropositive and chemically reactive. It is the eighth most abundant element; its concentration in the lithosphere is 20,900 grams per metric ton, and the percentage of its ions in seawater is 0.1272. Magnesium's density (only two-thirds that of aluminum) and the ease with which the element can be machined, cast, forged, and welded contribute to its commercial applications, as do the refractory properties of some of its compounds. China is the leading producer of primary (mined and processed) magnesium (627,000 metric tons in 2007), accounting for nearly 85 percent of magnesium production in the world. Russia and Canada are the world's other leading producers. However, from 2003 to 2007, Canadian production declined dramatically from 78,000 to 16,300 metric tons.

Magnesium is one of the most common minerals in the Earth's crust; its principal commercial source, however, is seawater. Extensive terrestrial deposits of magnesium are also found in the form of magnesite and dolomite. Magnesite, a magnesium carbonate, occurs as a hydrothermal alteration of serpentine,

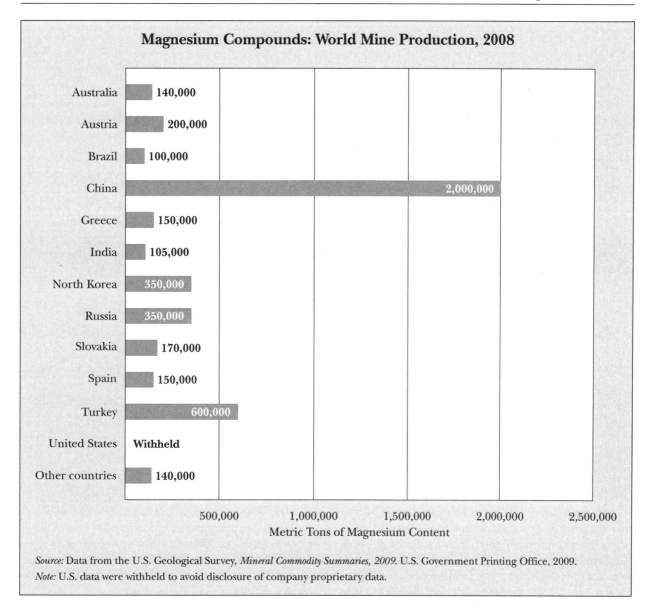

**Magnesium Compounds: World Mine Production, 2008**

| Country | Metric Tons of Magnesium Content |
|---|---|
| Australia | 140,000 |
| Austria | 200,000 |
| Brazil | 100,000 |
| China | 2,000,000 |
| Greece | 150,000 |
| India | 105,000 |
| North Korea | 350,000 |
| Russia | 350,000 |
| Slovakia | 170,000 |
| Spain | 150,000 |
| Turkey | 600,000 |
| United States | Withheld |
| Other countries | 140,000 |

*Source:* Data from the U.S. Geological Survey, *Mineral Commodity Summaries, 2009.* U.S. Government Printing Office, 2009.
*Note:* U.S. data were withheld to avoid disclosure of company proprietary data.

$(Mg,Fe)_3Si_2O_5(OH)_4$, a vein filling and a replacement mineral in carbonate rocks such as dolostone. Dolomite, or calcium magnesium carbonate, is the predominant mineral in dolostone, a widespread sedimentary rock similar to limestone. Most dolomites are thought to have originated from partial replacement of calcium in limestone by magnesium. Magnesium occurs in nature as a component of several common minerals. Important ores include magnesite, a white or grayish mineral found in crystalline or porcelain-like masses; dolomite, a white mineral that resembles limestone; and brucite, a pearly foliated or fibrous mineral that

resembles talc. Magnesium silicates are found in asbestos, serpentine, and talc. Magnesium chloride and magnesium sulfate occur in dissolved form in sea water and natural underground brines. Magnesium is also a constituent of chlorophyll in green plants.

HISTORY

Sir Humphry Davy discovered magnesia in 1808. In 1828, Antoine Bussy isolated pure magnesium by chemical reduction of the chloride, and in 1833, Michael Faraday isolated magnesium electrolytically. The earliest commercial production of the metal may

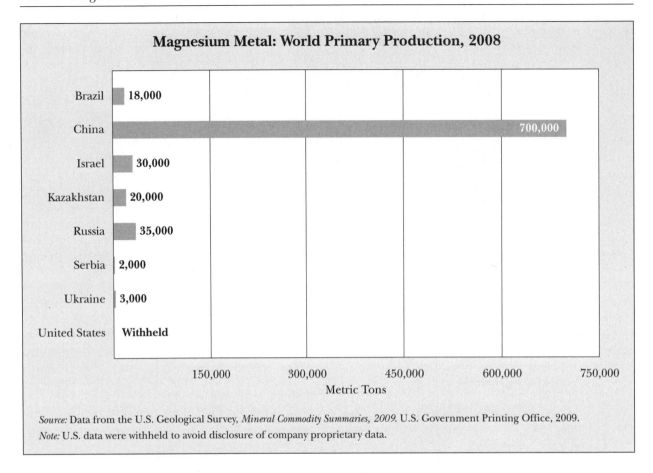

**Magnesium Metal: World Primary Production, 2008**

| Country | Production (Metric Tons) |
|---|---|
| Brazil | 18,000 |
| China | 700,000 |
| Israel | 30,000 |
| Kazakhstan | 20,000 |
| Russia | 35,000 |
| Serbia | 2,000 |
| Ukraine | 3,000 |
| United States | Withheld |

*Source:* Data from the U.S. Geological Survey, *Mineral Commodity Summaries, 2009.* U.S. Government Printing Office, 2009.

*Note:* U.S. data were withheld to avoid disclosure of company proprietary data.

have been in France during the first half of the nineteenth century, where a modification of the Bussy method was employed. At this time, magnesium metal was used primarily in photography. Around 1886, Germany developed an improved production process based on an electrolytic cell method devised by Robert Bunsen in 1852. Germany became the world's sole source for elemental magnesium. Magnesium alloys were used in Germany in the early 1900's in aircraft fuselages, engine parts, and wheels. In 1915, when a wartime blockade of Germany by the British interrupted the elemental magnesium trade, magnesium production began in the United States. Large-scale use of dolostone as a refractory material also commenced during World War I. In 1941, Dow Chemical Corporation introduced its process for extracting magnesium from seawater.

OBTAINING MAGNESIUM

Magnesium is obtained principally from seawater through the Dow seawater process. The water is treated with lime to produce magnesium hydroxide as a precipitate. This precipitate is mixed with hydrochloric acid to form magnesium chloride; the chloride, in turn, is fused and electrolyzed, producing magnesium metal and chlorine gas. From a liter of seawater, approximately 10 milligrams of magnesium can be extracted. Another common method for obtaining magnesium is the ferrosilicon (Pidgeon) process, which uses dolomite as a raw material. The dolomite is heated to produce magnesia, which is then reduced with an iron-silicon alloy.

USES OF MAGNESIUM

Dead-burned magnesite, produced by heating the mineral in a kiln at 1,500° to 1,750° Celsius until it contains less than 1 percent carbon dioxide, is a refractory material. Able to withstand contact with often corrosive substances at high temperatures, refractory materials are used to line furnaces, kilns, reaction vessels, and ladles used in the cement, glass, steel, and metallurgical industries. Magnesia refractories are materials particularly suited for the basic oxygen furnaces used in steelmaking. Dead-burned dolomite, produced by heating dolostone or dolomitic limestone at about 1,500° Celsius, is also a refractory material used for lining metallurgical furnaces.

In its elemental state, magnesium is soft and weak; its alloys, however, are sturdier and have a variety of uses. Magnesium is used extensively as an alloy metal, particularly in combination with aluminum, zinc, cadmium, and manganese. Magnesium alloys in general are lightweight, fatigue-resistant, free from brittleness, and able to withstand bending stresses; these qualities make magnesium alloys ideal for jet-engine parts, rockets and missiles, luggage frames, cameras, optical instruments, scientific equipment, and portable power tools. Duralumin, a lightweight alloy of aluminum, copper, magnesium, and manganese, is ductile and malleable before its final heat treatment; afterward, its hardness and tensile strength are increased. Its properties make duralumin especially useful to the aircraft industry. Magnalium, an alloy of aluminum and magnesium that is lighter and easier to work than aluminum, is used in metal mirrors and scientific instruments.

Pure magnesium is used in incendiary bombs, signals and flares, thermite fuses, and other pyrotechnic devices. It is an important component of photographic flashbulbs, a deoxidizing agent used in the preparation of some nonferrous metals, a rocket and missile fuel additive, and an agent for chemical synthesis. Magnesium reacts with organic halides to form Grignard reagents, an important class of extremely reactive chemical compounds that are used in synthesizing hydrocarbons, alcohols, carboxylic acids, and other compounds. Magnesium compounds are used in chemicals, ceramics, cosmetics, fertilizer, insulation, paper, leather tanning, and textile processing. Epsom salts (magnesium sulfate heptahydrate), milk of magnesia (magnesium hydroxide), and citrate of magnesium are used in medicines. Caustic-calcined magnesia (magnesite heated to between 700° and 1,000° Celsius to drive off 2 to 10 percent of its carbon dioxide) is mixed with magnesium chloride to create oxychloride (sorel) cement. This cement is used for heavy-duty floorings, stucco, and fireproof building materials. Dolostone, a rock composed chiefly of dolomite, is used as a building stone as well as a refractory material.

Magnesium is an essential element in all plants and animals. In green plants, it is a component of chlorophyll; in animals, it plays a role in carbohydrate metabolism and is an important trace element for muscle, nerve tissue, and skeletal structure. Serious dietary deficiencies of magnesium can bring on such symptoms as hyperirritability and soft-tissue calcification.

*Karen N. Kähler*

## FURTHER READING

Friedrich, Horst E., and Barry L. Mordike, eds. *Magnesium Technology: Metallurgy, Design Data, Applications.* New York: Springer, 2006.

Greenwood, N. N., and A. Earnshaw. "Beryllium, Magnesium, Calcium, Strontium, Barium, and Radium." In *Chemistry of the Elements.* 2d ed. Boston: Butterworth-Heinemann, 1997.

Henderson, William. "The Group 2 Elements: Beryllium, Magnesium, Calcium, Strontium, Barium, and Radium." In *Main Group Chemistry.* Cambridge, England: Royal Society of Chemistry, 2000.

Kogel, Jessica Elzea, et al., eds. "Magnesium Minerals and Compounds." In *Industrial Minerals and Rocks: Commodities, Markets, and Uses.* 7th ed. Littleton, Colo.: Society for Mining, Metallurgy, and Exploration, 2006.

Manning, D. A. C. *Introduction to Industrial Minerals.* New York: Chapman & Hall, 1995.

Seelig, Mildred S., and Andrea Rosanoff. *The Magnesium Factor.* New York: Avery, 2003.

Silva, J. J. R. Fraústo da, and R. J. P. Williams. "The Biological Chemistry of Magnesium: Phosphate Metabolism." In *The Biological Chemistry of the Elements: The Inorganic Chemistry of Life.* 2d ed. New York: Oxford University Press, 2001.

## WEB SITES

NATURAL RESOURCES CANADA
Canadian Minerals Yearbook, Mineral and Metal Commodity Reviews
http://www.nrcan-rncan.gc.ca/mms-smm/busi-indu/cmy-amc/com-eng.htm

U.S. GEOLOGICAL SURVEY
Magnesium: Statistics and Information
http://minerals.usgs.gov/minerals/pubs/commodity/magnesium

SEE ALSO: Alloys; Limestone; Metals and metallurgy; Steel.

# Magnetic materials

CATEGORY: Mineral and other nonliving resources

*Naturally occurring magnetic materials have been known and used for centuries. Materials that can be temporarily magnetized by an electrical current are widely used in applications ranging from simple electrical appliances and motors to sophisticated computer systems.*

## DEFINITION

Substances that respond to a magnetic field are called magnetic materials. The most common magnetic materials are iron (Fe), cobalt (Co), nickel (Ni), and their alloys. These three elements belong to Group VIIIB of the periodic table. Four varieties of magnetism are recognized: ferromagnetism, ferrimagnetism, diamagnetism, and paramagnetism. Iron, cobalt, nickel, gadolinium (Gd), and chromium dioxide ($CrO_2$) are examples of ferromagnetic materials. Ferroferric oxide ($Fe_3O_4$) is a ferrimagnetic material. Feeble magnetism is exhibited in certain alloys and elements. A substance that is magnetized in the opposite direction of the external magnetic field is called a diamagnetic material. Some examples are gold, silver, copper, and quartz. A substance that is magnetized in the same direction as the external magnetic field is called a paramagnetic material. Certain types of special alloys are paramagnetic.

*Magnetite is a type of magnetic material.* (USGS)

## OVERVIEW

Magnets attract materials or objects made of iron (and steel), cobalt, and nickel. A magnet's power is strongest at its two ends, called poles. One is called the north pole and the other the south pole. A compass is, in principle, a magnet pivoted at its center which orients itself in the direction of the Earth's magnetic field. A compass has long been one of the most important navigational instruments onboard ships and airplanes.

The largest deposits of the mineral magnetite ($Fe_3O_4$), magnetic iron ore, are found in northern Sweden. Sizable deposits of magnetite are also found in Australia, Italy, Switzerland, Norway, the Ural Mountains in Russia, and several other regions. In the United States, magnetite is found in Arkansas, New Jersey, and Utah. The Precambrian rocks of the Adirondacks contain large beds of magnetite.

The ancient Chinese discovered that a freely suspended lodestone (naturally occurring polarized magnetite) would always orient itself in the same geographical direction. This observation led to the development of the compass. In the West, historical records of magnetic materials date back to the ancient Greeks. By 500 B.C.E., the Greeks had discovered that certain rocks were attracted to iron nails on ships and boats. In 1600, William Gilbert, an English doctor, published *De Magnete*, in which he identified the Earth itself as a giant magnet.

A number of fundamental advances in the practical applications of magnetism occurred in the early nineteenth century. In 1820, the Danish scientist Hans Christian Ørsted discovered that a magnetic needle could be deflected by a current in a wire. In 1823, English scientist William Sturgeon wound an insulated copper wire around an iron bar and discovered that the iron bar became a strong magnet. Thus the electromagnet was born. In 1821, Michael Faraday demonstrated the first electric motor, the "magnetic rotation of a conductor and magnet." In 1828, Joseph Henry produced silk-covered wires and developed more powerful electromagnets.

Magnetic materials have a tremendous range of uses, from huge industrial electromagnets to the use of "magnetic bubbles" in highly advanced computer systems. Magnetic materials are classified into three major categories: hard, soft, and memory-quality materials. Hard magnetic materials have applications as permanent magnets in small motors, small direct-current generators (dynamos), measuring instruments, and speaker systems. Soft magnetic materials—those that are influenced by external fields—are widely used in transformers, generators, motors, and alternators of all sizes and rating capacities. Almost all appliances used in homes and industry, from shavers to washing machines to relays, contain electromagnets with soft magnetic materials. The materials used most often are iron, silicon-iron combinations, nickel-iron alloys, and ferrites. Memory-quality magnetic materials are used to record and store data, either in analog or digital form. Examples are magnetic tapes, drums, and disks.

Huge electromagnets are used to move automobiles or other metal objects in automobile recycling yards and junkyards. Gigantic electromagnets are essential to nuclear fusion experiments. Magnetic-levitation (maglev) trains are held above the ground by superconducting electromagnets. Superconducting electromagnets are also used in magnetic resonance imaging (MRI) body scanners, devices that produce detailed images of the inside of the body and provide diagnostic data to doctors.

*Mysore Narayanan*

SEE ALSO: Cobalt; Iron; Nickel; Steel.

# Manganese

CATEGORY: Mineral and other nonliving resources

*Manganese is one of the most abundant elements in the crust of the Earth and is usually a minor constituent in ordinary rocks. Its chemical and physical properties are similar to those of iron, and the two metals often occur together.*

## WHERE FOUND

Manganese oxides are abundant in nature; however, large, high-grade deposits are relatively rare. Concentrations of the element approximately 250 to 500 times greater than the average crustal abundance are required to produce ore. All the major ore deposits are sedimentary in origin and consist of various manganese oxide minerals. The major deposits of the world are sedimentary in origin and are located in Russia, Africa, and Brazil. The five leading manganese-producing countries in 2007 were South Africa, Australia, China, Gabon, and Brazil. Together these countries account for 70 percent of the world's total output.

## PRIMARY USES

Manganese plays a major role in steel production. Secondary uses of this mineral are in alloys, batteries, fertilizers, and the manufacture of chemicals.

## TECHNICAL DEFINITION

Manganese (atomic number 25, chemical symbol Mn) is the twelfth most abundant element in the crust of the Earth and makes up about 0.1 percent of the crust by weight. In its pure state, which does not occur in nature, it is a hard, brittle metal with a gray color, a melting point of 1,260° Celsius, a boiling point of 1,900° Celsius, and a density of 7.2 grams per cubic centimeter. It resembles iron in many of its properties and has oxidation states of +2, +3, +4, +6, and +7. As is true of iron, the reduced +2 form is quite soluble under near-surface conditions and is carried in solution by stream and groundwater.

## DESCRIPTION, DISTRIBUTION, AND FORMS

Because of its great crustal abundance, small amounts of manganese, in the form of dark-colored oxide minerals, are common in most rocks. For commercial production, however, ore bodies averaging at least 35 percent manganese and containing millions of metric tons of the metal are required. The highest-grade ore contains more than 48 percent manganese. Such deposits are not common. All the known major deposits are of sedimentary origin. There are several ore minerals of manganese, but the most important are all oxides: pyrolusite ($MnO_2$), psilomelane ($Mn_2O_3 \cdot 2H_2O$), and manganite ($Mn_2O_3 \cdot H_2O$).

Although manganese occurs in several oxidation states, the reduced +2 is most common in subsurface waters because of its solubility. Manganese oxide minerals precipitate readily at a boundary between oxidizing and reducing conditions, such as the reducing groundwater percolating into well-oxygenated stream water. As a result, manganese oxide coatings on stream pebbles and rocks are common, so common that they usually go unnoticed. Similar black coatings are also

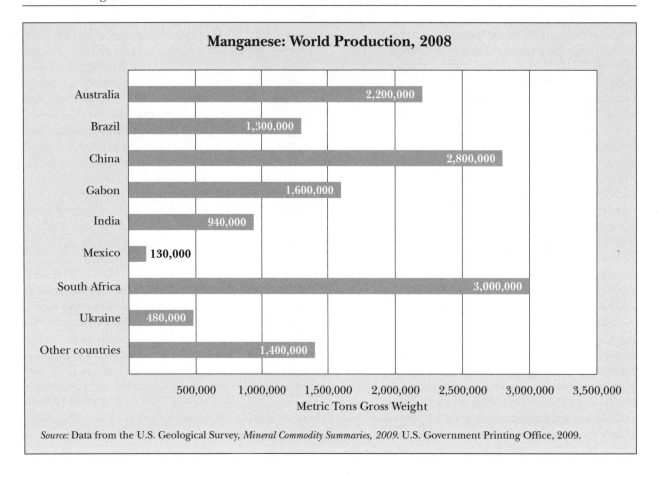

**Manganese: World Production, 2008**

| Country | Metric Tons Gross Weight |
|---|---|
| Australia | 2,200,000 |
| Brazil | 1,300,000 |
| China | 2,800,000 |
| Gabon | 1,600,000 |
| India | 940,000 |
| Mexico | 130,000 |
| South Africa | 3,000,000 |
| Ukraine | 480,000 |
| Other countries | 1,400,000 |

*Source:* Data from the U.S. Geological Survey, *Mineral Commodity Summaries, 2009.* U.S. Government Printing Office, 2009.

common in arid regions in the form of "desert varnish" and in deep freshwater lakes. In the ocean, large manganese oxide nodules occur. Changes from reducing to oxidizing conditions have been implicated as important in producing all of these common surface forms of manganese oxide, but it is also likely that manganese-oxidizing bacteria play an important role, particularly for desert varnish and stream pebble coatings.

The *Challenger* expedition in the 1870's discovered manganese oxide nodules in the deep-ocean basin, but their widespread occurrence and abundance did not become known until sampling in the 1960's. These nodules are black and rounded to irregular lumps of pebble and cobble size. They exist in all the world's oceans but are irregularly distributed. The origin of the nodules has been the subject of much research. Evidence indicates that the nodules are continually growing at a very slow rate by the addition of manganese and other metals from seawater. The absence of sediment to muddy the water increases their rate of

precipitation, a fact which explains why most nodules are found only in the deep-ocean basins, far removed from sediment eroded from landmasses.

Manganese is considered to be one of the least toxic of the trace elements. Several thousand parts per million of manganese in the diet of mammals and birds are usually required to develop symptoms of toxicity. The exact amount that is toxic varies from species to species and is also dependent on the form in which manganese is consumed and the age of the individual. The main symptom reported is a reduced rate of growth because of appetite depression.

While very high levels of manganese are required to produce toxic effects from oral consumption, mammals, including humans, appear to have a considerably low tolerance to the inhalation of manganese dusts. High levels of such dusts can occur in occupational settings such as steel mills, manganese mines, and certain chemical industries. The lungs apparently act as a sink from which manganese is continually absorbed. The main toxic effect produced is a serious neurological disease with many symptoms in common with Parkinson's disease. Such manganese-induced neurotoxicity has been the subject of considerable interest because manganese compounds have been used in gasoline as a replacement for lead compounds.

## HISTORY

Manganese oxide has been known since antiquity, when it was used in glass manufacture, but the metal itself was not isolated until 1770. There was little interest in the metal until 1856, when it was discovered that manganese could be used to remove sulfur and oxygen impurities as a slag from molten steel. All steel up to this time had been extremely brittle because of the presence of these impurities. An important world market for manganese quickly developed. The world's major deposit of manganese was discovered in the Nikopol' Basin in Ukraine in the 1920's. Subsequently, this area became the world's major producer. In the nineteenth century, the United States was self-sufficient in manganese, but these deposits are all exhausted.

## OBTAINING MANGANESE

Two types of sedimentary deposits account for most of the world's production. The first type, illustrated by the world's largest deposit at Nikopol' in southern Ukraine, consists of manganese in the form of earthy masses and nodules of manganese oxide in beds of sandy clay and limestone. This type of deposit is thought to have originated by a two-step process. First, manganese in its reduced form, derived from the weathering and erosion of continental areas, is carried by streams in solution to the open sea. Second, in the sea, reduced manganese undergoes oxidation, causing it to precipitate as manganese oxide minerals because of the strongly oxidizing conditions in the open ocean.

The second important type of deposit has resulted from the weathering of rocks containing small amounts of manganese silicate and carbonate minerals. These minerals are resistant to weathering, so their relative abundance increases as the less resistant minerals are dissolved. Eventually, a large, high-grade deposit of manganese may be produced. Geologists use the term "residual" to refer to any type of mineral deposit in which the valuable material has been concentrated by weathering. Important manganese deposits of this type occur in Brazil and China.

Mining companies became interested in deep-sea manganese nodules in the 1960's and 1970's. The richest area seems to be a portion of the deep Pacific floor extending 4,800 kilometers eastward from the southern tip of Hawaii. There are places in this region in which the nodules literally cover the seafloor. Interest in the nodules is high because, in addition to averaging 25 percent manganese, they also average about 1.3 percent nickel, 1 percent copper, 0.22 percent cobalt, and 0.05 percent molybdenum, all of which could be recovered as by-products. Between 1962 and 1978 several international consortia spent nearly $100 million studying methods for mining the nodules. At least two promising methods were identified, but no commercial mining of the deep seafloor occurred.

## USES OF MANGANESE

Most manganese is used during the manufacture of steel to remove sulfur and oxygen. There are no practical replacements for manganese in this essential role. Approximately 90 percent of the manganese

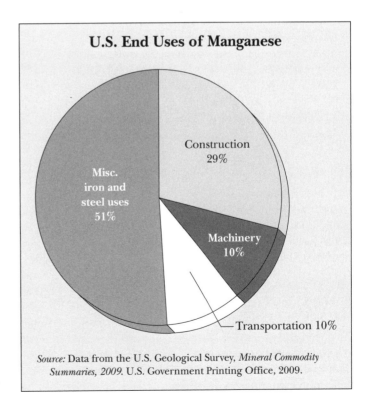

**U.S. End Uses of Manganese**

Misc. iron and steel uses 51%

Construction 29%

Machinery 10%

Transportation 10%

*Source:* Data from the U.S. Geological Survey, *Mineral Commodity Summaries, 2009.* U.S. Government Printing Office, 2009.

that is consumed each year in the United States is used in the manufacture of steel. Manganese is also used as a component in certain aluminum alloys and in dry cell batteries. Minor amounts are used as a colorant in glass, in fertilizers, and as a gasoline additive.

*Gene D. Robinson*

FURTHER READING

Adriano, Domy C. "Manganese." In *Trace Elements in Terrestrial Environments: Biogeochemistry, Bioavailability, and Risks of Metals.* 2d ed. New York: Springer, 2001.

Greenwood, N. N., and A. Earnshaw. "Manganese, Technetium, and Rhenium." In *Chemistry of the Elements.* 2d ed. Boston: Butterworth-Heinemann, 1997.

Howe, P. D., H. H. Malcolm, and S. Dobson. *Manganese and Its Compounds: Environmental Aspects.* Geneva, Switzerland: World Health Organization, 2004.

Klimis-Tavantzis, Dorothy J., ed. *Manganese in Health and Disease.* Boca Raton, Fla.: CRC Press, 1994.

Kogel, Jessica Elzea, et al., eds. "Manganese." In *Industrial Minerals and Rocks: Commodities, Markets, and Uses.* 7th ed. Littleton, Colo.: Society for Mining, Metallurgy, and Exploration, 2006.

Priest, Tyler. *Global Gambits: Big Steel and the U.S. Quest for Manganese.* Westport, Conn.: Praeger, 2003.

Sigel, Astrid, and Helmut Sigel, eds. *Manganese and Its Role in Biological Processes.* New York: Marcel Dekker, 2000.

Wolf, Karl H., ed. *Handbook of Strata-Bound and Stratiform Ore Deposits.* Vol. 2. New York: Elsevier Scientific, 1986.

WEB SITES

NATURAL RESOURCES CANADA
Canadian Minerals Yearbook, Mineral and Metal Commodity Reviews
http://www.nrcan-rncan.gc.ca/mms-smm/busi-indu/cmy-amc/com-eng.htm

U.S. GEOLOGICAL SURVEY
Manganese: Statistics and Information
http://minerals.usgs.gov/minerals/pubs/commodity/manganese

SEE ALSO: Bessemer process; Clean Air Act; Food chain; Iron; Marine mining; Sedimentary processes, rocks, and mineral deposits; Steel.

# Manhattan Project

CATEGORY: Historical events and movements

*The Manhattan Engineer District was created in August, 1942, to sponsor the Manhattan Project, a top-secret effort to produce the atomic bomb in time to be used during World War II. The Manhattan Project's legacy, in addition to the destruction wrought by the two atomic bombs the United States dropped on Japan, includes the proliferation of nuclear weapons and the peacetime development of nuclear power plants.*

BACKGROUND
During World War II, the United States, Germany, Great Britain, the Soviet Union, France, and Japan all had projects to examine the feasibility of constructing an atomic bomb. Japanese progress was minimal, and French progress halted with the German occupation of France. American efforts were spurred on by the British and by scientists such as Leo Szilard, Eugene Paul Wigner, and Enrico Fermi, who fled oppression in Europe. Since the Germans had a considerable head start in addition to formidable industrial and scientific resources, many feared that Adolf Hitler would develop the atomic bomb first.

DEVELOPING AND CONSTRUCTING THE BOMB
Enough work had been done prior to the Manhattan Project to convince those involved that the problems of producing a bomb could probably be surmounted if sufficient resources were made available. Because of the war mobilization, the Army Corps of Engineers was managing construction contracts amounting to $600 million a month, and funds for the top-secret Manhattan Project were hidden within that amount. The initial cost estimate for the project was $133 million; the actual cost was about $2 billion.

Before the Manhattan Project, American atomic bomb research was conducted by various scientists at several universities. Progress was intermittent. On September 17, 1942, Colonel (soon to be General) Leslie Richard Groves was appointed to head the Manhattan Engineer District. Groves was an engineer, and his supervision of the building of the Pentagon had demonstrated a knack for untangling bureaucratic messes. He was regarded as arrogant and abrupt but also as a person who could get the job done right.

Under Groves, the Manhattan Project proceeded

*Robert Oppenheimer, the scientific director of the Manhattan Project and architect of the atomic bomb, left, speaks with General Leslie Groves, the military director of the Manhattan Project, in Alamogordo, New Mexico.* (Popperfoto/Getty Images)

at breakneck speed. Factories were built before the machines they would house were fully worked out, and full-scale machines were built before prototypes were fully tested. While this approach did not always work, it worked well enough. At Hanford, Washington, fifty thousand construction workers built three large nuclear reactors to produce plutonium along with three separation plants to remove the plutonium from the used reactor fuel. A huge gaseous diffusion plant and an electromagnet separation plant were built at Oak Ridge, Tennessee, to separate uranium 235 from the more common uranium 238. Because of a copper shortage, more than 12,000 metric tons of silver were borrowed from the federal treasury and made into conductors for the electromagnets. The design and construction of the bombs were done at the Los Alamos weapons laboratory, headed by J. Robert Oppenheimer.

At the project's peak, more than 160,000 workers

were employed at twenty-five sites. Most of the Manhattan Project workers knew only that they were working on something very important and that it might help end the war. Many of those who knew that they were working on the atomic bomb hoped that it would help end the war and that it might make future wars unthinkable.

*Charles W. Rogers*

SEE ALSO: Isotopes, radioactive; Nuclear energy; Nuclear waste and its disposal; Plutonium; Uranium.

# Manufacturing, energy use in

CATEGORY: Obtaining and using resources

*Industrial processes consume roughly 46 percent of world energy each year. In the United States, about 80 percent of that energy goes to the basic production industries of iron, steel, aluminum, paper, chemicals, and nonmetallic minerals (cement, brick, glass, and ceramics).*

BACKGROUND

The sophistication of a society's technology can be judged by what it can make and how efficiently it can make those items. In ancient civilizations, rock and wood yielded to metal, fired pottery, and glass. Bronze and brass weapons swept aside stone. Then iron and steel replaced the softer metals.

Muscle power was sporadically aided by water power in antiquity, but the intensive use of water power began in Europe in the Middle Ages. Besides grinding flour, water mills supplied power for large-scale weaving, for sawmills, and for blowing air onto hot metal and hammering the finished metals. The gearing required to modify the motion and move it throughout a workshop also applied to wind power, and Dutch mills led manufacturing in the late Middle Ages.

A series of inventions led to James Watt's improved steam engine in 1782. The immediate goal was pumping water out of coal mines, but steam engines also allowed factory power to be located anywhere. Steam-powered locomotives allowed materials to be more easily moved to those locations.

At the beginning of the twentieth century, small electric motors allowed a further decentralization of industry. A small shop required only a power cable,

*A worker at the Kawasaki manufacturing plant in New York assembles a New York City subway car. Industrial manufacturing accounts for a significant portion of the energy used in the United States.* (AP/Wide World Photos)

the necessary equipment, and a flick of a switch rather than a large engine and the inconvenient (often dangerous) belts used to transfer power to various pieces of equipment.

Energy efficiency and materials efficiency grow as technology evolves. Often, increased efficiency is simply a by-product of increased production or quality. Each doubling of cumulative production tends to drop production costs, including energy costs, by 20 percent. These improvements are connected to control of heat, control of motion, and the development of entirely new processes.

### HEAT

Heat is the greatest component of manufacturing energy use. Heat (or the removal of heat) involves the same issues that space conditioning of a home does. One can add more fuel or reduce losses through increased efficiency. Efficiency can be increased by hav-

ing more insulation in the walls, a furnace that burns more completely, a furnace that uses exhaust gases to preheat air coming into it, a stove with a lighter rather than a pilot light, and controls that shut off heat to unused areas.

Manufacturing has the additional option of selling excess heat or buying low-grade heat for cogeneration. Often a manufacturing plant only needs low-grade heat of several hundred degrees for drying or curing materials. This heat production does not fully use the energy of the fuel. An electrical power plant running at 600° Celsius can generate electricity and then send its "waste heat" on to the industrial process.

A manufacturing plant also applies energy to materials, and in these processes there are many choices. Heat may be applied in an oven (large or small). Some energy may also be applied directly. For instance, oven curing of paint on car parts has been replaced by infrared ("heat lamp") radiation for quicker production. Some high-performance aerospace alloys are heated by microwave radiation in vacuum chambers.

There are a variety of other energy-saving approaches. Automated process controls are a major energy saver. In chemical industries, separating materials by their different boiling points with distillation columns requires much less steam than other methods. Also, the continuous safety flames at refineries are being replaced by automated lighters.

Another energy-efficient technique is to combine processes. For instance, steelmaking often comprises three separate heating steps: refining ore into blocks of pig iron, refining that into steel, and then forming the steel into products, such as I beams or wire. An integrated steel mill heats the materials only once to make the finished product. A steel "minimill" tends to be smaller, uses expensive electricity, and goes only a short distance in the production process—from iron scrap to steel. On the other hand, the minimill is recycling a resource, thereby saving both energy and materials. The recycling of paper, plastics, and some metals typically requires one-half the energy needed to produce virgin materials. The fraction for aluminum is about one-fourth.

## MOTION

Cutting, grinding, pumping, moving, polishing, compressing, and many other processes control the motion of materials and of heat. They use less energy than heating, but they often represent the high-grade energy in electricity.

Eighty percent of the electricity used by industry is used for motors. Motors can be made efficient in many ways, including controllers that match power use to the actual load, metal cores that drop and take electric charges more easily, and windings with more turns of wire. Easing the tasks of industrial motors requires many disciplines. For example, fixing nitrogen into ammonia ($NH_3$) is typically done with streams of nitrogen and hydrogen passing over a catalyst. An improved catalyst pattern increases the reaction rate and thus decreases the hydrogen and nitrogen pumping. Automated controls again can control pumping, using it only where and when it is needed.

## REDUCING ENERGY USE

Several processes can reduce energy use. For example, a lower-pressure process for making polyethylene plastic uses one-fourth of the energy used in the previous process. Plastics have replaced energy-intensive metals in many commercial products. Silica in fiber-optic cables is replacing copper for communications. Composites, made with plastics and glass, metal, or other plastic fibers, not only require less energy to fabricate than all-metal materials but also have greater capabilities. Composites in railroad cars and airplanes reduce weight and thus energy costs of operation.

Vacuum deposition of metals, ceramics, and even diamond provide cheaply attained materials that multiply savings throughout industry. Diamond-edged machine tools operate significantly faster or longer before replacement. Rubidium-coated heat exchangers withstand sulfuric acid formed when the exhaust from the burning of high-sulfur coal drops below the boiling point, which allows both harnessing that lower heat and recovering the sulfur.

Other new processes have been contingent on developments in entirely new, even radical, fields. In *Engines of Creation* (1986), K. Eric Drexler discussed the concept of "nanotechnology," proposing microscopic robots small enough to build or repair objects one molecule at a time. The "nanobytes" could manufacture items with unprecedented strength and lightness. Today society already sees the benefits of the miniaturization of nanotechnology in areas such as the electronics industry. The continuing improvement in data storage and processing speed made possible by smaller parts is just one example. Genetic engineering reduces energy costs in the chemical industry. Parasitic bacteria on legumes (such as peanuts and soy beans) fix atmospheric nitrogen into chemicals the plants can use. Breeding similar bacteria for other crops can largely eliminate the need for ammonia fertilizer (and thereby decrease nitrate runoff).

## ECONOMICS AND EFFICIENCY

Costs are the biggest factor affecting energy efficiency in manufacturing. When the price of natural gas was fixed by law at a low rate, for example, steam lines in some chemical plants had no insulation—it simply was not cost-effective to insulate.

Even after prices rise, there is often a long time lag. For example, the use of bigger pipes in a chemical plant means lower pumping costs, but the cost of installing big pipes is not justified when energy costs are low. When energy costs rise, new plants being built might use the larger pipes, but old plants might well run for many years before replacement or a major refit.

Similarly, highly efficient electrical motors are only about 25 percent more costly than conventional motors and are able to return the extra cost and start generating profit within three years. However, rebuilt conventional motors are available for one-third of the price of new motors. Thus the investment in efficient new motors might not pay for itself for several additional years.

Finally, social and political factors affect the adoption of energy-efficient technologies. Government policies have often discouraged recycling by granting tax subsidies to raw materials production and establishing requirements for their use rather than recycled materials. Tax policies have not allowed enough depreciation to encourage long-term investments in energy efficiency.

Government policies and programs can lead the way to decreased energy use in manufacturing. The U.S. Department of Energy, for example, supports the Save Energy Now program to partner with companies and provide an energy-use assessment at no cost to the participating company. This results in recommendations for how the company can reduce its energy consumption in the manufacturing process as well as in energy use in the workplace. Such programs on a global scale can make industry adopt a more energy-efficient manufacturing process.

*Roger V. Carlson*

FURTHER READING

Beer, Jeroen de. *Potential for Industrial Energy-Efficiency Improvement in the Long Term.* Boston: Kluwer Academic, 2000.

Drexler, K. Eric. *Engines of Creation: The Coming Era of Nanotechnology.* New York: Anchor Books, 1990.

Gopalakrishan, Bhaskaram, et al. "Industrial Energy Efficiency." In *Environmentally Conscious Manufacturing,* edited by Myer Kutz. Hoboken, N.J.: Wiley, 2007.

International Energy Agency. *Tracking Industrial Energy Efficiency and $CO_2$ Emissions: In Support of the G8 Plan of Action—Energy Indicators.* Paris: Author, 2007.

Kenney, W. F. *Energy Conservation in the Process Industries.* Orlando, Fla.: Academic Press, 1984.

Larson, Eric D., Marc H. Ross, and Robert H. Williams. "Beyond the Era of Materials." *Scientific American* 254, no. 6 (June, 1986): 34.

National Research Council. *Decreasing Energy Intensity in Manufacturing: Assessing the Strategies and Future Directions of the Industrial Technologies Program.* Washington, D.C.: National Academies Press, 2004.

Ross, Marc H., and Daniel Steinmeyer. "Energy for Industry." *Scientific American* 263, no. 3 (September, 1990): 89.

WEB SITE

U.S. DEPARTMENT OF ENERGY
Industrial Technologies Program
http://www1.eere.energy.gov/industry

SEE ALSO: Buildings and appliances, energy-efficient; Electrical power; Energy economics; Energy politics; Genetic prospecting; Industrial Revolution and industrialization; Petrochemical products; Recycling; Steel.

# Marble

CATEGORY: Mineral and other nonliving resources

WHERE FOUND
Marbles, geologically defined as metamorphically altered calcareous rocks, are found in the core areas of younger mountain chains formed by the collision of tectonic plates and the consequent uplift and distortion of carbonate sedimentary strata. They are also found in the exposed roots of ancient, very eroded mountain chains of continental shield areas. Important marble-producing areas include the Carrara area in the Italian Apennines and Vermont, Georgia, and Alabama in the United States.

PRIMARY USES
Marble is used in architecture as both an ornamental and a structural stone. It is also used as an artistic medium for three-dimensional art such as sculpture, interior furnishings, and mortuary and historical monuments.

TECHNICAL DEFINITION
Geologists define marble as a type of rock produced by metamorphic processes acting on either limestone or dolomite (dolostone), causing recrystallization through heat and pressure to produce a coarser-grained, harder rock. Stonemasons and quarriers have a more generic definition, which calls almost any hard rock that accepts a fine polish marble.

## DESCRIPTION, DISTRIBUTION, AND FORMS

As defined geologically, marble is a type of rock composed primarily of calcite. It can be, like limestone, monomineralic in nature—that is, a rock composed of only one, or nearly one, mineral. Thus it can be up to 99 percent calcite (calcium carbonate). True marble can be derived from either limestone or dolomite (sometimes called dolostone). Dolomite (calcium magnesium carbonate) is a carbonate rock in which much, if not most, of the original calcium carbonate has been replaced by magnesium. True marbles are formed by two types of metamorphism: regional and contact. Regional metamorphism is usually tectonic in nature and involves the slow compression and heating of rocks by large-scale crustal movements of the Earth over long periods of time. Contact metamorphism is caused by rocks coming into contact, or near contact, with sources of great geologic heat, such as intruding bodies of magma; in these cases change can be effected within a short period of time.

## HISTORY

Marble in its various forms has been known and admired since remote antiquity as a stone of choice for many applications. Some of the earliest known works of true architecture that have survived from ancient Mesopotamia, Egypt, and Greece featured marble as either decorative or structural elements. Sculptures, bas-reliefs, dedicatory columns, and triumphal arches have frequently featured various marbles. Thus marble has been in use at least five thousand years, dating back to the first civilizations, and its use continues up to the present. Many sculptors through the ages—among them such giants as Michelangelo, working in the fifteenth and sixteenth centuries in Italy—have preferred marble, especially the pure white varieties.

## OBTAINING MARBLE

Marble deposits are quarried in large operations that may involve hundreds of workers. In Europe marble is often obtained from quarries that have been worked continuously since antiquity. Until the last century or so, work was laboriously performed with age-old traditional tools and methods, but with the advent of power equipment the methodology and speed of extraction have greatly improved. Some constants have remained, such as the general strategy regarding extraction of large blocks of marble: removing the overburden (overlying sediments and rubble, if any), defining a quarry floor and front by quarrying monolithic blocks of marble parallel to their natural jointing planes, cutting away large blocks on all sides and removing the marble to the quarry floor, trimming, removing the marble from the quarry, and transporting it to the purchaser (often by use of specially built railroad systems).

Marble extraction has never had significant environmental effects, as the true marbles are chemically

*White marble is quarried from this site in Ticino, Switzerland.* (Karl Mathis/Keystone/Landov)

inert for all practical purposes. The metamorphism they underwent in their natural development stabilized their constituent minerals, including the trace minerals such as iron and magnesium from which colored marbles derive their patterns and hues.

## USES OF MARBLE

The primary importance of marble is its use in architectural columns, floorings, wall coverings, sculpture, vases and other receptacles, and monuments of all sorts. Beginning in the twentieth century, new minor uses were found for marble, including electrical outlet baseplates and other electrical insulators, as it is a good natural insulator.

*Frederick M. Surowiec*

## FURTHER READING

Dietrich, R. V., and Brian J. Skinner. *Gems, Granites, and Gravels: Knowing and Using Rocks and Minerals.* New York: Cambridge University Press, 1990.

Kogel, Jessica Elzea, et al., eds. "Decorative Stone" and "Dimension Stone." In *Industrial Minerals and Rocks: Commodities, Markets, and Uses.* 7th ed. Littleton, Colo.: Society for Mining, Metallurgy, and Exploration, 2006.

Mannoni, Luciana, and Tiziano Mannoni. *Marble: The History of a Culture.* New York: Facts On File, 1985.

Pellant, Chris. *Rocks and Minerals.* 2d American ed. New York: Dorling Kindersley, 2002.

Price, Monica T. *The Sourcebook of Decorative Stone: An Illustrated Identification Guide.* Buffalo, N.Y.: Firefly Books, 2007.

Robinson, George W. *Minerals: An Illustrated Exploration of the Dynamic World of Minerals and Their Properties.* Photography by Jeffrey A. Scovil. New York: Simon & Schuster, 1994.

Schumann, Walter. *Handbook of Rocks, Minerals, and Gemstones.* Translated by R. Bradshaw and K. A. G. Mills. Boston: Houghton Mifflin, 1993.

## WEB SITES

U.S. GEOLOGICAL SURVEY
Crushed Stone: Statistics and Information
http://minerals.usgs.gov/minerals/pubs/
    commodity/stone_crushed

U.S. GEOLOGICAL SURVEY
Dimension Stone: Statistics and Information
http://minerals.usgs.gov/minerals/pubs/
    commodity/stone_dimension

SEE ALSO: Aggregates; Calcium compounds; Carbonate minerals; Gypsum; Lime; Limestone; Metamorphic processes, rocks, and mineral deposits.

# Marine mining

CATEGORY: Obtaining and using resources

*The oceans cover 71 percent of the Earth's surface, and they represent a vast, largely untapped reservoir of natural resources. With advancements in imaging and other technologies, efforts to locate and retrieve the vast variety of mineral resources have expanded, although they continue to be mitigated by economic, ecological, and political offsets.*

## BACKGROUND

Ocean mining represents only a small percentage of the total mining done worldwide, because land deposits are more easily recognized and obtained than underwater deposits. Until the 1970's, deep-ocean deposits could not be mined commercially because precise navigation to survey deposits and guide dredges did not exist. Since then, ocean technologies have improved significantly. Moreover, competing land deposits are used (or paved over), and expanding economies are increasing demand. Thus the "mines of Neptune" are ripe for use. Marine mining can be divided into three categories: mining seawater, extending land mining along the continental shelves, and mining the ocean floors.

## MINING SEAWATER

Seawater can be seen as a massive ore body containing mostly water with an assortment of dissolved minerals. If seawater processing were efficient enough, more than sixty elements could be extracted. The major constituents of seawater are water ($H_2O$, 96.5 percent), sodium chloride (NaCl, 2.3 percent), magnesium chloride ($MgCl_2$, 0.5 percent), sodium sulfate ($Na_2SO_4$, 0.4 percent), and calcium chloride ($CaCl_2$, 0.1 percent).

Sodium chloride, or table salt, has been evaporated from seawater since antiquity, with sunlight and wind supplying the energy for the process. Modern table salt extraction begins with seawater in evaporation ponds that appear somewhat similar to those that have been used for centuries. However, the old single-step pond has been replaced by several ponds. A first pond settles out mud, iron salts, and calcium salts. At a second pond, slaked lime (calcium hydroxide, $Ca(OH)_2$) takes sulfur ions and precipitates out as gypsum plaster (calcium sulfate, $CaSO_4$). The table salt precipitates at a third pond, leaving a brine rich in salts of magnesium and potassium.

Magnesium was first extracted commercially in World War II. One method uses sea shells (calcium carbonate) baked to drive off carbon dioxide. Adding water produces (again) calcium hydroxide, from which the hydroxide combines with magnesium and precipitates out. Later, the precipitate is combined with hydrochloric acid (HCl), making magnesium chloride, which can be separated by electrolysis. Other systems go to magnesium carbonate ($MgCO_3$) or magnesium oxide (MgO). Bromine-rich brine is treated with acid to get elemental bromine. A similar process produces iodine.

Shellfish naturally extract calcium from seawater by growing (accreting) calcium carbonate ($CaCO_3$). This process can be mimicked by electrical accretion, in which a weak electrical charge on a wire screen accretes calcium carbonate, gradually making a sheet of artificial limestone while metal at the opposite electrode dissolves. Calcium carbonate accretion is experimental and expensive. However, it allows one to "grow" structures on site, and it may someday be used to build major oceanic structures.

Water, of course, is the prime constituent of seawater, and desalination (removal of salt from seawater or other salt solutions) was performed commercially beginning in the 1960's. The water and salts can be separated by distillation (much as evaporation and rain perform distillation in the hydrologic cycle), by low-pressure distillation (in which the water boils at lower temperatures), by refrigeration (in which ice freezes fresh, leaving concentrated brine), and by osmotic separation (in which pressure or electricity pulls water through a membrane, leaving concentrated brine). However, desalination is always expensive, and natural water sources are cheaper except in desert countries.

Extracting other minerals from seawater is theoretical. Although a cubic kilometer of seawater contains metric tons of many elements, those metric tons can be obtained only by pumping the water through some extraction process. The pumps and extraction process usually cost more than the extracted material is worth. After World War I, renowned German chemist Fritz Haber tried to extract gold from seawater to pay his nation's war debts but met with no success. Likewise, filtering for uranium has failed. Only plants and animals may be able to do such type of extractions: Certain shellfish and worms in the oceans are able to concentrate minerals hundreds or even thousands of times more than they are concentrated in the surrounding ocean.

### DEPOSITS ON THE CONTINENTAL SHELF

Where the continents meet the oceans, they generally slope gently for some distance before plunging into deep ocean waters. Worldwide, this shallow continuation (down to roughly 200 meters), called the continental shelf, covers an area equivalent to that of Africa.

Typical land minerals continue outward under the water on the continental shelf. In addition, the continental shelf has water-sorted deposits called placers along continuations of rivers "drowned" by changes in sea level and along beaches. Furthermore, many coastlines are somewhat like a set of stairs with drowned beaches and old beaches above the water line.

Tunnel mines have been extended from shore to obtain particularly desired ores, such as tin off England and coal off Japan. The Japanese have built artificial islands and tunneled from them to the surrounding deposits. Such methods can be extended. However, dredging is now the most common method of mining shallow deposits. A suction dredge (essentially a giant vacuum cleaner) can operate well to roughly 30 meters. Below that, economics shift toward lines of buckets or other exotic means.

The most commonly dredged materials are sand and gravel. Shells and coral are also dredged. These are cheap materials per unit, but the vast tonnage makes them important. More valuable ores are dredged in smaller tonnages throughout the world. For instance, gold is dredged off Alaska, and diamonds are dredged off the west coast of South Africa. Tin ore is dredged off Southeast Asia, and iron and titanium ores are mined off Australia.

### DEEP OCEAN DEPOSITS

The deeper waters of the ocean contain potential resources beyond imagining. To take only one example, the phosphorus-containing minerals glauconite and phosphorite, starting at the edge of the continental shelf, can easily be processed for fertilizer.

In tectonically active areas, water seeping down near volcanic rock is heated and eventually expelled back into the ocean. These hydrothermal vents, or marine vents, carry dissolved minerals, usually sulfides of zinc, lead, copper, and silver, along with lesser but still significant amounts of lead, cadmium, cobalt, and gold. Such deposits have been test mined in the Red Sea (where underwater valleys keep rich muds enclosed). In the deep ocean, such deposits make chimneys of metal sulfides that might eventually be mined.

The greatest deposits are in the deep ocean away from land. Rocks, sharks' teeth, and even old spark plugs provide settling points for the accretion of so-called ferromanganese nodules, which are oxides of mostly iron and manganese that also contain potentially profitable small amounts of copper, nickel, and cobalt. These potato-shaped ores cover millions of square kilometers and comprise billions of metric tons of metal.

## Economics, Ecology, and Politics

The difference between potential resources and what are termed mineral "reserves" is what people are willing to do and what it will cost to obtain them. This is particularly true of marine mining. The cost of shallow dredging is cheaper than land mining, but the advantage rapidly disappears as the waters grow deeper and the distance to the processing plant on shore becomes greater. For example, deep-ocean mining of ferromanganese nodules for copper might be much closer to reality if fiber-optics technology had not cut into the applications for copper cables. Finally, mining deep-sea ferromanganese nodules might yield the greatest profits from the small amounts of copper and nickel. However, ocean mining could also saturate the markets for cobalt and manganese, with unknown consequences—cobalt might directly replace nickel in stainless steel, making the stainless steel a cheaper competitor of copper.

Ecological concerns include the fact that dredging releases tremendous clouds of silt, killing wildlife and causing shallow waters to lose fish production. Dredging in cold, deep-ocean waters is worse, damaging areas of sparse, slowly reproducing life that require decades to heal. New types of neat dredges may be required if deep-ocean deposits are ever to be used commercially.

Politics is an even more powerful part of the picture. A political decision that required coal-burning plants on land to reduce emissions of sulfur oxide and sulfate created a glut of recovered sulfur. That glut largely destroyed offshore sulfur mining. Phosphorite mining off the California coast was canceled after it was discovered that the area had been used for dumping old bombs and shells. Tax incentives for recycling might delay the need for deep-ocean mining by decades, or requirements for electric cars might push ferromanganese-nodule mining forward in order to obtain nickel for batteries. Deep-sea mining controls from the Law of the Sea Treaty would prevent rival mining dredges from colliding, but the costs of future deep-ocean mining would probably include undetermined taxes and subsidies to potential mining rivals.

*Roger V. Carlson*

## Further Reading

Borgese, Elisabeth Mann. *The Mines of Neptune: Minerals and Metals from the Sea.* New York: H. N. Abrams, 1985.
Cronan, David S., ed. *Handbook of Marine Mineral Deposits.* Boca Raton, Fla.: CRC Press, 2000.
Earney, Fillmore C. F. *Marine Mineral Resources.* New York: Routledge, 1990.
Shusterich, Kurt Michael. *Resource Management and the Oceans: The Political Economy of Deep Seabed Mining.* Boulder, Colo.: Westview Press, 1982.
United Nations Division for Ocean Affairs and the Law of the Sea. *Marine Mineral Resources: Scientific Advances and Economic Perspectives.* New York: Author, 2004.

See also: Deep drilling projects; Desalination plants and technology; Integrated Ocean Drilling Program; Law of the sea; Manganese; Marine vents; Oceans; Oil and natural gas drilling and wells.

# Marine vents

Category: Geological processes and formations

*Marine vents are localized areas of the seafloor where cold seawater interacts with magma. The result of this interaction produces spectacular eruptions of hot seawater and enables the precipitation of sulfide minerals of iron, copper, and zinc.*

## DEFINITION

Marine vents, more commonly known as deep-sea hydrothermal vents, are produced along deep fractures in the seafloor. These fractures are associated with the mid-ocean ridges. The mid-ocean ridges are undersea mountain ranges that are sites of active volcanism. Despite their association with undersea volcanic mountain ranges, all marine vents occur at depths greater than 2 kilometers below the surface. Marine vents are studied primarily by deep submersible vehicles.

## OVERVIEW

Marine vents are formed when fractures in the seafloor develop and cold water flows in from above. As the seawater flows deeper into the fractures, it may encounter rocks heated by close proximity to magma; the rocks heat the seawater. The heated water begins to dissolve minerals from the surrounding rocks, and its chemistry changes from that of common seawater. If a critical temperature is reached, the hot water will rush to the surface. Although their appearance suggests an explosive volcanic eruption on land, marine vents are more like geysers than volcanoes.

As the hot seawater exits the vent, it begins to cool rapidly. Minerals which are in solution begin to precipitate out. This precipitation may give a dark, smoky appearance to the hot water exiting the marine vent. The name "black smoker" is commonly applied to these vents. The minerals which commonly precipitate out in these vents are metal sulfides (combinations of a metal and sulfur). The most common minerals found are sulfides of iron, copper, and zinc. These minerals form crusts around the opening and may precipitate into a tall "chimney" of minerals around the marine vent.

Marine vents are also the site of unique biologic communities. These communities thrive in the total absence of sunlight. The food chain is based on bacteria that derive their energy from chemosynthesis. This process enables the bacteria to derive their energy from chemicals dissolved in the hot water exiting the marine vents. Other animals depend on the bacteria. Some animals associated with the vent communities grow to very large sizes. Tube worms around marine vents may be larger than 3 meters in length. Because the communities depend on the vent waters for their source of energy, the animals live closely packed around the vent. When vents become inactive, the communities die. While not a likely source of food for humans, it has been suggested that the vent animals may contain unusual chemicals which may help develop new medicines.

There is a great deal of difficulty and expense involved in reaching deep marine vents. This fact, plus the cost of bringing minerals and animals to the surface and shipping them to shore, must be considered in deciding whether it is feasible to use these valuable resources. Despite the obstacles, marine vents remain the focus of much geologic, biologic, and oceanographic research.

*Richard H. Fluegeman, Jr.*

SEE ALSO: Biodiversity; Copper; Hydrothermal solutions and mineralization; Iron; Oceanography; Seafloor spreading; Zinc.

# Mercury

CATEGORY: Mineral and other nonliving resources

## WHERE FOUND

Mercury is generally found associated with volcanic rocks that have formed near subduction zones. The primary producing areas are in China, Kyrgyzstan, Spain, and Russia.

## PRIMARY USES

Mercury is used in the industrial production of chlorine and caustic soda. It is also used in dry cell batteries, paints, dental amalgams, gold mining, scientific measuring instruments, and mercury vapor lamps. Several of these uses are now banned in the United States.

## TECHNICAL DEFINITION

Mercury (chemical symbol Hg) is a silvery white metal that belongs to Group IIB (the zinc group) of the periodic table. It has an atomic number of 80 and an atomic weight of 200.5. It has seven stable isotopes and a density of 13.6 grams per cubic centimeter. Also known as quicksilver, mercury has a melting point of $-38.87°$ Celsius, making it the only metal that is liquid at normal room temperature. It boils at a temperature of $356.9°$ Celsius and has a constant rate of expansion throughout the entire range of temperature of the liquid. Mercury alloys with most metals and is a good conductor of electricity.

## DESCRIPTION, DISTRIBUTION, AND FORMS

Mercury is a relatively scarce element on Earth, accounting for only 3 parts per billion in crustal rocks. It is found both as free liquid metal and, more commonly, as the sulfide mineral cinnabar (HgS). It is generally found in areas of past volcanic activity. Mercury compounds are formed from mercury with either a +1 or +2 oxidation state. The most common mercury (I) compound is mercury chloride ($Hg_2Cl_2$), and the most common mercury (II) compounds are mercury oxide (HgO), mercury bichloride ($HgCl_2$), and mercury sulfide (HgS). (The Roman numerals refer to the valence state of the mercury.)

Mercury forms compounds that are used in agriculture, industry, and medicine. Some organic mercury compounds, such as phenylmercury acetate, are used in agriculture as fungicides to control seed rot, for spraying trees, and for controlling weeds. Because of their highly toxic nature, care must be used when applying or using such mercury compounds.

Mercury is a rare crustal element that is found both as liquid elemental mercury and combined with other elements in more than twenty-five minerals. Cinnabar is the primary ore mineral of mercury, and it is generally found in volcanic rocks and occasionally in associated sedimentary rocks. The volcanic rocks were generally formed as volcanic island arc systems near subduction zones. Since the deposits are concentrated in faulted and fractured rocks that were formed at or near the surface, they are extremely susceptible to erosion. Mercury is a highly volatile element, and it is usually lost to the atmosphere during the erosion of the ore deposits.

Mercury is also an extremely toxic element that can be easily released into the environment when mined, processed, or used. Mercury vapors can be inhaled, and mercury compounds can be ingested or absorbed through the skin. Mercury poisoning has been recognized in native peoples who used cinnabar as a face pigment, in gold miners who used mercury in processing gold ore, and in hat makers who used mercury compounds in producing felt.

Inorganic mercury compounds can be converted by bacteria into highly toxic organic mercury compounds such as methyl mercury. These organic mercury compounds become concentrated as they move up the food chain to higher-level organisms such as fish, birds, and humans. Because of this the disposal of inorganic mercury waste can become a major environmental hazard. In Japan the release of mercury waste from an industrial plant into the waters of Minamata Bay resulted in the deaths of forty-three people during the 1950's and early 1960's. In 1972, wheat seed treated with methyl mercury fungicide was used by farmers in rural Iraq. The wheat was enriched in methyl mercury, as was the bread made from the wheat. Animals and plants within the area also accumulated high concentrations of methyl mercury. As a result of this contamination, a total of 460 people died from mercury poisoning in 1972.

## HISTORY

Mercury has been known since at least the second century B.C.E. Chinese alchemists used mercury in futile attempts to transform the base metals into gold. Mercury was also used in ancient Egypt. Cinnabar, the red ore mineral of mercury, has long been used by aboriginal peoples as an important pigment. By Roman times the distillation of mercury was known, and a

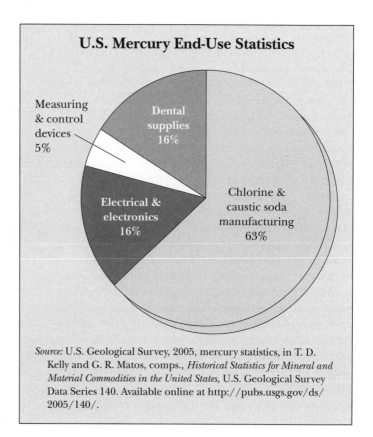

Source: U.S. Geological Survey, 2005, mercury statistics, in T. D. Kelly and G. R. Matos, comps., *Historical Statistics for Mineral and Material Commodities in the United States*, U.S. Geological Survey Data Series 140. Available online at http://pubs.usgs.gov/ds/2005/140/.

mercury trade between Rome and the rich Spanish cinnabar mines was well established. Beginning with the Renaissance and the scientific revolution in the sixteenth and seventeenth centuries, mercury became important for use in measuring devices such as thermometers and barometers. The major modern industrial, medicinal, and agricultural uses of mercury were developed in the nineteenth and twentieth centuries.

The toxicity of mercury compounds has been known since the early poisoning of cinnabar miners. Later, in the early nineteenth century, the mental effects that mercury had on felt makers gave birth to the phrase "mad as a hatter." The tragic effects of mercury poisoning were felt in Japan during the 1950's and Iraq in 1972, when hundreds died from ingesting organic mercury compounds.

In the United States, the Energy Independence and Security Act of 2007 will phase out the use of incandescent bulbs in federal buildings, to be replaced by mercury-containing compact fluorescent bulbs. Disposal of the new, energy-saving bulbs will therefore require special handling. The Mercury Market Minimization Act of 2008 forbids the sale, distribution, and export of elemental mercury and bans all U.S. exports as of January 1, 2013.

## OBTAINING MERCURY

The primary mercury deposits of the world are found in Spain, China, central Europe, and Algeria. Spain is estimated to have the greatest reserves, almost 60 percent of the world's total. In 2008, world production of mercury was approximately 950 metric tons. Mercury is also recovered through the recycling of batteries, dental amalgams, thermostats, fluorescent lamp tubes, and certain industrial sludges and solutions.

## USES OF MERCURY

In the past, the primary use of mercury in the world was in the industrial production of chlorine and caustic soda. However, beginning in the twenty-first century this usage was curtailed significantly, reflecting a general movement away from mercury usage. The United States has exported refined mercury for the production of chlorine and caustic soda, fluorescent lights, and dental amalgam. Mercuric sulfate and mercuric chloride have been used industrially to produce vinyl chloride, vinyl acetate, and acetaldehyde. Pharmacological uses of mercury compounds include mercury bichloride and mercurochrome as skin anti-

septics, and mercurous chloride (calomel) as a diuretic. Many of these uses have been curtailed, and a ban on U.S. exports was passed by Congress in 2008.

*Jay R. Yett*

## FURTHER READING

Adriano, Domy C. "Mercury." In *Trace Elements in Terrestrial Environments: Biogeochemistry, Bioavailability, and Risks of Metals.* 2d ed. New York: Springer, 2001.

Eisler, Ronald. *Mercury Hazards to Living Organisms.* Boca Raton, Fla.: CRC/Taylor & Francis, 2006.

Greenwood, N. N., and A. Earnshaw. "Zinc, Cadmium, and Mercury." In *Chemistry of the Elements.* 2d ed. Boston: Butterworth-Heinemann, 1997.

Harte, John, et al. *Toxics A to Z: A Guide to Everyday Pollution Hazards.* Berkeley: University of California Press, 1991.

Hightower, Jane M. *Diagnosis Mercury: Money, Politics, and Poison.* Washington, D.C.: Island Press/Shearwater Books, 2009.

Massey, A. G. "Group 12: Zinc, Cadmium, and Mercury." In *Main Group Chemistry.* 2d ed. New York: Wiley, 2000.

Risher, J. F. *Elemental Mercury and Inorganic Mercury Compounds: Human Health Aspects.* Geneva, Switzerland: World Health Organization, 2003.

## WEB SITES

NATURAL RESOURCES CANADA
Canadian Minerals Yearbook, Mineral and Metal Commodity Reviews
http://www.nrcan-rncan.gc.ca/mms-smm/busi-indu/cmy-amc/com-eng.htm

U.S. GEOLOGICAL SURVEY
Mercury: Statistics and Information
http://minerals.usgs.gov/minerals/pubs/commodity/mercury

U.S. GEOLOGICAL SURVEY
Mercury Contamination of Aquatic Ecosystems
http://water.usgs.gov/wid/FS_216-95/FS_216-95.html

U.S. GEOLOGICAL SURVEY
Mercury in the Environment
http://www.usgs.gov/themes/factsheet/146-00

SEE ALSO: China; Food chain; Hazardous waste disposal; Igneous processes, rocks, and mineral deposits; Plate tectonics; Russia; Spain; United States.

# Metals and metallurgy

CATEGORIES: Mineral and other nonliving resources; obtaining and using resources

*Enormous amounts of mineral resources are mined each year to supply society's requirements for metals. In addition, large amounts of carbon, oxygen, and electricity are consumed in the various metallurgical processes by which the raw materials are converted for use.*

## BACKGROUND

Although the term "metal" is difficult to define absolutely, there are two working definitions that include almost three-quarters of the elements of the periodic table classified as metals. Chemically, metals are those elements that usually form positive ions in solutions or in compounds and whose oxides form basic water solutions. Physically, metals contain free electrons that impart properties such as metallic luster and thermal and electrical conductivity. In the periodic table, all the elements found in Groups IA and IIA and in the B groups are metals. In addition, Groups IIIA, IVA (except carbon), VA (except nitrogen and phosphorus), and VIA (except oxygen and sulfur) are classified as metals. All the metals are lustrous and, with the exception of mercury, are solids at normal temperatures. Boron (IIIA), silicon and germanium (IVA), arsenic and antimony (VA), selenium and tellurium (VIA), and astatine (VIIA) show metallic behavior in some of their compounds and are known as metalloids.

The bonding in metals explains many of their physical characteristics. The simplest model describes a metal as fixed positive ions (the nucleus and completed inner shells of electrons) in a sea of mobile valence electrons. The ions are held in place by the electrostatic attraction between the positive ions and the negative electrons, which are delocalized over the whole crystal. Because of this electron mobility, metals are good conductors of electricity and thermal energy. This electron sea also shields neighboring layers of positive ions as they move past one another. Therefore most metals are ductile (capable of being drawn into wires) and malleable (capable of being spread into sheets). The absorption of electromagnetic radiation by the mobile valence electrons and its reemission as visible light explains the luster that is characteristic of metals.

## NATURAL ABUNDANCE

While all the known metals are found in the Earth's crust, the abundance varies widely, from aluminum (over 81,000 parts per million) to such rare metals as osmium and ruthenium (approximately 0.001 part per million). The metalloid silicon is the second most abundant element in the Earth's crust, with an abundance of more than 277,000 parts per million. Some of those metals found in low concentrations, such as copper and tin, are commonly used, while many of the more abundant metals, such as titanium and rubidium, are just beginning to find uses. The metal ore most important to modern industrial society, iron, is abundant and easily reduced to metallic form. The metals that were most important to early civilizations—gold, silver, mercury, lead, iron, copper, tin, and zinc—exist in large, easily recognized deposits and in compounds that are easily reduced to elemental form.

Very few metals occur "free" in nature. The form in which a specific metal is found depends on its reactivity and on the solubility of its compounds. Many metals occur as binary oxides or sulfides in ores that also contain materials such as clay, granite, or silica from which the metal compounds must first be separated. Metals are also found as chlorides, carbonates, sulfates, silicates, and arsenides, as well as complex compounds of great variety such as $LiAlSi_2O_6$, which is a source of lithium.

## METALLURGY

Metallurgy is a large field of science and art that encompasses the separation of metals from their ores, the making of alloys, and the working of metals to give them certain desired characteristics. The art of metallurgy dates from about 4000 B.C.E., when metalsmiths were able to extract silver and lead from their ores. Tin ores were obtained by 3000 B.C.E., and the production of bronze, an alloy of copper and tin, could begin. By 2700 B.C.E. iron was obtained. There is an obvious relationship between the discovery that metals could be refined and fabricated into objects such as tools and weapons and the rise of human civilizations. Early periods in the history of humankind have long been identified by the metals that became available. Throughout most of human history metallurgy was an art; the development of the science from the art has taken place gradually over the past few centuries.

The production of metals from their ores involves a three-step process: preliminary treatment in which impurities are removed, and possibly chemical treatment used to convert the metallic compound to a more easily reduced form; reduction to the free metal; and refining, in which undesirable impurities are removed and others are added to control the final characteristics of the metal.

The preliminary treatment involves physical as well as chemical treatment. Physical methods include grinding, sorting, froth flotation, magnetic separations, and gravity concentration. Chemical reactions may also be used for concentration. The use of cyanide solution to extract gold from its ores is an example of chemical concentration. In 1890, Karl Bayer devised a process which is based on the fact that aluminum trihydrate dissolves in hot caustic soda but other materials in bauxite do not. The result is almost pure $Al_2O_3$. Frequently, many metals present in small percentages are found in ores with more abundant metals. The processes used to concentrate the primary metal also concentrates the minor ones as well and makes their extraction possible. Most ores are mined and processed for more than one metal. Iron is a notable exception.

*A Saudi mine worker pours a stream of molten gold from the furnace into gold ingot molds.* (AFP/Getty Images)

Large-scale redox reactions are the means by which metals from ores are reduced to free metals. The particular method used depends on the reactivity of the metal. The most active metals, such as aluminum, magnesium, and sodium, are reduced by electrolytic reduction. Metal oxides are usually reduced by heating with carbon or hydrogen. This age-old process produces by far the greatest volume of free metals such as iron, copper, zinc, cadmium, tin, and nickel. Sulfides are usually roasted in air to produce oxides, which are then reduced to the free metal. Some sulfides, such as copper sulfide, produce the free metal directly by roasting.

The refining step encompasses an array of processes designed to remove any remaining impurities and to convert the metal to a form demanded by the end user. The major divisions of refining are pyrometallurgy, or fire refining, and electrometallurgy, or electrolysis. There are a few processes that do not fall into either of these major divisions such as the gaseous diffusion of uranium hexafluoride molecules to produce isotopically enriched uranium for the nuclear power industry.

Pyrometallurgy is a general name for a number of processes, including, but not limited to, roasting (heating to a temperature where oxidation occurs without melting, usually to eliminate sulfides); calcining (heating in a kiln to drive off an undesirable constituent such as carbon, which goes off as $CO_2$); and distilling (heating the mineral containing the metal to decomposition above the melting point of the metal, which is collected in a condenser).

Electrolytic refining involves immersing an anode of impure metal and a cathode of pure metal in a solution of ions of the metal and passing an electric current through it. Metal ions from the solution plate out on the cathode and are replaced in the solution by ions from the anode. Impurities either drop to the bottom as sludge or remain in solution. These byproducts, often containing gold, silver, and platinum, are later recovered by additional processes. Electrolytic refining is expensive in terms of the electricity required and of the often toxic solutions remaining to be safely disposed of.

## METALS AS CRYSTALS

When a metal solidifies, its atoms assume positions in a well-defined geometric pattern, a crystalline solid. The three most important patterns for metals are the body-centered cubic, the face-centered cubic, and the hexagonal. If atoms of one metal exist in the solid solution of another, the atoms of the minor constituent occupy positions in the crystal pattern of the major constituent. Since atoms of each element have characteristic size, the presence of a "stranger" atom causes distortion of the pattern and, usually, strengthening of the crystal. This strengthening is one of the major reasons that most metals are used as alloys—in solid solutions of two or more constituent metals.

Zinc is a hexagonal crystal, while copper atoms occupy the sites of a face-centered cubic lattice. As the larger zinc atoms occupy positions in the copper lattice, they distort the crystal and make it harder to deform. Brass, an alloy of copper and zinc, increases in hardness as the zinc concentration increases up to 36 percent, at which point the crystal changes to a body-centered cubic pattern with markedly different characteristics. Careful selection of various combinations of elements in differing concentrations can produce alloys with almost any desired characteristics.

The carbon steels are a good example of this variation. Various amounts of carbon and metals such as molybdenum are introduced into molten iron ore to create desired strength, ductility, or malleability in the finished steel product. Another example is the intentional doping of the semiconductor silicon with boron or phosphorus to create different conduction capabilities.

## METALS IN LIVING SYSTEMS

"Essential" metals are those whose absence will prevent some particular organism from completing its life cycle, including reproduction. These metals are classified, according to the amounts needed, as macronutrients or micronutrients. For animals the macronutrients are potassium, sodium, magnesium, and calcium. Sodium and potassium establish concentration differences across cell membranes by means of active transport and set up osmotic and electrochemical gradients. They are structure promoters for nucleic acids and proteins.

Magnesium, calcium, and zinc are enzyme activa-

tors and structure promoters. Magnesium is an essential component of chlorophyll, the pigment in plants responsible for photosynthesis. Calcium salts are insoluble and act as structure formers in both plants and animals. In muscles the calcium concentration is controlled to act as a neuromuscular trigger.

Among the important micronutrients are chromium and iron. In mammals, chromium is involved in the metabolism of glucose. The oxygen-carrying molecule in mammalian blood is hemoglobin, an iron-porphyrin protein. Many other metals are known to be important in varying amounts, but their specific activity is not yet clearly understood. This is and will continue to be an active field of research in biochemistry and molecular biology.

One of the interesting current techniques for studying the activity of metals on a cellular level is fluorescent imaging. Metals such as calcium interact with fluorescent dyes. The dyes have different fluorescent characteristics in the presence or absence of specific metal. Special cameras, called charge coupled devices (CCDs), are mounted on microscopes and feed electrical signals directly to a computer, which creates an image. Metal concentrations inside and outside cells can be studied in the presence and absence of other nutrients to establish relationships among the various materials that are needed to sustain viable cell activity.

## METALS AS TOXINS

Those materials that have a negative effect on metabolic processes in a specific organism are said to be toxic to that organism. Many metals fall into this category. Today toxic metals are found in the atmosphere and the waters of the Earth. Some are present because of natural processes such as erosion, forest fires, or volcanic eruptions, others because of the activities of humankind. The natural toxins are less problematic because many organisms, during the process of evolution, developed tolerances to what might be considered toxic.

Maintaining good air quality is a major problem for industrial nations. Highly toxic metals, whose long-term effects on the health of humans and the environment are of concern, have been released into the atmosphere in large quantities. The atmosphere is the medium of transfer of these toxins from the point of origin to distant ecosystems. Prior to the 1970's, attention was focused on gaseous pollutants such as sulfur dioxide ($SO_2$) and nitrogen oxide ($NO_x$) and on total particulate matter. Since that time, improved analytical techniques have provided improved data on trace metals in the atmosphere, making studies on health effects possible.

The largest contributors to trace metal pollution are vehicular traffic, energy generation, and industrial metal production. For some metals, such as selenium, mercury, and manganese, natural emissions on a global scale far exceed those from anthropogenic sources. However, local manganese emissions from human-made sources in Europe far exceed those from natural sources. This illustrates the problem facing humankind. Emission patterns must be studied for local, regional, and global effects. Global emission patterns have been studied and compared with statistical information of the world's use of ores, rocks, and fuels and to the production of various types of goods. These studies allow the major sources of various toxic metals to be identified.

Coal combustion has been identified as the chief emission source of beryllium, cobalt, molybdenum, antimony, and selenium. Nickel and vanadium come mainly from oil firing. Smelters and other noniron refining plants emit most of the arsenic, cadmium, copper, and zinc. Chromium and manganese are released as side products of iron refining and steel production. Finally, gasoline combustion is the main cause of lead pollution. Identification of the main culprits should point the way to the changes needed to reduce emission levels of these metals and to choices regarding future industrial growth. Installation of scrubbing devices for removal of toxic materials from gaseous emissions and replacement of old boilers will reduce some emissions. New coal technologies such as coal pyrolysis and in situ gasification should also reduce the contamination of the environment to some degree. Much more data on regional and local patterns are necessary to restore the health of the atmosphere.

*Grace A. Banks*

FURTHER READING

Chandler, Harry. *Metallurgy for the Non-Metallurgist.* Materials Park, Ohio: ASM International, 1998.

Craddock, Paul, and Janet Lang. *Mining and Metal Production Through the Ages.* London: British Museum, 2003.

Moniz, B. J. *Metallurgy.* 4th ed. Homewood, Ill.: American Technical Publishers, 2007.

Neely, John E., and Thomas J. Bertone. *Practical Metallurgy and Materials of Industry.* 6th ed. Upper Saddle River, N.J.: Prentice Hall, 2003.

Nriagu, Jerome O., and Cliff I. Davidson, eds. *Toxic Metals in the Atmosphere.* New York: Wiley, 1986.

Street, Arthur, and William Alexander. *Metals in the Service of Man.* 10th ed. London: Penguin, 1994.

Wolfe, John A. *Mineral Resources: A World Review.* New York: Chapman and Hall, 1984.

SEE ALSO: Alloys; Aluminum; Antimony; Arsenic; Brass; Bronze; Copper; Earth's crust; Gold; Iron; Magnetic materials; Mineral resource use, early history of; Minerals, structure and physical properties of; Nickel; Platinum and the platinum group metals; Silver; Smelting; Steel; Steel industry; Strategic resources; Tin.

# Metamictization

CATEGORY: Geological processes and formations

*Metamictization is the process of rendering crystalline minerals partly or wholly amorphous (glasslike) as a consequence of radioactive decay. Metamict minerals such as zircon are important as gemstones, and metamict minerals that do not lose their radioactive components during the process of metamictization may possibly be used for the disposal of high-level nuclear wastes.*

DEFINITION

The term "metamict" (meaning "mixed otherwise") was proposed in 1893 by W. C. Broegger when he recognized that some minerals, although they show crystal form, are nevertheless structurally very similar to glass. Metamict minerals fracture like glass, are optically isotropic (have the same properties in all directions) to visible and infrared light, and to all appearances are noncrystalline.

OVERVIEW

The discovery that all metamict minerals are at least slightly radioactive and that metamict grains contain uranium and thorium led to the conclusion that the process of metamictization results from radiation damage caused by the decay of uranium and thorium. Although all metamict minerals are radioactive, not all radioactive minerals are metamict. Many metamict minerals have nonmetamict equivalents with the same form and essentially the same composition.

Isotopes of uranium and of thorium decay, through a series of emissions of alpha particles (helium nuclei), into a stable isotope of lead. The alpha particle is emitted from the decaying nucleus with great energy, causing the emitting nucleus to recoil simultaneously in the opposite direction. In the final part of its trajectory, the alpha particle is slowed enough to collide with hundreds of atoms in the mineral, but since the larger recoil nucleus travels a much shorter path, it collides with ten times as many atoms. Consequently, the majority of radiation damage is caused by the recoiling nucleus. The immense amount of heat generated by both particles in a small region of the mineral structure produces damage, but some of the energy also serves to self-repair some of the damage spontaneously. Radioactive minerals that remain crystalline have high rates of self-repair, while metamict minerals do not.

Metamict minerals are not common in nature, and they are generally found in pegmatites associated with granites. Showing little resistance to metamictization, the largest group of metamict minerals includes the thorium-, uranium-, and yttrium-bearing oxides of niobium, tantalum, and titanium. The second-largest group of metamict minerals are silicates, with zircon (a zirconium-silicate mineral) occurring most frequently. The smallest group of metamict minerals are the phosphates, including xenotime (yttrium phosphate), which has the same crystal structure as zircon.

Since metamict gemstones, such as zircon, are isotropic and look clear inside, they are often of greater value than the crystalline varieties, because the anisotropic properties of crystalline gems make them look cloudy inside. In addition, radiation damage often imparts attractive color to the metamict gemstones. Metamict minerals may possibly have another important use in the future: Since some of them retain their radioactive elements over millions of years despite metamictization, they may provide the key for safe disposal of high-level nuclear wastes. Many geochemists believe that synthetic versions of these metamict minerals could be "grown" to produce rocks that would be able to contain hazardous nuclear wastes safely for tens of thousands of years.

*Alvin K. Benson*

SEE ALSO: Hazardous waste disposal; Igneous processes, rocks, and mineral deposits; Isotopes, radioactive; Niobium; Pegmatites; Silicates; Thorium; Uranium; Zirconium.

# Metamorphic processes, rocks, and mineral deposits

CATEGORIES: Geological processes and formations; mineral and other nonliving resources

*The word "metamorphism," based on Greek roots, translates as the "process of changing form." Existing sedimentary or igneous rocks are transformed in the solid state to metamorphic rocks as the temperature and pressure of their environment increase at various depths within the Earth. The numerous transformations that occur are collectively termed metamorphic processes.*

## BACKGROUND

Every metamorphic process relates either to the formation of new minerals, called neocrystallization, or to the formation of a new texture in the metamorphic rock. The new texture may simply be an increase in size and change in shape of existing minerals (recrystallization). The new texture may also involve the development of a "foliation," in which the elongate and platy minerals assume a parallel orientation. These general processes are further divided depending upon the specific chemical and mechanical changes occurring during the metamorphic transformation. Long periods of erosion can expose metamorphic rocks on the surface of the Earth; surface metamorphic rocks are often valuable resources, either because of their new minerals or because of the physical properties that the rocks themselves have as a result of their new textures.

## NEOCRYSTALLIZATION

New minerals form at the expense of old minerals. As the pressure and temperature increase on an existing igneous or sedimentary rock (called the protolith), the old minerals become unstable and break down into chemical components that recombine to form new minerals. Some of the chemicals, for example, $H_2O$ and $CO_2$, occur as gases at metamorphic temperatures. These gases mix to form a vapor that exists in the cracks and along the boundaries between the individual grains of the minerals. The gain and loss of gases from the vapor are part of the overall chemical reconstruction that takes place during metamorphism. The vapor inevitably escapes from the rock during the long period of cooling and erosion that exposes such rocks on the Earth's surface.

The neocrystallization process is usually expressed as a chemical reaction. The minerals of the protolith (existing rock) are the reactants, shown on the left side of the reaction, and the new metamorphic minerals that form are the products, listed on the right side. The reactions often will generate and/or consume chemicals residing in the vapor. The reactions illustrated in the figures accompanying this article are shown in triplicate, first as rock changes, second as mineral changes, and third as chemical recombinations. As an example, refer to the three parts of reaction 1. Reaction (a) is the conversion of the sedimentary rock (protolith) called dolostone, which commonly contains silica as chert nodules, to the metamorphic rock called marble. Reaction (b) is the same reaction with attention focused on the transformation of the minerals and the creation of the metamorphic mineral called tremolite, where the beginning vapor was water and the ending vapor is carbon dioxide. Reaction (c) shows how the individual chemical components have recombined, often changing from the mineral to vapor state during the transformation.

As with any chemical reaction, there are specific temperature and pressure conditions that must exist before the reaction can occur. Each metamorphic

## Reactions That Form Metamorphic Rocks

1.
 a. cherty dolostone + vapor $\rightarrow$ marble + vapor
 b. 5 dolomite + 8 quartz + water $\rightarrow$ tremolite + 3 calcite + 7 carbon dioxide
 c. $5CaMg(CO_3)_2 + 8SiO_2 + H_2O \rightarrow Ca_2Mg_5Si_8O_{22}(OH)_2 + 3CaCO_3 + 7CO_2$

2.
 a. peridotite + vapor $\rightarrow$ verde antique marble
 b. 4 olivine + 4 water + 2 carbon dioxide $\rightarrow$ serpentine + 2 magnesite
 c. $4Mg_2SiO_4 + 4H_2O + 2CO_2 \rightarrow Mg_3Si_2O_5(OH)_4 + 2MgCO_3$

3.
 a. peridotite + vapor (with dissolved silica) $\rightarrow$ serpentinite
 b. 3 olivine + 4 water + silica $\rightarrow$ 2 serpentine
 c. $3Mg_2SiO_4 + 4H_2O + SiO_2 \rightarrow 2Mg_3Si_2O_5(OH)_4$

4.
 a. cherty dolostone + vapor $\rightarrow$ soapstone + vapor
 b. 3 magnesite + 4 quartz + water $\rightarrow$ talc + 3 carbon dioxide
 c. $3MgCO_3 + 4SiO_2 + H_2O \rightarrow Mg_3Si_4O_{10}(OH)_2 + 3CO_2$

5.
 a. high-aluminum shales $\rightarrow$ kyanite schist
 b. kaolinite-clay $\rightarrow$ 2 kyanite + 2 quartz + 4 water
 c. $Al_4Si_4O_{10}(OH)_8 \rightarrow 2Al_2SiO_5 + 2SiO_2 + 4H_2O$

6.
 a. cherty limestone $\rightarrow$ marble + vapor
 b. calcite + quartz $\rightarrow$ wollastonite + carbon dioxide
 c. $CaCO_3 + SiO_2 \rightarrow CaSiO_3 + CO_2$

7.
 a. sodium-rich igneous felsite $\rightarrow$ blueschist
 b. albite (feldspar) $\rightarrow$ jadeite + quartz
 c. $NaAlSi_3O_8 \rightarrow NaAlSi_2O_6 + SiO_2$

8.
 a. sedimentary clay-rich shale $\rightarrow$ corundum-bearing garnet schist
 b. 6 staurolite $\rightarrow$ 4 garnet + 12 kyanite + 11 corundum + 3 water
 c. $6Fe_2Al_9Si_4O_{23}(OH) \rightarrow 4Fe_3Al_2Si_3O_{12} + 12Al_2SiO_5 + 11Al_2O_3 + 3H_2O$

mineral of interest forms within a specific temperature and pressure region in the Earth. The exact temperature and pressure conditions under which a metamorphic mineral or group of minerals will form can be determined by laboratory experiments; geologists then deduce that similar conditions must have existed whenever these minerals are found in the geological environment. The geological environment required for the development of a given metamorphic mineral is usually controlled by plate tectonic movements. Explorations for metamorphic resources are targeted to specific tectonic regions that correspond to the proper temperature-pressure environments for their formation.

There are three tectonic environments with specific pressure and temperature conditions that control the location for the development of metamorphic minerals. Burial metamorphism results from a high-pressure and low-temperature environment that occurs where two plates converge and one plate is actively subducted. During the recent geological past, the coastline along Oregon and Northern California experienced this tectonic environment. Contact metamorphism is a high-temperature, low-pressure environment occurring slightly farther inland from the region of burial metamorphism. Contact metamorphism results when magma generated during the sub-

duction of a plate rises into the overriding plate and solidifies as shallow igneous plutons. Contact metamorphism has occurred along the margins of the Sierra Nevada batholiths of eastern California. The third tectonic environment is regional metamorphism, often called dynothermal metamorphism, which corresponds to moderately high pressures and temperatures. Regional metamorphism is seen after extensive erosion of a contact metamorphism area has exposed deeper regions within the Earth's crust.

ISOCHEMICAL PROCESSES
Neocrystallization that occurs without any influx of new chemicals (other than the water and carbon dioxide from the vapor) is called isochemical metamorphism. Isochemical metamorphism produces about a dozen minerals that are considered valuable resources. The isochemical-neocrystallization processes responsible for the formation of some of these minerals are described below, with a brief indication of the tectonic environments that favor their formation.

SERPENTINE
When serpentine ($Mg_3Si_2O_5(OH)_4$) is the major mineral formed during the low-temperature, low-pressure metamorphism associated with the beginning of regional metamorphism, the resulting metamorphic

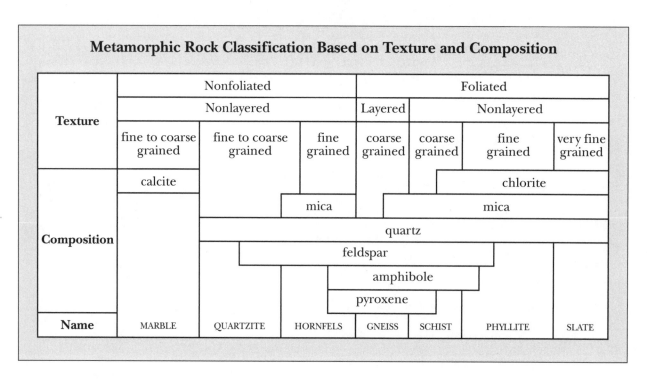

**Metamorphic Rock Classification Based on Texture and Composition**

| Texture | Nonfoliated | | | Foliated | | | |
|---|---|---|---|---|---|---|---|
| | Nonlayered | | | Layered | Nonlayered | | |
| | fine to coarse grained | fine to coarse grained | fine grained | coarse grained | coarse grained | fine grained | very fine grained |
| Composition | calcite | | | | | chlorite | |
| | | | mica | | mica | | |
| | | | quartz | | | | |
| | | feldspar | | | | | |
| | | | amphibole | | | | |
| | | | pyroxene | | | | |
| Name | MARBLE | QUARTZITE | HORNFELS | GNEISS | SCHIST | PHYLLITE | SLATE |

rock is called a serpentinite. Polished serpentinites are used widely as a facing stone in both interior and exterior applications. When the serpentinites contain some carbonate minerals they are marketed as "verde antique marble." Serpentine can occur in any one of three forms. The form called chrysotile is the most common asbestos mineral. Asbestos veins are common in serpentinites, and in many locations in eastern Canada and northern New England serpentinites have been mined for their asbestos.

Serpentine generally forms by metamorphism of ultramafic igneous rocks by one of two reactions. One type of serpentine reaction (see reaction 2) involves a mixed vapor phase of carbon dioxide and water, which produces some carbonate minerals. A second serpentine-forming reaction (see reaction 3) requires that some silica be dissolved in the water vapor.

## TALC

Talc ($Mg_3Si_4O_{10}(OH)_2$) can form large masses of randomly oriented interlocking small flakes to make a rock called soapstone, used extensively for carving and as a source of talcum powder for health and beauty applications. The term "steatite" refers to talc-rich rocks that are used because of talc's lack of chemical reactivity or its high heat capacity. Talc forms by regional metamorphism at low to moderate temperatures and low to moderate pressures. When the protolith is a sedimentary limestone or dolostone, the reaction for the formation of talc deposits is as shown in reaction 4.

A second common reaction that produces major talc deposits is the continuing metamorphism of a peridotite protolith. Talc forms by this reaction at temperatures slightly above 300° Celsius; however, the temperatures must remain below 700° Celsius to prevent the breakdown of talc.

## GRAPHITE

Graphite (a form of carbon, C) is used in a wide variety of applications from lubrication to high-temperature crucibles. Deposits of amorphous graphite form by contact metamorphism of coal beds, whereas deposits of flake graphite form by regional metamorphism of sedimentary rocks with the graphite being disseminated in mica schist and micaceous quartzite. Extensive weathering of these rocks assists in the release of the graphite. The graphite content of such metamorphic ores is usually 5 to 6 percent.

Clinker is a common term used by English miners for the graphite ore created by the contact metamorphism of coal beds. The reaction involves the breakdown of a wide variety of organic molecules. Continued high-temperature metamorphism of coal beds can transform the graphite into a natural coke, which has been mined in Wyoming and Utah.

## KYANITE

Kyanite ($Al_2SiO_5$) and the related minerals andalusite and sillimanite are used in the production of refractory ceramics, such as those used in spark plugs. Kyanite forms from aluminum-rich clay-shale protoliths during regional metamorphism at moderate to high temperatures (see reaction 5).

## WOLLASTONITE

Wollastonite ($CaSiO_3$) is used extensively in the manufacturing of tiles. It forms by high-temperature contact metamorphism of silica-bearing limestones. An example may be found in Willsboro, New York, where the wollastonite mine is in a metamorphosed limestone on the margin of the igneous intrusion that forms the Adirondack Mountains. This type of reaction is shown in example 6. This reaction normally occurs at temperatures around 650° Celsius.

## JADEITE

The pure form of the mineral jadeite ($NaAlSi_2O_6$) is the best quality of all materials called jade. Jade has been a valued material for sculpture and other art-and-craft applications for more than twenty-five centuries. It forms during burial metamorphism of alkali-rich igneous rocks that have been subjected to very high pressures and low temperatures. Such conditions are found in the mountains of the Coast Range in California, where jade has been mined (reaction 7).

## CORUNDUM

Corundum ($Al_2O_3$) is used extensively as an abrasive, and its pure colored variants known as ruby and sapphire are valued as gemstones. Corundum forms during regional metamorphism of aluminum-rich shale protoliths. The progressing metamorphism of the shale makes an intermediate mineral called staurolite, which commonly is sold in mineral shops and displayed in museums as "fairy crosses" because of its well-developed cruciform twining. Corundum forms when the staurolite breaks down at very high temperatures, as shown in reaction 8.

*Quartzite, pictured here in Dodge County, Wisconsin, is a type of metamorphic rock.* (USGS)

## METASOMATISM

A special type of metamorphism occurs whenever a major influx of new dissolved chemical components is added to the chemistry of the protolith. A water-rich fluid or vapor is the means of transport for this added chemistry. The process of adding chemistry to the rock through the vapor is called metasomatism. Metasomatism occurs chiefly in regions of contact metamorphism where highly volatile elements such as boron, fluorine, or chlorine are released into a water-rich fluid associated with the igneous pluton. The igneous-based fluid also carries dissolved silicon, aluminum, iron, magnesium, manganese, minor sodium, potassium, and often some tin, copper, tungsten, lead, and zinc. This saline fluid invades the adjacent limestone and reacts with calcium to form pronounced monomineralic zones at the contact between the pluton and the limestone.

The rocks produced by metasomatism are called skarns or tactites, and they are the coarsest grained of all metamorphic rocks. The garnet zone of a skarn may have individual grains of garnet that are as large as 20 centimeters in diameter. Skarns are mined throughout the world. Scheelite ($CaWO_4$), a major ore of tungsten, is mined from numerous metasomatized contact zones in California, Nevada, Idaho, and British Columbia. Other minerals that are mined from skarns are wollastonite, galena (an ore of lead), sphalerite (an ore of zinc), magnetite (an ore of iron), and chalcopyrite (an ore of copper).

## TEXTURE CHANGES AND RECRYSTALLIZATION

During metamorphism changes may occur in the size, the shape, and often the orientation of the mineral grains within the rock. There are at least six different processes related to texture changes; the exact process is dependent upon which of the texture variables are changed and the mechanics of the change.

A change in size and shape of an existing mineral without the formation of any new minerals is a process called recrystallization. Certain sedimentary protoliths may be monomineralic rocks; two common examples are a limestone that is made entirely of the mineral calcite and a silica-cemented sandstone that is made entirely of the mineral quartz. Such single-mineral rocks are unable to promote any form of neocrystallization, and recrystallization is the only result of metamorphism.

## MARBLE

The transformation from a sedimentary limestone to a metamorphic rock called marble often results in more than a thousandfold increase in the size of the calcite grains. The grains in the limestone protolith are commonly round in shape, whereas the grains in the marble interlock like a jigsaw puzzle to give a mosaic texture.

The interlocking texture in marble imparts a high coherence to the rock, yet its calcite mineralogy gives it a low hardness, allowing marble to be easily cut and polished. Pure white marble is used extensively for sculpting to form statues, as in the Lincoln Memorial; for building stone, as in the Greek Parthenon; and for ornamental carvings. Many marbles may contain an impurity that imparts a striking color pattern allowing their use in architecture as facings, tabletops, and flooring. Italy has more marble quarries than any other country. The United States quarries marble from both the Rocky and Appalachian mountain chains, with major quarries in Vermont and Colorado.

## FOLIATION: SLATE

A metamorphic rock in which the platy and elongate shaped minerals are parallel in their orientation is said to be foliated. A foliated texture can be seen in the rock by a tendency for the rock to break along parallel planes.

Slate is a foliated metamorphic rock in which the individual mineral flakes are so small that they can be seen only under the highest magnifications of a microscope. The foliation imparts to the slate the ability to break in near perfect planes. Slate is used as flagstones, roofing, floor tiles, hearthstones, and tabletops, especially billiard tables. A few slates are used not because of their foliation but because of their composition. Very clay-rich slates are ground because the smaller pieces will bloat when heated to form a material used as a lightweight aggregate.

## METAMORPHIC DIFFERENTIATION: GNEISS

At relatively high temperatures a metamorphic process occurs in which minerals segregate. The light-colored minerals such as quartz and feldspar move into zones parallel to the rock's foliation, leaving behind alternate zones of dark minerals such as biotite and amphibole. Metamorphic differentiations cause a marked dark versus light layering in the rock. Such rock is commonly called gneiss. Gneiss is quarried locally in many places as dimension stone.

## ANATEXIS: MIGMATITES

At the more extreme temperatures for regional metamorphism, partial melting will begin to occur within the light-colored layers of a gneiss. The process of partially melting a rock is called anatexis, and this process begins the transformation from metamorphic to igneous rocks. Migmatite is the name for such a mixed rock. Migmatites occur in regions that have experienced a great amount of erosion to reveal the highest levels of metamorphism. Migmatites are common in the shield regions of the major continents. The shield for the North American continent is exposed in the upper peninsula of Michigan, northern Wisconsin and Minnesota, and throughout most of Canada.

Migmatites are commonly used as monument stone. The contortions of pattern generated by the partial melting make each stone unique and generally quite handsome. Migmatites are quarried in Minnesota, New York, and Michigan and are used as building stone throughout the United States.

## CATACLASTITE

A special texture develops in rocks when the metamorphic pressure involves tectonic forces having a distinctly linear or planar orientation on the rock. Such opposing forces result in shear stress, and they cause mechanical breakage of the mineral grains in the rock. The name "cataclastite" refers to a metamorphic rock that exhibits a sheared texture containing many fragmented and distorted mineral grains that are often cemented together by a calcite matrix. Cataclastites are formed in tectonic regions that are experiencing active crustal movements. Some cataclastites are quarried and polished for use as a decorative "marble." A famous cataclastite, the "Fantastica di Lasa," is quarried from the northern Alps in Italy because of its attractive and unique appearance.

*Dion C. Stewart*

## FURTHER READING

Best, Myron G. *Igneous and Metamorphic Petrology.* 2d ed. Malden, Mass.: Blackwell, 2003.

Blatt, Harvey, Robert J. Tracy, and Brent E. Owens. *Petrology: Igneous, Sedimentary, and Metamorphic.* 3d ed. New York: W. H. Freeman, 2006.

Bowes, D. R., ed. *The Encyclopedia of Igneous and Metamorphic Petrology*. New York: Van Nostrand Reinhold, 1989.

Bucher, Kurt, and Martin Frey. *Petrogenesis of Metamorphic Rocks*. 7th completely rev. and updated ed. New York: Springer, 2002.

Philpotts, Anthony R., and Jay J. Ague. *Principles of Igneous and Metamorphic Petrology*. 2d ed. New York: Cambridge University Press, 2009.

Raymond, Loren A. *Petrology: The Study of Igneous, Sedimentary, and Metamorphic Rocks*. 2d ed. Boston: McGraw-Hill, 2002.

Winter, John D. *An Introduction to Igneous and Metamorphic Petrology*. 2d ed. New York: Prentice Hall, 2010.

WEB SITE

U.S. GEOLOGICAL SURVEY
Metamorphic Rocks
http://vulcan.wr.usgs.gov/LivingWith/
VolcanicPast/Notes/metamorphic_rocks.html

SEE ALSO: Asbestos; Corundum and emery; Garnet; Gneiss; Graphite; Kyanite; Marble; Mica; Plate tectonics; Slate; Talc.

# Methane

CATEGORY: Mineral and other nonliving resources

WHERE FOUND
Methane is found throughout the crust of the Earth. The United States, Canada, and Russia have the largest output of natural gas from methane deposits. Methane is also found in mud volcanoes. The decomposition of landfill materials has resulted in the production of significant amounts of methane, and several landfill sites in the United States have been drilled into as a source.

PRIMARY USES
The main use of methane is as a fuel source. It also has several industrial uses.

TECHNICAL DEFINITION
Methane is a naturally occurring gas composed of one atom of carbon and four atoms of hydrogen. This stable chemical compound has the formula $CH_4$ and is classified as a hydrocarbon.

DESCRIPTION, DISTRIBUTION, AND FORMS
Methane, a product of the decomposition of plant and animal remains, can be found throughout the Earth's crust in varying amounts. Where it is found in greater concentrations, methane is the primary constituent in natural gas deposits, which are the target of oil and gas exploration efforts worldwide. Methane is also found in coal deposits as an integral part of the coalification process and can be recovered from wells drilled into the coal in the same manner in which oil and gas are obtained.

HISTORY
Methane was considered a waste by-product of oil production in the past, and trillions of cubic meters escaped into the atmosphere in worldwide operations. Beginning in the 1950's methane-based natural gas was seen as a viable energy source. Several interstate pipelines have been constructed in the United States, primarily to deliver the gas from its origins in the Gulf Coast and Midwest to the metropolitan areas of the Northeast. As late as the 1960's, natural gas had little value in some areas, and wells drilled for oil that discovered natural gas instead were frequently abandoned for lack of markets.

Beginning in the 1980's, methane was touted by some as the fuel of the future. It is clean burning, relatively inexpensive, and fairly easily transported throughout the United States. Its supply is forecast to continue for hundreds of years. Research has attempted to substitute methane-based natural gas as a motor fuel in cars, trucks, and locomotives, and many vehicles have been converted to use it. Its use as a motor fuel will undoubtedly increase as more facilities are constructed to service existing and future vehicles.

OBTAINING METHANE
In spite of its advantages, methane has a significant disadvantage: It is explosive if mixed with air in a range of 5 percent to 15 percent by volume, and it has been blamed for several coal-mine disasters. As a result, modern coal-mining practice removes as much methane from coal deposits as possible in advance of mining and maintains the methane-air mixture in the mining environment below 1 percent by volume. Since methane is not life-sustaining, its accumulation in underground coal mines can also cause a condition known as "firedamp," which may asphyxiate mining personnel if undetected.

## USES OF METHANE

Methane is an excellent fuel for fuel cells. Fuel cells produce electricity directly from the interaction of hydrocarbon and a catalyst. This interaction is not dependent on combustion but is a heat-producer, giving rise to the utilization of waste heat in various ways. It is expected that future fuel cell research, together with advances in the transportation sector, will place a greater demand on methane resources.

*Charles D. Haynes*

### WEB SITE

U.S. ENVIRONMENTAL PROTECTION AGENCY
Methane
http://www.epa.gov/methane/

SEE ALSO: Fuel cells; Methanol; Oil and natural gas chemistry; Oil and natural gas reservoirs.

# Methanol

CATEGORIES: Energy resources; products from resources

*Methanol is manufactured by the oxidation of natural gas or the reaction of carbon dioxide with hydrogen. It has numerous chemical uses and has potential as a partial replacement for gasoline.*

## BACKGROUND

Methanol (also called methyl alcohol and wood alcohol) is a colorless liquid with little taste or odor. It boils at 64.51° Celsius and has a melting point (and triple point) of −97.56° Celsius. At 20° Celsius it has a vapor pressure of 97.60 torrs, a density of 0.7913 gram per milliliter, and an index of refraction of 1.3284. Its molar mass is 32.04 grams. Methanol is completely soluble in water and most organic solvents. It has a flash point of only 11° Celsius and is thus highly flammable. Methanol forms numerous binary and ternary azeotropic combinations with a variety of compounds, so it is difficult to purify.

Methanol is of considerable importance: It has long been considered a major industrial organic chemical, and it has more recently been identified as a likely automotive fuel source. The world production capacity for methanol is more than 22 million metric tons per year. By 2013, worldwide consumption of methanol is estimated to reach 58 million metric tons, more than one-half of which will be consumed in China, the world's largest producer and consumer of methanol.

## PRIMARY USES

A major portion of the methanol produced is used for the production of methyl esters such as methyl acrylate, methyl methacrylate, and methyl terephthalate, which are used in the manufacture of high-volume polymers. Methanol has been used to prepare formaldehyde, but now more direct formaldehyde synthetic methods have somewhat reduced that usage. Because formaldehyde is used in enormous quantities for production of synthetic water-based polymers, such as the phenolic and urea resins (employed in plywood manufacture, for example), even the reduced formaldehyde production from methanol is important. A growing use for methanol is its reaction with isobutene (2-methylpropene) for the synthesis of methyl tertiary-butyl ether, a gasoline additive that is used in winter in many large cities to reduce air pollution. Another group of major uses of methanol is for the chemical synthesis of acetic acid, methyl chloride, vinyl acetate, vinyl chloride, ethylene glycol (antifreeze), and other compounds. Methanol is also used as a solvent and extracting medium. Some methanol is used for the preparation of synthetic protein.

Methanol has an octane number value of 100; therefore, fuel uses for methanol have been proposed repeatedly. During the 1970's, as petroleum prices skyrocketed, a number of processes for producing methanol for fuel purposes from wood or other biomass sources were considered. Vehicles capable of using methanol or a gasoline-methanol mix were developed. As gas prices softened in the late 1990's, automakers shifted attention to ethanol, which is more economical to produce, as methanol prices rose. Methanol continues to be used as a fuel for drag race cars, and it is widely used in China as an automobile fuel. Even though methanol combustion products (almost entirely carbon dioxide and water) are nonpolluting and automobile engines can be easily modified to burn methanol, U.S. automakers have shifted their attention from methanol to hybrid and electric vehicles.

## METHANOL PRODUCTION

Before 1930 the most common production method was the anaerobic destructive distillation of hardwoods at temperatures below 400° Celsius. However, this method produced low yields (about 21 liters per metric ton of wood) of very impure methanol. Small amounts of relatively impure methanol produced in this manner are added to commercial ethanol to "denature" it and prevent the commercial alcohol's use as a beverage. Fermentation processes used to produce other alcohols have not been successful for methanol. However, because methanol is found in both plants and animals and is utilized by bacteria, fermentation appears to be a likely method if appropriate microorganisms could be identified or if genetically engineered bacteria could be developed for that purpose.

The most often used synthetic processes involve reactions of carbon monoxide and hydrogen (called synthesis gas), using catalysts such as copper, zinc, and chromium oxides at elevated pressures (above 300 atmospheres) and at temperatures higher than 300° Celsius. The high-pressure process is sometimes replaced with a lower-pressure one (below 100 atmospheres) at a somewhat lower temperature. The lower-pressure process requires more purified reactants and a more complex catalyst system but allows the reaction to proceed in simpler reactors. The synthesis gas is obtained by treating natural gas (methane) or petroleum fractions with high-pressure steam. Synthesis gas can also be obtained directly from coal, and if carbon dioxide is easily available, it may be more economically desirable to produce the synthesis gas from the prior reaction of the carbon dioxide with hydrogen.

## TOXICITY

Methanol, even in minute quantities, is a powerful poison, acting on many parts of the nervous system, particularly the optic nerves. Blindness, at least temporary, often results from its ingestion. Methanol is oxidized in the body to formaldehyde and formic acid, which are the major direct culprits in methanol poisoning. Coma and death frequently occur as a result of methanol consumption.

*William J. Wasserman*

## FURTHER READING

Blume, David. *Alcohol Can Be a Gas! Fueling an Ethanol Revolution for the Twenty-first Century*. Santa Cruz, Calif.: International Institute for Ecological Agriculture, 2007.

Cheng, Wu-Hsun, and Harold H. Kung, eds. *Methanol Production and Use*. New York: M. Dekker, 1994.

Kohl, Wilfrid L., ed. *Methanol as an Alternative Fuel Choice: An Assessment*. Washington, D.C.: International Energy Program, Foreign Policy Institute, the Paul H. Nitze School of Advanced International Studies, the Johns Hopkins University, 1990.

Lee, Sunggyu. *Methanol Synthesis Technology*. Boca Raton, Fla.: CRC Press, 1990.

Minteer, Shelley, ed. *Alcoholic Fuels*. Boca Raton, Fla.: CRC/Taylor & Francis, 2006.

Mousdale, David M. *Biofuels: Biotechnology, Chemistry, and Sustainable Development*. Boca Raton, Fla.: CRC Press, 2008.

Olah, George A., Alain Goeppert, and G. K. Surya Prakash. *Beyond Oil and Gas: The Methanol Economy*. Weinheim, Germany: Wiley, 2006.

Paul, J. K., ed. *Methanol Technology and Application in Motor Fuels*. Park Ridge, N.J.: Noyes Data, 1978.

Supp, Emil. *How to Produce Methanol from Coal*. New York: Springer, 1990.

## WEB SITE

ALTERNATIVE FUELS AND ADVANCED VEHICLES DATA CENTER, U.S. DEPARTMENT OF ENERGY
Methanol
http://www.afdc.energy.gov/afdc/fuels/methanol.html

*An Indy Racing League car refuels with methanol during a 2003 race.* (Getty Images)

SEE ALSO: Biofuels; Biotechnology; Energy economics; Ethanol; Methane; Petroleum refining and processing; Plant domestication and breeding; Synthetic Fuels Corporation; Wood and charcoal as fuel resources.

# Mexico

CATEGORIES: Countries; government and resources

*Mexico is second in worldwide silver production; the metal has been mined in the region since 1546. One-seventh of the annual global production of silver comes from Mexico. Mexico is the sixth largest producer of petroleum worldwide. The crude oil industry accounts for one-third of the nation's annual revenue and is controlled by a government-operated company.*

## THE COUNTRY

Mexico is located in North America, sharing a border with the United States to the north. It is bordered to the south by Belize and Guatemala in Central America. To the east, Mexico borders the Caribbean Sea and the Gulf of Mexico. The country's western shore meets the Pacific Ocean, the Gulf of California, and the Gulf of Tehuantepec. Only about one-third of Mexico is flat. A chain of volcanic mountains runs east-west across the country just south of Mexico City. Plateaus also dominate the landscape. The Sierra Madre mountain chains surround the region's plateau in a V shape. The Sonoran Desert covers the area east of the Gulf of California. Mexico's economy is the eleventh largest in the world. In 2007, the average annual income was $14,400. A large portion of Mexico's income results from oil production. The country is a leading producer of silver and also mines copper, lead, zinc, and gold.

## SILVER

Mexico is the second leading producer of silver in the world (2.8 million kilograms in 2007). Four of the top twelve silver mines (in terms of production) in 2007 were located in Mexico's silver belt in the center of the country. The majority of silver is taken from mines in Guanajuato, Pachuca, and Zacatecas.

The city of Taxco is one of the oldest mining sites in the Western Hemisphere. Within a year of conquering the Aztecs in 1521, the Spanish discovered the value of Taxco. By the beginning of the seventeenth century, silver mined in Taxco could be found throughout Europe. Taxco became known worldwide for its silver wealth. For the Spanish, it also was the primary mining site for several precious metals. However, as richer and more accessible veins were found, Taxco slowly faded in mining importance.

Don José de la Borda, known as the father of Taxco, rediscovered the city's silver wealth in 1716. He used part of the fortune he made to build schools, houses, roads, and Taxco's famous Santa Prisca Cathedral. Silversmithing and mining was forgotten again during Mexico's war for independence. The Spanish destroyed the silver mines so that Mexican revolutionaries could not gain their control.

William Spratling, an American professor of architecture, moved to Mexico in 1929. Spratling became interested in Taxco's silver history. He encouraged local artists to become silversmiths. Spratling also created an apprenticeship program for local silversmiths with promising artistic talent, training them using his own designs. Taxco again became world famous for its silver, this time primarily for the jewelry made from the metal. Silverware and jewelry are made out of sterling silver, which is 92.5 percent silver and 7.5 percent copper. Jewelry is often coated with a thin layer of 0.999 fine silver to give it extra shine. Britannia silver is also used for utensils and is 95.8 percent pure silver.

In the modern world economy, Taxco is the world leader in silver production. Numerous silver stores are located in and around the town's main plaza. Taxco is home to both the Spratling Museum and the Silver Museum. In 1937, Spratling created the silver fair as a party for local artists working with silver. The fair has become a national event, involving Mexico's finest silversmiths and some of the world's best artists. In 1953, Mexico's president created National Silver Day, which is celebrated the last Saturday of November. The silver fair starts that Saturday and ends the first Sunday of December each year.

## PETROLEUM

Petroleum and petroleum-related products have a long history in Mexico. Asphalt and bitumen, or pitch, has been used in Mexico since the time of the Aztecs. They are believed to have used asphalt to secure stone arrowheads on the ends of wooden spears. The first time oil was refined into kerosene was in 1876, near the city of Tampico on Mexico's eastern coast. By 1917, large quantities of Mexican oil were be-

## Mexico: Resources at a Glance

*Official name:* United Mexican States
*Government:* Federal republic
*Capital city:* Mexico City
*Area:* 758,505 mi²; 1,964,375 km²
*Population (2009 est.):* 111,211,789
*Language:* Spanish
*Monetary unit:* Mexican peso (MXN)

### ECONOMIC SUMMARY:

*GDP composition by sector (2008 est.):* agriculture, 3.8%; industry, 35.2%; services, 61%
*Natural resources:* petroleum, silver, copper, gold, lead, zinc, natural gas, timber
*Land use (2005):* arable land, 12.66%; permanent crops, 1.28%; other, 86.06%
*Industries:* food and beverages, tobacco, chemicals, iron and steel, petroleum, mining, textiles, clothing, motor vehicles, consumer durables, tourism
*Agricultural products:* corn, wheat, soybeans, rice, beans, cotton, coffee, fruit, tomatoes, beef, poultry, dairy products, wood products
*Exports (2008 est.):* $291.3 billion
*Commodities exported:* manufactured goods, oil and oil products, silver, fruits, vegetables, coffee, cotton
*Imports (2008 est.):* $308.6 billion
*Commodities imported:* metalworking machines, steel mill products, agricultural machinery, electrical equipment, car parts for assembly, repair parts for motor vehicles, aircraft, and aircraft parts
*Labor force (2008 est.):* 45.32 million
*Labor force by occupation (2005):* agriculture, 15.1%; industry, 25.7%; services, 59%

### ENERGY RESOURCES:

*Electricity production (2007 est.):* 243.3 billion kWh
*Electricity consumption (2007 est.):* 202 billion kWh
*Electricity exports (2007 est.):* 1.278 billion kWh
*Electricity imports (2007 est.):* 484.2 million kWh

*Natural gas production (2007 est.):* 55.98 billion m³
*Natural gas consumption (2007 est.):* 68.29 billion m³
*Natural gas exports (2007 est.):* 2.973 billion m³
*Natural gas imports (2007 est.):* 11.69 billion m³
*Natural gas proved reserves (Jan. 2008 est.):* 392.2 billion m³

*Oil production (2007 est.):* 3.501 million bbl/day
*Oil imports (2005):* 385,400 bbl/day
*Oil proved reserves (Jan. 2008 est.):* 13.68 billion bbl

*Source:* Data from *The World Factbook 2009.* Washington, D.C.: Central Intelligence Agency, 2009.
*Notes:* Data are the most recent tracked by the CIA. Values are given in U.S. dollars. Abbreviations: bbl/day = barrels per day; GDP = gross domestic product; km² = square kilometers; kWh = kilowatt-hours; m³ = cubic meters; mi² = square miles.

ing drilled and refined by American and British companies. The Mexican government then proclaimed in its constitution ownership of all the country's mineral rights. In 1938, strikes over wages from foreign-owned companies led to the creation of Petroleos Mexicanos (Pemex) by Mexican president Lázaro Cárdenas. This caused many of the foreign companies to leave Mexico. Pemex is the ninth largest oil company worldwide, and the largest in Latin America. Pemex is responsible for exploration, extraction, refining, transportation, distribution, and marketing of petroleum, petroleum products, and natural gas. Between heavy taxes and direct payments made to the government, Pemex is responsible for one-third of Mexico's annual revenues.

Mexico is the world's sixth largest producer of crude oil (3.5 million barrels per day in 2007) and is ninth in exports. It ranks seventeenth by amount of oil reserves. However, Mexico has passed peak production of oil, depleting its resources, and overall production has begun to decline. This could be a serious problem for the country because of how heavily the government relies on money from the petroleum industry. In April, 2009, oil production in Mexico was 1.37 million barrels per day, a figure that was under the target for the year. By 2010, Mexico's oil exports were expected to decline by 18 percent. Pemex has begun looking for new oil fields using seismic technology. Scientists send a seismic wave into the ground and can use computers to measure its reflection, which tells about the structure underground. Geologists can use this information to help determine the best places to drill for oil.

*In this 1952 photograph, a worker guides a rock crusher at the Real del Monte silver mine in Mexico. Mexico has long been a leader in silver production.* (Getty Images)

### NATURAL GAS

Methane is the main component of natural gas. In addition to methane, natural gas can include ethane, propane, butane, carbon dioxide, nitrogen, and helium. Natural gas, like petroleum and coal, forms from fossil fuels or in isolated natural gas fields. Extensive refining removes almost everything but methane. The natural gas industry in Mexico is run by Pemex. In 2008, Mexico ranked sixteenth in natural-gas production (55,980 million cubic meters) and thirty-fourth globally in proven reserves (392.2 billion cubic meters).

In 1995, some control of the natural gas industry was turned over to private industry. Pemex continued to control exploration, production, and firsthand sales. Pemex continues to own most of the pipelines throughout the country. Private companies handle transportation, storage, and distribution of natural gas. In 2005, several natural gas sites were found, which increased production and jobs. In 2007, natural gas pipelines became the target of attacks by the Ejército Popular Revolucionario (the People's Revolutionary Army), a small antigovernment terrorist group formed in the 1990's. The attacks resulted in the loss of hundreds of millions of dollars in production profits.

## COPPER

In the late nineteenth century, a series of copper deposits were found near Santa Rosalía. These mines have been mostly depleted. Remaining copper is produced from open-pit mines near Cananea and La Caridad. Mexico remains the twenty-second largest exporter of copper in the world. In 2007, copper exports brought in more than $320 million for Mexico. The top copper-exporting nation is Chile, where the industry made $5 billion in 2007. There are insufficient known reserves to maintain the world's current consumption of copper. Scientists estimate that the world population will deplete the Earth of known copper by about 2070 if the current rate of consumption continues. However, if the demand continues to increase, the world's copper might last until only 2035.

Mexico's largest mining company, Grupo Mexico SAB, has been fighting a lawsuit over control of the Southern Copper Corporation of Peru. American courts ruled that Grupo Mexico had to return 30 percent of its stock in Southern Copper to another mining company, Asarco. Asarco, a company based in Tucson, Arizona, was owned by Grupo Mexico until 2005, when it became board-managed, and the legal battle started. In 2009, Grupo Mexico appealed the judge's ruling. At the same time, Grupo Mexico was dealing with a strike among its workers at the country's largest copper mine, Cananea, near the U.S. border. The strike started over health and safety standards. The company was given permission to fire fifteen hundred striking workers in 2009. Mexico's labor board shut down the mine because idle machinery had been looted and damaged beyond repair. Grupo Mexico has worked to reopen the copper pit with plans to hire two thousand workers to make it operational.

## ZINC

In 2006, Mexico was ranked sixth in global zinc production, producing 453,893 metric tons. Mexico exported $172.8 million worth of zinc in 2007, ranking ninth worldwide. Canada is the world's leading zinc exporter, making more than $546 million in 2007. The largest producer of zinc in Mexico is the state of Chihuahua. The Charcas mine in the state of San Luis Potosí, in north-central Mexico, is the top zinc-producing mine. Production of zinc in the country has risen; new mines were opened in 2001, and others expanded in 2002. A Canadian company, Canasil Re-

sources, found a vein of zinc and silver in the state of Durango. The company was exploring a 29-square-kilometer patch of flatland with a geologic intrusion. Samples taken of the intrusion in 2006 were found to contain high levels of zinc. Canasil expanded its property in the area to include an addition 1,000 square kilometers to the north and east. Early stages of drilling began in 2007. Two zones containing high concentrations of zinc at relatively shallow depths were found with the potential to yield a new zinc district in Mexico.

## FORESTS AND TIMBER

Scientists estimate that in the mid-sixteenth century more than two-thirds of Mexico was forest. Today, the tropical forests of the southern and eastern parts of the country are largely all that remain. However, Mexico contains 1.3 percent of the world's total forest reserves, and one-quarter of the country is classified as forest. Mexico has more species of pine and oak trees than anywhere else in the world. Nonetheless, logging has depleted Mexico's forests severely. Some pine forests in the northern part of the country have been conserved, but the practice is not widespread. The national tree is the cypress, which is found near water in semiarid regions. Mexico also has a number of ceiba trees, which were sacred to the Mayas. The Mayas believed that a ceiba tree stood at the center of the Earth, connecting it with the spirit world overhead. Ceiba trees grow in tropical regions, tall with large canopies that house several different species. Even in modern deforestation, ceiba trees are often spared.

Mexico's rain forests along the gulf coast and throughout the country are being cut down, and the land burned by farmers to expand their fields. This rain forest is part of the Maya Forest, which covers the Yucatán Peninsula, northern Guatemala, and parts of Belize, 5.3 million hectares in total. Efforts to preserve the forest, and the Mayan ruins within, have been complicated by a rapidly growing population. In addition to use as farmland, the forests are being cut down to make room for roads, dams, and other accommodations needed to handle an influx of workers and tourists to the region. In 1978, the Mexican government set up an international sanctuary to protect 331,200 hectares of rain forest. However, the Montes Azules Biosphere Reserve continues to shrink each year. Support for the preservation of the reserve is worldwide: In 2004, the European Union pledged 31 million euros (approximately $44 million) for four years in an effort to aid the tribes that live in and near the sanctuary. Poverty and population growth have resulted in destruction of the forest.

Many valuable types of wood are found in the tropical forests, including hardwoods such as various oaks and mahogany. The forests also contain cedar and rosewood. Sapodilla trees are found in Mexico's rain forests and are the basis of chicle. Chicle is a form of latex that is used in chewing gum. In 2000, Mexico's forestry imports exceeded exports by $2.46 billion. However, many other products are found in the forests of Mexico, including gums, resins, fibers, oils, and waxes.

### Other Resources
Mexico is twenty-fourth in the world in exportation of nonmonetary gold. In 2007, gold exports amounted to more than $160 million. Gold is a popular metal used in jewelry, sculpture, and coins. Gold occurs naturally as granules, nuggets, and large deposits.

Lead is another metal that is heavily mined in Mexico. Bullets, pipes, pewter, radiation shields, batteries, and weights are all made from lead. Lead is also poisonous and can cause a variety of problems, including blood and brain disorders, nerve damage, even death. Mexico is also the sixth largest producer of salt in the world.

*Jennifer L. Campbell*

### Further Reading
Bowles, Ian, and Glenn Prickett, eds. *Footprints in the Jungle: Natural Resource Industries, Infrastructure, and Biodiversity Conservation.* New York: Oxford University Press, 2001.

Fernandez, Linda, and Richard Carson, eds. *Both Sides of the Border: Transboundary Environmental Management Issues Facing Mexico and the United States.* New York: Springer, 2002.

Ibarrarán, María, and Roy Boyd. *Hacia el Futuro: Energy, Economics, and the Environment in Twenty-first Century Mexico.* New York: Springer, 2006.

Joseph, Gilbert, and Timothy Henderson, eds. *The Mexican Reader: History, Culture, Politics.* Durham, N.C.: Duke University Press, 2003.

Meyer, Michael C., and William H. Beezley, eds. *The Oxford History of Mexico.* New York: Oxford University Press, 2000.

Nobel, John, ed. *Mexico.* 11th ed. Oakland, Calif.: Lonely Planet, 2008.

Primack, Richard, et al., eds. *Timber, Tourists, and Temples: Conservation and Development in the Maya Forest of Belize, Guatemala, and Mexico.* Washington, D.C.: Island Press, 1997.

See also: Copper; Forests; Gold; Oil and natural gas reservoirs; Silver.

# Mica

Category: Mineral and other nonliving resources

### Where Found
Micas are common rock-forming minerals and are widely distributed throughout the world. They occur in igneous, metamorphic, and sedimentary rocks. They are mined as sheets or flakes and scrap. Sheet mica is primarily found in Brazil, Madagascar, India, and Canada. Muscovite flakes are mined in the United States from igneous pegmatites and metamorphic schists located in North and South Carolina, Connecticut, Georgia, and New Mexico.

### Primary Uses
Muscovite sheets are used as electrical insulators in the electronic and computer industries. Scrap mica is ground and used primarily as a coating material and in the paint industry.

### Technical Definition
The mica group of minerals is composed mainly of muscovite, $KAl_2(AlSi_3O_{10})(OH)_2$; biotite, $K(Mg,Fe)_3(AlSi_3O_{10})(OH)_2$; phlogopite $KMg_3(AlSi_3O_{10})(OH)_2$; and lepidolite, $K(Li,Al)_3(AlSi_3O_{10})(OH)_2$; although there are thirty known mica minerals. Micas are hydrous aluminum silicate minerals that have a perfect basal cleavage. Micas have a hardness of 2.5 to 4 and show a vitreous to pearly luster. Muscovite is a type of mica that is colorless and transparent in thin sheets and white to light brown or light yellow in thicker blocks. Phlogopite is yellow to brown with a copper-colored reflection off cleavage surfaces. Biotite is primarily black but can appear dark green or brown. Lepidolite has a distinctive lilac to pink color.

### Description, Distribution, and Forms
Micas form monoclinic crystals that inevitably show a perfect basal cleavage. Crystals and their cleavage

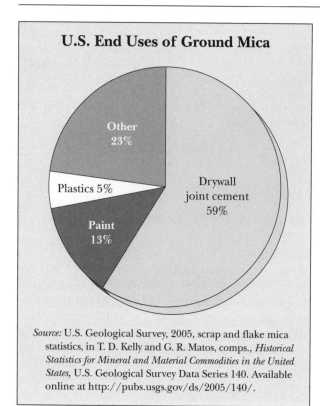

**U.S. End Uses of Ground Mica**

Other 23%

Plastics 5%

Paint 13%

Drywall joint cement 59%

*Source:* U.S. Geological Survey, 2005, scrap and flake mica statistics, in T. D. Kelly and G. R. Matos, comps., *Historical Statistics for Mineral and Material Commodities in the United States,* U.S. Geological Survey Data Series 140. Available online at http://pubs.usgs.gov/ds/2005/140/.

## OBTAINING MICA

The United States has limited supplies of sheet mica but is the largest producer of scrap mica. Although there are no environmental problems in mining mica, sheet mica is expensive to mine because of the intense hand labor needed to mine and process the sheets.

## USES OF MICA

Muscovite and phologopite remain important commercially because they have a low thermal and electrical conductivity and a high dielectrical strength. Sheet mica is used as electrical insulators, retardation plates in neon helium lasers, optical filters, and washers in the computer industry. The isinglass used in furnace and stove doors from the 1800's to the present is sheet muscovite. Lepidolite is the only mica mined and processed for its composition. It is a source of lithium, which is used in the production of heat-resistant glass.

Scraps and flakes of mica are processed into ground mica and used as a coating on rolled roofing, asphalt shingles, and waterproof fabrics. It is also used in wallpaper to give it a shiny luster, as a lubricant when mixed with oils, and as a pigment extender in paint. A magnesium-rich alteration product of biotite, vermiculite, is used as insulation, packing material, and an ingredient in potting soil.

*Dion C. Stewart*

## WEB SITE

U.S. GEOLOGICAL SURVEY
Mineral Information: Mica Statistics and
    Information
http://minerals.usgs.gov/minerals/pubs/
    commodity/mica/

SEE ALSO: Lithium; Metamorphic processes, rocks, and mineral deposits; Pegmatites.

sheets commonly display a hexagonal form. Muscovite and biotite can be found in thick "books" containing layer upon layer of thin cleavage sheets, which can be up to 3 meters across in pegmatites.

Micas are common throughout the world. Muscovite is characteristic of granites and pegmatites. In metamorphic rocks muscovite is the primary constituent of many mica schists. Biotite is found in igneous rocks ranging from granite pegmatites to diorites, gabbros, and peridotites. It also occurs in silica-rich lavas, porphyries, and a wide range of metamorphic rocks. Phlogopite occurs in metamorphosed magnesium limestones, dolomites, and ultrabasic rocks. Lepidolite occurs only in pegmatites.

## HISTORY

Mining of mica started as early as 2000 B.C.E. in India, where it was used as medicine, decoration, and paint. Commercial mining of mica in the United States began in 1803. Mica was used in store windows, shades for open light flames, and furnace viewing glass. When electronic vacuum tubes were developed in the early 1900's, mica was used as spacers and insulators in the tubes, thus beginning its use in the electrical industry.

**Mineral deposits.** *See* **Igneous processes, rocks, and mineral deposits; Metamorphic processes, rocks, and mineral deposits; Plutonic rocks and mineral deposits; Sedimentary processes, rocks, and mineral deposits**